Moulton's Grammar of
New Testament Greek:
Volume 3

Moulton's Grammar of New Testament Greek

Volume 3: Syntax

Nigel Turner
With a New Critical Introduction
by
Stanley E. Porter

t&tclark

LONDON • NEW YORK • OXFORD • NEW DELHI • SYDNEY

T&T CLARK
Bloomsbury Publishing Plc
50 Bedford Square, London, WC1B 3DP, UK
1385 Broadway, New York, NY 10018, USA

BLOOMSBURY, T&T CLARK and the T&T Clark logo are
trademarks of Bloomsbury Publishing Plc

First published in Great Britain 1906
This edition first published by T&T Clark 2019
Paperback edition published 2025

Copyright © T&T Clark

Introduction copyright © Stanley E. Porter, 2019

Stanley E. Porter has asserted his right under the Copyright,
Designs and Patents Act, 1988, to be identified as Author of this work.

All rights reserved. No part of this publication may be reproduced or
transmitted in any form or by any means, electronic or mechanical,
including photocopying, recording, or any information storage or retrieval
system, without prior permission in writing from the publishers.

Bloomsbury Publishing Plc does not have any control over, or
responsibility for, any third-party websites referred to or in this book.
All internet addresses given in this book were correct at the time of
going to press. The author and publisher regret any inconvenience
caused if addresses have changed or sites have ceased to exist,
but can accept no responsibility for any such changes.

A catalogue record for this book is available from the British Library.

A catalog record for this book is available from the Library of Congress.

ISBN: HB: 978-0-5674-7055-3
PB: 978-0-5677-1723-8
Pack: 978-0-5676-6242-2

Series: Biblical Languages: Greek

Typeset by Newgen KnowledgeWorks Pvt. Ltd., Chennai, India

To find out more about our authors and books visit
www.bloomsbury.com and sign up for our newsletters.

Contents

Introduction by Stanley E. Porter	ix
Preface	li
Chronological Bibliography	liii
Abbreviations	lvii

	PAGE
Introduction	1

BOOK ONE:
BUILDING UP THE SENTENCE: ANALYTICAL

I. Substitutes for Nouns in Subject, Object or Predicate   13

PART I. WORD-MATERIAL FOR SENTENCE-BUILDING

II. The Gender and Number of Nouns	21
III. The Comparison of Adjectives and Adverbs	29
IV. Vocatives	33
V. Substantival Article and Pronoun	36
VI. The Verb: Voice	51
VII. The Verb: Aspect and Tense	59
VIII. The Verb: Moods: Indicative and Subjunctive	90
IX. The Verb: Moods: Optative	118
X. The Verb: Noun Forms: Infinitive	134
XI. The Verb: Adjective-Forms: Participle	150

PART II. WORD-GROUPS DEFINING A NOUN OR ADJECTIVE

XII. The Adjectival and Predicative Definite Article	165
XIII. Attributive Relationship: Adjectives and Numerals	185
XIV. Attributive Relationship: Pronouns and Pronominal Adjectives	189
XV. Attributive Relationship: Substantives	206

PART III. WORD-MATERIAL WHICH DEFINES A VERB

XVI. Predicative Use of Adjectives and Adverbs	225
XVII. Case Additions to the Verb: Without a Preposition	230
XVIII. Case Additions to the Verb: With a Preposition	249
XIX. Negatives (especially the encroachment of MH upon the province of OY)	281

BOOK TWO: THE SENTENCE COMPLETE: SYNTHETIC SYNTAX
PART I. THE ORDINARY SIMPLE SENTENCE

XX. Subject and Predicate: Apparent Absence of Subject	291
XXI. Subject and Predicate: Absence of the Verb "To Be"	294
XXII. Congruence of Gender and Number	311
XXIII. The Subordination of Clauses	318
XXIV. Inconsistencies between Main and Dependent Clauses	324

PART II. CONNECTIONS BETWEEN SENTENCES

XXV. Co-Ordinating Particles	329
XXVI. Irregularity of Subordination	342
XXVII. Word Order	344

INDICES

Index to References	351
Index of Subjects	386
Index of Greek Words	402

Nigel Turner and Greek Syntax

An Introduction to Moulton's Third Volume, *Syntax*

Stanley E. Porter
McMaster Divinity College

Introduction

This essay is the third of four, each one accompanying a reprinted edition of one of the four volumes in the New Testament Greek grammar project conceived and instigated by James Hope Moulton, *A Grammar of New Testament Greek*, along with a reprinted edition of G. B. Winer's *A Treatise on the Grammar of New Testament Greek*, translated and edited by his father, William Fiddian Moulton. Of the four volumes, James Hope Moulton was the author of the first, entitled *Prolegomena*, and much of the second, entitled *Accidence and Word-Formation*, with the second completed by Moulton's student Wilbert Francis Howard. The third volume, *Syntax*, and the fourth, *Style*, were written some time later by Nigel Turner. These introductory essays attempt to provide biographical and related information to understand the contributions of the authors and their works to the larger field of study of New Testament Greek. Readers who wish to gain a more comprehensive picture of the entire four-volume grammar, as well as the translation of Winer's grammar, will want to read each of the five introductions. Even though there is some inevitable overlap among them, each introduction is uniquely tailored to the particular volume that it accompanies. This volume, containing Turner's *Syntax*, discusses the author and his work that led to the production of this third volume in *A Grammar of New Testament Greek*. I begin with the life and scholarly work of Turner, before offering a short summary and assessment of the volume.

The Life and Work of Nigel Turner

Nigel Turner (1916–1990) was born in Tuxford, England, on September 26, 1916, the year before Moulton died of exposure in the Mediterranean, a victim of the Great War.[1] Turner had no direct connection to Moulton, even though he lived to complete and even expand Moulton's grammar of New Testament Greek. Turner was educated at the Christ's Hospital School, a school founded in 1552 to educate the poor and that had moved from London to Horsham in West Sussex by the time Turner attended, where he received a traditional classical education with emphasis upon Greek. He proceeded to university and graduated from King's College of the University of London, where the major figure in New Testament studies was Professor R. V. G. Tasker, who, among other things, edited the Greek text used in the New English Bible, a translation project in which Turner was later involved (see below). Turner earned all three of his university degrees through the University of London, including the BD, the MTh, and the

---

[1] There is very little readily available biographical information on Nigel Turner. I have pieced together this account on the basis of bits and pieces gathered here and there, aided by the kind and generous efforts of a number of my students and colleagues, including especially my longtime friend Robert Morgan of Oxford, who gathered information from a number of different editions of *Crockford's Clerical Directory* (apparently not always consistent in their information on Turner); Professor Edward Adams of King's College London, who pursued enquiries for me; and correspondence with Mary Turner, Nigel Turner's widow, and their daughter, Elisabeth Sheehan, who provided many further details. I have also used a number of websites for factual information.

PhD, the last of which he received in 1953 while serving as a vicar. During his time at King's, Turner received a number of academic prizes. These include the Senior Wordsworth Prize for Latin in 1935 (Turner put his ability as a Latinist to good use later in his career in his work on Aquila), the Archbishop Robertson Prize in 1936 as the best second-year student, and the Plumptre Prize in 1938 for writing the best theology essay. He became an Associate of King's College in 1937 and, after an initial setback, received his BD in 1939. He then spent some time in Antigua as an assistant to the bishop of Antigua. Early in his academic career, Turner seems to have had an interest in eschatology, which was evidenced in an essay he apparently wrote on eschatology in the Old Testament.[2] His interest in eschatology was not strong throughout his career, with evidence in his further writings being relatively sparse.

Turner was educated for the Anglican ministry at Queen's College, an Anglican theological college in Birmingham, in 1938–9. He served several curacies before becoming a priest, and served in a variety of locations in the south of England especially during the war years. His younger brother, George, was a pilot during the Second World War and tragically died in a flying accident. Turner himself served as an air-raid warden during the war. His curacies during this time include Birmingham from 1939–42, Erdington (a suburb of Birmingham and also in the Birmingham diocese) from 1942–4, Aldridge (another suburb of Birmingham, but in the Litchfield diocese) from 1944–9, and Battle Abbey in East Sussex from 1949–51, near where the

---

[2] Nigel Turner, "Eschatology in the Old Testament Literature" (1936). I secured this reference from the online catalog of the library of Nigel Turner, cataloged by author, housed in the C. S. Lewis Institute Library (to which Turner's library was donated by his widow). However, the essay now appears to be missing, so at this point nothing further can be verified (e.g., whether this is the essay for which he was awarded the Plumptre Prize), and it does not appear to have been actively followed as a major interest later in his career. I wish to thank Tyson Rallens, the current caretaker of The Kilns, for helping try to locate the essay.

Battle of Hastings was fought in 1066, where Turner began his active scholarly career. Turner served as a vicar in the village of Diseworth, near Derby in Leicestershire, from 1951–8. During this time, he received his PhD for a thesis entitled "The *Testament of Abraham*: A Study of the Original Language, Place of Origin, Authorship, and Relevance" and began very actively publishing on the topic of the Greek language, the topic that would come to define his scholarly career. He then became a rector in Milton in Cambridgeshire, where he served for only two years, from 1958–60, during which time he was invited to preach a University Sermon in Cambridge in 1959. Turner left parish ministry in 1960 and settled in the ancient market town of Hitchen in Hertfordshire, where he remained until 1972. This was an important time for his scholarly career, as he published two of his major books on Greek language during this period and no doubt did work on his third. In 1972, Turner took up his only regular academic appointment, attaining the position of Reader in Theology at the University of Rhodesia in Salisbury, now the University of Zimbabwe,[3] where he remained until 1975, when he returned to England after suffering a slight stroke. He published several works that reflect his time in Africa. At that point, Turner returned to Britain and settled in Ely in Cambridgeshire, where he finished his third and fourth books on Greek and eventually died on May 21, 1990, leaving his widow, Mary, and two children, Elisabeth and Paul (to whom he dedicated the syntax volume). He is buried in the Ely Cathedral Cemetery, where his headstone succinctly describes him as both priest and scholar. This is a very apt description if it is taken in a chronological sense, as he served as a priest in the first half of his

---

[3] The University of Rhodesia was founded in 1955, and at first had an affiliation with the University of London. After the country gained independence, the University of Rhodesia became the University of Zimbabwe in 1980.

career and then devoted the second half to the publication of his major works of scholarship, especially on the Greek of the New Testament.

Turner's biblical scholarship follows two tracks, although one of the tracks is far more developed than the other. These two tracks encompass scholarship in biblical studies apart from Greek and, more importantly, scholarship in New Testament Greek. He published a significant amount of material in each area, but the second area dominated his attention throughout his scholarly career.

The area of biblical studies apart from Greek includes a number of different types of scholarly research. I enumerate three. The only major work that Turner wrote that was greatly removed from biblical topics was his book *The Art of the Greek Orthodox Church*, written while he was lecturing in Rhodesia.[4] At various points some of his extra-biblical scholarship overlaps or intersects with his Greek scholarship, but there are perhaps some hints at other areas of interest throughout his career. The first of these areas of scholarship, already mentioned, is his possible interest in eschatology and with it the book of Revelation. After his early thesis, if that is what it is, he also wrote the commentary on the book of Revelation for the revised *Peake's Commentary on the Bible*.[5] A second area of interest is some theological topics, such as the background to the use of Logos in John's Gospel being both Philonic and biblical, or the attitude of the church to the state within the New Testament where Turner sees Revelation as

---

[4] Nigel Turner, *The Art of the Greek Orthodox Church: A Study in Stylization* (University of Rhodesia Series in Humanities; Salisbury, Rhodesia: University of Rhodesia, 1976).

[5] Nigel Turner, "Revelation," in Matthew Black and H. H. Rowley (eds.), *Peake's Commentary on the Bible* (London: Thomas Nelson, 1962), pp. 1043–61.

not as stridently anti-state as others have argued.⁶ The third area is Turner's interest simply in various topics, people, and subjects within New Testament studies, what one might be tempted to call social and historical backgrounds. This interest is evidenced in the large number of dictionary entries that Turner wrote, particularly in *The Interpreter's Bible Dictionary*, on a wide variety of topics, ranging from Absalom to Trypho.⁷

Despite these interests, Turner directed his scholarship primarily toward describing the Greek of the New Testament and its relationship to other dialects of Greek used during the classical, Hellenistic, and Roman periods. Not only did Turner write four major works on Greek grammar and lexicography (see below for discussion),⁸ but he also published a number of other contributions in support of his distinctive hypothesis that the Greek of the New Testament constituted a definable form of Jewish or Biblical Greek.⁹ It is worth noting, however, that Turner's involvement in Moulton's *A Grammar of New Testament Greek* probably came about at least to some extent because of his interest and ability in Bible translation, an interest that he maintained throughout his scholarly career. Turner was involved in two major Bible translation projects, one organized by the British and Foreign Bible Society begun in 1954 and finally produced in 1973

---

6   Nigel Turner, "St. John's Eternal Word," *Evangelical Quarterly* 22 (1950), pp. 243–8; Turner, "The Church's Attitude to the State in the New Testament," *Journal of Theology for Southern Africa* 2 (1973), pp. 41–52, the latter a scholarly piece published while he was in Rhodesia.

7   See the bibliography at the end for the large number of dictionary and related entries.

8   Nigel Turner, *Syntax*, Volume 3 of *A Grammar of New Testament Greek* by James Hope Moulton (Edinburgh: T&T Clark, 1963); Turner, *Grammatical Insights into the New Testament* (Edinburgh: T&T Clark, 1965); Turner, *Style*, Volume 4 of *A Grammar of New Testament Greek* by James Hope Moulton (Edinburgh: T&T Clark, 1976); and Turner, *Christian Words* (Edinburgh: T&T Clark, 1980).

9   See also, e.g., Nigel Turner, "The Preposition *en* in the New Testament," *Bible Translator* 10.3 (July 1959), pp. 113–20; and Turner, "Modern Issues in Biblical Studies: Philology in New Testament Studies," *Expository Times* 71 (1960), pp. 104–7.

as *The Translator's New Testament*,[10] and the other the revision of the Revised Version that resulted in the New English Bible (see below). Although many of Turner's articles are only indirectly concerned with translation, a number of them are specifically addressed to it, especially the translation of the Hebrew Bible into Greek, the so-called Old Greek or Septuagint. As a result, Turner wrote an article on the Greek translators of the book of Ezekiel and was responsible for revising the edition by Joseph Reider of the index to Aquila's translation of the Greek Old Testament (which also demanded his ability in Latin).[11] However, Turner's interest in translation goes far beyond his interest in the Septuagint.

Turner's interest in translation is directly related to his view of the Greek of the New Testament as the special dialect of Greek of the early Christians. In reaction to the hypothesis of G. Adolf Deissmann, Albert Thumb, and Moulton regarding the Greek of the New Testament being koine or common Greek,[12] a number

---

[10] *The Translator's New Testament* (London: British and Foreign Bible Society, 1973).
[11] Nigel Turner, "The Greek Translators of Ezekiel," *Journal of Theological Studies* n.s. 7 (1956), pp. 12–24; Joseph Reider, *An Index to Aquila: Greek-Hebrew, Hebrew-Greek, Latin-Hebrew, with the Syriac and Armenian Evidence* (completed and revised by Nigel Turner; Supplements to Vetus Testamentum 12; Leiden: Brill, 1966).
[12] This position is represented in such works as G. Adolf Deissmann, *Bible Studies: Contributions Chiefly from Papyri and Inscriptions to the History of the Language, the Literature, and the Religion of Hellenistic Judaism and Primitive Christianity* (trans. Alexander Grieve; Edinburgh: T&T Clark, 1901); Deissmann, *Light from the Ancient East: The New Testament Illustrated by Recently Discovered Texts of the Graeco-Roman World* (trans. Lionel R. M. Strachan; London: Hodder and Stoughton, 1910); Albert Thumb, *Die Griechische Sprache im Zeitalter des Hellenismus: Beiträge zur Geschichte und Beurteilung der KOINE* (Strassburg: Karl J. Trübner, 1901); and James Hope Moulton, *Prolegomena*, Volume 1 of *A Grammar of New Testament Greek* (Edinburgh: T&T Clark, 1906; 2nd ed., 1906; 3rd ed., 1908). For a discussion of this viewpoint, as well as the other viewpoints referred to in the discussion that follows, in conjunction with representative essays by the various proponents, see Stanley E. Porter, "Introduction: The Greek of the New Testament as a Disputed Area of Research," in Porter (ed.), *The Language of the New Testament: Classic Essays* (Sheffield: Sheffield Academic, 1991), pp. 11–38. See also the introduction to the respective volumes, "James Hope Moulton and Koine Greek: An Introduction to Moulton's *Prolegomena*" and "James Hope Moulton and Wilbert Francis Howard and Greek Phonology and Morphology: An Introduction to Moulton and Howard's *Accidence and Word-Formation*."

of scholars have argued for a Semitic substrate hypothesis as a means of accounting for the Greek of the New Testament. These scholars argue that a Semitic substrate, either Hebrew or Aramaic, underlies various books of the New Testament. One can account for Semitic language influence and interference on the basis that the Greek of the New Testament reflects some level of translation of these underlying Semitic sources. Thus, there was earlier serious scholarly discussion of whether an Aramaic Gospel underlay Mark's Gospel or whether Matthew's Gospel was originally written in Hebrew or whether John's Gospel was a translation of a Semitic Gospel, and similar theories. In their more extreme forms, these theories were held by such scholars as the Yale Semiticist Charles Cutler Torrey, the Irish clergyman R. H. Charles, and the Oxford professor C. F. Burney. Torrey argued in a book entitled *Our Translated Gospels* that all four of the Gospels were translations out of Aramaic. He also argued in his *The Composition and Date of Acts* that Acts 1–15 was translated from an Aramaic source, and in *The Apocalypse of John* that it too was translated from an Aramaic original.[13] Charles in his work on the book of Revelation accounted for the well-known grammatical inconcinnities on the basis that the author thought in Hebrew while writing in Greek.[14] Burney argued for an Aramaic source for John's Gospel.[15]

---

[13] Charles Cutler Torrey, *The Composition and Date of Acts* (Harvard Theological Studies 1; Cambridge, MA: Harvard University Press, 1916); Torrey, *The Four Gospels: A New Translation* (London: Hodder and Stoughton, 1933); and Torrey, *The Apocalypse of John* (New Haven: Yale University Press, 1958).

[14] R. H. Charles, *Studies in the Apocalypse* (Edinburgh: T&T Clark, 1913), 79–102; Charles, *A Critical and Exegetical Commentary on the Revelation of St. John* (2 vols.; International Critical Commentary; Edinburgh: T&T Clark, 1920).

[15] C. F. Burney, *The Aramaic Origin of the Fourth Gospel* (Oxford: Clarendon, 1922). See also Burney, *The Poetry of Our Lord* (Oxford: Clarendon, 1925). Others to hold to similar positions were such scholars as J. A. Montgomery, *The Origin of the Gospel According to St. John* (Philadelphia, PA: John C. Winston, 1923); Klaus Beyer, *Semitische Syntax im Neuen Testament*, I (Göttingen: Vandenhoeck &

INTRODUCTION: SYNTAX xvii

A more nuanced position is taken by other, and often later, scholars such as Gustaf Dalman, Matthew Black, and Max Wilcox who argue that, while Semitic and especially Aramaic sources underlie the Gospels and especially the words of Jesus, the Gospels and Acts are not translations of these sources.[16] They nevertheless still believe that the Greek of the New Testament directly reflects various Semitic sources, sometimes to a high degree, on the basis of an underlying Semitic substrate. Turner, however, takes a view that is in a number of important ways distinct from the Semitic substrate hypothesis, even if, when examined, he too believes that the Greek in the New Testament reflects Semitic influence not because of the translation process but because of the creation of a unique Jewish and Christian dialect. Turner argues that the Greek of the New Testament does not reflect translation of underlying Semitic sources but was written in a form of Greek that encompassed Semitic influence so as to become a unified dialect of Semitic Greek used by

---

Ruprecht, 1962); Frans Zimmermann, *The Aramaic Origin of the Four Gospels* (New York: KTAV, 1979); Steven Thompson, *The Apocalypse and Semitic Syntax* (Cambridge: Cambridge University Press, 1985); Günther Schwarz, *"Und Jesu Sprach": Untersuchungen zur aramäischen Urgestalt der Worte Jesu* (Stuttgart: Kohlhammer, 1985); George Howard, *The Gospel of Matthew According to a Primitive Hebrew Text* (Macon, GA: Mercer University Press, 1987); and Maurice Casey, *Aramaic Sources of Mark's Gospel* (Cambridge: Cambridge University Press, 1998), among others.

[16] Gustaf Dalman, *The Words of Jesus: Considered in the Light of Post-Biblical Jewish Writings and the Aramaic Language* (trans. D. M. Kay; Edinburgh: T&T Clark, 1909); Dalman, *Jesus-Jeshua: Studies in the Gospels* (trans. Paul P. Levertoff; London: SPCK, 1929); Matthew Black, *An Aramaic Approach to the Gospels and Acts* (Oxford: Clarendon, 1946; 2nd ed., 1954; 3rd ed., 1967); and Max Wilcox, *The Semitisms of Acts* (Oxford: Clarendon, 1965). Others to hold to a similar position were such scholars as Joseph A. Fitzmyer, "The Languages of Palestine in the First Century AD," *Catholic Biblical Quarterly* 32 (1970), pp. 501–31 (and reprinted many times); and Adelbert Denaux, in Albert Hogeterp and Denaux, *Semitisms in Luke's Greek: A Descriptive Analysis of Lexical and Syntactical Domains of Semitic Language Influence in Luke's Gospel* (Wissenschaftliche Untersuchungen zum Neuen Testament 401; Tübingen: Mohr Siebeck, 2018), and, I would dare say, probably the vast majority of New Testament scholars (who, unfortunately, have not fully investigated the issue).

the Jews and early Christians.¹⁷ Hence Turner argues that the characteristics of Biblical Greek are not translationese or simply uneducated use but reflect the actual dialect used by Jews and Christians of the time. He argues this to the point where his position seems at times to hark back to the earlier Holy Ghost Greek hypothesis—that is, that the Greek of the New Testament is a special kind of theologically motivated, even if not divinely inspired, dialect of the language given for unique and even revelatory purposes. Or, to use the language of Black explicitly adopted by Turner, Biblical Greek was "a peculiar language, the language of a peculiar people."¹⁸

There are two important observations to make about Turner's position regarding the Greek of the New Testament, a position that he held almost from the outset of his scholarly publishing career. The first observation is that Turner's position is significantly different from the position of Moulton, whose grammar he completed. I note in the introduction to Volume 2 on *Accidence and Word-Formation* that Moulton perhaps moderated his view of the nature of Greek over the span of time from his *Prolegomena* to his *Accidence and Word-Formation*.¹⁹ However, I also note that he did not depart significantly from his original position

---

[17] Turner's position was held in similar ways by the Princeton Old Testament and Septuagint scholar Henry S. Gehman, "The Hebraic Character of Septuagint Greek," *Vetus Testamentum* 1 (1951), pp. 81–90, among several other articles, and more recently by Georg Walser, *The Greek of the Ancient Synagogue: An Investigation on the Greek of the Septuagint, Pseudepigrapha and the New Testament* (Stockholm: Almqvist & Wicksell, 2001), among others.

[18] Matthew Black, "The Biblical Languages," in Peter R. Ackroyd and C. F. Evans (eds.), *The Cambridge History of the Bible, Volume 1* (Cambridge: Cambridge University Press, 1970), pp. 1–11, quotation p. 111; cf. Nigel Turner, "Biblical Greek: The Peculiar Language of a Peculiar People," in Elizabeth A. Livingstone (ed.), *Studia Evangelica* VII (Berlin: Akademie-Verlag, 1982), pp. 505–12, although he alludes to this position elsewhere.

[19] James Hope Moulton and Wilbert Francis Howard, *Accidence and Word-Formation*, Volume 2 of *A Grammar of New Testament Greek* (3 parts; Edinburgh: T&T Clark, 1919–29 [one-volume edition published subsequently]), pp. 1–22.

regarding the New Testament Greek being koine Greek, even if he admitted Semitic influence especially through the Septuagint. In increasing contrast to Moulton, however, Turner appears to have strengthened his position regarding a Semitized Jewish and Christian Greek dialect over the course of his scholarly career. In his "Preface" to the volume *Style*, Turner notes that the volumes on syntax and style have been completed by a member of a younger generation than Moulton and Howard. "Because of that, and because the enterprise reflects so wide a passage of time, it is inevitable that the viewpoint of the Grammar upon the nature of New Testament Greek is not entirely a unity, and there are traces of the radical development to be expected as the state of these studies has progressed."[20]

Despite this statement, Turner also states that he believes that "despite the passage of time I have found my own views for the most part to be consistent with those of the Grammar's originator even at the distance of seven decades from its inception."[21] Howard and then Turner both seem to treat the Semitic hypothesis as an acceptable explanation of developments in New Testament Greek. This situation may have seemed to be the case at the time of Turner's writing, but already at the time of publication of the volume on style a strong movement back to the earlier koine Greek hypothesis was taking shape in the work of a number of scholars, anticipated by the writings of Joseph Fitzmyer[22] and seen more obviously in publications by more recent scholars such as Lars Rydbeck, Marius Reiser, G. H. R. Horsley, and Stanley Porter, among others, to the point where the koine Greek hypothesis is

---

[20] Turner, *Style*, p. vii.
[21] Ibid.
[22] Fitzmyer, "Languages of Palestine."

once more widely promoted.²³ The major contemporary response has been that a distinction needs to be made on the basis of the linguistic evidence in relation to the language system. Lars Rydbeck argues that the appropriate stratum of language for comparison with the Greek of the New Testament is a mid-level technical language, neither literary nor vulgar. This differentiation was more linguistically generalized by Moisés Silva in terms of *langue* and *parole*, and by Porter in terms of code and text.²⁴ Silva means that the *langue*, koine Greek, remained stable, even if instances of *parole*, or usage, have Semitic features, while Porter distinguishes between language as a shared meaning system or code and instances of this language or texts.

The second observation is to note how Turner outlines his developing position with regard to the nature of Greek.²⁵ Turner began his exploration of the topic with an essay on the question of whether the Gospels were written in Greek or Aramaic. This paper seems to begin from Moulton's position but already with some clear Semitic modifications, while clearly rejecting the translation hypothesis.²⁶ Turner's position is already made stronger in his essay that speaks of the "unique

---

[23] Lars Rydbeck, *Fachprosa, vermeintliche Volkssprache und Neues Testament: Zur Beurteilung der sprachlichen Niveauunterschiede im nachklassischen Griechisch* (Uppsala: n.p., 1967); Marius Reiser, *Syntax und Stil des Markusevangeliums im Licht der hellenistischen Volksliteratur* (Wissenschaftliche Untersuchungen zum Neuen Testament 2/11; Tübingen: Mohr Siebeck, 1984); G. H. R. Horsley, *New Documents Illustrating Early Christianity*, Volume 5: *Linguistic Essays* (Sydney: Ancient History Documentary Research Centre, Macquarie University, 1989), esp. pp. 5–40, a chapter entitled "The Fiction of 'Jewish Greek'"; and Stanley E. Porter, *Verbal Aspect in the Greek of the New Testament with Reference to Tense and Mood* (Studies in Biblical Greek 1; New York: Peter Lang, 1989), pp. 141–56.
[24] Moisés Silva, "Bilingualism and the Character of Palestinian Greek," *Biblica* 61 (1980), pp. 198–219; Porter, *Verbal Aspect*, pp. 151–2.
[25] An exception to this developing theory is Nigel Turner, "The Literary Character of New Testament Greek," *New Testament Studies* 20 (1974), pp. 107–14, where he focuses upon the influence of literary Greek.
[26] Nigel Turner, "Were the Gospels Written in Greek or Aramaic?," *Evangelical Quarterly* 21 (1949), pp. 42–8.

character" of Biblical Greek.[27] His article on the *Testament of Abraham*, pursuing some of the research for his doctorate, is a description of the Semitic Greek of that text as an example that extends beyond the Bible.[28] His essay on Luke 1 and 2 in relation to sources and Luke–Acts argues that those two chapters drew more heavily upon Semitized Greek than the rest of Luke–Acts, rather than being a translation as some have posited.[29] Turner's essay in *Peake's Commentary on the Bible* replaced the previous essay in the first edition by Moulton and then supplemented by Howard, and reflects Turner's different perspective, more in line with Black's.[30] The volume on *Syntax* provides a short, clear summary of Turner's position regarding Greek, a position that is also briefly summarized in the volume on *Style* (see summaries below). The final chapter in Turner's *Grammatical Insights into the New Testament* is "The Language of Jesus and His Disciples." Turner acknowledges but rejects the Semitic source hypotheses for a Greek hypothesis, but a Greek that is a "hybrid" Jewish-Christian Greek, not a temporary phenomenon but the normal language used by Jesus and many others.[31] In an essay that anticipated his *Christian Words*, Turner looks to various Jewish and Christian influences on the vocabulary of the New Testament.[32] Even the characteristics of Luke's so-called literary

---

[27] Nigel Turner, "The Unique Character of Biblical Greek," *Vetus Testamentum* 5 (1955), pp. 208–13.
[28] Nigel Turner, "The 'Testament of Abraham': Problems in Biblical Greek," *New Testament Studies* 1 (1955), pp. 219–23.
[29] Nigel Turner, "The Relation of Luke I and II to Hebraic Sources and to the Rest of Luke–Acts," *New Testament Studies* 2 (1955), pp. 100–9.
[30] Nigel Turner, "The Language of the New Testament," in Matthew Black and H. H. Rowley (eds.), *Peake's Commentary on the Bible* (London: Thomas Nelson, 1962), pp. 659–62.
[31] Turner, *Grammatical Insights*, pp. 174–88.
[32] Nigel Turner, "Jewish and Christian Influence on New Testament Vocabulary," *Novum Testamentum* 16 (1974), pp. 149–60.

style show the influence of various Semitisms.³³ In development of his earlier essay, Turner expands his view that both Judaism, especially through the Septuagint, and Christianity had an influence on New Testament vocabulary, giving words new and different meanings, although he seems to take the position to new lengths in his *Christian Words* (see summary below). In his final published statement, Turner responds to his critics and points to the characteristics of the Greek of the New Testament as a Semitized Greek characteristic of the early Christians.³⁴ Turner clearly represents a particular position in the study of the Greek of the New Testament, one that he had been developing since his earliest publication in 1949.

In the "Preface" to *Syntax*, Turner notes how he came to be involved in Moulton's *A Grammar of New Testament Greek*. To recapitulate the account offered in greater length in the introductions to the first two reprinted volumes of Moulton's grammar, Moulton himself was responsible for publishing the first volume, *Prolegomena*, in 1906, with two further editions soon to follow. In this grammar, Moulton, rather than continuing the grammatical thought of Georg Winer's rationalist approach or even the Semitized view of Greek that he himself had held earlier, argues that the Greek of the New Testament represents the koine or common vernacular found in the recently discovered Greek documentary papyri. Moulton began on the second volume in his grammar, *Accidence and Word-Formation*, and wrote roughly three-fourths of it before undertaking a missionary and teaching

---

³³ Nigel Turner, "The Quality of the Greek of Luke–Acts," in J. K. Elliott (ed.), *Studies in New Testament Language and Text: Essays in Honour of George D. Kilpatrick* (Supplements to Novum Testamentum 44; Leiden: Brill, 1976), pp. 387–400.
³⁴ Turner, "Biblical Greek," pp. 505–12. This paper does not seem to take his view as far as the opinion expressed in *Christian Words*, but this paper was written in 1973 even though not published until 1982.

INTRODUCTION: SYNTAX   xxiii

trip to India during the Great War. He unfortunately was killed on his return trip and completion of the volume was turned over to one of his accomplished students, Wilbert Francis Howard. Howard completed Moulton's preface, a major chapter in part three on suffixation, and added a very important appendix on Semitisms in the New Testament that Moulton had originally intended to coauthor with a Semiticist colleague. Howard wrote this appendix to respect Moulton's original intention to write such an appendix in response to criticisms of his position, even though his position did not change materially but had developed by recognizing more fully the possibility of some Semitisms used by some writers of the New Testament especially under Septuagintal influence. There remains some question about what Moulton himself would have written in such an appendix on the basis of his remaining writings, but Howard appears to have pushed Moulton and his position along a trajectory that was in some ways more compatible with a Semitic influence hypothesis regarding the nature of New Testament Greek. Howard was also commissioned to write the third and at that time final volume of the grammar on syntax. However, Howard died in 1952 before writing that volume.

The task of completing Moulton's grammar then fell to Henry George Meecham. Meecham, who had taught at the Methodist Hartley Victoria College since 1930[35] and lectured in New Testament in the University of Manchester, was himself a

---

[35] Victoria College was founded in 1881 as a Primitive Methodist institution and renamed Hartley Victoria College in 1934, and finally closed in 2015. A. S. Peake, who was also at the University of Manchester and the first holder of the position of Rylands Professor of Biblical Exegesis, was at this institution. See John James William Edmondson, "The Doctrines of Hell and Judgment and the Need for Personal Conversion as an Index to the Development of Liberal Theology within the Theological Colleges of the Methodist Church in England from 1907 to 1932" (MA thesis, University of Durham, 1990), pp. 32–68.

former student of Moulton (Meecham received his MA, BD, PhD, and DD from Manchester) who had revised the fifth editions of Moulton's introduction to and reader in New Testament Greek[36] and had himself published a number of scholarly works in the area of Greek language and literature.[37] Meecham agreed to take on the task of writing the third volume if he were to have an assistant.[38] It appears that, at the time, G. D. Kilpatrick, Dean Ireland's Professor of the Exegesis of Holy Scripture at Oxford University, was on the New Testament Committee for the New English Bible, and this may have provided the link by which he knew both Meecham and Turner, who at various times worked on the translation (as did Tasker, with whom Turner must have studied in London).[39] At this time in the early 1950s, Turner had not yet published very many scholarly articles (to say nothing of books), even though the trajectory of his view of Biblical Greek was already emerging in those publications. In any case, Kilpatrick suggested Turner for the task of assistant to Meecham, and Turner had successfully compiled what he calls a "provisional bibliography" when in 1955 Meecham too died.[40] The publishers, who by this time must have been wondering whether anyone

---

[36] James Hope Moulton, *An Introduction to the Study of New Testament Greek* (London: Epworth, 5th ed., 1955); Moulton, *A First Reader in New Testament Greek* (London: Epworth, 5th ed., 1955).

[37] Henry G. Meecham, *Light from Ancient Letters: Private Correspondence in the Non-Literary Papyri of Oxyrhynchus of the First Four Centuries, and Its Bearing on New Testament Language and Thought* (London: George Allen and Unwin, 1923); Meecham, *The Oldest Version of the Bible: "Aristeas" on Its Traditional Origin. A Study in Early Apologetic with Translation and Appendices* (London: Holborn, 1932) (dedicated to his teachers, Peake and Moulton, and with thanks to Howard); Meecham, *The Letter of Aristeas: A Linguistic Study with Special Reference to the Greek Bible* (Manchester: Manchester University Press, 1935); and Meecham, *The Epistle to Diognetus: The Greek Text with Introduction and Notes* (Manchester: Manchester University Press, 1949).

[38] See Turner, *Syntax*, p. v.

[39] Geoffrey Hunt, *About the New English Bible* (Oxford: Oxford University Press; Cambridge: Cambridge University Press, 1970), pp. 80, 81.

[40] Turner, *Syntax*, p. v.

would live long enough to complete Moulton's grammar, commissioned Turner with the completion of the third volume, which he did, before suggesting that a fourth volume on style be included. In the "Preface" to the fourth volume, Turner notes that Moulton himself, although not specifically envisioning such a fourth volume, had in fact anticipated it in his introduction to *Accidence and Word-Formation*, in which he began to distinguish the linguistic usage of the different biblical writers (even if Howard completed this analysis drawing on other works by Moulton and others).[41] Moulton indicated his interest in style not only in that introduction but also in his major article on "New Testament Greek in the Light of Modern Discovery,"[42] in which he engaged in a much fuller exposition of what might well be called the stylistic characteristics of the various authors, as well as possibly other places in his works where he singles out the characteristics of individual New Testament writers. In any case, in 1963 Turner published the third volume on *Syntax*, followed by publication of *Style* in 1976.

Before turning to the individual grammatical volume with which we are concerned here, *Syntax*, we should note the other major Greek grammatical and lexicographical publications by Turner. Apart from the works on related biblical topics already noted above, Turner's major publications are directly concerned with the Greek of the New Testament. In the course of his scholarly career, he published four major volumes on Greek grammar and lexicography in its various parts.

---

[41] Turner, *Style*, p. vii.
[42] James Hope Moulton, "New Testament Greek in the Light of Modern Discovery," in Henry Barclay Swete (ed.), *Essays on Some Biblical Questions of the Day by Members of the University of Cambridge* (London: Macmillan, 1909), pp. 461–506.

The first of these volumes is the volume on syntax, which was his first major book publication. This volume took Turner just under ten years to complete, from the time he joined the writing project as an assistant to Meecham until it was published in 1963. A summary and discussion of the volume is found in the next section of this essay, after completing the treatment of Turner's other major scholarly works.

Turner's second scholarly volume on matters of Greek was entitled *Grammatical Insights into the New Testament*, published in 1965, only two years after *Syntax* and clearly benefiting from the research that he had completed on the previous volume. Turner frames this second volume as designed both for the interested person without technical competence in Greek (hence he uses transliteration as a means of ostensive accommodation) and for the specialist. His overriding purpose in the volume is to address the relevance and importance of matters of Greek grammar, including finer points of syntax, especially as they may inform Biblical Theology. Turner claims to share the perspective of James Barr that theology does not occur at the level of the word but at the level of the sentence,[43] with Turner emphasizing that the Semitic influence upon the use of Greek by the early Christian authors is even greater in syntax than in the language's lexicon. Turner makes clear that he is not advocating either a fundamentalist or neo-fundamentalist approach and he is certainly not advocating for an approach that takes an approximate view of the text through relying upon translation. Turner cites an appropriate quotation from the Manchester Old Testament scholar H. H. Rowley made already in 1963 concerning the importance of knowledge of the

---

[43] See James Barr, *The Semantics of Biblical Language* (Oxford: Oxford University Press, 1961), p. 233.

Greek or Hebrew language for study of the Bible: "One who made it his life's work to interpret French literature, but who could only read it in an English translation, would not be taken seriously; yet it is remarkable how many ministers of religion week by week expound a literature that they are unable to read save in translation!"[44] In a statement as timely in 1960 as it would be today, Turner cites R. A. Ward as stating that "he has been told by ministers that there is no need to 'waste time on Greek. It is all in the commentaries.'"[45] Turner's book is an attempt to show the value of Greek grammatical study by offering insights into the text by means of sometimes focused and specific and other times more general grammatical observations.

Turner includes forty-six relatively short studies, most of them subdivided into a number of even smaller studies, under six major chapter headings, before concluding with a chapter on "The Language of Jesus and His Disciples." It is impossible here to summarize even a small number of these short articles, although virtually all of them contain matters of interest to the Greek student. Some of the positions advocated by Turner have become well known, while others arguably merit further consideration than they have received to date. The first section is on what he calls the "grammar of God." In this chapter, with three studies included on "God," "Jesus is God," and "A holy spirit and the Holy Ghost," Turner discusses a variety of grammatical constructions that have

---

[44] H. H. Rowley, "Recent Foreign Theology," *Expository Times* 74 (September 1963), p. 383, cited in Turner, *Grammatical Insights*, p. 3.

[45] R. A. Ward, "The Preacher's Use of the Aorist," *Expository Times* 71 (June 1960), pp. 267–70, here p. 267, cited in Turner, *Grammatical Insights*, p. 3. Ward taught at Wycliffe College in Toronto, Ontario, Canada. One might, in this day and age, indeed think that "it is all in commentaries" on the basis of their size and attempt to be comprehensive in scope in virtually all regards (apart possibly from Greek, one notes), but we know from simple examination of them that this is hardly the case.

implications for understanding God, many of them related to the use of the article.[46] He directly responds to modern theology as represented by the biblically conservative but theologically liberal scholar J. A. T. Robinson[47] by showing how the use of the Greek article is important for establishing the subject and predicate of a Greek clause, all in the service of clear theology. In a discussion of Jesus as God, Turner sees Greek grammar supporting such a notion in several key passages (although he does not refer to Granville Sharp). Chapter two concerns Jesus of Nazareth. The largest chapter, this one includes fifteen subordinate studies. The first is on the census in Luke 2, where Turner argues that the word often translated "first" should be translated "before," indicating that the Lukan census is the one before Quirinius's in AD 6. This is an argument that merits further consideration. Turner argues for a reformulation of Mark 1:1 and 4 by placing vv. 2–3 in parenthesis. He also argues for a reformulation of Mark 1:9 as "Jesus of Nazareth in Galilee came." Turner claims that John 2:4 should be "Madam, leave this to me" on the basis of Semitic influence and implication. His survey of the meaning of the ἵνα clause in Mark 4:12 is insightful, as is his conclusion regarding human deliberation. He argues for the kingdom of God being a human condition in Luke 17:21, and for "he went outside" for the verb ἐπιβαλών in Mark 14:72, based on the parallel in Matthew. Jesus may not have given a clear "yes" to the question of his identity at his trial, thus maintaining the messianic secret despite his personal beliefs (Matt 26:64). Turner argues for a past and

---

[46] I note that many times, although not always, Turner refers to the "definite article" in *Grammatical Insights*, whereas in *Syntax* he usually refers simply to the "article." One wonders if this is inadvertent, or whether there is some theological significance he is attaching to the terminology in *Grammatical Insights*.

[47] John A. T. Robinson, *Honest to God* (London: SCM, 1963).

present understanding of the perfect in Matt 16:19 as a means of alleviating human responsibility.

Chapter three contains five shorter studies. The first concerns Acts 22:3 and 26:4, where Turner believes they both point to Tarsus as the place of Paul's upbringing, not Jerusalem. He is probably correct on this point. Turner also takes the reference to "I" in Romans 7 and elsewhere as a rhetorical device. He believes that a distinction can be made regarding "hearing" on the basis of case in Acts 9:4. He further argues that Paul's purpose for going to Rome was to preach his own point of view (Rom 1:15). Turner even entertains the idea that Gal 6:11 in context implies that Paul had literally rather than metaphorically been crucified. Chapter four on Paul's teaching contains twelve shorter studies. He sees Paul as arguing for reconciliation or freedom from an unbelieving spouse in 1 Cor 7:10–16, and 1 Cor 7:21 indicating a slave should take the opportunity to be free. Turner argues for both objective and subjective genitive in "faith of God." He also argues for Pauline soteriology being corporate, and so the conjunction in Rom 5:12 is "in" or "by whom," not "because." He further argues for a mystical use of the preposition ἐν. 2 Corinthians 5, Turner argues, is about being unclothed in an intermediate state. Chapter five has six subunits on John. Turner argues here that in John 1:40 the Other Disciple is John the son of Zebedee, the traditionally ascribed author of the Gospel. As for John 1:3–4, Turner follows the early church fathers in rendering it "as to that which has been made, he was its life," interpreting the construction as an independent nominative. "Born of bloods" in John 1:13 refers to a joint contribution to birth, either of both male and female or of human and spiritual. John 3:16 using the indicative rather than the infinitive with ὥστε is about the incarnation rather than about God's love. Turner argues for an imperatival use of ἵνα in

John's Gospel (e.g., in John 9:3). The contrast in 1 John 2:1 and 3:9, based upon tense-forms, is between committing a sin and becoming a sinner. Chapter six has five subsections on other New Testament writers. However, Turner returns to Acts 4:2 to find unity in use of the preposition ἐν. He also examines two instances from Revelation, three from James, several from 1 Peter, and one from Hebrews. Some of Turner's explanations are concerned with lexical items, some with entire clauses, some with verbal aspect, and some with the rendering of idioms, and a number with other grammatical issues. Sometimes he argues for Markan parenthesis, and sometimes he is not certain of the linguistic significance, even if he observes the usage, as in the rendering of the perfect imperative in Mark 4:39.

Turner concludes his grammatical insights with his essay on the language of Jesus and his disciples, in which he argues that the disciples certainly spoke Aramaic but they also spoke and wrote in a dialect of Greek with sufficient Semitic influence, especially from the Septuagint, to be called Jewish Greek. As a result, Jesus may have spoken Greek in such situations as his conversation with the Syro-phoenician woman, his encounter with the Roman centurion, and his trial before Pilate. Rather than this being a sign of bilingualism or only a temporary linguistic situation, Turner argues for this usage as what he calls "the normal language of Jesus, at least in Galilee—rather a separate dialect of Greek than a form of the Koine, and distinguishable as something parallel to classical, Hellenistic, Koine and Imperial Greek."[48] He is skeptical about how much Hebrew Jesus would have known and used. Turner is more inclined to accept the view of T. K. Abbott from 1891 that Greek was Jesus's primary language, based upon the

---

[48] Turner, *Grammatical Insights*, p. 183.

argument that selective and limited instances of use of Aramaic in Mark's Gospel probably reflect those occasions when Jesus used Aramaic, possibly with those who only spoke Aramaic.[49] The fact that this Greek has resemblances to the documentary papyri may be because the papyri themselves reflect Semitic influence. However, none of the papyri have the sustained style of usage found in the Greek of the New Testament. This language has its own linguistic unity and consistency and character whose effect is "to evoke a sense of the holy and to point the reader beyond," with the book of Revelation reflecting this "hieratic tongue" most sublimely.[50] *Grammatical Insights* draws upon examples from the Greek New Testament informed throughout by Turner's findings in his *Syntax*, which relies upon his theory of Jewish Greek used by early Christians, a position summarized in his final essay in the volume. This volume is worth revisiting, whether one agrees with Turner's conclusions or not, to benefit from his provocative analyses.

In his *Style*, Turner produced the fourth and final volume in Moulton's *A Grammar of New Testament Greek*. This volume was published in 1976. In the "Preface" to *Style*, Turner recognizes that his perspective is different from that of Moulton and even Howard, and hence does not represent a unified position on the nature of New Testament Greek within the set of grammar volumes.[51] However, as mentioned above, Turner rightly notes that Moulton did in some ways envision not just a third volume on syntax, which he himself had originally intended to write, but also a fourth volume on style. Turner also claims, however,

---

[49] T. K. Abbott, *Essays, Chiefly on the Original Texts of the Old and New Testaments* (London: Longmans, Green, 1891), pp. 129–82, esp. 147–61.
[50] Turner, *Grammatical Insights*, p. 188.
[51] Turner, *Style*, p. vii.

that his views have, despite the passage of seven decades from the origination of the grammar project, been consistent with Moulton's, to the point that Moulton's son, Harold K. Moulton, had approved of the fourth volume on style being included within *A Grammar of New Testament Greek*. Turner does not reconcile these positions.

The first and most important matter for a volume on style is definition of it. For his treatment, Turner begins his "Introduction" with the question regarding the nature of the Greek of the New Testament, that is, regarding the "dialect" of its Greek, and whether that dialect is unified.[52] For Turner, this question is inextricably joined to the question of what he defines as style. He also notes that style is closely related to syntax and admits that some duplication between the two is inevitable. Style, for Turner, "concerns itself with grammatical and other linguistic features which distinguish the work of one author from that of another," that is, he attempts "to isolate comparative tendencies and differing techniques."[53] To this point, style appears to be a reconfiguration of syntax. However, it is more than this. It also involves "wider categories, such as word-order, rhetoric, parallelism and parenthesis."[54] He continues by noting that it also involves "the irregularities in sentence-construction which result from Semitic influence," in order "to investigate the ways in which the dialect or variety of Greek found here is distinctive from the main stream of the language."[55] He believes that there is much evidence of such Semitic influence at every turn, due to the

---

[52] Ibid., p. 1.
[53] Ibid. Turner favorably quotes the definition by K. J. Dover "that style is 'a group of aspects of language,' a contrasting of linguistic facts among various authors" (*Greek Word Order* [Cambridge: Cambridge University Press, 1960], p. 66).
[54] Turner, *Style*, p. 1.
[55] Ibid.

fact that early Christians were probably bilingual with Aramaic and Greek, and possibly Hebrew. Turner recognizes that there is the possibility of confusion over his definition of style, and so he clarifies by noting that, even though each biblical author has a distinct style, "the styles are not so far apart as to impair the inner homogeneity of Biblical Greek," that is, the unity of his Jewish Greek is not compromised by authorial variation.[56] Further, he notes that he rejects the notion of Semitic sources, apart from in rare instances. Turner concludes the introduction with a brief summary of his findings for the New Testament authors.

The rest of the volume on style is organized around thirteen chapters. The first concerns sources behind the individual Gospels, followed by chapters on the sub-corpora of the New Testament: Mark, Matthew, Luke–Acts, John, Paul, the Pastoral Epistles, Hebrews, James, 1 Peter, the Johannine letters, Jude and 2 Peter, and Revelation. The first chapter, on sources for the Gospels, constitutes in many ways a defense of the author's Jewish Greek hypothesis. Turner first gives credence to various circumscribed theories arguing for written Semitic sources behind various parts of the New Testament (but dismissing those that claim this for the entire New Testament), to the point that he accepts a multilingual, possibly even a trilingual, linguistic environment, certainly with Aramaic among the Jews of Palestine, with Greek at least for trade with Gentiles, and possibly with Hebrew being used in the time of Jesus. Turner moves from this to his Jewish Greek hypothesis: "Since the quality of New Testament Greek is decidedly Semitic in varying degrees, there may well have been a spoken language in common use among these trilingual Jews which would render superfluous the hypothesis of source-translation as an explanation

---

[56] Ibid., p. 2.

of certain phenomena in New Testament Greek," to the point of suggesting that what he calls "uncommon Greek idioms" are common in Aramaic and Hebrew and indicate "that such a body of idiom, as is exposed everywhere in this volume [*Style*], comprised a distinct dialect or branch of the Koine Greek."[57] He extends his theory further by noting ancient evidence of the use of Greek, indicating that "Greek was a living tongue among first-century Jews even around Jerusalem."[58] This came about as a result of the conquests of Alexander in the fourth century BC including Palestine, with a range of epigraphical and literary evidence in support. "It should not be considered improbable, therefore, that Jesus normally spoke in Greek, albeit a simple Semitic kind of speech."[59] This Semitic Greek was influenced by both Hebrew and Aramaic. Whereas Jesus's language may reflect Aramaic, the evangelists sometimes reflect both. Turner's "Semiticized Biblical Greek" as a unified dialect, he claims, may remove the feeling of certainty sought by some interpreters who wish to go back to original Aramaic sources, but it is what Turner believes is to be found in the New Testament.[60]

In discussing the individual books of the New Testament, Turner often follows a common pattern. That pattern is, usually after a relatively short introductory section, to discuss Aramaisms, Hebraisms, and then Semitisms, before concluding with discussion of features of the sub-corpus. This general pattern is followed, for example, for Mark, Matthew, Luke-Acts, John in a slightly different configuration, James along

---

[57] Ibid., p. 7. Turner claims as his ally in this position Gerhard Mussies, *The Morphology of Koine Greek* (Leiden: Brill, 1971), pp. 96–7.
[58] Turner, *Style*, p. 8.
[59] Ibid.
[60] Ibid., p. 9. He refers in particular to Vincent Taylor, *The Gospel According to St. Mark* (London: Macmillan, 1955), p. 65, as one of those expositors.

with several other prior discussions, the Johannine letters again with several other prior discussions, and Revelation again with several other prior discussions. The treatment of Mark includes an extended discussion of Mark's so-called "mannered style" and Latinisms mostly in Mark. The chapter on Matthew compares the Semitic "quality" of Matthew and Mark, arguing for Matthew's "smoother style" and some distinctive Matthean features. Discussion of Luke–Acts includes treatment of Lukan sources, literary features, a section on Semitisms where Luke is least likely to have originated with sources, and a final section on Christian elements of Lukan style (see Turner's subsequent book on this topic, *Christian Words*, treated below). The study of John includes discussion of sources, the influence of the Septuagint, then discussion of types of Semitisms, before concluding with brief discussion of such elements as clause ordering, particles, prepositions, John's constrained vocabulary, and what Turner thinks are needless stylistic varieties. James treats authorship, several form-critical issues, and its close relationship to wisdom literature, before discussing types of Semitisms and concluding with another chapter on Christian style. Treatment of the Johannine letters discusses authorship, unity with the Gospel, and its own integrity, before discussion of Semitic elements. Finally, examination of Revelation begins with sections on sources, grammatical solecisms, redundant expressions, and discussion of various views of the Greek found in Revelation, before discussing types of Semitisms.

By contrast with these chapters, the chapters on the other sub-corpora are arranged individually. The chapter on Paul excludes the Pastoral Epistles and divides the remaining ten letters into four groups, with group two being the four main letters. The character of this group is treated first, seeing them as private letters but with literary features, and then the style of Ephesians is contrasted with this major group. After a chapter on harsh elements in Paul's style, Turner refutes a Hellenistic hypothesis regarding Paul and discusses Paul's Semitic style. He treats Paul's biblically influenced syntax, biblical vocabulary, Biblical Greek word order, and Biblical Greek style, before concluding with discussion of Paul's amanuensis. The Pastoral Epistles are treated separately, beginning with a discussion of what Turner characterizes as an elevated koine style relatively free from Semitic influence, even if it is not elegant Greek. Turner's discussion of Hebrews begins with such literary characteristics as rhythm and other features, but he still discerns an underlying influence of Jewish Greek, which is tied to speculation on authorship by a Jew or Jewish proselyte. Treatment of 1 Peter discusses the issues of integrity, the role of an amanuensis, and some literary features along with significant Semitic characteristics. Finally, the chapter on Jude and 2 Peter includes a section on Jude's literary language and Jewish features, and then 2 Peter's literary features and Jewish character, before comparing the two. One sees a number of common major areas of discussion within Turner's examination of sub-corpora of the New Testament, such as various types of Semitisms, the issue of Christian language including both syntax and vocabulary, and debate over literary features and their relationship to Jewish Greek. Turner also includes a number of other features not always treated in every book, usually in support of his Jewish Greek hypothesis.

Turner's fourth and final book on Greek language, as well as his last written book, is entitled *Christian Words* and was published in 1980. As mentioned above, this volume seems to contain in some ways the most categorical of Turner's statements regarding the Greek of the New Testament. He lays out his viewpoint

INTRODUCTION: SYNTAX   xxxvii

in his "Introduction." Turner begins where he left off with his earlier statement from Barr in *Grammatical Insights* regarding a syntactical over a lexicographical approach to New Testament theology, by claiming that exegesis must take into account the larger context (what he calls the "total environment"): "The paragraph determines the gist of the individual words within it."[61] However, Turner then takes a turn toward endorsing the value of the individual word, especially a word of Holy Scripture. His concern is with Christianity communicating in the context of the contemporary world, a context in which, at least figuratively speaking, there are conflicting biblical and secular languages, and the Christian must be knowledgeable about the language of the Bible. Turner, endorsing an infalliblist view of the Scriptures, argues that those who were inspired to write the Bible were given the task of conveying God's language through the earthly language of Biblical Greek, which we must understand to understand the Bible. "More than fifteen years ago," Turner states, "my studies in syntax led me to ask whether the Biblical language was not unique, and since then investigation of the style of Biblical Greek has confirmed that impression."[62] Turner thus reinforces his view of the unique Greek of the Bible, a position tied very closely to his view of inspiration and coming exceptionally close to advocacy of Holy Ghost Greek. Having dealt with syntax and style, he continues, "Now, in turn, the vocabulary of the same kind of Greek has come under discussion, only to strengthen it."[63] This volume contains examples of what he calls Christian Words. He deals with a surprisingly large number of words within this volume (although it is difficult to specify the number, as his

---

[61] Turner, *Christian Words*, p. viii.
[62] Ibid., p. ix.
[63] Ibid.

headings are English concepts, under which Greek words are listed and treated—the estimate on the back cover is over 450; see below on this mixing of concepts and words).

For this volume, Turner defines his Christian Words under four categories.[64] At the outset, he states, "By 'Christian words' I have in mind Greek terms which so far as I know the first believers devised for themselves."[65] Turner recognizes that recent New Testament Greek lexicography (he cites Walter Bauer, but this actually goes back much further to Deissmann) has reduced the number of such words to a very small number. He offers as examples (in English rendering) newly formed compounds such as "little-faith," "eye-service," "double-minded," and "respect of persons."[66] Turner, however, has three further categories that greatly re-expand the categories. The second category includes words "which acquire a deeper sense and a new consecration within the Christian vocabulary."[67] He includes here the words "truth," "church," "parable," "way," "covenant," "Word," "saint," and "angel." He also includes words heightened in frequency, such as "goodness," "reverence," "evangelist," and "beloved." Finally, he includes words used with a different sense than in their secular sources, such as "Bishop," "Presbyter," "Deacon," "brother," "gospel," "koinōnia," "parousia," and "salvation." The third category is reserved for those words that, "through their Biblical

---

[64] For an assessment of Turner's view of Christian words, see Stanley E. Porter, "Is *dipsuchos* (James 1,8; 4,8) a 'Christian' Word?," *Biblica* 71 (1990), pp. 469–98, which I draw upon here. Some of the questions raised include Turner's disregard of Barr's admonitions regarding biblical theology and lexical fallacies (such as confusion of word and concept, among others), his not noting other linguistic explanations of semantic shifts, and his apparent lack of differentiation between *langue* and *parole* or code and text, along with some questions of whether his analyses of individual words are correct.

[65] Turner, *Christian Words*, p. ix.

[66] Ibid., p. x. Turner concedes Hellenistic influence even upon these words, although he seems to confine it to spelling.

[67] Ibid.

association, had deployed a new level of meaning in addition to their gist hitherto."⁶⁸ Words included by him here include *doxa* adding the meaning of "glory," *homologō* adding "praise," *glōssai* adding "nations," and *diathēkē* adding "covenant." The fourth and final category that Turner posits is where Christian usage has "quite changed their former meaning."⁶⁹ Examples here include "hypocrite" not being used of an actor, "peace" not being used to indicate the ceasing of strife, "tender mercies" not indicating one's intestines, and "parable" not being a maxim.

The question becomes how one determines such meanings. Turner posits several steps. The first, he claims, is to return to the notion of context or "their immediate linguistic environment."⁷⁰ However, this proposal is intriguing, as Turner wishes to call into question, to the point of virtual outright rejection, both Jewish usage contemporary with that of the New Testament and, perhaps more importantly, the evidence from the Greek documentary papyri especially from Egypt. The theological reason for this is clear: God chose not to communicate in this way. In explicitly rejecting Moulton's position on koine Greek,⁷¹ Turner directly states, "God seems not to have used the contemporary vernacular speech [as Moulton believed, and before him J. B. Lightfoot posited]⁷² without revolutionizing it, whether in style (or lack of

---

⁶⁸ Ibid.
⁶⁹ Ibid.
⁷⁰ Ibid.
⁷¹ Ibid., p. xi, quoting and rejecting Moulton, *Prolegomena*, p. 5. One cannot help but notice that this calls into question the continuity that Turner posits between Moulton's and his views of Greek, as stated in Turner, *Style*, p. vii. See further below.
⁷² Turner cites the well-known statement by J. B. Lightfoot, who wrote before the discovery of the Greek documentary papyri in Egypt, that "if we could only recover letters that ordinary people wrote to each other without any thought of being literary, we should have the greatest possible help for the understanding of the language of the New Testament" (J. B. Lightfoot from notes of lectures given in 1863, cited by Moulton, *Prolegomena*, p. 242).

it), whether in sentence construction [as evidenced in Turner's *Syntax* and *Style*], or whether in vocabulary."[73] Turner thus claims that "the early Christians had their own form of speech, and I account it to be as 'sacred' in vocabulary as I found it in syntax and style."[74]

Turner recognizes, however, that the language he is examining is still recognizably Greek, with many words still used with recognizably Greek meanings. This leads him to attempt to tie his view of Greek to the view promoted by Deissmann and Moulton. He states that what he is calling "Christian Greek is essentially the old Attic dialect of the secular language extended and popularized by contact with other dialects and by its employment among the conquered peoples of the Greek and Roman empires."[75] Such a position, as advocated by Deissmann, Moulton, and others who have followed them, is supported by abundant papyrological evidence—although such a position, Turner argues, is also directly linked to a socioeconomic view of early Christianity that links vernacular language with the lowest socioeconomic classes. Rather than looking to such secular origins for the nature of Greek, Turner posits, one must look to the religious environment of early Christianity formed by the Greek Old Testament, which itself preceded the Greek of the New Testament and had already evidenced religious transformation. The basis of determining the Christian vocabulary of the New Testament is not its socioeconomic or any other secular environment but its Christian thought-world that was already thoroughly biblical in its orientation. In the numerous examples that follow, Turner proceeds alphabetically—in English—through the vocabulary of

---

[73] Turner, *Christian Words*, p. xi.
[74] Ibid.
[75] Ibid., p. xii.

the New Testament. Although he often recognizes the meaning of the word in secular Greek, he then proceeds to examine the word as Biblical or Christian Greek.

Syntax

Although Turner's volume on syntax was his first major book publication, it was the third volume in Moulton's *A Grammar of New Testament Greek* and was designed to move beyond the prolegomena, phonology, and morphology of the first two volumes and to provide a syntax of the language. This volume took Turner just under ten years to complete, from the time he joined the writing project as an assistant to Meecham until it was published in 1963. By this time, Turner's perspective on Greek had come to full (although arguably not its most categorical) development, so there are major differences between Moulton and him not just regarding the character of the Greek of the New Testament but also how one attempts to describe it. Turner opens the volume with an "Introduction" that essentially makes two major related points regarding specifically the Greek of the New Testament. The first point is regarding what he calls "the almost complete absence of classical standards in nearly every author" of the New Testament.[76] His second point is that the distinctions made in the classical language have been virtually eliminated in the Greek of the New Testament. Such conclusions raise the legitimate question of how to describe the Greek of the New Testament. Turner contends that "it is not that Biblical Greek has no standards at all, but pains must be taken to discover

---

[76] Turner, *Syntax*, p. 2.

them outside the sphere of classical Greek, even outside secular Greek altogether, although the living Koine must be kept in mind always."[77] Turner clearly positions Biblical Greek, including the Greek of the New Testament, as consciously following patterns that are recognizably Greek but moving beyond or outside of those of the secular Greek of the time. To explore this situation, Turner examines the influence of the Septuagint and of what he calls "Semitic idiom" on New Testament Greek.[78] His research as found in this volume "does suggest that Bibl[ical] Greek is a unique language with a unity and character of its own,"[79] to the point that the Septuagintal influence has resulted in the biblical books having a similar linguistic character different from that of earlier classical or contemporary documentary papyri, with some resemblances of books reflecting clear Semitic sources. After citing a number of examples, Turner closes by claiming not to wish to try to exceed the evidence in his conclusions, although he draws attention to Biblical Greek having a "remarkable unity within itself" that might well have contemporary relevance for those contemplating the question of the existence of a "Holy Ghost language."[80] This almost divine character is apparently to be expected, since both the content and the language of the Scriptures are unique. This introductory statement aptly describes Turner's perspective and places his subsequent description of Greek into an appropriate context.

When he turns to the description itself, Turner follows what he calls "a natural linguistic pattern: the building up of the sentence from its independent elements right to the complicated

---

[77] Ibid., p. 3.
[78] Ibid., p. 4.
[79] Ibid.
[80] Ibid., p. 9.

co-ordinations and subordinations of the period [meaning here compound sentence]."[81] Turner follows this linguistic pattern of building the sentence, a feature not found in many other Greek grammars, except perhaps for Edwin Mayser's grammar of the papyri.[82] However, his abbreviated discussion seems to assume basic knowledge of standard Greek syntax as he discusses how the Greek of the New Testament differs from either classical Greek or other Hellenistic or extra-biblical Greek. The resulting grammar is divided into two portions or what are called books. The first book—the larger of the two—concerns building up the sentence and is what Turner calls analytical. This first book is divided into three parts. Before he begins part one, however, Turner dedicates the first chapter to various types of substitution for nouns, including the article with various other elements. Some may find this initial chapter oddly placed, as none of the linguistic components of the sentence have yet been discussed. Part one in ten chapters addresses words used to build the sentence, with chapters on gender and number of nouns, comparison of adjectives and adverbs, vocatives, substantival use of the article and pronoun, and then six chapters on the verb, with chapters on voice, aspect and tense, the indicative and subjunctive moods, optative mood, infinitive as noun form of the verb, and participle as adjective form of the verb. This chapter treats the major parts of speech as components within the sentence. A number of the categories within this section seem to reflect similar categories as are found in earlier grammars influenced by comparative philology, although at places Turner is cognizant of more recent

---

[81] Ibid., p. 1.
[82] Edwin Mayser, *Grammatik der griechischen Papyri aus der Ptolemäerzeit* (3 vols.; vol. 1.1 rev. Hans Schmoll; Berlin: de Gruyter, 1906–70), volume 2 (in three parts). See Horsley, *New Documents*, pp. 50–2.

twentieth-century developments. This is evident in the chapter on aspect and tense, in which Turner refers to both verbal aspect and lexical aspect. He claims that the Greek tense-forms express both "kind of *action*" or *Aktionsart* and "the state of the subject" or aspect (he uses the German "Aspekt"). However, he states that *Aktionsart* or "kind of action" is used to express the notion that "the tense-stems indicate the point of view from which the action or state is regarded,"[83] apparently conflating the two concepts under the term *Aktionsart*. The subsequent descriptions of use of verbs utilize a mix of both *Aktionsart* and aspect terminology, including "continuous" ("linear") and "instantaneous" ("punctiliar") as the major kinds of action, and traditional categories.[84] However, the voice and mood systems are not linguistically defined, with, instead, categories of usage being exemplified.

Part two in four chapters addresses word-groups used to define nouns or adjectives. Turner apparently divides the major parts of speech into nominals and verbals and in this chapter treats expansion of the nominal category. This includes chapters on adjectival and predicative use of the article (Turner uses the term "definite article" in the title but simply "article" in most other places), and then three relatively short chapters on the attributive relationship, with one chapter each for adjectives and numerals, for pronouns and pronominal adjectives, and for substantives. The third and final part of book one concerns words used to define a verb, with four chapters. This part is concerned with expansion of the verbal category. These chapters include predicative usage,

---

[83] Turner, *Syntax*, p. 59. See note 1, where Turner includes a relatively full bibliography including Jens Holt, *Études d'Aspect* (Copenhagen: Universitetsforlaget I Aarhus, 1943), during Turner's time one of the only and latest books on aspect. The only other was Mártin Sánchez Ruipérez, *Estructura del Sistema de Aspectos y Tiempos del Verbo Griego Antiguo: Análysis Funcional Sincrónico* (Salamanca: Colegio Trilingue de la Universidad, 1954).

[84] Turner, *Syntax*, p. 59 and following.

cases without a preposition in relation to a verb, cases with a preposition in relation to the verb, and negatives. Thus, book one describes words and word-groups and how they are related to each other.

Book two—roughly only one-fifth of the entire volume—is concerned with the complete sentence, what Turner calls synthetic. There are two parts. Part one on the simple sentence contains five short chapters. These chapters focus upon subject and predicate without a subject, subject and predicate without a form of the verb "be," congruence, clausal subordination, and inconsistencies in complex sentences. Part two concerns connections between sentences. These three short chapters address coordinating particles, irregular subordination, and word order. Thus, book two concerns sentences and sentence compounding, along with the semantic relationships between and among these sentences. With that, the volume closes with indexes. Throughout the volume Turner makes clear his perspective on the nature of the Greek of the New Testament, by drawing attention to various Semitic elements at various points.

Greg Horsley has provided the fullest critique of Turner's volume on syntax.[85] This is not the place to engage in a full assessment of Turner's *Syntax* in light of Horsley's criticism, except to note the three major areas of concern for further consideration elsewhere. These three areas mentioned by Horsley are that Turner's volume was already dated at the time of its publication, since it reflected, for the most part, language study of the nineteenth century; that Turner was highly dependent upon Mayser's grammar of the Ptolemaic papyri, not just in his

---

[85] Horsley, *New Documents*, pp. 49–62; cf. pp. 5–40, with his criticism of the "Jewish Greek" hypothesis as well.

overall outline (which in fact has some advantages of building up the sentence from its constituents) but in his use of Mayser's and others' data in imprecise and potentially unhelpful ways; and that his Semitic Greek hypothesis, especially regarding its unique linguistic nature, is questionable in light of further research. These are serious criticisms that must be considered. One cannot help but notice that Turner's *Syntax* represents a position that is divergent from Moulton's so that one must be cautious and not assume that the volumes in the same series represent a similar perspective. The two positions represent very different perspectives on language, on the context of early Christianity, and on the social, cultural, and linguistic background of early Christianity. Turner's volume also seems to assume that the reader has a firm grasp of standard Greek syntax, as his discussion often entails description of features claimed to be unique to his Biblical Greek. In that sense, his *Syntax* is not a syntax of the entirety of the Greek of the New Testament but a selective treatment of matters of syntax, seen through his perspective on the nature of this Greek. Turner's comparative philological approach, with some acknowledgeable exceptions such as his attempt to consider verbal aspect, does not reflect developments in modern linguistics of the twentieth century, with its synchronic emphasis upon language as system. The arguably most important comment to make on Turner's *Syntax* is that his description of Jewish Greek has been questioned, as it posits a stable hybrid form of language that is linguistically unparalleled as a dialect. Turner wants to emphasize the instances of Semitic phenomena over consideration of the Greek language and thus does not adequately address the differences between *langue* and *parole*, or code and text. Some New Testament authors may evidence Semitic language influence, especially in their lexical choice, without this affecting the Greek language system. Nevertheless, in light of the history of discussion of Moulton's grammar and Turner's having not just brought it to completion but also extended it to a fourth volume, we should be grateful and beholden to Turner for his diligence in writing this volume on syntax.

Nigel Turner Select Bibliography

This bibliography is organized roughly chronologically, so that one can trace the progress of Turner's intellectual thought. As a result, some works without his authorship appear within this list.

Turner, Nigel. "Eschatology in the Old Testament Literature." Unpublished paper, 1936.
Turner, Nigel. "Were the Gospels Written in Greek or Aramaic?" *Evangelical Quarterly* 21 (1949), pp. 42–8.
Turner, Nigel. "St. John's Eternal Word." *Evangelical Quarterly* 22 (1950), pp. 243–8.
Turner, Nigel. "The Unique Character of Biblical Greek." *Vetus Testamentum* 5 (1955), pp. 208–13.
Turner, Nigel. "The 'Testament of Abraham': Problems in Biblical Greek." *New Testament Studies* 1 (1955), pp. 219–23.
Turner, Nigel. "The Relation of Luke I and II to Hebraic Sources and to the Rest of Luke–Acts." *New Testament Studies* 2 (1955), pp. 100–9.
Turner, Nigel. "An Alleged Semitism." *Expository Times* 66 (1955), pp. 252–4.
Turner, Nigel. "The Translation of Μοιχᾶται ἐπ' Αὐτήν in Mark 10:11." *Bible Translator* 7.4 (1956), pp. 151–2.
Turner, Nigel. "The Greek Translators of Ezekiel." *Journal of Theological Studies* n.s. 7 (1956), pp. 12–24.

Turner, Nigel. "The Style of St. Mark's Eucharistic Words." *Journal of Theological Studies* n.s. 8.1 (1957), pp. 108–11.

Turner, Nigel. "The New-Born King (Matthew ii. 2)." *Expository Times* 68 (1957), p. 122.

Turner, Nigel. "The Preposition *en* in the New Testament." *Bible Translator* 10.3 (July 1959), pp. 113–20.

Turner, Nigel. "The Minor Verbal Agreements of Mt. and Lk. against Mk." In *Studia Evangelica*. Texte und Untersuchungen 73. Berlin: Akademie-Verlag, 1959. pp. 223–34.

Turner, Nigel. "Modern Issues in Biblical Studies: Philology in New Testament Studies." *Expository Times* 71 (1960), pp. 104–7.

Turner, Nigel. "The Language of the New Testament." In Matthew Black and H. H. Rowley (eds.), *Peake's Commentary on the Bible*. London: Thomas Nelson, 1962. pp. 659–62.

Turner, Nigel. "Revelation." In Matthew Black and H. H. Rowley (eds.), *Peake's Commentary on the Bible*. London: Thomas Nelson, 1962. pp. 1043–61.

Turner, Nigel. "Absalom" (I, pp. 22–3), "Acraba" (I, p. 28), "Agia" (I, p. 55), "Alexander" (I, pp. 77–8), "Alexandra" (I, pp. 78–9), "Asphar" (I, p. 260), "Attharias" (I, p. 317), "Calamolalus" (I, p. 482), "Callisthenes" (I, p. 490), "Chadiasans" (I, p. 549), "Chaereas" (I, p. 549), "Chaphenatha" (I, p. 552), "Charax" (I, p. 552), "Cos" (I, p. 701), "Daphne" (I, p. 769), "Dathema" (I, p. 771), "Delos" (I, p. 815), "Dionysia" (I, p. 844), "Elasa" (II, p. 71), "Epiphanes" (II, p. 123), "Esdras, Books of" (II, pp. 140–2), "Eumenes" (II, p. 179), "Eupolemus" (II, p. 181), "Gymnasium" (II, p. 502), "Hanukkah" (II, p. 523), "Hasmoneans" (II, pp. 529–35), "Hyrcanus" (II, p. 669), "Indian Driver" (II, p. 700), "Joakim" (II, p. 909), "Joseph, Prayer of" (II, p. 979), "Kedron" (III, p. 5), "Ladder of Tyre" (III, pp. 57–8), "Lysias (Syrian)" (III, p. 193), "Maccabeus" (III, p. 215), "Machaerus" (III, pp. 217–18), "Menelaus" (III, pp. 349–50), "Myndos" (III, p. 478), "Nicanor" (III, pp. 546–7), "Orthosia" (III, p. 609), "Phaselis" (III, p. 781), "Sampsames" (IV, p. 198), "Seat, Moses" (IV, p. 260), "Seleucia" (IV, pp. 263–4),

"Seleucia in Syria" (IV, pp. 264–6), "Seleucus" (IV, pp. 266–7), "Sicyon" (IV, p. 343), "Side" (IV, p. 343), "Symeon" (IV, p. 476), "Tephon" (IV, pp. 573–4), "Toparchy" (IV, pp. 672–3), "Touch" (IV, p. 675), "Tribune" (IV, p. 710), "Trypho" (IV, p. 717). In George Arthur Buttrick (ed.), *The Interpreter's Dictionary of the Bible*. 4 vols. New York: Abingdon, 1962.

Turner, Nigel. *Syntax*, Volume 3 of *A Grammar of New Testament Greek* by James Hope Moulton. Edinburgh: T&T Clark, 1963.

Turner, Nigel. "The Transmission of the Text: B. New Testament." In T. W. Manson (ed.), *A Companion to the Bible*. Second edition edited by H. H. Rowley. Edinburgh: T&T Clark, 1963. pp. 163–82.

Turner, Nigel. "Beatitudes" (pp. 93–4), "Beloved" (pp. 95–6), "Love" with GGF (pp. 593–5), "Lovely" (p. 595), "Lover" (p. 595). In Frederick C. Grant and H. H. Rowley (eds.), *Dictionary of the Bible*. Edinburgh: T&T Clark, 1963.

Turner, Nigel. "Second Thoughts: VII. Papyrus Finds." *Expository Times* 76 (1964), pp. 44–8.

Turner, Nigel. *Grammatical Insights into the New Testament*. Edinburgh: T&T Clark, 1965.

Reider, Joseph. *An Index to Aquila: Greek-Hebrew, Hebrew-Greek, Latin-Hebrew, with the Syriac and Armenian Evidence*. Completed and revised by Nigel Turner. Supplements to Vetus Testamentum 12. Leiden: Brill, 1966.

Turner, Nigel. "Q in Recent Thought." *Expository Times* 80 (1969), pp. 324–8.

Turner, Nigel. "The Church's Attitude to the State in the New Testament." *Journal of Theology for Southern Africa* 2 (1973), pp. 41–52.

The Translator's New Testament. London: British and Foreign Bible Society, 1973.

Turner, Nigel. "Jewish and Christian Influence on New Testament Vocabulary." *Novum Testamentum* 16 (1974), pp. 149–60.

Turner, Nigel. "The Literary Character of New Testament Greek." *New Testament Studies* 20 (1974), pp. 107–14.

Turner, Nigel. *The Art of the Greek Orthodox Church: A Study in Stylization*. University of Rhodesia Series in Humanities. Salisbury, Rhodesia: University of Rhodesia, 1976.

Turner, Nigel. *Style*, Volume 4 of *A Grammar of New Testament Greek* by James Hope Moulton. Edinburgh: T&T Clark, 1976.

Turner, Nigel. "The Quality of the Greek of Luke–Acts." In J. K. Elliott (ed.), *Studies in New Testament Language and Text: Essays in Honour of George D. Kilpatrick*. Supplements to Novum Testamentum 44. Leiden: Brill, 1976. pp. 387–400.

Turner, Nigel. *Christian Words*. Edinburgh: T&T Clark, 1980.

Turner, Nigel. "Biblical Greek: The Peculiar Language of a Peculiar People." In Elizabeth A. Livingstone (ed.), *Studia Evangelica* VII. Berlin: Akademie-Verlag, 1982. pp. 505–12.

PREFACE

THIS volume on Syntax has been doomed to be delayed. Perhaps providentially, for after the revolution in Biblical studies during the first half of this century the time is most opportune to make a detailed survey of New Testament idiom. It is now over fifty years since the first edition of the Prolegomena appeared, and Dr. Moulton had perished at sea before completing Volume II. His pupil, Dr. W. F. Howard, saw that volume through the press in parts, from 1919 to 1929, but before he had opportunity to lay many plans for Volume III he himself died in 1952; and then, on condition that he had the assistance of someone who would collect the necessary material, Dr. H. G. Meecham assumed responsibility for the Syntax. It was on Dr. G. D. Kilpatrick's suggestion that I was permitted to help at this point, and we had done no more than compile a provisional bibliography when Dr. Meecham died in 1955. By the kind invitation of the publishers I then worked alone and broke the spell by living to complete Volume III. It was a privilege for me, both to bring Dr. Moulton's task to fruition in a new age, and to be associated with the distinguished name of Messrs. T. and T. Clark.

My care has been lightened by the publishers' trust in me, their generosity and wise guidance; and I am grateful to the specialist printers who, faced with many typographical problems, so promptly achieved such excellent craftsmanship.

NIGEL TURNER.

Hitchin, *Corpus Christi*, 1962.

CHRONOLOGICAL BIBLIOGRAPHY

General works on syntax. See separate chapters for detailed bibliography.

1. G. Pasor, *Grammatica Graeca Sacra Novi Testamenti Domini nostri Jesu Christi*, Amsterdam 1655 (the first NT Grammar; wise use is made of the LXX).
2. G. B. Winer, *Grammatik des neutestamentlichen Sprachidioms*^{7}, Leipzig 1867 (1st ed. 1822; the first scientific NT Grammar).
3. A. Buttmann, *Grammatik des neutestamentlichen Sprachgebrauchs*, Berlin 1859 (Eng. tr. by Thayer 1873). Good use of LXX.
4. W. Schmid, *Der Attizismus in seinen Hauptvertretern* (4 vols. and Index), Stuttgart 1887–97.
5. J. Viteau, *Étude sur le grec du NT. Le verbe: Syntaxe des propositions*, Paris 1893.
6. E. de W. Burton, *Syntax of the Moods and Tenses in NT Greek*, Edinburgh 1894.
7. G. B. Winer, *Gramm. des nt. Spr.* (see 2): 8th ed. by P. W. Schmiedel, I.1894, II 1.1897, II 2.1898.
8. A. N. Jannaris, *An Historical Greek Grammar*, London 1897.
9. W. W. Goodwin, *Syntax of the Moods and Tenses of the Greek Verb*, London 1897.
10. J. Viteau, *Étude sur le grec du NT comparé avec celui des Septante. Sujet, complément et attribut*, Paris 1897.
11. R. Kühner, *Ausführliche Grammatik der griechischen Sprache*, I, 3rd ed. by F. Blass, Hannover 1890.
12. R. Kühner, *Ibid.*, II, vols. 1 and 2, 3rd ed. by B. Gerth, Hannover and Leipzig 1898–1904.
13. H. Reinhold, *De graecitate Patrum Apostolicorum librorumque apocryphorum Novi Test. quaestiones gramm.* (Diss.), Halle 1898.
14. B. L. Gildersleeve, *Syntax of Classical Greek from Homer to Demosthenes* (2 vols.), New York 1900, 1911.
15. K. Meisterhans, *Grammatik der att. Inschr.*, 3rd ed. by E. Schwyzer, Berlin 1900 (previous ed. referred to sometimes).

16. P. Giles, *A Short Manual of Comparative Philology*, London 1901.
17. T. Nägeli, *Der Wortschatz des Ap. Paulus*, Göttingen 1905.
18. F. E. Thompson, *A Syntax of Attic Greek*, London 1907.
19. J. M. Stahl, *Kritisch-historische Syntax des griechischen Verbums der klassischen Zeit*, Heidelberg 1907.
20. A. Boatti, *Grammatica del grec del Nuovo Testamento*^{2} (2 vols.), Venice 1908–1910.
21. G. A. Deissmann, *Bible Studies* (Engl. tr., A. Grieve)^2, Edinburgh 1909.
22. H. St. J. Thackeray, *A Grammar of the OT in Greek according to the Septuagint*, I, Cambridge 1909.
23. W. Warning, *De Vettii Valentis sermone* (Diss.) Münster 1909.
24. M. Johannessohn, *Der Gebrauch der Kasus und der Präp. in der Septuaginta*, I Gebrauch der Kasus (Diss.) Berlin 1910.
25. A. Thumb, *Handbuch der neugriech. Volkssprache*^{2}, Strassburg 1910.
26. J. H. Moulton, *A Grammar of NT Greek: Prolegomena*, Edinburgh 1906.
27. J. H. Moulton, *Einleitung in die Sprache des NT. Auf Grund der vom Verf. neu bearbeiteten 3 engl. Aufl. übersetzte deutsche Ausgabe*, Heidelberg 1911. (This amounts to a 4th edition of the *Prolegomena*).
28. M. Arnim, *De Philonis Byzantii dicendi genere* (Diss.), Greifswald 1912.
29. H. B. Swete, *An Introduction to the OT in Greek*, rev. by R. R. Ottley, Cambridge 1914.
30. J. H. Moulton and W. F. Howard, *A Grammar of NT Greek*, vol. II, Edinburgh 1919–1929.
31. L. Radermacher, *Neutestamentliche Grammatik*^{2}, Tübingen 1925.
32. H. G. Liddell and R. Scott, *A Greek–English Lexicon*, 9th ed. rev. by H. S. Jones, Oxford 1925–1940.
33. M. Johannessohn, *Der Gebrauch der Präpositionen in der LXX*, Berlin 1926.
34. H. Ljungvik, *Studien zur Sprache der apokrüphen Apostelgeschichten* (Diss.), Uppsala 1926.
35. E. Mayser, *Grammatik der griechischen Papyri aus der Ptolemäerzeit*, II vol. 1, Berlin 1926; II vol. 2, 1934; II, vol. 3, 1934.

36. J. Wackernagel, *Vorlesungen über Syntax mit besonderer Berücksichtigung von Griechisch, Lateinisch und Deutsch*², I, Basel 1926; II, 1928.
37. P. F.-M. Abel, *Grammaire du grec biblique suivie d'un choix de papyrus*, Paris 1927.
38. H. Pernot, *Études sur la langue des Évangiles*, Paris 1927.
39. R. Helbing, *Die Kasussyntax der Verba bei den LXX*, Göttingen 1928.
40. G. Sacco, *La koinè del Nuovo Testamento e la trasmissione del sacro testo. Lezioni preliminari per lo studio del NT greco con introduzione e crestomazia*, Rome 1928.
41. A. A. Tzartzanos, Νεοελληνική σύνταξις ἤτοι Συντακτικὸν τῆς νέας ἑλληνικῆς γλώσσης ..., Athens 1928.
42. J. H. Moulton and G. Milligan, *The Vocabulary of the Greek Testament*, London 1930.
43. J. Psichari, *Essai sur le grec de la Septante*, 1930.
44. A. T. Robertson, *A Grammar of the Greek NT in the Light of Historical Research*⁵, New York 1931.
45. H. Ljungvik *Beiträge zur Syntax der spätgriechischen Volkssprache*, Uppsala 1932.
46. B. F. C. Atkinson, *The Greek Language*², Cambridge 1933.
47. G. Kittel and G. Friedrich, *Theologisches Wörterbuch zum NT*, Stuttgart 1933—.
48. G. Bonnacorsi, *Primi saggi di philologia neotestamentaria*, I, Turin 1933.
49. M. Zerwick, *Untersuchungen zum Markus-Stil*, Rome 1937.
50. S. G. Kapsomenakis, *Voruntersuchungen zu einer Grammatik der Papyri der nachchristl. Zeit*, Munich 1938.
51. M. Soffray, *Recherches sur la syntaxe de Saint Jean Chrysostome*, Paris 1939.
52. J. Humbert, *Syntaxe grecque* (Collection de Philologie Classique), Paris 1945.
53. M. Black, *An Aramaic Approach to the Gospels and Acts*, Oxford 1946, 2nd ed. 1954.
54. M.-J. Lagrange, *S. Matthieu*, Paris, 8th ed. 1948.
55. E. Schwyzer, *Griechische Grammatik*, vol. II, Munich 1950 (based on K. Brugmann).
56. C. F. D. Moule, *The Language of the NT* (inaugr. lect.), Camb. 1952.
57. C. F. D. Moule, *An Idiom Book of NT Greek*, Cambridge 1953.

58. F. Blass and A. Debrunner, *Grammatik des nt. Griechisch*[9], Göttingen 1954.
59. M. Zerwick, S.J., *Graecitas Biblica*[3], Rome 1955
60. R. Morgenthaler, *Statistik des nt. Wortschatzes*, 1958.
61. W. Bauer, *Griechisch-Deutsches Wörterbuch zu den Schriften des NT und der übrigen urchr. Literatur*[5], Berlin 1958.

ABBREVIATIONS

(The numbers refer to the Bibliography)

Abel: 37
anarthr.: anarthrous
Beginnings: F. J. Foakes Jackson and Kirsopp Lake, *The Beginnings of Christianity*, London 1920–33
Bibl. Greek: Biblical Greek
Black AAGA²: 53
Blass-Debr.: 58
Burton: 6
class.: classical
Expos. T. and *Exp. T.* and *E.T.*: Expository Times
Gild. or Gildersleeve: 14
Goodwin: 9
Helbing DKVS: 39
Hell. Greek: Hellenistic Greek
Humbert: 52
ICC: International Critical Commentary
JBL: Journal of Biblical Literature
JThS: Journal of Theological Studies
Jannaris: 8
Johannessohn DGKPS: 24
Johannessohn DGPS: 33
K-Blass: 11
K-G: 12
Kittel WB: 47
LXX: Septuagint
Ljungvik BSSVS: 45
Ljungvik SSAA: 34
LS: 32
MGr: Modern Greek
MT: Massoretic Text
MM Vocab: 42
Mayser: 35
Meisterhans-Schwyzer: 15
Moulton Proleg.: 26
Moulton Einl.: 27
Moulton-Howard: 30
Moule: 57
NEB: New English Bible, Oxford and Cambridge 1961
NT: New Testament
NTS: New Testament Studies

O': Septuagint
OT: Old Testament
pap.: papyri
Pernot *Études*: 38
Radermacher² or Rad.²: 31
RSV: Revised Standard Version, Nelson 1946
Schmid Attizismus: 4
Schwyzer: 55
Soffray: 51
Stahl: 19
Thackeray: *OT Gr.*: 22
Vet. Test.: Vetus Testamentum
Wackernagel: 36
Winer-Schmiedel: 7
Zerwick: 59
Zerwick *Untersuchungen*: 49

A GRAMMAR OF NEW TESTAMENT GREEK

VOLUME III

INTRODUCTION

Dr. Moulton's own plan for the Grammar was that it should be not only a learned assessment of this field but also a practical guide to the student. I have designed volume III specially for three classes of reader: first, the teacher with an interest in exegesis, or the Bible translator either in Europe or among the young native churches who wishes to know the exact significance of every construction; then, the textual critic whom characteristic differences in the author's style may help to decide between variants; and also the student of comparative philology whose concern is the relationship of Biblical Greek to classical and Hellenistic.

The plan of this work follows a natural linguistic pattern: the building up of the sentence from its independent elements right to the complicated co-ordinations and subordinations of the period. The student who likes to have all his pronouns or all his prepositions dealt with together in one chapter must console himself by making good use of the index, for he will find that the various parts of speech are treated in the appropriate place as they contribute to the construction of the sentence. His compensation will be a better understanding of syntax in the true sense and not as a mere catalogue of parts of speech.

Space is very limited, and I wish I could have treated more fully (1) the syntax and style of Paul, (2) the study of word-order, and (3) the syntactic idiosyncrasies of the various authors, as I believe that all these are of great value for illuminating textual problems and difficult exegesis. During the course of the work those points have been constantly in mind, but their fuller treatment will yield ampler rewards. Some authors repeatedly confuse εἰς and ἐν, but others keep them carefully distinct. Knowledge of this kind brings deeper insight, as also does the study of Paul's use of the adnominal genitive, whether it is largely subjective or largely objective. We will never be at home with the fourth evangelist until we observe his peculiar performance with tenses and make allowance for his love of the perfect and pluperfect. What C. H. Turner once commenced to do for Markan syntax needs completing and carrying out for other authors too. Light has been thrown on the Infancy narrative and even on the elusive Q from a careful study of Luke's characteristic style [1]. Without a complete guide to his syntactical predilections, we will never know whether a writer is true to himself or whether he is going out of his way to impress.

I have tried to expose consistently the almost complete absence of classical standards in nearly every author. A tendency to use the active voice wherever possible in place of the declining middle [2], a tendency to give to certain transitive verbs like ἄγω and στρέφω an intransitive sense [3], to give an object to some intransitive verbs (e.g. βασιλεύω, εὐαγγελίζω), and to use the present in reported speech referring to the past; [4] the retreat of the Koine imperfect before the aorist and its confusion with the aorist; [5] the disappearance of the perfect through its assumption of aoristic functions and aoristic " weak " endings; [5] the even greater departure from classical standards in moods [6], especially the optative and infinitive, where the infin. of purpose after verbs of motion and the articular infinitive are on the increase (in spite of the retreat of the infin. before ἵνα and ὅτι in other respects [7]); the less rigid connection between the mood and the conjunction, so that the subjunctive may stand more often without ἄν and conversely ἄν (including ἐάν and ὅταν) stands with the indicative; the articular neuter of the adjective for an abstract noun [8] (τὸ ἅγιον, τὰ καλά); the non-classical use of the definite article generally; fluidity in the meaning and use of prepositions; weakening of the ἵνα-construction; indifference to the case after ἀκούω; lack of distinction between ἴδιος and αὐτοῦ, εἰς and ἐν, ὅστις and ὅς—these are well-known aberrations. More subtle, but as decisive for exegesis, is the infiltration of the comparative into the old preserves of the superlative, so that the

---

[1] *NTS* 2, 100–109; *Studia Evangelica*, Berlin 1959, 223–234.
[2] Ch. 6 § 4.   [3] Ch. 6 § 2.   [4] Ch. 7 § 1.
[5] Ch. 7 § 3.   [6] Ch. 8.   [7] Ch. 10.
[8] Ch. 1.

alert translator will not lose the opportunity of translating the one as the other, if necessary, and will not forget how philological study has made it essential to look at the superlative in the elative sense of *very*, and even to suspect the comparative in this way: πυκνότερον must be *very often* and ἀκριβέστερον *very accurately*. On the other hand, it is probably a unique feature of Bibl. Greek, under Hebraic influence, to put the positive for the superlative: e.g. *greatest* (not *great*) *in the kingdom of heaven*. So also the use of παρά and ὑπέρ with the positive, which is a Hebraic survival in Modern Greek; and since the general trend of the language was towards more emphatic comparison μᾶλλον is added to the normal comparative [1]. The translator will avoid over-translating, because nearly all ancient distinctions are blurred. He will look askance at the " theology of prepositions " and will remember that Hellenistic writers much prefer to add prepositions, especially composite prepositions, to the simple case and also confuse the nice distinctions between prepositions and between the cases, so that the exegete must always look at the context [2]. It is not that Biblical Greek has no standards at all, but pains must be taken to discover them outside the sphere of classical Greek, even outside secular Greek altogether, although the living Koine must be kept in mind always. Mark at least has simple rules which he carefully observes and, to a less extent, so have the others.

Biblical and Hellenistic Greek share the non-classical tendency to omit ὦ in the vocative. With the less cultured writers in post-Christian papyri the NT also shares the tendency to supply nominative forms for the vocative [3]. The popular love of emphatic speech demands a more extended use of pronouns of all kinds, both substantival and attributive [4], in the NT and Koine. Αὐτός becomes simply *he*. Personal pronouns are inserted where they would be unnecessary in class. Greek, and the genitives follow their nouns with a consistency which points to the influence of the Hebrew suffix. Possibly on an Aramaic model, the evangelists use the proleptic pronoun followed by a resumptive noun. But it is a Hellenistic tendency to use the simple personal pronoun for a reflexive; and in the

---

[1] See ch. 3.   [2] See ch. 18.   [3] See ch. 4.
[4] See ch. 5 and 14.

LXX and illiterate papyri we find the 3rd. pers. reflexive used for all persons in the plural, as in the NT. Indirect pronouns are going out of use, and the direct interrogative pronouns like τίς find themselves serving in indirect questions; Hellenistic also is the confusion of relative and interrogative pronouns [1]. The genitive of the pers. pronoun (μου, etc.) is preferred in the Koine to the possessive pronoun (ἐμός, etc.). Εἷς is a post-classical substitute for τις. Ἴδιος becomes no more than ἑαυτοῦ or even αὐτοῦ (simple possessive); and, in the Imperial period at any rate, the anarthrous demonstrative pronoun is not necessarily predicative [2]. The nice distinctions between οὐ and μή in class. Greek have gone, and μή is encroaching [3]. Bibl. Greek shares with the Koine the tendency to misuse and extend the scope of the gen. absolute; [4] and, aided by Semitic precedent, to insert the personal pronoun pleonastically; [5] moreover, the popular tendency towards forceful expression is seen in the forming of new compound particles, and Semitic simplicity in the reduced number and use of particles [6].

In view of the Appendix to volume II, I have not supplied a separate chapter on "Semitisms", which raise a vexed question bedevilled by the objection that nearly all of them appear in the papyri; but the discussion of the influence of the LXX and Semitic idiom arises in every chapter of the book. To some future work I leave discussion whether this influence supports the hypothesis of a spoken Jewish Greek. The present work does suggest that Bibl. Greek is a unique language with a unity and character of its own. It does not follow that if a construction occurs as frequently in the epistles as in the gospels it will be less likely to have a Semitic origin [7], for direct translation is not the only possible medium of Semitic influence. When the LXX was established its idioms powerfully influenced free compositions of Biblical Greek [8]. The idiosyncrasies of Bibl.

---

[1] See ch. 5.   [2] See ch. 14 § 1.   [3] See ch. 19.
[4] See ch. 23 § 3f.   [5] See ch. 24 § 3.   [6] See ch. 25.
[7] See *Exp. T.* LXVII, 247. As a contrast to what this writer found in the Loeb *Select Papyri*, vol. i, concerning the repetition of prepositions, attention should be drawn to Mayser's considered opinion on the Ptolemaic papyri which he had examined: "In der weitaus überwiegenden Mehrzahl der beobachteten Fälle, zumal im Stil privater Urkunden, wird bei καί, τε ... καί, οὐ μόνον ... ἀλλά usw. die Präposition nur einmal gesetzt." (II 2, 516).
[8] Moulton-Howard 478.

Greek syntax are shared in varying degrees by almost all the NT writers, whether they were translating or not. There is a family likeness among these Biblical works, setting them apart from the papyri and from contemporary literary Greek, although the books with Semitic sources may have these features to an especial degree. This is so in the relation between the independent and attributive use of ἐκεῖνος, in which colloquial usage is entirely opposed to the Biblical; it is so with the position of ἕνεκα (-εν) [1], in the Bible the reverse of that of Polybius and the papyri; and with the three broad types of construction with πᾶς.

As to verbs, there was a Hellenistic tendency to use the historic present λέγει, etc., but its popularity in the NT is considerably helped by Aramaic precedent [2]. The perfective aorist is Hebraic. Although development of the perfect tense in the NT has reached a stage closely corresponding with that in the vernacular, there are very important respects in which it is different, and the NT represents a new development. The number of resultative perfects is few indeed compared with secular literary and vernacular texts, and the use of this form is limited to a small number of verbs, except in the emphatic, solemnly strained style of the fourth evangelist. Moreover, although a few examples of εἰμί with the perfect ptc. as a periphrastic tense appear in the Ptolemaic pap., they cannot be compared with the galaxy which is apparent in the LXX and NT [3]. Mayser's exx. are very few. Even Chantraine will not dismiss the probability of Aramaic influence. The perfect tense in general is much rarer in the NT than in the popular language, and it preserves a good deal more of its old force. While the old intransitives have almost all disappeared in the Koine, ἕστηκα and γέγονα being the only living forms, in the NT we do still have a few, especially where they can be understood with a *present* meaning (e.g. the two above, and τέθνηκα, ἤγγικα, πέποιθα, ἀνέῳγα). Some perfects are still true perfects, and not aorists, in spite of the universal confusion in the Ptolemaic and Imperial pap. Even in " colloquial " Mark, a significant distinction is sometimes made (15[44]), and this is true of Paul (1 Co 15[3]). The oft repeated γέγραπται is correctly used, and other perfects retain their true present force.

---

[1] *Vet. Test.* 5, 1955, 208.   [2] See ch. 7 § 1.   [3] See ch. 7 § 9.

The history of the optative mood in the literary and colloquial Greek of the post-classical period is first a gradual decay and subsequently a revival of this mood; in the first place, the revival was due to atticistic influence, but popular Greek followed the fashion in time. Now, the period in which this mood was least in favour in secular writers is the period of the NT and the later books of the LXX, which contrariwise display a comparative fondness for the mood. Is it the conservatism of religion? It might only be that atticizing scribes confused like-sounding endings. But the old Volitive optative is admirably suited to the pious aspiration and longing of religious books. Volitive optatives could owe their preservation to their incidence in the solemn diction of Christian devotion and synagogue liturgy. They appear in the LXX, and that version became the Church's book. It is a form of speech well fitted for pious lips.

Some characteristically Biblical prepositions hardly occur at all in the papyri; e.g. ὀπίσω (over 300 times in LXX and 26 in NT), ἀπέναντι and κατέναντι. And ἔμπροσθεν is extremely rare outside Biblical Greek. The use of cases with prepositions is not that of the Koine, or the Biblical books show a more rapid tendency to drop one or more of the cases, e.g.

		LXX	NT	Polybius	Papyri	Herodotus
ἐπί	(g:d:a)	1·5:1:3·7	1·2:1:2	1·5:1:3	4·5:1:2·5	
παρά	(g:d:a)	2·5:1:1·5	1·6:1:1·2		22·5:1:2·5	1·8:1:3·5
πρός	(g:d:a)	·23:1:43	·16:1:116	·2:1:15	·02:1:4	2:1:6
μετά	(g:a)	3·8:1	3·6:1	1·2:1	1·6:1	

The wider use of ἐν is remarkable in Bibl. Greek, e.g.:

	LXX	NT	Papyri
ἐν : παρά	1 : ·06	1 : ·07	1 : ·43
ἐν : περί	1 : ·06	1 : ·12	1 : ·28

It is a peculiarity of Bibl. Greek, and not of the Koine, to use the feminine for neuter in certain expressions like εἰς κρυπτήν and ἀπὸ μιᾶς, but the variations in the gender of λιμός are shared by the Koine [1].

A distributive *singular*, in preference to the plural, is distinctly Biblical, like τὸ σῶμα ὑμῶν, although we have κατὰ γεωργόν once in the papyri. The plural *worlds* and *heaven* belongs to Bibl. Greek, and is normal Greek only poetically. The allusive plural is normal Greek, but late: of Herod it is said, *They are dead who sought the child's life*; and *the prophets* (Mt 2²³) is simply Hosea; while ὄχλοι πολλοί is one vast crowd [2].

The use of *soul* for the reflexive pronoun must be uniquely Biblical. The use of αὐτός as a demonstrative (which has significance for exegesis) is doubtfully Koine and more likely to be due to Semitic influence; so also extra-Biblical examples of οὐ ... πᾶς are rare [3]. Biblical Greek uses παρά and ὑπέρ for comparison in place of ἤ or the genitive and is fond of the genitive of quality. The dative is beginning to decline in Hell. Greek but the popularity of ἐν in Bibl. Greek gives it a false appearance of life [4].

The NT is not in line with the Koine in the use of cases after certain verbs. It uses the dat. as well as the acc. after προσκυνέω [5], and reverts to the Attic dat. after πειθαρχέω [6]. The acc. is invariable in the LXX (except atticistic 4Km 2²⁴, Ep. Je 65), and in the NT after καταράομαι, against the dat. of secular style [7]. The only two instances of acc. after ἐπηρεάζω which I can find, occur in NT, while secular Greek has the dative [8].

A partitive expression is often used in NT and LXX as subj. or obj. of the verb, e.g. θανατώσουσιν ἐξ ὑμῶν, without the help of τινας, in Lk 21¹⁶. This plays small part indeed in the non-Biblical language [9], and clearly reflects the Hebrew מן. In partitive expressions the Ptolemaic papyri much prefer ἀπό to ἐκ [10], but NT writers prefer ἐκ and also often use ἐν in a partitive sense which is extremely rare in the papyri [11].

---

[1] See ch. 2. [2] See ch. 2. [3] Ch. 14 § 1.
[4] Ch. 17.
[5] Mayser II 2. 256; MMVocab.s.v. The dat. becomes increasingly common in LXX: Helbing DKVS 296-298.
[6] Mayser II 2, 208. Ptolemaic pap. all gen.; dat. in A.D. 260 (MMVocab.s.v.).
[7] Kittel WB I 449; Helbing DKVS 71; Bauer s.v.
[8] Mayser II 2, 265.
[9] See ch. 15 § 2,1, I b; Mayser II 2, 351.
[10] Mayser II 2, 352. [11] Mayser II 2, 353.

The position of the attributive adjective (and participle) in relation to the noun and article is in the Ptolemaic pap. quite different from that in Bibl. Greek. There are three possible positions: I. ὁ ἀγαθὸς ἀνήρ, II. ὁ ἀνὴρ ὁ ἀγαθός, III. ἀνὴρ ὁ ἀγαθός. The art. before the noun is often omitted in Hell. Greek and particularly in the papyri, but that is very rare in Bibl. Greek [1]. I can find only one instance in the first twenty chapters of Genesis, and there are very few in the NT. As to the other two possible positions, if we take as a sample of iii/B.C. papyri the Hibeh Papyri nos. 27–120, there are twenty exx. of position I and ten exx. of the repeated article. The Tebtunis Papyri nos. 5–124 will serve for ii–i/B.C.: they have the first position with over 140 exx., but only four or five exx. with repetition of the article [2]. This is not like the picture in Bibl. Greek. In the Pauline and General epistles [3] (where direct rendering of a Hebrew text is ruled out) the proportion is: position I 24, position II 23, position III one only. Clearly the tendency in the papyri of the NT period is for the second position to be practically negligible (140 : 5), while Biblical writers are fond of the usage even when there is no emphasis. In LXX Ge 1–19 the proportion between positions I and II is 18 : 56, the very reverse of the proportion in iii/B.C. papyri. In 1 Km 1–6 the proportion is 1 : 16.

The construction ἐν τῷ with infin. occurs so often in Lk-Ac that to Dr. Howard it was "one more evidence of the great influence of the LXX on the style of Luke." [4] It occurs in the papyri occasionally [5], but this expression, like εἰς τό and τοῦ c.infin. (of which Paul and Luke are specially fond) belongs almost exclusively to Bibl. Greek through the influence of Hebrew [6]. Dr. Howard observed that the use of ἵνα "had already gained great flexibility in the Κοινή" (p. 470). If one cannot claim that its even greater flexibility of use in the NT [7] was entirely due to Semitic influence, one must at least underline the difficulty of finding anywhere but in Biblical books such a

---

[1] See ch. 13 § 1.   [2] Mayser II 2, 25ff.
[3] The first chapters of the following books have been read: Ro, 1 and 2 Co, Ga, Ph, Col, Phm, 1 and 2 Th, 1 and 2 Ti, Ti, Heb, Jas, 1 and 2 Pt, 1 Jn.
[4] See the Appendix to vol. II of this Grammar, p. 451.
[5] Mayser II 1, 328.
[6] Mayser II 1, 321ff, 330; I 3, 43. See below ch. 10 § 2b.
[7] See e.g. Radermacher² 193. See below ch. 8 § 2 B2.

wide variety in the use of ἵνα, imperatival, causal, consecutive, epexegetical, within so small a space.

Other instances of the unique character of Bibl. Greek abound in peculiarities of word-order [1], in asyndeton [2] and parataxis [3], in the use of proleptic pronouns [4], and in the pleonastic insertion of personal pronouns [5], as well as in many other smaller and less significant ways.

I do not wish to prove too much by these examples, but the strongly Semitic character of Bibl. Greek, and therefore its remarkable unity within itself, do seem to me to have contemporary significance at a time when many are finding their way back to the Bible as a living book and perhaps are pondering afresh the old question of a "Holy Ghost language". The lapse of half a century was needed to assess the discoveries of Deissmann and Moulton and put them in right perspective. We now have to concede that not only is the subject-matter of the Scriptures unique but so also is the language in which they came to be written or translated. This much is plain for all who can see, but the further question arises, whether such a Biblical language was the creature of an hour and the *ad hoc* instrument for a particular purpose, or whether it was a spoken language as well, something more than an over-literal rendering of Semitic idioms, a permanent influence and a significant development in the language. Students of Greek await the answer with interest.

---

[1] See ch. 27.   [2] See ch. 25 § 3.   [3] See ch. 26 § 1.
[4] See ch. 5 § 2 (a) 3; ch. 14 § 1. 2.   [5] See ch. 24 § 3.

BOOK ONE

BUILDING UP THE SENTENCE: ANALYTICAL

The minimal form of the sentence is Subject and Predicate. The Subject is usually expressed by a noun and the Predicate by a verb; and this verb may need a direct or indirect Object. But often the Predicate too may be a noun or its substitute.

CHAPTER ONE

SUBSTITUTES FOR NOUNS IN SUBJECT, OBJECT OR PREDICATE

§ 1. The Article with Adjectives [1]

A subject, object or predicate may be expressed without using a noun. The usual substitute for it in cultured speech is a non-substantival neuter expression, but sometimes also a masculine or feminine one. We find the article with a non-predicate adjective, and used in both (a) an individual and (b) a generic sense. By this method is represented a quality *par excellence*.

(a) Of God: Jn 5⁴⁴ ὁ μόνος BW, 1 Jn 5²⁰ ὁ ἀληθινός. Of Christ: Lk 4³⁴ ὁ ἅγιος, Ac 22¹⁴ ὁ δίκαιος. Of Satan: ὁ πονηρός. Also ἡ ἔρημος. *the desert*, Jas 2⁶ τὸν πτωχόν *beggar*. Also ὁ σόφος.

(b) οἱ πλούσιοι and οἱ ἅγιοι. οἱ πολλοί either *the majority*, or *the many* previously indicated. 1 Pt 4¹⁸ ὁ δίκαιος, ὁ ἀσεβής. Mt 25⁴ αἱ φρόνιμοι. Also οἱ μαλακοί.

But the substantival expression is more usually neuter. In the pre-Christian papyri are τὸ ἅγιον, τὸ ἄξιον, τὸ δίκαιον, τὰ καλά, τὸ στρατιωτικόν *the army*, τὸ ἱππικόν, τὸ ναυτικόν, etc. (Mayser II 1, 1ff). Again we have (a) individual, (b) generic, more often; and (c), especially in Paul, the equivalent of an abstract noun; the latter is a class. idiom (Hdt. Thuc.) and higher contemporary Koine (Strabo, Joseph., I Cl.), as well as Biblical (LXX).[2] In the NT it is characteristic of Paul and Luke and not often in the Gospels. This abstract usage followed by the gen. does not appear in the papyri.

(a) Individual concrete expressions: 2 Co 8¹⁵ OT τὸ πολύ, τὸ ὀλίγον, Philem¹⁴ τὸ ἀγαθόν *a good deed*, Ro 8³ τὸ ἀδύνατον *the one thing the Law could not do*. 1 Co 3¹⁰ θεμέλιον, sc. λίθον, 7⁵ ἐκ συμφώνου. Also τὸ

---

[1] K.-G I 266ff., Gild. I § 36, Mayser II 1, 1ff. Ljungvik SSAA 24f. Schmid, Attizismus IV 608.
[2] Also Apost. Fathers, e.g. Mart. Petri 82²⁰ τὸ παράδοξον τοῦ θεάματος, and Pass. Andr. alt. 28¹·⁴ff.

καλόν. Never τὸ συνειδός for συνείδησις, but τὸ σωτήριον for ἡ σωτηρία (Lk 2³⁰ 3⁶, Ac 28²⁸, Eph 6¹⁷ all OT), and often τὸ μαρτύριον for ἡ μαρτυρία. Neut. sing. is also used collectively to denote persons: τὸ ἔλαττον ... τοῦ κρείττονος = οἱ ἐλάττονες ... τῶν κρειττόνων; also neut. pl. with a gen. 1 Co 1²⁷ᶠ τὰ μωρὰ τοῦ κόσμου, etc. Papyri: τὸ δυνατόν, τὸ λοιπόν, τὰ ἴδια, τὰ καλά, τὰ ὑπάρχοντα.

(b) Generic: Mt 6¹³ τοῦ πονηροῦ (but masc?), 12³⁵ = Lk 6⁴⁵ τὰ (B al om.) ἀγαθά ... πονηρά, Lk 6⁴⁵ τὸ ἀγαθόν, Ro 3⁸ τὰ κακά, τὰ ἀγαθά 13³ τὸ ἀγαθόν *good works*, Gal 6¹⁰ same, Mt 13⁴⁸ τὰ καλά ... τὰ σαπρά *fish*.

(c) Abstract ideas; usually with a following gen.: Ro 1¹⁹ τὸ γνωστὸν τοῦ θ. *knowledge concerning God* (Chrysost.) or *what is known* (or *can be known*) *about God* (Origen) or *God in his knowableness* (Kittel WB I 719), 1²⁰ τὰ ἀόρατα αὐτοῦ *he the Invisible* (ib.) 2⁴ τὸ χρηστὸν τοῦ θ. = χρηστότης (which precedes) or more definitely *God in his kindness* (ib.), 9²² τὸ δυνατὸν αὐτοῦ *how powerful he is*, 1 Co 4⁵ τὰ κρυπτὰ τοῦ σκότους¹ *the darkness which hides*, 1²⁵ τὸ μῶρον τοῦ θ. = μωρία (which precedes) or *God seeming to be foolish;* τὸ ἀσθενὲς τοῦ θ. similarly. 7³⁵ τὸ εὔσχημον καὶ εὐπάρεδρον τῷ κυρίῳ, 2 Co 4¹⁷ τὸ παραυτίκα ἐλαφρὸν τῆς θλ. ἡμῶν, 8⁸ τὸ τῆς ... γνήσιον *what is genuine with respect to* ..., Ph 3⁸ τὸ ὑπερέχον τῆς = ὑπεροχή, 4⁵ τὸ ἐπιεικὲς ὑμῶν, Col 1¹⁶ τὰ ὁρατὰ καὶ ἀόρατα (no gen.), Heb. 6¹⁷ τὸ ἀμετάθετον τῆς, 7¹⁸ τὸ αὐτῆς ἀσθενὲς καὶ ἀνωφελές, 1 Pet 1⁷, Jas 1³ τὸ δοκιμεῖον = *something tested* (Deiss. BS 259ff. Mayser 1² 3, 52). Cp. Strabo's τὸ εὐμεταχείριστον τῆς θήρας. LXX. 2 Mac 4⁴ τὸ χαλεπὸν τῆς, 3¹⁶ τὸ τῆς ... παρηλλαγμένον, 2³¹ τὸ σύντομον τῆς ..., τὸ ἐξεργαστικὸν τῆς, 4 Mac 6¹³ ἐν θαυμαστῷ τῆς, 18⁸ τὰ ἁγνὰ τῆς.

§ 2. The Article with (1) Attributive Adverbs

This is like the class. τὰ εἰς τὸν πόλεμον *things belonging to war*. Thus in pre-Christian papyri: πᾶν τὸ ἑξῆς *all other contributions*, τὸ ἐφαύριον, ἐν τῷ μεταξύ, ἀπὸ τοῦ νῦν, ἕως ..., μέχρι ..., τὸ πρότερον, τὸ πρωΐ, τὰ ἄνω, τὰ ἐνταῦθα, τὰ ἐπάνω, εἰς τὰ μάλιστα, ἐκ τοῦ ὀπίσω (Mayser II, 1, 13). In the NT: εἰς τὸ μέσον, ἐν τῷ μέσῳ, ἐκ τοῦ μέσου (without art., if a gen. follows), Lk 16²⁶ οἱ (S*BD om.) ἐκεῖθεν, Mt 24²¹ ἕως τοῦ νῦν, 23²⁶ τὸ ἐντός, Jn 8²³, 1 Co 14¹⁶ τὸ ἀμήν, 2 Co 1²⁰ τὸ ναί, τὸ ἀμήν, Rev 3¹⁴ ὁ ἀμήν, Col 3¹ᵗ τὰ κάτω, τὰ ἄνω, 2 Co 1¹⁷ Jas 5¹² τὸ ναί, τὸ οὔ. Sometimes the noun so formed is used as an adverbial accusative: τὸ πρωΐ, τὸ ἑπτάκις Lk 17⁴D, τὸ ἀνὰ δηνάριον Mt 20¹⁰ SCLNZ *everyone a penny*.

The Article with (2) *prepositional phrases*. Mayser II 1, 9–13: τὰ ἐκ τῆς γῆς *offspring* or *product*, hence Ro 12¹⁸ τὸ ἐξ ὑμῶν *so far as it originates from you*; papyri τὸ κατ' ἄνδρα distributive, hence pap. and NT τὸ καθ' ἡμέραν *daily*; but also in pap., Ac and Paul τὰ κατά τι expresses general relationship, so τὸ κατὰ σάρκα

---

¹ Cp. Ex Actis Andr. 45²⁶ᶠ τὸ κρυπτόμενον αὐτοῦ τῆς φύσεως.

§ 2] SUBSTITUTES FOR NOUNS

Ro 9⁵ = *as far as the material side is concerned*; Ph 1¹² Col 4⁷ τὰ·κατ' ἐμέ = *what concerns me*; but the same phrase Ac 25¹⁴ τὰ κατὰ Παῦλον is obviously *Paul's case* in the courts and this may be the correct interpretation in Ph and Col (*my lawsuit*); so Ac 16³⁹ D τὰ καθ' ὑμᾶς = *we acted amiss at your trial in court* (πρᾶγμα). But 2 Co 10⁷ τὰ κατὰ πρόσωπον = *what is in front of you* (spatial); Ro 12⁵ τὸ καθ' εἷς a stereotyped adv. Ac 28⁷ τὰ περὶ τὸν τόπον ἐκεῖνον (local), Herm V iii 3¹ τὰ περὶ τὸν πύργον. Local in the papyri, but sometimes of general relationship like κατά; hence probably *my circumstances* in Ph 2²³ τὰ περὶ ἐμέ, and not *my surroundings*. The gen. τὰ περί τινος is frequ. in pap. and in Luke and Paul, e.g. Lk 24²⁷ τὰ περὶ ἑαυτοῦ, Ac 18²⁵ τὰ περὶ τοῦ 'Ι. Mk 5²⁷ (but τά om. by S^cAC²DLW al) *things concerning*.... With παρά: Mk 5²⁶ δαπανήσασα τὰ παρ'· (παρ' om. DW) ἑαυτῆς class., Lk 10⁷ πίνοντες τὰ παρ' αὐτῶν, Ph 4¹⁸ δεξάμενος... τὰ παρ' ὑμῶν. In the pap. τὸ παρά τινος (sing.) is a sum of money to be paid by someone, esp. taxes due (Mayser II 1, 12), but τὰ παρά τινος (pl.) is something sent, an answer, a mandate, an errand, an ordinance. With Ph 4¹⁸ cp. P. Alexandr. 4, 15 (iii/B.C.) εἴλεφεν τὰ παρὰ σοῦ = *he received what you sent*, but P. Teb. I 12, 23 (118 B.C.) ἀποδέχομαι τὰ παρὰ σοῦ = *your instructions*. Cp. Jos. BJ. 2, 124, Ant. 8, 175.

These were all neuter but we have masc. and fem. also with prepositional phrases: Mayser II 1, 14–20 ἀπό, διά g., ἐκ, εἰς, ἐν, ἐπί g., κατά acc., μετά g., παρά g. acc., περί acc., πρό, πρός dat., ὑπό acc. ἀπό: Heb 13²⁴ οἱ ἀπὸ τῆς 'Ιτ. *Italians*. Inscr. 60 B.C. (Preis. Samm. 4980, 6) οἱ ἀπὸ τῆς πόλεως. Pap. i/B.C. (ib. 5216, 11) οἱ ἀπὸ 'Αλεξανδρείας, etc., very frequ. to represent a person's home or extraction. In the pap. also to denote a class: οἱ ἀπὸ τῆς τραπέζης are *bank officials* PSI IV 383, 8 (248 B.C.), like Ac 12¹ οἱ ἀπὸ τῆς ἐκκλησίας *church folk*, 15⁵ οἱ ἀπὸ τῆς αἱρέσεως.

ἐκ: very frequ. in Paul as we use *-ists* of members of a sect or persuasion: Ro 3²⁶ οἱ ἐκ πίστεως 'Ι. *believers in J.*, 4¹⁴·¹⁶ οἱ ἐκ νόμου *who live by the Law*, ὁ ἐκ πίστεως 'Α. *who shares A's faith* (a persuasion), Ac 6⁹ οἱ ἐκ τῆς συναγωγῆς (a sect). Class. use of a country: Isocr. 4³² οἱ ἐκ τῆς 'Ασίας *Asians*. Papyri of descendants, members of a family or class, residents (like ἀπό); members of a family in Ro 16¹¹ οἱ ἐκ τῶν Ναρκίσσου.

εἰς: Mk 13¹⁶ ὁ εἰς τὸν ἀγρόν. Ac 2³⁹ οἱ εἰς μακράν local.
ἐν: Mk 13¹⁴ οἱ ἐν τῇ 'Ι. local.
ἐπί: Mk 13¹⁵ ὁ ἐπὶ τοῦ δώματος local.
κατά: Ac 25²³ οἱ κατ' ἐξοχήν *eminent men*. Eph 5³³ οἱ καθ' ἕνα *as individuals*.

παρά g.: in class. Gk. *those sent out by*. In pap. usually someone's *agent* or assistant, a *proxy*, but less often of relatives and friends (as Mk 3²¹) W. Chr. 10, 6 (130 B.C.) etc., esp. ἡ μήτηρ καὶ οἱ παρ' ἡμῶν πάντες in a private letter BGU VI 1300, 4 (iii–ii/B.C.), 1 Cl. 12⁴ *king's messengers*, 1 Esd 1¹⁵ 1 Mac 2¹⁵ *a king's proxy*, Mk 3²¹ (see J. Moulton in *ET* 20, 1909, 476) οἱ παρ' αὐτοῦ but not DW and Lat. *his kinsfolk*, LXX Su³³ *her family and friends*, 1 Mac 9⁴⁴ vl⁵⁸ *his men*. Cf. Jos. Ant. 1, 193. περί: Mk 4¹⁰ Lk 22⁴⁹ οἱ περὶ αὐτόν *his disciples*; *J. and his disciples* is impossible. Ac 13¹³ 21⁸TR οἱ περὶ (τὸν) Π. *Paul and his party* (class.); *the escorts alone* is impossible. Later than class. οἱ περί τινα was often a periphrasis for the person alone: Plu. Pyrrh. 20, 1 οἱ περὶ Φαβρίκιον = *Fabricius*; Tiber. Gracch. 2, 3 οἱ περὶ Δροῦσον = *Drusus*; so in Polyb. 4, 36; 6, 21; 11, 2; Diod. Sic. 1, 16; 1, 37; 19, 19; Ep. Arist. 51; Philo vi cont. 15; Jos. Ant. 13, 187; 15, 370; c. Ap. 1, 17. Probably we have this in NT: Jn 11¹⁹ τὰς περὶ M. καὶ M. = *Martha and Mary* only (p⁴⁵ AΘ al.). There is little if any support in the pap., unless P. Flind. Petr. I 29, 4 τὰ περὶ τὴν ἀναδενδράδα (Radermacher 2, 118).

The Article with (3) *genitives of Nouns*. In the pre-Christian papyri this neuter expression denotes (a) residence, possessions, property, house or home of the person in the genitive (Mayser II 1, 8); (b) with impers. genitive the phrase is largely periphrastic: τὰ τῆς γεωργίας = *field work*.

(a) *personal*: Lk 20²⁵ τὰ Καίσαρος, τὰ τοῦ θεοῦ *property of*, 1 Co. 1¹¹ ὑπὸ τῶν Χλόης (strictly ὑπὸ τῶν τῶν Χλόης *by them of Chloe's house*).

(b) *impersonal*. Nothing more subtle than periphrasis is involved: Mt 21²¹ τὸ τῆς συκῆς *the fig tree*, Ro 14¹⁹ τὰ τῆς εἰρήνης *peace*, Jas 4¹⁴ τὸ (τὰ A) τῆς αὔριον *tomorrow*, 2 Pt 2²² τὸ τῆς ἀληθοῦς παροιμίας *the true proverb*.

§ 3. The Ellipse of Various Nouns

The absence of the noun (although its idea is quite necessary, in contrast to § 1 above) occurs in adjectival and other kinds of attributes (pronominal, participial, adverbial), and the context supplies its lack [1].

Certain nouns are liable to ellipse in this way in NT and contemporary Greek. So ὁδός is to be supplied in the papyri as in Lk 3⁵ OT εἰς εὐθείας, 5¹⁹ ποίας, 19⁴ ἐκείνης, and also γῆ or χωρά very frequently: Mt 3⁵ etc. ἡ περίχωρος (Plut. LXX), 23¹⁵ ἡ ξηρά (Xen. LXX), Mk 15³⁹ ἐξ ἐναντίας (D substitutes ἐκεῖ and W omits), Lk 1³⁹· ⁶⁵ ἡ ὀρεινή, ἡ ἔρημος, ἡ

---

[1] K-G I 265ff. Gild. I §§ 32–35. Mayser II 1, 20ff.

οἰκουμένη (*world*; class., pap., MGr.), 17²⁴ or better scil. μερίδος (T. Levi 18⁴), Heb 11²⁹ D*c*KLP διὰ ξηρᾶς (but SAD*E p¹³ p⁴⁶ supply γῆς).

In dates in the pap. ἡμέρα is almost always omitted: Mt 11²³ etc. μέχρι τῆς σήμερον (elsewhere with ἡμέρα), Mt 27⁶² (Mk, Lk, Jn, Jas) τῇ (ἐπ) αὔριον like P. Hamb. I no. 27, 4 (250 B.C.) τῆι ἐφαύριον. Lk 13³² Ac 27¹⁹ τῇ τρίτῃ (elsewhere τῇ τρ. ἡμ.) like P. Eleph. 5, 17 (284 B.C.) τρίτηι. Lk–Ac τῇ ἑξῆς. Lk 13³³ τῇ ἐχομένῃ, cp. P. Hal. 1, 30 (iii/B.C.) τῆι ἐπιομένηι, but in Ac 21²⁶ with no ellipse of ἡμ. Ac 16¹¹ 20¹⁵ 21¹⁸ τῇ ἐπιούσῃ, like P. Petr. III 56(b) 12 (260 B.C.), but no ellipse of ἡμ. in Ac 7²⁶. Ac 20⁷ etc. τῇ μιᾷ τῶν σαββάτων. Heb 4⁴ ἡ ἑβδόμη, but same verse has ἡμ. Herm. S. VI 5³ (Clem. Hom. IX.1) πρὸ μιᾶς. Possibly ἀφ᾽ ἧς (Ac 24¹¹ 2 Pt 3⁴ 1 Mac 1¹¹: *since*)¹, is an ellipse of ἡμ. (or ὥρα in Lk 7⁴⁵). There is no ellipse of ἡμ. at Col 1⁶·⁹ Herm. M. IV 4³, but the phrase is virtually a conjunction.

Χείρ is frequ. omitted in phrases like ἡ δεξιά, ἡ ἀριστερά Mt 6³ etc., ἐν δεξιᾷ Ro 8³⁴ etc. (unless we assume ἐνδέξια, class., in view of the fact that NT writers have ἐκ δεξιῶν, not ἐν δ.). Herm. S. IX 12³ has δεξιά and εὐώνυμα. MGr. also. Ptolemaic pap.: δεξιάν P. Petr. II 45 (248 B.C.), but χείρ is inserted also in pap.

It is probable that we should supply περίοδος with -μηνος and -ήμερος ending adjectives. For νυχθήμερος see Blass-Debr. § 121. Hdt 2, 124 ἡ τρίμηνος. Polyb. VI 34³ ἡ δίμηνος, XXVII 7² ἡ ἕκμηνος. LXX Ez 39¹⁴ τὴν ἑπτάμηνον. 4 Mac 16⁷ ἑπτὰ δεκάμηνοι. Jg 19²A 20⁴⁷A τετράμηνον anarthrous. Ditt. Syll³ 410⁴·²⁴ (c 274 B.C.), 442³·¹⁷ (c 250 B.C.). In preChristian papyri: Petr. III 78, 13 (iii/B.C.) etc. ἡ πενθήμερος. PSI IV 380, 6 (249 B.C.) ἡ δίμηνος. 408, 9 (iii/B.C.) ἡ τετράμηνος (Mayser II 1, 23). Jn 4³⁵ τετράμηνος anarthrous (-νον HW al). Heb 11²³ OT τρίμηνον (= Ex 2² μῆνας τρεῖς) (-ος p⁴⁶).

The ellipse of ὥρα is probable in other similar examples (e.g. PSI IV 391, 4 (241 B.C.) τῆι δευτέραι τῆς νυκτός): ἐξαυτῆς *at once*. Not class. are πρωΐα and ὀψία in Mt Mk Jn Herm. Mk 11¹¹B ὀψίας οὔσης (other MSS either add τῆς ὥρας or substitute ὀψέ), with which cp. BU II 380³ (iii/A.D.) ὀψ(ε)ίας τῆς ὥρας, P. Ox. III 475¹⁶ (A.D. 182) ὀψίας.

Other less frequ. noun-ellipses are the following:

Ἄνεμος: Ac 27¹⁵ τῷ πνέοντι (Western).

Ἄγαλμα: 19³⁵ τὸ διοπετές.

Αὔρα: 27⁴⁰ τῇ πνεούσῃ (indicated by Arrian ep. ad Traj. 5 ταῖς αὔραις ταῖς . . . πνεούσαις). Lucian Herm. 28, Char. 3 τῷ πνέοντι.

Γλῶσσα: Rev 9¹¹ ἐν τῇ ἑλληνικῇ (S ἑλληνιδι), or supply διάλεκτος or φωνή LXX.

Δραχμή: Ac 19¹⁹ ἀργυρίου (sc. δραχμῶν, but we would expect ἀργυρίων).

Ἱμάτιον: Mt 11⁸ ἐν μαλακοῖς. Jn 20¹² Herm. V. IV 2¹ ἐν λευκοῖς. Rev 18¹²·¹⁶ βυσσίνου, πορφύρας etc. Pap. (Mayser II 1, 26).

Μέρος: not class. but pre-Chr. pap (τὸ τρίτον, τέταρτον passim) Rev: τὸ τρίτον, τέταρτον, δέκατον. Mk 16⁵? ἐν τοῖς δεξιοῖς.

---

¹ And in weak variants in Herm. S. VIII 1⁴A (but read ἄφες with P. Mich. See below p. 94.) 6⁶A (but read ἀφότε with P. Mich.).

Πληγή: Lk 12⁴⁷ᶠ δαρήσεται πολλάς... ὀλίγας. 2 Co 11²⁴ τεσσεράκοντα παρὰ μίαν.
Πύλη: Jn 5² but this could not be supplied by the general reader without local knowledge; it is suspect, being om. by Syr^{cur. pesh.}
'Ράβδος: Heb 5⁷ ἱκετηρίας (or sc. ἐλαία). Büchsel in Kittel WB III 297f traces the origin to the olive branches of the suppliant, whence after Isocr. the adj. came to mean *earnest supplication*.
Ὕδωρ: Mt 10⁴² ψυχροῦ. Jas 3¹¹ τὸ γλυκὺ καὶ τὸ πικρόν. Aristoph. Nub. and pap: θερμόν (Gild. I § 38).
Ὑετόν: Jas 5⁷ πρόϊμον καὶ ὄψιμον (S)B.
Ἐλαία: Ro 11²⁴ ἡ ἀγριέλαιος, καλλιέλαιος. Ἔλαιον supplied in papyri (Mayser II 1, 24).

It remains only to notice under this head some stereotyped phrases where there is noun-ellipse:

Ἀπὸ μιᾶς: Lk 14¹⁸ sc. γνώμη or ὁρμή or φωνή, or more probably γλῶσσα in view of Philo V 170⁸ ἀπὸ μιᾶς καὶ τῆς αὐτῆς γνώμης = with one mind or voice. And some would supply φορά *impetus*. It may be Aramaism rather than ellipse (*min ch'dā*) = at once, but it occurs in secular PSI II 286²² (iii–iv/A.D.) = at once, and Wilcken. Chrest. 46, 15 (A.D. 338) μίαν ἐκ μιᾶς (sc. ἡμέρα), and in MGr. Lagrange (*S. Luc* 404) suggests that ὁδός or φωνή or preferably γνώμη be understood.
Κατὰ μόνας: There is no knowing what noun to supply. Mk 4¹⁰ Lk 9¹⁸, LXX Ge 32¹⁶ Ps 4⁹ Je 15¹⁷ 1 Mac 12³⁶. Thuc. I 32.5. Xen. Mem. 3.7.4. Menander. Polyb. 4.15.11. Diod. Sic. 4.51.16. Jos. BJ 6, 326; Ant. 17, 336, etc. Herm. M. XI 8. MGr καταμόναχο. BGU III 813, 15 (ii/A.D.).
Κατ' ἰδίαν: Mt 14¹³·²³, 17¹·¹⁹, 20¹⁷, 24³, Mk 4³⁴ 6³¹ᶠ 7³³ 9². ²⁸ 13³, Lk 9¹⁰ 10²³, Ac 23¹⁹, Ga 2². 2 Mac 4⁵ 14²¹. Ign Sm. 7². Hellenistic, not class.: Plut. 2, 120d. Polyb. 1, 71, 1; 4, 84, 8. Diod. Sic. 1, 21. Philo sacr. Abel. 136. Jos. BJ. 2, 199. Pap: P. Or. gr. 51, 9 (239 B.C.); 737, 7 (ii/B.C.). Insc: Dit. Syll³. 1157, 10, and see L.S. s.v. ἴδιος. Uncertain what noun to supply.
Ἰδίᾳ: the class. equivalent of the last. 1 Co 12¹¹ PSI IV 434¹² (261 B.C.).
Δημοσίᾳ: Ac 16³⁷ etc. = *openly*. Dit. Syll. 807⁹ (A.D. 138) = *publicly*. Vettius Valens p. 71²² *publicly*. Different meaning in class. Attic: *at the public expense* or *by public consent*.

PART I
WORD-MATERIAL FOR SENTENCE-BUILDING

CHAPTER TWO

THE GENDER AND NUMBER OF NOUNS

§ 1. The Gender of Nouns [1]

As in class. Greek [2] the neuter gender may refer to a person (e.g. τὸ γεγεννημένον Jn 3⁶ 1 Jn 5⁴, cp. masc. 5¹), provided that the emphasis is less on the individual than on some outstanding general quality like *foolishness*; [3] πᾶν is often added to make this clear (1 Jn 5⁴, Jn 17² πᾶν ὅ like Heb. כָּל אֲשֶׁר, 6³⁷ πᾶν ὅ resolves itself into τὸν ἐρχόμενον. Ga 3²² τὰ πάντα but τοὺς πάντας in Ro 11³². Jn 12³² πάντα S*D p⁶⁶ lat Aug; rest masc.)

Mt 12⁶ μεῖζον *something greater*? 12⁴¹ᶠ πλεῖον. Lk 1³⁵ τὸ γεννώμενον (was τὸ τέκνον in mind?). Jn 17²⁴ the gift is depicted first in its unity = ὅ, then individually = κἀκεῖνος. 1 Co 1²⁷ᶠ τὰ μῶρα . . . τὰ ἀσθενῆ . . . τὰ ἰσχυρά, pl. not to confuse with sing. in 1²⁵. 2 Th 2⁶ neut. synonymous with ὁ κατέχων 2⁷. 1 Co 11⁵ *she* is one and the same as if (ἐν καὶ τὸ αὐτό). Heb 7⁷ τὸ ἔλαττον 9⁵ χερουβείν as neut. pl. (or sing. AP). See Bauer s.v. for discussion and bibliography. Neut. pl. used adverbially Ph 2⁶ τὸ εἶναι ἴσα θεῷ (ἴσα Thuc. III 14. Abel § 41a).

A direct Hebraism is fem. for neut. [4]: Mt 21⁴² LXX = Mk 12¹¹ = Ps 117 (118)²³ αὕτη = זֹאת i.e. τοῦτο. LXX Ps 27³·⁴ 32⁶ 74¹⁸ 102¹⁹ 119⁵⁰·⁵⁶ αὕτη. 1 Km 4⁷ τοιαύτη. Etc.

Perhaps an Aramaism is Lk 11³³ εἰς κρυπτήν, where fem. pass. ptc. = a neuter, *hidden*; Bauer on the other hand takes the view = εἰς κρύπτην (see s.v.).

Note also the use of fem. to form adv. phrases: Lk 14¹⁸ ἀπὸ μιᾶς (see ch. 1). Mk 4¹⁰ κατὰ μόνας (ch. 1). LXX Jg 7⁵.

A masc. for a fem. is Mk 5¹⁵ λεγιών (because demon's name).

A fem. for a masc. is ἡ βάαλ.

Note the variation in the gender of λιμός Lk 4²⁵; Lk 15¹⁴ Ac 11²⁸; same variation in a papyrus ii/B.C.

---

[1] K-Blass I 358ff. Schwyzer II 27-38. Mayser II 1, 28-34. R. Meister, "Genus bei den LXX" (Wien Stud. 34, 77ff). H. Roensch, *Itala und Vulgata*, 1869, 452.
[2] Examples in K-G I 14,
[3] M. J. Lagrange, *S. Matthieu*, Paris 1948, 233, on Mt 12⁶.
[4] P. Katz, *Philo's Bible*, Cambridge 1950, 25f. Swete Intr.³ 307.

Inscriptions give a parallel for ἡ θεός and ἡ θεά Ac 19²⁷. Also papyri: θεοί ... πᾶσαι P. Eleph. 23¹³ (223 B.C.). SB 3444 (iii/B.C.). Or. gr. 132¹² (130 B.C.). θεὰς πάσας P. Grad. = SB 5680 (229 B.C.). Attic θεός was common gender, but later -α indicated a fem. deity ¹.

Sometimes a pl. masc. noun covers masc. and fem. subjects: Lk 2⁴¹ οἱ γονεῖς. To 10¹² B τοὺς πενθερούς. So οἱ ἀδελφοί, οἱ παῖδες. Thus οἱ κύριοι (Lk 19³³ Ac 16¹⁶·¹⁹) may cover a man and woman owner ².

The form πέτρος (Mt 16¹⁸ σὺ εἶ πέτρος καὶ ἐπὶ ταύτῃ τῇ πέτρᾳ) which is usually masc. (but in Hell. period also fem., probably in accordance with λίθος) means a *boulder*, a *stone*, and as a simplex it is restricted on the whole to poetic and elevated diction. On the other hand, the generally preferred πέτρα means chiefly *rock*; it is also a kind of collective or augmentative to πέτρος, and later it takes also the meaning a *fragment of rock*, a *stone*. The name of the apostle Πέτρος, if it actually means *rock* and corresponds to Aram. Κηφᾶς, cannot be connected directly with πέτρος, since this was out of general use; it does not mean *rock* but is a masculinizing of πέτρα (Wackernagel op. cit. 14f).

§ 2. The Number of Nouns ³

SINGULAR: (1) In LXX and pre-Christian papyri, a generic sing. may appear with persons or races, and in the pap. with numbers (like our *six foot*). The usage is not unclass., especially in the historians, and dates from Homer (Schw. II 41): with ὁ Ἰουδαῖος Ro 3¹ (*the Jew* as a Jew) cp. ὁ Συρακόσιος and ὁ Ἀθηναῖος Thuc. 6, 78, 1, ὁ Χαλκιδεύς 6, 84, 3, ὁ Ἕλλην Hdt 1, 69, and the proverb *Romanus sedendo vincit*, etc. With ὁ ἀγαθὸς ἄνθρωπος and ὁ πονηρὸς ἄ. Mt 12³⁵, ὁ ἀσθενῶν Ro 14¹, τὸ ἀγαθὸν ἔργον 13³, and ὁ δίκαιος and ὁ ἀσεβής 1 Pt 4¹⁸, cp. ὁ δικαστής Lycurg. 79. Generic also are the class. κέραμος Thuc. 2, 4, 2 and ἄμπελος 4, 90, 2. With class. ἡ ἵππος Hdt 1, 80, cp. LXX Ge 14¹¹ *cavalry*, Ex 8⁶ ἀνεβιβάσθη (ὁ)ἡ βάτραχος *frogs*. 1 Pt 2²⁴ LXX τῷ μώλωπι ἰάθητε Rev. 11⁸ πτῶμα αὐτῶν.

---

¹ Wackernagel II², 25.
² So Souter in *Expos.* VIII, 1914, 94f; IX, 1915, 94f.
³ K-G I, 13–20. Schwyzer II 38–46. Gild. I §§ 37, 42–59. Mayser II 1, 34–45. Wackernagel I 73–105. U. Holzmeister, "De 'plurali categoriae' in Novo Testamento et a Patribus adhibito," *Biblica* 14, 1933, 68–95.

§ 2] GENDER AND NUMBER OF NOUNS 23

It is not possible to classify here ὁ πτωχός Jas 2⁶ or ὁ δίκαιος 5⁶; these refer to an individual example (e.g. 2²).

We demur also at 1 Co 6⁵ ἀνὰ μέσον τοῦ ἀδελφοῦ αὐτοῦ: it is less likely to be generic than a combined result of Semitic influence and abbreviation thereof (full: *between brother and brother*), because in LXX we find e.g. ἀ.μ. ὕδατος καὶ ὕδατος Ge 1⁶ and ἀ.μ. ποίμνης καὶ ποίμνης 32¹⁶. It is not a great step to omit the repeated noun.

(2) Contrary to normal Greek and Latin practice, the NT sometimes follows the Aram. and Heb. preference for a distributive sing. Something belonging to each person in a group of people is placed in the sing.: as τὸ σῶμα ὑμῶν 1 Co 6¹⁹, ἐν τῇ καρδίᾳ αὐτῶν Lk 1⁶⁶. On the other hand, NT does frequ. exhibit the pl., e.g. καρδίαι Mt 9⁴.

	καρδία sing. of a group (Sem.)	Pl. of a group (normal)
Mt. Mk.	Mt 13¹⁵ LXX 15⁸ LXX = Mk 7⁶. Mk 3⁵ 6⁵² 7²¹ 8¹⁷	Mt 9⁴ 18³⁵ (sing. Syr. Coptᵇᵒ) Mk 2⁶·⁸ (sing. Syrᵖᵉ. Coptᵇᵒ 2MSS)
Lk. Ac	Lk 1⁵¹·⁶⁶ 8¹²·¹⁵ 9⁴⁷ 12³⁴ 24³²·³⁸ Ac 2³⁷ 28²⁷ LXX bis	Lk 1¹⁷ 3¹⁵ 5²² 16¹⁵ 21¹⁴·³⁴ Ac 7³⁹·⁵¹ vl⁵⁴ 14¹⁷ 15⁹
Jn	12⁴⁰ LXX 14¹·²⁷ 16⁶·²²	
Paul	Ro 1²¹ 2 Co 3¹⁵ 6¹¹ LXX Eph 1¹⁸ 4¹⁸ 5¹⁹ 6⁵ Ph 1⁷ Col 3¹⁶ DᶜEKL	Ro 1²⁴ 2¹⁵ 5⁵ 16¹⁸ 2 Co 1²² 3² 4⁶ 7³ Ga 4⁶ Eph 3¹⁷ 6²² Ph 4⁷ Col 2² 3¹⁵·¹⁶ 4⁸ 1 Th2⁴ LXX 3¹³ 2 Th 2¹⁷ 3⁵
Heb	8¹⁰ LXX vl.	3⁸LXX ¹⁵LXX 4⁷LXX 8¹⁰ LXX vl. 10¹⁶ LXX ²²
Jas	3¹⁴	4⁸ 5⁵·⁸
Jn. Epp	1 Jn 3¹⁹ vl. ²⁰bis ²¹	3¹⁹ S lat Syrʰ
Pet.		1 Pt 3¹⁵ 2 Pt 1¹⁹
Rev		17¹⁷

κεφαλή sing. of a group		Pl. as normal
Mt. Mk.	Mt 10^{30} = Lk 12^7	Mt 27^{29} = Mk 15^{29}
Lk. Ac	Lk 12^7 = Mt 10^{30} Lk 21^{18} Ac 18^6 21^{24}	Lk 21^{28}
Rev		4^4 $9^{7,17,19}$ 18^{19}
LXX	Ps $21(22)^7$ 37^4 Je 14^4 18^{16} Ziegler La 2^{15} etc.	Ps $108(109)^{25}$ etc.

ὀσφύς sing. of a group		Pl. as normal
Lk. Ac		Lk 12^{35}
Paul	Eph 6^{14}	
1 Pt		1^{13}

σῶμα sing. of a group		Pl. as normal
Mt. Lk	6^{25} = Lk 12^{22}	
Paul	Ro 8^{23} 1 Co $6^{19,20}$ 2 Co 4^{10}	1 Co 6^{15} Eph 5^{23}
Jas	3^3	

χείρ with preposition (metaph.) εἰς, ἐκ, ἐπί, διά		Plural
Mt. Mk		Mt 17^{22} = Mk 9^{31} = Lk 9^{44} Mt 26^{45} = Mk 14^{41} = Lk 24^7
Lk. Ac	Lk $1^{71,74}$ Ac 2^{23} (but C³EP pl) 15^{23}	Ac 5^{12} 14^3 24^7 vl 28^{17}
Jn	10^{39}	
Rev	13^{16} 20^4	

§ 2] GENDER AND NUMBER OF NOUNS 25

In addition we find ἀπὸ προσώπου and similar Semitisms always sing.: Lk 2³¹ Ac 3¹⁸·²¹ 7⁴⁵; κατὰ πρ. Lk 2³¹; διὰ στόματος Lk 1⁷⁰ Ac 3¹⁸·²¹ Eph 4²⁹ Col 3⁸ Rev 11⁵. We find distrib. sing. τύπον 1 Th 1⁷ (see Milligan's note) 2 Th 3⁹; στολὴ λευκή Rev 6¹¹. Distrib. sing. also in papyri: κατὰ γεωργόν (Mayser II 1, 45 n. 6).

PLURAL: Exceptionally the pl. may be used in the NT for one person or thing in both a Semitic and a normal Greek manner [1].

(1) *Semitic.* עוֹלָמִים is behind αἰῶνες[2], which means both *world* (Heb 1² 11³ 1 Ti 1¹⁷? 1 Cl 35³ 55⁶ 61² To 13⁷·¹¹) and *eternity* (Sext. Emp. phys. 1, 62. Orac. Sib. 3, 767. Barn 18² To 13² Si 18¹ Da 6²⁷Θ Lk 1³³ Ga 1⁵ Eph 2⁷ 3¹¹ Jude²⁵ Rev 14¹¹, and often), esp. in εἰς τοὺς αἰῶνας (Ps 60⁵ 76⁸ 88⁵³ Mt 6¹³ vl Lk 1³³ Ro 1²⁵ 9⁵ 11³⁶ 2 Co 11³¹ Heb 13⁸), εἰς πάντας . . . (To 13⁴ Da 3⁵² Enoch 9⁴ Or. Sib. 3⁵⁰ Jude ²⁵), and εἰς τοὺς αἰῶνας τῶν αἰώνων (Ps 83⁵ ZP 4, 1038, 22b 15, Ro 16²⁷ Ga 1⁵ Ph 4²⁰ 1 Ti 1¹⁷ 2 Ti 4¹⁸ Heb 13²¹ 1 Pt 4¹¹ 5¹¹ Rev 4⁹ᵗ 10⁶ 15⁷ 19³ 20¹⁰ 22⁵, 1 Cl 20¹² 32⁴ 38⁴ 43⁶). Thus we have *end of the world* τὰ τέλη τῶν αἰώνων in 1 Co. 10¹¹, as in T. Levi 14¹, but it may be the normal pl. of αἰών: *the fulfilment of the ages* or *the frontiers of the ages* (i.e. the limits dividing one of the seven *ages* from the ensuing one); Or. Sib. 8³¹¹ τέλος αἰώνων *end of time.*

שָׁמַיִם is behind οὐρανοί: but here again, following a Jewish idea, the pl. of seven heavens may be intended, esp. in 2 Co 12² Eph 4¹⁰. In the material sense of *sky* the sing. predominates: the exceptional plurals are Mt 24³¹ (contrast Mk 13²⁷, LXX De 30⁴), 3¹⁶·¹⁷ = Mk 1¹⁰·¹¹ (but Lk has sing.), Ac 7⁵⁶. In the less common figurative sense of *heaven* as God's abode the pl. predominates, as Mt 5¹⁶·⁴⁵ 6¹ etc.: the exceptional singulars (like ὁ μέγας ἐν οὐρανῷ Ζεύς Plat. Phaed. 246E) are Lk 10²⁰D (rest pl) 11¹³ (exc. p⁴⁵) Eph 6⁹S (rest pl) Col 4¹S* BAC (rest pl) 1 Pt 14S (rest pl), everywhere in Jn and Rev (exc. 12¹² LXX) Did 8². Taken as a whole, the sing. is more normal Greek, and scribes would correct to the sing. There is a significant variant at Mk 13²⁷: pl. is found in some MSS and some Old Latin, which is perhaps original in view of the tendency of scribes. In LXX the sing. is normal (Ge 1¹ 14¹⁹·²² To 7¹⁷BA Da Bel⁵ 1 Mac 2³⁷ al), with pl. in poetic passages (Jth 9¹², esp. Pss). For the LXX see P. Katz, *Philo's Bible* 141-146; H. Traub in Kittel WB V 510f.

(2) *Normal Greek but late.* Class. poetic sometimes: ἄρματα of one only (K-G I 18, n. 2). The allusive pl. is sometimes used when a class or variety rather than number is stressed. This is so in post-class. Greek and always the importance of the individual's action appears to be emphasized, not that of a group: Mt 2²⁰ τεθνήκασιν οἱ ζητοῦντες

---

[1] Kummerer. *Über den Gebrauch des Plur. statt des Sing. bei Soph. und Eur.*, 1869. Wackernagel I 97ff.
[2] H. Sasse in Kittel WB I 197-208 (αἰῶνες).

(Herod), Ostr. Berol. P. 10987 = SB 4631 (106 B.C.) τῶν οἴνων *the wine*, P. Hib. 54, 23 (245 B.C.) *send us the cheese* (τυρούς). P. Petr. II 20 col. 2, 5 πλήθη σίτου *a quantity of corn* (250 B.C.). PSI VI 584, 30 (iii/B.C.) γράψον μοι ... ἀντίγραφα *an answer* (Mayser II 1, 34f, 39).

A difficult pl. which may be explained in this way is Mt 2²³ *prophets*: the reference is to one prophet only. Zerwick calls it *pluralis categoriae* (§ 4a) and he further suggests it as an explanation of Mt 27⁴⁴ (after Jerome, Aug., Ambrose): both robbers are said to reproach Jesus whereas it was only one, and we need not call in another tradition to help us out. Other difficulties are thus solved: Mt 14⁹ Mk 6²⁶ ὅρκους *oath* (Xen. Hell 5, 4, 54. 2 Mac 4³⁴ 7²⁴ 14³². Ep. Arist. 126. Jos. Ant. 3, 272; 7, 294; see J. Schneider in Kittel WB V 458–467). Mt 21⁷ ἐπεκάθισεν ἐπάνω αὐτῶν (scribes soften the harshness), 22⁷ *army*, Mk 4¹⁰ *parable*, 7³⁷ *deaf* ... *dumb* (sing.), Lk 5²¹ βλασφημίας sing, Jn 6¹⁴ σημεῖα B al. Old Lat a boh, 6²⁶ σημεῖα 8²⁴ *sin*, 9¹⁶ *sign*, 10²¹ *blind man*. Zerwick (§ 4b) suggests that the women of Mt 28⁹ is a pl. of category referring only to Magdalene, in view of Jn 20¹⁴⁻¹⁸. Abel suggests (§ 41d) that this pl. of species is used in Ac 21²⁸ Ἕλληνας = only Trophimus! 19³⁸ ἀνθύπατοί εἰσιν too, because there was but one proconsul. Matthew uses the pl. of ὄχλος where we do not find the word at all in Mark: 5¹ 7²⁸ 9⁸·³³ 12⁴⁶ 13³⁴·³⁶ 14¹⁵. In this respect he is supported by Luke in Mt 11⁷ 12²³ 14¹³. In addition, Matthew has ὄχλοι πολλοί 4²⁵ 8¹·¹⁸ vl 13² 15³⁰ 19². It seems that ὄχλοι πολλοί means no more than ὄχλος or ὄχλος πολύς (or πλεῖστος) or πολὺ πλῆθος (Mk 3⁷), and is not intended to be understood of separate groups, in view of the Mk and Lk parallels. Therefore πολλοί must be taken in the unusual sense (as with χρόνοι) of *great* (= ἱκανοί or μεγάλοι). The usage is not quite confined to Mt (see Lk 5¹⁵ 14²⁵). But the motive for using the pl. of ὄχλος is not clear; it is confined to Mt Lk and Ac 1–17 (apart from a vl in Mk and Jn, and Rev 17¹⁵ where more than one crowd is meant). Probably it betrays the influence of the later Greek meaning of the pl., i.e. *the masses*.

(3) *Classical*. The directions *north, south*, etc. are pl. Mt 2¹ 24²⁷ Lk 13²⁹ ἀπὸ ἀνατολῶν. Pl. also in Diod. Sic II 43, Dio Cass. 987. 32, Jos. c. Ap. 1, 77, Philo spec. leg. 3, 187, Lucian peregr. 39, 1 Cl. 10⁴, LXX Ge 13¹⁴ Nu 23⁷. But sometimes sing. in NT: Mt 2²·⁹ ἐν τῇ ἀνατολῇ (or is the sing. astronomical rather than geographical? See Bauer s.v. = *rising*). Rev 7², 16¹² ἀνατολῆς (-ῶν A). 21¹³ ἀνατολῆς (even alongside pl. δυσμῶν; but Bᵣ ἀνατολῶν). Dit. Syll³ 1112, 25. Jos. Ant. 1, 37 al. Herm. V. I 4, 1.3. Also δυσμαί *west*, which is sing. in LXX, Enoch, Philo, Jos., Or. Sib., but generally pl. in Biblical Greek: BGU 1049, 8. LXX Ps 106³. T. Jud 5². Mt 8¹¹ 24²⁷ Lk 13²⁹ 12⁵⁴ Rev 21¹³. In MGr some place-names exist in the pl., referring to the region around; thus Ἀνατολάς = various parts of Asia Minor (Thumb Handbook² 27f); it may be that here we have a clue to the pl. ἀπὸ ἀνατολῶν Mt 2¹ (also LXX Ge 11²).

Right and *left* are pl., but also (as class.) sometimes sing: Ro 8³⁴ Eph 1²⁰ etc. *District* is pl. τὰ μέρη Mt 2²² etc., and *beyond* ἐπέκεινα Ac 7⁴³ LXX Am 5²⁷ probably (better vl ἐπὶ τὰ μέρη D*). Names of

§ 2]   GENDER AND NUMBER OF NOUNS   27

festivals are formed on the class. principle, as in the papyri (Mayser II 1, 39): Mt 14⁶ Mk 6²¹ Jn 10²². *Sabbath* pl. for sing.: Zen. P. Cairo 762.6 (iii/B.C.), Plu. mor. 169c, Mt 12¹·⁵ 28¹ Mk 1²¹ Lk 4¹⁶ Ac 13¹⁴·16¹³ Col 2¹⁶, LXX Ex 20¹⁰ Le 23³², Philo Abr. 28, Jos. Ant. 1, 33, Diog. 4, 3. That is unless we take σάββατα as a sing. (formed from שַׁבָּת with -α added to make it easier Greek). Other pl. festivals: τὰ ἄζυμα Mt 26¹⁷ Lk 22¹ Ac 12³ etc. Mk 14¹ (D om); οἱ γάμοι *wedding* (feast) poet. class., frequent in papyri (where sing. = *wedlock*, as sing. in Heb 13⁴): Preisigke s.v. (ii/A.D.), P. Ox I 111 (iii/A.D.), BGU III 909.3 (A.D. 359); also Diog. L. 3.2; it is suggested that the pl. is a Latinism from *nuptiae*; Mt 22² 25¹⁰ etc., Est 2¹⁸ 9²². Sing.: Mt 22⁸ Jn 2¹ᶠ and LXX. To 6¹³ 8¹⁹ 1 Mac 9³⁷ 10⁵⁸. Τὰ πάσχα Mt 26¹⁸W may be a mistake for τὸ πάσχα. Τὰ γενέσια (γενέθλια class. papyri; Mayser II 1, 39) Mt 14⁶ Mk 6²¹. Τὰ ἐγκαίνια LXX and Jn 10²².

Further class. plurals: πύλαι Mt 16¹⁸ only Wi 16¹³ (elsewhere sing. for one gate); θύραι in NT of one door in fixed idioms only, ἐπὶ θύραις Mt 24³³ = Mk 13²⁹, πρὸ τῶν θ. fig. Jas 5⁹, πρὸ τῆς θ. lit. Ac 12⁶, elsewhere several doors Jn 20¹⁹·²⁶ Ac 5¹⁹ 16²⁶ 21³⁰ (5²³ sing. or pl.?); κόλποι Hell. Lk16²³ (sing.²²); αἵματα¹ shed blood of several persons, LXX Hab 2⁸ etc. Rev 16⁶S (sing. BACP) 18²⁴B (sing. p⁴⁷ SACP), ancestral Jn 1¹³ (of husband *and* wife); ὕδατα Mt 14²⁸ᶠ Jn 3²³ Rev 1¹⁵ 14² 17¹·¹⁵ etc.

Less usual in class. Greek: ἀργύρια Mt 26¹⁵ 27⁵ 28¹²; ὀψώνια Hell. LXX pap. (sing. and pl. iii/B.C.; Mayser II 1, 37) Lk 3¹⁴ Ro 6²³ etc., sing. 2 Co 11⁸; κέντρα². Hell. Ac 9⁵ TR 26¹⁴ (perhaps pl. because the goad was double-pointed); ἱμάτια *upper garment* Jn 13⁴ 19²³ Ac 18⁶·⁷ (but *clothes* pl. Mk 5³⁰ et al.); χιτῶνες Mk 14⁶³; τὰ ἄγια *temple*, or part of, LXX, e.g. 3 Km 8⁶ Jdt 4¹² 16²⁰ 1 Mac 3⁴³ etc. Or. Sib. 3³⁰⁸ Heb 8² 9²·³·²⁴ᶠ 13¹¹ Philo Jos.; αἱ κριθαί Rev 6⁶ SACP (sing. B), sing. in post-cl. and LXX (Bauer s.v.; Mayser II 1, 35, several papyri iii/B.C.); αἱ διαθῆκαι Eph 2¹² Ro 9⁴ SCK (sing. p⁴⁶ BDE), sing. elsewhere in LXX NT; names of towns, Φίλιπποι, Ἀθῆναι, Πάταρα, Ἱεροσόλυμα (P. Zen. 259 B.C.), Τὸ AB, 1 Esd A (see Abel § 41); αἱ ἐπιστολαί 1 Co 16³?; ἡμέραι Mk 2²⁰ (and one day in same verse) but probably a Hebraism; καιροί *period* Rosetta stone 20 (196 B.C.) P. Petr. II 45 (246 B.C.) PSI IV 432, 5 (iii/B.C.), P. Par. 46, 7 (153 B.C.) etc. Mt 16³ this (*end-*) *period*, 21⁴¹ Lk 21²⁴ (T. Naphth. 7¹), Ac 1⁷ 17²⁶ *the allotted span*, Ac 3¹⁹ Messianic *period* (so 1 Th. 5¹ 1 Ti 4¹); χρόνοι Lk 8²⁷ TR (rest sing.) 20⁹ 23⁸ Ac 1⁷ Ro 16²⁵ 1 Th 5¹ 2 Ti 1⁹ Ti 1² 1 Pt 1²⁰ Jude¹⁸ Pol 1², not quite *years*, as in much later Greek, but advancing that way, certainly *period*, as in τῶν ἐπάνω χρόνων (*the earlier period*) P. Hib. 96, 6.23 (259 B.C.), Mayser II 1, 38, 2 Cl. 19⁴ οἱ νῦν χρ. = *the present period*, Herm. S. IX 20, 4 οἱ πρότεροι χρ. = *the earlier period*, M. Pol. XVI 2 οἱ καθ' ἡμᾶς χρ. = *our own period*.

Sometimes NT uses the Pluralis Poeticus for abstract subjects in a class. way³: e.g. φόνοι P. Teb I 5, 5 (118 B.C.), μοιχεῖαι, πορνεῖαι,

---

¹ See Behm in Kittel WB I 172 n. 6.
² See K. L. Schmidt in Kittel WB III 664, 18ff.
³ E.g. θρόνοι μάχαιραι σκῆπτρα in the tragedians: Menge, *De poetarum scaenic. Graec. sermone*, Göttingen 1905, 32ff.

κλοπαί Mt 15¹⁹ Mk 7²¹ᶠ; ἔρεις, ζῆλοι (vl in 2 Co 12²⁰) Ga 5²⁰ᶠ, with several other abstract nouns; ὑποκρίσεις 1 Pt 2¹ vl, with other abstracts, 4³, 1 Co 7² Jas 2¹ Jude¹³. These plurals may imply *cases of*... (Katz, op. cit. 112). In 2 Co 11²³ 2 Co 1¹⁰ (p⁴⁶ Syr) θάνατοι may imply ways of dying, i.e. *deadly perils*. Similar examples are μεθοδεῖαι Eph 6¹¹ *astuteness*; οἰκτιρμοί Ro 12¹ etc. (Hebrew), sing. Col 3¹² (K pl.); ἄναγκαι 2 Co 6⁴ 12¹⁰; θελήματα *that which (I) wish* Ac 13²² Eph 2³; μάχαι 2 Co 7⁵ Ti 3⁹; φόβοι 2 Co 7⁵ Xen. hier. 6, 5. Behind these plurals may be the thought of the diversity of words or expressions involved, although the Atticists resorted to the pl. to avoid hiatus.

The Pluralis Sociativus, or letter writer's plural (or *modestiae* or *auctoris*), is frequent in Paul especially with personal and possessive pronoun, but mainly where he seems to be writing on behalf of a group: Col 1³ (but sing. Eph 1¹⁵ᶠ) Ro 1⁵. See also Mk 4³⁰ Heb 5¹¹ 6¹·³·⁹·¹¹ 13¹⁸ᶠ·²²ᶠ 1 Jn 1⁴. This is common enough in all periods of Greek from Homer onwards and does not call for much comment. One can safely judge only by the context what number the writer really intends, since sing. and pl. alternate as capriciously in Paul as in contemporary letters. In 1 Jn the writer seems to identify himself very closely with other members of the fellowship; hence *we*.[1]

---

[1] On this subject see K. Dick, *Der schriftst. Pl. bei Paulus*, Halle 1900, Wackernagel I 98f, Stauffer in Kittel WB II 341A, 354f, Moule 118f.

CHAPTER THREE

THE COMPARISON OF ADJECTIVES AND ADVERBS

Comparison in Biblical Greek [1] is affected by the double influence of Semitic usages and the general trend of the Greek language. This resulted in more emphatic comparison, the positive adjective with παρά (= Heb. adj. and מן), a levelling of comparative and superlative, and a moving down one stage in the use of each of the three degrees. The disappearance of the Dual number is in line with this popular inability to distinguish between comparative and superlative (Zerwick § 112).

§ 1. Heightening of Comparison

As in the papyri the genuine comparative is still in wide use but the opportunity is frequently taken to heighten comparison by the addition to the comparative of particles like ἔτι and adverbs like πολύ and πολλῷ and even accumulations like πολλῷ μᾶλλον much more than in class. Greek [2]. Note also the comparative form of a comparative: 3 Jn[4] and Archiv f. Pap. (Wilcken) iii 173 (iv/A.D.) μειζοτέραν.

Πολύ or πολλῷ: PSI IV 435, 19 (258 B.C.), Ros. stone 31 (196 B.C.), Jn 4[41] 2 Co 8[22]; πολλῷ μᾶλλον P Par 26, 48 (163 B.C.) Ph 1[23] *much more better!*; μᾶλλον: 1 Cl 48[6], Herm. S. IX 28[4], 2 Co 7[13]; μᾶλλον περισσότερον Mk 7[36]; πολύ μᾶλλον: P. Tor. VIII 65 (119 B.C.), inscr. Preiss. Samm. 5827, 17 (69 B.C.); ἔτι: P. Petr. II 13(18b)11 (255 B.C.), Ph 1[9] *still more greatly*, Heb 7[15] *still more* manifest.

§ 2. Comparative for True Superlative

Mt 8[12] τὸ σκότος τὸ ἐξώτερον, 11[11], 18[1. 4] ὁ μείζων (or elative: *very*). In Apollodorus, of Odysseus tied under the *largest* ram: τῷ μείζονι (Radermacher[2] 68); μέγιστος is almost obsolete by this time, but appears

---

[1] K-G I 20ff, II 301ff. Schwyzer II 183–185. Gild. §§ 28–39. Mayser II 1, 45–54. Jannaris 315–317. Radermacher[2] ch. VII. M. Zerwick S.J., *Graecitas Biblica*[3], Rome 1955, §§ 107–116. Otto Schwab, *Historische Syntax der griechischen Comparation in der klassischen Litteratur* (Beitr. zur histor. Syntax der griech. Spr. herausg. v. M. Schanz. IV 1–3), 1893–95.
[2] Hesiod Erga 127 πολύ χειρότερον.

in Atticistic 2 Peter. Mk 9³⁴ τίς μείζων, Lk 7²⁸ ὁ μικρότερος *the least*, 9⁴⁸ ὁ μικρότερος ἐν πᾶσιν ὑμῖν, 1 Co 12²³ Heb 8¹¹, LXX 1 Km 17¹³A ¹⁴A Jg 6¹⁵, Barn 12² ὑψηλότερος πάντων *highest of all*.

§ 3. Comparative for Elative Superlative

In many instances where the comp. form indicates an unusually high degree of comparison in the NT and papyri (but not in Hermas), one may speak of an *elative* sense which normally belongs to the superlative. This is not class. usage and is characteristic of the inferior popular speech (Mayser II 1, 49f).

Add to Mayser's examples: P Teb. 33 (ii/B.C.) ἐν μίζονι ἀξιώματι, BU II 417, 28 (ii–iii/A.D.), 451, 11 (i–ii/A.D.), 615, 9.28 (ii/A.D.) ταχύτερον Ac 24²⁶ πυκνότερον *very often* or *so much the more often*, 2 Cl 17³ *as often as possible*, also Clem. Hom. ep. ad Jac 9, Ga 4¹³ τὸ πρότερον = τὸ πρῶτον *originally* (but the true compar. sense is possible: *the first time*), Ac 27¹³ ἆσσον *as near as possible* (or read θᾶσσον), 24²² ἀκριβέστερον *very accurately*, 18²⁶ 23¹⁵· ²⁰ same, P Petr. II 16.13 (iii/B.C.), PSI IV 444, 11 (iii/B.C.), Epict. I 24, 10, Herm. V. III 10¹⁰, Philo, Jos., BU II 388 II 41 (ii–iii/A.D.), Ac 25¹⁰ κάλλιον *very well* (or merely pos.), 2 Ti 1¹⁸ βέλτιον same (Ac 10²⁸D), Ac 4¹⁶D φανερότερον *extremely obvious*, 17²² δεισιδαιμονεστέρους not class. *rather* but probably popular elative *extremely god-fearing* (strengthened by ὡς), 2 Co 8¹⁷ σπουδαιότερος *very zealous*, Ph 2²⁸ adv., Clem. Hom. 1¹⁴ τάχιον *as quickly as possible*, 11¹³ same (distinguish from 9²³). But in some instances these might well be comp. for pos.

§ 4. Comparative for Positive

Especially τάχιον *quickly*: Jn 13²⁷ (but could be elative) 1 Ti 3¹⁴ SKL 0142 (WH ἐν τάχει) 2 Ti 4⁹ I 33 (rest τάχεως or ἐν τάχει) Heb 13¹⁹ (but prob. a true comp.) 13²³ *soon* Herm. M.X 1, 6.

Other examples are νεώτερος and καινότερος, often positive however in class. Greek; so in NT πρεσβύτερος is simply a religious official; Ac 17²¹ καινότερον *something new* (but possibly an Atticistic refinement: *newer*), 25¹⁰ κάλλιον (but perhaps under § 3), Ro 15¹⁵ τολμηρότερον *boldly*; PSI V 484, 7 (258 B.C.) πρεσβύτεροι = no longer young, *old* (older than they used to be, not older than others); Mayser II 1, 47f; Or. gr. 48, 15 (iii/B.C.) οἱ νεώτεροι *the young*, P. Petr. I 21 (237 B.C.) μείζω more than normally *large*; very often in Ptolemaic papyri πλείονες = *many, more than one*: Lk 11⁵⁴ περὶ πλειόνων (vulg. *de multis*), 1 Co 9¹⁹ 10⁵ 15⁶ Ac 19³² β-text 27¹² 2 Co 2⁶ 4¹⁵ 9² Ph 1¹⁴ Heb 7²³ (RSV *many in number*); Ac 2⁴⁰ ἑτέροις τε λόγοις πλείοσιν and M. Pol. 12¹ ταῦτα καὶ ἕτερα πλείονα exclude *majority* and *more* (it must be *many* or *several*);

§ 4-7] COMPARISON OF ADJECTIVES AND ADVERBS 31

P. Madg. 21, 6 (222 B.C.) τοῖς φυλακίταις καὶ ἄλλοις πλέοσιν *many others*. We suggest *many* for all the above NT examples of πλείονες, rather than the class. *more* or *the majority of*.

§ 5. Elative Superlative

Not so prominent in pre-Christian papyri as in NT and Christian texts: αἱ πλεῖσται Mt 11[20] *very numerous* Ac 19[32]D *very many*; ὁ πλεῖστος ὄχλος Mt 21[8] Mk 4[1] *very large*; σὺν ἄλλοις πλείστοις = *with very many others* P. Teb I 45, 17; 46, 14; 47, 11 (113 B.C.). Τιμιώτατος *most rare* Rev 18[12] 21[11] Jos. Ant. 17, 225. Κράτιστε *Most Excellent* Lk 1[3] Ac 26[25] Dion. Hal. opusc. I 3, 6. Ἐλάχιστος *very small* Mt 5[19] 25[40. 45] Lk 12[26] 16[10] 19[17] 1 Co 4[3] Jas 3[4]. Ἥδιστα Ac 13[8]D. Ἱλαρώτεραι Herm. S. IX 10, 7. The elative superlative may be intensified by the addition of ὡς, ὅτι, ᾖ, οἷος, and sometimes ἐν τοῖς (sc. δύνασθαι or οἷος ἦν): e.g. ὡς τάχιστα Ac 17[15], culminating in MGr ὅσον τὸ (τά) μπορεῖς γληγορύτερα *as quickly as you can*. On the other hand the true superlative, less frequent now but still active enough in the less uncultured papyri (Mayser II, 1, 51), is virtually dead in NT through Semitic influence. But see Ac 26[5] ἀκριβεστάτην, Eph 3[8] ἐλαχιστότερος (a compar. superlative: *less than least*). Mk 12[28] πρώτη πάντων. Mt 2[6] 5[19] 1 Co 6[2] 15[9] ἐλάχιστος. 1 Co 14[27] τὸ πλεῖστον *at most*.

§ 6. Positive for Superlative

We have no NT example of repetition of the positive, as in pre-Christian papyri, but the positive itself is used in a superlative sense under Hebraic influence (although there are class. poet. examples with gen.: κακὰ κακῶν, K-G I 21, 339): Mt 22[36] μεγάλη *greatest* (not *the great one*; equivalent to πρώτη πάντων in the parallel Mk 12[28], 5[19] Jn 2[10] τὸν καλὸν οἶνον *best*, Lk 9[48] μέγας *greatest*, Lk 1[42] εὐλογημένη σὺ ἐν γυναιξίν, LXX Ca 1[6] ἡ καλὴ ἐν γυναιξίν, Heb 9[2f] LXX τὰ ἅγια c. gen. *holiest*.

§ 7. Positive for Comparative

Mk 9[42] καλόν . . . μᾶλλον *better*. Lk 5[39] ὁ παλαιὸς χρηστός ἐστιν *is better*. Then the frequent οἱ πολλοί which is class., the *majority*, even without οἱ (as a vl) in Mk 6[2] 9[26]. Then Mt 20[28]D ἔτι κάτω = κατώτερον, cp. MGr κόμ (= ἔτι) καλός *better*. Where comparison is introduced by ἤ, μᾶλλον (ἤ), παρά or ὑπέρ (or ἀπό LXX) on the Semitic pattern, the adj. may be positive as well as comparative (although the adj. with μᾶλλον and μάλιστα had already occurred in Ionic prose and Attic poetry to a small extent): Ac 20[35] μακάριον . . . μᾶλλον . . . ἤ *happier than*, Ga 4[27] LXX πολλά . . . μᾶλλον ἤ *more than*, 1 Co 12[22] πολλῷ μᾶλλον . . . ἀναγκαῖα *much more necessary*, Lk 13[2] ἁμαρτωλοὶ παρά *more sinful than*, 18[14] SLB δεδικαιωμένος παρά (D adds μᾶλλον) (ἤ in W Θ, like LXX Ge 38[26] δεδικαίωται . . . ἤ ἐγώ); Mt 18[8f] Mk 9[43. 45. 47] 1 Cl 51[3] καλὸν ἤ *better than*; Mk 10[25] Clem. Alx. εὐκόλως . . . ἤ (it is suggested that this is the true pre-MSS text which was amended to εὐκοπώτερον); Ap. Const. 4³ μακάριος ἤπερ; LXX Ge 49¹² λευκοὶ ἤ; Ex 18¹¹ μέγας παρά (Philostr. Ap. III 19), Nu 12³ πραΰς παρά, 1 Km 1⁸ Ec 2⁹ 9⁴ ἀγαθὸς ὑπέρ, Hag 2⁹ μέγας ὑπέρ. The pos. with παρά is also MGr: see Pernot *Études* 75, who sees in this the ultimate influence of Hebrew on MGr. Germane to this is the frequent reduction of μᾶλλον ἤ to simple ἤ or παρά: LXX Ps 45(44)⁸ ἔχρισεν ... παρά, Lk 15⁷ χαρὰ ἔσται ... ἤ; 1 Co 14¹⁹, Just. Ap. 15⁸, BU III 846¹⁵ (ii/A.D.), Epict. III 22 θέλω ... ἤ; Lk 17² To 3⁶ λυσιτελεῖ ... ἤ; Mk 3⁴ ἔξεστιν ἤ; LXX Nu 22⁶ ἰσχύει ... ἤ; 2 Mac 14⁴² θέλω ἤπερ (but βούλομαι ἤ in Homer and often); it is a Semitism but there are some class. parallels: Andoc. 1, 125 λυσιτελεῖν ἤ, Hdt 9, 26 δικαῖόν ἐστιν ... ἤπερ (K–G II 303), Aesop 121 συμφέρει ἤ. Even without ἤ in Mt 5²⁹·³⁰ συμφέρει σοι ... καὶ μή.

§ 8. Superlative for Comparative

To complete the picture, πρῶτος and ἔσχατος must be mentioned here. Πρῶτος = πρότερος Aelian Anim. II 38; VIII 12, P. LPw (ii–iii/B.C.), Plut. Cat. min § 18, IG XII 5, 590, Kaibel Epigr. 642, 10 (iii–iv/A.D.), Mt 21²⁸·³¹ *elder*, Jn 1¹⁵·³⁰ *superior to* or *before me*, 15¹⁸ *before us*. Πρῶτος meaning *former* and ἔσχατος meaning *latter* occur in Mt 27⁶⁴. Thus πρῶτος in Ac 1¹ is ambiguous: either Luke is guilty of a popular Hellenistic mannerism or he intended to write three volumes. Similarly difficult is Lk 2² αὕτη ἡ ἀπογραφὴ πρώτη. It is the first census of a series (if class. Greek); or first of two (if Hellenistic). And if Hellenistic it could mean either *the first census of the two made by Quirinius*, or *the census before the (greater) census made by Quirinius*; see Lagrange *S. Luc* in loc.

With this popular Hellenistic failure to appreciate the significance of the Dual, we may compare the confusion of ἄλλος and ἔτερος, τίς and πότερος (Mt 9⁵ τί γάρ ἐστιν εὐκοπώτερον), and the use of ἀμφότεροι for more than two. See below, ch. 14 § 2.

CHAPTER FOUR
VOCATIVES [1]

§ 1. The use of ὦ

Whereas in class. Greek it was only exceptionally that ὦ was omitted, the reverse is now the case. Semitic and Koine influences once again united in their effect upon the NT, for in the Hell. period ὦ was reserved for emotional or stilted speech. " So erscheint ὦ bei Epiktet neben Eigennamen nur da, wo es sich um Grössen der Vergangenheit handelt " (Johann. DGKPS 13). In pre-Christian papyri it apparently occurs nowhere for certain except in an Artemis curse of iv/B.C. (Mayser II 1, 55). In Luke and Paul it occurs with only four out of seventeen vocatives. There will therefore be some special reason for each occurrence in the NT. Surprisingly we never find it used in prayer invoking the deity; but its use is confined to

(a) the beginning of a sentence where emotion is expressed: Mt 15²⁸ (not D) ὦ γύναι, μεγάλη (emph. position, increasing the emotion) σου ἡ πίστις (contrast γύναι alone: Lk 22⁵⁷ Jn 2⁴ 4²¹ etc.); Mt 17¹⁷ Mk 9¹⁹ ὦ γενεὰ ἄπιστος (great emotion); Lk 24²⁵ ὦ ἀνόητοι (exasperation); Ac 3¹⁰ ὦ πλήρης (indignation); Ga 3¹ ὦ ἀνόητοι Γαλάται (anger); 1 Ti 6²⁰ ὦ Τιμόθεε (affection). But there is no great emotion in: Ro 2¹·³ 9²⁰ Jas 2²⁰, and in fact simple ἄνθρωπε is found Lk 12¹⁴ 22⁵⁸·⁶⁰. Never ὦ πάτερ in NT, but in Josephus and Corpus Hermeticum. See Schrenk in Kittel WB V 985, n. 251;

(b) exclamations (= ὤ): Ro 11³³ ὦ βάθος;

(c) Acts, the only NT book where ὦ cannot be said to involve some emotion: 18¹⁴ ὦ Ἰουδαῖοι (not the first word, but correct position of the vocative in Attic style), 27²¹ ὦ ἄνδρες same. (Without ὦ: ἄνδρες ἀδελφοί 1¹⁶ 13²⁶ etc.; ἀνδ. Ἰσραηλεῖται 3¹²; ἄνδρες 7²⁶ etc.; ἀνδ. Ἰουδαῖοι 2¹⁴; βασιλεῦ 26⁷). There is no emotion, and everything that is classically correct, even to position after the first main verb, about ὦ Θεόφιλε 1¹; and yet Luke relapses into κράτιστε Θ. in Lk 1³, perhaps by a Latinism; cp. Dion. Hal. Orac. Vett. 1 ὦ κράτιστε Ἀμμαῖε. See Schwyzer op. cit. on this subject. The only other Biblical book which has unemphatic or unemotional ὦ (i.e. not corresponding to Heb. exclam. יהּ) is 4 Mac.; see Johannes. DGKPS 8-13.

---

[1] K.-G. I 47ff. Schwyzer II 59-64. Gild. I §§ 14-25. Humbert §§ 417-424. Wackernagel I 305-312. Mayser II 1, 55ff. Johannessohn DGKPS 7-15. Moulton Einl. 108ff. Abel § 42. Zerwick §§ 22-24.

§ 2. Nominative form instead of Vocative

Although there is no certain example in the pre-Christian papyri, yet in the less educated writers of the post-Christian papyri there is a tendency for nominative forms to usurp the vocative. In the NT generally, when adjectives are used alone, it is the nominative form : Ac 13¹⁰ ὦ πλήρης; Lk 12²⁰ 1 Co 15³⁶ ἄφρων (vl. ἄφρον). In class. Attic the articular nominative of a single noun sometimes accompanied rather harsh address to inferiors, somewhat impersonally and with particular definiteness (almost pointing) : ὁ παῖς, ἀκολούθει Aristoph. Ra. 521.

There is no vocative of the article in Greek, and so if the article was required the nom. form was used, the noun taking the nom. ending, if this was different, in sympathy with the article: Ga 4²¹ οἱ ὑπὸ νόμου θέλοντες εἶναι, Col 3⁵ τὰ μέλη *members, mortify earthly things*, 3¹⁸ᵗᵗ αἱ γυναῖκες, ... οἱ ἄνδρες, ... τὰ τέκνα, etc., 4¹ οἱ κύριοι, Eph 5¹⁴ ὁ καθεύδων. Some NT examples owe themselves to Hebraic influence, the Semitic vocative being constituted by articular nominative; thus LXX Ps 21² Lk 18¹¹ ὁ θεός, cp. ὁ πατήρ, etc., Lk 8⁵⁴ ἡ παῖς, ἔγειρε, Mk 5⁴¹ τὸ κοράσιον (= Aramaic emphatic state טַלְיְתָא), Mt 11²⁶ Mk 14³⁶ Ro 8¹⁵ Ga 4⁶ 'Αββα, ὁ πατήρ (Aram.), Jn 17²¹ πατήρ (anarthr.), Jas 5¹ οἱ πλούσιοι, Jn 13¹³ ὁ διδάσκαλος καὶ ὁ κύριος, 20²⁸ ὁ κύριός μου καὶ ὁ θεός μου perhaps because the vocative form κύριε is lightly used in the Gospels as almost *sir*[1]; hence the emphatic form here takes its place, *my Lord*; 19³ χαῖρε, ὁ βασιλεύς (S βασιλεῦ) (where Mt 27²⁹ BD Mk 15¹⁸ SBD have χαῖρε, βασιλεῦ . . .) said by Moulton to be due to "the writer's imperfect sensibility to the more delicate shades of Greek idiom"; actually it is an artist's stroke, the def. article pointing the finger of scorn; Rev 15³ ὁ βασιλεύς (S βασιλεῦ) τῶν ἐθνῶν (but Ac 26⁷ etc. βασιλεῦ, which, Moulton felt, admitted the royal prerogative whereas ὁ βασιλεύς in the mocking of Jesus does not); Lk 18¹¹ Heb 10⁷ OT etc. ὁ θεός (in Heb 1⁸ it is only just conceivable that ὁ θεός is nom. = *thy throne IS God*); Rev 11¹⁷ 15³ OT κύριε ὁ θεός (but Mt 27⁴⁶ θεέ μου, and seldom articular in LXX[2]), cp. Epict. II 16, 13 κύριε ὁ θεός which is from Jewish–Hellenistic magic; Rev 6¹⁰ ὁ Δεσπότης ὁ ἅγιος; Lk 12³² Mk 9²⁵ Rev 18⁴ ὁ λαός μου: Mt 9²⁷ 20³⁰·³¹ (p⁴⁵ υἱέ) υἱὸς Δαυίδ, anarthr. because of Heb. construct state (but Mk 10⁴⁷ υἱὲ Δαυίδ); Ac 7⁴² οἶκος Ἰσραήλ anarthr. because of construct state (LXX

---

[1] Κύριε of Jesus: Mk 7²⁸ 10⁵¹; Mt 72¹ᶠ 8². 6. 8. 21. 25 14²⁸. 30 15²². 25. 27 16²² 17⁴. 15 18²¹ 20³⁰ᶠ. 33 25³⁷. 44 26³²; Lk 5⁸. 12 6⁴⁶ 7⁶ 9⁵⁴. 59 vl 61 10¹⁷. 40 11¹ 12⁴¹ 13²³. 25 14²² 17³⁷ 18⁴¹ 19⁸ 22³³. 38. 49; Jn 4¹¹. 15. 19. 49 57 6³⁴. 68 9³⁶. 38 11³. 12. 21. 27. 32. 34. 39 13⁶. 9. 25. 36. 37 14⁵. 8. 22 21¹⁵. 16. 17. 20. 21. Of others: Mt 11²⁵ 13²⁷ 21²⁹ 25¹¹. 20. 22. 24 27⁶³; Lk 10²¹ 13⁸. 25 14²¹ 19¹⁶. 20. 25; Jn 12²¹. 38 20¹⁵.

[2] Helbing DKVS 34. Thackeray OT Gr. § 10, 10. Katz, *Philo's Bible* 59f, 152f.

Am 5²⁵); Jn 17¹¹B ²¹BDW ²⁴·²⁵AB πατήρ; Jn 12¹⁵ABDW OT Lk 8⁴⁸ BKLW Mt 9²² DGLW Mk 5³⁴ BDW LXX Ru 2²² ABL Jg 11³⁵ B, etc. θυγάτηρ anarthr. How are we to explain the anarthrous nominatives among the above? They probably never had the article, but scribes fell into the contemporary way of substituting nom. forms in the 3rd declen. for the special forms of the vocative. E.g. BGU II 423.11 (ii/A.D.) κύριέ μου πατήρ, P. Ross. Georg. III 2, vol. 27 (iii/A.D.) μήτηρ.

Moreover the nominative is common, as in class. Greek to a less extent, when additions other than an adjectival epithet, and especially participles, are made to the vocative, including a second or a third vocative: Mk 9¹⁹ D Lk 9⁴¹ D ὦ γενεά ἄπιστε (but other MSS and Mt 17¹⁷ ἄπιστος), Jn 17¹¹ πάτερ ἅγιε, Lk 11³⁹ ὑμεῖς οἱ Φαρισαῖοι, Mt 6⁹ πάτερ ἡμῶν ὁ ἐν τοῖς οὐρανοῖς, Lk 6²⁵ ὑμῖν, οἱ ἐμπεπλησμένοι, Ac 13¹⁶ ἄνδ. Ἰσρ. καὶ οἱ φοβούμενοι τὸν θεόν; cp. Xen. Cyr. III 3, 20 ὦ Κῦρε καὶ οἱ ἄλλοι Πέρσαι, Ro 2¹·³ ὦ ἄνθρωπε ὁ κρίνων, Rev 12¹² οὐρανοὶ καὶ οἱ ἐν αὐτοῖς σκηνοῦντες, 18²⁰ οὐρανὲ καὶ οἱ ἅγιοι καὶ οἱ ἀπόστολοι, 19⁵ αἴνετε..., πάντες οἱ δοῦλοι αὐτοῦ, LXX Hag 2⁴ Sach 3⁸ Ἰησοῦ ὁ ἱερεὺς ὁ μέγας. Zerwick (§ 23) suggests that the speech of Elisabeth in Lk 1⁴⁵ becomes more intelligible if we understand ἡ πιστεύσασα as a vocative, as implied in the Vulgate's 2nd person: *Blessed are you because you have believed.* The difficulty is the αὐτῇ which soon follows, making the whole into 3rd person; of course, Vulg. alters this. Artemis pap. 1 (iv/B.C.) θεοὶ οἱ μετὰ Ὀσεράπιος καθήμενοι, P. Par. 51.39 (159 B.C.) εὐφράνεσθαι (= εὐφραίνεσθε), οἱ παρ' ἐμοῦ πάντες, J. Chrysostom *Hom. Stat.* 467, 17 (387 A.D.) ὁ θεός, ὁ μὴ θέλων τὸν θάνατον τοῦ ἁμαρτωλοῦ. " Cette construction devint fréquente à l'époque romaine, si bien que le nominatif avec l'article a fini par être l'équivalent du vocatif (σύ)."[1]

---

[1] Soffray p. 1.

CHAPTER FIVE

SUBSTANTIVAL ARTICLE AND PRONOUN

§ 1. Substantival Article[1]

The def. art. has always preserved its demonstrative force; this is apparent even in MGr. in τὸ καὶ τό, τὰ καὶ τά *this and that* and πρὸ τοῦ *previously*. In the beginning the def. art. grew out of the old demonstrative pronoun in Homer: *this one, he*. It separates some from others, individualizing something as this and not that. Considering the total use of the article, it is true that the higher the type of Greek above ordinary speech the less prolific is the use of the article, so that whereas Atticistic style keeps fairly close to the norm established by Attic prose popular speech uses the article freely. However this does not apply to the special use of the article considered in this section, the pronominal use, that is, the substantival use as opposed to the adjectival; this is much reduced in the NT. Only in Ac 17²⁸, a quotation, does τοῦ = τούτου, and there is no trace of καὶ τόν *and him*, τὸν καὶ τόν *such and such a one*, or πρὸ τοῦ *before this*. All we have is occasional occurrences of ὁ μὲν ... ὁ δέ *the one ... the other* and indefinite *one ... another*, and ὁ δέ *but he*, and ὁ μὲν οὖν *now he*.

(a) ὁ μὲν ... ὁ δέ: Ptol. pap. very rare (Mayser II 1, 56f); 1 Co 7⁷ (ὅς ... ὅς p⁴⁷ S°KL), Eph 4¹¹, Heb 7²⁰ᶠ·²³ᶠ 12¹⁰. Lk 8⁵ᶠ ὁ μὲν ... καὶ ἕτερος, Mt 13²³ ὁ μὲν ... ὁ δὲ ... ὁ δέ (but accent ὅ neut., cp.⁸). Mt 22⁵ C² X, Mk 4⁴ W τὸ μέν. Jn 7¹² οἱ μὲν ... ἄλλοι δέ. Its place is usually taken by a non-class. use of the relative: Lk 23³³ ὃν μὲν ... ὃν δέ, Mt 13⁴ ἃ μὲν ... ἄλλα δέ (D ἃ δέ) 13⁸ 16¹⁴ οἱ μὲν ... ἄλλοι δὲ ... ἕτεροι δέ, 21³⁵ 22⁵ 25¹⁵, Mk 4⁴ 12⁵ Lk 8⁵ Ac 14⁴ 17¹⁸ (τινὲς ... οἱ δέ) 27⁴⁴ 28²⁴, Ro 9²¹ 14² ὃς μὲν ... ὃ (ὃς FG) δέ, 14⁵, 1 Co 11²¹ 12⁸·²⁸ 2 Co 2¹⁶ Ph 1¹⁶, 2 Ti 2²⁰, Jude ²²ᶠ. Papyri: P. Teb. I 61(b) 29 (118 B.C.) τὴν μὲν ... ἣν δέ, P. Ox. IX 1189, 7 (c. A.D. 117) ἣν μὲν ... ἣν δέ). There are also Semitic substitutes: ὁ εἷς ... ὁ ἕτερος Mt 6²⁴ Lk 16¹³, εἷς ... καὶ εἷς Mt 20²¹ 24⁴⁰·⁴¹ Mk 10³⁷. Even Luke has ὁ εἷς ... ὁ ἕτερος.

---

[1] K-G I 583–588. Gild. II §§ 515ff. Schwyzer II 19–27. F. Völker, *Syntax d. griech. Papyri* I. Der Artikel, Münster 1903, § 1. Winer-Schmiedel § 17. Moulton Einl. 129.

§ 1-2]   SUBSTANTIVAL ARTICLE AND PRONOUN   37

(b) ὁ δέ, ἡ δέ, οἱ δέ. In class. Attic ὁ δέ rarely refers to the subject of the preceding sentence (Gild. II § 518). It occurs frequently in NT to continue a narrative, even in Jn where it occurs least often: 5¹¹ ὁ δὲ ἀπεκρίθη SC*GKL (ὃς δέ AB, as Mk 15²³ SD and P. Ryl. II 144, 14 (A.D. 38), P. Soc. It. IV 313, 8 (iii–iv/A.D.) ὃς δέ). Mt 26⁶⁷ 28¹⁷ οἱ δέ. It usually marks a change of subject for the new sentence, as in Attic (e.g. Mk 1⁴⁵ and throughout Mk). In Mk 10³² where οἱ δέ does not mark a change of subject the reading is probably to be rejected in favour of καί. On its rare appearances in papyri it is sometimes followed by a participle.

(c) ὁ μὲν οὖν. Acts only: 5⁴¹. With ptc. 1⁶ 2⁴¹ 8⁴ 11¹⁹ 15³· ³⁰ 23¹⁸ 28⁵.

There is no instance of the article as a relative pronoun in the NT.

§ 2. Substantival Pronouns[1]

(a) *Personal*. These are very frequent in the NT.

1. The nominatives ἐγώ σύ ἡμεῖς ὑμεῖς were usually not employed in class. Greek except for emphasis or antithesis; this principle is not strictly observed in NT and papyri (Mayser II 1, 33), e.g. the stock phrases in letters ὡς ἐγὼ θέλω, ὡς ἐγὼ ἀκούω, etc., cp. Tit 1⁵ ὡς ἐγώ σοι διεταξάμην. But in the following examples at least there is some sort of emphasis or antithesis:

ἐγώ Mk 14²⁹ Lk 11¹⁹ Jn 10³⁰ Ro 7¹⁷ 1 Co 7¹² Eph 4¹ (but prob. simply to carry an apposition) 2 Ti 4⁶; if ἐγώ occurs in the papyri it is usually emphatic. Σύ Mt 6¹⁷ 26⁶⁴ 27¹¹ Jn 2¹⁰ (cp. with πᾶς ἄνθρωπος) 4⁹ (but simply to carry a phrase in apposition, rather than emphatic: also 10³³ Lk 1⁷⁶ Ac 1²⁴ Ro 14⁴) 4¹⁰ 18³⁷ (*you have said it, not me*) 21²², Ac 10¹⁵ 11¹⁴, 2 Ti 4⁵ Jas 2³. Ἡμεῖς Mt 6¹² 17¹⁹ Ac 15¹⁰ Ga 2⁹. Ὑμεῖς Mk 6³⁷.

Without much emphasis are the following: Mk 13⁹ βλέπετε δὲ ὑμεῖς ἑαυτούς, ²³ ὑμεῖς δὲ βλέπετε, Lk 1¹⁸ ἐγὼ γάρ εἰμι πρεσβύτης, 9⁹ ἐγώ, Jn 1³⁰ (c Syrᶜ om ἐγώ), 18³⁸ superfluous ἐγώ, 1 Co 2³ κἀγώ, 11²³ ἐγώ, Ph 4¹¹ ἐγώ. Mt 11²³ σύ, 27¹¹ σύ, Jn 1⁴² σύ, 6³⁰ τί οὖν ποιεῖς σὺ σημεῖον; 18³³ σὺ εἶ ὁ βασιλεύς; Ro 2³ σύ. Ac 4⁷ τοῦτο ὑμεῖς are together stylistically but it is fanciful to suppose the meaning is *people like YOU doing a miracle like THIS*; the simple question was angry, not subtle. Jn 5³⁸· ³⁹· ⁴⁴ (some correctors have om. ὑμεῖς). Eph 5³² (it is straining things to say that ἐγώ = *I as an apostle*; the corresponding phrase in

---

[1] K-G I 555f. Gild. I §§ 68ff. Schwyzer II 186–207. Wackernagel II 84–101. Mayser II 1, 62–73. Winer-Schmiedel § 22. Moulton Einl. 135. G. Dronke, " Beiträge zur Lehre vom griech. Pron. aus Apollonius Dyscolus," *Rh. M.* 9, 107ff.

1 Co 1¹² is simply λέγω δέ). Lk 10²³ᶠ (there cannot be any difference between ἃ βλέπετε and ἃ ὑμεῖς βλέπετε standing side by side). 2 Co 11²⁹ (the sudden insertion of ἐγώ is gratuitous and meaningless in τίς ἀσθενεῖ καὶ οὐκ ἀσθενῶ; τίς σκανδαλίζεται καὶ οὐκ ἐγὼ πυροῦμαι;). Mt 10¹⁶ 11¹⁰ ἰδοὺ ἐγώ is the Heb. הִנְנִי, but the Aram. 'anāh is used unemphatically, especially with the participle. Thus there are no grounds for thinking that scribes have inserted the pronouns; we should retain them in the variant readings.

2. The difference between the enclitic and the accented forms of pers. pronouns in the oblique cases, like μου and ἐμοῦ, is once again the fact that the accented form tends to mark a contrast, as in class. Greek: P. Rein. 18, 5 (108 B.C.) γραψαμένου ἐμοῦ τε καὶ τῆς μητρός. But in Biblical Greek, and particularly the LXX (Johannessohn DGPS 369ff) there is a large number of these accented and enclitic forms, especially in the genitive, occurring without emphasis; clearly this is due in some part to Semitic influence and the resultant tendency to attach pronouns like suffixes to substantival and verbal forms with a liberality and casualness which offends classical taste. So the redundancy in the NT also is obviously a Semitism (Lagrange, S. Matth. XCVI); Hebrew and Aramaic employ this pronoun so often in the form of a suffix that it would be surprising if Jewish writers did not carry the habit into their Greek. The MSS show many variants but we do well to prefer the reading which retains the superfluous αὐτοῦ, etc. The general tendency of the language was certainly in this direction, and unliterary Gentiles indulge in the repetition of μου, σου, αὐτοῦ and the other oblique cases (Moulton-Howard 431f), but this will not explain the 34 instances of αὐτοῦ in Lk 1 where the Semitic background is so obvious, and the Semitic Matthew's usage is no more abundant than Mark's or Luke's. His extreme ἀποκριθεὶς δὲ ὁ κύριος αὐτοῦ εἶπεν αὐτῷ (25²⁶) is in line with the rest of NT. Of course, the writers vary in the degree to which they depart from the Greek norm of economy in this respect, some equipping every verb with a pronoun when it can be readily inferred from the context.

Very close to the Greek norm: Jn 8³⁸ παρὰ τῷ πατρί (SD add μου) and ὁ πατήρ often in Jn without pronoun, unless he means simply *the Father*. Mt 27²⁴ ἀπενίψατο τὰς χεῖρας, 15² τὰς χεῖρας (αὐτῶν add CDEF). Ac 7⁵⁸ τὰ ἱμάτια HPS (viii–xi/A.D. uncials; but rest have pronoun), 16¹⁵ παρεκάλεσεν λέγουσα, 13³ ἐπιθέντες τὰς χεῖρας αὐτοῖς ἀπέλυσαν, Mk 6⁵ ἐπιθ. τ. χεῖρας. Ph 1⁶ ἐπιτελέσει (sc. αὐτό). Eph 5¹¹ (sc. αὐτά). 1 Ti 6² (sc. αὐτούς). Jn 10²⁹ (sc. αὐτούς). Lk 14⁴ (sc. αὐτόν).

Less Greek: Lk 24³¹ αὐτῶν δὲ διηνοίχθησαν οἱ ὀφθαλμοί, Herm. S.V 7, 3 αὐτοῦ γάρ ἐστιν πᾶσα ἐξουσία A, VIII 7, 1 ἄκουε καὶ περὶ αὐτῶν. Ac 7²¹ superfluous αὐτόν bis, as scribal activity indicates. Mt 6³ superfl. σου. Mt 8¹ vl Mk 5² superfl. αὐτῷ; and same kind of repetition occurs in Mt 4¹⁶ OT 5⁴⁰ 8¹ 26⁷¹ Col 2¹³ Ph 1⁷ Jas 4¹⁷ Rev 6⁴. On the other hand, such repetition is not unknown in class. authors (K-G II 579, n. 2 and 3) where the first pronoun forms part of a preceding participial clause: eg. Mk 10¹⁶, ἐναγκαλισάμενος αὐτὰ κατευλόγει τιθεὶς τὰς χεῖρας ἐπ' αὐτά, and 9²⁸ Lk 1⁶² Ac 7²¹ 2 Pt 3¹⁶ and especially in Rev; see also Acta Thomae 198¹⁷ ἀνθρώποις ὑμῖν οὖσιν ὥσπερ τοῖς ἀλόγοις ζώοις ἐπιτιθέασιν ὑμῖν φόρτους (Ljungvik SSAA 27 gives further examples from apocryphal Acts). The question of rhythm may play some part in the repetition, e.g. Mt 22³⁷ (as in Engl.: *with all thy heart and with all thy soul and with all thy strength*); Rev 9²¹ οὐ... αὐτῶν οὔτε... αὐτῶν οὔτε ... αὐτῶν. And there is insertion for emphasis, e.g. P. Oxy. VIII. 1162 (iv/A.D.) τὸν ἀδελφὸν ἡμῶν Ἀμμώνιον παραγινόμενον πρὸς ὑμᾶς συνδέξασθαι (=σθε) αὐτὸν ἐν ἰρήνῃ; Passio Barth. 141³¹ τούτους πάντας τοὺς κατακειμένους ἐνθάδε ἀπὸ βαρέων νοσημάτων τίς ἐστιν ὁ καταβλάπτων αὐτούς; Jn 18¹¹ τὸ ποτήριον... οὐ μὴ πίω αὐτό; Mt 6⁴ ὁ πατήρ σου... ἀποδώσει σοι, 1 Pt 5¹⁰ PHL ὁ καλέσας ὑμᾶς... καταρτίσαι ὑμᾶς, Rev. 21⁶ 046 ἐγὼ τῷ διψῶντι δώσω αὐτῷ.

For accus. and infin. instead of plain infin., see pp. 147f.

For superfluous αὐτοῦ etc. after a relative, see p. 325.

See also Lk 12⁴⁸ Jn 6³⁹ 15².

It is usual to find that the accented forms of 1st p. sing. pronoun in oblique cases are used for special emphasis in the NT, especially after a preposition (with the notable exception of πρός: e.g. Mt 25³⁶ πρός με (S ἐμέ), Mk 9¹⁹ πρός με (p⁴⁵ S ἐμέ), Ac 22⁸ (S*AB ἐμέ)¹⁰, even emphatically Mt 3¹⁴ σὺ ἔρχῃ πρός με; however nearly all MSS read πρὸς ἐμέ in Jn 6³⁷ first time, and SE al the second time; inscr. from Magnesia 19¹⁰ πρὸς ἐμέ, 22⁵ πρός με, PSI IV 326, 4 πρὸς ἐμέ (261 B.C.), P. Hib. 63, 3 πρός με (265 B.C.)).

Quite in keeping with the animated style of Paul's letters is the usage of ἐγώ and σύ (all cases) which is first found in the late class. Greek of Demosthenes and which is actually more a matter of rhetoric than syntax. Paul instances both himself and his reader in a vivid way to illustrate a point, not intending to apply what is said literally to himself or his reader: Ro 2¹⁷ 7⁷ff. ⁹f 8²

11¹⁷ 14⁴ etc. 1 Co 10³⁰ Ga 2¹⁸. We must refer to Bauer s.v. ἐγώ (end); Stauffer in Kittel WB II 355ff.

Normal in secular Greek is the sense-construction with pronouns: Ac 8⁵ *Samaria* foll. by αὐτοῖς, similarly Mt 4²³ 9³⁵ 11¹ Lk 4¹⁵ Ac 16¹⁰ 20² 2 Co 2¹²ᶠ Ga 2² 1 Th 1⁹ etc.; Jn 8⁴⁴ αὐτοῦ can only refer to a general conception like *falsehood* which has been no more than implied (it is unhelpful to translate *his father*; this needs at least a change of subject just before, as RVᵐᵍ, and the whole thing becomes confused at once; it might refer to a mythological *devil's father*, but even this author could scarcely be so credulous); Ro 2²⁶ αὐτοῦ has no expressed antecedent but again is vague in reference; Eph 5¹² αὐτῶν too has but a general reference which must be drawn from σκότος just before; Theodoret I 914 τοῦτο τῆς ἀποστολικῆς χάριτος ἴδιον· αὐτοῖς γάρ (ἀποστόλοις must be inferred); 2 Co 5¹⁹ αὐτοῖς after κόσμος; Mt 1²¹ αὐτῶν after λαός; Jn 17² αὐτοῖς after πᾶν (but S*W correct to αὐτῷ); Mt 14¹⁴ Mk 6⁴⁵ αὐτοῖς after ὄχλος; 3 Jn⁹ αὐτῶν after ἐκκλησία; Mt 28¹⁹ Rev 19¹⁵ LXX Ex 23²⁷ Dt 4²⁷ 18¹⁴ al Ac 15¹⁷ OT ἔθνη foll. by αὐτούς; Ro 2¹⁴ by οὗτοι, Ac 16¹⁷ OT by οὕς; Lk 23⁵⁰ᶠ αὐτῶν of members of Council, inferred; LXX Jon 1³ εὗρε πλοῖον βαδίζον εἰς Θαρσίς . . . καὶ ἀνέβη εἰς αὐτὸ τοῦ πλεῦσαι μετ' αὐτῶν; Mt 8⁴ Mk 1⁴⁴ Lk 5¹⁴ αὐτοῖς after ἱερεύς, unless it is a general ref., not to the priests but to the public; Mt 14¹¹ Mk 6²⁸ αὐτῆς after κοράσιον; Mk 5²³ αὐτῇ after θυγάτριον (p⁴⁵ AK correct to αὐτῷ); Lk 2²¹ᶠ αὐτόν after παιδίου: Col 2¹⁵ αὐτούς after ἀρχάς, ἐξουσίας; Rev 17¹⁶ after κέρατα, θηρίον. This is fairly common in class. Greek and very common in LXX: Dt 21⁸, 1 Km 14³⁴ Wis 16²⁰ αὐτοῖς after λαός; Jdt 5³ αὐτῶν after λαός; Wis 16³ αὐτοί after λαός, Si 16⁸ αὐτῶν after παροικίας.

3. In MGr αὐτός has become the pers. pronoun *he* (not *himself*). The beginnings of this development appear already in pre-Christian papyri (Mayser II 1, 64), in LXX (e.g. Ge 12¹²), and in NT especially in Luke; e.g. 1¹⁷ αὐτὸς προελεύσεται αὐτοῦ,²² καὶ αὐτός, 2²⁸ καὶ αὐτὸς ἐδέξατο αὐτό,⁵⁰ καὶ αὐτοί,³ ²³, 4¹⁵ καὶ αὐτός, 6³⁵ 7⁵, 9³⁶ καὶ αὐτοί, 11¹⁴ καὶ αὐτό, 16²³ 24²¹. It is possible to argue that the emphasis is still present even in the NT examples, but even here in place of αὐτός a class. Attic writer would use ἐκεῖνος. The LXX appear to use αὐτός without emphasis but not αὐτή or αὐτό; perhaps Lk 11¹⁴ shows αὐτό so used, if καὶ αὐτὸ ἦν is genuine; as to αὐτή, the editors of the NT text are divided in preference for αὐτή and αὕτη (Lk 2³⁷ 7¹² 8⁴² Heb 11¹¹). The text is uncertain in Lk 4¹⁵ καὶ αὐτὸς ἐδίδασκεν (Ae om. αὐτός), 5¹⁷ 19².

It is not easy to decide, but probably the pronoun has some emphasis in all the following: Mt 1²¹ Col 1¹⁷ *he* and no other, Mt 8¹⁷ (Isa 53⁴)

§ 2] SUBSTANTIVAL ARTICLE AND PRONOUN 41

αὐτός ... ἔλαβεν *he himself carried*, 12⁵⁰, Mk 1⁸, 2²⁵ *he |himself*, 5⁴⁰ αὐτὸς δέ (ὁ δὲ AMW), 14⁴⁴ αὐτός ἐστιν *he is the man*, Lk 5³⁷ 6⁴² 10¹ 18³⁹, Jn 4² 6⁶ 9²¹ 16²⁷, Ac 3¹⁰ αὐτός (BDEP οὗτος), 14¹² 18¹⁹ Ro 8²³ 16² καὶ γὰρ αὐτή *she herself*, 1 Co 3¹⁵, 1 Th 3¹¹ 4¹⁶ 5²³, 2 Th 2¹⁶ 3¹⁶, Col 1¹⁸ καὶ αὐτός ἐστιν ἡ κεφαλή ... *he himself* (alone).

The proleptic pronoun followed by resumptive noun is an Aramaic peculiarity [1]: Mt 3⁴ αὐτὸς δὲ ὁ (ὁ om. D) Ἰωάννης *he, i.e. John*; Mk 2²¹ (see below under partitive ἀπό), 6¹⁷ αὐτὸς γὰρ ὁ (ὁ om. D) ʽΗρ. *he, i.e. Herod*, ²²AC τῆς θυγατρὸς αὐτῆς τῆς Ἡρωδιάδος *her daughter, i.e. Herodias's*, Jn 9¹³ ἄγουσιν αὐτὸν πρὸς τοὺς Φαρισαίους, τόν ποτε τυφλόν. Probably also: Mk 6¹⁷·¹⁸·²² 12³⁶·³⁷. It appears particularly in codex Bezae [2]: Mt 12⁴⁵ D αὐτοῦ τοῦ ἀνθρώπου ἐκείνου; Mk 5¹⁵! D καὶ θεωροῦσιν αὐτὸν τὸν δαιμονιζόμενον ... διηγήσαντο δὲ πῶς ἐγένετο αὐτῷ τῷ δαιμονιζομένῳ; 6¹⁸ D αὐτὴν γυναῖκα τοῦ ἀδελφοῦ σου. Ac 3² D (but mistake for παρὰ τῶν?). This hypothesis of Aramaic influence could explain the apparent use of αὐτός = οὗτος in a demonstrative sense: see p. 194.

(b) *Reflexive.* These pronouns do not share in the general increase in the use of pronouns in Hell. Greek. In the NT and pre-Christian papyri as in Hellenistic generally, even in the old colloquial Attic (but not class. Attic), the simple personal pronoun often serves as a reflexive; otherwise the regular reflexive is a formation of αὐτός like ἐμαυτοῦ, σεαυτοῦ, ἑαυτοῦ, αὐτοὺς ἡμᾶς (2 Th 1⁴), ὑμῶν αὐτῶν (e.g. Ac 20³⁰ 1 Co 5¹³ OT), ἑαυτῶν. In the NT sometimes αυτον may be αὐτόν, but if so, it is difficult to see why this abbreviated form should be used instead of ἑαυτόν when it obviously causes confusion with αὐτόν. The contracted form is dying out in Hell. Greek (Blass-Debr. § 64.1) and in the NT period αὑτοῦ is virtually dead. It is therefore precarious to read αὑτοῦ where the uncials have ΑΥΤΟΥ, and so with αὑτόν and αὑτούς (Lk 23¹² Jn 2²⁴ Ac 14¹⁷ Ph 3²¹).

1. *Direct reflexives.* Used as a direct complement of the verb (Jn 14²¹ ἐμφανίσω αὐτῷ ἐμαυτόν) referring back to the subject, we have in the NT usually these compound -αὐτός

---

[1] C. F. Burney, *The Aramaic Origin of the Fourth Gospel*, Oxford 1922, 85ff. Moulton-Howard 431.
[2] M. Black, *An Aramaic Approach to the Gospels and Acts* ², Oxford 1953, 70–74.

forms, but sometimes the simple pronoun (e.g. Mt 6¹⁹ᶠ θησαυρίζετε ὑμῖν (for ἑαυτοῖς) θησαυρούς; 17²⁷ ἀντὶ ἐμοῦ καὶ σοῦ (Aram. influence for ἐμαυτοῦ?): Ac 26⁹ ἔδοξα ἐμαυτῷ (= class. μοι), 1 Co 4⁴ ἐμαυτῷ σύνοιδα. Pre-Christian papyri exhibit examples of both emphatic and unemphatic reflexives formed from αὐτός (Mayser II 1, 66). But although personal pronouns have greatly increased in number in Biblical Greek, reflexive pronouns are retreating. The process is held up by the fact that the disappearance of ἐμός and σός often calls for the substitute of a refl. pronoun. In Luke ἑαυτοῦ is more frequent (60 times) than in Matthew (31). Note that Luke has altered Matthew's θησαυρίζετε ὑμῖν (6¹⁹ᶠ) to ποιήσατε ἑαυτοῖς (12³³). Instead of the reflexive, Mt has ἔλεγξον ... μεταξὺ σοῦ καὶ αὐτοῦ (18¹⁵) and δὸς ἀντὶ ἐμοῦ καὶ σοῦ (17²⁷). But Luke uses the reflexive gen. without emphasis (ἑαυτοῦ 15²⁰, Ac 14¹⁴). The confusion has a Semitic explanation, in that Hebrew-Aramaic pronominal suffixes allow no distinction between personal and reflexive (Zerwick § 156).

Another development in the LXX, NT and illiterate papyri is the use of the 3rd person reflexive in place of 1st or 2nd person. In the plural we have e.g. for 2nd pers.: Jn 12⁸ μεθ' ἑαυτῶν, Lk 17³ προσέχετε ἑαυτοῖς, Ph 2¹², Heb 10²⁵ ἑαυτῶν, Mt 3⁹ ἐν ἑαυτοῖς, 23³¹ ἑαυτοῖς, Ac 13⁴⁶, Heb 3¹³ ἑαυτούς, Mt 25⁹ Ro 6¹³ 1 Jn 5²¹. 1st pers.: Ro 8²³ ἐν ἑαυτοῖς, 1 Co 11³¹ ἑαυτούς, 2 Co 1⁹ ἐν ἑαυτοῖς, Ac 23¹⁴ 2 Co 10¹² ἑαυτούς. In the sing. the substitution is even more commonly found; for 2nd pers.: Mt 23³⁷ Lk 1⁴⁵ 13³⁴ Mk 12³¹ vl ὡς ἑαυτόν, Jn 18³⁴ ἀφ' ἑαυτοῦ σύ..., corr. to ἀπὸ σεαυτοῦ by SBC*L, Ro 13⁹ FGLP, Ga 5¹⁴ FGLN*P (OT) ὡς ἑαυτόν (but σεαυτόν, as in Mt 22³⁹ LXX, is prob. to be preferred), Ac 25²¹ αὐτόν for σαυτόν. For 1st pers.: Herm. V IV 1⁵ ἠρξάμην λέγειν ἐν ἑαυτῷ S*a s (corr. to ἐμαυτῷ by Sᶜ), Herm. S. II 1 τί σὺ ἐν ἑαυτῷ ζητεῖς, IX 2⁵, Clem. Hom. XIV 10, XVII 18 ἑαυτοῦ, BU 86 (ii/A.D.) ἑαυτοῦ.

Although after a preposition we find ἑαυτοῦ etc. (as Jn 8¹⁸ ἐγώ εἰμι ὁ μαρτυρῶν περὶ ἐμαυτοῦ), yet often in NT and Koine a simple personal pronoun will be used, and this is certainly so in Mt: 5²⁹ᶠ 18⁸ᶠ βάλε ἀπὸ σοῦ, 6² μὴ σαλπίσῃς ἔμπροσθέν σου, 11²⁹ *take my yoke* ἐφ' ὑμᾶς, 18¹⁶ παράλαβε μετὰ τοῦ BDIW (but σεαυτοῦ SKLM); and especially where two pronouns are connected: 18¹⁵ μεταξὺ σοῦ καὶ αὐτοῦ, 17²⁷ δὸς ἀντὶ ἐμοῦ καὶ σοῦ. But even Mt has the reflexive form too: 9³. ²¹ εἶπον ἐν ἑαυτοῖς, 12²⁵ *divided* καθ' ἑαυτῆς, 15³⁰ ἔχοντες μεθ' ἑαυτῶν. P. Petr. II 40(a) 27 (223 B.C.) περὶ ὑμῶν ἐντείνεσθε, PSI IV 443, 19 (iii/B.C.) ὑμᾶς παρεξόμεθα, etc. (Mayser II 1, 67). Ph 2²³ τὰ περὶ ἐμέ, Eph 2¹⁶ ἐν αὐτῷ either *by himself* or *by it* (the cross): similar ambiguity Col 1²⁰, 1 Jn 5¹⁰, Jas 5²⁰.

There is the Semitic periphrasis for reflexive pronoun [1] by means of נֶפֶשׁ, e.g. Lk 9²⁴ ἀπολέσῃ τὴν ψυχὴν αὐτοῦ is the same as ²⁵ ἑαυτὸν δὲ ἀπολέσας ἢ ζημιωθείς, and cp. Mt 20²⁸ (Mk 10⁴⁵) with 1 Ti 2⁶. Mt 16²⁵ᶠ (Mk 8³⁵⁻³⁷) in this sense: at least, Luke seems to have understood it so, for he writes ἑαυτὸν δὲ ἀπολέσας 9²⁵. So also OT quotations: Mt 12¹⁸ ἡ ψυχή μου (= ἐγὼ αὐτός), Ac 2²⁷ Heb 10³⁸. But clearly the contexts intend us to feel the force of the double meaning of נֶפֶשׁ as *soul* and *life* which cannot be rendered so neatly in Greek.

2. *Indirect reflexives.* There are NT examples, though comparatively few, of the use of the reflexive pronoun where there is little or no dependence on the verb, because of the intervention of a noun or a phrase: Mt 12⁴⁵ πονηρότερα ἑαυτοῦ (DE*W αυτου), Mk 5²⁶ τὰ παρ' ἑαυτῆς (ABL αυτης), 8³⁵ τὴν ψυχὴν ἑαυτοῦ σῶσαι (first time) B Orig. D², (second time) C³ WXYΘ fam¹³ (the rest correct to αὐτοῦ), Lk 11²¹ τὴν ἑαυτοῦ αὐλήν, 13³⁴ τὴν ἑαυτῆς νοσσιάν·(D αὐτῆς), 14²⁶ τὸν πατέρα ἑαυτοῦ B, τὴν ψυχὴν ἑαυτοῦ, ³³τοῖς ἑαυτοῦ ὑπάρχουσιν (DW correct to αὐτοῦ), 16⁸ τὴν γενεὰν τὴν ἑαυτῶν, 24²⁷ τὰ περὶ ἑαυτοῦ (DEL αυτου); often in Paul, e.g. Ro 4¹⁹ 5⁸ 16⁴· ¹⁸, 1 Co 10²⁹ συνείδησιν δὲ λέγω οὐχὶ τὴν ἑαυτοῦ (emph. and contrast),³³ τὸ ἐμαυτοῦ συμφέρον; Heb 10²⁵ τὴν ἐπισυναγωγὴν ἑαυτῶν (= ἡμῶν). This is quite common in the papyri (Mayser II 1, 67ff). The use of the simple pers. pronoun is more common in the NT.

(c) *Reciprocal pronouns.* As in the papyri and to some extent in earlier Greek, ἑαυτῶν serves for ἀλλήλων in NT.: P. Petr. II 45 (246 B.C.), P. Par. 46, 12 (153 B.C.), etc.; 1 Co 6⁷ having lawsuits μεθ' ἑαυτῶν, Eph 5¹⁹ speaking ἑαυτοῖς, Col 3¹⁶ admonishing ἑαυτούς, 1 Th 5¹³ be at peace ἐν ἑαυτοῖς (SD*FGP αυτοις, clearly = αὐτοῖς); but Mk 9⁵⁰ εἰρ. ἐν ἀλλήλοις. Often side by side with ἀλλ. for variety: Lk 23¹² μετ' ἀλλήλων ... πρὸς

---

[1] Schwyzer II 192 n. Huber 67. Mayser II 1, 65-72; II 2, 65-74. Winer-Schmiedel § 22, 18b. Lagrange, *S. Matth.* XCVII. Zerwick § 160.

ἑαυτούς (SBLT αυτους, clearly = αὐτούς), Col 3¹³; Ph 2³ is precise: ἀλλήλους ἡγούμενοι ὑπερέχοντας ἑαυτῶν; so Mk 9⁵⁰ ἔχετε ἐν ἑαυτοῖς ἅλα καὶ εἰρηνεύετε ἐν ἀλλήλοις. Other alternatives for ἀλλ.: Ac 2¹² ἄλλος πρὸς ἄλλον (ἄλλος ἄλλον in Mayser II 1, § 26 n.2). For "Semitic" εἰς τὸν ἕνα. see p. 187.

(d) *Demonstrative pronouns.* On the article as demonstr. pronoun, see pp. 34, 36f. The usual pronouns are οὗτος, ἐκεῖνος, less often ὅδε.

1. Ὅδε, fading rapidly in the Koine and lacking in the i/B.C. papyri (Mayser II 1, 73f), especially in its substantival use, in the NT it is almost confined to τάδε λέγει Ac 21¹¹ Rev 2¹· ⁸· ¹²· ¹⁸ 3¹· ⁷· ¹⁴, P. Giss. I 36, 10 (135 B.C.), 37 II 11 (134 B.C.), etc. It is commoner in LXX, especially in the more literary parts (Thackeray OT Gr. 11). It tends to belong to official writing and not to living literature. See also Lk 10³⁹ καὶ τῇδε ἦν ἀδελφή not = ταύτῃ but *behold there was,* as LXX use τῇδε to render הִנֵּה Ge 25²⁴ = 38²⁷ καὶ τῇδε ἦν δίδυμα *behold there were,* 50¹⁸ οἵδε ἡμεῖς σοι οἰκέται *behold we are,* Ex 8²⁹⁽²⁵⁾ ὅδε ἐγὼ ἐξελεύσομαι *behold I go,* Je 3²² οἵδε ἡμεῖς ἐσόμεθά σοι *behold we shall be.*[1] See also, in this light, Lk 16²⁵ fam¹ Marc. ὅδε = *this man* (not *he . . . here;* it was misunderstood by very early scribes as Hellenistic for *here* and therefore corrected to ὧδε, in the same way as in LXX ὅδε is corrupted to ὧδε Ex 8²⁹⁽²⁵⁾ Le 10¹⁶ DaΘ 3⁹²⁽²⁵⁾, and οἶδε to ὧδε, ἴδε, etc. Num 14⁴⁰).

2. Οὗτος is very frequent in papyri and NT and as in earlier Greek refers to someone actually present (often contemptuously Lk 15³⁰ ὁ υἱός σου οὗτος, 18¹¹ οὗτος ὁ τελώνης; also Mt 26⁶¹· ⁷¹ Mk 2⁷ Jn 6⁴² 9²⁴ 12³⁴ Ac 5²⁸ 7⁴⁰ 17¹⁸), not necessarily referring to the noun which is nearest, but to the noun which is most vividly in the writer's mind (deictic). Mt 3¹⁷ οὗτός ἐστιν ὁ υἱός μου, Ac 4¹¹ οὗτος Jesus (although *God* is the nearest noun), 8²⁶ αὕτη ἐστὶν ἔρημος the road (not Gaza, though G. is the nearer noun), Mt 3³ οὗτος (refers right back to ¹), 1 Jn 5²⁰ (God, not Christ, is the true God). It often refers back to a previous description or introduction of a person (anaphoric): Mt 27⁵⁷ᶠ

---

[1] J. Ziegler's conclusion; the MSS nearest to this are Marchalianus and Venetus (ιδου οιδε). but the great uncials (SB) have a corrupted text (ιδου δουλοι) which bears no relation to לי אתנו הננו. See *Beiträge zur Ieremias-Septuaginta,* Göttingen 1958, 38–39.

§ 2] SUBSTANTIVAL ARTICLE AND PRONOUN 45

ἄνθρωπος . . . οὗτος προσελθών, etc., Lk 23^50f ἀνήρ . . . οὗτος οὐκ ἦν, Ac 1^16ff Ἰούδα . . . οὗτος, Heb 7^1.

Indeed οὗτος in the apodosis referring back to the protasis is a favourite usage in various NT writers (but Luke often gets rid of it): Mt 10^22 24^13 ὁ δὲ ὑπομείνας . . . οὗτος σωθήσεται = Mk 13^13 (Lk alters), Mk 12^40 = Lk 20^47 κατέσθοντες τὰς οἰκίας . . . οὗτοι λήμψονται, Jn 6^46 ὁ ὢν παρὰ τοῦ θεοῦ οὗτος ἑώρακεν, 7^18 ὁ δὲ ζητῶν τὴν δόξαν . . . οὗτος ἀληθής ἐστιν, 15^5 ὁ μείνων ἐν ἐμοί . . . οὗτος φέρει καρπόν, Mt 5^19 ὃς δ᾽ ἂν ποιήσῃ . . . οὗτος μέγας κληθήσεται, 2 Jn^9 ὁ μένων . . . οὗτος . . . Mt 21^42 = Mk 12^10, Mt 13^20. 38 15^11 18^4 26^23, Mk 3^35 6^16 Lk 9^24 Ro 7^15 ὁ μισῶ τοῦτο ποιῶ, Jas 3^2 εἴ τις . . . οὗτος . . .

A characteristic usage in Paul and John is οὗτος in the preceding clause with ἵνα, ὅτι, or infin. or a noun to follow: Lk 1^43, Jn 3^19 αὕτη . . . ὅτι, 8^47 etc. διὰ τοῦτο . . . ὅτι, 13^35, 1 Jn 2^3 ἐν τούτῳ γινώσκομεν . . . ἐάν, 3^11, 5^2 ἐν τούτῳ ὅταν, 2 Jn^6, 1 Co 7^37 τοῦτο κέκρικεν . . . infin., 2 Co 2^1 ἔκρινα ἐμαυτῷ τοῦτο, τὸ μή . . . ἐλθεῖν, 13^9 τοῦτο καὶ εὐχόμεθα, τὴν ὑμῶν κατάρτισιν, 1 Ti 1^9 εἰδὼς τοῦτο, ὅτι . . . , Heb 2^15 ἀπαλλάξῃ τούτους, ὅσοι . . . (examples in Pernot *Études* 50f, 62, 119, 144f), P. Petr. II 13 (19) (252 B.C.) τοῦτο . . . ὅτι, P. Par. 63 (165 B.C.) τοῦτο . . . ὅτι, PSI V 495, 23 (258 B.C.) same. Antecedent of a relative: Mt 11^10 οὗτος περὶ οὗ, Jn 7^49 Ac 7^40 οὗτος ὅς, Ph 2^5 τοῦτο . . . ὅ. We find various adverbial usages: αὐτὸ τοῦτο = Pauline *just this* Ro 9^17 OT 13^6 Ph 1^6 2 Pt 1^5; τοῦτο αὐτό = *just for this reason* 2 Co 2^3. See Bauer s.v. αὐτός 1 h. In Attic and literary Koine there is τοῦτο μέν . . . τοῦτο δέ *on the one hand . . . on the other* Heb 10^33. καὶ τοῦτο = *and indeed* Ro 13^11 1 Co 6^6. 8 Eph 2^8; pl. class. Heb 11^12. τοῦτ᾽ ἔστιν is formal and literary, mostly in Ac, Paul, Heb (besides Mt 27^46 Mk 7^2).

3. Ἐκεῖνος, which in its substantive use is almost never found in pre-Christian papyri, refers to the remoter person or thing, and is rarer in NT than οὗτος (except in John), with which it is practically interchangable; it very seldom marks an opposition to οὗτος, as it does in Herm. M. III 5 : ἐκεῖνα (*the past*) . . . ταῦτα (*the present*), but there is Lk 18^14 οὗτος . . . παρ᾽ ἐκεῖνον, Jas 4^15 τοῦτο ἢ ἐκεῖνο, Jn 5^38 ὃν ἀπέστειλεν ἐκεῖνος, τούτῳ . . . . However, in Jn 21^23 οὗτος and ἐκεῖνος are not so much for contrast as for variety. Ἐκεῖνος denotes persons in their absence deictically : ἐκεῖνοι opposed to ὑμεῖς Mt 13^11 Mk 4^11 Jn 5^39 Ac 3^13

2 Co 8¹⁴; opposed to ἐγώ or ἡμεῖς Jn 3²⁸· ³⁰ 1 Co 9²⁵ 10¹¹ 15¹¹. As οὗτος was seen to represent the person nearest to the author's mind, so ἐκεῖνος represents the remoter person, e.g. Jn 1⁶*tt*: οὗτος (John) ἦλθεν . . . ἵνα πάντες πιστεύσωσιν δι' αὐτοῦ; Jesus has now been mentioned and John becomes in thought the remoter person; hence οὐκ ἦν ἐκεῖνος τὸ φῶς. 7⁴⁵ the officers (who were away from the scene of action) came to the priests καὶ εἶπον αὐτοῖς ἐκεῖνοι. 13²⁴*t* νεύει τούτῳ (*John*) . . . περὶ οὗ λέγει (*Jesus* subject) . . . ἐκεῖνος (*John*, the remoter person, now Jesus has been introduced). Contemptuously like οὗτος: Jn 7¹¹ 9²⁸ 19²¹ *this fellow*. More often anaphorically, in the apodosis like οὗτος: Mk 7²⁰ τὸ . . . πορευόμενον, ἐκεῖνο κοινοῖ τὸν ἄνθρωπον, Jn 1³³ ὁ πέμψας . . . ἐκεῖνος, 5¹¹, 9³⁷ ὁ λαλῶν μετὰ σοῦ ἐκεῖνός ἐστιν, 10¹ ὁ μὴ εἰσερχόμενος . . . ἐκεῖνος . . ., 14²¹ ὁ ἔχων . . . ἐκεῖνος . . ., Ro 14¹⁴ τῷ λογιζομένῳ . . . ἐκείνῳ κοινόν, 2 Co 10¹⁸ οὐ γὰρ ὁ ἑαυτὸν συνιστάνων, ἐκεῖνος . . ., Xen. Cyr. 6, 2, 33 ὁ . . . ἀκούων, ἐκεῖνος . . ., Herm. M. VII 5. It is dependent on the personal whim of the writer whether οὗτος or ἐκεῖνος is used in this anaphoric way, Matthew preferring οὗτος, John liking both. Ἐκεῖνος is even, like οὗτος, used in the protasis with resumptive ὅτι, relative pronoun, etc.: Mt 24⁴³ ἐκεῖνο δὲ γινώσκετε ὅτι, Jn 13²⁶ ἐκεῖνός ἐστιν ᾧ ἐγὼ βάψω (Judas was not even absent, and by any rule we would expect οὗτος, as in Mt's parallel), Ro 14¹⁵ ἐκεῖνον . . . ὑπὲρ οὗ, Heb 11¹⁵ ἐκείνης ἀφ' ἧς. Thus, like οὗτος, its meaning is often weakened (especially in Jn) to *he* or *they*: Mk 16¹⁰· ¹³· ²⁰ Jn 10⁶ *they* (S* om), 5³⁷ 8⁴⁴ 9⁹· ¹¹· ²⁵· ³⁶ 11²⁹ 12⁴⁸ 14²¹· ²⁶ 16¹⁴ etc. So it is inadvisable to build any theories of authorship on the notorious ἐκεῖνος (= *he*, the eye-witness) in Jn 19³⁵.

4. Τοιοῦτος and τοσοῦτος are several times used substantivally in the pre-Christian papyri, especially with the article (Mayser II 1, 76), as also in the NT: τοιοῦτος Lk 9⁹ anarthr.; Mt 19¹⁴ Ac 19²⁵ Ro 1³² 1 Co 7²⁸ 2 Co 10¹¹ etc. articular. Τοσοῦτος Ac 5⁸ Ga 3⁴ Heb 1⁴ etc. anarthr.; none articular. Articular τοιοῦτος may be weakened into a more indefinite term for οὗτος: 1 Co 5⁵ 2 Co 2⁶· ⁷ 12²· ³· ⁵. In correlative clauses we have Ac 26²⁹ τοιούτους . . . ὁποῖος *qualiscunque*; Heb 1⁴ τοσούτῳ . . . ὅσῳ.

<small>Other less class. (more popular and Semitic) uses of correlatives include: Mk 9³ οἷος . . . οὕτως; 13¹⁹ οἵα . . . τοιαύτη; Rev 12⁶· ¹⁴ ὅπου . . . ἐκεῖ; 16¹⁸ οἷος . . . τηλικοῦτος; 17⁹ ὅπου . . . ἐπ' αὐτῶν. We can</small>

best explain Ro 9⁶ (οὐχ οἷον δὲ ὅτι ἐκπέπτωκεν) as a mixture of οὐχ οἷον (Hell. for οὐ δήπου Phryn. 372) and οὐχ ὅτι (see p. 298).

(e) *Relative pronouns.* Already in the Koine the distinction between the relative pronoun of individual and definite reference (ὅς and ὅσος) and that of general and indeterminate reference (ὅστις and ὁπόσος) has become almost completely blurred. Indeed in general relative clauses ὅς is the rule, and although ὅστις is still used occasionally in its proper sense of *whoever*, it is nearly always misused, by Attic standards, of a definite and particular person (Mayser II 1, 76. Pernot *Études* 150–180). Moreover the use of ὅστις for ὅς is very old in Ionic Greek (e.g. Hdt II 99).

The same development proceeds in the NT. Complete indifference to the distinction is shown by Matthew who writes ἀνθρώπῳ βασιλεῖ ὅς in one place (18²³) and ἀνθρώπῳ βασιλεῖ ὅστις in another (22²) after exactly the same phrase; and by Luke who writes πόλιν Δαυὶδ ἥτις καλεῖται Βηθλέεμ (2⁴) where to translate *utpote quae* (class.) is obviously wrong. Ὅστις is almost limited to the nominative in all writers, though least of all in John who uses ὅς (sing. and pl.) nom. 16, acc. 50, gen. 6, dat. 2 times. Ὅσος is restricted, except in Hebrews, to nom. and acc. In LXX ὅστις is confined to nom. and accus. In Luke the indef. forms are restricted to ἥτις οἵτινες αἵτινες; this may have been a general rule (perhaps to avoid confusion with the article) since we note the following interchange in Heb 9² ἐν ᾗ . . . ἥτις,⁹ ἥτις . . . καθ'ἥν, 13⁷ οἵτινες . . . ὧν, Eph 5⁵ ὅς (ὅ vl) becoming in Col 3⁵ ἥτις, Ro 4¹⁶ ὅς ἐστιν πατήρ becoming in Ga 4²⁶ᶠ ἥτις ἐστὶν μήτηρ. Heb 11³³ οἵ is the sole exception in that book. Cadbury [1] explains the few exceptions to this rule in Lucan writings as due in part to doubtful readings, in part to Luke having drawn some of his material from Mark (e.g. Lk 8¹³ = Mk 4¹⁶), and in part to euphonic considerations for avoiding a clash with a previous τινες (e.g. Lk 8² γυναῖκές τινες αἵ ἦσαν . . .). The rule is effective for Paul too, except that he has ἅτινα for ἅ: Ro 16³ᶠᶠ is particularly revealing, viz. οἵτινες . . . οἷς . . . ὅς . . . ἥτις . . . οἵτινες . . . (οἵ in ⁷, but notice the vl ὅς p⁴⁶ and τοῖς DG) . . . ἥτις. It is effective for John, except that he has ὅ τι and ἅτινα; and except for ὅστις 8⁵³ (D ὅ τι),

---

[1] *JBL* 42 (1923) 150–157.

where however it might be excused by class. standards (Zerwick § 165). As to Matthew, in general relative clauses he observes the rule in respect of ὅς in 10^{14} $23^{16.18}$, but not in respect of ὅστις in $5^{39.41}$ $7^{15.24}$ 10^{33} etc. [1], nor πᾶς ὅστις 7^{24} 10^{32} 19^{29}. He breaks the rule with πᾶν ῥῆμα ἀργὸν ὅ 12^{36}, πᾶσα φυτεία ἥν 15^{13}. The Ptolemaic pap. follow the same rule, irrespective of general or individual reference. The conclusion is that we must not in exegesis read into ὅστις any shade of meaning like *quippe qui* (*because*); e.g. Ac 17^{11} they were not more noble *because* they received the message, but simply *who* received the message, whatever the context or theology may demand. Care must be taken also not to read in too much of consecutive (Mt 2^6) or concessive (Lk 1^{20}) meaning.

Ὅσπερ, which still flourishes a little in pre-Christian papyri (Mayser II 1, 77) has been abandoned in NT, except for Mk 15^6 CΘEFG, and Jn 10^{16} ἅπερ p^{45}

Ὅ ἐστιν = *i.e.* Mt 1^{23} 27^{33} Mk 3^{17} 5^{41} $7^{11.34}$ 12^{42} $15^{16.42}$ Col 1^{24} Heb 7^2 Rev $20^{2.12}$ 21^{17}; P. Petr II 13 (17) 4 (258 B.C.), W. Chr. 167, 21 (131 B.C.), P. Goodsp. 6, 5 (129 B.C.), P. Lond. III no. 879 (p. 9) 21 (123 B.C.).

(*f*) *Interrogative pronouns* [2]. (The adjectival use is also, for convenience, discussed here.)

1. The direct interrog. pronouns τίς ποῖος πόσος ποταπός now find themselves used in indirect questions, since the indirect pronouns are going out of use. The confusion was not unknown in class. Greek, but the interchange is much more freely employed in the Koine.

Indirect use: P. Hib. 29, 41 (265 B.C.) γράφων τι ὀφείλεται, P. Eleph. 13, 7 (223 B.C.) γράφειν τί..., PSI IV 425, 28 (iii/B.C.) εἰδήσωμεν τίνες οὐκ εἰλήφασιν, P. Par. 34, 9 (157 B.C.) ἠρώτησάν με ἐν ποίῳ καταλύματι ... (= ἐν τίνι), P. Par. 60, 4 (154 B.C.) ἀπόστιλόν μοι πόσον ἔχει καὶ ὑπὸ ποίου χρόνου (= τίνος). For ποῖος = τίς op. also Dit. Syll³ 344, 59 (303 B.C.) ἐκ ποίας πόλεως, Ac 23^{34} ἐπερωτήσας ἐκ ποίας ἐπαρχείας (= τίνος), 1 Pt 1^{11} ἐραυνῶντες εἰς τίνα ἢ ποῖον καιρόν (tautologous for emphasis), Lk 7^{39} ἐγίνωσκεν ἂν τίς καὶ ποταπή ἡ γυνή..., 2 Pt 3^{11} ποταποὺς δεῖ..., P. Oxy. XIV 1678, 16 (iii/A.D.) γράψον μοι ποταπὸν θέλεις.

---

[1] In 7^{15} in fact the class. meaning *utpote qui* is quite appropriate (οἵτινες ἔρχονται ... ἐν ἐνδύμασι προβάτων).

[2] K-G II 515ff, Schwyzer II 212ff. Wackernagel II 110-125. Mayser II 1, 78-80. Winer-Schm. § 25. W. Petersen, "Greek pronominal adjectives of the type ποῖος," *Trans. and Proc. Amer. Philol. Assoc.* XLVI. 59.

§ 2] SUBSTANTIVAL ARTICLE AND PRONOUN 49

2. Confusion of relative and interrogative pronouns is usual in Hellenistic Greek, although sometimes Luke appears to be correcting Matthew.

(α) In the same sentence both types of pronoun may occur: P. Par. 62, 2, 6 (ii/B.C.) ὅσα ... ἐστιν καὶ τίνες ... καὶ ὅσας, 1 Ti 1⁷ μήτε ἃ ... μήτε περὶ τίνων, 2 Cl 1² πόθεν ... ὑπὸ τίνος ... εἰς ὃν τόπον ... ὅσα.

(β) The relative pronoun was used in indirect questions and after verbs of knowing, sometimes even in class. Greek (K–G II 438f), and frequently in the Koine: P. Goodsp. 3 (iii/B.C.) ὅπως εἰδῇς ὃν τρόπον οἱ θεοί σε οἴδασιν, P. Petr. II 11 (1) (iii/B.C.) ἵνα εἰδῶμεν ἐν οἷς εἶ, etc. ..., Mt 6⁸ οἶδεν ... ὧν χρείαν ἔχετε (see Bauer s.v. οἶδα 1 f.g.). But ὅστις ἥτις ὅ, τι hardly ever occur in this way in the Koine or NT as they did in class. Greek: Jn 5²⁷ κρίσιν ποιεῖν ὅ, τι υἱὸς ἀνθρώπου ἐστιν *to judge what a man is* (? or read as ὅτι), Ac 9⁶ ὅ τι SBAC (but vl. τί), Herm. S. VIII 1, 4 δηλωθήσεται σοι ὅ, τι ἐστίν (A τό τί). We do however find ὁποῖος: 1 Co 3¹³ Ga 2⁶ 1Th 1⁹ Jas 1²⁴. Οἷος may occur: Lk 9⁵⁵ οἴου πνεύματος (but ποίου D 700 al; p⁴⁵ W al om the whole). Ὅπως Lk 24²⁰.

(γ) Τίς = ὅστις or ὅς as a relative (perhaps as old as Sophocles) is Hellenistic: Athen. X 438 fin τίνι ἡ τύχη δίδωσι, λαβέτω (saying of Ptolemy Euergetes); Ptol. pap.: five exx. in Mayser II 1, 80, a papyrus (Cnidus ii–i/B.C.) ὅτι τί θέλ(ε)ις πράξω *that I will do what you want*, BU III 822, 4 (iii/A.D.) εὗρον γεωργὸν τίς αὐτὰ ἑλκύσῃ, LXX Le 21¹⁷, Mt 10¹⁹ δοθήσεται τί λαλήσητε (= διδάξει ὑμᾶς ἃ δεῖ εἰπεῖν in Lk 12¹²), 15³² οὐκ ἔχουσιν τί φάγωσιν, 26⁶², Mk 2²⁵ οὐδέποτε ἀνέγνωτε τί ἐποίησεν Δαυίδ (= Lk 6³ ὅ), 14³⁶ οὐ τί ἐγὼ θέλω, ἀλλὰ τί σύ (D corrects to οὐχ ὅ ... ἀλλ' ὅ ...), ⁶⁰ οὐδὲν ἀποκρίνῃ τί (= ὅ) οὗτοί σου καταμαρτυροῦσιν (but this involves understanding πρός before οὐδέν; we must therefore divide into two sentences οὐδὲν ἀποκρίνῃ; τί οὗτοι ...;), Lk 17⁸ ἑτοίμασον τί δειπνήσω, Ac 13²⁵ τίνα με ὑπονοεῖτε εἶναι, οὐκ εἰμὶ ἐγώ p⁴⁵? CD (τί ἐμέ SAB), Jas 3¹³ (but probably interrog.), Ign. Rom. 5³ τί μοι συμφέρει, ἐγὼ γινώσκω, BU III 948, 13 (iv–v/A.D.) οὐδὲν ἔχω τί ποιήσω σοι.

(δ) The confusion goes to extreme lengths in NT when we find ὅστις introducing *direct* questions, unless we are to understand ὅ, τι *why* as an abbreviation of τί (ἐστιν) ὅτι: Mt 16⁷ ὅτι ἄρτους οὐκ ἐλάβομεν, Mk 2¹⁶ ὅτι μετὰ τῶν τελωνῶν ... ἐσθίει; BL 33 (AC correct to τί ὅτι, and SDW harmonize with Mt and Lk διατί), 9¹¹ ἐπηρώτων αὐτὸν λέγοντες· ὅτι λέγουσιν οἱ γραμματεῖς ... (W harm. with Mt τί οὖν); this could be ὅτι after λέγοντες, but the parallel Mt 17¹⁰ has the question τί οὖν; and the Lat. vns. have *quare* and *quia*; 9²³ ἐπηρώτων αὐτόν· ὅτι ἡμεῖς οὐκ ἠδυνήθημεν (ADHII διατί, harm. with Mt); Jn 8²⁵ τὴν ἀρχὴν ὅτι καὶ λαλῶ ὑμῖν (Bodmer p⁶⁶ ειπον υμιν την αρχην is simply an insertion to make things easier) *why do I speak to you at all?* (class. τὴν ἀρχήν = ὅλως Hdt 4, 25; Dem. 23, 93; Lucian Eunuch. 6; P. Oxy. 472, 17 (A.D. 130); Philo spec. leg. 3, 121; Jos. Ant. 1, 100 etc.; Philostr. 1, 356, 17; Hom. Clem. 6¹¹ τί καὶ τὴν ἀρχήν ... διαλέγομαι, 19⁶ ἐπεὶ τί καὶ τὴν ἀρχήν ζητεῖ;); LXX Ge 18¹³ A ὅτι (τί ὅτι DM), 2 Km 7⁷ B ὅτι (Luc. τί ὅτι), 12⁹, 4Km 8¹⁴ AB ὅτι why (rest τί), 1 Ch 17⁶ ὅτι why, Barn. 8⁵ ὅτι δέ (presumably same meaning as διατί δέ in ⁴· ⁶), 10¹ ὅτι δὲ Μωϋσῆς εἶπεν Gr. Enoch 3¹ δι' ὅτι why?

It may not be too bold to go a step further and claim interrogative status¹ for ὅ in the notorious ἑταῖρε ἐφ' ὅ πάρει Mt 26⁵⁰ *what have you come for?* (vulg. *ad quid*). Certainly the gen. of ὅστις occurs in this way in eccles. Greek e.g. ἀνθ' ὅτου dir. question (Jannaris § 2038), and so also of ὅς, e.g. ὧν ἕνεκα Euseb. Praep. Ev. VI 7 p. 257d (Usener, *Der hl. Tychon*, 50); possibly Arr. Epict. IV 1, 120 ἦν δοκεῖς; the abbott Arsenius asks himself Ἀρσένιε, δι' ὅ ἐξῆλθες; (Migne PG 65, 105c. Zerwick § 169).

(*g*) *Interrogative pronouns used as exclamations.* Whereas class. Greek employs the relatives οἷος, ὅσος, ἡλίκος, etc. in this way (K-G II 100f), as the NT also employs οἷος in 1 Th 1⁵ 2 Ti 3¹¹ and ἡλίκος in Col 2¹ (possibly ὅσα in Ac 9¹⁶ 14²⁷) ², yet in the NT the interrogatives are used as exclamations just as they are used in indirect questions (see p. 49):

Mt 27¹³ (B*ὅσα), Mk 15⁴ ἴδε πόσα . . . Ac 21²⁰, Ga 6¹¹ ἴδετε πηλίκοις (p⁴⁶ B corr. to ἡλίκοις), 2 Co 7¹¹ (direct), Heb 7⁴; Acta Phil 62⁹ σὺ ἀγαπητὲ τοῦ θεοῦ Ἰωάννη, πόσα αὐτοῖς διελέξω καὶ οὐχ ὑπηκούσθης, 59¹²·¹⁷; Acta Thom. 235⁸; Acta Joh. 170¹²ᶠ; Mart. Petri et Pauli 158¹⁷ᶠ πόσων καλῶν πραγμάτων τε καὶ σημείων ὑπ' ἐμοῦ σοι δεικνυμένων θαυμάζω πῶς ἀμφισβητεῖς. The usage is not generally recognized as pre-Hellenistic, in spite of the contention of O. Lagercrantz, *Eranos* 18, 1918, 26–113.

On the whole then two points are notable in the NT and contemporary use of pronouns: 1. a great increase, to the extent of redundancy, and 2. " subtiliorum distinctionum abolitio " (Zerwick §§ 146, 161-169, who rightly insists that, for correct interpretation of the NT text, canons of classical and literary taste must be laid aside).

---

¹ Other interpretations, making ὅ a relative: (1) the ὅ refers to the kiss; paraphrase. " Friendly? You give me a kiss, for *which* I presume you have come here? " (2) Wellhausen has to supply too much, i.e. " By this kiss you are accomplishing the purpose for which you are here." (3) More simply, supply a verb, e.g. " *Do* that for which you are here." (E. C. E. Owen in *JThS* 29, 1928, 384–386; and Klostermann, *Zschr. f. nt. Wiss.* 29, 1930, 311, who adduces ἐγὼ δὲ ἐφ' ὅ πάρειμι, sc. ποιήσω). (4) Supply a ref. to the kiss: " *Is this* the reason why you are here? " (Radermacher² 78). (5) Emend to ἑταῖρε, αἶρε " *Take* what you have come for " (Blass).
² In Lk 5³D, Heb 10³⁷, Philitas 7D, ὅσον ὅσον = ὀλίγον ὀλίγον (Hesychius) *very little* or *how little!*

CHAPTER SIX

THE VERB: VOICE [1]

§ 1. Absolute Verbs (Mayser II 1, 80ff)

Many transitive verbs are used in an absolute sense, apparently as intransitive, the object understood from the context:

Mk 10¹⁹ μὴ ἀποστερήσῃς, P. Par. 26, 35 (163 B.C.) ἀποστεροῦσιν = *they deprive* a person, 1 Co 6⁸ ἀδικεῖτε καὶ ἀποστερεῖτε (MM Vocab. s.v.); Col 2¹⁵ ἐδειγμάτισεν (unless we take the previous object), cp. PSI IV 442, 18 (iii/B.C.) *arranged an inspection*, Mk 13¹⁷ ἐν γαστρὶ ἔχειν, P. Magd. 4, 6 (222 B.C.) ὗν λευκὴν ἐν γαστρὶ ἔχουσαν *be pregnant*; Mt 23¹⁶·¹⁸ ὀφείλει: Semitic חַיָּב is not needed to explain this absol. use, as we have Rev L. 5, 1 (259 B.C.).

§ 2. Transitive and Intransitive Verbs (Mayser II 1, 82–87)

Transitive verbs have a noun-object either in the accus. or in an oblique case; in intransitive verbs the verbal idea is entirely realized in the subject itself.

(a) Hellenistic Greek extensively gives to trans. verbs an intrans. sense and substitutes a reflexive idea for the object. The most frequent instance of this in the Koine is ἄγω and βάλλ-· with their compounds, compounds of στρέφω, and less often ἀνακάμπτω, κλίνω, λύω- and ἔχω- compounds.

ἄγω: Mt 26⁴⁶ etc. ἄγωμεν *let us go*, class. phrase ἄγε *come!*; παράγω *pass by* Mt 9²⁷ 20³⁰ Mk 15²¹ etc., Polyb. V 18, 4, P. Tebt. I 17, 4 (114 B.C.); *disappear* 1 Co 7³¹; περιάγω *go about, traverse* (not cl.) Mt 4²³ Ac 13¹¹; ἐπανάγω *return* Mt 21¹⁸ Xen. etc., P. Vat. A 15 (168 B.C.); in P. Par. 12, 20 (157 B.C.) = *return home*, but Lk 5³·⁴ *put out to sea* sc. boat; προάγω *go forward* 2 Jn⁹ vl, P. Lond. I no. 21 (p. 13) 15 (162 B.C.); *to go before* (τινα) Mt 2⁹ and *passim*, 1 Ti 1¹⁸ Heb 7¹⁸, P. Tor. I 8, 21 (116 B.C.); ptc. = *previous*; προσάγω *draw near* Ac 27²⁷ Xen. Hellenistic; συνάγε ἔτι ἄνω *move up* (but *assemble* in Or. gr. 130, 5 (146–116 B.C.) Mt 20²⁸ D; ὑπάγω Jn 3⁸ (and esp. often in Jn) = simplex as in MGr, especially in imperative, and only in pres. tense, P. Par. 15 (p. 225) 4 (121 B.C.) bis.

---

[1] K-G I 89–259. Gild. I 61–190. Schwyzer II 216ff. J. M. Stahl, *Kritisch-historische Syntax des griechischen Verbums der klassischen Zeit*, Heidelberg 1907. Jannaris 356–364. Wackernagel I 105–294. Mayser II 1, 80–130.

αἴρω: Ac 27¹³ *set sail*; μεταίρω *depart* Mt 13⁵³ 19¹, Aqu. Ge 12⁹.

βάλλω: Ac 27¹⁴ ἔβαλεν . . . ἄνεμος *rushed*; Mayser gives no parallels but there are Aesch., Eurip., Aeschin., and Enoch 18⁶, and ῥίπτω in the same sense (Radermacher², 23); Mk 4³⁷ class. ἐπιβάλλω *rush upon*; Lk 15¹², P. Lille 3, 64/5 (241 B.C.) τὸ ἐπιβάλλον μέρος; P. Grenf. I 33, 33 (103 B.C.) ἡ ἐπιβάλλουσα μερίς a fixed formula *belonging to* (Mayser II 1, 84); Mk 14⁷² ἐπιβαλὼν ἔκλαιεν is controversial: *begin* is possible in later Greek (Migne PG 93, 1708) supported by DΘ 565 ἤρξατο κλαίειν, gloss of Theophylact and Euthymius ἀρξάμενος; Diog. Laert. VI 27 ἐπέβαλε *begin*; P. Tebt. I 50, 12 (112 B.C.) ἐπιβαλὼν συνέχωσεν, exx. in Mayser II 1, 84 meaning *set to work and*; but *consider* is also possible (Marc. Ant. X 30 ἐπιβάλλων τούτῳ sc. νοῦν *consider this*).

βρέχω: Mt 5⁴⁵ Jas 5¹⁷ = ὕειν (class.) as in vernacular.

ἐγείρω: Lk 8⁵⁴ ἔγειρε (= ἐγέρθητι 7¹⁴) *be roused*.

ἔχω: Ac 21¹³ 2 Co 12¹⁴ etc. *to be* in a certain condition (class.), often in pap. letters with καλῶς *be well*, like Mk 16¹⁸; ἀπέχω *be distant* Lk 15²⁰ etc. (pp. 291, 336 for impers. use); ἐνέχω Mk 6¹⁹ Lk 11⁵³ *hate, persecute*; ἐπέχω *tarry* Ac 19²², P. Rev. L. 4, 2; 17, 6 (259 B.C.); προσ- *listen to* Ac 8⁶ 16⁴ Heb 2¹ 2 Pt 1¹⁹ pap. (τὸν νοῦν no longer inserted, as in class. Attic); *stands written* 1 Pt 2⁶ περιέχει ἐν γραφῇ¹; Jos. Ant. 11, 104 ἐν αὐτῇ περιέχει; ὑπερ- *excel* Ro 13¹ 1 Pt 2¹³ Ph 2³ 3⁸ Wis 6⁶ (Johannessohn DGKPS 69: 2 Mac 11²² ἡ δὲ τοῦ βασιλέως ἐντολὴ περιεῖχεν οὕτως).

ἀνακάμπτω: *return* Mt 2¹² Lk 10⁶ Ac 18²¹ Heb 11¹⁵; often in papyri (Mayser and MM Vocab.).

κλίνω: *decline* Lk 9¹² 24²⁹, Hell., Polyb. P. Hib. 38, 8 (252 B.C.), MGr.; ἐκκλίνω *turn aside* Ro 16¹⁷ etc., P. Tor. I 2, 17 (116 B.C.).

προκόπτω: Ro 13¹² Hell.

ἀναλύω: *go home* Lk 12³⁶ Ph 1²³, P. Par. 22, 29 (165 B.C.) etc. See Bauer s.v. and Büchsel in Kittel WB IV 338.

ἀπορίπτω: Ac 27⁴³, class. poet., Hell.

στρέφω: *turn* intr. Ac 3¹⁹ 7⁴²? 1 Pt 2²⁵ C (rest pass.), Jn 12⁴⁰ LXX WKLMX (rest pass.), Polyb.; ἐπιστρέφω *turn round*, P. Par. (Mayser II 1, 87), but the Bibl. context requires *be converted*; ἀναστρέφω *return* Ac 5²² 15¹⁶, P. Strass. II 111, 23 (iii/B.C.); ἀποστρέφω *return* Ac 3²⁶ P. Magd. 29, 9 (219 B.C.).

καταπαύω *take rest* Heb 4⁴· ¹⁰ LXX (Ge 2² Ex 31¹⁸ etc.), Com. Att. fragm. III no. 110⁸ p. 425 Kock (see Helbing DKVS 169f), but largely trans. in class.

ἐπιφαίνω: *show oneself* (of stars) Lk 1⁷⁹ Ac 27²⁰, Hell.

(b) Sometimes a causative sense is given to intrans. verbs, so that they may have an object. Thus in LXX βασιλεύω = *cause to reign*, ἐξαμαρτάνω = *cause to sin*, and some translators, esp. Lamentations, have gone very far in this direction ², but the

---

¹ The reading of C corrects it and makes it transitive again: ἡ γραφή.
² Thackeray OT Gr. 24; J. Ziegler, *Beiträge zur Ieremias-Septuaginta*, Gött. 1958, 53.

process is advanced also in NT: ἀνατέλλω *cause to rise* Mt 5⁴⁵ (but intr. oft.) class. poet. Ionic, LXX Ge 3¹⁸ (Helbing DKVS 78) 1 Cl 2⁴, Diog. 12¹, Ev Naas.²; ἀναφαίνω *cause to appear* (a Hell. peculiarity) Ac 21³ SB*, Lucian dial. mar. X 1 ἀνάφηνον; εὐαγγελίζω Ac 16¹⁷ D* Rev 10⁷ 14⁶ (but p⁴⁷S have middle, as elsewhere in NT), Hell. (see Friedrich in Kittel WB II 708, 710); μαθητεύω *make a disciple of* (for *be a disc.*, as Mt 27⁵⁷, Plut.) Ac 14²¹; κατακληρονομέω Ac 13¹⁹ OT *cause to inherit*; θριαμβεύω *lead in triumph* (for *celebrate a triumph*; class. intr.) 2 Co 2¹⁴, Plut., MGr τονὲ σπουδάζω *I make him study*, τονὲ ζῶ *I make him live*, μὲ πέθανε *he has caused me to die* (see Psichari 185).

§ 3. The Active Voice (Mayser II 1, 89ff. Jannaris 356 ff. Abel § 52)

The intransitive active is used in a passive sense with παρά and ὑπό c. gen., e.g. ἀποθνήσκω ὑπὸ τῆς λύπης *died in grief* P. Par 23, 12 (165 B.C.). It was the rule in Attic Greek, and the pass. of ἀποκτείνω was τελευτάω or ἀποθνήσκω, as in NT, although we find the pass. form ἀπεκτάνθη in Mk 9³¹ etc. Hdt 6, 92 ἐτελεύτησαν ὑπ' Ἀθηναίων. The pass. of (εὖ, κακῶς) ποιέω was (εὖ, κακῶς) πάσχω, as in Ga 3⁵ ἐπάθετε εἰκῆ, and we find in Mt 17¹² an excellent example of act. and pass. together: ἐποίησαν ἐν αὐτῇ ... μέλλει πάσχειν ὑπ' αὐτῶν (see P. Amh. 78, 4 βίαν πάσχων ... ὑπὸ Ἐκύσεως). See Ac 27¹⁷·²⁶·²⁹ for ἐκπίπτω as pass. of ἐκβάλλω (in Ptolemaic papyri πίπτω as pass. of ἐπι-, προβάλλω; Mayser II 1, 90). The intr. ἕστηκα *I still stand* (= I have been placed), pass. in meaning though act. in form, is well established in class. Greek, as also ἔστην, intr. but active in form (*stand*). The simply conceived expressions ἐξεληλύθει Lk 8² (as pass. of ἐκβάλλω) and τὸν ἀναβάντα πρῶτον ἰχθύν Mt 17²⁷, may be due to Aramaic influence (Wellhausen Einl.² 19), but they are not foreign to Koine ways of speech either: e.g. P. Giss. I 39, 9 (130 B.C.) ἐὰν δέ τις ὅρκος ἢ τεκμήριον ... ὑπὲρ τοῦ δικαίου πέσηι (sc. εἰς σε) *be imposed* (*on you*). The use of 3rd. p. pl. act. instead of pass. will be discussed pp. 292f.

§ 4. The Middle Voice (Mayser II 1, 91–116; Abel § 53)

MGr retains merely an active and a passive-deponent voice. The trend of the language in our period may have moved only very slightly away from the class. norm but it was in this direction: where class. writers preferred the middle voice to express a somewhat loose connection between the subject and the action of the verb, in Hell. Greek the active voice is preferred. The forms of the middle and passive voices are tending to merge. The fut. and aor. tenses of the middle are declining; they alone anyway remained distinct from the passive in form even during the class. period. Now deponent verbs prefer passive forms, and ἀπεκρίθη in the NT is used (about 195 times) in place of ἀπεκρίνατο, while ἐγενήθημεν (*we were*, not *we were made*) displaces ἐγενόμεθα. Moreover, where there was formerly a fut. act. with a fut. mid. form, very often it conforms now with the active (e.g. ἀκούσω for ἀκούσομαι).

(a) The middle voice has sometimes been described as reflexive, and there are many instances of this in pre-Christian papyri (Mayser II 1, 94–105), but Hell. Greek will as soon use the active with a reflexive or personal pronoun in order to express a reflexive idea. Theoretically the middle involves the whole subject in the verb's action and expresses the subject in some special relationship to himself; e.g. 1 Co 6[11] ἀπελούσασθε *you were washed*, i.e. got yourselves washed. But in our period there is not always any significance in the writer's choice of middle or active, and the reflexive middle in the NT is relatively rare: Mt 6[17] ἄλειψαί σου τὴν κεφαλήν, 27[5] ἀπήγξατο, Mk 14[54] θερμαινόμενος, Jn 19[24] OT διεμερίσαντο ... ἑαυτοῖς, 2 Pt 2[22] ὗς λουσαμένη (Radermacher[2] 147). The reciprocal middle is even rarer: perhaps Mt 26[4], Jn 12[10] *took counsel with one another*.

(b) There is much confusion in the use of middle and active in NT. Of some verbs there is the middle form only, no active, both in Hell. and earlier Greek (e.g. αἰσθάνομαι); but of others the middle form is often used where we expect the active in spite of what has been noted as to the tendency of the language to allow the middle to disappear. There was enough deadening of linguistic sensitivity to make this possible. So much so that in the papyri and NT we can find even the active and middle of the same verb together in the same phrase; some distinction may have been intended, but none is apparent. E.g.:

    1. αἰτέω *and* αἰτέομαι: an attempt was often made by exegetes to distinguish these in the NT, the active being described as a simple requesting and the middle an asking for what is due by contract. It is

true that the middle has a commercial or contractual flavour where the active serves for requests to God. "Commercial": Mt 27²⁰· ⁵⁸ etc. (mid.), Mk 6²² (act., but mid. in SW), ²³ (act.), ²⁴ (mid.), ²⁵ (mid.). Simple requests of a beggar or son: Mt 7⁹ᶠ Ac 3² 16²⁹ (act.) 1 Co 1²² (act.). But, although in the pre-Christian papyri the middle prevails in the official style (Mayser II 1, 109f), there is often no principle either here or in the NT. For instance, prayer to God can be middle: Mt 18¹⁹ etc., Ac 13²¹ LXX 1 Km 8⁵. And yet "contractual" requests can be active or, rather, even vary in the same context: Mt 20²⁰ (act.), ²² (mid.), Mk 10³⁵ (act.), ³⁸ (mid.). No rule applies to that or the following: Jas 4²ᶠ οὐκ ἔχετε διὰ τὸ μὴ αἰτεῖσθαι ὑμᾶς· αἰτεῖτε καὶ οὐ λαμβάνετε διότι κακῶς αἰτεῖσθε, 1 Jn 5¹⁴ᶠ αἰτώμεθα ... ὃ ἐὰν αἰτώμεθα, οἴδαμεν ὅτι ἔχομεν ... ἃ ᾐτήκαμεν. The change may have significance, but what? For the papyri see Mayser II 1, 109 n. 3, who quotes the ancient grammarian Ammonius to the effect that the active is used of requesting without reference to repayment, whereas the middle is to request with a view to using the thing requested and repaying it. But this hardly illuminates NT usage.

2. καρποφορέω and καρποφορέομαι: can there be significance in the contrast between the active in Col 1¹⁰ and middle καρποφορούμενον in 1⁶? The middle is rare, but there seems to be no difference (see Bauer s.v., but also Lightfoot in loc.).

3. *Some other verbs* appear in the middle where one expects active, since they have a transitive sense: the mid. of τίθημι in an act. sense has some class. precedent (e.g. Demosth. 56, 4 θέσθαι ἐν φυλακῇ like Ac 4³), 1 Co 12²⁸ οὓς μὲν ἔθετο, 1 Th 5⁹ ἔθετο ἡμᾶς; for pap. see Mayser II 1, 111; in view of Koine parallels, σπασάμενος in Mk 14⁴⁷ can easily be changed to act. in Mt 26⁵¹ ἀπέσπασεν; further the following appear in the NT in the middle with apparently the same meaning as the active: ἀμύνω aid (see Bauer), ἀπειλῶ, ἐπιδεικνύω, ἀπεκδύομαι Col 2¹⁵ (ICC in loc.) *strip* or *spoil*, but *divesting oneself* is the more usual meaning for mid., συνκαλέομαι Lk 9¹ 15⁶ DF ⁹ ADEGW 23¹³, Ac 10²⁴ 28¹⁷, ἐμβάπτομαι Mk 14²⁰ (Mt alters to act.), ἐπιδείκνυμαι *display* Ac 9³⁹, ἐπιτελέομαι *pay in full* 1 Pt 5⁹ P. Teb. 61 (b) 35 (118 B.C.) (ἐὰν μὴ ἐπιτελῶνται οἱ γεωργοὶ τὰ ἐκφόρια), ζηλόομαι Ga 4¹⁸ (or passive? Moule 25f), φανερόω Eph 5¹³ *that which illuminates*, or pass.?, φυλάσσομαι *observe* Mk 10²⁰ (parallels make it act.) LXX Ge 26⁵ Le 20⁸. Πληρόω is controversial: it appears in the act. Eph 4¹⁰ *fill*, but is this the same as the mid. in 1²³? AV and RV take it so, but some take it as pass., of Christ's being filled. Other words never appear in the act. in the NT but have an act. in the earlier Attic: προβλέπομαι Heb 11⁴⁰ *foresee*, περιβλέπομαι Mk 9⁸ etc. (mainly Mk, except for Lk 6¹⁰) *look around*, ἁρμόζομαι 2 Co 11² (no direct parallel, but see Moulton Pr. 160, MM Vocab. s.v.), ἐκδίδομαι Mt 21³³· ⁴¹ Mk 12¹ Lk 20⁹ (here Mt retains Mk's mid.) frequ. in pap.: P. Giss. I 1 col. 1, 8 (173 B.C.), καταλαμβάνομαι Ac 4¹³ 10³⁴ 25²⁵ Eph 3¹⁸ *apprehend mentally*, Dion. Halic. etc., παρατηρέομαι *watch closely* Lk 6⁷ 14¹ Ac 9²⁴, *observe scrupulously* Ga 4¹⁰. Ἐκλέγομαι *choose* Mk 13²⁰ Lk 10⁴² (11 times in Lk-Ac) Jn 6⁷⁰ (4 times) Eph 1⁴ 1 Co 1²⁷· ²⁸ Jas 2⁵, P. Magd. 29, 4

(221 B.C.) ἐγλεξάμενος τὸν βέλτιστον τόπον. The following middles are active with intrans. sense, and also have an active form in NT: ἀπορέομαι *be in doubt* Lk 24⁴ Jn 13²² Ac 25²⁰ Ga 4²⁰ 2 Co 4⁸; ὑστερέομαι *be inferior* 1 Co 12²⁴; ἐνεργέομαι Ro 7⁵ (8 times Paul) Jas 5¹⁶ *operate* (in act reserved for God or divine δυνάμεις in NT); see Lightfoot Gal. 204f., Milligan Thess. 28f., Mayor Jas. 177ff; but πολύ might be object in Jas 5¹⁶, thus making the verb trans. προέχομαι Ro 3⁹ (see Field Notes 152f., ICC in loc., Vaughan in loc.).

The evidence makes it difficult to claim, as Zerwick does (§ 178), that many of the above instances display a special use of the middle voice in which the subject is indicated as acting "ex se ipso", much less that ἔθετο in Ac 12⁴ indicates that Herod locked Peter up *very carefully*, i.e. for himself. The general lack of nice distinctions in use of the middle rules it out.

(c) On the other hand, some verbs appear in the active where we would expect the middle in class. Greek. The context supplies all that is required in the way of a reflexive idea. This is notably true of ποιέω with a verbal noun.

The middle of ποιέω is so rare in NT that its few (mainly Lucan) examples are worth studying (see Abel § 53 e): it is followed by ἀναβολήν, λόγον, μνείαν, πορείαν, σπουδήν; Lk 5³³ δεήσεις ποιοῦνται, 13²² πορείαν ποιούμενος, Ac 1¹ λόγον ἐποιησάμην (class., not same usage in pap.), 20²⁴ οὐδενὸς λόγον ποιοῦμαι τὴν ψυχήν, 25¹⁷ ἀναβολὴν μηδεμίαν ποιησάμενος, P. Amh. 34(c) 6 (157 B.C.), Ac 27¹⁸ ἐκβολὴν ἐποιοῦντο (techn.). The middle was the rule in class. Greek, and in some instances there is a variant correcting to the middle of ποιέω where the active appears in the stronger text: Mk 3⁶ συμβούλιον (mid. W), Jn 14²³ μονήν (mid. vl.), Ac 8² κοπετόν (mid. EHP), 23¹³ HP συνωμοσίαν (mid. vl). But the active, unchallenged, appears where we expect the middle: Mk 2²³ ὁδόν, 3⁶ συμβούλιον, Lk 1⁷² 10³⁷ ἔλεος (Hebraism; LXX Ge 24¹²), 18⁷· ⁸ ἐκδίκησιν, Ac 8² κοπετόν, 23¹² συστροφήν, 25³? ἐνέδραν; Jn 5²⁷ Jude ¹⁵ κρίσιν, Rev 11⁷ etc. πόλεμον.

This is true too of (κατα-) δουλόω: Ac 7⁶ OT 1 Co 9¹⁹ 2 Co 11²⁰ Ga 2⁴ 2 Pt 2¹⁹; and of εὑρίσκω *obtain* (where Attic prose had middle): Mt 10³⁹ 11²⁹ Lk 1³⁰ Ac 7⁴⁶ 2 Ti 1¹⁸ etc. Attic poets. See also Mt 26⁵¹ ἀπέσπασεν τὴν μάχαιραν (but correctly σπασάμενος Mk 14⁴⁷ Ac 16²⁷), 18²³⁽²⁴⁾ 25¹⁹ συναίρω λόγον (Moulton Pr. 160), 26⁶⁵ διέρρηξεν τὰ ἱμάτια, Ac 7³³ OT λῦσον (mid. LXX), 16¹⁶ παρεῖχεν ἐργασίαν (mid. C), 19²⁴ A* DE (mid. vl), 28² παρεῖχον φιλανθρωπίαν, ³ καθῆψεν (mid. C). See Deissmann NB 81ff; Moule 24–26. The middle is on its way out.

(d) Other verbs are passive in form but with middle or deponent meaning (middle-passive). These are also in the papyri: αἰσχύνομαι ᾐσχυνήθην, γίνομαι ἐγενήθην, δύναμαι ἠδυνήθην, ἀποκρίνομαι ἀπεκρίθην, ὀργίζομαι ὠργίσθην, φοβέομαι ἐφοβήθην, ἀνάγομαι ἀνήχθην, ἐνθυμέομαι ἐνεθυμήθην.

This is all part of the general Hellenistic tendency to substitute either the passive or active forms for the declining middle. The confusion of ἐβαπτίσθην and ἐβαπτισάμην has long puzzled expositors, but there is no mystery; both the middle and passive are now being used in the sense of *to allow oneself to be*..., and both voices become at times virtually an intransitive active: cp. ἀναστὰς ἐβαπτίσθη Ac 9[18]. In the variant readings therefore there is no prima facie evidence either way: Lk 11[38] 1 Co 10[2]. The development is fairly advanced in NT, where ἠγέρθη for instance is passive only in form and is used of the resurrection with a very active nuance: Mk 14[28] 16[6] Mt 27[64] etc. There is simply no difference between this and ἀνέστη, where the action of the Father is assumed no more and no less (Zerwick § 175). No one *placed* the Pharisee in the Temple in Lk 18[11] or Paul on Mar's Hill in Ac 17[22]; although σταθείς is used, they *stood* there. Translate *stand* also in Mt 18[16] Ac 5[20] Ro 14[4] Col. 4[12].

The following also are intrans. active in idea, rather than passive or middle: ἀπογράφομαι Lk 2[1, 3, 5] *register*; κείρασθαι, ξύρασθαι 1 Co 11[6] *cut her hair*; ὄφελον καὶ ἀποκόψονται Ga 5[12] (MM Vocab. s.v.); ἀδικέομαι *submit to fraud*, ἀποστερέομαι *submit to loss* 1 Co 6[7]; δογματίζομαι Col 2[20] *submit to rules*; γαμίζομαι Mt 22[30] 1 Co 7[38] etc. *get married*; συσχηματίζομαι Ro 12[2] *conform*; ἱλάσθητι Lk 18[13] *be merciful*; ἁγνισθῆναι Ac 21[24, 26] *purify oneself*.

§ 5. The Passive Voice (Mayser II 1, 116–130; Abel § 54)

(a) In common with class. Attic, when NT authors transfer certain verbs with a genitive or dative object to the passive, the indirect object becomes the subject of the verb; there may also be an impersonal indirect object in the accusative, and this remains so. E.g.:

With dative: ἐγκαλέομαι *be accused* Ac 19[40] etc., P. Magd. 21, 6 (1 B.C.) τοὺς ἐγκεκλημένους, also 33, 11 (221 B.C.) etc. (Mayser II 1, 120); διακονέομαι *be served* Mt 20[28] Mk 10[45]; μαρτυρέομαι *be well spoken of* Ac 6[3] 1 Ti 5[10] Heb 7[8] etc. (Deissmann NB 93); but this construction is not followed in 3 Jn[12] Δημητρίῳ μεμαρτύρηται, Dion. Hal. de Thuc. 8); πιστεύομαι *be entrusted with* Ro 3[2] etc. Polyb. etc.; *find belief, be believed in* 1 Ti 3[16] of Christ, 2 Th 1[10] of his witness; χρηματίζομαι *be warned* Mt 2[12] etc. Lk 2[26] D (different construction in the rest: ἦν αὐτῷ κεχρηματισμένον); εὐαρεστέομαι *be pleased* Heb 13[16], Diodor., Diog. Laert.; ἀρκέομαι Lk 3[14]

1 Ti 6⁸ He 13⁵ 1 Cl 2¹, Ign. Pol. 5¹, P. Par. 22, 20 (165 B.C.), 38, 11 (160 B.C.), BGU VI 1247, 13 (149 B.C.) etc.; ἐπιτρέπομαι *be permitted* Ac 26¹ 28¹⁶ 1 Co 14³⁴, Thuc. 3, 22 (οἷς ἐτέτακτο παραβοηθεῖν), P. Magd. 27, 6 (220 B.C.), but here the verb becomes impersonal when it is passive and the object of the act. remains still in the dative.

With genitive: καταγινώσκω *stand condemned* Ga 2¹¹ (Field Notes 188f) Diodor., M. Aurel.; κατηγορέομαι *be accused* Mt 27¹² Ac 22³⁰ 25¹⁶; πληρόομαι Jn 18⁹.

(b) Many trans. deponent verbs may be used with passive sense (see K-G I 120, 4; Stahl 73, 3) in both class. and later Greek. In the Koine this extends to all tenses with certain verbs, like βιάζομαι, ἐργάζομαι, λογίζομαι, but the pres. tense is rare, as in class. and NT.

Aorist: these passives are easy to detect as the two voices differ in form in the aorist (and future). κατειργάσθην 2 Co 12¹² *be performed*, several pap. (Mayser II, 1, 121); ἐλογίσθην λογισθήσεται *be reckoned* Lk 22³⁷ Ac 19²⁷ Ro 2²⁶ 4³ etc., pap.; ἰάθην ἰαθήσεται Mt 8⁸ etc.; ἀπαρνηθήσεται Lk 12⁹; ἐχαρίσθην Ac 3¹⁴ etc.; ἐρρύσθην Lk 1⁷⁴ etc.; ἐμνήσθην *be remembered* Ac 10³¹ Rev 16¹⁹ LXX, not class. or pap. See A. Prévot, *L'aoriste grec en* -θην, Paris 1935, 148–153.

Perfect: ἴαται Mk 5²⁹; ἐσμὲν εὐηγγελισμένοι Heb 4²; ἐπήγγελται Ga 3¹⁹ 1 Cl 35⁴, LXX 2 Mac 4²⁷; ἐπιλελησμένον Lk 12⁶.

Present: rare in NT, class. λογίζομαι Ro 4⁴· ⁵· ²⁴ 9⁸; εὐαγγελίζομαι Mt 11⁵ Lk 7²² 16¹⁶; βιάζομαι Mt 11¹² (not Lk 16¹⁶), P. Tebt. I 6, 32 (140 B.C.), Stahl 73, 3; ἰάομαι Ac 5¹⁶ D Barn 8⁶.

(c) The passives of verbs like ὁράω ὀπτάνω φαίνω γινώσκω εὑρίσκω may attach the person concerned by means of the dative, rather than ὑπό c. gen., and then they have an intransitive meaning:

ὀφθῆναι c. dat. P. Cair. Zen. 28, 3 (255 B.C.), P. Par. 63, 11, 56 (165 B.C.), Mt 17³ Mk 9⁴ Lk 1¹¹ 22⁴³ etc.; ὀπτάνομαι Ac 1³, Eurip. Bacch. 914 (ὀφθητί μοι), P. Par. 49, 33 (160 B.C.); φαίνομαι Mt 2⁷ Lk 9⁸ Ph 2¹⁵ Heb 11³ etc., frequ. in pap. (Mayser II 1, 122) *appear*; γινώσκομαι *become known* Ac 9²⁴ etc., Eurip. Cycl. 567, Xen. Cyr. 7, 1, 44 (but with ὑπό 1 Co 8³); εὑρίσκομαι[1] Ro 10²⁰ LXX (vl. ἐν), Ac 8⁴⁰ ε. εἰς Ἄζωτον 2 Co 12²⁰ *come to* (Heb. infl.), LXX Est 1⁵, Herm S. IX 13, 2; = *in regnum dei venire* (vet. lat.); Acta Thom. 175²ᶠ; also 116⁴ᶠ πῶς νῦν εὑρέθης ὧδε; Acta Andr. et Matth. 90⁹ᶠ πῶς εὑρέθης ἐνταῦθα; *what are you doing here? or how have you got in here?* (Wright II, p. 103); Gesta Pil. 12²; see de Boor's index to Theophanes: P. Ox. I 131 (vi–vii/A.D.); Acta Xanth. 76³²ᵗᶠ ἡ δὲ Πολυξένη ἐξελθοῦσα τῆς πόλεως καὶ μὴ ἐπισταμένη διὰ ποίας ὁδεύσῃ ὁδοῦ, εὑρέθη εἰς ἐρήμους τόπους ὁρέω (a striking parallel to Ac 8⁴⁰); Migne PG 65, 377c; MGr μοῦ εὑρέθη εἰς τὴν ἀνάγκην μου *he came to me in my need*; θεάομαι Mt 6¹ 23⁵ *appear*; σταθῆναι see Blass-Debr. §§ 97, 1; 191.

---

[1] See Sophocles Lexicon s.v. for its use in later Greek in this sense.

CHAPTER SEVEN

THE VERB: ASPECT AND TENSE [1]

IN SOME places in the NT interpretation is affected by a consideration which is important for understanding the verb. Originally in Indo-Germanic speech the tense-stems of the verb were not intended to indicate kinds of *time*, e.g. present, past or future. That came later, and incidentally can usually be assumed in Greek; but essentially the tense in Greek expresses the kind of *action*, not time, which the speaker has in view and the *state* of the subject, or, as the Germans say, the *Aspekt*. In short, the tense-stems indicate the point of view from which the action or state is regarded. The word *Aktionsart* (kind of action) has been taken over in all countries to express this essential idea. The chief kinds of action are: (1) continuous, which grammarians call *linear*, and (2) instantaneous, which they call *punctiliar*. By their very meaning some verbs can express only either one or the other *Aktionsart*, but the majority may be used in both ways. The aorist stem expresses punctiliar, and the present expresses linear action. Sometimes however the aorist will not even express momentary or punctiliar action but will be non-committal; it regards the action as a whole without respect to its duration; time is irrelevant to it. Now the augment (ἐ-) is a different matter. It was this which in Greek indicated the time as distinct from the *Aktionsart*, and the augment was added to both present (which becomes imperfect) and aorist action-stems

---

[1] K.-G I 129–200. Gild. I 79–143. Stahl 74–220. Schwyzer II 246–269. Wackernagel I 149–210. Jannaris 433–444. W. W. Goodwin, *Syntax of the Moods and Tenses of the Greek Verb*, Lond. 1897. E. W. Burton, *Syntax of the Moods and Tenses in New Testament Greek*[4], Chicago 1909. A. Svensson, *Zum Gebrauch der erzählenden Tempora im Griech*, Lund 1930, J. Holt, *Études d'Aspect*, Copenhagen 1943 (a hist. of *Aspekt*-theories). J. W. Carpenter, *The Aktionsart of the Aorist in Acts* (Diss. of S. Baptist Theol. Sem.) 1943. Gildersleeve, *AJP* 23, 1902, 241–53. E. Purdie, "The Perfective *Aktionsart* in Polybius." *IF* 9, 1898, 63–153. Moulton Einl. 176–237. O. E. Johnson, *Tense Significance as the Time of Action*, Language Diss. no. 21, 1936. J. Humbert, "Verbal Aspect: Has it evolved from Ancient to Modern Greek?" *The Link*, Oxford 1938, 1, 21–28. Zerwick §§ 180–214a. Moulton Proleg. ch. VI.

to show that the time had passed, from the speaker's standpoint. If there is no augment to the stem we may assume that the speaker refers either to some contemporary action or else that he is not concerned with the time as such at all. Besides the augment, the future tense too indicates a temporal relationship with the speaker and considerations of *Aktionsart* do not often intrude.

§ 1. Present Indicative

It normally expresses linear action and, until the augment has transferred this tense to the imperfect, the linear action is understood as taking place at the same time as the speech. The equivalent in English might be the periphrastic present: *I am walking*. There is however a complication, because Greek has no present stem with a punctiliar root. In order to say *I walk* without reference to time, English can be unambiguous; not so Greek. It must use the indicative of the present, with all the disadvantages of ambiguity arising from its linear stem; if the aor. indic. were used it would but confuse still more by bringing in the augment which indicates past time. Thus in Greek one seldom knows apart from the context whether the pres. indic. means *I walk* or *I am walking*. In other moods than indic., of course, the problem does not arise, there being no complicating augment, and so the aorist stem is freely used to indicate punctiliar action in *present* time. One must always bear that in mind for exegesis.

(*a*) The *Historic Present* is common to cultured and unliterary speech, to class. Greek, the papyri, LXX, Josephus, and MGr., especially in vivid narrative where the speaker imagines himself present [1]. In spite of the present being the tense of linear action, the hist. present is an instance where *Aktionsart* and tense-forms do not coincide; this present usually has punctiliar action. Mark and John are particularly fond of it, and their narrative is made vivid thereby. Mk has 151 exx. (72 verbs of speaking: λέγει and pl., and φησίν); Mt has 93 exx. (68 verbs of speaking); Lk only 9, and the Hellenistic 2 Maccabees only two (14¹⁶ συμμίσγει, 15⁵ φησίν). Luke markedly

---

[1] K. Eriksson, *Das Praesens Historicum in der nachclassischen griechischen Historiographie*, Diss. of Lund, 1943. Wackernagel I 162ff. Zerwick *Untersuchungen*, 49–57. Hawkins Hor. Syn.² 143f, 213ff.

§ 1]   THE VERB: ASPECT AND TENSE   61

tries to avoid it, as vulgar if used to excess. Were it not for the universal precedent in Greek we would be tempted to allege that the influence of the Aramaic participle accounts for this (see Moulton-Howard 456f). As Lagrange points out (*S. Matth.* XCII), it is Aramaic to use λέγει or pl. at the beginning without connecting particle: " en grec on dirait ἔφη, après un mot quelconque." In Daniel we have ענה ואמר, and this appears already in Pap. Eleph. 45 1. 16, but one also finds in these papyri the asyndetic אמר at the beginning. Mt has this λέγει 17 times: 8[7] 16[15] 17[25] 18[22] 19[8. 18. 20. 21] B⊖ 20[7. 21. 23 2]1[31. 42 22]4[3 26]2[5. 35. 64] 27[22]. Jn extensively uses it and varies it with the aorist quite naturally, sometimes keeping the main events in the present and the incidentals in the aorist (e.g. 1[29-43]). In all speech, especially the least educated, forms like λέγει and φησίν appear in reports of conversation: Mt Mk Jn prefer the former, Lk the latter. Sometimes it indicates that an event took place simultaneously with, or immediately after, a point of time already given: e.g. Mt 2[13] Mk 14[17], Herm. V. I 1[3], but the hist. pres. is so universal that it is impossible to theorize. We can only say that in post-class. Greek there is an increasing tendency to find it with λέγει and verbs of speaking, with verbs of seeing (this is frequent in the LXX Pent.), and with verbs of motion, especially coming and going (also frequ. in LXX later historical books). Thus there are 1145 pages in the eleven books of the Archaeology of Dionysius of Halicarnassus and 1000 historic presents—almost one each page (Eriksson op. cit. 39). And at its most frequent in Josephus we find: Ant. 5 (245/68 pp.), 6 (280/82 pp.), 18 (273/71 pp.), BJ 1 (379/140 pp.) (Eriksson op. cit. 76). The proportion in Arrian's *Anabasis* is 162/100 pp., as compared with Xenophon's *Anabasis* 165/100 pp. (Eriksson op. cit. 83). But doubtless the frequence of the picturesque participle in Heb. narrative, which tended to be translated by the present indic., contributed to its popularity in Biblical Greek.

It occurs about 337 times in LXX, of which 232 are in 1-4 Kms (Horae Synopticae[2], 213). Here, according to Thackeray (Schweich Lectures p. 21), it introduces a new scene in dramatic narrative, especially a new character or change of locality or a turning-point. "Even the colloquial λέγει . . . may be brought under the same head. It is the *loquitur* introducing a new speaker. It marks the exact point where *oratio recta* begins, the past tense being retained even in the verb immediately preceding; 'he answered and saith,' ἀποκριθεὶς λέγει in St. Mark, ὑπολαβὼν λέγει in Job LXX. The main function is this, I maintain, to introduce a date, a new scene, a new character, occasionally a new speaker; in other words, a fresh paragraph in the narrative." In what Thackeray called Early Reigns "the clearest instance of the date-registering use is the present βασιλεύει, which, along with θάπτεται, is constant in the recurrent decease-and-accession formula " in 3 Kms. "With this mannerism of the Alexandrian translators we should contrast the later fourth book, where the formula consistently runs ἐκοιμήθη—ἐτάφη—ἐβασίλευσεν." Thackeray suggested that the presents in Mark (except λέγει) were used in a similar way for new scenes and characters (p. 22). "They generally coincide with chapter-openings in the capitulary system in Codex Alexandrinus." But the very fact that Thackeray's later translator does not observe this canon is overwhelming evidence that if there was such a rule it was not universally observed. At most, it may be a tendency.

Mayser divides the use of hist. pres. in the pre-Christian pap. into three: (a) the dramatic: and a typical example is given, showing the variation with the aorist, in the same way as in Mk and Jn: P. Par 23, 9ff (165 B.C.) (II 1, 131), (b) in reports of dreams, obviously for drama and vividness, and (c) in making records, especially on letters and documents.

(b) The *Perfective Present* is rare.

It occurs in NT with ἀδικέω Ac 25[11] (Mt 20[13] is the usual sense of pres.) almost = *be worthy of death, be in the wrong*, P. Tebt. I 22, 11 (112 B.C.) γράψον ἡμῖν τίς ἀδικεῖ.—Ἥκω Lk 15[27] Jn 8[42] etc. *be here*, Or. gr. 186, 6 (58 B.C.) ἥκω καὶ πεποίηκα τὸ προσκύνημα.—Ἀπέχω Mt 6[2] etc. (Deissmann L. v. 0[4·88]) = ἀπείληφα or ἔσχηκα, v. frequ. in the Koine (Mayser II 1, 132f).—Ἀκούω Lk 9[9] 1 Co 11[18] 2 Th 3[11], class. Xen. Mem. 3, 5, 26, P. Hal. 1, 167, 177 (250 B.C.), P. Amh. II 37, 8 (ii/B.C.) etc. *have heard*.—Νικάω Ro 12[21] Rev 2[7] 15[2] etc., class. *be a conqueror*. Πάρεισιν Ac 17[6] *have come* (Burton 10).—Πειθόμεθα Heb. 13[18] (corr. to perf. in S[c]C[c]D[bc] IK).—Κεῖται Mt 3[10].—Πάρεστιν Jn 11[28].—Ἥττωνται 2 Pt 2[20].

(c) The Present which indicates the continuance of an action during the past and up to the moment of speaking is virtually the same as Perfective, the only difference being that the action is conceived as still in progress (Burton § 17). It is frequent in the NT: Lk 2[48] 13[7] (ἰδοὺ τρία ἔτη ἀφ᾿ οὗ ἔρχεται) 15[29] (τοσαῦτα ἔτη δουλεύω σοι, and I still do), Jn 5[6] 8[58] (εἰμί) 14[9] (μεθ᾿ ὑμῶν εἰμί) 15[27] (ἐστέ), Ac 15[21] (Μ. γὰρ ἐκ γενεῶν ἀρχαίων κατὰ πόλιν τοὺς κηρύσσοντας αὐτὸν ἔχει, and still has) 26[31] (πράσσει, his manner of life still continues), 2 Co 12[19], 2 Ti 3[15] (οἶδας), 2 Pt 3[4], 1 Jn 2[9] 3[8].

§ 1] THE VERB: ASPECT AND TENSE 63

(d) Concerning the *Futuristic* use of the *Present*, Moulton [1] suggested that these presents differed from the future tense " mainly in the tone of assurance which is imparted "; they are confident assertions intended to arrest attention with a vivid and realistic tone or else with imminent fulfilment in mind, and they are mainly restricted to the vernacular. In English it would be *I am to* . . . or *I am about to* . . . . It is oracular sometimes in class. Greek (e.g. Hdt 8, 140) and so it is not surprising that it is used so much in the NT of the Coming One, with the verb ἔρχομαι: Mt 11³ ὁ ἐρχόμενος *the Messiah*, 17¹¹ 'Ηλίας ἔρχεται, Jn 14³ ἔρχομαι (immediately foll. by a verb in the fut.), Lk 12⁵⁴ᶠ same, 1 Co 16⁵ᶠ ἐλεύσομαι . . . διέρχομαι (*I am going through* . . .) . . . διαμενῶ; but in other languages too verbs of going employ a futuristic present (Wackernagel I 161).

In a prophetic or oracular sense other verbs too: Mk 9³¹ παραδίδοται (periphr. fut. in Mt-parallel) foll. by fut. καὶ ἀποκτενοῦσιν, Mt 26² παραδίδοται, 27⁶³ ἐγείρομαι, Jn 11⁴⁸ ἐλεύσονται καὶ αἰτοῦσιν p⁴⁵ (Θ ἔρουσιν; rest fut.), 20²³ ἀφίενται WΘ eschat. fut.? (J. Jeremias in Kittel WB III 753), Lk 13³² ἐκβάλλω . . . ἀποτελῶ . . . τελειοῦμαι, 1 Co 15³² OT ἀποθνῄσκομεν. In other senses: Mt 2⁴ γεννᾶται *is to be born or about to be born*, 24⁴³ Jn 4³⁵ ἔρχεται, Mt 26² γίνεται, P. Par. 51, 39 (159 B.C.) [ἀφ']εσίς μοι γίνεται ταχύ, Mt 20¹⁸ Jn 20¹⁷ ἀναβαίνομεν, P. Par. 47 (153 B.C.) ἀναβαίν⟨ει⟩αὔριον, O. P. 1157, 25f (iii/A.D.), largely rhetorical and poet. in class. Greek, Lk 14¹⁹ Jn 14². ¹². Ac 20²² πορεύομαι. This use appears in the papyri; it is not always easy to decide whether there is futurity, e.g. in wills καταλείπω *I leave*, as in English (Mayser II 1, 134). See also: Mt 18¹² ζητεῖ (alongside a fut.), 26¹⁸ ποιῶ τὸ πασχα *I am about to celebrate*, Lk 3⁹ ἐκκόπτεται καὶ βάλλεται, 19⁸ δίδωμι καὶ ἀποδίδωμι, Jn 10¹⁵ τίθημι, 21²³ οὐκ ἀποθνῄσκει, 1 Co 15²⁶ καταργεῖται, Rev 9⁶ φεύγει. See K-G I 137, 5. Stahl 88, 4. Wackernagel I 159, 161f.

(e) A *Conative Present*, having the same nuance as the imperfect, is conceivable where there is the notion of incompleteness and attempt: Jn 10³² *do they want to stone me?* 13⁶ *are you trying to wash* . . .? Ro 2⁴ *try to lead* or *tend to lead*, Ga 5⁴ *try to be justified*, 6¹² *try to compel*, Jn 13²⁷ *what you want to do*, Ac 26²⁸ *you try to persuade me*, 2 Co 5¹¹ Ga 2¹⁴. Incohative (*begin*): Mk 11²³ 4¹⁷.

(f) Burton (12) discusses a *Gnomic Present* used in generalizations or proverbs: Mt 7¹⁷ Jn 7⁵² 2 Co 9⁷ Jas 1¹³⁻¹⁵.

---

[1] *Einleitung*, 196.

(g) The *Aktionsart* is often difficult to determine in the present because of the lack of a punctiliar stem in the indic. which does not indicate past time. As already explained, the Greek pres. indic. must serve for *I walk* as well as *I am walking*. The following however are thought to be punctiliar actions taking place at the moment of speaking (Burton 9): Mt 5$^{22, 28}$ etc. *I tell you*, 14^8, 26^{63}, Mk 2^5 Mt 9^2 *sins receive forgiveness herewith*, Lk 7^8 *off he goes*, 12^{44}, Jn 5^{34}, 9^{25}, Ac 8^{23}, 9^{34} ἰᾶταί σε *he heals you* (not *is healing you*) or ἴαται perf.?, 16^{18} παραγγέλλω σοι herewith *I bid you*, 26^1 ἐπιτρέπεται almost = *herewith receive permission*.

(h) Present in reported speech referring to the past. Not only after verbs of speaking, but also perception and belief, the NT prefers the pres. tense in indirect discourse reported in the past; class. Greek has it only when the point of view of the original speaker (not the narrator) is adopted.

Mt 2^{22} ἀκούσας ὅτι 'Α. βασιλεύει, 18^{25} πάντα ὅσα ἔχει B Orig. (rest εἶχεν), 21^{45} ὅτι περὶ αὐτῶν λέγει (but past in Mk-parallel 12^{12}), Mk 8^{16} διελογίζοντο ὅτι ἄρτους οὐκ ἔχουσιν p^{45} B (D corrects to εἶχαν), but rest make it orat. recta, Ac 22^2 ἀκούσαντες ὅτι προσφωνεῖ DEH (rest. corr. to προσεφώνει). Exceptions in NT, conforming to class. precedent: Mk 12^{12} ἔγνωσαν ὅτι τὴν παραβολὴν εἶπεν (see Mt-parallel above), Jn 16^{19} ἔγνω ὅτι ἤθελον (vl. ἤμελλον) αὐτὸν ἐρωτᾶν.

§ 2. Imperfect

The contrast between the indicatives of the imperfect and aorist illustrates the difference between linear and punctiliar *Aktionsart* in its most acute form, for the imperfect is the tense of incomplete action, duration and continuity; the presence of the augment indicates that all this is in past time. Although imperfects are retreating before aorists in the Koine, they are still in wide use and the class. distinctions are still being observed. There is a certain interplay between the tenses; indeed we can find no difference between ἔλεγεν and εἶπεν in the NT. Although it is usual to distinguish various kinds of imperfect, and for convenience we preserve these divisions, the classification is not inelastic and the chief determining factor for translators will be the context itself.

1. Behind its use with verbs of asking, requesting, and commanding is the idea of incomplete action in the past. It is

§ 2]   THE VERB: ASPECT AND TENSE   65

close to the conative idea. Such verbs, in their very nature "imperfect", await a fulfilment in a further action by another agent: ἀξιόω, κελεύω, παρακελεύομαι, (ἐπ-)ερωτάω, πέμπω, ἀποστέλλω, πυνθάνομαι, etc.; and in the Koine also ἀπαιτέω, λέγω, προσμαρτυρέω, προσφέρομαι.

Mt 2^4 ἐπυνθάνετο; so also Lk 15^{26} 18^{36} Ac 4^7 10^{18} (BC aor) 21^{33} 23^{19}. Mk 8^5 ἠρώτα; so Ac 3^3 16^{39}. Mk $8^{23.\ 27.\ 29}$ ἐπηρώτα. Mt 8^2 προσεκύνει = request; so 9^{18} 15^{25} S*BDM, as distinct from the aorist which means worship (Mt 2^{11} 14^{33} etc.), but Mt 18^{26} προσεκύνει could mean prostrated, and this is its usual meaning in NT. Lk 8^{29} παρήγγελλεν the unclean spirit to come out (aor. is expected). Ac 15^{38} ἠξίου requested not to take with them, cp. P. Tor. I 4, 73 (116 B.C.): it may mean that Paul's suggestion about Mark was only tentative at first. Ac 16^{22} ἐκέλευον to beat them (breaks the rule about unfulfilled action, as magistrates would be certain their command would be obeyed: vulg. iusserunt). Ac 27^{33} παρεκάλει to take food (but Iterative?). Where the aorist is found the request is usually peremptory, demanding obedience (see Zerwick § 202 on the difference between Mk 5^{10}: "rogatio vana est, ideo imperfectum": and 5^{12} request successful and therefore aorist. Vulg. neglects the distinction): Ac 10^{48} προσέταξεν to be baptized (essential), 23^{18} ἠρώτησεν (-αν) me to bring this young man to you (demand), Mt 8^{34} παρεκάλεσαν to go away, 18^2 begged, 26^{53} demanded, Mk 9^{16} (merely a dir. question, but by Jesus), Lk 8^{37} insisted, Ac 8^{31} he made Ph. come up (not invited), 16^{15} insisted (παρεβιάσατο shows how insistent he was). In Jn 4^{52} ἐπύθετο is merely a question, but an urgent one, and the answer known.

2. A *Conative* or *Desiderative* imperfect [1], of incomplete or interrupted action, which sometimes softens the harshness of a remark or makes it more diffident, is discernible in NT but rare in the Koine. Mt 3^{14} Mk 9^{38} (vl. aor.) Lk 9^{49} p^{45} SBL *wished to hinder*, Lk 1^{59} *wished to name him Z.* (Abel cites Xen.), Ac 7^{26} *tried to reconcile them*, 25^{22} ἐβουλόμην ... ἀκοῦσαι *would like to listen*, 26^{11} ἠνάγκαζον *tried to make them blaspheme* (2 Mac 6^{18} ἠναγκάζετο *the attempt was made to force him to eat*), where to misinterpret this tense with AV is serious, 27^{41} ἐλύετο *the surf seemed to be trying to break up the prow* (or Incohative), Ro 9^3 ηὐχόμην γὰρ ἀνάθεμα εἶναι *I could almost pray*, Ga 4^{20} ἤθελον ... παρεῖναι, Phm ^{13} ἐβουλόμην, Heb 11^{17} *tried to offer*, Mk 15^{23} *tried to give*, Ac 18^4 *tried to persuade*.

3. An impf. with a linear *Aktionsart* is used in descriptions in narrative to portray and set in relief the manner of the action;

---
[1] K-G I 141. Stahl 100, 3. Mayser II 1, 135f. Burton § 23.

it is common in the Koine of the Imperial period, less so in the Ptolemaic (Gild. I 93; Mayser II 1, 136). It seems to represent a past event as still taking place at the time when an event in the aorist suddenly intervenes to cap it. In fact, the aorist advances the bare story and the imperfect supplies the picture's details, when the two tenses are woven together in narrative. On the other hand, sometimes the change of tense is prompted by no other motive than avoidance of monotony, as when Mt changes Mk's οὐχ ηὕρισκον into οὐχ εὗρον (Mt 26⁶⁰ Mk 14⁵⁵). There is a papyrus parallel to Mk's two imperfects: P. Hamb. no. 27, 4 (250 B.C.) ἐπεζήτουν καὶ οὐχ ηὕρισκον, but by capping it with an aor. Mt is probably more stylistically correct: they *were* seeking a long time and in spite of that there was no sudden solution. So in Lk 7⁶ ὁ δὲ Ἰησοῦς ἐπορεύετο *he was going when* ἔπεμψεν *the centurion sent friends.* Correct too is Ac 21²⁰ ἐδόξαζον τὸν θεόν, εἶπόν τε, *they kept praising God and finally said,* 5²⁷¹ ἦγεν αὐτοὺς ... ἀγαγόντες δὲ αὐτοὺς ἔστησαν; the impf. indicates action which proceeded until finally they were presented to the Sanhedrin, 21³ (*we kept on our course to Syria* [impf.] *and finally landed at Tyre* [aor.]), 21³⁰ they were in process of dragging P. out of the Temple (impf.) when suddenly the gates were shut (aor.), Mt 8²⁴ ἐκάθευδεν he kept on sleeping till finally ἤγειραν αὐτόν, 26⁶³ ἐσιώπα Jesus kept silent till the High Priest εἶπεν, 3⁴ John's dress (impf.), ⁵ his audience (impf.), ⁶ his baptizing (impf.): all contributes to a vivid picture against the background of which John utters his rebukes (⁷ aor.), Mk 5³² περιεβλέπετο Jesus was looking around him until the woman came ἦλθεν, 9²⁰f ἐκυλίετο he kept rolling about, and presumably they watched him awhile until Jesus spoke ἐπερώτησεν. There are many instances of descriptive impf., however, without a finalizing aorist to follow. These apparently are intended to make the narrative interesting and continuous until some action is expected in the aor. to give point to the whole description; but more often than not the description is left without climax: Mk 14³⁵ ἔπιπτεν καὶ προσηύχετο (vivid details of Gethsemane), Mt 7²⁸ ἐξεπλήσσοντο, 26⁵⁸ ἠκολούθει καὶ ἐκάθητο, Lk 2⁴⁷ ἐξίσταντο, 16¹⁹ ἐνεδιδύσκετο, 15¹⁶ ἐπεθύμει ... καὶ οὐδεὶς ἐδίδου, 17²⁷ describing Noah's times, 24¹⁴ ὡμίλουν, ²¹ ἠλπίζομεν Jn 11³⁶ ἐφίλει, 19³ ἤρχοντο, Ac 5⁴¹ ἐπορεύοντο, 15³ διήρχοντο ... ἐποίουν, 14¹⁹ ἔσυρον, 18¹⁹ D διελέγετο (rest aor.), 21²⁹ ἐνόμιζον.

But how to account for Mt 4¹¹ ἄγγελοι προσῆλθον (aor.) καὶ διηκόνουν (impf.), 13⁸ the seed ἔπεσεν (aor.) and yet it ἐδίδου (impf.) καρπόν, 25⁵ the maids ἐνύσταξαν (aor.) and yet ἐκάθευδον (impf.), 1 Co 10⁴ in the same verse and context ἔπιον and ἔπινον, 10⁶·¹¹ in the same context ταῦτα τύποι ἡμῶν ἐγενήθησαν (aor.) and ταῦτα τυπικῶς συνέβαινεν (impf.)? Is it anything more subtle than a desire for variety? If the impfs. are descriptive, so must the aorists be, in these particular contexts. The most we can say is that the aor. records the action without stressing its execution, e.g. *angels, who had come, ministered to him; the seed, which had fallen, bore fruit.*

4. The *Iterative* or customary imperfect represents interrupted continuance or repetition, rather than an action that was done once and for all. In Mk 6⁴¹ Lk 9¹⁶ Jesus gives thanks and breaks the bread (punctiliar), but the next verb ἐδίδου reveals that the disciples kept returning to Jesus for more food (linear iterative).

Mk 1³¹ διηκόνει *began to wait on them*, 5¹³ ἐπνίγοντο, 7²⁶ ἠρώτα αὐτόν, 12⁴¹ ἔβαλλον (or Descriptive?), 15⁶ ἀπέλυεν, Lk 21³⁷ ηὐλίζετο *he used to spend the night*, 2⁴¹ ἐπορεύοντο κατ' ἔτος, 8²⁹ ἐδεσμεύετο ... ἠλαύνετο, Jn 4³¹ ἠρώτων, Ac 2⁴⁵ ἐπίπρασκον καὶ διεμέριζον (often but spasmodic), 4³⁴ ἔφερον ... καὶ ἐτίθουν, 18⁸ ἐπίστευον καὶ ἐβαπτίζοντο. But the Markan use of this impf. is full of uncertainty. Mark keeps his aorists in proper use, but does he his imperfects? Very often he uses the periphrastic tense for the customary imperfect, and therefore in 1⁷ ἐκήρυσσεν λέγων the reference may be to some definite occasion and actual saying. 14⁶⁰·⁶¹, where ἐπήρωτα = ἐπηρώτησεν confirms this view.

5. The impf. often occurs where in English we would use the pluperfect: that is, to express past time relative to the time of the main action after verbs of perception and belief. Greek tenses do not so much express relative time, which emerges from the context, as indicate *Aktionsart*. If punctiliar action is intended, it will be aorist. Mk 6¹⁸ ἔλεγεν γὰρ ὁ Ἰωάννης *John had been saying*, 11³² *that John had been a prophet*, Lk 8²⁹ παρήγγελλεν *he had been commanding*, Jn 6²² *had been there*, 9¹⁸ *that he had been blind and made to see* (the latter aor., because punctiliar action), Mk 9⁶ Θ οὐ γὰρ ᾔδει τί ἐλάλει *what he had said*. Papyri: Mayser II 1, 137 (f).

6. Habit rather than logical principle appears to govern the choice of impf. or aor. with verbs of speaking. In the papyri

ἔλεγον *I said* is found in close conjunction with a series of verbs in the aorist, even εἶπα P. Par. 51, 9 and 17–21 (159 B.C.). In the NT ἔλεγεν occurs in Mk 4 [21. 24. 26. 30] 7⁹. ²⁰ Lk 5³⁶ 6⁵ 9²³ etc., in contexts where εἶπεν performs exactly the same function in Lk 6³⁹ 15¹¹ etc. MGr has this variation (Thumb *ThLZ* 1903, 422f; Schwyzer II 277f). It is too much to claim any difference in *Aktionsart*, so that εἶπεν would be for simple reference to an utterance already made while ἔλεγεν introduced the detailed content of a speech. In Jn 11³⁶ᶠ there is no perceptible difference between ἔλεγον οὖν οἱ Ἰουδαῖοι and τινὲς δὲ ἐξ αὐτῶν εἶπαν: each introduces speech in the same way, and indeed scribes have standardized the εἶπαν to ἔλεγον (AK II). The general practice too was to use λέγων, not εἰπών, after another verb of saying. For imperfect in conditional clauses see pp. 91f.

§ 3. Aorist Indicative

See previous section for the relationship between impf. and aorist.

(*a*) The "Aoristic Perfect" and the boundary between aorist and perfect. The choice between perfective aorist and perfect seems to have become a matter of the personal feeling of the writer, depending on whether, in a past action, its fulfilment in the present was to be more or less prominently expressed. In the Hellenistic period, as Chantraine demonstrates (see below, pp. 81f.), the perfect increasingly trespassed on the sphere of the aorist as a narrative tense (aoristic perfect), and thereby committed suicide. By listing together the instances where both tenses occur side by side Mayser (II 1, 139ff) shows for the uneducated Koine that the perfect at first represented an action or phenomenon with great emphasis on the fact that it was past and with clear reference to its fulfilment in the present; and yet at the same time he gives plenty of evidence that decadence soon set in and that both tenses were used "promiscuously". This is true especially of papyri in the Imperial period (Moulton Prol. 143). We have to ask whether NT usage is in line with the uncultured mass of the papyri rather than with the educated in this respect. The "promiscuous" use increased in the first three cc. A.D., and the aorist was used increasingly for the perfect, as well as vice versa, to such an extent that eventually in iv/A.D. the perfect as a distinct tense is altogether eclipsed. Its doom had already been written in iv or iii/B.C. when the perfect left its first estate to become an active conjugation alongside that of the present and aorist, whereas it had originally been entirely intransitive. Such a climax led directly to its ruin, since it could not compete in the popular language with the pres. and aor. which now seemed to fulfil all its functions. Spoken language tends to eliminate superfluous elements, and having ceased to express *the state arrived at* and having assumed an active force as well it made itself redundant by sharing the meaning of the aorist. Its reduplicated stems had no chance against the simpler formations of the aorist. In MGr it has disappeared and a periphrasis takes its place. Although in Byzantine texts it is no longer distinguishable from the aorist in meaning, care must still be taken to ascertain whether the mingling in the NT is not by design, with the distinctions correctly observed. What is taken for "aoristic perfect" is often a true resultative perfect denoting a past action of which the results still vividly survive.

1. Mark is very careful when Pilate marvels that Jesus *is already dead* τέθνηκεν; Pilate then enquires when *he died* ἀπέθανεν (15^44f). So is Paul: 1 Co 15^3 *Christ died* ἀπέθανεν *and was buried* ἐτάφη *and has risen again* ἐγήγερται. Mt 9^22 *your faith has made you whole* σέσωκεν; *from that very hour received her wholeness* ἐσώθη. Mk 5^19 *what the Lord has done* πεποίηκεν *and that he showed mercy* ἐλέησεν. Ac 21^28 *he brought in* εἰσήγαγεν *and has defiled* κεκοίνωκεν. There are many instances of such careful distinction in the pre-Christian papyri (Mayser II 1, 139f), e.g. *he did us no wrong* οὐθὲν ἡμῖν κακὸν ἐποίησεν, *but has always taken care of us* ἀλλ' ἐκ τῶν ἐναντίων ἐπιμεμέληται P. Grenf. II 36 (95 B.C.).

2. But undoubtedly there are exx. in NT where, either alone or in conjunction with another verb in the aorist, a verb in the perfect functions in a clearly aoristic sense in narrative; and often the perfect stem assumes aoristic endings in the papyri and NT—a disguise which helped it to survive a little longer:

(α) Narrative perfect with an aorist: Rev 5^7 ἦλθεν καὶ εἴληφεν, (Dan O' 4^30b εἴληφα) 8^5 εἴληφεν ... καὶ ἐγέμισεν, 7^14 εἴρηκα (B εἶπον) ... καὶ εἶπεν (having no visible reduplication, the forms of εἴληφα and εἴρηκα may have appeared to the uneducated like aorists), 3^3 εἴληφας καὶ ἤκουσας, 11^17 εἴληφας ... καὶ ἐβασίλευσας, Mt 25^20 ὁ τὰ πέντε

τάλαντα λαβών, and yet ²⁴ ὁ τὸ ἓν τάλαντον εἰληφώς, Jn 12⁴⁰ τετύφλωκεν
... καὶ ἐπώρωσεν AB*Θ fam¹³ (corr. to perf. by B°Δ fam¹) or ἐπήρωσεν
Bodm. pap. SW (LXX Isa 53⁵ ἐτραυματίσθη καὶ μεμαλάκισται, 57¹⁸
ἑώρακα καὶ ἰασάμην, 66⁸ ἤκουσεν ... καὶ ἑόρακεν, Ex 5²² ἐκάκωσας ...
ἀπέσταλκας, ²³ πεπόρευμαι ... ἐκάκωσεν, 6⁴ παρῴκήκασιν ... παρῴκησαν
(all in first part of Exodus), Col 1¹⁶ ἐν αὐτῷ ἐκτίσθη τὰ πάντα ... καὶ
εἰς αὐτὸν ἔκτισται (any subtle distinction here is doubtful, but the
exegete could hardly be blamed for suspecting it), P. Oxy. III 482, 1–2
(ii/A.D.) ἀπεγρκψάμην καὶ πέπρακα (and see Moulton Prol. 143), Mt 13⁴⁶
πέπρακεν (perhaps because there is no aor. from the same root?) ...
καὶ ἠγόρασεν, Jn 1³ χωρὶς αὐτοῦ ἐγένετο οὐδὲ ἕν· ὃ γέγονεν, 2 Co 12¹⁷
ἀπέσταλκα ... ἐπλεονέκτησα (DE corr. to ἔπεμψα, some cursives to
ἀπέστειλα), 11²⁵ νυχθήμερον ἐν τῷ βυθῷ πεποίηκα, after a succession
of aors., 1 Co 2⁸ ἔγνωκεν ... ἔγνωσαν, Ac 7³⁵ κατέστησεν ... ἀπέσταλκεν
(CHP corr. to -στειλεν), 22¹⁵ ἑώρακας καὶ ἤκουσας, Jn 3³² ὃ ἑώρακεν καὶ
ἤκουσεν, 17² ἔδωκας ... δέδωκας, 18²⁰ᶠ λελάληκα (corr. to aor. by C³DΓ)
... ἐδίδαξα ... ἐλάλησα. 1 Jn 4¹⁰. ¹⁴ ἀπέστειλεν ... ἀπέσταλκεν, Justin
M. Ap. I 22 πεποιηκέναι ... ἀνεγεῖραι, also 32 ἐκάθισε καὶ εἰσελήλυθεν
(Moulton Prol. 143).

(β) Isolated narrative perfects: the MSS show that there was a
certain indeterminateness in the use of the two tenses which dates from
an early period in textual transmission. Mk 11² κεκάθικεν A(W)XY
ΠΦD (rest corr. to aor. like Lk 19³⁰), 14⁴⁴ δεδώκει (Mt. aor.), Rev 2²⁸
εἴληφα, 8⁵ εἴληφεν, 19³ εἴρηκαν (aor. termination), 2 Co 11²¹ ἠσθενήκαμεν
p⁴⁶ SB (corr. to aor. by DGIᵛⁱᵈ), 2¹³ ἔσχηκα, 7⁵ ἔσχηκεν (p⁴⁶ BFGK
corr. to ἔσχεν), 1⁹, Ro 5² ἐσχήκαμεν (a true pf., as we still possess it?),
Mk 5¹⁵ τὸν ἐσχηκότα τὸν λεγιῶνα, 3 Mac 5²⁰ ἔσχηκα, Lives Proph. Mal. 2
καλὸν βίον ἔσχηκε *he led a good life.* Moulton's view of ἔσχηκα was that
it took the place of a constative aor. of ἔχω, which is lacking since ἔσχον
is almost exclusively the ingressive aor. = *got, received* (Prol. 145). It
is also very like the aors. ἔθηκα and ἀφῆκα. For secular use of pres.
ἔσχηκα see Schmid II 53; for Polybius see Schoy 75–77.

The pf. γέγονα is commonly in the Gospels = γίνομαι or ἐγενόμην.
For aor.: Mt 1²² 21⁴ (see Jn 19³⁶ ἐγένετο), 24²¹ BLWZ (but corr. to
ἐγένετο by SDΘ 700 e Geo¹ Eus Hipp², while the rest harm. with Mk),
26⁵⁶, Mk 5³³ 9²¹ 13¹⁹ οὔπω γέγονεν (corr. to aor. by D 299 565 184 *b* Old
Lat. vulg. Aug Arm), 14⁴ (but om γέγονεν D 64 Old Lat (*a ff i*) Syrˢ, to
harm. with Mt 26⁸), Dan 12¹ Θ οὐ γέγονεν (Ο' οὐκ ἐγενήθη), Lives Proph.
Jer. 13f, Dan 6, Nah. 2, Elisha 2 (pap. exx. in Moulton Prol. 146).

Lk 9³⁶ ἑώρακαν, Jn 13¹⁵ δέδωκα S fam¹ fam¹³ (rest aor.), 13³ 6³²
δέδωκεν vl, 13¹ ἐλήλυθα EFG (vl. aor.), Ga 3¹⁸ κεχάρισται ὁ θεός,
4²³ γεγέννηται, Heb 7⁶ δεδεκάτωκεν ... εὐλόγηκεν, ⁹δεδεκάτωται,
8⁵ κεχρημάτισται.

LXX evidence: Ge 16⁵ δέδωκα τὴν παιδίσκην, 24³⁰ οὕτως λελάληκέν
μοι, 26²³ ἑωράκαμεν (cp. Lk 9³⁶ Jn 3³²), 29³⁴ Α τέτοκα, 31¹ εἴληφεν,
38²³ ἀπέσταλκα, 41⁵⁵ ἐκέκραξεν, 42³⁰ λελάληκεν, and some dubious
ones. Isai 3⁹ βεβούλευνται, 13⁴ ἐντέταλται, 20³ πεπόρευται, 22³
πέφευγασιν, 48¹⁰ πέπρακα, ¹⁷ δέδειχα, 48¹⁶ SAQΓ ἀπέσταλκεν (Β aor.),

49⁶ δέδωκα, 51²² εἴληφα, 54⁶ κέκληκεν, 60¹ ἀνατέταλκεν, 61¹ ἀπέσταλκεν, 66⁹ δέδωκα, ¹⁹ ἀκηκόασιν ... ἑοράκασιν. Dan O' (all corr. to aor. or impf. in Θ): 2⁸ ἑωράκατε, ³¹·³⁴·⁴¹·⁴⁶ ἑώρακας.

Chantraine¹ argues that the pf. in Mt is puristic, but cp. ἡλίκος οὐδείς πω γέγονεν Demosth. 1, 9, similarly Isocr. 15, 30.

In view of the evidence from the Koine and LXX we cannot claim that the confusion of aor. and pf. is due to Latin influence. We find it also to a small extent in Polyb. (3, 10, 1; 4, 1, 1: δεδηλώκαμεν and ἐδηλώσαμεν) and more so in Diodorus (16, 1, 6) and Strabo 2, 5 p. 133 γέγονε = ἦν) who are further from the class. model.

(b) The *Aktionsarten* of the aorist. The rules concerning this which we have already described (above, pp. 59f.) must be viewed with great caution; the rules appear to collapse with the "linear" aorists in Ac 1²¹ (συνελθόντων, εἰσῆλθεν καὶ ἐξῆλθεν) and with Lk 9³² διαγρηγορήσαντες, Mt 27⁸ ἐκλήθη ... ἕως τῆς σήμερον (perhaps praegnans: *was called* [and kept the name] *until to-day*). Nevertheless, assuming as a working hypothesis the essential punctiliar and momentary meaning of the aorist stem, one will find various ways of using the indicative. They depend largely on the meaning of the verb itself and vary according to whether the preliminaries (Ingressive) or consequences (Perfective) of an action or state are chiefly in mind when the verb is used; or indeed whether the action is conceived on its own without reference to its progress and result (Constative). There are the following ways, and yet there is fundamentally but one kind of aorist action or aspect and that is punctiliar.

1. The *Ingressive* (Incohative) aorist ² or *Inceptive* aorist may be found with verbs expressing a state or condition; it indicates the point of entrance into such a state: βασιλεύω *became a king*, δουλεύω *became a slave*, πιστεύω *put his trust*, etc. The tense is to be distinguished from presents in -σκω, which indicate not so much the beginning of a state but are linear and indicate a gradual becoming, to become *more and more*; which is different from *began to be silent, a hush came upon it* (ἐσίγησεν Ac 15¹²), he ceased to be rich and *became poor* (ἐπτώχευσεν 2 Co 8⁹), *he sprang to life* (νεκρὸς ἦν καὶ ἔζησεν Lk 15³²; the same translation in Ro 14⁹ Rev 2⁸ 13¹⁴ 20⁴), they did not cease to be ignorant or *begin to recognise* (οὐκ ἔγνωσαν Jn 1¹⁰ 16³), *he burst into*

---

¹ *Histoire du Parfait Grec*, Paris 1907, 235f.
² K-G I 155, 5. Stahl 137, 3. Goodwin 16. Moulton Einl. 177ff. Zerwick §§ 185f. M. W. Humphreys, "The Ingressive Second Aorist", *Transactions and Proceedings, Amer. Philol. Association*, 23, 62.

tears ἔκλαυσεν Lk 19⁴¹, ἐδάκρυσεν Jn 11³⁵), *they said no more* (ἐσίγησαν Lk 20²⁶, ἡσύχασαν Ac 11¹⁸). Sometimes this aor. will vitally distinguish the meanings of a word: ἁμαρτάνω *be a sinner*, but ἥμαρτον *commit a sin*, and so the apparent conflict between 1 Jn 2¹ and 3⁹ can be reasonably explained (Zerwick § 186), cp. Ro 6¹ with 6¹⁵.

Other exx. of Ingressive are probably: Mt 5¹⁶ λαμψάτω, 2¹⁶ ἐθυμώθη, 21¹ ἤγγισαν, 22⁷ ὠργίσθη, Mk 10²¹ ἠγάπησεν, Lk 6²² μισήσωσιν, 8²³ ἀφύπνωσεν, Jn 4⁵² κομψότερον ἔσχεν *started to mend*, Ac 7⁶⁰ ἐκοιμήθη *fell asleep*, 1 Co 4⁸ ἐβασιλεύσατε *become kings*, 2 Co 7⁹ ἐλυπήθητε, 8⁹ ἐπτώχευσεν *became poor*, πλουτήσητε, Heb 6¹⁸ κρατῆσαι (cp. pres. 4¹⁴), papyri Mayser II 1, 142. Possibly also: Mk 1¹¹ ἐν σοὶ εὐδόκησα *joy comes at thought of you* (but may be infl. of Heb. stative pf.), Lk 12³² *it was his happy inspiration to give you*, Mt 13²⁶ ἐποίησεν.

2. *Perfective* (or effective, or resultative) aorist (Stahl 128, 2), in which the emphasis is all on the conclusion or results of an action. Again the meaning of the verb makes this clear (e.g. shut, persuade, hide, fall, hinder, learn, save, escape). It is the reverse of the Conative impf. Mt 23² ἐπὶ τῆς M. καθέδρας ἐκάθισαν they took their seat and still sit (another explanation in Moulton-Howard 458) but it may be a Hebraism (perfective), 27²⁰ *they succeeded in persuading* (cp. the Conative pres. infin. in Ac 13⁴³ where Paul and Barn. could only *urge*, not succeed in persuading), Mt 27⁴⁶ Mk 15³⁴ (LXX Ps 21²) ἐγκατέλιπες, the present results of the action are much in mind, Mt 28¹⁵ διεφημίσθη . . . μεχρὶ τῆς σήμερον ἡμέρας, Ac 27⁴³ *succeeded in preventing*, 28¹⁴ *we were prevailed upon*.

3. *Constative* (summary) or *Complexive* aorist conceives the idea as a whole without reference to the beginning, progress, or end; it is a total yet punctiliar aspect, for it must not be supposed that punctiliar *Aktionsart* necessarily involves a brief space of time. The action is represented as complete, an assumption which must be made from the context, which indicates that no further action of the same kind is contemplated. E.g. Jn 7⁹ ἔμεινεν, Ac 14³ ἱκανὸν χρόνον διέτριψαν, 18¹¹ ἐκάθισεν, the limits of the action being defined by *eighteen months*, 28³⁰ ἐνέμεινεν *two whole years*, 10³⁸ διῆλθεν, Ro 15² ἤρεσεν constantly, 2 Co 11²⁵ ἐραβδίσθην. Infin. Ac 11²⁶; imper. Mt 6³⁴.

4. The aorist in *Epistolary* style (as in Latin) is logical, since the action so described will be past at the time the letter

is read (Schwyzer II 281). Ac 23³⁰ etc. ἔπεμψα (ἀπέστειλα in the papyri, Mayser II 1, 144), Eph 6²², Ph 2²⁸ Col 4⁸ Phm¹². It is notable, however, that one never finds ἔγραψα (Koine) but always γράφω, and always ἀσπάζεται. 1 Co 5⁹ ἔγραψα probably refers to an earlier letter; 1 Co 5¹¹ Ro 15¹⁵ to an earlier place in the same letter. In Ga 6¹¹ it might be taken either way: if epistolary, the picture is of P. taking his pen and finishing the letter himself. Note that he does not use the epistolary aor. in 2 Co 13¹⁰ (γράφω). It may be epistolary in 2 Co 8¹⁷·¹⁸·²² 9³·⁵. In 1 Jn 2¹²·¹⁴ γράφω occurs three times, then ἔγραψα three times (perhaps for the sake of variety; the author of Jn is fond of varying his tenses) which may refer back to some earlier writing.

5. *Gnomic* aorist [1] is a timeless and almost futuristic aorist, expressing axioms which avail for all time. The explanation may be that, the present stem in Greek being linear, it would not be suitable for expressing generalities; the timeless tense is therefore used, but the augment denoting past time cannot be jettisoned and has to go with it. We must look rather to the stem than the augment. This is more likely to be the correct assumption than that the writer had in mind a single specific instance after the manner of fables and parables (" a certain man *went* ... "). It is true however that in the NT the Gnomic aorist is found almost only in conjunction with comparisons (perfect with similar meaning: Mt 13⁴⁶ Jas 1²⁴). Mt 13⁴⁴·⁴⁶·⁴⁸ (but these could well be ordinary aorists; see Moule p. 13), 18¹⁵ (vulg. fut.), 5²⁸, Mk 11²⁴ ἐλάβετε SBCLW (AN pres.; D fut.), Lk 7³⁵ ἐδικαιώθη *wisdom is justified* (general statement), Jn 1⁵, 15⁶ ἐβλήθη ἔξω ... καὶ ἐξηράνθη (the latter aor. may suggest the immediacy of the result of excision), ⁸, Ga 5⁴, 1 Pt 1²⁴ (LXX Isai 40⁷) ἐξηράνθη ὁ χόρτος, καὶ τὸ ἄνθος ἐξέπεσεν, Jas 1¹¹ ἀνέτειλεν γὰρ ὁ ἥλιος ... καὶ ἐξήρανεν τὸν χόρτον ...; these may incidentally be Gnomic but they also would render the Heb. perfect too literally, unless we see in the aoristic punctiliar *Aktionsart* a graphic picture of the fading of the grass and flower; Moule includes also Jas 1²⁴ κατενόησεν ... ἐπελάθετο *no sooner has he looked ... than he has gone away and ... forgotten* (p. 12) and aptly quotes Ign. Eph. 5³ ἑαυτὸν διέκρινεν forthwith

---
[1] K-G I 161. Schwyzer II 286. Zerwick § 191. H. C. Elmer, "A Note on the Origin and Force of the Gnomic Aorist", *Trans. and Proceedings, Amer. Philol. Association*, 25, 59–63 (1894). Wackernagel I 181.

excommunicates himself; Herm. V. III 12, 3; 13, 2; M. III 2; S. IX 26, 2; Epict. IV 10, 27 (aor. and pres. together: ὅταν θέλῃς, ἐξῆλθες καὶ οὐ καπνίζῃ). See Jannaris § 1852 for MGr. The aorists in the Magnificat may be Gnomic (Lk 1⁵¹⁻⁵³); they possibly also help to explain the popularity of this kind of aorist in Biblical Greek—what God did in the past is evidence of what he will always do. Lk 16⁴ ἔγνων τί ποιήσω may be Gnomic, or merely an example of the way Greek more exactly interprets the *Aktionsart*: *the idea occurred to me, what to do*.

6. *Proleptic* aorist looks like a future, taking place after some actual or implied condition, e.g. Jn 15⁶ if a man will not abide in Christ ἐβλήθη ἔξω . . . καὶ ἐξηράνθη *he will be cut off and withered*, 15⁸ ἐδοξάσθη *he will be glorified if you bear fruit*. The timeless aor. is a suitable tense to express this projection of the future into the present as if some event had already occurred. Ga 5⁴ if you are going to be justified by the Law κατηργήθητε ἀπὸ Χριστοῦ *you will be severed from Christ*; see also 1 Co 7²⁸.

§ 4. Moods of Present and Aorist in relation to their Time and Aktionsarten.

(a) *Present and aorist Imperative and prohibitive Subjunctive* [1]

The same distinction holds in the imperative as in the indicative; the present is durative or incomplete or iterative and the aorist punctiliar or constative. It affects commands in this way, that the aorist imper. is more or less restricted to precepts concerning conduct in specific cases; and this applies also to prohibitions, which in the aorist are subjunctive. Somewhat peremptory and categorical, they tend to be ingressive, giving either a command to commence some action or a prohibition against commencing it. On the other hand, present imperatives give a command to do something constantly, to

---

[1] K-G I 189C. Gild. I §§ 401–422. Stahl 148–152, 363. Schwyzer II 339–344. Mayser II 1, 145–150. Moulton Einl. 198ff, 271ff. Zerwick §§ 181–183, 189. Georges Cuendet, *L'impératif dans le texte grec et dans les versions gotique arménienne et vieux slave des Évangiles*, Paris 1924. E. Kieckers, *Zum Gebrauch des Imperativus Aoristi und Praesentis*, Idg. Forsch. XXIV, 1909, 10–16. F. W. Mozley, "Use of the Present and Aorist Imperative", *JThS* 4, 1903, 279ff. L. A. Post, "Dramatic Uses of the Greek Imperative", *AJP* 59, 1938, 31ff. W. Heidt, "Translating New Testament Imperatives", *Catholic Biblical Quarterly*, 13, 1951, 253ff.

continue to do it; or else a prohibition against its continuance, an interruption of an action already begun. But they are less pressing, less rude, less ruthless, than the aorist. Requests to the deity are regularly aorist, for they aim to gain a hearing for specific matters rather than to bind continually. These distinctions are broadly observed in all periods and even in MGr. On the other hand there are passages which do not conform: in 2 Co 13[11, 12] after a chain of *present* imperatives we find the aor. ἀσπάσασθε without being aware of anything significant in the change. The problem of the *Aktionsarten* of the tenses is by no means solved as yet for the NT, and possibly John gives a clue when he seems to vary the tense according to the verb he is using. Why is the same prohibition, however, μὴ ὀμόσῃς in Mt 5[36] and μὴ ὀμνύετε in Jas 5[12]?

1. *Present Imperative:*

(α) *Positive.* Mt 26[38] Mk 14[34] do not go away (aor.) but be on guard always (γρηγορεῖτε). Lk 22[40, 46] Heb 13[18] *keep praying* προσεύχεσθε. Pres. of περιπατέω and στοιχέω *go on walking*: 1 Co 7[17] Ga 5[16, 25] Eph 4[17] 5[2, 8] Ph 3[16] Col 2[6] 4[5] 1 Th 4[12]. See Lk 11[9] αἰτεῖτε, ζητεῖτε, κρούετε: *petite perseveranter . . . quaerite indefesse . . . pulsate iterum atque iterum* (Zerwick § 181). But ἔρχου and ἐλθέ do not seem to conform, for the pres. = *start to come* Jn 14[7] ἔρχου καὶ ἴδε, while the aor. ἐλθάτω = *continue to come* Mt 6[10] (the Kingdom being present already as a grain of seed). In Mt 14[29] however ἐλθέ conforms: either ingressive *start to come!* or perfective *come here!* 1 Co 7[36] *let him go on doing what he wants* ποιείτω. But except for Jn 21[10] ἐνέγκατε, we find always φέρε, φέρετε, whatever the context. Mt 5[24] *first be reconciled* (aor.) *and then come and offer as many gifts as you like* πρόσφερε (but 8[4] προσένεγκε τὸ δῶρον). Another exception is ἔγειρε, ὕπαγε, πορεύου and pl., which are used perhaps for politeness, as less peremptory, regardless of the *Aktionsart*: Ac 22[10] πορεύου where the rule demands aor. Mt 2[20] 25[9] Lk 5[24] also. But πορεύθητι correctly Mt 8[9] *be off!* We usually find πιστεύω in the pres. also: Mk 1[15] *persevere in repentance* μετανοεῖτε *and belief* πιστεύετε, 5[36] *stop being frightened* μὴ φοβοῦ, but *go on having faith* πίστευε (perhaps corrected in Lk 8[50]: *start to have faith* πίστευσον). In Mk the command is to continue to have as much faith as before; in Lk, it is to begin having faith, or to have a better faith than before the child died. Perhaps Luke felt the subtle difference.

(β) *Negative*. Mt 6¹⁹ *stop laying up* μὴ θησαυρίζετε,²⁵ *cease being anxious* μὴ μεριμνᾶτε (but ³⁴ *never be anxious* μὴ μεριμνήσητε). Mk 5³⁶ 6⁵⁰ etc. Lk 1¹³. ³⁰ 2¹⁰ 5¹⁰ 8⁵⁰ etc. *stop being frightened!* μὴ φοβοῦ and pl. Lk 8⁵² they were weeping, and he said *Weep not* (or *Stop weeping*) μὴ κλαίετε. Jn 2¹⁶ μὴ ποιεῖτε *stop making*, 5⁴⁵ μὴ δοκεῖτε *cease to imagine*, 19²¹ μὴ γράφε *stop writing*, i.e. *alter what you have written*, 20¹⁷ μή μου ἅπτου *stop touching me!* 6⁴³ μὴ γογγύζετε. Ro 6¹² μὴ βασιλευέτω *continue to reign*, ¹³ *do not continue yielding your members to sin* μὴ παριστάνετε, *but start yielding yourselves to God* παραστήσατε. 2 Co 6¹⁷ μὴ ἅπτεσθε (SAQ in LXX Isai 52¹¹, B aor.). Eph 4²⁶ μὴ ἁμαρτάνετε, 5¹⁸ μὴ μεθύσκεσθε, Col 3⁹ μὴ ψεύδεσθε. Jas 1⁷ *he must stop thinking* μὴ οἰέσθω, 5¹² μὴ ὀμνύετε (aor. Mt 5³⁶). 1 Pt 4¹⁵ *let none of you ever suffer* πασχέτω; the writer prefers pres. to aor. imper.; we might expect aor. at 1¹³. ¹⁵. ¹⁷. ²² 2². ¹³. ¹⁷ 3¹⁰. ¹¹. ¹⁴. ¹⁵ 4⁷ 5². ⁵. ⁶. ⁸. ⁹. See also Mt 6¹⁶ 1 Ti 4¹⁴ 5²². PSI IV 353, 16 (254 B.C.) μὴ ἐπιλανθάνου ἡμῶν *do not forget us in future*. P. Tebt. I 6, 43 (140 B.C.) μηθενὶ ἐπιτρέπετε πράσσειν τι τῶν προδεδηλωμένων *stop allowing anyone to do what we have ordered previously*.

2. *Aorist imperative or Prohibitive subjunctive*.

(α) *Positive*. Important for exegesis is the aor. imper. in 1 Co 7²¹ μᾶλλον χρῆσαι; the Corinthian Christians are urged to make use once and for all of the opportunity to be free; only with a pres. imper. ought the interpretation to be *use your present state* to the glory of God. Mt's χαίρετε in 5¹² is altered by Luke to aor. because he adds *in that day*. Mt 5⁴² δός of a definite occasion and person, where Lk 6³⁰ δίδου to *anyone* who asks. Mt 6²⁸ καταμάθετε is a command now, once and for all, to look at the lilies, probably during a walk in the fields, Lk. 9²³ ἀρνησάσθω ἑαυτὸν καὶ ἀράτω τὸν σταυρὸν αὐτοῦ (aor.) καὶ ἀκολουθείτω μοι (pres.); the self-denying is a decision, once and for all (om. the harmonizing vl. καθ' ἡμέραν), but the *following* is a continuous discipline. 12⁵⁸ δὸς ἐργασίαν. 19³⁰ λύσαντες αὐτὸν ἀγάγετε. 14²³ ἔξελθε. Jn 2¹⁹ λύσατε. 4¹⁶. ³⁵. Ro 13¹³ *now let us walk* περιπατήσωμεν. Jas 4⁹ *start to be wretched and mourn and weep* ταλαιπωρήσατε πενθήσατε κλαύσατε, ¹⁰ *start to humble yourselves* ταπεινώθητε, 5⁷·⁸ *be patient* (as a precept) μακροθυμήσατε. Mt 26⁴⁸ κρατήσατε *arrest him!* (but 2 Th 2¹⁵ κρατεῖτε *go on preserving*; Rev 2²⁵ aor. misused). Aorists for precepts until the coming of Christ: Mt 5³⁹ στρέψον, 6⁶, 1 Ti 6¹²·¹⁴·²⁰, 2 Ti 4²·⁵ 1¹⁴ 2²·³·¹⁵. 1 Pt 1¹³·¹⁷·²² 2¹⁷ 5², 1 Jn 5²¹, 2 Cl 8⁶. Prayer: Mt 6¹⁰ δός (aor. because Mt adds *this day*) Lk 11³ δίδου *continue to give* because *day by day* is added (SD harm. with Mt); aor. in all petitions of Lord's Prayer (ἁγιασθήτω γενηθήτω δός ἄφες), and in prayer in papyri (Mayser II 1, 145f). Greetings: ἀσπάσασθε, but also pres. in papyri, against NT usage.

(β) *Negative.* Mt 5¹⁷ μὴ νομίσητε *never think!* 6² μὴ σαλπίσῃς *never sound!* Categorical prohibitions: Mt 7⁶ μὴ δῶτε, 6³⁴ μὴ μεριμνήσητε, Jn 3⁷ μὴ θαυμάσῃς. In 3rd. pers. prohibitions occur in aor. imper. and occasionally in the form μή τις with aor. subjunctive: 1 Co 16¹¹ 2 Co 11¹⁶ 2 Th 2³.

But there are exceptions to what seems a fairly definite principle: Jn 3⁷ has μὴ θαυμάσῃς, which sounds unnatural as *cease to marvel* (but perhaps like our *Never marvel!*). In Mt 1²⁰ 10²⁶ we expect *stop fearing* (pres.) instead of μὴ φοβηθῇς and pl. = *never fear.* We have some aorists too in prayer to the deity: Mt 6¹³ Lk 11⁴ μὴ εἰσενέγκῃς, Ac 7⁶⁰ μὴ στήσῃς, but a suggested reason has already been given. In general, some writers prefer the pres. (Paul) and others the aor. (1 Pt) imper.

3. Difference in *Aktionsart* is best seen when both tenses lie together.

Ac 12⁸ *put your cloak on* περιβαλοῦ (punctiliar) *and keep behind me* ἀκολούθει (linear). Jn 5⁸ ἆρον (ingressive) ... καὶ περιπάτει (linear), 9⁷ ὕπαγε (exclam. and invariable) καὶ νίψαι, 2⁵⁻⁸ φέρετε alongside ποιήσατε γεμίσατε ἀντλήσατε (see above for invariable φέρετε), 2¹⁶ ἄρατε ταῦτα ἐντεῦθεν *get these things out of here!* μὴ ποιεῖτε *stop making ....* Ro 6¹³ *do not continue* παριστάνετε, *but once and for all* παραστήσατε. Mt 26³⁸ Mk 14³⁴ *do not go away* μείνατε ὧδε (constative), but *continue to watch* γρηγορεῖτε, Lk 10⁴ *cease carrying* μὴ βαστάζετε, *never salute* ἀσπάσησθε, 17⁸ ἑτοίμασον τί δειπνήσω *get something ready,* περιζωσάμενος διακόνει μοι *continue to wait.* P. Petr. II 40(a) 12 μὴ ὀλιγοψυχήσῃτε *stop being faint-hearted,* ἀλλ' ἀνδρίζεσθε *continue to be brave* (223 B.C.).

To Moulton the general agreement of Mt and Lk in the use of tense in their parallel passages showed "how delicately the distinction of tenses was observed "[1]. That is not the only possible conclusion to be drawn, and Moulton seems to many today to be a little over confident in the rules of *Aktionsart* [2]. There is a case for Luke having known Mt and having followed his use of tenses. In any case the NT use of tenses is not so strikingly standardized or logical.

Before the prohibitive aor. subjunctive we often find in the NT ὅρα ὁρᾶτε βλέπετε, which do not, however, affect the construction: Mt 8⁴ 18¹⁰ Mk 1⁴⁴ 1 Th 5¹⁵.

The prohibitive aor. imperative is later than the NT: Horn quotes the first as iii/A.D.

(b) *Infinitive of Present and Aorist* [3]

In general the same distinction holds. When the infin. indicates a direct command, which is rare in the NT, though very frequent in the papyri (and χρή or δεῖ may perhaps be assumed), the tense is always present:[4] Lk 9³ μηδὲν αἴρετε . . . μήτε ἀν δύο χιτῶνας ἔχειν [5]; Ac 15²³ 23²⁶ Jas 1¹ (χαίρειν, the wish-infin. of epistolary style), Ro 12¹⁵ (χαίρειν, κλαίειν), Ph 3¹⁶ (στοίχειν), 2 Ti 2¹⁴ (μὴ λογομαχεῖν, which may however depend on διαμαρτυρόμενος; AC* λογομάχει); aor. Ign. Eph. 11¹.

The consecutive, final and epexegetical infin. maintains the same distinctions in the pap. and NT (Mayser II 1, 151f); *pres.*: Mk 3¹⁴ to proclaim continually, Ac 20²⁸ to shepherd continually; more often with *aor* (see below p. 136). In sentences with πρίν, πρὶν ἤ, πρὸ τοῦ the infin. again indicates *Aktionsart* rather than time; *aor*. Mt 1¹⁸ *before ever they came together*, 26³⁴ *before the cock start to crow*. Kind of action rather than of time is also differentiated by the independent articular infin. The distinction holds after verbs of which the meaning requires punctiliar action in the dependent infin.; they are θέλω, βούλομαι, αἱρέομαι, δοκεῖ, κρίνω, δύναμαι, δυνατός, κελεύω and verbs which concentrate on the fulfilment of the desired course. There are exceptions in the Koine: Jn 9²⁷ pres. with θέλω, Ac 16²² with κελεύω, in

---

[1] *Einleitung* 274.
[2] But the brilliant ch. VI of the Prolegomena is still vitally important for the student of tenses.
[3] K-G I 192ff. Stahl 180ff. Mayser II 1, 150–168. Moulton Proleg. 204.
[4] Unless, as seems likely, κηρυχθῆναι Lk 24⁴⁷ is imperatival.
[5] An alternation of imperat. and infin. which is paralleled in the papyri, but always 3rd pers.: Mayser II 1, 303f.

pap. with βούλομαι (but proportion of 2:1 for aor.) and θέλω, κρίνω, δεῖ.

With μέλλω the fut. infin. was most frequent in class. Greek, but is restricted to Ac in NT; in the more official language as well as in the colloquial speech of the pap. there is the aor., and occasionally the fut. in official style, but in the less educated and in the NT the pres. prevails [1]. NT has 3 fut., 5 aor., 84 pres. Aorist: Lk 20³⁶ D Marc., Ac 12⁶ AB, Ro 8¹⁸ Ga 3²³ Rev 3². ¹⁶ 12⁴. Fut. infin. also for ἐλπίζω in NT, although class. fut. is found in papyri (Mayer II 1, 216). Note the subtle nuance in 1 Co 7⁹ κρεῖττον γάρ ἐστιν γαμεῖν ἢ πυροῦσθαι *to be in a married state* (not *to marry*). Note also that when Barnabas wished to take Mark (παραλαβεῖν), all Paul may have objected to was παραλαμβάνειν (Mark's being with them throughout the journey) Ac 15³⁷ᶠ.

(c) *Participle of Present and Aorist* [2]

Like the infin., the ptc. had originally no temporal function but simply indicated the kind of action [3]. The *time* of action was inferred from the context. But eventually the aorist ptc. came to denote a time which was past in relation to the main verb, and the present ptc. time which was contemporaneous (Mayser II 1, 175f). The reason for this may have been the difficulty of thinking of an act as a simple event (aor. ptc.) without also conceiving of it as taking place in the (immediate) past. The pre-position or post-position of the ptc. has little to do with this: Mk 1³¹ ἤγειρεν αὐτὴν κρατήσας τῆς χειρός (relative past time in spite of post-position). Yet in spite of that development there are numerous examples of the aor. ptc. denoting coincident action [4], where the time of the action is not antecedent to that of the main verb; there is the common phrase ἀποκριθεὶς εἶπεν which is the same as ἀπεκρίθη εἰπών,

---

[1] K-G I 177n. 4. Stahl 195. Moulton Einl. 184, 2. Mayser II 1, 166.
[2] K-G I 197. Stahl 209ff. Gild. I §§ 329ff. Mayser II 1, 168–176. Schwyzer II 385–409. Moulton Einl. 211ff. C. D. Chambers, "A Use of the Aorist Participle in some Hellenistic Writers," *JThS* 24, 1923, 183ff. A. T. Robertson, "The Aorist Participle for Purpose in the Κοινή," *JThS* 25, 1924, 286ff.
[3] Zerwick § 184 goes so far as to distinguish ὁ ἀκούων (he who hears with lasting effect) from ὁ ἀκούσας (who hears ineffectively and momentarily): Lk 6⁴⁷⁻⁴⁹.
[4] For the pre-Christian papyri, see Mayser II 1, 173f.

and also Ac 1²⁴ προσευξάμενοι εἶπαν and its reverse Mk 14³⁹ προσεύξατο ... εἰπών. The meaning of the ptc. is not always that of the main verb : Mt 27⁴ ἥμαρτον παραδούς, Ac 10³³ καλῶς ἐποίησας παραγενόμενος, 18²⁷ προτρεψάμενοι οἱ ἀδελφοὶ ἔγραψαν, Lk 15²³ φαγόντες εὐφρανθῶμεν; Heb 2¹⁰ ἀγαγόντα is more suitably interpreted of coincident action (*by bringing in*). So 1 Ti 1¹² Heb 6¹³. Usually the main verb is aorist, but sometimes future : Lk 9²⁵ 3 Jn⁶; sometimes pres. and impf. Mk 8²⁹; sometimes perf. Ac 13³³.

Even time which is *future* to the main action seems to be denoted by the aor. ptc. ¹ : Mt 10⁴ Judas who was to betray him ὁ καὶ παραδοὺς αὐτόν, Jn 11² Mary who was to anoint ² ἡ ἀλείψασα, Ac 16⁶ διῆλθον ... κωλυθέντες (= ἐκωλύθησαν δέ?), 25¹³ κατήντησαν ... ἀσπασάμενοι = καταντήσαντες ... ἡσπάσαντο (vl ἀσπασόμενοι to correct this anomaly) but we might by straining this make it an aor. of coincident action, the arrival and greeting being timed together! Wilcken Chr. 26 II³² (A.D. 156), LXX 1 Mac 15²⁸ ἀπέστειλε ... ἕνα ... κοινολογησάμενον (Lucianic; rest fut.).

Equally unexpected is the pres. ptc. expressing action relatively future in time. It is characteristic of Jn, e.g. 5⁴⁵ ἐστὶν ὁ κατηγορῶν ὑμῶν Μωϋσῆς (where the parallel κατηγορήσω just before makes it inevitable that this ptc. has future sense).

Ac 14²¹ᶠ ὑπέστρεψαν ... ἐπιστηρίζοντες *they returned ... to strengthen*, 15²⁷ ἀπεστάλκαμεν ἀπαγγέλλοντας *we have sent ... who will tell you*, 18²³ ἐξῆλθεν διερχόμενος τὴν Γαλατικὴν χώραν *he went from A. to go through*, 21¹⁶ συνῆλθον ... ἄγοντες *went with us ... in order to bring us*. Pre-Christian papyri, Mayser II 1, 170. Post-Christian also, e.g. P. Oxy. I 120 11 (iv/A.D.) ἀπόστιλόν μοι τινα ... παραμένοντά μοι.

It is debatable whether we may go so far as to see in the pres. ptc. an indication of time prior to the time of the main

---

¹ See Chambers, op. cit., for passages in support; also W. F. Howard ibid. 403–6; and *per contra* A. T. Robertson op. cit. For another explanation see Zerwick § 198 : " fortasse potest intellegi de actione simpliciter subsequente (loco καί cum verbo coordinato : κατήντησαν καὶ ἠσπάσαντο)." There may be analogous cases in Ac, which Z. admits to be doubtful, but we are in danger, according to some grammarians, of making nonsense of grammar if we see fut. action in the aor. ptc. Nevertheless Z. draws a good example of ἐλών of posterior action from Philostr. vit. Ap. I 22.

² Unless a previous anointing is referred to, viz. Lk 7³⁸, in which case Mary of Bethany is identified with the sinful woman from the street. The aor. ptc. is usually explained however of time *past* in relation not to the events described but to the time of writing.

verb [1]. Mayser gives some possibilities from the papyri and there are instances in class. Greek. The prior action which is thus indicated is usually continued action, so that the ptc. amounts to an impf.:

> Mt 2²⁰ *they who were seeking* 23¹³ *those who were entering* (trying to enter?) τοὺς εἰσερχομένους, 27⁴⁰ *you who were trying to destroy* ὁ καταλύων ... *and rebuild* οἰκοδομῶν, Jn 9²⁵ *I was blind* τυφλὸς ὤν *but now I see*, 12¹⁷ *the crowd that was with him* ὁ ὤν, Ac 4³⁴ *they sold* πωλοῦντες, Ga 1²³ *who persecuted* ὁ διώκων, Eph 4²⁸ *who stole* ὁ κλέπτων, Rev 20¹⁰ *who deceived them* ὁ πλανῶν αὐτούς, 2 Jn ⁷ ἐξῆλθον ... οἱ μὴ ὁμολογοῦντες. Pres. and aor. together: Lk 2⁴² ἀναβαινόντων αὐτῶν ... καὶ τελειωσάντων.

§ 5. Perfect Indicative [2]

The following are the significant trends of the Hellenistic period, as they are exemplified in the NT probably better than in any other single text of the time.

(1) By extending its sphere to cover the functions of the aorist, the perfect tends eventually to disappear and be confused with the aorist (see above under Aoristic Perfect). There is, particularly in the less cultured papyri, a tendency to emphasize the connection of a past action with the present, and in consequence to favour the perf. tense.

(2) The confusion is well illustrated by the introduction into the perf. system of the " weak " endings of the aorist.

(3) The perf. participle middle is developed and gradually assumes the strength of an adjective.

(4) A periphrastic conjugation becomes established.

In common with the Koine generally the NT and Ptolemaic papyri significantly extend their use of the perfect to a greater extent than do the literary writers of the period. They allow it to trespass seriously on the territory of the aorist. The *Aktionsart* belonging properly to the tense is either fulfilment in the present of a process begun in the past or else the contemplation of an event having taken place in the past with an interval

---

[1] H. G. Meecham, "The Present Participle of Antecedent Action. Some N.T. Instances." *Exp. T.* 64, June 1953, 285. Mayser II 1, 170f.

[2] K-G I 146-150. Stahl 107-119. Gild. I §§ 226-34. Schwyzer II 286-288. Mayser II 1, 176-207. P. Chantraine, *Histoire du Parfait Grec*, Paris 1907. Moulton Einl. 220ff. Zerwick §§ 209-212. J. E. Harry, "The Perfect Forms in later Greek from Aristotle to Justinian," *Proc., Amer. Philol. Association* XXXVII 53. H. J. Cadbury, "A Possible Perfect in Acts ix, 34," *JThS* 49, 1948, 57ff. M. S. Enslin, "Perfect Tense," *JBL* 55, 121-31.

intervening, whereas the English perfect is used when no interval intervenes. It is therefore a combining of the *Aktionsarten* of aorist and present. Originally it had no resultative force but simply expressed the subject's state; this had been arrived at by some previous activity, but the state arrived at was represented by the perfect as so permanent that the perfect can be said from long before the NT period to have present meaning [1]. Several examples of this present perfect have survived in the Ptolemaic papyri (Mayser II 1, 177f) and NT: οἶδα, ἕστηκα, πέποιθα *trust*, κεῖμαι, μέμνημαι, τέθνηκα *be dead*, πέπεισμαι *be sure*, ἤλπικα *hope*, ἥγημαι *believe* (cl.), κέκραγα, ὄλωλα, πέφηνα, εἴωθα. They have in fact become independent presents, each one divorced from its own present stem. Among these ἀπόλωλα was disappearing (Mt has 2, Lk 5), the popular style of Mk being innocent of it and the "literary" Luke having most; it was giving way to ἀπολλύω. Τέθνηκα is still *to be dead* but its distinction from ἀπέθανον is disappearing. Ἀνέῳγα survives at Jn 1⁵¹ 1 Co 16⁹ 2 Co 6¹¹ but is already being displaced by ἀνέῳγμαι in cl. Attic, and Paul falls back on ἀνεῳγμένης 2 Co 2¹². Πέποιθα Gospels: Mt has 2, Lk 3, Mk 10²⁴ τοὺς πεποιθότας ἐπὶ (τοῖς) χρήμασιν DAΘ fam¹ fam¹³ lat syr bo (but SBW k sa om), Paul. Ἕστηκα Gospels: Mt has 13, Lk 10, Jn 16, Mk ptc. only ἑστηκώς 9¹ 11⁵ (vl ἑστώτων) 13¹⁴ (vll. ἑστός and στῆκον), ἑστώς 3³¹ (vl στήκοντες), and usually in NT, but a new pres. form is being coined from this perf. i.e. στήκω (8 times, and in variants for ἕστηκα). Οἶδα the old pres. pf., is preserved. Ἐγρήγορα is archaic, but a new verb γρηγορέω has been built on it. Ἤγγικα *to be here* appears as well as ἐγγίζω Mk 1¹⁵ 14⁴² (SC aor.); conceivably it is a true pf. *to have drawn near*. Ἧκα Mk 8³ (vl εἰσίν) Atticistic correction? Εἴωθα Mk 10¹ εἰώθει = impf.

But not all these intrans. perfects became independent presents. Some of them still survive with their resultative force in the Koine and Bibl. Greek: ἀκήκοα, κεκάθικα, ἠκολούθηκα, κέκραγα, εἴωθα, διαμεμένηκα, συμβέβηκα, τετελεύτηκα, μεμαρτύρηκα, κεκοπίακα, πεπίστευκα, σέσηπα, πέπονθα, εἴληφα, τέτυχα.

Four books from LXX: Ge (παρ-) ἕστηκα 18²² 24¹³. ³⁰. ³¹. ⁴³ 45¹; γέγονα 3²² 18¹² 44²⁸ 47⁹ : κεκόπακα 8⁷. ⁸. ¹¹; προβέβηκα 18¹¹ 24¹; γεγήρακα 18¹³ 27²; συνῴκηκα 20³; προσώχθεικα 27⁴⁶A; παρεμβέβληκα 32¹; ἐκπεπόρνευκα 38²⁴; ἧκα 42⁷ 45¹⁶ 47³; συμβέβηκα 42²⁹ AD; ἡμάρτηκα 43⁹; ἐκλέλοιπα 47¹⁵. ¹⁸; τέθνηκα 50¹⁵.

---

[1] For ἔσχηκα, πέπονθα, and πεποίηκα in a present sense in Polyb., see A. Schoy, *De perfecti usu Polybiano*, Bonn 1913, 75f.

§ 5] THE VERB: ASPECT AND TENSE 83

Ex (παρ-) (συν-) ἕστηκα 3^5 7^{19} $17^{6.\ 9}$ 24^{10} $33^{8.\ 10}$ 9^{31} $18^{13.\ 14}$ 20^{21} 24^{13}; οἶδα $3^{7.\ 19}$ 5^2 10^{26} $32^{1.\ 22.\ 23}$ $33^{12.\ 17}$ 23^9; τέθνηκα 4^{19} 14^{30} 21^{35}; κέκραγα 5^8; γέγονα 8^{15} $9^{18.\ 24}$ $10^{6.\ 14}$ 11^6 $32^{1.\ 23}$ 34^{10}; ἡμάρτηκα 9^{27} 10^{16}; πέφευγα 14^5; καταβέβηκα 19^{18}; τετέλευκα 21^{34} 22^1; πέπτωκα 23^5; κεχρόνικα 32^1.

Isa (συν-)πέπτωκα 3^8 9^{10} 21^9 23^{13}; (ἀφ-) (παρ-) ἕστηκα 6^2 5^{29} 17^5 $59^{11.\ 14}$; πέπτωκα 9^{10} 21^9 23^{13}; πέφευγα 22^3; γέγονα 23^2; ἀπόλωλα 23^{14}; πέποιθα $30^{15.\ 32}$ 33^2 36^7 37^{10} 50^{10} 59^4; κεκοπίακα 47^{13} ἤγγικα 56^1; ἀνατέταλκα 60^1; ἥκα 60^4; παραβέβηκα 66^{24}.

Dan O' ἕστηκα and compounds 2^{31} 3^{91} 7^{10} $8^{3.\ 6}$ 10^{13} 11^2 $12^{1.\ 5}$; ἡγνόηκα 9^{15}.

Thus the old intrans. perfect was giving way before the active, transitive and resultative pf. The resultative was already popular in the Attic orators and continued to be so in the literary texts of the Hellenistic period, and subsequently in Atticistic texts. Many *new* perfects of a resultative kind appear. The vernacular shows the same tendency, and by iii/B.C. the verbal balance between the intrans. and resultative is reached. The decline of the resultative perfect did eventually set in (see above, pp. 68f.) and by i/A.D. as revealed by the NT the number of such perfects has shrunk, except in the literary traditions; its form is limited to only a few verbs (cp. the variety in the LXX books just examined) and its meaning is difficult to distinguish from the aorist. There is an instructive exception: in the Johannine writings, by contrast especially to the Synoptists and Paul, the resultative pf. is frequent. There are 77 examples; Mk has only 8, Lk 14, and Mt 7. The intrans. perfects are not less frequent: there are still 100 in the Joh. writings. We may ascribe this to the peculiar style of the Fourth Gospel, its love of emphasis and solemnity, its stress on the abiding significance of everything. Generally, however, the NT writers use only a perfect which is already well established by tradition, the same verbs being employed repeatedly. Let us take Mk as an example: 5^{15} ἐσχηκότα (om D 17* 27 Old Lat. vulg^p1 syr^s bo), 5^{34} 10^{52} σέσωκεν, 14^{44} δεδώκει, δέδωκεν Θ (aor. in D *ackr*^{1} vulg^1: scribes did not like the "Latin" plupf. in Greek), 15^{10} παραδεδώκεισαν (aor. DWΘ fam^{13} fam^1 700 *a c* vulg^1), 5^{19} πεποίηκεν (aor. DKΦ fam^1 517 565 700), 7^{37} πεποίηκεν, 11^{17} πεποιήκατε BLΔΨ 892 1342 orig (aor. rest), 15^7 pf. or plupf., 5^{33} διὸ πεποιήκει λάθρᾳ DΘ28 565 700 *a ff* geo arm (but neither διό nor λάθρᾳ is Marcan!). In Mt εἴρηκα occurs twice, but the following only once : ἔγνωκα, ἡτοίμακα, εἴληφα, πέπρακα, σέσωκα. Lk (who is more flexible) has : δέδωκα, συνήρπακα, συνείληφα, σέσωκα once; ἀπέσταλκα, κέκληκα, ἑώρακα, πεποίηκα 2. 1 Co κέκρικα, εἴληφα, μεμέρικα, ἑώρακα once, κέκληκα 2, ἔγνωκα 3. The resultative pf. is however often used with what seems to be aoristic force. So the MSS show many variations with the aorist. Although the resultative pf. is so frequent in Jn the same verb occurs over and over again : ἤντληκα, βέβληκα, βέβρωκα, ἐλήλακα, τεθέαμαι, πεπλήρωκα, τετύφλωκα, πεφίληκα once; ἀκήκοα, γέγραφα, μεμίσηκα twice; ἀπέσταλκα, εὕρηκα, τετήρηκα 3; ἔγνωκα, πεποίηκα 4; εἴρηκα, μεμαρτύρηκα 5; λελάληκα 10; δέδωκα 14; ἑώρακα 17.

To a slightly less degree, as we have seen, there is the same limitation in the LXX. Thus, Ge κεκόπακα 3; δέδωκα (NT) 5; τέθεικα, πέπρακα (NT), ἀνενήνοχα, ἐκπεπόρνευκα, ἐκλέλοιπα, σέσωκα (NT), λελάληκα (NT) once; εἴληφα (NT) 3; πεποίηκα (NT) 5; (ἐπ-) ἀκήκοα 4; τέτοκα 3; ἑώρακα (NT) 4; εἴρηκα (NT) 3; ἀπέσταλκα (NT) 3; εὕρηκα 3. Ex καταλέλοιπα, ἐμπέπαιχα, συνκέκλεικα, λελάληκα (NT), ἠγάπηκα, κέκραξα, προσκεκύνηκα, ἦσαν πεποιηκότες once; (εἰσ-) ἀκήκοα 3; ἑώρακα (NT) 5; ἀπέσταλκα (NT) 5; δέδωκα (NT) 2; εἴρηκα (NT) 4; παρῴκηκα 2; πεποίηκα (NT) 2; ἡμάρτηκα 3; εὕρηκα 4. Isa συνῆκα, ἀποβέβληκα, πεπότικα, ἔσπαρκα, ἐζωγράφηκα, εἴληφα (NT), κέκληκα (NT), πεποίηκα (NT), ἐγκαταλέλοιπα, ἀκήκοα, κέκληκα once; ἀπέσταλκα (NT) 3; λελάληκα (NT) 2; ἀπολώλεκα 2; ἑόρακα (NT) 2; δέδωκα (NT) 4, πέπρακα (NT) 2. Dan ἑώρακα (NT) 8; εὕρηκα, σέσωκα (NT), εἴρηκα (NT) once. This is enough to show that the resultative pf. was becoming lifeless, fossilized in a few verbs only. Comparing the situation, for instance, in Thucydides book II we find only εἴρηκα and δέδωκα among the resultatives which are so common in LXX and NT, and hardly any of the resultatives in that book are repetitions of the same verb. By iii and iv/A.D. the perfect has greatly declined, and in the collection of Christian papyri of this date by G. Ghedini [1] we find only εὕρηκα, ἐνήνοχα, (παρα-)δέδωκα, ἐπέσταλκα, προστέθεικα, ἠπάντηκα, εἴρηκα.

We may glance at some exegetically interesting examples of the perfect in the NT. It expresses a present state in πέπεισμαι *I am persuaded*, but it may not be simply a pres. pf., as the processes involved are important, as well as the resultant state ; and the same is true of ἤλπικα. But truly present are τέθνηκα and ἥγημαι. Illustrative of a tense which expresses action begun in the past but fulfilled in the present is the series of resultative perfects in 2 Ti 4⁷ : *I have fought* ἠγώνισμαι, *I have*

---

[1] *Lettere cristiane dai papiri greci del III e IV secolo*, Milan 1923.

finished τετέλεκα, *I have kept* τετήρηκα, i.e. until now. It is remarkable that ἑώρακα occurs so often in the NT and ἀκήκοα comparatively seldom; but to explain the aor. of the latter side by side with the perf. of the former by the theory that to have seen the Lord was a more abiding experience than merely to have heard him, is utterly fantastic (Jn 3³², Ac 22¹⁵ Clem. Hom. 1⁹). Of the two perfects used by Pilate (Jn 19²² ὃ γέγραφα γέγραφα) the first must be simply for euphony, as it is aoristic.

Although a very large number of perfects in the NT cannot fairly be distinguished from aorists, there are still some which retain true resultative, and some a present, meaning.

§ 6. Other Moods of the Perfect in relation to Time [1]

(a) Of perfects with present meaning there are in NT and Koine the *imperatives* ἔρρωσο, ἔρρωσθε (Ac 15²⁹ 23³⁰ SELHP) and the periphrasis with ἴσθι. In Eph 5⁵ τοῦτο ἴστε γινώσκοντες may be a Hebraism (cp. γινώσκων οἶδεν LXX 1 Km 20³, and ἴστε γινώσκοντες Sym Je 49(42)²²). In Jas 1¹⁹ ἴστε may be imper. or indic. (S* ἴστω); so also Heb 12¹⁷. In Mk 4³⁹ (as opposed to φιμώθητι in DW, and 1²⁵ Lk 4³⁵) πεφίμωσο is probably a solemn stereotyped phrase used in adjurations.

(b) On the other hand, the *infinitive* is fairly common. In indirect speech (antecedent action): Lk 10³⁶ 22³⁴, Jn 12¹⁸· ²⁹, Ac 12¹⁴ 14¹⁹ 16²⁷ 25²⁵ 27¹³, Ro 15⁸, Col 2¹, 1 Ti 6¹⁷ 2 Ti 2¹⁸, Heb 11³. Subject or object (its time is coincident with the main verb): Lk 12⁵⁸ Ac 19³⁶ Ro 15¹⁹ Ac 26³² 2 Co 5¹¹, 1 Pt 4³ 2 Pt 2²¹. With prepositions διά εἰς μετά (antecedent action): Mk 5⁴ Lk 6⁴⁸ Ac 8¹¹ 18² 27⁹ Eph 1¹⁸ Heb 10⁹· ¹⁵ 11³ (Mayser II 1, 186ff).

(c) The *participle* also is fairly common, and its time is relative to that of the main verb, either antecedent or coincident. E.g. coincident: Jn 4⁶ 19³³ Ro 15¹⁴. Antecedent: Mt 26⁷⁵ Lk 16¹⁸ Jn 11⁴⁴ 18¹⁸ (Mayser II 1, 192ff). It is here, as well as in the indicative, that a difference from class. Greek is apparent: there was a distinct tendency in the Hellenistic period to connect very closely a past action with its present consequences. Hence Mt 5¹⁰ οἱ δεδιωγμένοι. It was preferable to say "who has been here a week" than to say "who came here a week ago." Aquila came from Italy recently (Ac 18²), but in Hellenistic they thought, "he has been here since coming from Italy recently." Hence the perfect where class. Greek would have aorist. Thus there can be no difference between preaching Christ ἐσταυρωμένον (as he has been since Good Friday) and preaching Christ σταυρωθέντα (as he was on Good Friday): the one is rather more classical than the other.

---

[1] K-G I 192ß. Stahl 152f. Gild. I §§ 406–409. Mayser II 1, 185–207. Moulton Einl. 277.

§ 7. Pluperfect [1]

The tense was never very frequent in the class. period—much less so than in Latin or English—and in the Ptolemaic papyri it shrank to an inconsiderable number of verbs, and was restricted largely to epistolary style. It still appears in NT, but many of the plupfs. of the Latin Bible translate the aorist: e.g. Ac 14²⁷. When it occurs it is simply the perfect placed in past time, relative to the time of speaking: Lk 16²⁰ *he lay* (we might use the impf. *he was lying*), Jn 9²² *the Jews have agreed* put into the past, 11⁴⁴ past of *his face is swathed in a towel*.

§ 8. Future [2]

(*a*) *Indicative*. This is the one tense which does not express the *Aktionsart*, but simply states the time of action relative to the speaker. However, it is usually punctiliar, the periphrastic future being used when it is required to indicate linear action (Moulton Proleg. 149f), but the question is really a matter of opinion (Moule p. 10).

The future expresses a command, both in secular (Mayser II 1, 212f) and Biblical Greek. In the Mosaic Law this is particularly so, and prohibitions are formed by the addition of οὐ. All from the OT are: Mt 5²¹· ⁴³· ⁴⁸ 1 Pt 1¹⁶. Otherwise it occurs: Mt 6⁵ οὐκ ἔσεσθε, 20²⁶ οὐχ οὕτως ἔσται, 21³ ἐρεῖτε, ¹³ κληθήσεται, 27⁴ σὺ ὄψῃ (Latin?), ²⁴ ὑμεῖς ὄψεσθε (Latin?), Ac 18¹⁵ ὄψεσθε αὐτοί (Latin?); also Mk 9³⁵ Lk 1³¹; 1 Cl 60² καθαρεῖς, Herm V. II 2, 6 ἐρεῖς; several times in Barn. 19²ᶠᶠ, Herm. M. XII 3, 1, Did. 11⁷. But Jesus' own commands are imperative: Mt 5⁴⁴ ἀγαπᾶτε, 10¹³ ἐλθάτω ἡ εἰρήνη ὑμῶν ἐπ' αὐτήν (D fut). The MSS often vary between fut. ind. and imper. (Cuendet op. cit. 124), e.g.: Mt 20²⁷ Lk 17⁴.

Entirely due to Semitic influence is Rev 4⁹¹ καὶ ὅταν δώσουσιν τὰ ζῷα δόξαν . . . πεσοῦνται . . . καὶ προσκυνήσουσιν . . . καὶ βαλοῦσιν *when they gave glory . . . they fell . . . worshipped . . . threw*; we suspect literal rendering of the Heb. impf. which can be future under some circumstances.

Apparently Gnomic are: Ro 5⁷ *will die* = *is willing to*, 7³ χρηματίσει almost imper. *let her be called*. Deliberative: Mt 11¹⁶ *am I to compare*.

(*b*) *Infinitive*. It expresses time which is future in relation to the main verb; it has died out in colloquial speech, for the pap. examples are nearly all very early (Mayser II 1, 216), but it is still found in Ac and Heb: Jn 21²⁵ SBC (rest aor.) οἶμαι, Ac 11²⁸ 24¹⁵ 27¹⁰ (μέλλω), 23³⁰ (μηνύω), 26⁷ B (rest aor.) ἐλπίζω, Heb 3¹⁸ (ὄμνυμι).

(*c*) *Participle*. The same applies. Independent use: Lk 22⁴⁹ τὸ ἐσόμενον (D γενόμενον), Jn 6⁶⁴ παραδώσων (D pres., S μέλλων), Ac 20²² τὰ συναντήσοντά μοι, Ro 8³⁴ ὁ κατακρινῶν? 1 Co 15³⁷ τὸ σῶμα τὸ

---

[1] K-G I 151ff. Stahl 119–123. Gild. I §§ 235–237, Mayser II 1, 207–211. Moulton Einl. 232ff.
[2] K-G I 170ff. Stahl 140ff. Gild. I §§ 265–284. Mayser II 1, 211ff. Keith. " The Future in Greek," *Class. Q.*, 1912, 6, 121.

§ 8-9] THE VERB: ASPECT AND TENSE 87

γενησόμενον, 1 Pt 3¹⁸ τίς ὁ κακώσων ὑμᾶς, 2 Pt 2¹³ κομιούμενοι (S*B arm ἀδικούμενοι), Heb 3⁵ τῶν λαληθησομένων. Dependent: very rare, the pres. ptc. or infin. or a clause taking its place: Mt 27⁴⁹ ἔρχεται σώσων (W σώζων, S* σῶσαι, D καὶ σώσει), Mk 11¹³ vl ὡς εὑρήσων, Ac 8²⁷ ἐληλύθει προσκυνήσων, 22⁵ ἐπορευόμην ἄξων, 24¹¹ ἀνέβην προσκυνήσων, ¹⁷ ποιήσων . . . παρεγενόμην, Heb 13¹⁷ ὡς λόγον ἀποδώσοντες (probably genuine only in Ac and Heb). Instead, perhaps under Heb. or Aram. influence, we have the pres. ptc. for fut., e.g. Ἰούδας ὁ παραδιδούς (Mt 26²⁵), ἀποδημῶν (25¹⁴), περὶ τῶν πιστευόντων (Jn 17²⁰); also Mt 20²⁰ 22¹⁶, Lk 1³⁵ 2³⁴ 14³¹ 22¹⁹ᶠ, Ac 21²ᶠ 26¹⁷. In all these, translate as a final clause or a future (Zerwick §§ 208, 208ᵃ).

§ 9. Periphrastic Tenses [1]

As Lagrange notes, it is a "construction très usitée en araméen, connue des Grecs mais surtout avec le participe au parfait." (*S. Matth.* XCI.)

(a) *Present and Imperfect* [2]. For this εἰμί serves (but never γίνομαι in Ptol. pap. and rarely in NT) with pres. ptc. In NT it is rarely the pres. ind. of εἰμί but usually ἦν ἔσομαι εἶναι or ἴσθι. Scribes of a later age did not like the periphr. tense and altered it at e.g. Mk 1³⁹ 2⁴ 3¹ 5¹¹, ⁴⁰ 9⁴ 13²⁵ 14⁴ 15²⁶. But the development is not far advanced in Hell. Greek, not even in the popular style of the papyri (Mayser II 1, 223f). Due acknowledgement must therefore be given to the influence of Semitic speech [3] for the popularity of the usage in NT: so many of the examples occur in Mt, Lk, and the first part of Ac. In Jn the ἦν cannot always be considered independently, even with a little straining: 1⁹. ²⁸ 2⁶ 3²³ 18³⁰ ἦν κακὸν ποιῶν (vl κακοποιός). What possible distinction can there be between ἐβάπτιζεν and ἦν βαπτίζων in Jn 3²². ²³, or between ἐν τῷ εἶναι αὐτὸν προσευχόμενον and ἐν τῷ προσεύχεσθαι αὐτόν in Lk 9¹⁸. ²⁹ᶠ? Björck (op. cit. 68f) argues against Semitic influence and (op. cit. 53f) urges that sometimes the instances are only apparently periphrastic, the ptc. being adjectival. Indeed it is probably a supplementary predicate in Mk 1⁴ ἐγένετο Ἰωάννης ὁ βαπτίζων ἐν τῇ

---

[1] K-G I 38n. 3. Gild. I § 191. 285–290. 291. 293. Stahl 144–147. Schwyzer II 407 (ζ). Mayser II 1, 223ff. Moulton Einl. 357ff. Radermacher², 102. Bauer s.v. εἰμί 4. P. F. Regarde, *La Phrase Nominale dans la Langue du NT*, Paris 1919, 111–185.

[2] G. Björck, Ἦν διδάσκων. *Die periphr. Konstruktionem im Griech.*, Uppsala 1940.

[3] Aramaic in particular; de Zwaan in *Beginnings* II 62 mentions the Aram. imperfect.

ἐρήμῳ κηρύσσων . . . (= ἐγένετο καὶ ἐκήρυσσεν), 9³· ⁷, Mt 5²⁵, Lk 1²⁰, Ac 9⁹. No doubt in some instances the copula really means *there is* or *there are*, but not in the vast majority.

Present: Mt 1²³ 7²⁹ 19²² 27³³ etc., Mk 5⁴¹ 15²². ³⁴ Lk 6⁴³ 8³² SBD, Jn 1⁴² 5², Ac 1¹² 4³⁶ 14¹⁵ 25¹⁰, Ro 13⁶ 15⁴, 1 Co 8⁵, 2 Co 2¹⁷ 9¹² 10¹¹, Ga 1¹⁰· ²²ᶠ 4²⁴, Col 1⁶ 2⁵· ²³ 3¹, Eph 5⁵ DEKL, 1 Ti 5²⁴, Jas 1¹⁷ 3¹⁵, 2 Pt 3⁷, Rev 1¹⁸ 3¹⁷. Πρέπον ἐστιν Mt 3¹⁵ 1 Co 11¹³. Δέον ἐστιν Ac 19³⁶ 1 Cl 34². 'Εξόν (sc. ἐστιν) Ac 2²⁹ 2 Co 12⁴. Συμφέρον (sc. ἐστιν) 2 Co 12¹ p⁴⁶ SBFGP (συμφέρει DEKL).

Imperfect: in Mk there is abundance of periphr. tenses (29): 1⁶· ¹³· ²²· ³³· ³⁹ 2⁴· ⁶· ¹⁸ 3₁ 4³⁸ 5⁵· ¹¹· ⁴⁰ 6⁵² 9⁴ 10²². ³²ᵇⁱˢ 14₄. ⁴⁰· ⁴⁹· ⁵⁴ 15⁷· ²⁶· ⁴⁰· ⁴³; Mt 7²⁹ 12⁴ 14²⁴ SCE (B differs) 17³ 19²² 24³⁸ 27⁵⁵· ⁶¹ Lk 1¹⁰· ²¹· ²² 2⁸· ³³· ⁵¹ 3²³ 4²⁰· ³¹· ³³· ³⁸· ⁴⁴ 5¹⁶· ¹⁷· ²⁹ 6¹² 8³² SBD (ACEFG diff) ⁴⁰ 9³⁰· ⁵³ 11¹⁴ 13¹⁰· ¹¹ 14₁ 15₁ 19⁴⁷ 21³⁷ 23⁸· ⁵¹ 24¹³· ³²· ⁵³; Jn 1²⁸ 2⁶ 3²³ 5⁵ 10⁴⁰ 13²³ 18¹⁸· ²⁵· ³⁰ 19⁴¹ ἦν τεθειμένος SB (AD |ἐτέθη|); Ac 1¹⁰· ¹³· ¹⁴ 2²· ⁵· ⁴² 8₁· ¹³· ²⁸ 9⁹· ²⁸ 10²⁴· ³⁰ 11⁵ 12⁵· ⁶· ¹²· ²⁰ 14⁷ 16⁹· ¹² 18⁷ 19¹⁴ 21³· ⁹ 22¹⁹· ²⁰; 2 Co 5¹⁹; Ga 1²²· ²³ᶠ 2¹¹; Ph 2²⁶; Eph 2¹²; Ti 3³; 1 Pt 2²⁵; Rev 1¹⁶ 10² 17⁴ 21¹¹· ¹⁴.

(b) *Perfect and Pluperfect*. We have an illustration of the principle that when a grammatical form tends to disappear, having lost its characteristic force, the language will find a substitute; often that substitute is a periphrasis. Class. Greek furnishes numerous examples of periphrastic optative and subjunctive, and the periphrasis began to extend to other parts so that εἰμί with perf. ptc. is very common in NT. No real difference can be detected between ἐπεγέγραπτο Ac 17²³ and ἦν γεγραμμένον Jn 19¹⁹. Even in the same book within a few lines we find γεγραμμένα ἐστίν Jn 20³⁰ and ταῦτα δὲ γέγραπται 20³¹. Cp. 1 Jn 4¹² τετελειωμένη ἐστιν, 2⁵ τετελείωται; Herm. S. IX 4 ὑποδεδυκυῖαι ἦσαν alongside ὑποδεδύκεισαν. Although it may be possible occasionally to trace the presence of the class. force of *insistence* [1], as when Paul separates ἑστώς (a pres. pf.) from εἰμί with great emphasis, referring to his position as a suitor for Imperial justice (Ac 25¹⁰), yet usually there is no emphasis and the question of Semitic background is immediately raised. The same construction occurs in the early part of Acts, where there are grounds for supposing Semitic influence (5²⁵ εἰσίν . . . ἑστῶτες). Mayser does not give many exx. from secular Greek. Nevertheless, whatever its origin, the periphrastic

---

[1] Thucydides book II: 4³· ⁵ 6² 10³ 12² 49³ 78³ (often with expressive force).

§ 9] THE VERB: ASPECT AND TENSE 89

perfect persisted in the mainstream of the language and is in regular use at the present day with the force of the Latin and English perfect.

LXX. Ge 27^{33} 30^{33} 40^6 41^{36} 43^9 44^{32}. Ex 12$^{6.\ 34}$ 17^{12} 21$^{23.\ 36}$ 32^{15} 33^{13} 34^{30} 39^{23}. Isa 1^{11} 8$^{14.\ 17}$ 9^{19} 10^{20} 11^5 bis 12^2 13$^{3.\ 15}$ 17$^{7.\ 8.\ 9}$ 20$^{5.\ 6}$ 22$^{3.\ 14.\ 24}$ 27^{10} 28^7 30^{12} 33^{12} 36$^{4.\ 5}$ 42^{20} 54^{11} 58^{14}. Dan. 2$^{20.\ 42}$ 35$^{2.\ 53.\ 54.\ 56}$ 6^3 8^{26} 10^9 12^9.

Pre-Christian papyri: 5 in iii/B.C., 11 in ii/B.C. (Mayser II 1, 224f).
NT: Mt 1^{23} 9^{36} 10^{30} 18^{20} 26^{43}; Mk 1$^{6.\ 33}$ 6^{52} 14^{21} D 15$^{7.\ 26.\ 46}$; Lk 1^7 2^{26} 4$^{16.\ 17}$ 5$^{1.\ 17.\ 18}$ 8$^{2.\ 3}$ 9^{45} 12$^{2.\ 6}$ 15$^{24.\ 32}$ 18^{32} 20^6 23$^{15.\ 51.\ 53.\ 55}$ 24^{38}; Jn 1^{24} 2^{17} 3$^{21.\ 24.\ 28}$ 6$^{31.\ 45}$ 10^{34} 12$^{14.\ 16}$ 13^5 18$^{18.\ 25}$ 19$^{11.\ 19.\ 20}$ 20^{30}; Ac 1^{17} 2^{13} 4^{31} 8^{16} 9^{33} 12$^{6.\ 12}$ 13^{48} 14^{26} 16^9 17^{23} 18^{25} 19^{32} 20$^{8.\ 13}$ 21$^{29.\ 33}$ 22$^{20.\ 29}$ 25$^{10.\ 14}$ 26^{26}; Ro 7^{14} 13^1 15^{14}; 1 Co 1^{10} 5^2 7^{29} 14^8 15^{19}; 2 Co 1^9 4^3; Ga 2^{11} 4^3; Eph 2$^{6.\ 8.\ 12}$; Col 2^{10}; Heb 4^2 7$^{20.\ 23}$ 10^{10}; Jas 5^{15}; 2 Pt 3$^{5.\ 7}$; 1 Jn 4^{12}; Rev 7^5 17^4 21^{19}.

(c) Future Perfect periphrasis is very rare too (Mayser II 1, 225): Mt 16^{19} 18^{18} Lk 12^{52} Heb 2^{13} (Isa 8^{17}); but it takes the place of the normal fut. pf.

(d) Periphr. Future, normally linear in *Aktionsart*, is expressed by θέλω and μέλλω with infin. or by the fut. of εἰμί with the ptc. Mt 10^{22} 24^9 Mk 13^{13}, Lk 21^{17} ἔσεσθε μισούμενοι, 21^{24}. Mk 13^{25} (corr. by Mt 24^{29}) Lk 5^{10} 12^{52} 22^{69} Ac 6^4 D 13^{11} 1 Co 14^9 Jude ^{18}; Lk 1^{20} ἔσῃ σιωπῶν. Μέλλω Mk 13^4 Lk 7^2 22^{23} Jn 12^4 Ac 18^{14} 20^3 28^6.

(e) Periphrasis with aorist ptc. (= plupf.): Lk 23^{19} B ἦν βληθείς (Engl. impf. or plupf.?) vl. perf., Jn 18^{30} S*, 2 Co 5^{19} ἦν θέμενος. No more in NT, but in post-Christian Greek (K-G I 38f. Gild. I 125f. Radermacher^2, 102).

(f). Periphrasis with verbal adjectives in -τος : Lk 4^{24} δεκτός ἐστιν (= δέχεται), Ac 11^{17} ἤμην δυνατός, 28^{22} γνωστόν ἐστιν, Jn 18^{15} ἦν γνωστός, 6^{45} ἔσονται διδακτοί, Ro 1^{25} ἐστιν εὐλογητός.

(g) Periphrasis with γίνομαι: Mk 9^3 (9^7), 2 Co 6^{14} Col 1^{18}, Heb 5^{12}, Rev 1^{18} 3^2 16^{10}, Did 3^8, LXX Isa 30^{12}.

(h) Other periphrases: pres. subjunctive Eph 4^{14} Jas 1^4. Perf. subj. Lk 14^8 Jn 3^{27} 6^{65} 16^{24} 17$^{19.\ 23}$ 1 Co 1^{10} Ph 1^{10} 2 Co 1^9 9^3 Jas 5^{15} 1 Jn 1^4, LXX Isa 8^{14} 10^{20} 17^8 20$^{5.\ 6}$. Pf. imper. Lk 12^{35}. Pf. ptc. Eph 4^{18} Col 1^{21}. Infin. Lk 9^{18} = 11^1. Imper. Mt 5^{25} Lk 19^{17} Hom. Clem. ep. ad Jac^3, Mart. Pelag. 26^{15}. Eph 5^5?

It is well to note that in true periphrastic tenses the copula keeps very close to the participle; there are hardly more than four exceptions to this rule in Mark.

CHAPTER EIGHT

THE VERB: MOODS: INDICATIVE AND SUBJUNCTIVE

IN THE use of moods Hellenistic Greek moves further away from class. Greek than in its use of tenses. The optative mood is less used, although there is a considerable survival in the LXX and NT. The infinitive has retreated on some flanks and advanced on others.

§ 1. The Indicative [1]

1. The imperfect indicative (without ἄν), in main clauses, to express necessity really concerns only ἔδει, since χρή is not Hellenistic [2]. The time is either *past* (*it would have been necessary*, but did not happen) or else *present* (*it were necessary*, but is not happening); in English *ought* serves for both and we make the second verb carry the time-indication.

(a) *Past*: Lk 24²⁶ *would it not have been necessary* οὐχὶ ταῦτα ἔδει παθεῖν τὸν Χριστόν, Heb 9²⁶ *it would then have been necessary* ἔδει αὐτὸν πολλάκις παθεῖν. Mt 18³³ *ought you not to have pitied*, 23²³ Lk 11⁴² *ought you not to have done*, Mt 25²⁷, Lk 13¹⁶. Ptol. papyri (dates): 266, iiim, 258, 258, 258, 258, 165, 107.

(b) *Present*: Ac 24¹⁹ *they ought to be here* οὓς ἔδει ἐπί σου παρεῖναι. P. Hib. 46, 13 (258 B.C.) ἔδει πάλαι τὰ ἐνέχυρα αὐτῶν ὧδε εἶναι καὶ πεπρᾶσθαι, also iiim.

Other imperfects are used in a similar sense for the pres. in NT, but not the papyri: καθῆκεν Ac 22²² (D² καθῆκον), ἀνῆκεν Eph 5⁴ (DE τὰ οὐκ ἀνήκοντα) Col 3¹⁸, ἐδύνατο Mt 26⁹ Jn 9³³ Ac 26³², ὤφειλον 2 Co 12¹¹, καλὸν ἦν Mt 26²⁴, κρεῖττον ἦν 2 Pt 2²¹. It is not suggested that the past obligation was not lived up to; it is simply a present obligation expressed for some reason in the imperfect. The reason may be the same as that which

---

[1] K.-G I 202–216. Stahl 351ff. Gild. I §§ 361–368. Schwyzer II 301–309. Mayser II 1, 226–229. R. Law, "Imperfect of Obligation in the NT", *Exp. T.* 30, 330ff. For fut. ind. as a command, see above.

[2] In NT only Jas 3¹⁰; in LXX only Pr 25²⁷ 4 Mac 8²⁵ A. There are two uncertain examples in the Ptol. pap.: Mayser II 1, 226.

prompts the English past tense *ought* instead of present *owe*: simply because the obligation logically conceived is anterior to the implied fulfilment of the obligation. What we do not find in NT are: ἐξῆν *it were possible*, ἦν with the verbal adj. in -τέος, ὀλίγου with aor. ind. for something that nearly happened, and προσῆκει.

2. In the same way an unfulfilled or impossible wish can be expressed by ὤφελον or ἐβουλόμην, etc., as a regret. 1 Co 4⁸ ὄφελον (ὤφελον DᶜEL) ἐβασιλεύσατε, 2 Co 11¹ ὄφελον (ὤφ. DᶜEFGKL) fut. ind., Rev 3¹⁵ ὄφελον (ὤφ. BP) ψυχρὸς ἦς ἢ ζεστός, Ign. Sm. 12¹, LXX and Epict. have ὄφελον (and ὤφ.) with indic., Gr. Enoch 10⁶⁻¹⁰ ὄφελον subj. Nothing in papyri. In class. Greek a wish relating to the past which can no longer be fulfilled is expressed by εἴθε with ind.; a wish which cannot be fulfilled, relating to past or present, by ὤφελον or εἴθε (εἰ γάρ) ὤφελον, with inf. But the pap. and NT have no instance of εἴθε and εἰ γάρ used in this way.

By omitting the apodosis, a protasis with εἰ may become a wish clause (Lk 19⁴² Ac 23⁹).

Ac 26²⁹ SᶜAB εὐξαίμην ἄν (class.), Ro 9³ ηὐχόμην ἀνάθεμα εἶναι. Ἐβουλόμην: Arist. Ran 866, P. Flor. I 6, 7 (A.D. 210) Ac 25²² Phm¹³. Ἤθελον: Soph. Ajax 1400, Epict. (= *I must*), Ga 4²⁰, Clem. Hom. 1⁹, BU IV 1078⁸ (A.D. 39), P. Lond III 897²⁰ (p. 207) (A.D. 84), MGr ἤθελα.

In cl. Attic the aor. (rarely the impf.) was used with ἄν to denote what would have happened at a past time if the attempt had been made, and therefore what *might, could,* or *should* have taken place. Thus ἠβουλόμην ἄν = *I should (could) have wished* (under other circumstances), Lat. *vellem*. But already in Attic orators the ἄν is dispensed with (K-G I 205; Stahl 358).

3. The " unreal " indicative (impf. for what *should be* now; aor. for what *should have been*) is found in conditional sentences; the ἄν which is the characteristic of " unreal " usage may not even be present. The tenses maintain their proper *Aktionsarten* (NB. plupf. Ac 26³² 1 Jn 2¹⁹).

(a) Apodosis with ἄν [1]: Mt 11²¹ εἰ ... ἐγένοντο (*had been*

---

[1] Whether Mt 15⁵ Mk 7¹¹ comes here is debatable. It might be an apodosis, with a protasis to be supplied like " if it had not been δῶρον." Thus translate, Δῶρον *is the benefit which you would have received from me*. But ἐάν is not elsewhere used for ἄν in " unreal " use (hence D's correction to ἄν).

done) ... ἄν ... μετενόησαν (*would have repented*), Jn 18³⁰ εἰ μὴ ἦν ..., οὐκ (syr^lew οὐδ') ἄν σοι παρεδώκαμεν *if he were not ... we would not have*, 18³⁶ (see below). Ptol. pap: iii/B.C. (6), ii/B.C.
(1) We have pres. indic. in the protasis in P. Par. 47 (153 B.C.) ἰ μὴ μικρόν τι ἐντρέπομαι, οὐκ ἄν με ἴδες τὸ π⟨ο⟩ρσωπόν μου πόποτε, which is parallel to Lk 17⁶ εἰ ἔχετε πίστιν ..., ἐλέγετε ἄν *if you have faith, you would say* (the "real" condition, pres. indic., may be due to politeness, for the disciples had claimed to have *some* faith, when they asked for it to be increased. *If you had faith* would seem to deny this too bluntly.)

The position of ἄν: it goes back as far as possible, and often there is οὐκ ἄν; note the following: Lk 19²³ κἀγὼ ἐλθὼν σὺν τόκῳ ἂν αὐτὸ ἔπραξα, Jn 18³⁶ οἱ ὑπηρέται ἄν οἱ ἐμοὶ ἠγωνίζοντο (B*om ἄν; SB^mg LWX have ἠγωνίζοντο ἄν), 8¹⁹ εἰ ἐμὲ ᾔδειτε καὶ τὸν πατέρα μου ἂν ᾔδειτε BLW (ᾔδειτε ἄν LΓΔ), Ga 1¹⁰ χρ.δοῦλος οὐκ ἂν ἤμην, Heb 10² ἐπεὶ (*otherwise*) οὐκ ἂν ἐπαύσαντο.

(*b*) Apodosis without ἄν: Mk 9⁴² Lk 17² DW καλόν ἐστιν αὐτῷ μᾶλλον εἰ περιέκειτο (vl. περίκειται) μύλος ὀνικὸς ... καὶ ἐβλήθη (vl. βέβληται), but the "real" indic. of the other MSS may have some point: "If such a man as that is drowned, it is just as well!" So also Ga 5¹¹ εἰ ... ἔτι κηρύσσω, τί ἔτι διώκομαι. Mt 26²⁴ Mk 14²¹ καλὸν (ἦν) αὐτῷ εἰ οὐκ ἐγεννήθη. Jn 9³³ εἰ μὴ ἦν ... οὐκ ἠδύνατο, 15²⁴ εἰ τὰ ἔργα μὴ ἐποίησα ... ἁμαρτίαν οὐκ εἴχοσαν, 19¹¹ οὐκ εἶχες B (ἔχεις SA) ἐξουσίαν ... εἰ μὴ ἦν..., 8³⁹ εἰ τέκνα ... ἐστε, τὰ ἔργα ... ἐποιεῖτε SB² DΓWΘ fam¹³ (+ ἄν S^cKL) (ποιεῖτε p⁶⁶ B*700 Old Lat syr^s), Ac 26³² ἀπολελύσθαι ἐδύνατο ... εἰ μὴ ἐπεκέκλητο Καίσαρα, Ro 7⁷, Ga 4¹⁵ (S^cD^cEKLP add ἄν), 2 Cl 20⁴, Gosp. Petr. 2⁵, LXX 2 Mac 5¹⁸, 3 Mac 5³², Ptol. pap. (dates): 141 116 2.

4. The augment-indicative with ἄν stands in dependent clauses in an iterative sense (= class. optative). It is certainly found in class. Greek in *main* clauses to denote a customary past action [1]. But in NT and simple Koine it never occurs in main clauses; in temporal and conditional relative clauses it may be a remnant of the class. usage [2] in main clauses. The class. ὃς ἄν (ὅταν) βούλοιτο ἐδύνατο becomes in later Greek ὃς ἄν (ὅταν) ἐβούλετο ἐδύνατο.

---

[1] *He would often do it, he used to do it*; Goodwin § 162. The only exception seems to be Soph. Ph. 442ff. ὃς οὐκ ἂν εἵλετο (Schwyzer II 350).
[2] Burton § 26.

Again ἄν stands early, as near as possible (if not actually joined) to the conjunction or relative: Mk 3¹¹ τὰ πνεύματα, ὅταν αὐτὸν ἐθεώρουν, προσέπιπτον, 6⁵⁶ ὅπου ἐάν (ἄν) εἰσεπορεύετο ... ἐν ταῖς ἀγοραῖς ἐτίθεσαν..., 15⁶ ὃν ἂν ᾐτοῦντο DG rightly, Ac 2⁴⁵ 4³⁵, 1 Co 12² ὡς ἂν ἤγεσθε; LXX Ge 38⁹, Ex 33⁸ ἡνίκα δ' ἂν εἰσεπορεύετο, Ps 119 (120)⁷ ὅταν ἐλάλουν αὐτοῖς ἐπολέμουν με δωρεάν *each time I spoke to them*, 1 Mac 13²⁰, Nu 21⁹ (A aor.): see Ottley, *Introduction to OT in Greek*, 1914, 306. Polybius 4, 32, 5 ὅταν ... ἐν πειρασμοῖς ἦσαν, Herm S. IX 6, 4.

The aor. is found, as well as impf. Mk 6⁵⁶ ὅσοι ἂν (SΔ om) ἥψαντο SBDLΔW (ἥπτοντο ANXΓΠ) αὐτοῦ, ἐσῴζοντο: von Soden accepts impf., the more normal construction, but aor. is not without precedent. Mk 11¹⁹ ὅταν SBCKL (ὅτε AD) ὀψὲ ἐγένετο, ἐξεπορεύετο ἔξω τῆς πόλεως = *whenever it was evening, every evening*, not as some translators take it *when it was evening* (of that day); by class. standards it is what Field called a "solecism" (Notes 35), but not by Hellenistic, in which it is normal iterative indic. with ἄν. Ac 3² ὃν ἐτίθουν καθ' ἡμέραν πρὸς τὴν θύραν τοῦ ἱεροῦ. It would suggest, in Rev 8¹ (ὅταν ἤνοιξεν), that the Lamb's breaking of the seals was a repetitive performance, in spite of the aor. Aor. elsewhere: Polyb. 4, 32, 6 ὅταν ... ἐτράπησαν, 13, 7, 8. 10. LXX Ge 30⁴² vl, Ez 10¹¹. Herm. S. IX 4, 5; 17, 3. Barn 12². P. Lond. IV 1394 (A.D. 709) ἀπόστειλον πρὸς ἡμᾶς εἴ τι δ' ἂν συνῆξας χρυσίου ἀπὸ τῶν αὐτῶν δημοσίων For ὅταν with indic. however in a non-iterative meaning see pp. 112f. For pres. and fut. indic. with ἄν see p. 110.

§ 2. The Subjunctive[1]

(*A*). MAIN CLAUSES

1. *A substitute for the Imperative*

The difference in meaning between pres. and aor. imper. has already been discussed (pp. 74–78); for the perfect imper. see pp. 85, 89. All that remain are the substitutionary forms of the imperative, of which we have already discussed the pres. and aor. infinitive and fut. indic. (pp. 78, 86). There remains the subjunctive, both positive and negative.

---

[1] K-G I 217–225. Gild. I §§ 369–386. Stahl 228, 364ff. Schwyzer II 309ff. Wackernagel I 230ff. F. Slotty, *Der Gebrauch des Konjunktiv und Optative in den griechischen Dialekten*, I. 1915.

(a) *The Jussive*. This use of 2nd and 3rd p. subjunctive in positive sentences was never acceptable to Ionic and Attic writers (K-G I 220) and probably does not appear in NT[1] although there are examples from inscriptions of v–iii/B.C. (Slotty op. cit. 22ff) and post-Christian Greek [2]. They are all aor. and so could be confused with fut. through the phonetic resemblance of -σει and -σῃ, -σομεν and -σωμεν, etc. Moreover, confusion was already apparent in Attic Greek poetry between the subjunctive and optative for wishes (K-G I 225), and all the time the opt. was generally losing ground; thus the way was prepared for the jussive use of the subjunctive in the popular Koine (exx. in Slotty op. cit. 34, Mayser II 1, 230), while the analogy of the prohibitive subjunctive was ever at hand to suggest this development.

The hortative subj. in 1st p. does however occur in NT (as in class. Greek); Jn 14³¹ Ga 5²⁶ 1 Co 11³⁴ διατάξωμαι ADEFG (-ξομαι p⁴⁶ SBC). Also, where cl. Greek used ἄγε, φέρε or δεῦρο, Hellenistic has ἄφες (ἄς with 1st and 3rd p. subj. in MGr as an imper.) and δεῦρο with 1st p.: Mt 7⁴ 27⁴⁹ Mk 15³⁶ SDV 12⁷ Lk 6⁴² Ac 7³⁴ OT Rev 17¹ 21⁹, Lk 2¹⁵ διέλθωμεν δή, Epict. 1, 9, 15 ἄφες δείξωμεν, P. Oxy. III 413, 184 (ii/A.D.).

(b) *Negative*. In prohibitions, as have seen (pp. 74–78), it depends on the *Aktionsart* of the verb whether the pres. imper. or aor. subj. with μή is used; never probably the pres. subj. in NT [3] but Herm. S. IV 5 (A pap^(mich)) οὐδὲν διαμάρτης. In neg. hortatory sentences, e.g. 1 Co 16¹¹ μή τις ... ἐξουθενήσῃ *let no one despise*, 2 Co 11¹⁶ 2 Th 2³.

Ὅπως (ἄν) and ὅπως μή with subj. or fut. ind. occur in the Ptol. pap. like the class. ὅπως and fut. ind., but not the NT.

(c) *Imperatival* ἵνα. However the NT does display exx. of ἵνα with subj. in 2nd and 3rd p. [4] Mt 20³³ κύριε, ἵνα ἀνοιγῶσιν,

---

[1] Possible exceptions at 1 Co 7³⁹ FG γαμηθῇ (3rd p), 11³³ ἐκδέχησθε (2nd p).
[2] Reinhold, *Apost. Väter* 104; Ign. Pol 8³ διαμείνητε; Barn. 19¹ σπεύσῃ; Ljungvik BSSV 71 (ἐν νόῳ ἔχῃς ὅτι BGU II 5, ii–iii/A.D.).
[3] Possibly except Col 3⁹ p⁴⁶ μὴ ψεύδησθε.
[4] Schwyzer II 318. Horn 120ff. Radermacher² 170. Pernot *Études* 63, 97ff, 123, 148f. Moulton Einl. 281. C. J. Cadoux, "The Imperatival Use of ἵνα in NT," *JThS* 42, 1941, 165ff. H. G. Meecham, ibid. 43, 1942, 179f. A. R. George, ibid. 45, 1944, 56ff. (criticism of Cadoux and Meecham). H. G. Meecham *Exp. T.* 52, Aug. 1941, 437. Mayser II 1, 231f. Ljungvik SSAA 38.

Mk 5²³ ἵ᾽ α... ἐπιθῇς (or it depends on παρακαλεῖ), 10⁵¹ 'Ραββουνεί ἵνα ἀνα[λέψω. Lk 18⁴¹. Jn 6³⁹ ἵνα... μὴ ἀπολέσω, 9³ ἵνα φανερωθῇ, 13¹⁸ ἵνα ἡ γραφὴ πληρωθῇ, 15²⁵. 1 Co 5² ἵνα ἀρθῇ ἐκ μέσου ὑμῶν ὁ τὸ ἔργον τοῦτο πράξας usually taken as final, but only imperat. ἵνα will make good sense, as RSV (but not quite NEB), 7²⁹ ἵνα... ὦσιν, 2 Co 8⁷ ἵνα περισσεύητε, 9⁴ ἵνα μὴ λέγωμεν (p⁴⁶ C*DG it λέγω) *not to say*, Col 4¹⁶ ἵνα... ἀναγνωσθῇ *see that it is read*, Ga 2¹⁰ ἵνα μνημονεύωμεν *we must remember*, Phm¹⁹, Eph 5³³ ἡ δὲ γυνὴ ἵνα φοβῆται τὸν ἄνδρα. 1 Ti 1³ ἵνα παραγγείλῃς (or depends on παρεκάλεσα), 1 Jn 2¹⁹ (final in RV, NEB) ἵνα φανερωθῶσιν *they must be manifest*. Doubtful in Jn 1⁸ *he must bear witness*, 14³¹ *the world must learn*, 18⁹·³² 19²⁴, Mk 14⁴⁹ *the Scripture must be fulfilled*, 1 Co 7⁵·¹⁰·²⁹ 2 Co 8⁷·¹³ 9⁴ Col 2⁴. None in Ac, Past, Heb, Jas, 1, 2 Pt, Rev. The use is popular (Slotty 35), although it is found also in LXX 2 Mac 1⁹ ἵνα ἄγητε τὰς ἡμέρας τῆς σκηνοπηγίας. Note νά with 2nd and 3rd p. subj. as imper. in MGr. Ptol. pap.: pos. iii/B.C. (2), neg. iii/B.C. (1).

LXX displays a great many exx. because of the influence of its Semitic background: Ge 18²¹ ἵνα γνῶ *I must know*, 30⁸? ἵνα εὕρῃ ὁ παῖς σου χάριν, 44³⁴ ἵνα μὴ ἴδω *let me not see*, 47¹⁹ *let me not die before you*. Ex. Le none. Nu 11¹⁵ *let me not see my wretchedness*, 21²⁷ *let the city be built*. Dt 5¹⁴ *your servant must rest*. Josh 22²⁴ *let not our children say*. Jg Ru Km none. 1 Ch 21³ ἵνα μὴ γένηται εἰς ἁμαρτίαν τῷ Ἰσραήλ *let him not be accused of sin*. 1 Esd. none. 2 Es Ne. To S none. To B 8¹² ἵνα θάψωμεν αὐτὸν καὶ μηδεὶς γνῷ (Β ὅπως). Est. Jdt. none. Ps 38⁵ ἵνα γνῶ *let me know*. Pr Eccl Ca Wi Si Isa Je Ba. none. Ezk 37²³ *they must no longer be defiled* pres. subj. Dan O' none. 2 Mac 1⁹ ἵνα ἄγητε *see that ye keep*. 3 4 Mac none. Jb 32¹³ (cp. Eph 5³³ Mk 5²³) 1 Mac 1⁹? Acta Petri et Pauli 209¹⁴ ἵνα γνῷς, βασιλεῦ, Acta Phil. 39¹ff ἵνα λαλῶσιν ὁμοιότητα ἄνθρωπον (following an imperat.), 86²¹ff μὴ καλυψάτω με... ἀλλ᾽ ἵνα διαπεράσω... Before an imperat.: Acta Thom. 253⁶ff ἵνα... πέμψῃ... καὶ εὐφραινέσθωσαν..., 253¹⁰f ἵνα μὴ ἀπόληται ἡ πεποίθησίς μου καὶ ἡ ἐλπίς μου ἡ ἐν σοὶ μὴ καταισχυνθῇ, 254⁶ff.

In view of this wealth and the secular poverty of examples, we may claim the imperatival ἵνα as virtually a Semitism, illustrating the homogeneity of Biblical Greek and its distinction from the Koine.

2. *Emphatic Denial and Prohibition with* οὐ μή

Besides the imperatival use of the subj. in main clauses, we have the following:

The use of οὐ μή [1] to express emphatic denial or a strong

---

[1] Which also occurs as *nonne* in questions expecting answer yes (see below ch. 19 § 2).

prohibition [1], not so strongly as in class. Greek [2], is in NT almost restricted to quotations from LXX, to sayings of Jesus, and to Rev. The fut. ind. is also used in NT but not in Ptol. pap. The subj. is very strongly attested in the papyri, and this seems to rule out an exclusively Semitic influence. For theories on the origin of the οὐ μή construction, see Moulton Proleg. 188ff, Goodwin 389ff, Thompson *Syntax* 431–438. It was probably οὔ (*no!*)· μή (*it is not*), then punctuated οὐ μή.

(a) *In Denials*

1. *Aorist.* Aor. subj. occurs in class. Greek. L.S. (s.v. οὐ μή) gives exx from Aesch. Soph. Eurip. Hdt. Thucyd. Aristoph. Plato, Xen. Demosth. Post-cl.: Aelius Aristides (ii/A.D.), Diogenes; Epict. III 22, 33 οὐ μὴ ἀποθάνωσιν; Ep. Barn. 17² οὐ μὴ νοήσητε *you will not understand*; Ep. Clem. 27⁵ καὶ οὐδὲν μὴ παρέλθῃ τῶν δεδογματισμένων ὑπ' αὐτοῦ. Ptol. Pap.: many exx., esp. Zen. P. 59084. 9 (257 B.C.) οὐ μὴ κινηθῶ *that will certainly make no impression on me*; 59396. 4 (iii/B.C.) πρὸς δέ σε οὐθὲν μὴ διενεχθῶμεν *we will certainly not quarrel with you*. Imperial: P. Oxy. 119 (ii–iii/A.D.) οὐ μὴ φάγω, οὐ μὴ πείνω. LXX: (Ge οὐ μή 15 times in 337 negs; Ex 13 in 302; Dt 33 in 499) Ge 6³ οὐ μὴ καταμείνῃ τὸ πνεῦμά μου etc. (9), Ex (6), Le (6) Nu (11), Dt (33), Isa (88), Je α (28) β (50); also, e, g, Jb 7⁹, Wi 1⁸·SA 3¹ 6²² 12¹⁰; Ps. Sol. I 5; Vit. Proph. Jer. 14. NT:—Mt 5¹⁸·²⁰·²⁶, 15⁶ οὐ μὴ τιμήσῃ E*FGK (rest fut.), 16²⁸ οἵτινες οὐ μὴ γεύσωνται θανάτου, 21¹⁹, 24²·³⁴·³⁵ οὐ μὴ παρελθῶσιν (Mk 13³¹ ACDᶜ a harmonization), ²¹ οὐδὲ οὐ μὴ γένηται, 26²⁹·³⁵ οὐ μή σε ἀπαρνήσωμαι AEGK (rest fut.), Mk 9¹·⁴¹, 13² οὐ μὴ ἀφεθῇ ὧδε λίθος ἐπὶ λίθον ὃς οὐ μὴ καταλυθῇ, ¹⁹·³⁰, 14²⁵·³¹ (-σωμαι SEFGK), 16¹⁸, Lk 9²⁷ 12⁵⁹ o.μ. ἐξέλθῃς, 13³⁵ o.μ. ἴδητε. 1¹⁵ o.μ. πίῃ, 6³⁷ᵃ·ᵇ·, 8¹⁷ o.μ. γνωσθῇ . . ., 18⁷ οὐ μὴ ποιήσῃ; ¹⁷·²⁹ᶠ οὐχὶ μὴ ἀπολάβῃ, 21¹⁸·³² 22¹⁶ οὐκέτι οὐ μή, ¹⁸·⁶⁷·⁶⁸, Jn 4⁴⁸ 6³⁵ (vl. fut. ind.), 8¹² (vl. fut. ind.) ⁵¹·⁵², (vl. fut. ind.), 10²⁸, 11²⁶·⁵⁶, 13⁸ οὐ μὴ νίψῃς (D fut. ind.), 18¹¹ οὐ μὴ πίω αὐτό; Ac 13⁴¹ (LXX Hab1⁵), Ga 4³⁰ οὐ μή (p⁴⁶ FG om) κληρονομήσῃ ACFG (rest fut.), Ro 4⁸ (Ps 31²) οὐ μὴ λογίσηται, 1 Co 8¹³ Heb 8¹² (Je 38³⁴), 13⁵ οὐ μή σε ἀνῶ οὐδὲ p⁴⁶ (rest οὐδ' οὐ) μή σε ἐγκαταλίπω D (rest-λείπω) very emph., Rev 2¹¹

---

[1] K-G I 176f, II 221–223. Jannaris § 1827. Slotty *Konj. und Opt.* 42 § 90. Gild. *AJP* 3, 1882, 202–205. C. D. Chambers, *Cl. Rev.* 10, 1896. 150–153; 11, 1897, 109–111; Wharton ibid. 10, 1896, 239; R. Whitelaw ibid. 239–244; A. Y. Cambell ibid. 57, 1943, 58–61. Mayser II 1, 233. R. Ludwig, *D. prophet. Wort* 31, 1937, 272–279. Moulton Proleg. 187–192.

[2] Very rare indeed in Hell. Greek. I read the following books without finding a single οὐ μή among 1370 negatives: Aratus *Phaenomena* (iv–iii/B.C.), Callimachus *Hymns* and *Epigrams* (iii/B.C.). Lycophron *Alexandra* (iii/B.C.), Aelian *Letters of Farmers* ii–iii/A.D.), Philostratus *Love Letters* (ii–iii/A.D.), Alciphron *Fishermen, Farmers, Parasites, Courtesans* (iv/A.D.). But in *Didache* (ii/A.D.), there were 2 out of 124 negs., and in Ep. Clem. (i/A.D.) 1 out of 95 negs.; in Eps. Ign. 1 out of 217.

§ 2] THE VERB: MOODS 97

οὐ μὴ ἀδικηθῇ, 3¹², 7¹⁶, 15⁴ τίς οὐ μὴ φοβηθῇ; 18²¹· ²³ etc. 1 Pt 2⁶ (Isa 28¹⁶).

2. *Present.* Classical: Xen. Plato, Soph. Is. Ptol. Pap: comparatively rare, e.g. Zen. P. 59610. 21 οὐ μὴ βούλωνται φυλάσσειν (iii/B.C.), Mich. Zen. 77. 13 οὐ μὴ ἕξηις αὐτῶι ἐγκαλέσαι (iii/B.C.). No true ex. occurs in NT, a vl. only Heb 13⁵ p⁴⁶. LXX, e.g. Ge 28¹⁵ Dt 15¹¹ AF, Isa 10²⁰ οὐκέτι μὴ πεποιθότες ὦσιν, 11⁹ οὐ μὴ κακοποιήσουσιν οὐδὲ μὴ δύνωνται, 16¹² οὐ μὴ δύνηται ἐξελέσθαι αὐτόν, 24²⁰ οὐ μὴ δύνηται ἀναστῆναι 36¹⁴ οὐ μὴ δύνηται ῥύσασθαι ὑμᾶς, Je 1⁹ 15²⁰ 29¹¹ 30¹² 43⁵.

3. *Future.* Class.: Aesch. Soph. Aristoph. Xen. Aeschin. NT:— Mt 15⁶, 26³⁵, 16²² οὐ μὴ ἔσται σοι τοῦτο, Lk 21³³ οἱ δὲ λόγοι μου οὐ μὴ παρελεύσονται apparently a conflation of Mt-Mk: Mt 24³⁵ οὐ μὴ παρέλθωσιν, Mk 13³¹ οὐ παρελεύσονται. (ACDᶜ harmonize Lk with Mt; such details make it likely that Luke knew Mt.¹), Lk 10¹⁹ οὐδὲν οὐ μὴ ὑμᾶς ἀδικήσει.

Jn 4¹⁴ οὐ μὴ διψήσει, 6³⁷ οὐ μὴ ἐκβαλῶ ἔξω, 10⁵ οὐ μὴ ἀκολουθήσουσιν (vl. aor. subj.), Mk 14³¹ οὐ μή σε ἀπαρνήσομαι, Jn 20²⁵ οὐ μὴ πιστεύσω, Ga 4³⁰ οὐ γὰρ μὴ κληρονομήσει (Ge 21¹⁰), Heb 10¹⁷, Rev 9⁶ οὐ μὴ εὑρήσουσιν, 18¹⁴ οὐκέτι οὐ μὴ εὑρήσουσιν Herm. M. IX 2; IX 5; S. I 5. Barn 11¹ πῶς τὸ βάπτισμα . . . οὐ μὴ προσδέξονται, 19⁷ μήποτε οὐ μὴ φοβηθήσονται (cp. Did. 4¹⁰). LXX:— e.g. Ge 21¹⁰ A οὐ γὰρ μὴ κληρονομήσει ὁ υἱός . . . (D om μή), Nu 35³³ A (rest οὐ), Dt 4³¹ οὐκ ἐνκαταλείψει σε οὐδὲ μὴ ἐκτρίψει σε, 28³⁰ AF οὐ μὴ τρυγήσεις αὐτόν (B om μή). Isa (12), Je α (9), β (4). Enoch 98¹² 99¹⁰.

(b) *In Prohibitions* ²

1. *Fut. Ind.* In class. Greek "interrogative": Soph. *Tr.* 978, Eurip. *Supp.* 1066, *Andr.* 757, *El.* 982, *Hipp.* 213, Aristoph. *Ach.* 166, *Nu.* 367, *V.* 397. Editors and MSS vary between fut. ind. and aor. subj. Probably both were allowed, but subj. may have been commoner in denials and fut. ind. in prohibitions. LXX: Le 11⁴³ οὐ μὴ κοιμηθήσεται ὁ μισθὸς τοῦ μισθωτοῦ . . . Dt 1⁴² οὐκ ἀναβήσεσθε οὐδὲ μὴ πολεμήσετε (F aor. subj.), 6¹⁴ AF οὐ μὴ πορεύσεσθε (B om μή), 7¹⁶ AF οὐ μὴ λατρεύσεις τοῖς θεοῖς (B om μή), 2 Km 24¹⁴ οὐ μὴ ἐμπέσω *let me not fall*, Je 11²¹ οὐ μὴ προφητεύσεις . . . (-σης A). Mt 16²² οὐ μὴ ἔσται σοι τοῦτο. Barn 10⁴ οὐ μή, φησίν, κολληθήσῃ οὐδὲ ὁμοιωθῇς, 5.

2. *Aor. Subj.* LXX:—Ge 3¹ οὐ μὴ φάγητε, ³ οὐδὲ μὴ ἄψησθε, 21¹⁶ οὐ μὴ ἴδω τὸν θάνατον τοῦ παιδίου μου, Ex (7), Le (1), Nu (3), Dt (13). NT:—Mt 13¹⁴ Ac 28²⁶ (LXX Isa 6⁹) Jn 13⁸ οὐ μὴ νίψῃς μου τοὺς πόδας. Ep. Barn. 10⁶ οὐ μὴ γένῃ παιδοφθόρος οὐδὲ ὁμοιωθήσῃ,⁷· ⁸ οὐ μή, φησίν, γενηθῇς τοιοῦτος, 19² οὐ μὴ ἐγκαταλίπῃς ἐντολὰς κυρίου (cp. Did. 4¹³), ⁴ οὐ μή σου ὁ λόγος τοῦ θεοῦ ἐξέλθῃ ἐν ἀκαθαρσίᾳ τινῶν, ⁵ οὐ μὴ διψυχήσῃς, ⁵ οὐ μὴ ἄρῃς τὴν χεῖρά σου ἀπὸ τοῦ υἱοῦ σου, ⁶ οὐ μὴ γένῃ

---

¹ See *Studia Evangelica* (Texte und Untersuchungen, LXXIII) 1959, pp. 223–234.
² W. W. Goodwin, *Trans. American Philol. Assocn.* 1869–70, 52. Slotty op. cit. 43. Mayser II 1, 233 (very rare in papyri, and never prs. subj. or fut. ind.).

ἐπιθυμῶν τὰ τοῦ πλησίον σου ... οὐ μὴ γένῃ πλεονέκτης,[7] οὐ μὴ ἐπιτάξῃς δούλῳ σου (contrast Did. 4[10]).

3. *A Cautious Statement.*

Μή with subjunctive to express a cautious statement in a main clause [1] is rare in NT: Mt 25⁹ μήποτε οὐκ ἀρκέσῃ SALΣ (μήποτε οὐ μὴ ἀρκ. BWC; D ἀρκέσει), 1 Th 5¹⁵ ὁρᾶτε μή τις ἀποδοῖ ἀλλά ... διώκετε, 2 Ti 2²⁵ μήποτε δῷ αὐτοῖς ὁ θεός *perhaps God will give.* Fairly frequ. in Platonic dialogue, e.g. *it would be rude* μὴ ἀγροικότερον ᾖ, *it would not be right* μὴ οὐ θεμιτὸν ᾖ. Only rarely in Ptol. pap. (e.g. P. Par. 32, 162 B.C.) μὴ οὐκ ἀποδώσοι. It is similar to the prospective or future subj. [2] without μή.

Foreign to class. Attic, this substitute for fut. ind. emerges in later Greek (K-G I 218). It was understandable that the like-soundings -ῃ and -ει should be confused in fut. and aor., but ἀφεθῇ αὐτοῦς ἡ ἁμαρτία (LXX Isa 33²⁴) and εἴπω σοι (for ἐρῶ σοι)[3] go beyond that. So also Ptol. pap. UPZ 31, 7 (162 B.C.) εὐδοκῶ ... ἐπέλθω. Exx. from post-Christian pap. in Moulton Einl. 292, 2. LXX Isa 10¹⁶ S ἀποστείλῃ. Hom. Clem. 11³ δυνηθῇ.

4. *Deliberative Subjunctive* [4].

The dubitative subj., the interrogative form of the hortatory, occurs in class. Greek (K-G. I 174, 233; Slotty 51) sometimes in 3rd p., but generally 1st p., negatived by μή and introduced immediately by βούλει, βούλεσθε, etc. Incidentally the fut. ind. (see above p. 86) is found sometimes in class. Greek (Plato *Crito* 50B) and NT: Lk 16¹¹ᶠ τίς πιστεύσει; τίς δώσει; Mt 16²⁶ τί δώσει (for Mk 8³⁷ τί δοῖ, which p⁴⁵ ACDW harm. with Mt), Lk 22⁴⁹ εἰ πατάξομεν (-ωμεν GH), Mk 6³⁷ ἀγοράσωμεν ... καὶ δώσομεν p⁴⁵ AB (-σωμεν SD fam¹³ 28 565; δῶμεν WΘ fam¹), Ro 3⁵ 4¹ etc. τί ἐροῦμεν. Sometimes even pres. ind. in NT: Jn 11⁴⁷ Herm. S. IX 9, 1 τί ποιοῦμεν, 1 Jn 3¹⁷ μένει (or μενεῖ fut.). Plato *Symp.* 214A πῶς ποιοῦμεν.

---

[1] K-G I 224, 7. Stahl 366, 3. Gild. I § 385. Moulton Einl. 303ff. Slotty §§ 84–86, 318, 331. Schmid Attic. III 90. Mayser I 1, 234.
[2] Schwyzer II 313f. Slotty § 130. Mayser II 1, 234–5. Moulton Einl. 292, 2. Reinhold 101–103. Sophocles Lexicon p. 45.
[3] P. Würthle, *Die Monodie des Michael Psellos auf den Einsturz der Hagia Sophia,* 1917, 22f.; Mayser II 1, 235.
[4] Mayser II 1, 235. Schwyzer II 318. A. W. McWhorter, "A Study of the so-called Deliberative Type of Question (τι ποιήσω;) " *Trans. and Proc., Amer. Philol. Association,* 41, 1910, 157ff.

Subjunctive: Mt 6²⁵ φάγητε, etc. 23³³ πῶς φύγητε: 26⁵⁴ πῶς... πληρωθῶσιν; Mk 12¹⁴ δῶμεν ἢ μὴ δῶμεν; Lk 11⁵ ἕξει... πορεύσεται... καὶ εἴπῃ (AD a fut.), ⁷ κἀκεῖνος εἴπῃ (D ἐρεῖ), 23³¹ ἐν τῷ ξηρῷ τί γένηται (DK fut.); γένηται also in Epict. IV 1, 97; 100. Ro 10¹⁴ᶠ ἐπικαλέσωνται (p⁴⁶ KLP -σονται), πιστεύσωσιν (vl. -σουσιν), ἀκούσωσιν SᶜA²B (L -σουσιν, S*D -σονται, p⁴⁶ -σωνται), κηρύξωσιν (vl. -ουσιν), Hom. Clem. 19² πῶς... στήκῃ (from Mt 12²⁶), Herm. S. V 7, 3 πῶς σωθῇ A (P. Mich. -θήσεται), Pass. Perp. et Felic. 1¹ διὰ τί μὴ... γραφῇ παραδοθῇ LXX 2 Km 23³ πῶς κραταιώσητε. In Ptol. pap. only in dependent clauses, e.g. οὐκ εἴχομεν ὅθεν αὐτῶι δῶμεν, (dates): 254 247 248 iiim (3) 257; once infin. (251); see Mayser II 1, 235f. Introduced by θέλεις, βούλεσθε etc. as in class. Greek (K-G I 221f): Mt 13²⁸ Lk 9⁵⁴ 18⁴¹ Jn 18³⁹.

(B) Subordinate Clauses.

1. *Fearing.*

The subj. appears as in class. Greek after expressions of anxiety with μή or μήποτε or μήπως, e.g. P. Magd. 9, 3 (iii/B.C.) φοβουμένη μὴ συμπέσηι, MGr φοβοῦμαι μήπως. It occurs after φοβοῦμαι in Luke, Paul and Heb. as a semi-literary feature, rather than popular. Pres. subj.:—Heb 4¹ μήποτε δοκῇ, 12¹⁵ μή τις ἐνοχλῇ (after ἐπισκοπέω). Fut. ind.:— Ro 11²⁰ᶠ φοβοῦ... μήπως οὐδὲ σοῦ φείσεται p⁴⁶ DFG (φείσηται in minusc. only; SABCP om μήπως). Aor. subj.:— Ac 23¹⁰ φ. (or εὐλαβηθείς HLP) μὴ διασπασθῇ, 27¹⁷, ²⁹ μήπως. 2 Co 11³ 12²⁰. Past indic.:—Ga 4¹¹ μήπως εἰκῆ κεκοπίακα (p⁴⁶ 1739 ἐκοπίασα).

After other words than φοβοῦμαι:—Lk 12⁵⁸ δὸς ἐργασίαν... μήποτε κατασύρῃ σε... καὶ παραδώσει (note change to fut. ind.), 14⁸ᶠ *do not sit... μήποτε...* ᾖ κεκλημένος (D ἥξει), Ac 5³⁹ *we cannot kill them* μήποτε καὶ θεομάχοι εὑρεθῆτε. 2 Ti 2²⁵. Perhaps Mt 25⁹ *go and buy... μήποτε...* PSI V 495, 8 εὐλαβεῖσθε μήποτε (subj.?) (258 B.C.). P. Tebt. 43, 22 προορώμενοι μήποτε... συκοφαντηθῶμεν (118 B.C.). P. Par. 45 προσέχων μὴ εὕρῃ (153 B.C.). Μή alone (Lat. *ne*): Mk 13³⁶ Col 2⁸ μή τις ἔσται (final?). Μήπως 2 Co 9⁴. Like cl. Greek, NT Greek distinguished between fear of an uncertain thing in the future (subj.) and fear regarding a present inevitable reality (indic.). Note the difference even in the same verse: Ga 2² *I laid before them the Gospel* μήπως εἰς κενὸν τρέχω ἢ ἔδραμον. 1 Th 3⁵ *I have sent...* μήπως ἐπείρασεν ὑμᾶς ὁ πειράζων καὶ εἰς κενὸν γένηται ὁ κόπος ἡμῶν.

2. Purpose

(a) *Use of* ἵνα, ἵνα μή, *and* μή [1].

The purpose clause has increased its modes of expression in Hell. Greek. Here we are simply concerned with ἵνα. Its mood was always subjunctive in class. Greek (or oblique optative), and it is generally so in the Koine, even after a secondary tense. The alleged opt. δώῃ Eph 1¹⁷ is probably a subj. Hell. Greek also has fut. ind., and we have this in NT, especially in Rev and Paul, quite profusely but always with evidence that scribes have corrected to aor. subj. The addition of κἄν in two instances (Mk 6⁵⁶ Ac 5¹⁵) supplies a modifying or conditional element: *so that even if*.

Fut. indic.

Mt 12¹⁰ ἵνα κατηγορήσουσιν SWX (rest corr. to -σωσιν). Lk 14¹⁰ ἵνα ... ἐρεῖ (ADW corr. to εἴπῃ), 20¹⁰ ἵνα δώσουσιν (CDW δῶσιν). Jn 7³ ἵνα θεωρήσουσιν (B³ X -σῶσιν). 17² ἵνα δώσει (var. corr.: δώσῃ SᶜCG; δώσω S*; δῷς W; ἔχῃ D). Ac 5¹⁵, 21²⁴ ἵνα ξυρήσονται SB*D*E. 1 Co 9¹⁵ ἵνα τις κενώσει, 18 ἵνα θήσω, ³¹, 13³ ἵνα καυθήσομαι (CK -σωμαι; p⁴⁶ SAB καυχήσωμαι), Ga 2⁴ ἵνα καταδουλώσουσιν SAB* CDE (vl. subj.), Eph 6³, Ph 2¹¹ ἵνα κάμψῃ ... ἐξομολογήσονται (ACDG -σεται). 1 Th 5¹⁰ ἵνα ζήσομεν A (D*E corr. to ζῶμεν; S to ζήσωμεν). 1 Pt 3¹ ἵνα ... κερδηθήσονται. Rev 3⁹ ἵνα ἥξουσιν (B -ωσιν) καὶ προσκυνήσουσιν (B -σωσιν), 6⁴ ἵνα σφάξουσιν, ¹¹ ἵνα ἀναπαύσονται AP 046 1 (SC -σωνται), 8³ ἵνα δώσει (BP -σῃ), 9⁴ ἵνα ἀδικήσουσιν (SP 046 1 -σωσιν), ⁵ ἵνα βασανισθήσονται (vl -σθῶσιν), 9²⁰ 13¹² ἵνα (μὴ) προσκυνήσουσιν (vl -σῶσιν), 14¹³ ἵνα ἀναπαήσονται (P -παυσῶνται) (ὅτι p⁴⁷), 13¹⁶ ἵνα δώσει ΔΩΣ 1, 22¹⁴ ἵνα ἔσται ... καὶ εἰσέλθωσιν (causal ἵνα, like 14¹³?). On causal ἵνα see below p. 102. There are instances also where, after ἵνα, ὅπως, or μή, with subj., there follows καί with fut. ind. to indicate further result: Mt 5²⁵, 13¹⁵ OT, 20²⁸ D μήποτε ... ἐπέλθῃ ... καὶ καταισχυνθήσῃ, Mk 5²³ A, Lk 22³⁰ (many vll), 12⁵⁸, Jn 12⁴⁰ OT, 15⁸ ἵνα καρπὸν ... φέρητε καὶ γενήσεσθε (BDL corr. to γένησθε), Ac 21²⁴ (see above), Ro 3⁴ OT SADE, Eph 6³ OT, Barn 4³ S, Herm. M. VI 2¹⁰; S. IX 7⁶, 28⁵, LXX Je 29¹¹ DaSu²⁸. (Other exx. in Radermacher² p. 216).

Pres. ind.

Jn 5²⁰ ἵνα θαυμάζετε SL, 17²⁴ ἵνα θεωροῦσιν W (rest subj.), Ga 6¹² ἵνα ... μὴ διώκονται p⁴⁶ ACGKL (subj. BSD), Eph 1¹⁸ FG ἵνα

---

[1] K-G II § 553. Mayser II 1, 240ff. Schwyzer II 671ff. W. B. Curry, *The Nature and Use of the ἵνα-clause in the NT* (Diss. of S-W Bapt. Sem., 1949). E. Stauffer in Kittel WB III, 327ff (NT in general); in *Theol. Stud. u. Krit.* 102, 1930, 232–257 (purpose-ἵνα in Paul). H. Diel, *De enuntiatis finalibus apud Graecarum rerum scriptoribus posterioris aetatis*, Munich 1895.

οἴδατε, Ti 2⁴ ἵνα σωφρονίζουσιν S*AGF, Rev 16¹⁵ ἵνα βλέπουσιν p⁴⁷, Ign Eph 4³ ἵνα... ᾄδετε... μετέχετε. Very rare in Ptol. pap.: P. Par. 23, 23 εἵνα διακονεῖ (165 B.C.), Or. gr. 139, 21 ἵνα... ὑπάρχει (146–116 B.C.); even these are doubtfully indicative and may be bad spelling for subj. (Mayser II 1, 244); later BU IV 1081³ (ii–iii/A.D.) ἐχάρην ἵνα σε ἀσπάζομαι (causal ἵνα?).

Pres. subj.

Mt none.—Mk 3⁹·¹⁴·¹⁴ 4¹² 6⁴¹ 8⁶.—Lk 5¹⁴ 8¹⁶ 9⁴⁰ aor.? 11³³ 18⁵·¹⁵ 22³⁰.—Jn 3¹⁵·¹⁶ 4³⁶ 5²⁰·²³·⁴⁰ 6²⁸·³⁸ (8⁶) 9³⁹ 10¹⁰·³⁶ 13¹⁵·¹⁹ 14³·¹⁶ 15²·¹¹·¹⁶ 16⁴·²⁴·³³ 17¹¹·¹³·¹⁹·²²·²³·²³·²⁴·²⁶ 20³¹.—Ac 8¹⁹ 24⁴.—Ro 9¹¹ 11²⁵ 15⁴·⁶·²⁰.—1 Co 1²⁷·²⁷ 5⁷ 7³⁴ 14³¹ 15²⁸.—2 Co 1⁹·¹⁷ 4⁷ 5¹²·¹⁵ 9³·⁸ 12⁷ 13⁷.—Ga 1¹⁶ 4¹⁷ 6¹².—Eph 4¹⁴·²⁸ 5²⁷.—Ph 1¹⁰·²⁶·²⁷ 2¹⁹.—Col 2⁴ 3²¹.—1 Th 4¹²·¹³.—1 Ti 2² 4¹⁵ 5⁷·²⁰ 6¹.—2 Ti 3¹⁷.—Ti 1⁹·¹³ 2⁴·⁵·¹⁰ 3¹³·¹⁴.—Heb 5¹ 6¹⁸ 9²⁵ 13¹⁷.—Jas 1⁴.—1 Pt 4¹¹.—1 Jn 1³·⁴ 2¹ 4¹⁷.—Phm ¹³·¹⁴·¹⁵.—Rev 3¹⁸ 7¹ 11⁶ 12¹⁴ 16¹⁵ (Total: = 111).

LXX Ge 6¹⁹ 21³⁰ 42³ 43⁸.—Ex 11⁹ 20²⁰ 26¹³ 27²⁰ 36²⁹ 38¹⁶·²⁷.—Dt 5¹⁶·²⁹ 10¹³ 16²⁰ 29⁹ 30⁶.—Jos 1⁷ 3⁴ 4⁶·²⁴ 22²⁵·²⁷ 23⁶.—Jg 5¹⁵ A.—2 Esd 6¹⁰ 7²⁵.—To 14⁹ BᵇA.—Est 4¹⁷.—Pr 3⁶·²³ 5⁹ 6⁵·³² 26⁵ 27¹¹·²⁶·²⁶.—Wi 9² 12²² 13⁹ 14¹⁷ 16³.—Si 8⁴·¹⁵ 17⁹ 22¹³ 30²³·³⁶ 35².—Isa 40²⁰ 44¹⁵.—Je 39¹⁴.—Ezk 14¹¹.—1 Mac 12³⁶.—2 Mac 1¹⁸ 6¹⁵ 11³⁶.—3 Mac 2³⁰.—Jb 2⁸ 33³⁰ (Total:—62). Ptol. pap. (dates): 223 251 241 iii 255 iii 240 iii 258 241 iii 250 223 261 250 222 255 241 iii 241 258 iii 240 260 253 251 258 261 248; 153 99 163 154 113 57 165 118 ii 161 131 110 103 152 95 168 5 2 166 153 164 118 114 ii 168 115 76 117 (Total:—57).

Aor. Subj.

Mt 1²² 2¹⁵ 4¹⁴ 5²⁹·³⁰ 7¹ 9⁶ 12¹⁰ (fut. ind.) ¹⁷ 14¹⁵ 17²⁷ 18¹⁶ 19¹³·¹⁶ 21⁴ 23²⁶ 26⁵·⁵⁶ 27²⁶.—Mk 1³³ 2¹⁰ 3²·¹⁰ 4¹² (see below) ²¹·²² 5¹²·²³ 6³⁶·⁵⁶ (ἵνα κἄν) 7⁹ 9²² 10¹³·¹⁷ 11²⁵ 12²·¹³·¹⁵ 14⁴⁹ 15¹¹·¹⁵·²⁰·³² 16¹.—Lk 1⁴ 5²⁴ 6⁷·³⁴ 8¹² 9¹² 11⁵⁰·⁵⁴ 12³⁶ 14²³·²⁹ 15²⁹ 16⁴·⁹·²⁴·²⁸ 19⁴·¹⁵ 20¹⁰·¹⁴·²⁰ 22⁸.—Ac 2²⁵ 4¹⁷ 5¹⁵ ἵνα... κἄν 9²¹ 16³⁰ 22⁵·²⁴ 23²⁴.—Jn 1⁷·⁸·¹⁹·²²·³¹ 3¹⁷·²¹ 4⁸ 5³⁴·³⁶ 6⁵·¹⁵·³⁰·⁵⁰ 7³² 8⁵⁹ 9³⁶ 10¹⁰·¹⁷·³¹·³⁸ 11⁴·¹¹·¹⁵·¹⁶·¹⁹·³¹·⁴²·⁵²·⁵⁵ 12⁹·²⁰·³⁶·³⁸·⁴⁷·⁴⁷ 14¹³·²⁹·³¹ 15¹⁶ 17¹·¹² 18⁹·²⁸·³²·³⁷ 19⁴·¹⁶·²⁴·²⁸; negative: 3¹⁶·²⁰ 4¹⁵ 5¹⁴ 6¹²·⁵⁰ 7²² 12³⁵·⁴⁰·⁴²·⁴⁶ 16¹ 18²⁸·³⁶ 19³¹.—Ro 1¹¹·¹³ 3⁸ 5²⁰·²¹ 6¹·⁴·⁶ 7⁴·¹³ 8⁴·¹⁷ 11¹¹·¹⁹·³¹·³² 14⁹ 15¹⁶.—1 Co 1²⁸ 2¹² 3¹⁸ 4⁶·⁸ 5² (imperatival?) ⁵ 7⁵·³⁵ 9¹⁵·¹⁹·²⁰·²⁰·²²·²³·²⁴·²⁵ 10³³ 11¹⁹ 14⁵·¹⁹ 16⁶·¹¹; neg.: 1¹⁵·¹⁷ 8¹³ 9¹² 11³²·—2 Co 1¹¹·¹⁵·²⁴·⁹ 4¹⁰·¹¹·¹⁵ 5⁴·¹⁰·²¹ 7⁹ 8⁹·¹⁴ 11⁷·¹²·¹⁶·¹⁶ 12⁹ 13⁷; neg.: 2³·⁵·¹¹ 6³ 9³·⁴ 10⁹ 13¹⁰.—Ga 2⁵·⁹·¹⁶·¹⁹ 3¹⁴·²²·²⁴ 4⁵ 6¹³.—Eph 2⁷·¹⁰·¹⁵ 3¹⁰·¹⁸·¹⁹ 4¹⁰·²⁹ 5²⁶·²⁷ 6³·¹³·²²; neg.: 2⁹.—Col 1¹⁸·²⁸ 2² 4⁴·⁸.—Ph 2¹⁰·¹⁵·²⁸·³⁰ 3⁸; neg.: 2²⁷.—1 Th 2¹⁶ 5¹⁰.—2 Th 2¹² 3⁹·¹⁴.—1 Ti 1¹⁶·²⁰ 3¹⁵ 5¹⁶ 6¹⁹.—2 Ti 1⁴ 2⁴·¹⁰ 4¹⁷.—Ti 1⁵ 2⁸·¹⁴ 3⁷; neg.: 1 Ti 3⁶·⁷.—Heb 2¹⁴·¹⁷ 4¹⁶ 10⁹·³⁶ 11³⁵ 12²⁷ 13¹²·¹⁹; neg.: 3¹³ 4¹¹ 6¹² 11²⁵·⁴⁰ 12³·¹³.—Jas 5⁹·¹² 4³.—1 Pt 1⁷ 2²·¹²·²¹·²⁴ 3¹·⁹·¹⁶·¹⁸ 4⁶·¹³ 5⁶.—2 Pt 1⁴.— 1 Jn 2²⁸ 3¹·⁵·⁸ 4⁹ 5¹³.—Rev 2¹⁰ 3¹¹·¹⁸ 6² 8¹² 9¹⁵ 12⁴·⁶·¹⁵ 13¹⁵ 16¹² 19¹⁵·¹⁸ 21¹⁵; neg.: 3¹⁸ 8¹² 18⁴ 20³. (Total:—322).

LXX Ge 26, Ex 37, Le 7, Nu 4, Dt 43, Jos 4, Jg Ru 3, Km 8, Chr 3, 1 Esd 1, 2 Esd-Ne 2. To S 2, To B 5, Jdt 6, Est 1, Ps 6, Pr 35, Eccl. 5, Wi 23, Si 25, Jb 16, Isa 26, Je 9, Ba 2, La 1, Ezk 3, DaO′ 7, Θ 4, 1 Mac 3, 2 Mac 3, 3 Mac 1, 4 Mac 2. (Total:—112).

It is difficult to decide between telic and ecbatic force for ἵνα in the formula with πληρόω, ἀναπληρόω, τελειόω. It is probably telic, since ὅπως is occasionally substituted for ἵνα in the formula, and especially in view of the Jewish theology probably lying behind it. But in Lk 9⁴⁵ ἵνα μὴ αἴσθωνται αὐτό is probably consecutive rather than final. In Col 2⁴ ἵνα may be final: *I say this in order that* . . . , but equally possible is an imperatival sense: *Let no one* . . . . 2 Co 1¹⁷ is similarly controversial. The ἵνα in Jn 9² (τίς ἥμαρτεν . . . , ἵνα) is consecutive, but the weak variant ὅτι indicates that scribes took it for causal ἵνα. It is like Epict. III 1, 12 τί εἶδεν ἐν ἐμοὶ ὁ Ἐπίκτητος, ἵνα . . . περιίδῃ; So also the ἵνα in Mk 15³² καταβάτω ἵνα ἴδωμεν καὶ πιστεύσωμεν is obviously consecutive. For instances of ecbatic ἵνα elsewhere, see Jannaris §§ 1758, 1951; Radermacher² 191f.

The question of causal sense for some instances of ἵνα in NT has also been raised [1]. In Rev 22¹⁴ it is claimed that μακάριοι . . . ἵνα is parallel with μακάριοι ὅτι in Mt 5³ᶠᶠ; but the possibility of telic force cannot be ruled out. In Rev 14¹³ the question of imperatival ἵνα arises: *They shall rest!* The ἵνα of Mk 4¹² = Lk 8¹⁰ is transformed into causal ὅτι in the Mt-parallel, but this would not prove identity of meaning. In 1 Pt 4⁶ (ἵνα κριθῶσιν . . . καὶ ζῶσιν) it would be possible to assume that ἵνα is causal and that a second ἵνα (telic) has fallen out before ζῶσιν— or that we are to take ἵνα first as causal and then as telic. The causal as well as final use of ἵνα was acknowledged by the grammarian Apollonius Dyscolus (ii/A.D.) and no doubt this was so in NT. The causal makes excellent sense in Jn 8⁵⁶ (Abraham rejoiced *because* . . .). The real crux is Mk 4¹². The consecutive of NEB is not so good as final (OT background) or causal (good precedent and excellent sense). Lohmeyer in

---

[1] On causal ἵνα see Jannaris § 1714; Pernot *Études* 90–95; H. Windsich, " Die Verstockungsidee in Mk 4.12 und das kausale ἵνα der späteren Koine," in *ZNW* 26, 1927, 203ff; A. T. Robertson, " The Causal Use of ἵνα," *Studies in Early Christianity* 1927, 49ff; C. H. Dodd, in *JThS* 23, 1922, 62f; U. Holzmeister, in *Biblica* 17, 1936, 512ff; LS s.v.; Bauer s.v. (II2).

his commentary (Göttingen 1937, in loc) states truly " ἵνα bedeutet in der Koine . . . auch, wenngleich seltener, ' weil ' ".

Ἵνα instead of almost any infinitive [1], for epexegetic infinitive, in demands after verbs of willing and the like, and also in an ecbatic sense, marks the beginning of a process which ended in the disappearance of the infinitive and substitution of νά with subj. in MGr.

Subjunctive:

Mt 4³ εἰπὲ ἵνα . . . γένωνται, 16²⁰ ἐπετίμησεν B*D (διεστείλατο SCΘ) ἵνα . . . εἴπωσιν.—Mk 5¹⁰ παρεκάλει . . . ἵνα μὴ . . . ἀποστείλῃ, 3⁹ εἶπεν . . . ἵνα . . . προσκαρτερῇ. 6²⁵ θέλω ἵνα . . . δῷς, 9³⁰ ἤθελεν ἵνα τις γνοῖ, 10³⁵ θέλομεν ἵνα . . . ποιήσῃς, ⁵¹. Mk. command: 3⁹·¹² 54³ 6⁸·¹² 7³⁶ 8³⁰ 9⁹ 10⁴⁸ 12¹⁹ 13³⁴ 15²¹; grant 10³⁷ 11¹⁶·²⁸; beseech 5¹⁰·¹⁸ 6⁵⁶ 7²⁶·³² 8²² 9¹⁸ 14³⁵·³⁸ 13¹⁸.—Mt 7¹² θέλητε ἵνα ποιῶσιν, 18¹⁴ θέλημα . . . ἵνα ἀπόληται, 20²¹ εἰπὲ ἵνα καθίσωσιν, ³¹ ἐπετίμησεν . . . ἵνα σιωπήσωσιν, 27³² ἠγγάρευσαν ἵνα ἄρῃ, 28¹⁰ ἀπαγγείλατε . . . ἵνα ἀπέλθωσιν, 12¹⁶ ἐπετίμησεν . . . ἵνα μὴ . . . ποιήσωσιν, 14³⁶ παρεκάλουν . . . ἵνα aor. subj., 24²⁰ 26⁴¹ προσεύχεσθε . . . ἵνα aor. subj., 27²⁰ ἔπεισαν . . . ἵνα aor. subj.—Lk 6³¹ θέλετε ἵνα ποιῶσιν, 1⁴³ *whence is this to me* ἵνα ἔλθῃ; command: 4³ εἰπὲ . . . ἵνα, 10⁴⁰ εἰπὸν ἵνα, 18³⁹ ἐπετίμων . . . ἵνα; 20²⁸ ἔγραψεν . . . ἵνα; request: 7³⁶ ἠρώτα . . . ἵνα, 8³² παρεκάλεσαν . . . ἵνα, 8³¹ παρεκάλουν . . . ἵνα, 9⁴⁰ ἐδεήθην . . . ἵνα, 16²⁷ ἐρωτῶ . . . ἵνα, 21³⁶ δεόμενοι . . . ἵνα, 22³² ἐδεήθην . . . ἵνα, ⁴⁶ προσεύχεσθε . . . ἵνα; completing verbal idea 7⁶ ἱκανὸς . . . ἵνα, 17² *better for him* ἵνα; Ac. command: 16³⁶ ἀπέσταλκαν . . . ἵνα ἀπολυθῆτε, 17¹⁵ λαβόντες ἐντολὴν . . . ἵνα, 19⁴ λέγων . . . ἵνα, plot: 27⁴² βουλὴ ἐγένετο ἵνα. Jn, will: 6⁴⁰ θέλημα . . . ἵνα . . . ἔχῃ, 17²⁴ θέλω ἵνα . . . ὦσιν, command: 11⁵⁷ δεδώκεισαν . . . ἐντολὰς ἵνα, 13²⁹, ³⁴ ἐντολὴν καινὴν δίδωμι ἵνα, 15¹² ἡ ἐντολὴ ἡ ἐμὴ ἵνα, ¹⁷ ἐντέλλομαι . . . ἵνα, 17⁴ τὸ ἔργον . . . ὃ δέδωκάς μοι ἵνα ποιήσω, beseech: 4⁴⁷ ἠρώτα ἵνα καταβῇ, 17¹⁵·²¹ ἐρωτῶ ἵνα, 19³¹ ἠρώτησαν ἵνα, agree: 9²² συνετέθειντο . . . ἵνα, 11⁵³ 12¹⁰ ἐβουλεύσαντο ἵνα, allow: 12⁷ ἄφες . . . ἵνα, epexegetic: 6²⁹ τοῦτό ἐστιν τὸ ἔργον τ. θεοῦ ἵνα πιστεύητε, 8⁵⁶, 12²³ 13¹ 16²·³² ἡ ὥρα ἵνα, 15⁸ ἐν τούτῳ ἐδοξάσθη . . . ἵνα καρπὸν πολὺν φέρητε, ¹³ *greater love* . . . ἵνα (= *i.e.*), 17³ *this is eternal life* ἵνα, 18³⁹ *there is a custom* ἵνα; consecutive: 9² τίς ἥμαρτεν . . . ἵνα τυφλὸς γεννηθῇ; completing verbal action 1²⁷ ἄξιος ἵνα, 2²⁵ χρείαν εἶχεν ἵνα, 4³⁴ ἐμὸν βρῶμά ἐστιν ἵνα, 5⁷ ἄνθρωπον οὐκ ἔχω ἵνα, 6⁷ οὐκ ἀρκοῦσιν αὐτοῖς ἵνα ἕκαστος βραχὺ λάβῃ, 11⁵⁰ 16⁷ συμφέρει ὑμῖν ἵνα, 13² *put it in the heart* ἵνα, 16³⁰ οὐ χρείαν ἔχεις ἵνα; after ποιέω 11³⁷.—Ro command 16²; pray 15³¹·³².—1 Co 16¹⁰ βλέπετε ἵνα; seek 14¹·¹²; say 7²⁹; epex. 4³; a small thing ἵνα 9¹⁸ (fut. ind.); beseech 1¹⁰ 14¹³ 16¹²·¹⁶; it is required 4²; 14⁵ θέλω . . . λαλεῖν . . . ἵνα προφητεύητε,

---

[1] Even subject infinitive, e.g. Jn 16⁷ συμφέρει ὑμῖν ἵνα ἐγὼ ἀπέλθω, and 1 Co 9¹⁸.

16^{12} θέλημα ἵνα νῦν ἔλθῃ.—2 Co beseech 12^8 παρεκάλεσα ἵνα; exhort 8^6 9^5.—Ga consecutive 5^{17}.—Eph pray 1^{17} 3^{16} $6^{19}.$ ^{20} δεήσει ἵνα.—Ph pray 1^9 epex. 2^2 *namely* ἵνα.—Col pray 1^9 αἰτούμενοι ἵνα $4^{3.12}$; βλέπε ἵνα 4^{17}; after ποιέω 4^{16}.—Th beseech 1 Th $4^{1.\ 1}$ 2 Th 3^{12} παρακαλέομαι; pray 2 Th 1^{11} $3^{1.\ 2}$; consec. 1 Th 5^4.—1 Ti exhort $1^{3.\ 18}$ 5^{21} Ti 2^{12} 3^8.— 2 Pt 3^{17} φυλάσσομαι.—Joh epp. command 1 Jn 3^{23} 4^{21} 5^{16} 2 Jn $^{5.\ 6}$; opex. 1 Jn 1^9 (cp. Heb 6^{10}) faithful and just ἵνα; 2^{27} χρείαν ἔχω ἵνα, 3^{11} the message ἵνα, 5^3 love of God ἵνα; 2 Jn ^{6} love ἵνα; 3 Jn^4 joy ἵνα; 2 Jn^8 βλέπετε ἵνα.—Rev command 6^{11} 9^4 ἐρρέθη ἵνα (fut. ind.); 9^5 ἐδόθη αὐταῖς ... ἵνα 19^8; 14^{13} ναί λέγει τὸ πνεῦμα ἵνα (fut. ind.); completing verbal action 2^{21} χρόνος ἵνα; 8^6 prepare ἵνα; 21^{23} οὐ χρείαν ἔχει ... ἵνα; epex. (or consec?) 9^{20} repented ἵνα (fut. ind.); 13^{13} ἵνα = *i.e.*; after ποιέω (cp. Mt 24^{24} ὥστε) 3^9 13^{12} (fut. ind.) $^{15.\ 16.\ 17}$.

LXX: Ge 22^{14} consec., 24^8 ἐξόρκισε σε κύριον ... ἵνα μή λάβῃς.—Ex 6^{11} λαλέω.—Dt command 6^2 ὅσα ἐνετείλατο ἵνα φοβῆσθε κύριον; swear 4^{21}.— 3 Km 6^2 (5^{17}) command ἐνετείλατο ἵνα B^{ab}.—1 Ch 21^{18} command εἰπεῖν ... ἵνα.—2 Ch 18^{15} adjure ὁρκίζω σε ἵνα μή λαλήσῃς (A fut. ind.).— 1 Esd command 4^{47} ἔγραψεν ... ἵνα προπέμψωσιν, ^{50} ἔγραψεν ... ἵνα ... ἀφίουσι (B pres. ind., A pres. subj.), 6^{31} προστάξαι ἵνα, 8^{19} προσέταξα ... ἵνα ... διδῶσιν pr. ind.; beseech 4^{46} δέομαι ... ἵνα ποιήσῃς τὴν εὐχήν; care 6^{27} ἀτενίσαι ἵνα συνποιῶσιν.—Ne 7^{65} εἶπεν ... ἵνα μή φάγωσιν.— To S command 14^9 ἐνυποταγήσεται ... ἵνα ὦσιν...; beseech 6^{18} δεήθητε ... ἵνα ἔλεος γένηται (not B); completing verbal idea 3^{15} *he has no other child* ἵνα κληρονομήσῃ αὐτόν (not B), 5^7 χρείαν ... ἔχω ἵνα βαδίσῃς (not B), ^{9} πιστός ... ἵνα πορευθῇ μετὰ σοῦ (B τοῦ and inf.), 6^{15} *they have no other son* ἵνα θάψῃ αὐτούς (not B).—To B beseech 8^4 προσευξώμεθα ἵνα ἡμᾶς ἐλεήσῃ ὁ κύριος (S ὅπως).—Jdt 7^{28} μαρτυρόμεθα ὑμῖν ... ἵνα μή ποιήσῃ.—Mal 1^9 beseech δεήθητε ... ἵνα ἐλεήσῃ ὑμᾶς S^{ca}.—Ps allow 38^{14} ἄνες μοι ἵνα ἀνυψύξω.—Ca beseech 5^1 αἰτεῖται ... ἵνα καταβῇ S.—Wi consec. 14^4.—Si beseech 37^{15} δεήθητι ... ἵνα εὐθύνῃ, 38^{14} δεηθήσονται ἵνα εὐοδώσῃ; promise 44^{18} διαθῆκαι αἰῶνος ἐτέθεσαν ... ἵνα μή ἐξαλειφθῇ, 45^{24} ἐστάθη ... διαθήκη ... ἵνα ... ᾖ.—Isa command 36^{12}; βουλεύομαι 42^{21}.—Ba pray 1^{11} προσεύξασθαι ... ἵνα ὦσιν.—Ezk after ποιέω 36^{27} ἵνα ... πορεύησθε.—Da O' command 3^{10} προσέταξας καὶ ἔκρινας ἵνα πᾶς ... προσκυνήσῃ (Th. μή and aor. subj.), 3^{96} κρίνω ἵνα ... διαμελισθήσεται fut. ind. (no ἵνα in Th), 6^{12} οὐχ ὁρισμὸν ὥρισω ἵνα πᾶς ἄνθρωπος μή εὔξηται εὐχήν (Th ὅπως), adjure 6^{12} ὁρκίζομέν σε ... ἵνα μή ἀλλοιώσῃς ... καί ... ἐλαττώσῃς (Th om); fear 1^{10} ἵνα μή ἴδῃ (Th μήποτε); request 1^8 ἠξίωσεν ... ἵνα μή συμμολυνθῇ (Th ὡς οὐ μή), 2^{16} ἠξίωσεν ἵνα δοθῇ (Th ὅπως), 2^{49} ἠξίωσεν ... κατασταθῶσιν (co-ord. in Th).—Da Θ be ready 3^{15} (LXX infin).—Jb command 37^6 A.—1 Mac command 4^{59} ἔστησεν ... ἵνα ἄγωνται, 11^{41} ἀπέστειλεν ... ἵνα ἐκβάλῃ; write 15^{19} γράψαι... ἵνα μή συμμαχῶσιν.—2 Mac command 2^2 ἐνετείλατο ... ἵνα μή ἐπιλάθωνται; beseech 2^8 ἠξίωσεν ἵνα ... καταγιασθῇ.—4 Mac beseech 16^{12} οὐδ' ἵνα μή ἀποθάνωσιν ἐπέτρεπεν....

In the Greek Bible the books which use ἵνα in a non-final sense at least equally as often as in a final sense are: Ch, 1 Esd, To S, Dan O', 1 Mac, Mt, Mk.

As to order of clauses, the ἵνα-clause generally follows the governing main clause, except where a second clause depends on the main verb; the exceptions in pre-Christian papyri are (dates): iii 244 iii 164 152 (all pre-positive).

(b) *Use of* ὅπως (μή), ὡς, *etc.*[1]

In NT ὅπως is rather strictly confined to final sentences and to its use after *beseech* (e.g. παρακαλέω). In class. Attic it was also used with fut. ind. after *strive, take care*, but that is restricted to ἵνα in NT. In both NT and Koine[2] ἵνα and ὅπως alternate for the sake of variety: Jn 11⁵⁷, 1 Co 1²⁹ ἵνα ... καταργήσῃ, ὅπως μὴ καυχήσηται 2 Co 8¹⁴ ἵνα γένηται ... ὅπως γένηται; 2 Th 1¹². John restricts himself almost entirely to ἵνα, in spite of the return of ὅπως in Hell. Greek; in the Ptol. papyri it is almost as frequent as ἵνα (302 : 260), although most exx. of ὅπως occur in official writing (Mayser II 1, 247–52, 256, 261). The figures of R. C. Horn (p. 31) corroborate Mayser:

Period	ἵνα	ὅπως	Proportion
Ptolemaic	222	200	same
Imperial	436	88	5 : 1
Byzantine	153	41	4 : 1

For class. Greek, see the figures in Goodwin, appendix III.

Ὅπως has largely lost its ἄν in NT, in spite of many instances in the early papyri and older inscriptions, especially in official writings (Mayser II 1, 254–57; II 3, 50; Meisterhans 254; Horn 31); exceptions in the NT are Lk 2³⁵ Ac 3²⁰ 9¹²vl 15¹⁷ OT (Am 9¹² where no ἄν), Ro 3⁴ (Ps 50 (51)⁶), 9¹⁷ (Ex 9¹⁶ where our text has no ἄν).

The only place in NT where final ὡς occurs is Ac 20²⁴ (vl. ὅπως). It is rare also in the Koine. R. C. Horn gives only P. Tebt. 56, 11ff (ii/B.C.), P. Prk. 5232, 35 (A.D. 14), P. Path 1 (99 B.C.), P. Prk 5357, 9 (prob. Byz.).

Other ways of expressing purpose in the later Koine are: ὑπὲρ τοῦ c. inf. (P. Giess. ii/A.D.), πρὸς τό c. inf. (P.B.M. A.D. 187,

---

[1] K-G II 375, 2; 385, 5. Schmid Attic. IV 621. Mayser II 1, 254–8.
[2] Mayser II 1, 245; Diogen. of On. I 8 οὐχ ἵνα ... ἀλλ' ὅπως ... Cp. in 1 Clem ὅπως and εἰς τό.

P. Flor. A.D. 514, O.P. A.D. 335, P.B.M. A.D. 345). εἰς τό c. inf. (O.P. A.D. 190, O.P. A.D. 427), ὥστε c. inf. (P. Flor. iii/A.D. bis). See pp. 135f., 141-144. In Hellenistic colloquial speech there was much overlapping in the use of ἵνα (or ὅπως) and ὥστε (or ὡς); so much so that ἵνα (ὅπως) are even used with the inf. and ὥστε with subj., with their final and consecutive rôles respectively reversed (see Ljungvik BSSVS 46f).

Certain writers like Aristophanes, Plato and the orators, favoured ἵνα, but Homer, Thucydides, Xenophon, Herodotus, and Attic inscriptions of v–iv/B.C. favoured ὅπως. Polybius always chooses ἵνα and this development is reflected in NT and inscriptions and papyri of i/A.D., until the Atticistic revival of ὅπως set in about iii–iv/A.D.

	ἵνα	ὅπως
Homer	9	145
Thuc. (whole)	53	156
Xen. (i–iii)	32	52
Herodotus	17	107

	ἵνα	ὅπως
Polybius (i–v)	62	0
NT	746	58
Test. Sol.	16	10
Ep. Arist.	28	17
Pap. i/A.D.	2	0
ii/A.D. *	17	3
iii–v	21	3

* From P. Bouriant, P. Lug. Bat. 1, 2, 3, P. Oslo 1, 2, 3.

Ac is the only NT book with much stylistic pretence in this respect (as with τε). Where there is a variant, except in Ac, we should probably accept ἵνα, e.g. Mt 6¹⁸D. However, ὅπως seems to be preferred with verbs of *beseeching*: Mt 8³⁴ παρεκάλεσαν, 9³⁸ δεῖσθαι, Lk 7³ ἐρωτᾶν, Ac 8¹⁵ προσεύχεσθαι, Jas 5¹⁶ εὔχεσθαι.

3. *Relative clauses* [1]

A futuristic subjunctive (neg. μή) in relative clauses introduces an element of uncertainty and supposition. Sometimes

---

[1] K-G II § 559. Stahl 521ff. Meisterhans-Schw. 236f. Moulton Einl. 259ff. Mayser II 1, 261–267. M. L. Earle, " Subjunctive of Purpose in Relative Clauses in Attic Greek," *Trans. & Proc. American Philol. Assocn.*, 23, 17; J. E. Harry, " The Use of οἷος, ποῖος, and ὁποῖος,", ibid. 38, 18. A. W. Argyle, " The Causal Use of the Relative Pronouns in the Greek N.T.", *Bible Translator* 6, 1955, 165–169 (repetition is not a Semitism). H. J. Cadbury, " Relative Pronouns," *JBL* 42, 150–7.

the clause is the equivalent of a condition (ὅς ἄν = ἐάν τις); sometimes of a final clause. The main verb is usually future or an imperative, but the general idea may be timeless. These general relative clauses almost invariably contain the particle ἄν (even if the verb is in the indic. mood[1]), and it stands as near to the rel. pronoun as possible, though δέ, γάρ, etc., may intervene. Its presence was virtually essential in classical prose and is only very rarely omitted in NT and Egyptian Koine. Of course, the conditional particle ἐάν is gaining on ἄν from iii/B.C. In the papyri it becomes more frequent at the end of ii/B.C. and during i/B.C. (ἄν:—iii 130; ii–i 78. ἐάν:—iii 4; ii–i 16). The use of pres. or aor. subj. bears little or no relation to the *Aktionsart*. In the papyri, the difference appears to be that the pres. indicates that the time of the subordinate clause is coincident with that of the main (or durative action, if relatively past), while the aor. indicates a relatively past time. To take the half-dozen instances of pres. tense in Mt: in 7[12] the main verb is *do so to them* and the rel. clause is *what you wish them to do to you*, i.e. at the time when you are doing it to them; 11[27] the Father is known only to that man *to whom the Son has been willing* (from time to time, durative) *to reveal him* ᾧ ἐάν βούληται; 16[25] 20[26, 27] *that man will lose his life who is desirous* (at that moment) *to save it* (whereas also in 16[25] is the aor., meaning *who by that time has already lost it, he will save it*); 20[4] *I will pay you whatever* (at that time) *is the right payment* ὃ ἐάν ᾖ δίκαιον. By way of contrast, we discover from the more abundant aorists in Mt that the relative action is always antecedent to the main action: 5[19] *he will be called least, who* (by that time shall have) *relaxed*; [32] *he makes his wife an adulteress who divorces* (i.e. has already divorced) *her*.

1. *Pres. subj.*

(a) with ἄν: (α) coincident time, e.g., LXX Ge 39[8], Mk 9[37] ὃς ἄν ἐμὲ δέχηται BL 892; Jn 2[5] ὅ τι ἂν λέγῃ *whatever he will be saying to you*: do it at the time he is saying it (for a different explanation, making it equivalent to universal ἄν c. subj. in conditional clauses, see Zerwick

---

[1] It is a feature of Hell. Greek that the connection between the mood and the conjunction (e.g. subj. after ἄν) is becoming less determined, and so we have εἰ with subj., ἐάν with indic., ὅτε with subj., ὅταν with indic., etc. In MGr only the fuller conjunctions ἐάν and ὅταν remain; and they have both indic. (real) and subj. (probable).

§ 235: *whatsoever at any time he says to you.*) (β) antecedent continuous or iterative time, e.g. Mt 20²⁷ Mk 10⁴³ᵗ ὃς ἂν θέλῃ ... ἔσται ὑμῶν (δοῦλος).

(b) with ἐάν: (α) coincident, e.g. LXX Ge 6¹⁷ ὅσα ἐὰν ᾖ, 20¹⁵, 21²² (durative), 30³³, 44¹; Mt 7¹² ὅσα ἐὰν θέλητε (or continuous), 11²⁷ ᾧ ἐὰν βούληται, 20⁴ ὃ ἐὰν ᾖ δίκαιον, Mk 6²² αἴτησόν με ὃ ἐὰν θέλῃς. (β) antecedent cont. or iterat., e.g. Mt 16²⁵ 20²⁶ Mk 8³⁵ ὃς ... ἐὰν θέλῃ.

(c) without ἄν or ἐάν, e.g. Mt 10³³ ὅστις δὲ ἀρνήσηται BLW (rest ἄν).

2. Aor. subj.

(a) with ἄν: LXX Ge 2¹⁷ 3⁵ 11⁶ 12¹ 21⁶ 22² 24¹⁴· ⁴³ 26² 42³⁸ 44⁹· ¹⁰ 48⁶ AB. Mt 5¹⁹ ὃς δ' ἂν ποιήσῃ, ²¹ φονεύσῃ, ²² 15⁵ εἴπῃ, 5³¹ 19⁹ ὃς ἂν ἀπολύσῃ (OT Dt 24¹), 10¹¹ εἰς ἣν ἂν πόλιν ... εἰσέλθητε, ¹⁴ ὃς ἂν μὴ δέξηται, ³³ ὅστις δ' ἂν ἀρνήσηται vl., 12⁵⁰ ὅστις ... ἂν ποιήσῃ, 16²⁵ ὃς δ' ἂν ἀπολέσῃ, 18⁶ ὃς δ' ἂν σκανδαλίσῃ, 19⁹ ὃς ἂν ἀπολύσῃ, (21⁴⁴ ἐφ' οὗ ἂν πέσῃ), 23¹⁶· ¹⁸ ὃς ἂν ὀμόσῃ, 26⁴⁸ ὃν ἂν φιλήσω. Mk 3³⁵ ὃς ἂν ποιήσῃ, 3²⁸ ὅσα ἂν βλασφημήσωσιν SD (ὅσας ἄν AFΦ fam¹ 22 28 157 700), 3²⁹ ὃς δ' ἂν βλασφημήσῃ, 6¹¹ ὃς ἂν (τόπος) μὴ δέξηται, 9³⁷ ὃς ἂν ... δέξηται DWΔΘ (corr. to ἐάν by 565 579 700), ⁴¹ ὃς γὰρ ἂν ποτίσῃ (S ἐάν; ΗΓΔ Ψ 28 ποτίσει), ⁴² ὃς ἂν σκανδαλίσῃ (ACX ἐάν), 10¹¹ ὃς ἂν ἀπολύσῃ (ANX 700 ἐάν), ¹⁵ ὃς ἂν μὴ δέξηται (ANX 700 ἐάν), 11²³ ὃς ἂν εἴπῃ. 14⁴⁴ ὃν ἂν φιλήσω (LNΔΨ ἐάν).

(b) with ἐάν: LXX Ge 15¹⁴ 20¹³ 21¹² 28¹⁵· ²² 31³² 34¹¹ 41⁵⁵ 42³⁸ 48⁶ (Rahlfs). Mt 5¹⁹ ὃς ἐὰν ... λύσῃ, ³² ὃς ἐὰν ... γαμήσῃ, 10⁴² ὃς ἐὰν (vl) ποτίσῃ, 11⁶ ὃς ἐὰν (vl) μὴ σκανδαλισθῇ, 12³² ἐὰν (vl) εἴπῃ. 14⁷ ὃ ἐὰν αἰτήσηται (an apparent exception: she had not asked anything yet, but would have done so before he was able to make the gift), 15⁵ ὠφεληθῇς, WHT (rest aor. ind.), 16¹⁹ δήσῃς, 18⁵ δέξηται, ¹⁹ οὗ ἐὰν αἰτήσωνται ¹⁸ ὅσα ἐὰν δήσητε, 21²² ἐὰν (vl) αἰτήσητε, 22⁹ ὅσους ἐὰν εὕρητε, 23³ πάντα ... ὅσα ἐὰν εἴπωσιν.—Mk 3²⁸ ὅσα ἐὰν βλασφημήσωσιν ΒΔΘ, ὅσας ἐὰν βλ. CFΣ 33 565 892 1071, 6²³ ὅτι ἐάν με αἰτήσῃς ΒΔ p⁴⁵ 118 124 435, ὅτι ὃ ἐὰν μ.α. SAC Θ fam¹³ 33, 7¹¹ ὃ ἐὰν ἐξ ἐμοῦ ὠφεληθῇς (DW 28 ἄν), 8³⁸ ὃς γὰρ ἐὰν ἐπαισχυνθῇ SBC Θ p⁴⁵ (ἄν GHKSUWΠΦ fam¹· ¹³ 22 543 28 33 700 Cl. Alx D), 9³⁷ ὃς ἐὰν ἐμὲ δέξηται ACNXΓΣΦ, 10³⁵ ὃ ἐὰν αἰτήσωμεν (ἄν DW 6369 C*; αἰτήσομεν SᶜA), 13¹¹ ὃ ἐὰν δοθῇ (ἄν ADW 229 1342).

(c) neither ἄν nor ἐάν: Mt 10³³ BLW ὅστις δὲ ἀρνήσηται.

3. Pres. and Aor. side by side

Mt 16²⁵ ὃς ... ἐὰν θέλῃ — ὃς δ' ἂν ἀπολέσῃ.

Thus in Mt the situation is different from that in pre-Christian papyri, and precisely the same as in LXX Ge (Rahlfs' text).

PAPYRI / MATTHEW

PAPYRI						MATTHEW					
Present			Aorist			Present			Aorist		
ἄν	ἐάν	neither	ἄν	ἐάν	neither	ἄν	ἐάν	neither	ἄν	ἐάν	neither
118	12	3	85	8	2	1	5	–	18	14	1

LXX GE / MARK

LXX GE						MARK					
Present			Aorist			Present			Aorist		
ἄν	ἐάν	neither	ἄν	ἐάν	neither	ἄν	ἐάν	neither	ἄν	ἐάν	neither
1	5	–	13	10	–	2	2	–	12	7	–

Also in contradistinction to the papyri [1], the NT sometimes employs the subj. in relative clauses, in a final sense, where class. Greek used the fut. ind. : Mk 14¹⁴ Lk 22¹¹ ποῦ ἐστιν τὸ κατάλυμα ὅπου φάγω (D corr. to fut.), Lk 11⁶ ὃ παραθήσω αὐτῷ *something to set before him*, 9⁵⁸ οὐκ ἔχει ποῦ τὴν κεφαλὴν κλίνῃ *nowhere to lay*, Ac 21¹⁶ ἄγοντες παρ' ᾧ ξενισθῶμεν Μνάσωνι. LXX Je 11⁶ ἐπικατάρατος ὁ ἄνθρωπος, ὅς ... ἔχει ... καὶ στηρίσει ... καὶ ... ἀποστῇ.

In the papyri too, qualitative-consecutive relative sentences employ the indicative, not the subjunctive. Like Latin, NT sometimes uses subj. : Heb 8³ ἔχειν τι ... ὃ προσενέγκῃ *something to offer* (but also Isocr. IV 44 ἔχειν ἐφ' οἷς φιλοτιμηθῶσιν), 1 Clem 38² ἔδωκεν δι' οὗ ἀναπληρωθῇ.

The difference between indic. and subj. in these general relative clauses is ideally and approximately that between εἰ c. indic. and ἐάν c. subj. in true conditional clauses. The former indicates an assumption which is actual and realized, while the latter points to future probabilities which may not actually be realized. But in the papyri which concern official decrees and statutes, as Mayser remarks, the distinction is often effaced and in fact the two moods can be used quite promiscuously (II 1, 266). This applies equally to the NT :

---

[1] Mayser II 1, 214, 267. But not necessarily to Hellenistic Greek generally. See examples in Radermacher² 170.

Mt 13¹² ὅστις γὰρ ἔχει (ind.), Mk 4²⁵ ὃς γὰρ ἔχει ΑΕ²G ὃς ἂν ἔχῃ (subj.) DE*F ὃς ἂν ἔχει (ind.), 4²⁵ ὃς οὐκ ἔχει (ind.), E*G ὃς οὐκ ἔχῃ (subj.), Lk 8¹⁸ ὃς γὰρ ἂν ἔχῃ (subj.), δοθήσεται αὐτῷ, καὶ ὃς ἂν μὴ ἔχῃ (subj.), καὶ ὃ δοκεῖ (ind.) ἔχειν, ἀρθήσεται ἀπ' αὐτοῦ.—Mt 10³² ὅστις ὁμολογήσει (ind.), ³³ ὅστις δ' [ἂν] ἀρνήσηται (subj.).—Lk 12⁸ πᾶς ὃς ἂν ὁμολογήσῃ (subj.) p⁴⁵ SΘ (B*D Mcion. harm. with Mt 10³²). Thus the moods fluctuate for no good reason, and only the context can really decide whether the rel. clause is definite or indefinite.

Very occasionally the indic. occurs with ἄν in NT and LXX (see pp. 91, 92f): Future Mk 3²⁸ ὅσας ἐὰν βλασφημήσουσιν L, 8³⁵ SBCD² ἀπολέσει (ALW -σῃ), Lk 12⁸ ὁμολογήσει AB*DR, 17³³ SAL (BDEW -σῃ), Ac 7⁷ δουλεύσουσιν ACD. LXX Le 27¹² καθότι ἂν τιμηθήσεται. Barn 11⁸ SC ὃ ἐὰν ἐξελεύσεται. Present Mt 11²⁷ LW ᾧ ἐὰν βούλεται, Rev 14⁴ ὅπου ἂν ὑπάγει.

There are a few exx. of subj. without ἄν (ἐάν) in the papyri— five, all told, in Mayser—but all the NT exx. are textually suspect: Mt 10³³ BWL, Ga 6¹⁶ p⁴⁶ ὅσοι στοιχήσωσιν, Jas 2¹⁰ SBC ὅστις . . . τηρήσῃ, 2¹⁰ SABC πταίσῃ, Herm. S. II 3 bis.

4. *Temporal Clauses* [1]

A special kind of relative clause, they follow the same construction with regard to relative time in the use of subj. with ἄν. As with the relative conjunction, ἄν stands as near as possible to the temporal conjunction. It is only with ἕως, and then largely in the aor., that ἄν can be omitted. In post-Christian papyri these particles have a final sense (Ljungvik BSSVS 43–46).

(a) *Clauses with* ἄχρι, ἕως *and* μέχρι.

Pres. subj. = *as long as*, of indefinite continuance in either past or future.

With ἄν: none in NT. Ptol. pap. (dates): 237 285.

Without ἄν: none in NT. Ptol. pap.: 140.

Pres. indic.: Mt 5²⁵ ἕως ὅτου εἶ *while.* Jn 9⁴ ἕως ἡμέρα ἐστίν. Ptol. pap. (dates): 223 iii 164.

We may note ἕως with pres. indic. in a futuristic sense: Mk 6⁴⁵ SBL ἕως αὐτὸς ἀπολύει (vl. ἀπολύσῃ, -σει, D αὐτὸς δὲ

---

[1] K-G II § 567. Stahl 444ff. Mayser II 1, 268ff. Meisterhans-Schwyzer 242, 9; 247, 1; 251b. Schwyzer II 648ff. A. Tschuschke, *De πρίν particulae apud scriptores aetatis Augusteae prosaicos usu* (Diss. of Breslau), 1913.

ἀπολύει), Jn 21²². ²³ ἕως ἔρχομαι *until I come*, also 1 Ti 4¹³. This can hardly mean *as long as*, any more than in Herm. S. IX 11, 1 ἕως ἔρχεται, V 2, 2; IX 10, 5. 6. The papyri have ἕως with pres. subj. on two occasions with possible meaning *until*, but never pres. ind., or even fut. ind. like Lk 13³⁵ vl.

Aor. subj. (ἕως and μέχρι) = *until*, of a punctiliarly conceived future event preceded in time by the action of the main clause:

with ἄν: Mt 2¹³ ἕως ἄν εἴπω, 5¹⁸ 24³⁴ ἕως ἄν πάντα γένηται, 5²⁶ ἕως ἄν ἀποδῷς, 10¹¹ ἕως ἄν ἐξέλθητε, 12²⁰ ἕως ἄν ἐκβάλῃ (Isa 42³)k 16²⁸ ἕως ἄν ἴδωσιν, 22⁴⁴ ἕως ἄν θῶ (Ps 110¹), 23³⁹ ἕως ἄν εἴπητε.—Mk 6¹⁰ ἕως ἄν ἐξέλθητε, 9¹ ἕως ἄν ἴδωσιν, 12³⁶ ἕως ἄν θῶ.—Lk 9²⁷ ἕως ἄν ἴδωσιν, 20⁴³ ἕως ἄν θῶ (Ps 110¹), 21³² ἕως ἄν πάντα γένηται.—Ac 2³⁵ (Ps 110¹).— 1 Co 4⁵ ἕως ἄν ἔλθῃ.—Ga 3¹⁹ ἄχρις ἄν ἔλθῃ (vl. ἄχρις οὗ).—Heb 1¹³ (Ps 110¹).—Μέχρις ἄν none.

without ἄν: Mt 10²³ ἕως ἔλθῃ, 14²² ἕως ἄν ἀπολύσῃ (-σει ΚΓ), 17⁹ ἕως οὗ ἐγερθῇ, 18³⁰ ἕως ἀποδῷ, ³⁴ ἕως οὗ ἀποδῷ, 26³⁶ ἕως οὗ... προσεύξωμαι *while, as long as* (fut. subj.?).—Mk 13³⁰ μέχρις οὗ... γένηται (Β μέχρις ὅτου; S μέχρι; W ἕως; D ἕως οὗ), 14³² (-ξομαι D).—Lk 12⁵⁰ ἕως ὅτου τελεσθῇ, ⁵⁹ ἕως ἀποδῷς 13⁸ ἕως ὅτου σκάψω, ³⁵ ἕως εἴπητε (vl.), 15⁴ ἕως εὕρῃ, ⁸ ἕως οὗ εὕρῃ, 17⁸ ἕως (+ ἄν ΑΚ) φάγω καὶ πίω *while, as long as*, 21²⁴ ἄχρι (οὗ) πληρωθῶσιν, 22¹⁶ ἕως ὅτου πληρωθῇ, ¹⁸ ἕως οὗ... ἔλθῃ, ³⁴ ἕως... ἀπαρνήσῃ, 24⁴⁹ ἕως οὗ ἐνδύσησθε.—Jn 13³⁸ ἕως οὗ ἀρνήσῃ. —Ac 23¹² ἕως οὗ ἀποκτείνωσιν, ¹⁴ -ωμεν (final, as in later papyri), ²¹ ἕως οὗ ἀνέλωσιν, 25²¹ ἕως οὗ ἀναπέμψω.—Ro 11²⁵ ἄχρι οὗ... εἰσέλθῃ.— 1 Co 11²⁶ ἄχρι οὗ ἔλθῃ, 15²⁵ ἄχρι οὗ θῇ (Ps 110¹).—2 Th 2⁷ ἕως (+ ἄν FG) ... γένηται.—Heb 10¹³ ἕως τεθῶσιν.—Jas 5⁷ ἕως λάβῃ.—2 Pt 1¹⁹ ἕως οὗ ... διαυγάσῃ.—Rev 6¹¹ ἕως πληρωθῶσιν, 7³ ἄχρι σφραγίσωμεν, 15⁸ ἄχρι τελεσθῶσιν, 17¹⁷ Β ἄχρι τελεσθῶσιν (vl τελεσθήσονται), 20³, ⁵ ἄχρι τελεσθῇ.—Ga 4¹⁹ μέχρις οὗ μορφωθῇ.—Eph 4¹³ μέχρι καταντήσωμεν.

	Present subjunctive			Aorist subjunctive					
	ἕως	ἕως ἄν	μέχρι ἄν	ἕως	ἕως ἄν	μέχρι	μέχρι ἄν	ἄχρι	ἄχρις ἄν
Ptol. pap.	1	4	1	7	44	–	3	–	–
NT	–	–	–	28	18	3	–	9	1

In the earlier papyri ἕως ἄν predominates, but in the Imperial period ἕως is preferred.

(b) *Clauses with* ἐπάν, ὅταν, ὡς ἄν.

With pres. subj.

(1) Usually of an iterative action, indefinite, in the past or future. By far the most frequent, in secular and Biblical Greek, is ὅταν. The main clause has most often the present or future, but also the aorist. *Whenever.* See pp. 92f.

"Οταν:—Mt 6² ὅταν οὖν ποίῃς ἐλεημοσύνην, ⁵ ὅταν προσεύχησθε, ⁶·¹⁶, 10²³ 15².—Mk 11²⁵ ὅταν στήκητε BWG (ACD -κετε; S στῆτε) 13⁴·¹¹ 14⁷·²⁵.—Lk 11² (AWCH προσεύχεσθε), ²¹·³⁴ 12¹¹ 14¹²·¹³ 21⁷.— Jn 7²⁷ (SHXΔ* ἔρχεται) 8⁴⁴ 9⁵ 16²¹.—Ro 2¹⁴.—1 Co 3⁴ 14²⁶.—2 Co 12¹⁰ 13⁹.—1 Th 5³.—1 Jn 5².—Rev 4⁹ SQ δώσωσιν (vl. δώσουσιν 10⁷.) Ἡνίκα:—2 Co 3¹⁵ ἕως σήμερον ἡνίκα ἂν ἀναγινώσκηται Μωϋσῆς.

(2) Of a definite action occurring in the future: *when*.

"Οταν:—Mt 26²⁹.—1 Co 15²⁴.—Rev 18⁹.—Pap (A.D. 270).

Ὡς ἄν:—Ro 15²⁴ πορεύωμαι εἰς τὴν Σπανίαν. Only in Ptol. pap., not in later Koine (Horn 133). Its use in Paul (so also 1 Co 11³⁴, Ph 2²³) might be due to his familiarity with LXX; more probably he is using the spoken language of his day (Horn 136): P. Fay. I 111 16 (A.D. 95) ὡς ἐὰν βλέπῃς.

Ἐπάν *after*:—Lk 11³⁴ ἐπὰν δὲ πονηρὸς ᾖ (D ὅταν).

"Οτε c. subj. is late (Jannaris § 1988), but see Lk 13³⁵ AD ὅτε εἴπητε.

With aor. subj.

(1) Most commonly of a definite action taking place in the future but concluded before the action of the main verb. Thus the main verb is usually fut. ind., but it may be imper. The particles are ὡς ἄν, ὅταν, and ἐπάν.

Ἐπάν:—Mt 2⁸ ἐπὰν δὲ εὕρητε ἀπαγγείλατέ μοι (D ὅταν).—Lk 11²² νικήσῃ (D ἐάν), ³⁴ ᾖ (D ὅταν). BU 523, 17 ἐπὰν ἀναβῇς *after you have been.*

"Οταν:—Mt 5¹¹, 9¹⁵ ἐλεύσονται ἡμέραι ὅταν ἀπαρθῇ, 10¹⁹ 12⁴³ 13³² 19²⁸ 21⁴⁰ 23¹⁵ 24¹⁵·³²·³³ 25³¹.—Mk 2²⁰ 4¹⁵·¹⁶·²⁹·³¹·³² 8³⁸ 9⁹ 12²³·²⁵ 13⁷ ὅταν ἀκούσητε (vl. ἀκούετε), ¹⁴·²⁸·²⁹.—Lk 5³⁵ ὅταν ἀπαρθῇ, 6²⁶ 8¹³ 9²⁶ 13²⁸ S ἴδητε (B*DX ὄψεσθε; ABcorr W -ησθε), 16⁴·⁹ 17¹⁰ 21⁹·²⁰ 23⁴².—Jn 4²⁵ 5⁷ 7³¹ 8²⁸ 10⁴ 14³⁹ 15²⁶ 16⁴·¹²·²¹ 21¹⁸.—Ac 23³⁵ 24²².— Ro 11²⁷.—1 Co 13¹⁰ 15²⁴·²⁴·²⁷·²⁸·⁵⁴ 16²·³·⁵·¹².—2 Co 10⁶.—Col 3⁴ 4¹⁶.—2 Th 1¹⁰.—1 Ti 5¹¹.—Ti 3¹².—Heb 1⁶.—Jas 1².—Rev 11⁷ 12⁴ 17¹⁰ 20⁷.

Ὡς ἄν:—1 Co 11³⁴ τὰ δὲ λοιπὰ ὡς ἂν ἔλθω διατάξομαι.—Ph 2²³ ὡς ἂν ἀφίδω:—LXX Ge 12¹² ὡς ἂν ἴδωσίν σε ... ἐροῦσι.—P. Hib. I 59, 2 (247 B.C.), UPZ I 7I, 18 (152 B.C.); Horn 133, Mayser II 1, 271f, 274f.

(2). Much rarer are the instances where the action is indefinite or iterative:

'Επάν:—(= בכל־עת אשר) LXX Est 5¹³ S¹ ἐπὰν ἴδω Μαρδ. *all the while that*, Da O' Bel¹² ἐπὰν κλεισθῇ *after it has been.*
"Οταν:—Lk 6²² 11²⁴ 12⁵⁴ 14⁸·¹⁰ 21³⁰·³¹.—Jn 2¹⁰.—Rev 9⁵.
'Ηνίκα:—LXX Ex 1¹⁰ καὶ ἡνίκα ἂν συμβῇ ἡμῖν πόλεμος *each time.*—Dt 7¹².—2 Co 3¹⁶ (Ex 34³⁴) ἡνίκα δὲ ἐὰν ἐπιστρέψῃ.
For ὅτε, ὅταν, and ἐπάν with indic., see pp. 92f.

	Pres. subj.		Aor. subj.				
	ὅταν	ὡς ἄν	ὅταν	ὡς ἄν	ἐπάν	ἐπειδάν	ὁπηνίκ' ἄν
Ptol. pap.	20	10	19	49	3	2	3
NT	33	1	82	2	1	–	–

(c) *Clauses with* πρίν.

Neither πρίν nor πρὶν ἄν occur with subj. in the Ptol. pap., but πρίν c. subj. occurs in papyri from ii–v/A.D. (Horn 128). Πρίν was possible without ἄν in class. Greek and it so occurs in LXX and NT. Lk 2²⁶ πρὶν ἢ ἂν ἴδῃ (S* ἕως ἂν ἴδῃ; B om ἤ; ADW om ἄν), 22³⁴ πρὶν ἢ ἀπαρνήσῃ AWΓ (SBL ἕως; K ἕως οὗ; D ἕως ὅτου). With optative Ac 25¹⁶ (see next ch.). LXX Si 11⁷ πρὶν (+ἤ SA) ἐξετάσῃς; Sym. Ps 57 (58)¹⁰ πρὶν ἤ (LXX πρὸ τοῦ c. inf.); Sym. Je 40 (47)⁵ πρὶν ἢ ἀπαλλάγω ἐγώ.—Herm. S. V 7, 3 πρὶν ἀκουσθῶσι τὰ ῥήματα.

5. *Conditional Sentences* [1]

The subjunctive occurs in the hypothetical protasis which is introduced by ἐάν. This is often written εἰάν and sometimes ἤν in the papyri, never in NT. Moreover, we find ἄν for ἐάν, as there was interchange at this time between the two particles; and this occurs six times in Jn especially in connection with τις (cp. ἄν τις ὑμῶν κακῶς ἐρεῖ in a very badly written papyrus from the Fayum, SB 5627, 11).

---

[1] K-G I § 399, 2; II § 575. Meisterhans-Schwyzer § 89. Stahl 390. Schwyzer II 682–688. Mayser II 1, 275–288. Moulton Einl. 292ff. E. B. Clapp, " Conditional Sentences in the Greek Tragedies," (*Trans. and Proc. Amer. Philol. Assn.* 22, 81). J. Sterenberg, *The Use of Conditional Sentences in the Alexandrian Version of the Pentateuch.* (Diss. of Munich, 1908.)

Parallel with relative and temporal clauses, the aor. subj. denotes a single event taking place in the future, and the pres. subj. a general or iterative occurrence which may or may not be expected to take place at any time. The pres. denotes also coincident action with the main verb, whereas the aor. is like the Latin future, and is fut. perf. in its relation with the main clause.

(a) Ἐάν *with pres. and aor. subjunctive.*

(1) *Present:* very common in Koine. In a general and iterative sense, as " condicio universalis " (Zerwick § 227c), the pres. subj. denotes a hypothesis which can occur over and over again (present *Aktionsart*). The most common example of this condition in the Ptol. pap. is stereotyped phrases in decrees and punishments, having a continual validity. In the main clause is a pres. ind. (or even optative), mainly an imperative or jussive of some kind.

Mt 5²³ ἐὰν οὖν προσφέρῃς *as often as you*, 6²². ²³, 8² ἐὰν θέλῃς, δύνασαι (how tentative, cp. with Peter's εἰ θέλεις 17⁴!), 10¹³. ¹³ 15¹⁴ 17²⁰ 21²¹.—Mk 1⁴⁰ 9⁴⁵. ⁴⁷ 14³¹ ἐὰν δέῃ ... οὐ μή σε ἀπαρνήσομαι (S ·σωμαι).—Lk 5¹² 6³³ 10⁶ 13³ ἐὰν μὴ μετανοῆτε is not distinguishable from ⁵ ἐὰν μὴ μετανοήσητε (as scribes realized, correcting to μετανοῆτε), 19³¹.—Jn 3². ²⁷ 5³¹ 6⁶². ⁶⁵ 7¹⁷ 8¹⁶. ³¹ 9³¹ 11⁹.¹⁰ 12²⁶. ²⁶ 13¹⁷. ³⁵ 14¹⁵. ²³ 15⁴. ⁴. ⁷. ¹⁴ 21²² ἐὰν αὐτὸν θέλω μένειν ... τί πρὸς σέ; (difficult because so definite; class. would be εἰ), ²³.—Ac 5³⁸ (see Zerwick §§ 219–220: Gamaliel seems strangely biased. He says doubtfully *If it should be of men* (ἐὰν ᾖ) but confidently *If (as it seems) it is of God* (εἰ ... ἐστιν), the one hypothetical, the other "real". Luke has composed the speech and is giving his own conviction, not Gamaliel's), 13⁴¹ 26⁵.—Ro 2²⁵. ²⁵. ²⁶ 9²⁷ 11²². ²³ 12²⁰. ²⁰ 13⁴ 14⁸. ⁸. ⁸.—1 Co 4¹⁵ 5¹¹ 6⁴ 7³⁶ 9¹⁶. ¹⁶ vl. 11¹⁴. ¹⁵ 13¹. ² 14¹⁴. ²⁴. ²⁸ 16⁴.—Col. 3¹³.—1 Th 2⁸.—1 Ti 1⁸ 3¹⁵.— 2 Ti 2⁵.— Jas 2¹⁴. ¹⁵. ¹⁷ 4¹⁵ (vl. aor. subj.).—1 Pt 3¹³.— 1 Jn 1⁷. ⁹ 2³ γινώσκομεν ... ἐὰν ... τηρῶμεν (S* φυλάξωμεν), ¹⁵ 3²⁰. ²¹ 4¹².—Heb 6³ ἐάνπερ.

(2) *Aorist:* This represents a definite event as occurring only once in the future, and conceived as taking place before the time of the action of the main verb. It is expectation, but not fulfilment as yet. It is very near the meaning of ὅταν, and is often more than mere probability (see LXX Isa 24¹³ *when*; Am 7²). In the apodosis occurs fut. and pres. indic., or imper. or jussive.

Mt 4⁹ 5¹³. ²⁰. ⁴⁶. ⁴⁷ 6¹⁴. ¹⁵ 9²¹ 12¹¹. ²⁹ 16²⁸ 18³. ¹². ¹³. ¹⁵. ¹⁶. ¹⁷. ¹⁹ ἐὰν συμφωνήσωσιν (SD fut. ind.) ... γενήσεται FGKMW, ³⁵, 21³. ²¹. ²⁵. ²⁶

§ 2] THE VERB: MOODS 115

22^{24} $24^{23. \ 26. \ 48}$ 26^{42} 28^{14}.—Mk $3^{24. \ 25. \ 27}$ 5^{28} $7^{3. \ 4. \ 11}$ 8^2 $9^{43. \ 50}$ $10^{12. \ 30}$ $11^{3. \ 31}$ 12^{19} OT 13^{21}.—Lk 4^7 6^{34} $12^{38. \ 45}$ 14^{34} 15^8 $16^{30. \ 31}$ 17^3. $^{3. \ 4}$ 19^{40} ἐὰν οὗτοι σιωπήσωσιν (SBALWR fut. ind.; D σιγήσουσιν) κράξουσιν ΓΔΘ 20^5. $^{6. \ 28}$ $22^{67. \ 68}$.—Jn 3^3. $^{5. \ 12}$ 5^{43} 6^{51} 7^{37} $8^{36. \ 51. \ 52. \ 54. \ 55}$ 9^{22} 10^9 $11^{40. \ 48}$ $12^{24. \ 24. \ 32. \ 47}$ 13^8 $14^{3. \ 14}$ (vl. pres. subj.), 15^{10} $16^{7. \ 7}$ 19^{12} 4^{48} $6^{44. \ 53}$ 7^{51} 8^{24} 20^{25}.—Ac 15^1 27^{31}.—Ro $7^{2. \ 3. \ 3}$ $10^{9. \ 15}$ 14^{23} 15^{24}.—1 Co 4^{19} $7^{8. \ 11. \ 28. \ 39. \ 40}$ $8^{8. \ 10}$ 9^{16} (vl. pres. subj.) 10^{28} $12^{15. \ 16}$ $13^{3. \ 3}$ (vl. fut. ind.), 14^6. $^{6. \ 7. \ 9. \ 11. \ 16. \ 23. \ 30}$ 15^{36} $16^{7. \ 10}$ (see Allo in loc., but this type of condition does not express mere probability: Zerwick § 226).—2 Co 5^1 10^8 ἐάν... καυχήσωμαι (SLP fut. ind.)... οὐκ αἰσχυνθήσομαι p^{46} BGH 33, 12^6, 13^2.—Ga 1^8 5^2.—Col 4^{10}.—2 Th 2^3.—1 Ti 2^{15}.—2 Ti $2^{5. \ 21}$.—Heb 3^6. ^{7} OT 4^7 10^{38} OT.—Jas 2^2 5^{19}.—1 Jn $1^{6. \ 8. \ 10}$ 2^1 ἐάν τις ἁμάρτῃ ... ἔχομεν $2^{24. \ 28. \ 29}$. 3^2 4^{20} 5^{16}.—Rev 2^5 $3^{3. \ 20}$ $22^{18. \ 19}$.—Heb 3^{14} ἐάνπερ.

(b) Εἰ *with fut. indic.*

This sometimes conveys the same idea but occurs very seldom in Ptol. pap. The feeling of definiteness and actual realization accompanies it. It is almost causal. Mt 26^{33} Mk 14^{29} εἰ (καὶ) πάντες σκανδαλισθήσονται (i.e. granting the assumption: *let us suppose that all will actually be offended*).— Lk 11^8 εἰ καὶ οὐ δώσει *although*.—1 Co 9^{11} μέγα εἰ ἡμεῖς... θερίσομεν (i.e. we are in fact doing it).—1 Pt $2^{20. \ 20}$ εἰ ὑπομενεῖτε. The difficulty about this view is 2 Ti 2^{12} εἰ ἀπαρνησόμεθα, where the condition was surely conceived as no more than hypothetical.

With pres. indic.

Si igitur. Mt 5^{29} εἰ ὁ ὀφθαλμός σου σκανδαλίζει σε (altered from ἐάν c. subj. in Mk 9^{43-47}), 6^{30} εἰ... ὁ θεὸς οὕτως ἀμφιέννυσιν *since he clothes*, 17^4 (a foregone conclusion for Peter). Lk 22^{42} εἰ βούλει.—Mt 19^{10}.—Lk 6^{32}, Jn 7^4 εἰ ταῦτα ποιεῖς, Jn 11^{12}D εἰ κοιμᾶται.—Ac 5^{38f}.—Ro 2^{17ff} $7^{16. \ 20}$ 8^{11} 11^{17}.—1 Co 7^{36} εἰ δέ τις... νομίζει (Paul knows this is actually happening). —Ga 1^9 2^{18}.—Heb 7^{15}.

(c) Ἐάν *with pres. ind.*

This calls for some comment; it is an abnormal use in the Ptol. pap., confined to ἐὰν δεῖ and ἐὰν φαίνεται, for other exx. are of doubtful reading or capable of different explanation (Mayser II 1, 284f). But Horn quotes BGU 597 (A.D. 75). From ii/A.D. the construction makes more frequent appearance, as εἰ and ἐάν are beginning to be confused (we have exx. in ii/A.D., iii/A.D., and late Imp. period), and increases in Byzantine Greek. It seems to bear a causal sense: 1 Co 4^{15} ἐὰν... ἔχετε (perhaps a half-way-house of actuality between ἐὰν ἔχητε *you may have* and εἰ ἔχετε *since you have*), 13² ἐὰν ἔχω ... καὶ εἰδῶ?, Jn 5³¹ ἐὰν ... μαρτυρῶ?, 1 Jn 5¹⁵ ἐὰν οἴδαμεν (S corr. to ἴδωμεν).—1 Th 3⁸ ἐὰν ... στήκετε (S*DE corr. to -ητε).— Mk 11¹³ D (ειδειν εαν τι εστιν). *Fut. indic.* too: Ac 8³¹ πῶς γὰρ ἂν δυναίμην ἐὰν μή τις ὁδηγήσει με SB*GE, Rev 2²² SA.—Herm. M. V 1, 2; IV 3, 7.

Apparent use of ἐάν with impf. (ἦν, ἦσθα, ἦσαν) in papyri and LXX (also p⁴⁶ 1 Co 7³⁶ 14²⁸) is probably an illusion, since these forms are intended as subjunctive (see Debrunner *Glotta* 11, 1920, 25f).

	ἐάν		εἰ	ἐάν
	Pres. subj.	Aor. subj.	Fut. ind.	Indic.
Ptol. pap.	246	218	9	5 ?
NT	88	159	8	6 ?

(d) *Εἰ with subjunctive.*

It appears to encroach on the province of ἐάν. This is unusual in Ptolemaic times (there are two exx. from iii/B.C.) but it becomes increasingly common in papyri from ii/A.D. onwards (see confusion mentioned in previous section): BGU (c. A.D. 100), P. Giess. (ii/A.D.), P. Ryl. (ii/A.D.), P. Lips. (A.D. 240), P. Grenf. (late iii/A.D.), P. Rein. (iv/A.D.), PSI (iv–v/A.D.), OP (v/A.D.), PR (v–vi/A.D.), OP (v–vi/A.D.), OP (A.D. 583), P. Cair. (Byz.), etc.[1]

There is therefore nothing surprising in Rev 11⁵ καὶ εἴ τις θελήσῃ SA (p⁴⁷ θελήσει; C θέλει; καὶ η in S* = κἄν?), Lk 11¹⁸ εἰ μερισθῇ p⁴⁵Γ (rest (δι)εμερίσθη). On 1 Co 14⁵ see p. 321 (ἐκτὸς εἰ μή is a fixed formula).

6. *Indirect Questions*

Greek, unlike Latin, keeps the mood and tense of *direct* speech, e.g. Mk 6⁵⁵ ὅπου ἤκουον ὅτι ἐστίν. Therefore these

---

[1] R. C. Horn op. cit. p. 31; Reinhold op. cit. 107; Jannaris §§ 1988f; Radermacher² 199.

subjunctives in indirect speech will also have been subjunctive in direct speech. Thus Mt 6[25] is an indir. deliberative question: μὴ μεριμνᾶτε τί φάγητε; also Mk 9[6] οὐ γὰρ ᾔδει τί ἀποκριθῇ (according to Latin standards this would be *he did not know what he was saying*, as in the Lk-parallel 9[33] ὃ λέγει); Heb 8[3] after ἔχω is ὃ προσενέγκῃ; Mk 8[1f] Lk 12[17]; Mayser II 1, 214, 235. Mt 10[19] δοθήσεται ὑμῖν τί λαλήσητε; Mk 6[36]. We may have fut. ind. in an indir. delib. question: Ph 1[22] (p[46] B subj.), or else punctuate τί αἱρήσομαι;. In relative past time (for class. optative) NT keeps subj. as a rule: Ac 4[21] μηδὲν εὑρίσκοντες τὸ πῶς κολάσωνται αὐτούς; but see under Optative (next ch.). This is so in Hell. Greek generally (e.g. Epict. Ench. 7; Marc. Ant. 9, 3, 7).

CHAPTER NINE

THE VERB: MOODS: OPTATIVE

THE MOOD was declining [1] during the last three centuries B.C. It is still used fairly widely to indicate a wish in the papyri, LXX and NT, in spite of the popularity of the imperative, in curses as well as requests. It was probably never used much in conversation, even in Athens; Xenophon was addicted to it but it is scarce in Attic inscriptions. The figures per 100 pp. are approximately Alciphron (*Letters*) 109, Xenophon (*Mem.*) 350, Plato (*Phaedo*) 250, Strabo 76, Polybius 37, Diodorus Siculus 13, Callimachus 49 (in 49 pp.), Aratus 94 (in 46 pp.). Even Dionysius of Halicarnassus (30 B.C.) and Diodorus Siculus (i/B.C.) who maintain the Attic tradition tend to dispense with it. In fact, the fut. optative, never more than a substitute in indirect speech for the future indic., is quite extinct in Hellenistic Greek. The aor. opt. proved toughest, lasting until viii/A.D. The optative to express a wish (volitive) was the most persistent, surviving particularly in set phrases like μὴ γένοιτο; whereas the potential optative, in main and conditional clauses, was rare in the Ptolemaic, and almost extinct and awkwardly used, in the

---

[1] Hilaire Vandaele, *L'Optatif Grec. Essai de Syntaxe historique*, Paris 1897. F. G. Allinson, "On Causes Contributory to the Loss of the Optative in Later Greek," *Studies in Honor of B.L. Gildersleeve*, Baltimore, 1902, pp. 353-356. K. Reik, *Der Optativ bei Polybius und Philo von Alexandria*, Leipzig 1907. C. Mutzbauer, *Die Grundbedeutung des Konjunctiv und Optativ und ihre Entwicklung im Griechischen* (Ein Beitrag zur historischen Syntax der griechischen Sprache), Leipzig-Berlin 1908. C. Harsing, *De optativi in chartis Aegyptiis usu*, Diss. Bonn 1910. J. Scham, *Der Optativgebrauch bei Klemens von Alexandrien in seiner sprach- und stilgeschichtlichen Bedeutung. Ein Beitrag zur Geschichte des Attizismus in der altchristl. Literatur*, Diss. Tübingen 1913. F. Slotty, *Der Gebrauch des Konjunktivs und Optativs in den griechischen Dialekten*. I. Teil: Der Hauptsatz, Göttingen 1915. D. C. Fives, *The Use of the Optative Mood in the Works of Theodoret, Bp. of Cyrus* (Patristic Studies of the Cath. Univ. of America) 1937. R. de L. Henry, *The Late Greek Optative and Its Use in the Writings of Gregory Nazianzen* (Patr. Stud. Cath. Univ. America, 68) 1943 (on pp. 95-99 are bibliographies of LXX, NT, and Papyri). E. L. Green, "The Optative Mood in Diodorus Siculus," *Proc. & Trans. Amer. Philol. Assn.* 62. Mayser II 1, 288ff. Schwyzer II 338ff.

Imperial papyri [1]. The reason for the decline probably lies in the " syntactical weakness " (Schwyzer II 337) of the optative. No one can or could quite define its essential function. The two chief functions, volitive and potential, were too dissimilar to give a unity to the mood, and the subjunctive was always at hand for a substitute for either. Moreover, the refinements inherent in the use of the optative were beyond the powers of uneducated Greeks and most barbarians. Those later writers who sought to revive the mood found it difficult to recapture the ancient subtleties. Horn has demonstrated that the optative did gain a new lease of life in the Byzantine period, usually in set phrases or interchangeably with the subjunctive, and its revival in ii/A.D. in the vulgar texts merely followed the earlier learned reaction against its disappearance. Literary writers, especially the Atticists, affected it. Even the ii–iii/A.D. papyri follow suit and the scribes of some NT MSS favoured it. Alongside this went a growing confusion in its use, indicating that the revival was artificial; even an educated writer like Procopius of Caesarea (Schwyzer II 338) confuses it with subjunctive, uses it excessively, and in a non-Attic way.

Optatives which do occur in Hell. authors may be classified:

	MAIN			SUBORDINATE				
	Volitive	Potential		Condition	Oblique	Comparat.	Final	Temporal	Total
Ptol. pap.	54	127	*Total* 181	13	17				30
LXX	434	41	475	26	7	18	13		64
NT	39	3	42	8	16			2	26

The NT thus shows only a slight decrease from the LXX. There is a tendency to replace optatives with the subjunctive, and optatives occur only in Lk-Ac (28), Paul (31), 1 Pt, 2 Pt (4), Jude (2), Mk (2), Heb (1).

---

[1] Thus it is used after *primary* tenses in the main clause: A.D. 249 ἵνα τοῦτο εἰδέναι ἔχοις, ἐπιστέλλεταί σοι; iv/A.D. ὁπόταν βουληθείης; A.D. 345 ἐὰν δέ τις αὐτῶν ἀφυστερήσειεν καὶ μὴ παραστήσωμεν.

§ 1. Main Clauses

Its disappearance was slightly slower than in dependent clauses. In main clauses it has two distinct functions: to express a wish, usually in set phrases (where the mood survived longest), and to express a rather mild affirmation, generally with ἄν but occasionally without in uncultivated speech. The addition of ἄν to the latter does not infallibly distinguish the two functions, although in the papyri and NT ἄν is not usually lacking with potential optative.

(a) Wish

There is no ἄν. Gradually the subjunctive, fut. indic., and 3rd p. imperat. encroach upon this usage, but here the optative held out the longest. Even in class. times it was not easy to dissociate *wish* (opt.) from *exhortation* to others to fulfil the wish (subj.) or even from positive command (imper.). A cultured writer like auct. ad Heb. has the optative of wish only once. Radermacher (p. 160) illustrates this "struggle of the moods" by referring to a curse-table of 4 B.C. with μὴ τύχῃ εὐιλάτου in the fourth line but μὴ τύχοι in the eighth; and to Acta Thomae 129 συντμήθεισαν καὶ γένωνται. Even in good literary texts ἠξίουν, ἤθελον, ἐβουλόμην often take the place of the older ἀξιοίην ἄν, βουλοίμην ἄν, θέλοιμι ἄν (Ac 25²² ἐβουλόμην; Ga 4²⁰ ἤθελον); and ἵνα c. subj. will now express a wish. However, the opt. εἴη occurs at all periods in the papyri and is common in Biblical Greek.

Mayser and Horn illustrate by the following occurrences the decline and revival of the wish optative in papyrus texts; it was weakest in the NT period. iv/B.C. (2), iii/B.C. (5), ii/B.C. (23), i/B.C. (1) i/A.D. (1), ii/A.D. or ii–iii/A.D. (8), iii/A.D. or iii–iv/A.D. (6), iv/A.D. (4), later (8, all γένοιτο). By contrast, let us look at their incidence in Biblical Greek: LXX. Ge 9²⁷ 19⁹ vl. 27²⁸ 28³ 31⁴⁹. ⁵³ vl. 34¹¹ 43¹⁴. ¹⁴. ²⁹ 44⁷*¹⁷* 48¹⁶. ¹⁶ 49 ⁶. ⁶. ⁸.—Ex 15¹⁶.—Lev 5¹⁶.—Nu 5²² 6²⁴. ²⁴. ²⁵. ²⁵. ²⁶. ²⁶ 23¹⁰. ¹⁰.—Dt 27¹⁵ (same phrase in ¹⁶. ¹⁷. ¹⁸. ¹⁹. ²⁰. ²¹. ²². ²³. ²³. ²⁴. ²⁵. ²⁶ 28¹². ¹³. ²⁰. ²¹. ²². ²⁴. ²⁵. ²⁷. ²⁸. ³⁵. ³⁶ 29¹⁹⁽¹⁸⁾ 33⁷. ¹⁶. ²⁷.—Jo 7²⁵ 22²². ²⁹* 24¹⁶*.—Jg 5²⁴. ²⁴. ³¹ 9¹⁹. ¹⁹. ²⁰ quat. (ter A) 13¹⁷ (not A).—Ru 1⁹. ⁹ (not A) ¹⁶. ¹⁷ 2⁴. ¹². ¹². ¹³ 3¹¹. ¹².—1 Km 1¹⁷ 2²⁰ 3¹⁷ 14⁴⁴. ⁴⁴ 20¹³. ¹³. ¹⁶ 24¹³. ¹³. ¹⁶ quat. 25²². ²². ²⁶. ³¹ 26¹⁹. ¹⁹A ²⁰. ²⁴. ²⁴. ²⁴ A (B ind.)—2 Km 3⁹. ⁹. ²⁹. ³⁵. ³⁵ 7²⁶ 14⁷ 16⁴ 18³² 19¹³⁽¹⁵⁾ bis 23⁴ 24²³.— 3 Km 1³⁷. ³⁷. ⁴⁷ 2²³. ²³. ³³ 8⁵⁷ ter 10⁹ 19². ² 20(21)³* 21(20)¹⁰. ¹⁰.— 4 Km 6³¹. ³¹ (Analysis:

---

* μὴ γένοιτο.

§ 1] THE VERB: MOODS 121

α, ββ, γγ = 41; βγ, γδ = 12).—1 Ch $12^{17}B^{17}B$ bis (S sec. ἐλέγξατο, A sec. ἐλέγξαι, 21^3 $22^{12.\ 12}$.—2 Ch 7^{41} 24^{22}.—1 Esd $6^{32(33)}$.—2 Esd $15(5)^{13}$.—Ps 6^{11} quat. (R imper.) $7^{5.\ 6.\ 6}$. ^{6}B 11 (12) ^{4}B (AR fut. ind.) $16(17)^2$ $17(18)^{36}$R^{vid} (B imper.) $19(20)^{2.\ 2.\ 3}$. ^{3}B (R*^{vid} imper.)$^{4.\ 5.\ 5}$B (AR fut. ind.) $20(21)^{9.\ 9}$ $24(25)^2$. ^{2}U (B imper.)^{20} $30(31)^{2.\ 18}$ ter $32(33)^{22}$ 34 $(35)^4$ B bis (SAU imper.) $^{19.\ 24.\ 25}$ B^{ab} $^{26.\ 26.\ 27.\ 27.\ 27}$ B (SAR imper.) 35 $(36)^{12}$ B (S^{ca}R fut. ind.) 36 $(37)^{15}$ B (R imper.)^{15} 39 $(40)^{12}$ A (B ind.) $^{15.\ 15.\ 15}$ B (R* imper.) $^{15.\ 17}$ 40 $(41)^3$ ter ^{4} B (AR fut. ind.)^{14} 51 $(52)^{6.\ 6}$ (R sec. indic.)^6 B^c (B ind.) 62 $(63)^6$ (R ind.) 66 $(67)^2$ ter $^{7.\ 8}$ 67 $(68)^3$ 68 $(69)^{7.\ 7.\ 15.\ 25}$ 69 $(70)^3$ quat. (SR imper.)^4 (SR imper.) $70(71)^1$ $71(72)^{19}$ 73 $(74)^{23}$ (S^{ca} RT indic.) 84 $(85)^8$ 88 $(89)^{53}$ 89 $(90)^{5.\ 6}$ quat. 103 $(104)^{34.\ 35}$ 105 $(106)^{48}$ 108 $(109)^{7.\ 7.\ 13}$ S^{ca} T (S imper.)$^{14.\ 14.\ 15}$ 112 $(113)^2$ 113^{16} (115^8) ^{22} (115^{14}) 118 $(119)^{5.\ 41.\ 170.\ 172}$ (AR* ind., T subj.) 120 $(121)^3$ (subj?)^7 (ART fut. ind.) 127 $(128)^5$ ter (AR ind.; T subj.) 133 $(134)^3$ A (S fut. ind., T aor. subj.) 134 $(135)^{18}$ 136 $(137)^{5.\ 6}$ 146 $(147)^1$.—Pr 4^{27b} A (B fut. ind.) 11^{26} 24^{52} $(30^{17.\ 17})$.—Eccl. 5^7 B (ACS^{ca} ind.).—Jb 1^{21} $3^{3.\ 4.\ 5.\ 5.\ 6}$ quat. $^{7.\ 7.\ 8.\ 9}$ ter 5^4 B (A ind.)$^{4.\ 5.\ 14.\ 15.\ 15.\ 16.\ 16}$ $6^{10.\ 29}$ $12^{25.\ 25}$ 13^6 $15^{6.\ 6}$ C (B fut. ind.)$^{28.\ 28.\ 30}$ B (A ind.)$^{33.\ 33}$ $16^{6(5).\ 19(18)}$. $21(20).\ 21\ (20)$ B ^{22} (21) 17^8 B (A ind.) $^{9.\ 9}$ $18^{7.\ 7.\ 8.\ 8}$ A (B pf. ind.) $^{9.\ 11.\ 11.}$ $^{13.\ 14.\ 14.\ 17.\ 18}$ 19^{26} $20^{10.\ 10.\ 15}$ C (B ind.) $^{16.\ 16}$ B (A fut. ind.) $^{17.\ 23.\ 23.}$ $^{24.\ 25.\ 25.\ 26.\ 27.\ 27.\ 28.\ 28}$ $21^{20.\ 20}$ 22^{22} S* 23^4 (S^{ca} ind.) ^{5} ter $24^{18.\ 19.\ 20.\ 20}$ $27^{5.\ 7}$ 29^{13} 30^{24} $31^{8.\ 8.\ 10.\ 10.\ 21.\ 22.\ 28.\ 30.\ 30.\ 40}$ (A subj.) $24^{10.\ 11}$ (A ind.).— Wi 7^{15}.—Si 22^2 C (A fut. ind.) $25^{19\ (26)}$ 33 $(36)^{4.\ 11}$ 38^{15} $43^{21\ (23)}$ S* (B fut. ind.) $45^{26\ (31)}$ $46^{11\ (14).\ 12\ (14)}$ $49^{10\ (12)}$ $50^{23\ (25)}$ $51^{29\ (37)}$ bis.—Jdt $10^{8.\ 8}$ $13^{20\ (26)}$ $15^{11\ (12),\ 10\ (11)}$ B (SA aor. ind.).—To B $3^{9.\ 11}$ $5^{14\ (19).}$ $^{17.\ (22).\ 19\ (24)}$ $7^{17\ (20)}$ 10^{12} 11^{17} $13^{10\ (12)}$ bis.—To S 3^9 $5^{10.\ 14.\ 14.\ 17}$ quat. ^{19} $7^{7.\ 12.\ 17}$ 9^6 $10^{11.\ 11.\ 12}$ quat. $11^{14.\ 17}$ $13^{10.\ 10}$.—Ob^{12} A.—Jon 2^8.—Zach 3^2.—Isa 14^{29} 25^1 28^{22}.—Je 3^{19} $11^{5.\ 20}$ 15^{11} 17^{18} ter 20^{12} 36^{22} (29^{22}).— La 1^{22} 2^{18}.—Da O' $3^{39.\ 44.\ 44.\ 44.\ 98}$ (4^1) $4^{16\ (19).\ 34c}$.— Da Θ $3^{39.\ 44}$ ter 9^8 (4^1) $7^{25\ (26)}$.—1 Mac $8^{23.\ 23}$ 9^{10*} 13^{5*}.—2 Mac 1^2 V (A inf.) $^{3.\ 4.\ 4.\ 5}$ ter 15^{24}.—4 Mac 6^{15} S (A imper.) $^{17.\ 21}$ 13^9 A (SV subj.).

NT. Mk 11^{14} (vl. subj.).—Lk 1^{38} $20^{16*.\ 16*}$.—Ac 8^{20} (the only pres. tense among the volitives).—Ro $3^{4*.\ 6*.\ 31*}$ $6^{2*.\ 15*}$ $7^{7*.\ 13*}$ 9^{14*} $11^{1*.\ 11*}$ $15^{5.\ 13}$.—1 Co 6^{15*}.—Ga 2^{17*} 3^{21*} 6^{14*}.—1 Th $3^{11.\ 12.\ 12}$ 5^{23}.—2 Th $2^{17.\ 17}$ $3^{5.\ 16}$.—Phm ^{20} ὀναίμην.—2 Ti $1^{16.\ 18}$ 4^{16}.—Heb 13^{21}.—1 Pt 1^2 5^{10}.— 2 Pt 1^2.—Jude $^{2.\ 9}$.

Ps. Sol 4^7 ἐξάραι (or imper?) $^{8.\ 9.\ 16*.\ 18.\ 18.\ 19.\ 21}$ KPM (not AV) $^{22.\ 28.\ 29*}$ 11^9 $12^{4.\ 4.\ 5.\ 6.\ 6.\ 8.\ 8}$ $17^{10.\ 27.\ 27.\ 51}$ 18^6 (The only other opt. in this book renders the Heb. frequentative impf.: ὁ πλοῦτος αὐτῶν διέλθοι *went forth*).—Vit. Proph. (only final, after ἵνα).—T. Sol. D 6^1 βασιλεῦ Σολομῶν, χαίροις.—Clem. ad Cor. tit. 23^1 45^7 54.—Ign. ad Eph. 2^1 $11^{2.\ 2}$ 12^2, ad Magn. 11, ad Trall. 13^3, ad Smyrn. 5^3.

Some Hell. authors: Aratus *Phaenomena* (1154 lines): 16 (χαίροιτε), 100, 154, 155, 304, 324, 460, 637, 758, 823, 824, 824, 1049, 1050, 1086, 1088, 1090.—Callimachus *Hymn* I (Zeus) 64, 68; II (Apollo) 113; III (Artemis) 84, 137 (εἴην), 137; IV (Delos) 98, 162, 195, 240, 326 (χαίροι);

---

* μὴ γένοιτο.

VI (Demeter) 116 (εἴη).—Alciphron *Letters* II 2^1 5^3 (μὴ ... γένοιτο) 14^1 16^1 17^{4*} 20^3 25^3; III $12^{1.1}$ (εἴη) [5] (εἴη) [5] 15^4 (γένοιτο) 26^2 28^4 $32^{1.1}$ 35^3 37^2 38^3 41; IV 3^2 (γένοιτο) 5^1 (εἴη) 9^2 (γένοιτο) $18^{3.3*16.16}$ $19^{21.21}$.

It is clear then that the optative can still express a wish or prayer, nearly always in 3rd p. and especially in the formula μὴ γένοιτο (15 in NT). Only two of the NT instances are imprecations (prayers for evil): Mk 11^{14} Ac 8^{20}. In fact, there is a strong tendency to use the imperative: ἀνάθεμα ἔστω Ga 1^{8t} 1 Co 16^{22}. The author of Ac uses λαβέτω instead of LXX λάβοι when citing the Psalms (1^{20}). In spite of this, there still remain 39 instances of wish-optative. The LXX does not contain any more on an average per page.

(b) *Potential*

The opt. with ἄν indicates a potential mood; sometimes it is described as an " urbane " or " deliberative " optative.

It frequently helped the writer to express what would happen on the fulfilment of some supposed condition; to express, in fact, an apodosis without a protasis. It was becoming a luxury of speech and was beginning to disappear in favour of the subj. or fut. ind. with ἄν. As with the volitive, it was largely in set phrases that it survived: thus καλῶς ἄν ἔχοι. Already in Polybius it seems to be confined to these. Careful authors use it more frequently than the NT authors, but they are in doubt whether to use ἄν or some other particle like ἴσως or δήπουθεν. The vagaries of scribal transmission may be partly responsible for the omission of ἄν, but Reinhold (*de Graecitate patrum Apost.* p. 110) brings forward enough examples to show that there was confusion here at the close of the Hellenistic period. In the Attic inscriptions investigated by Meisterhans (p. 247f), opt. c. ἄν is found only in some poetry (iv/B.C.) but in decrees, etc., there would be little occasion for it. In the iii/B.C. papyri however this opt. is widespread in certain epistolary phrases:

καλῶς ἄν ποιήσαις 264. 257. 245. iii.—χαρίζοιο ἄν *be so good* 258 ter. 250 bis. iii quat.—καλῶς ἄν ἔχοι 25 times in iii/B.C.—εἴη ἄν ὡς θέλω 260. 252. 223, 257.—βούλομαι P. Petr. III.—εἴη ἄν ὡς ἡμεῖς θέλομεν 257. 256. iii–ii.—εἴη ἄν τὸ δέον. 242 ter.—Other phrases 258 (Horn). iii (Horn). 223. 260 bis. 255.

ii/B.C.: χαρίζοιο ἄν 156.—χαρίζοι⟨ο⟩ δ' ἄν 156.—εἴη ἄν ὡς θέλω ii (Horn). 170 (Horn). 153 (Horn).—εἴη ἄν ὡς βούλομαι 168. 153 ter.

---

* μὴ γένοιτο.

164 (cp. 2 Mac 11²⁸).—εἴη ἂν ὡς εὔχομαι BGU IV.—εἴη ἂν ὡς αἱρούμεθα Goodsp.—εἴη ἂν τὸ δέον P. Par. (156 B.C.).—Other phrases 160 (Horn). BU, P. Par. 63 (164 B.C.), 64. 64, P. Par. (156 B.C.), P. Lond. I (168 B.C.), Cairo (123 B.C.).

i/B.C.—none.
i/A.D.: εὖ ποιήσαις (no ἄν) 95.
ii/A.D.: c. 130. 167.
iii/A.D.: 274. 298. late. iii–iv.
Later: 346. iv. 591. vi–vii.

It should be said that some of the above are not a fair sample of the popular speech, but are part of the florid style of officials or the affectation of literary aspirants. The less stereotyped phrases had been dropped from the living speech by the close of iii/B.C. All that was retained thereafter were certain polite set phrases which die very hard.

Unless we include 4 Mac, this optative is not common in the LXX, although we might include the deliberative optative in questions under this head. Apart from the latter there is only 2 Mac 11²⁸ outside 4 Mac (1¹· ⁵· ⁷· ⁸ no ἄν, ¹⁰ 2⁶· ²⁴ 3⁴ S [AV ind.] 5⁶· ¹³ no ἄν, 7¹⁷· ²² 8⁶ 9⁶· ²⁴). But there are questions of a potential or deliberative or futuristic kind: with ἄν: Ge 23¹⁵ 44⁸.—Dt 28⁶⁷· ⁶⁷.—Jb 19²³ 25⁴ 29² 31³¹ 41⁴ ⁽⁵⁾.— Pr 20¹⁸ ⁽²⁴⁾.—Si 25³ ⁽⁵⁾.—Ezk 15².

without ἄν: Nu 11²⁹.—Jg 9²⁹.—2 Km 18³³ (19¹).—Ps 119 (120)³· ³.—Ca 8¹.—Jb 23⁸ (A ἄν) 31³⁵ 38²⁰· ²⁰.—4 Mac 8¹⁷ 14¹⁰ (Sᶜᵃ ἄν) 15⁴.

In NT there seems to be but one genuine instance which is not a question (Ac 26²⁹ ABSᶜ), and this is where in the royal presence of Agrippa, Paul employs the stilted εὐξαίμην ἄν. Luke makes the Athenians to say τί ἂν θέλοι οὗτος λέγειν; (Ac 17¹⁸), and the Ethiopian to ask *how could I?* πῶς γὰρ ἂν δυναίμην; (8³¹). Perhaps also Ac 2¹²E. It was old-fashioned in the NT age, and the writers prefer a mere future (Ro 3⁶ 1 Co 15³⁵) or other device. But we must also include here many dependent questions of a deliberative kind which are only incidentally dependent, and are still deliberative when transformed into direct speech: Lk 1⁶² 6¹¹ (not D) 9⁴⁶ 15²⁶ (vl. om ἄν).—Jn 13²⁴ vl.—Ac 5²⁴ 10¹⁷ 17²⁰ vl. 21³³ (EHLP add ἄν). But opinions may legitimately differ whether the following have opt. simply because of the class. rules of sequence: Lk 1²⁹ (but D ἄν) 8⁹ (vl. om opt.) 18³⁶ (vl. + ἄν) 22²³ (vl. ind.). In Lk 3¹⁵ (διαλογιζομένων μήποτε αὐτὸς εἴη ὁ χριστός) what they actually asked themselves may be expressed by opt. The presence of ἄν would seem to decide in favour of an original potential in these doubtful cases.

In this respect LXX and NT are much of a unity, and

because of the infrequence of this opt. the LXX should be classified with the papyri of i/B.C.–i/A.D. rather than with those of iii/B.C.

T. Sol. D 4⁴ διαπορῶν τί ἄρα ἀποκρίνοιτο.—Ign. ad Eph. 2², ad Magn 2, 12, ad Rom 5², ad Polyc. 6².

Some Hell. authors: Alciphron *Letters* I 11³ (εἴποις ἄν *you might say*), 13¹ (ἠπόρουν ὅ τι πράξαιμι *I didn't know what to do*), 14³ (πῶς ... ὑπομείναιμεν *how could we endure?*), 22¹ ἄν; II 2² (εἴπαις ἄν *you might say*), 10³ ἄν, 15² ἄν; III 2² (εἴποι τις ἄν *you might say, as it were*), 11¹ ἄν; IV 2³ ἄν, 3³ ἄν, 8¹ ἄν, 10⁴, 11⁵ ἄν, 13⁶·⁷ ἄν, 16⁷ ἄν, 18² ἄν ²·³ ἄν, 19³ ἄν.— Callimachus *Hymns* I 15. 15. 91 κεν; II 26. 27. 31 ἄν, 35 κε; III 15. 104, 155 κεν, 177 κεν, 250; IV 25 κε, 126 κε; V 103.—Aratus *Phaenomena* 12 κε, 78 ἄν, 142 ἄν, 169, 195 κεν, 211 κεν, 451 κε, 456 ἄν, 463 κε, 495 κε, 530 κε, 559 κεν, 562 ἄν, 566 ἄν, 579 ἄν, 607 ἄν, 712 κε, 729 κε, 731, 782 κε, 793 ἄν, 797 κεν, 798 ἄν, 802 κε, 815 ἄν, 816 ἄν, 818 κε, 827 κεν, 839 κεν, 839, 850 κε, 857 ἄν, 873 κεν, 876 ἄν, 879 ἄν, 888 κε, 904, 915, 1006 κε, 1066, 1085, 1144, 1144 κε, 1145 ἄν, 1148, 1148, 1154 κεν.

§ 2. Dependent Clauses

Here is a still more rapid decline in the Hell. period, and the opt. has become almost entirely alien to the popular speech. In more artificial language it still serves in indirect speech and final and conditional clauses, whereas in class. Greek it regularly appeared in dependent clauses after a historic tense where the subj. would have appeared had the clause depended on a primary tense. The NT retains the subj. even in historic sequence, in common with popular Greek in general from the mid-ii/B.C. The class. rule is rarely observed in the Ptolemaic papyri (Mayser II 1, 288).

(a) Iterative

This is the regular class. function of the opt. in dependent clauses following a historic tense. It expresses reiteration, best rendered in English by *ever* (*whoever, whenever, if ever*). The impf. ind. or aor. ind., sometimes with ἄν (see above, Indic. Mood), was substituted for this in the later period. The LXX and NT have ὅταν and ὁπόταν with impf. or aor. ind., but Mayser can find no instance of this in the Ptolemaic papyri, while Radermacher finds one or two instances in Polybius. The iterative opt. was soon confused with the potential, and ἄν was consequently added, as is seen in Aristeas 59 (Wendland) τὴν διάθεσιν εἶχεν ὥστε, καθ' ὃ ἂν μέρος στρέφοιτο, τὴν πρόσοψιν εἶναι τὴν αὐτήν.

Clear instances of iterative opt. are found in the Ptol. pap., Philo, and NT, especially with εἰ τύχοι *for example* (1 Co 14¹⁰ 15³⁷). Papyri:—

iv/B.C.: UPZ no. 1. 12f ⟨δ⟩ ς δ' ἀν[ελοι] τὰ γράμματα ταῦτα [κα] ἰ ἀδικοῖ 'Ἀρτεμισίην. ὁ θεὸς αὐτῶι τὴ⟨ν⟩ δίκην ἐπιθ[είη]. This is a potential opt. within a hypothetical relative clause, hardly distinguishable from the iterative.

iii/B.C.: Petr. II 18 (2b) 15 ἔτυπτεν αὐτὸν κατὰ τοῦ τραχήλου καὶ εἰς ὃ μέρος τύχοι τοῦ σώματος (246). Formal language of a bill of complaint. Magd. 42 πληγάς μοι ἐνέβαλεν καὶ πλείους εἰς ὃ τύχοι μέρος τοῦ σώματος (221).

ii/B.C.: 162 (Horn). 118 (Horn). 117 (Horn). PSI III 167 18 (118 B.C.) formal language. Teb 24. 65 τύχοι (117 B.C.). BGU VI 1253. 10 (but Lobel's emend. does away with opt. here).

i/ A.D.: 18 (Horn)
ii/A.D.: 131 (Horn)
iii/A.D.: c 376 (Horn)

later: 409 and eleven other exx. of temporal, to viii/A.D. Stylistic revival of opt. in Byzantine Greek: v–vi/A.D., vi/A.D., c 551. 616. In an iterative temporal clause this revival appears to have begun already in 2 Clem 12³ ὅταν λαλῶμεν . . . καὶ . . . εἴη.

Except for εἰ τύχοι the iterative opt. is no longer in use in LXX and NT, having quite disappeared from the colloquial language by this time [1]. Mark's method of filling the gap (ὅταν with past ind.) is found elsewhere with extreme rarity [2]. More frequently ἄν is added [3] to the indicative.

(b) Conditional

The reaction in favour of the opt. influenced a wider circle than the Atticists, particularly in conditional and final clauses in the case of non-atticizing cultured writers. After ii/A.D. the influence spread to more popular authors. Rademacher observes that the text Περὶ Ἑρμηνείας (prob. i/A.D., not atticistic)

---

[1] In literary writers, e.g.: Aratus *Phaenomena* 823 ὅτ' εὐδίου κεχρημένος ἤματος εἴης *whenever you desire a fair day*, 1141 ὅτ' ὄμβρου σήματα φαίνοι (mice build nests) *whenever Zeus shows signs of rain*,— Callimachus *Hymns* III 136 τῶν εἴη μὲν ἐμοὶ φίλος ὅστις ἀληθής *whoever is a true friend of mine*. VI 68 ὅσσα πάσαιτο τόσων ἔχεν ἵμερος αὖτις.

[2] Polyb. IV 32.5f.—LXX Ex 17¹¹·¹¹, Nu 11⁹ 21⁹, Jg 6³ (A ὅταν; B ἐάν), 1 Km 17³⁴, Ps 77³⁴ 118⁸² 119⁷, Jb 20²² (A ὁπότε; B ὁπόταν). NT Mk 3¹¹.

[3] LXX Le 27¹² καθότι ἄν c. fut. ind., To 7¹¹B ὁπότε ἄν εἰσεπορεύοντο. NT Mk 6⁵⁶ ὅσοι ἄν ἤψαντο, Ac 2⁴⁵ 4³⁵ καθότι ἄν χρείαν εἶχεν. 1 Co 12² ὡς ἄν ἤγεσθε.

employs as a typical form of conditional sentence εἰ c. opt. in the protasis and fut. indic. in the apodosis. So also Philo [1], Herm. S. IX 12, 4 (οὐδεὶς εἰσελεύσεται, εἰ μὴ λάβοι: Harnack λάβῃ), Theophilus ad Autolycum I 6. The atticizing influence must have been wide. Epictetus, and Diodorus (Kapff, p. 88) use opt. after εἰ quite extensively. It is rare in LXX and papyri (Harsing 38f; Mayser II 1, 293); none of the instances adduced by Horn appear to be earlier than i/A.D. and the majority are Byzantine. Radermacher notes that the Pergamum inscriptions have but one instance and prefer ἐάν c. subj. in the protasis and fut. ind. in the apodosis. Moreover in most examples from the Ptolemaic papyri εἰ c. opt. stands obliquely for the direct form ἐάν c. subj., and so ought strictly to be considered as indirect speech. Besides, most of them betray the stilted language of official letters or decrees.

Of true conditions with opt., there are only three in NT: Ac 24[19] ἔδει... κατηγορεῖν, εἴ τι ἔχοιεν πρὸς ἐμέ, 1 Pt 3[14] εἰ καὶ πάσχοιτε ..., μακάριοι, [17] κρεῖττον..., εἰ θέλοι τὸ θέλημα τοῦ θεοῦ, πάσχειν... There are about 25 in LXX, which is almost the same percentage, especially if 4 Mac is ignored: 1 Km 24[20.20] εἰ εὕροιτό τις τὸν ἐχθρὸν... καὶ ἐκπέμψαι αὐτόν (fut. ind. in apodosis) (A εὑρών... ἐκπέμψαι), 14[6] εἴ τι ποιήσαι ἡμῖν Κύριος (sc. *it would be well*); hardly conditional: *Perhaps the Lord will.*—2 Km 16[12] εἴ πως ἴδοι Κύριος: *perhaps the Lord*... (see above).—4 Km 6[27] μή σε σώσαι Κύριος·πόθεν σώσω σε; Ps 138 (139)[9] S*ca (BR* subj.) ἐὰν λάβοιμι τὰς πτέρυγάς μοι (apodosis fut. ind.).— Jb 6[2] εἰ γάρ τις ἱστῶν στῆσαι μου τὴν ὀργήν, τὰς δὲ ὀδύναι μου ἄραι ἐν ζυγῷ (apod. fut. ind.), 6[8] εἰ γὰρ δῴη, καὶ ἔλθοι μου ἡ αἴτησις, καὶ τὴν ἐλπίδα μου δῴη ὁ Κύριος (no apodosis): *if only God would give me...!* 20[23] εἴ πως πληρώσαι γαστέρα αὐτοῦ (apod. opt.), 34[14] εἰ γὰρ βούλοιτο συνέχειν (apod. fut. ind.), 38[20] εἰ ἀγάγοις με εἰς ὅρια αὐτῶν (a question; not a true condition).—Isa 49[15]. εἰ δὲ καὶ ταῦτα ἐπιλάθοιτο γυνή (apod. fut. ind.) (S* ind.).—2 Mac 9[24] Α ὅπως ἐάν τι παράδοξον ἀποβαίη (V ind.).— 4 Mac 2[8] κἂν φιλάργυρός τις εἴη..., 4[17] εἰ ἐπιτρέψειεν... (apod. aor. ind.), [23] εἴ τινες αὐτῶν φάνοιεν, 5[3] εἰ δέ τινες μὴ θέλοιεν, [19] εἰ μιεροφαγήσαιμεν, 6[18] εἰ νῦν μεταβαλοίμεθα [19]Α γενοίμεθα τοῖς νέοις ἀσεβείας τύπος (S γενώμεθα), 8[2.2] εἰ μὲν μιεροφαγήσαιεν... εἰ δὲ ἀντιλέγοιεν, 9[2] εἰ μή... γνώσει χρησαίμεθα, [27] ὡς δ' εἰ φαγεῖν βούλοιτο, 12[4]Α εἰ μὲν μὴ πεισθείης (S πισθείς), 14[17] εἰ δὲ καὶ μὴ δύναιτο κωλύειν.

The use of slightly antique language in the presence of Felix, rather than εἴ τι ἔχουσιν, is understandable. The only way to account for the apparently impeccable Attic of the

---

[1] K. Reik, *Der Optativ bei Polybius and Philo*, Leipzig 1907, 154.

Petrine optatives is to suppose them to have been abstracted from the archaic periods of a solemn exhortation; even here the potential clause (opt. c. ἄν) which might have been expected in a classical apodosis does not occur, for the genius of living speech has forcibly interposed the pres. tense since persecution is at hand. Zerwick ascribes the opt. to the writer's tactfulness of heart and a reluctance to mention sufferings except very tentatively to those who were actually destined to meet them (§ 228d). The other instances of εἰ c. opt. are not so much real conditions as final clauses (Ac 17²⁷ 27¹²)¹, and there are parenthetical phrases introduced by εἰ = *if possible* or *as it were*: εἰ δυνατὸν εἴη (vl. ἦν), εἰ δύναιντο (Ac 20¹⁶ 27³⁹) and εἰ τύχοι (1 Co 14¹⁰ 15³⁷). Other clauses introduced by εἰ and dependent on a verb like ζητεῖν are virtually indirect questions, a class. survival: Ac 17¹¹ 25²⁰. The LXX also uses εἰ c. opt. in these several ways—another indication of kinship in style and syntax with the NT. In neither LXX nor NT is there an instance of εἰ c. opt. in the protasis and opt. c. ἄν in the apodosis; and notice εἴ πως in 2 Km 16¹² Jb 20²² Ac 27¹². However, the LXX has εἰ c. opt. to express a wish, Hebrew אִם; Mk 8¹² uses εἰ c. fut. ind.

The constructions of εἰ c. opt. in conditions is still common in literary writers, but the style is very affected and poetic:

Aratus *Phaenomena* 563 ἀτὰρ εἰ νεφέεσσι μέλαιναι γίνοιτ᾽ *if they be dark with clouds,* 564 ἢ ὄρεος κεκρυμμένα ἀντέλλοιεν *or if they rise hidden behind a hill,* 825 εἰ δ᾽ αὕτως καθαρόν μιν ἔχοι *if he be so pure again,* 826 δύνοι δ᾽ ἀνέφελος *and if he set cloudless,* 838 εἴ γε μὲν ἀμφοτέροις ἄμυδις κεχρημένος εἴη *if he is draped both in black and red,* 855 καὶ εἴ ποτε χείματος ὥρῃ ὠχρήσαι κατιὼν *if in winter his hue wax wan at evening,* 858 εἰ δ᾽ ὁ μὲν ἀνέφελος βάπτοι *but if cloudless he dip,* 872 εἰ μὲν κεῖναι μᾶλλον κνέφαος φορέοιντο ἀκτῖνες *the more those beams are borne in shadow,* 874 εἰ δ᾽ ὀλίγος τανύοιτο περὶ δνόφος ἀκτίνεσσιν *but if but faint the dust that veils his beams,* 887 εἰ δὲ μὲν ἐκ βορέαο μι᾽ οἴη φοινίσσοιτο *but if only one shine purple to the north,* 905 εἰ δ᾽ ὁ μὲν ἐκ βορέω Φάτνης ἀμενηνὰ φαείνοι *if the Ass shine feebly to the north of the Manger.*—Callimachus *Hymn* III 178 καὶ εἰ Στυμφαλίδες εἶεν *even if they were,* IV 129 καὶ εἰ μέλλοιμι ῥοάων διψαλέην ἄμπωτιν ἔχων *even if I must wander.*—Especially frequent in the atticistic Alciphron's *Letters*: I 1. 5 εἰ χειμὼν ἐπιλάβοιτο *in case of bad weather,* 10, 4 ἵν᾽ εἰ πού τι ... εὑρεθείη σῶμα *if any corpse is found* (oblique), 12, 2 εἰ ...

---

¹ Ac 17²⁷ ζητεῖν τ. θεόν, εἰ ἄρα γε ψηλαφήσειαν αὐτὸν καὶ εὕροιεν, 27¹² ἔθεντο βουλὴν ἀναχθῆναι ... εἴ πως δύναιντο ... παραχειμάσαι.

πύθοιτο *if he should hear* (+ fut. ind.), 13, 4; 16, 3; 20, 2: II 12; 14, 2; 15, 1; 18, 3 εἰ δὲ μάθοι *if he finds out* (+ fut. ind.); 21, 3; 28, 2; 37, 2; III 5, 2 εἰ μὴ τὸ χωρίον πρὸς τοῖς ἀργυρίοις λάβοι (says she will not bestow her favours) *unless she gets the landed estate in addition to the cash* (oblique); 5, 3; 8, 2; 10, 3. 4; 14, 3; 16, 1; 26, 4; 28, 4; 34, 1; 38, 1. 2. 3; 42, 2; IV 3, 3; 10, 3. 3; 17, 6; 19, 3. 19. 21. Often in an oblique sense after a historic tense.

(c) *Final*

This is another atticism which is very rare in the papyri. Class. authors had used the opt. after a secondary tense, but apart from the doubtful Mk 12²S (ἵνα λάβοι) we find it neither in the NT nor Koine generally; it is almost absent from Polybius. The Atticists went so far as to use the opt. where the classical rule preferred subj. After ii/A.D., less literary authors followed suit, e.g. Vettius Valens and some later papyri. Radermacher finds odd examples as early as Plutarch and the apocryphal Acts of Apostles. Attic inscriptions of the period invariably have subj. after ἵνα, although they occasionally have opt. after ὅπως. Diodorus Siculus, who is distinctly a literary man, has only about eight final optatives compared with 179 subjunctives. Epictetus, who has potential opt. four times, has it only once in a final clause. Meisterhans shows it once in Attic inscriptions, iv/B.C. fin. (p. 247). Examples in the Ptol. pap. are difficult to establish: there may be a fut. opt. in ii/B.C. ἠξίωσα ἵνα χρηματισθήσοιτο P. Tebt I. There is nothing else before ii/A.D. fin. The discarding of the final opt. in post-class. Greek represents one of the furthest departures of that Greek from the Attic model.

Opt. after ἵνα, ὅπως: percentage, as compared with subj.					
Biblical	ii/ B.C.	i/B.C.	i/A.D.	ii/A.D.	iii/A.D.
2 Mac 71% (atticist) LXX 1·7% NT nil	Polyb. 7%	Diod. Sic. 5%	Josephus 32% Plutarch 49%	Arrian 82% Appion 87%	Herodian 75%

It is safe to say that there is nothing of this atticistic elegance in NT. It is unlikely that the pointing in Eph 1¹⁷ is δῴη (WH text); B has δῷ (WH mg); and in any case the ἵνα may be imperatival; final opt. does not come very well after a present tense, except with the Atticists and much later writers, and makes the achievement of the purpose more remote than the author could have intended. The same δωη occurs in 2 Ti 2²⁵ (vl. δῷ) after μήποτε and balances a subj., but it must be admitted that in the same epistle δωη cannot be anything else than an opt. (1¹⁶·¹⁸)¹. There is textual uncertainty in two other places in Eph (3¹⁶ 6¹⁹) and in Jn 15¹⁶, but the opt. always rests on slender evidence. These optatives, like that in Mk 12², are probably the learned corrections of atticistic scribes. In Eph 6¹⁹ moreover the ἵνα is epexegetical rather than final. It may seem that the class. rule of sequence in oblique clauses is being followed in Mk 14¹⁰ᶠ where παραδοῖ (as if from an -ω verb) is used in a final and a relative clause, but we must remember that οι and η were often confused and this may be a scribe's correction of παραδῇ. This could also be the explanation of ἵνα τις γνοῖ Mk 9³⁰ (a correction of a corrupt γνῇ).

Kinship in syntax between LXX and NT is further indicated by the fact that, apart from 4 Mac, there is no sure example of this optative.

LXX: Ps 37 (38)¹⁷ R* μήποτε ἐπιχαρείησάν μοι οἱ ἐχθροί μου (B subj.).—Pr 22¹⁷ S* τὴν δὲ σὴν καρδίαν ἐπίσημον ἵνα γνοῖς (vl. subj.), ¹⁹ S* ἵνα γνώρισον τὴν ὁδόν σου (vl. subj.).—Jb 21² A ἀκούσατε... ἵνα μὴ εἴη μοι (B ᾖ).—4 Mac 4⁶ ὅπως ... λάβοι, ²³ ὅπως ... θάνοιεν, 5⁶ ὅπως ... σῴζοιο, 6⁸ AS^ca ὅπως ἐξανισταῖτο (S* ἐξανίστατο), 8¹² ὅπως ... πείσειεν, 10¹ ὅπως ἀπογευσάμενος σῴζοιο, 12⁶ ὅπως ... παρορμήσειεν, 12⁶ V* ὅπως ποιήσαιεν (A ποιῆσαι), 17¹ ἵνα μὴ ψαύσειεν τι τοῦ σώματος.

Aratus *Phaen.* 381. 496. 1127 (after primary tense).—Callimachus *Hymn* I 34. 53, III 27. 61. 89. 108. 167.—Alciphron *Letters* I 15, 1 (after primary tense), II 3, 2 (primary), III 7, 5 (primary), IV 18, 3 (primary).

(d) *Indirect Statements*

The Atticists took this opt. too under their special protection, even after a primary tense; e.g. Alciphron IV 7, 5 τὰς νεφέλας ὁπόθεν εἶεν καὶ τὶς ἀτόμους ὁποῖαι ἀγνοοῦμεν. After a secondary tense in indirect speech the opt. was employed in class.

---

¹ Moreover the argument about balance is weaker in view of 2 Mac 9²⁴ where an opt. does in fact balance a subj.

Greek but there was never any constraint about it; direct speech was legitimate within the dependent clause. Hellenistic writers took advantage of the concession, and, although Diodorus Siculus uses the opt. 29 times like this, he leaves the direct speech as it is in 475 instances [1]. Even Atticists, like Dionysius of Halicarnassus, shared this preference. On the whole it would not appear that the opt. in, and because of, indirect speech, even after a secondary tense, was favoured in Hell. Greek. In the papyri, most of the Hellenistic examples are early (9 out of 10 are iii/B.C.) and the rest are nearly all in the Byzantine period of optative-revival (A.D. 117. 265. 336. 345. 543. 583. 583).

In the LXX and NT therefore it is a sign of atticizing style, and only a few books display it: Jb 23³ (γινώσκειν) ὅτι εὕροιμι αὐτὸν ἔλθοιμι εἰς τέλος.— 2 Mac 4¹ ἐκακολόγει ... ὡς οὗτός τε εἴη.—4 Mac 4²².—Ac 25¹⁶ ἀπεκρίθην ὅτι οὐκ ἔστιν ἔθος ... χαρίζεσθαι ... πρὶν ἢ ... ἔχοι ... τε ... λάβοι (but οι and η were often confused).

Alciphron I 13, 1 ἠπόρουν ὅ τι πράξαιμι, II 5, 2 τοῦ προξένου φήσαντος ὡς δεοίμην χρημάτων *when my sponsor said that I needed money*, III 2, 1 κατεμέμφετο ὅτι μὴ θαμίζοιμι παρ' αὐτόν *blamed me for not coming to see him more often*, 2, 2 φράσας παρ' ὅτου καλοῖτο *told her who had invited her*.

(e) Indirect Questions

This opt. also is rare, and here too in class. Greek it was permissible to retain the form of the direct question. Strangely, although it had disappeared in pre-Christian times, Luke is fond of this opt. Excluding deliberative questions, which are incidentally indirect [2], Luke has opt. six times. Thus in Lk 9⁴⁶ τὸ τίς ἂν εἴη μείζων αὐτῶν we have an indirect question and must not translate εἴη *might be*; it is not indefinite, deliberative, or future, but means *was*. Only Est. and 2 Mac (A-text) betray any traces of it in LXX, and there is sometimes the excuse of a

---

[1] See the tables in Kapff op. cit. p. 63.
[2] These probably owe their origin to a dir. delib. question: Lk 1⁶² ἐνένευον ... τὸ τί ἂν θέλοι, 3¹⁵ διαλογιζομένων πάντων ... μήποτε αὐτὸς εἴη ὁ χριστός, 6¹¹ διελάλουν πρὸς ἀλλήλους τί ἂν ποιήσαιεν τῷ Ἰησοῦ. 15²⁶ ἐπυθάνετο τί ἂν εἴη ταῦτα.—Jn 13²⁴ vl. πυθέσθαι τίς ἂν εἴη.— Ac 5²⁴ διηπόρουν ... τί ἂν γένοιτο τοῦτο, 10¹⁷ διηπόρει ... τί ἂν εἴη τὸ ὅραμα, 17²⁰ βουλόμεθα οὖν γνῶναι τί ἂν θέλοι (B τίνα θέλει ταῦτα εἶναι), 21³³ ἐπυνθάνετό τις εἴη καὶ τί ἐστιν πεποιηκώς (vl. τίς ἄν).

doubly dependent clause (Est 3³ 2 Mac 3³⁷A). The only other examples, besides Clem ad Rom 14³, are in the papyri, mostly in iii/B.C.¹, and in the atticistic revival of such writers as Alciphron ².

LXX: Est 3 (13)³ πυθομένου ... πῶς ἂν ἀχθείη τοῦτο ἐπὶ πέρας (potential?).—2 Mac 3³⁷ Α ἐπερωτήσαντος ... ποῖός τις εἴη ἐπιτήδειος (V ἦν).—4 Mac 11¹³ πυνθανομένου τοῦ τυράννου εἰ βούλοιτο ...
NT: Lk 1²⁹ διαλογίζετο ποταπὸς εἴη ὁ ἀσπασμός, 8⁹ ἐπερώτων ... τίς αὕτη εἴη ἡ παραβολή, 18³⁶ ἐπυνθάνετο τι εἴη τοῦτο, 22²³ συνζητεῖν .. τὸ τίς ἄρα εἴη, Ac 17¹¹ ἀνακρίνοντες τὰς γράφας εἰ ἔχοι ταῦτα οὕτως, 25²⁰ ζήτησιν ἔλεγον εἰ βούλοιτο.

It is not clear why Luke should have indulged in this galaxy of atticisms. It lends at least some weight to the suggestion that the Lucan writings were finally written up not earlier than the second century.

We are led directly to a final point. Why all these optatives in Biblical Greek, if the Scriptures were written and rendered in the language of the people? The opt. was dead, as far as popular language was concerned, except for a few set phrases. It would appear from our survey that all the LXX books which have the opt. to a considerable extent must either be dated early in the Hellenistic period or else must be supposed to have been affected by the atticistic revival of this mood. Job uses it extensively, and it should be remembered that this book belongs to the Kethubim, and for a long time such works were not regarded with the reverence accorded to those of the first and second division of the Canon. As a translation the Greek Job is free enough to be called a paraphrase, and much of the Hebrew is omitted. Similar conditions apply to the Greek Proverbs, and that book, on account of its preference of οὐδείς

---

¹ P. Petr. III 51, 9 ἐρωτώμενος, «πόσον» εἴ «η» αὐτὸς εἴη (iii/B.C.); note that πόσον and η are added by the scribe himself and should not be read; doubly dependent.—II 20 πυνθανομένου ... εἴ τι συντεθεικὼς αὐτῶι εἴης (252 B.C.); doubly dependent.—BGU VI 1246, 3 πυθομένου ... εἰ δυναίμην (iii/B.C.); doubly dependent.—P. Eleph. 13, 3 ἐπυνθανόμην ... εἴ τι βούλοιτο (223/B.C.).—Wilcken Theb. Book XII 12 ὑπεδείξαμεν ταυτὴν τὴν ὠνὴν αὐτία, εἴ πως δύναιντο προσεπιδέξασθαί τι (ii/B.C.). —P. Par 35, 29 πυνθανομένων δ' ἡμῶν, τοῦ τίνος χάριν εἴησαν (163 B.C.). —Insc. Magnes. 215.—An inscr. i/A.D.—BGU 347².10.—Post-Christian papyrus A.D. 170—Harsing appears not to be able to find any post-Christian instances: p. 31.
² I 17, 1 ἠρόμην ... ὅτου εἴη. ἠρόμην ... τίνα τρόπον ... ἀποκέοιτο. III 17, 1 ποῖ καταχθείην ... καὶ εὐκαίρως ἐμφάγοιμι μόνος. 24, 2 εἴ πού τι τῶν κόκκων ἐπιδράξασθαι δυνηθείη.

to οὐθείς, could not be much earlier than 100 B.C. The opt. in these books, therefore, is more likely to be due to the atticistic revival than to survival from the class. usage in the early stages of Hell. Greek.

On the other hand, it is significant that we find the quota of optative in Comparative clauses almost exclusively in the Pentateuch, Psalms, Proverbs, and Isaiah [1], which is an argument for grouping these books closely. Moreover, we find support for their early date in the fact that Mayser can only find one instance of this construction, and this is in iii/B.C. (P. Cair. Zen. 14, 18 κέχρηται ἡμῖν, ὡς ἂν εἴ τις ἐχθρῶι χρήσαιτο, 256 B.C.). There is no evidence that this construction is due to atticism, but it could well be a survival in iii/B.C. of the quite common class. construction, aided by the similar idiom in Hebrew (כַּאֲשֶׁר אִישׁ with impf.).

On the whole, it is more likely that the dependent optatives in Job, Psalms, and Proverbs (Kethubim) are due to a stylistic or atticistic influence rather than to a date in iii/B.C. or early ii/B.C. Isaiah, however, which has a volitive opt. and a comparative opt. once in 40 pages, and yet does not in other ways display an atticizing influence, but is good Koine Greek, may be supposed to date from iii/B.C. or early ii/B.C., if the use of the opt. is any criterion, and assuming that the needs of the synagogue lectionary would demand an early translation of this Prophetical book. The Prophets were read in the synagogues, in addition to the Pentateuch, and there was no distinction of " former " and " latter " until much later; so that the optatives in Jg, Kingdoms, Isaiah and Ezek. α might seem to be reasonably accounted for by the early date of their translation, which in turn was due to the desire to hear them in the synagogues.

There is much to be said for the suggestion that this apparent lingering of the indirect opt. into the NT period and beyond may be due to scribal activity in confusing like-sounding endings, and in addition to this, in the case of indirect questions, the potential idea may enter into each instance far more deeply than would appear at first; hence it is not the class. rule of sequence which is surviving so much as the old potential opt.—

---

[1] With ἄν: Ge 33[10], Isa 66[20], Ezk 1[16]. Without ἄν: Ex 33[11] AF, Nu 22[4. 7] (AF fut. ind.), Dt 1[31]AF (B ind.)[44] 8[5]B (AF subj.) 28[29] 32[11], Jg 16[9] (A ind.), Ps 82 (83)[15] (R fut. ind.), Pr 23[7] 25[26. 26], Isa 11[9] 21[1].

admirably suited to Christian aspiration and piety! Indeed, one must not reject too lightly the possibility that the optatives in NT owed their preservation in some measure to their incidence in the pompous and stereotyped jargon of devotion. These opt. phrases are decidedly formal (e.g. εἰ τύχοι = *e.g.*); εἴη, θέλοι and γένοιτο occur again and again. Because the LXX came to be a Church book, the same consideration should be given to the problem there. The optatives may reflect a date of translation early in the Hell. period. But if by any chance, as seems likely on other grounds, there was a new recension of some part at least of the LXX made much nearer to the Christian age, the retention of the optatives at a time when everywhere they were diminishing need not surprise us in view of their value for the liturgy, Jewish and Christian.

CHAPTER TEN

THE VERB: NOUN FORMS: INFINITIVE

IN SOME DIRECTIONS the infinitive [1] is now enlarging its sphere, especially in the infin. of purpose after verbs of motion; and, particularly in the more cultured Hell. writers, the articular infin.—a development which by chance coincides with Semitic partiality for the infin. with prepositions and thus explains its popularity in NT. In other directions the infin. is retreating, especially in face of ἵνα and ὅτι, the latter being prevalent after verbs of speaking, perceiving and believing—some of which kept very strictly to infin. in class. Greek.

§ 1. With the Function of a Dative

(a) Final-consecutive

This use with verbs of moving, sending, and giving, etc., or in loose connection with a whole clause which it supplements, has strongly increased in Hellenistic in comparison with class. prose. Malalas has especial preference for the final infin. after εἶμι, ἔρχομαι, ἵσταμαι, ὁρμάω, περιτρέχω, πέμπω, ἀπάγω, κατάγω, καλέω. In NT this development is even more pronounced. Sometimes the infin. is used alone, sometimes with ὥστε and more rarely ἐφ' ᾧ.

1. The simple infin. of purpose (class. with *giving, permitting*, etc.) is used with still more verbs of motion than in class. Greek and became really popular from c. 150 B.C.:

With ἔρχομαι Mt 2² ἤλθομεν προσκυνῆσαι, 4¹ ἀνήχθη πειρασθῆναι, 5¹⁷, 11⁷ ἐξήλθατε ... θεάσασθαι, 20²⁸ ἦλθεν διακονηθῆναι, 27⁵⁵ W ἠκολούθησαν διακονῆσαι (rest ptc.), Lk 9⁵², 18¹⁰ ἀνέβησαν προσεύξασθαι,

---

[1] K-G II 3–46. Stahl 596–680. Jannaris 480–89. Wackernagel I 257–76. Meisterhans-Schwyzer § 90. Schwyzer II 357–384. Mayser II 1, 296–339. F. H. Allen, *The Infin. in Polybius compared with the use of the Infin. in Biblical Greek*, Diss. Chicago 1907. Abel §§ 69–71. Zerwick §§ 266–279ᵇ. Ljungvik SSAA 40–45. Moulton Einl. 319ff. Pernot *Études* 31ff. 69ff. 102ff. 124ff. P. Aalto, *Studien zur Geschichte des Infinitiv im Griech.*, Helsinki 1953.

Ac 10³³ πάρεσμεν ἀκοῦσαι, Jn 4⁷ ἔρχεται... ἀντλῆσαι ὕδωρ, 14² πορεύομαι ἑτοιμάσαι τόπον, 21³ ὑπάγω ἁλιεύειν, Ro 10⁶ 1 Co 10⁷ 16³ Heb 9²⁴ Herm. S. IX 9, 1, Mart. Petr. 88, 7, Acta Petri et Pauli 186, 4. But John is very fond of parataxis with verbs of motion, rather than the infin.; e.g. ἔρχεσθε καὶ ὄψεσθε 1⁴⁰; also 1⁴⁷ 11³⁴ 14³ 19³⁸ 20¹⁹ etc. The Atticists themselves quite often used the infin.: exx. in Schmid, *Der Attizismus*, 1887-1897, II 56, III 79, IV 81, e.g. ἀφίκετο, ἀκοῦσαι. Radermacher² (p. 152) draws several exx. from apocryphal Acts of the Apostles. Pernot is exhaustive for the Gospels, and shows (pp. 103ff) that Mt often prefers infin. after verbs when Mk does not, thus, ὁμολογέω 14⁷ (cp. Mk 6²³), θέλω 15³² (cp. Mk 8³), δίδωμι 13¹¹ (cp. Mk 4¹¹), ἑτοιμάζω 26¹⁷ (cp. Mk 14¹²); and Mt tends to substitute an infin. for Mk's final ἵνα, thus ἀποστέλλω 21³⁴ (cp. Mk 12²), ἔρχομαι 28¹ (cp. Mk 16¹); or else εἰς τό c. inf. 26² for Mk's final ἵνα (cp. Mk 15²⁰). The fut. ptc. would have been more usual in class. Attic but it is scarcely used in NT.[1] In the Ptolemaic papyri ἀναβαίνω, διαβαίνω, ἀπέρχομαι, κατάγω are followed by infin. of purpose (Mayser II 1, 297). Witkowski ep.² 38, 34 ἐὰν ἀναβῶ κἀγὼ προσκυνῆσαι.—Xenophon of Ephesus p. 393, 29 ἐληλύθει προσεύξασθαι τῷ θεῷ.—Acta Petri et Pauli 17 ἀπῄει ποιῆσαι.—Mart. Petr. VI εἰσέρχομαι... σταυρωθῆναι.—Mart. Pauli IV ἔρχεται... κρῖναι. In the LXX there is a marked tendency to use the infin. after verbs of coming, going, and sending: e.g. Le 14⁴⁹ 17¹¹ 21¹⁷ Isa 61¹ᶠ. It is used also with verbs like δίδωμι, ἀποστέλλω, as in class. Attic: Mt 25³⁵ ἐδώκατέ μοι φαγεῖν, Mk 3¹⁴ ἀποστέλλῃ κηρύσσειν, 7⁴ παρέλαβον κρατεῖν, Ac 12⁴ 16⁴ παραδιδόναι φυλάσσειν.—Often δίδωμι, φαγεῖν, or πιεῖν.—Ac 1²⁴ᶠ ἐξελέξω... λαβεῖν, 20²⁸ ἔθετο ἐπισκόπους ποιμαίνειν, Jn 6³¹ ἄρτον... ἔδωκεν αὐτοῖς φαγεῖν (LXX Ps 78²⁴) 6⁵²; 4⁷·¹⁰ δός μοι πεῖν, 4³⁸ ἀπέστειλα ὑμᾶς θερίζειν. Ἔχω (cp. Byz. Greek): Jn 4³² βρῶσιν ἔχω φαγεῖν, (8⁶) 8²⁶ πολλὰ ἔχω... λαλεῖν, 16¹². Πέμπω: Jn 1³³ ὁ πέμψας με βαπτίζειν.

The construction with ἵνα is sometimes substituted for infin. in the papyri, as in the phrase δέξασθαι τὸν υἱὸν αὐτῆς εἶνα διακονεῖ ἡμῖν (P. Par 23, 22) which comes shortly after προσλάβεσθαι τὸν υἱὸν διακονεῖν ἡμῖν (22, 25) (165 B.C.), So also in NT: 1 Co 9¹⁵ ἀποθανεῖν ἤ... ἵνα... κενώσῃ, 14⁵ λαλεῖν... μᾶλλον... ἵνα προφητεύητε. It raises a question where the MSS differ between the constructions: have scribes and commentators introduced ἵνα or have atticistic correctors preferred the shorter form with the infin.? Mt 27²⁶ Mk 15¹⁵ Jn 19¹⁶ παρέδωκεν ἵνα σταυρωθῇ, Jn 5³⁶ δέδωκεν... ἵνα τελειώσω (Tert. corr. to τελειῶσαι), 11³¹ ὑπάγει... ἵνα κλαύσῃ (Chrys. corr. to κλαῦσαι), 55 ἀνέβησαν... ἵνα ἁγνίσωσιν (Chrys. ἁγνίσαι), 12²⁰ ἀναβαινόντων ἵνα προσκυνήσωσιν (Chrys. προσκυνῆσαι).

2. The infin. of purpose is helped by ὥστε (and ὡς?) in LXX, NT, and occasionally in the papyri (Mayser II 1, 298) and Josephus; it is common after NT, down to Byzantine period;

---

[1] Ac 24¹¹ ἀνέβην προσκυνήσων. Cp. Lk 18¹⁰ Ac 8²⁷.

it helped to give the dying infin. of purpose a little longer life in this period:

Mt 10¹ ἔδωκεν ἐξουσίαν ὥστε, 27¹ συμβούλιον ἔλαβον ὥστε θανατῶσαι αὐτόν (D corr. to ἵνα θανατώσουσιν), Lk 4²⁹ ἤγαγον... ὥστε κατακρημνίσαι (AC εἰς τό) 9⁵² εἰσῆλθον ὥστε ἑτοιμάσαι (vl. ὡς p⁴⁵ SB), 20²⁰ ἵνα ἐπιλάβωνται αὐτοῦ λόγου, ὥστε παραδοῦναι αὐτὸν τῇ ἀρχῇ τοῦ ἡγεμόνος (AWΓ εἰς τό), Ac 20²⁴ AHLP ὡς τελειῶσαι (E ὥστε, probably -τε has fallen out before τελ-). LXX Ge 15⁷ 1 Mac 4². ²⁸ 10³, 2 Mac 2⁶ Mart. Dasii 5 δέδοκται... ὥστε... προσαχθῆναι. Epict. IV 6, 8. ἐσπούδακας... μανθάνειν ὥστε ἄλυπος εἶναι. Final ὡς: Clem. Hom 12¹.

3. Ὥστε also appears with finite verb, imperative and subjunctive (Mayser II 1, 300): Ga 2¹³ ὥστε συναπήχθη (vl. συναπηχθῆναι) Jn 3¹⁶. Ὡς with indic.: Clem. Hom. 2²⁵; ὡς with subj. 12¹⁷.

4. Ὥστε c. infin. in a consecutive sense is more widely used than in class. Attic. Class. Greek would have indic. in Ac 15³⁹ ἐγένετο παροξυσμὸς ὥστε ἀποχωρισθῆναι αὐτοὺς ἀπ' ἀλλήλων. Clem. Hom. ὡς c. inf. 8¹¹ 20¹³.

5. Infin. without ὥστε, to express result. Lk 1⁵⁴ ἀντελάβετο Ἰσραὴλ... μνησθῆναι ἐλέους, 7² ποιῆσαι ἔλεος. The influence of Heb. infin. is likely in Lk 1–2 and the infin. is best rendered as a ptc. or gerundive (so also Mt 21³² Ac 7¹⁹ 15¹⁰ Ga 3¹⁰ Ph 3¹⁰).— Ac 5³ διὰ τί ἐπλήρωσεν... τὴν καρδίαν σου ψεύσασθαί σε, Heb 6¹⁰ οὐ γὰρ ἄδικος ὁ θεὸς ἐπιλαθέσθαι, Rev 5⁵ ἐνίκησεν... ἀνοῖξαι (B ὁ ἀνοίγων), 16⁹ οὐ μετενόησαν δοῦναι αὐτῷ δόξαν. Class.: Hdt V 76, Xen Hell. V 1, 14. Hellenistic: Epict. IV 1, 50, P. Oxy III 526, 3 (ii/A.D.), Herm. M. VIII 2, Did 4³. For ἵνα possibly expressing result, see p. 102.

6. The so-called Infinitive Absolute (class. ὡς ἐμοὶ δοκεῖν) is literary and very rarely found in papyri or NT: PSI IV 392, 6 (242 B.C.) ὅπερ σὺν θεῶι εἰπεῖν πεπείσμεθα. Cair. Zen. 11, 7 (256 B.C.) σὺν θεοῖς ἐλπίζω σε στεφανωθήσεσθαι.—NT: Heb 7⁹ ὡς ἔπος εἰπεῖν (frequent class.).—Ign. Trall. 10; Sm 2 τὸ δοκεῖν.—Diogn. 6¹ ἁπλῶς εἰπεῖν (see Schwyzer II 379).

(b) *Imperatival Infinitive:* see above, p. 78.

§ 2. Infinitive with Various Case-functions

(a) *Without Article*

To supplement verbs of perception, belief, saying, etc., it was usual in class. Greek to have the infin. as the object, but the ptc. was also possible; and with all but verbs of believing it was also permissible to have a ὅτι construction. Very prominent in NT is the vast reduction in the use of infin. and an extension of the ὅτι construction, which now becomes usual except in the more educated writers, Luke, Paul, Hebrews. Even verbs of believing now have this construction. Ὡς is nearly confined to Luke and Paul[1], and πῶς is now being confused with ὡς. Later on, πῶς absorbs all the functions of ὅτι, ὡς, and finally drives them out altogether. The beginnings of this seem to be appearing already in NT[2]. We notice too a reluctance to use the class. indirect speech form of accusative and infinitive; even Luke prefers the direct form (Ac 1⁴ 25⁴ᶠ). For Mark, see Zerwick *Untersuchungen* 24ff. Later on, ὡς ὅτι too becomes the equivalent of ὅτι (Mayser II 3, 45 n. 1; Jannaris § 1754; Sophocles Lex. s.v. ὡς): Hom. Clem. 1⁷ 11²⁸ 14⁷ 16⁶·⁷, P. Oxy XVI 1831, 1; 1833, 1 (v/A.D.) ὡς ὅτιπερ. The beginnings of this (although without a verb of speaking to introduce it) may lie in NT use of ὡς ὅτι (*i.e., viz., to the effect that*), 2 Co 5¹⁹ (RV *to wit*; RSV *that is*; NEB *what I mean is, that . . .*) 11²¹, 2 Th 2².

1. *Infinitive* as a Direct Object. *Verba putandi* in strong contrast to class. Greek now commonly are followed by ὅτι in Hell. Greek (Radermacher² 190). But δοκέω c. accus. and infin. 1 Co 12²³ 2 Co 11¹⁶; ἡγέομαι c. accus. infin. Ph 3⁸; λογίζομαι c. inf. Ro 3²⁸ 6¹¹ 14¹⁴ 2 Co 11⁵ Ph 3¹³; νομίζω c. inf. Lk 2⁴⁴ etc. and Paul; οἴομαι c. inf. Jn 21²⁵ Ph 1¹⁷ 1 Clem 30⁴ OT 2 Clem 14²; πείθομαι c. accus. inf. Ac 26²⁶; πέποιθα and πέπεισμαι Lk 20⁶ Ro 2¹⁹ 2 Co 10⁷, Ign Trall 3²; πιστεύω c. infin. Ac 15¹¹ Ro 14²; ὑπονοέω c. accus. inf. Ac 13²⁵ 27²⁷ Herm. V. IV 1, 6. In general the infin. with these verbs is confined to Luke, Paul and Heb., as a mark of literary style (Mayser II 1, 312). Ὀμνύω ὅτι (Mt 26⁷⁴ Mk 14⁷¹ Rev 10⁶) is unclassical; see by contrast Heb 3¹⁸ (fut. infin.). With *verba volendi* and *iubendi*, in class. Greek ὥστε was often

---

[1] Mk 12²⁶ vl. πῶς, Lk 6⁴ vl. πῶς, 8⁴⁷ (D ὅτι), 23⁵⁵ 24⁶ (D ὅσα) ³⁵ (D ὅτι), Ac 10²⁸·³⁸ 20²⁰ (πῶς at ¹⁸), Ro 1⁹, Ph 1⁸, 1 Th 2¹⁰. The Hellenistic use of ὡς = ὅτι is the true explanation of Mk 14⁷² Lk 22⁶¹, not that in *Nov. Test.* 2, 1958, 272ff.

[2] Πῶς after ἀνέγνωτε Mt 12⁴ Mk 2²⁶ 12²⁶ vl.; after ἐθεώρει Mk 12⁴¹; after ἐπέχων Lk 14⁷; after ἀπαγγέλλω Ac 11¹³ 1 Th 1⁹. See also perhaps Mk 10²³ (A. Pallis, *Notes on St. Mark*, new ed. Lond., 1932, 35), and Pallis also includes Mk 10²⁴ λέγει αὐτοῖς· Τέκνα, πῶς δύσκολόν ἐστιν, which he explains as hyperbaton for λέγει πῶς (= ὅτι) δυσκ. ἐστιν, τέκνα. See also Barn. 11¹ 14⁶, 1 Clem 19³ 21³ 34⁵ 37² 50¹. Epict. IV 13, 15: δεῖξόν μοι σεαυτὸν πιστόν . . . καὶ ὄψει ὅτι πῶς οὐκ ἀναμένω (yet ὄψει in II 12, 4).

added to the infin. or ὅπως and fut. ind. substituted, and later ἵνα which we find often in NT except in Luke, Paul and Hebrews. Ἵνα after ἐρωτάω is Hellenistic (Mk 7³⁶ etc., Ptol. pap. Mayser II 1, 243). The accus. of the object with infin. after παραινέω is a mark of literary style (only Ac 27²²). Θέλω usually has accus. and infin., as in Ptol. papyri (Mayser II 1, 160), but ἵνα in Mt 7¹²; 1 Co 14⁵ has both (θέλω ὑμᾶς λαλεῖν ..., μᾶλλον δὲ ἵνα προφητεύητε); cp. MGr θά = θενά = θέλω ἵνα. In Jn 8⁵⁶ ἵνα follows ἠγαλλιάσατο (*was glad that he should*), just as it follows ἐχάρην in pap. BU IV 1081, 5 (ii–iii/A.D.), whereas the ptc. follows χαίρω in Ptol. pap.-(Mayser II 1, 175, 353). Different from class. Greek is the passive construction (as in Latin) instead of active after *verba iubendi*: Mt 18²⁵ ἐκέλευσεν αὐτὸν πραθῆναι, Ac 5²¹ ἀπέστειλεν ἀχθῆναι αὐτούς (P. Tebt. 331. 16 [A.D. 131] ἀξιῶ ἀχθῆναι αὐτούς), 23³ κελεύεις με τύπτεσθαι, Herm. S. IX 8, 3 ἐκέλευσε διὰ τῶν παρθένων ἀπεχθῆναι (P. Oxy I 33. col. II 14 [end ii/B.C.] ἐκέλευσεν αὐτὸν ἀπεχθῆναι, Mart. Matth. 243, 18ff ἐκέλευσεν πλῆθος ἀνθρακιᾶς ἐνεχθῆναι; followed by active φέρειν δέ. Mk 6²⁷ ἐπέταξεν ἐνεχθῆναι (but SBCΔ act.: ἐνέγκαι) τὴν κεφαλὴν αὐτοῦ (cp.³⁹), Ac 22²⁴ εἴπας μάστιξιν ἀνετάζεσθαι αὐτόν (but act. in D* ἀνετάζειν), Mk 10⁴⁹ εἶπεν αὐτὸν φωνηθῆναι ADWX (but in SBCLΔ corr. to direct command). But active (like class. Greek): Ac 23¹⁰ 16²² Mk 6³⁹ ἐπέταξεν αὐτοῖς ἀνακλῖναι πάντας (SB*G ἀνακλιθῆναι, to harm.¹ with Mt 14⁹), 5⁴³ D δοῦναι (rest δοθῆναι). There is textual variation in Mk 8⁷ between παραθεῖναι, παρατεθῆναι, and numerous examples of alternation in apocryphal Acts (Ljungvik SSAA 42, n. 2). For LXX, see Bonnaccorsi 553, Abel § 309.

2. *Infin.* in looser dependence on main verb, without any apparent case-relationship.

a. Adverbial: with *be able, know how, begin, must*, etc., the Ptolemaic papyri and NT have only the infin.: δύναμαι, ἰσχύω, ἔχω (*must* Lk 12⁵⁰), ἄρχομαι. The latter never occurs with ptc. in NT, as in class. Greek (see pp. 154f); it is very frequent in the Syn. Gospels especially in a Semitic pleonastic sense as ἤρξατο, ἤρξαντο (see *JThS* 28, 352f), as it has very little force; in no instance must it definitely mean *begin to*, and often it is plainly better to ignore the auxiliary; it appears to be a periphrasis for both aor. and impf. It is liked by Mark (26 times, + 3 in D) more than Matthew (6 times) where it may even have some point (4¹⁷ 16²¹). Also with infin. are προλαμβάνω Mk 14⁸ (= class. φθάνω c. ptc.), κινδυνεύω Ac 19²⁷· ⁴⁰, προσποιέομαι Lk 24²⁸, προστίθεμαι *to do more* (see p. 227); verbs meaning to *instigate, compel* (but πείθω, ποιέω, ἀγγαρεύω also have ἵνα); *to be on guard, be ashamed, be frightened* (but ἵνα with βλέπετε, φυλάσσομαι, προσέχω), *to allow* (but ἀφίημι with ἵνα Mk 11¹⁶), and there is in general a larger freedom to use the infin. in loose connection

---

¹ Nevertheless, this accus. c. infin. construction after a verb which already has an object has ample precedent: Pass. Barth. 133, 29f σὺ κελεύεις ἡμᾶς λυθῆναι αὐτήν; Mart. Andr. alt. 58, 14f κελεύσας τοῖς δημίοις ἀδιατμήτους αὐτοῦ τὰς ἀγκύλας καταλειφθῆναι; also Acta Joh. 170. 29f; Acta Thom. 218, 25ff.

with the verb perhaps under Semitic influence: e.g. *to see to cast out* (Mt 7[5] Lk 6[42]), *looked round to see* (Mk 5[32]), *be a long time in coming* (Lk 12[45]).

  b. Nominal. An infin. or ἵνα will follow not only a personal verb but also an adj. or noun, or an impersonal verb.

  (i) *Nouns*: the Ptolemaic papyri have infin. after ἐξουσία (NT), κήρυγμα, πρόσταγμα, σχολή, χρεία (NT), ὥρα (NT) etc. The NT has ἵνα after συνήθεια (Jn 18[39]), ὥρα (Jn 12[23] 13[1] 16[2]); ὥρα followed by infin. as in class. Greek (Ro 13[11]); καιρὸς τοῦ c. inf. (1 Pt 4[17]); καιρός c. inf. (Heb 11[15] Rev 11[18]); καιρός c. ὅτε (2 Ti 4[3]), ὥρα c. ὅτε (Jn 4[21. 23] 5[25] 16[2. 25]), ὥρα ἐν ᾗ (Jn 5[28]). Apparently the use of ὥρα and καιρός with ὅτε or ἐν ᾗ is confined to definite prophecy; the inf. indicating a nearer imminence. The NT also has infin. after ἐξουσίαν ἔχω (Jn 10[18] 1 Co 9[4ff] Heb 13[10] Rev 11[6]); δίδωμι ἐξουσίαν c. infin. (Jn 1[12] Rev 13[5]), c. ὥστε (Mt 10[1]), c. ἵνα (Ac 8[19]), and χρείαν ἔχω c. infin. (Mt 3[14] etc. Jn 13[10] same subject, and ἵνα where there is a new subject [1], 1 Th 4[9] S°D*H), τοῦ c. accus. infin. (Heb 5[12]), c. ἵνα (Jn 2[25] 16[30] 1 Jn 2[27]).

  (ii) *Adjectives and adverbs.* The Ptol. pap. display ἄξιος (NT), δυνατός (NT), ἐπιτήδειος, ἕτοιμος (NT), ἑτοίμως (NT), ἱκανός (NT), πιστός, ὥριμος: all with infin. In the NT: ἱκανός c. ἵνα (Mt 8[8] Lk 7[6]), c. infin. (elsewhere), ἄξιος c. ἵνα (Jn 1[27]), c. infin. often, c. τοῦ and infin. (1 Co 16[4]), c. relative clause (Lk 7[4]), ἕτοιμος, ἑτοίμως ἔχω c. inf. (Ac 21[13] 2 Co 12[14] 1 Pt 4[5]), ἐν ἑτοίμῳ ἔχω c. inf. (2 Co 10[6]).

  3. *The Infinitive as Subject.*

  Impersonal verbs: δεῖ, συμφέρει, ἔξεστιν, ἐγένετο, γίνεται, συνέβη —usually (acc. c.) infin., but sometimes ἵνα (e.g. συμφέρει ἵνα Mt 5[29f] 18[6] etc., ἔδει ἵνα πάθῃ Barn 5[13]). For the Ptol. pap. Mayser II 1, 307f (infinitive).

  Neuter adjectives or nouns with the copula or without: Ptol. pap. ἀναγκαῖον, δίκαιον, ἔθος, ἐπιτήδειον, etc. (Mayser II 1, 306f) mainly infinitives. NT: δυνατόν c. infin. (Ac 2[24]), ἀρκετόν c. ἵνα (Mt 10[25]), καλόν c. infin. (1 Co 9[15]), ἐλάχιστον ἵνα (1 Co 4[3]), βρῶμα ἵνα (Jn 4[34]).

  Preceding demonstrative pronoun: in Jn particularly, the infin. gives way to ἵνα (1 Jn 5[3] αὕτη ... ἵνα ...), especially if the epexegesis is theory rather than fact (Jn 15[8] ἵνα καρπὸν πολὺν φέρητε). For fact he often substitutes ὅτι (1 Jn 2[3] 3[16] 5[2]).—Infin.: Ac 15[28] 1 Th 4[3] Eph 3[8] Jas 1[27].—But ἵνα: Lk 1[43] (although the epexegesis is fact) Jn 6[40] 17[3] 1 Jn 3[11. 23] 4[21] 2 Jn[6].

  In Hebraistic figures of speech: Lk 21[14] Ac 19[21] τιθέναι (τίθεσθαι) ἐν τῇ καρδίᾳ (τῷ πνεύματι): Hebraism. Ac 16[14] ἧς διήνοιξεν τὴν καρδίαν (Hebraism) προσέχειν (cp. τοῦ inf. Lk 24[45]). Lk 2[1] δόγμα ... ἀπογράφεσθαι πᾶσαν τὴν οἰκουμένην. Ac 14[5] ἐγένετο ὁρμή.—On the other hand we find ἵνα following: Mt 18[14] etc. θέλημά ἐστιν, Jn 13[34] Ac 17[15] ἐντολὴ ἵνα, Ac 27[42] βουλὴ ἐγένετο, Jn 13[2] *put into the heart* ἵνα παραδοῖ αὐτόν.

---

[1] Hence Jn 16[30] the vl. of Syr[lew] is not likely to be correct, having ἵνα introducing the same subject: οὐ χρείαν ἔχεις ἵνα τινά ἐρωτᾷς. Nor can οὐ χρείαν ἔχετε γράφειν be correct in S*AD° at 1 Th 4[9].

4. The Infinitive with πρίν, πρὶν ἤ.

Πρίν occurs three times (all iii/B.C.) and πρὶν ἤ five times in Ptol. pap. in Mayser's list. In NT and Koine generally we do not find the indic. but (a) after a positive sentence, accus. c. infin.: Mt 26³⁴.⁷⁵ (A adds ἤ) Mk 14⁷² Lk 22⁶¹ (B adds ἤ) Jn 4⁴⁹ 8⁵⁸ (not D and lat)¹ 14²⁹ Ac 2²⁰ OT (WH text); ἤ c. infin. Mt 1¹⁸ πρὶν ἤ συνελθεῖν αὐτούς, Mk 14³⁰ (SD om ἤ), Ac 2²⁰ (WHᵐᵍ) 7². (b) after a negative sentence: ἤ c. subjunctive Lk 2²⁶; ἤ c. optative Ac 25¹⁶; ἤ c. infin. Diogn. 2³. In LXX and NT πρίν is being superceded by πρὸ τοῦ, but it occurs mainly in To, Si, Isa, and 2-4 Mac.

(b) Articular Infinitive ²

Essentially the function of an article with an infin. is the same as with a noun since the infin. is probably in origin a noun, except that with the infin. the article often appears for no reason except to supply the case-ending which is lacking. The cult of the articular infinitive was promoted by the Atticists but it is already seen in Luke, Paul, Hebrews, James and Peter, and especially in the higher kinds of Koine writing ³. Votaw ⁴ shows in his thesis that in the OT translation books the anarthrous and articular infinitives are about equal in number, whereas in NT the articular is rarer. It is almost absent from the Johannine writings, but in the Ptol. pap. its use is not confined to literary or official texts (Mayser II 1, 321).

It serves the purpose of almost every kind of subordinate clause.

A. Without Preposition.

1. Τό c. infin. serves the purpose of a mere infin. comparatively rarely in the Ptol. pap. and almost exclusively in the bureaucratic style. It is hardly used in the NT outside Paul:

Mt 15²⁰ τὸ ... φαγεῖν (subject), 20²³ τὸ καθίσαι obj., Mk 9¹⁰ τὸ ἀναστῆναι (subject), 12³³ τὸ ἀγαπᾶν (subject),' Ac 25¹¹ τὸ ἀποθανεῖν, Ro 4¹³ τὸ κληρονόμον αὐτὸν εἶναι, 7¹⁸ τὸ θέλειν ... τὸ κατεργάζεσθαι, 13⁸ τὸ ... ἀγαπᾶν, 1 Co 11⁶ τὸ κείρασθαι ἤ ξύρασθαι, 14³⁹, 2 Co 8¹⁰ᵗ τὸ θέλειν, Ph 1²⁴ τὸ δὲ ἐπιμένειν τῇ σαρκί, 2⁶ 4¹⁰ τὸ ὑπὲρ ἐμοῦ φρονεῖν, Ga 4¹⁸ (SABC om τό), Heb 10³¹. 1 Co 7²⁶ 2 Co 7¹¹ 9¹ περισσόν μοι ἐστιν τὸ γράφειν, 10² δέομαι τὸ μὴ παρὼν θαρρῆσαι, Ro 14¹³ τὸ μὴ

---

¹ For πρίν without verb, used as preposition, see pp. 260, 270.
² Goodwin 315. Moulton Einl. 343. H. F. Allen, op. cit. 29ff.
³ There is but one instance of the very literary practice of adding an adj. (Heb 2¹⁵ διὰ παντὸς τοῦ ζῆν) as in 2 Mac 7⁹ ἐκ τοῦ παρόντος ζῆν, and class. Greek.
⁴ C. W. Votaw, *The Use of the Infin. in Biblical Greek*, Chicago 1896.

τιθέναι πρόσκομμα, ²¹, 2 Co 2¹, 1 Th 3³ τὸ μηδένα σαίνεσθαι, 4⁶ τὸ μὴ ὑπερβαίνειν, Ac 4¹⁸ τὸ καθόλου μὴ φθέγγεσθαι (S*B om τό).—LXX 2 Esd 6⁸ τὸ μὴ καταργηθῆναι.

2. Τοῦ c. infin.¹ is used often in LXX (Hebrew Infin. Construct), more rarely in the Ptol. pap.; it belongs to a higher level of the Koine, and is mainly found in Paul (13) and Luke (44) in NT, and scarcely elsewhere except in Mt and Mk ².

(i) Epexegetical: after nouns like χρόνος (Lk 1⁵⁷ τοῦ τεκεῖν), καιρός (1 Pt 4¹⁷), ἐπιποθία (Ro 15²³), ἐξουσία (Lk 10¹⁹), εὐκαιρία (Lk 22⁶), γνώμη (Ac 20³) *to be of opinion that*, also ἐλπίς and χρεία. See also Lk 2⁶ Ac 27²⁰ 1 Co 9¹⁰ Heb 5¹². But John on the contrary sometimes introduces ἵνα instead of τοῦ c. infin. after nouns like χρεία, ὥρα, χρόνος. Rev 12⁷ is possibly epexegetical or appositional ὁ Μιχαὴλ καὶ οἱ ἄγγελοι αὐτοῦ τοῦ ACP (p⁴⁷ SB om τοῦ) πολεμῆσαι; on the other hand, it is more probably a translation of Semitic imperatival ל c. infin. (Moulton-Howard 448f); note the subjects of the infin. in the nom., which is not Greek at all; in support of imper. cp. LXX Hos 9¹³ Ἐφραίμ τοῦ ἐξαγαγεῖν *Ephraim must* . . ., Eccl 3¹⁵ 1 Ch 9²⁵; elsewhere in Rev τοῦ c. inf. is also never sure (9¹⁰ p⁴⁷ SAP om τοῦ; quite weak vl. 14¹⁵); Debrunner suggested that the author was following his tendency elsewhere to use the nom. in preference to another case, so here instead of gen. or dat.³—After adjectives, as class. (Xen. Anab. 7, 7, 48; Polyb. 39, 9, 12): Lk 17¹ ἀνένδεκτον . . . τοῦ . . . μὴ ἐλθεῖν *impossible that*, 24²⁵, Ac 23¹⁵ ἕτοιμοί ἐσμεν τοῦ ἀνελεῖν αὐτόν, 1 Co 16⁴ ἄξιον . . . τοῦ πορεύεσθαι.—After verbs which in class. Greek took the gen.: Lk 1⁹ ἔλαχε τοῦ θυμιᾶσαι (so LXX 1 Km 14⁴⁷; but class. has inf. only), 2 Co 1⁸ ἐξαπορηθῆναι . . . τοῦ ζῆν.

(ii) Consecutive or final sense, especially Luke and Paul, and the most common type in NT; on the whole, however, Paul prefers εἰς τό or πρὸς τό for final and consec.: Mt 13³ ἐξῆλθεν . . . τοῦ σπείρειν, 2¹³ ζητεῖν τοῦ ἀπολέσαι, 21³² μετεμελήθητε τοῦ πιστεῦσαι (consec.), 3¹³ 11¹ 24⁴⁵ (D om τοῦ); Lk 2²¹ *eight days* τοῦ περιτεμνεῖν (fin. or consec.), Ro 8¹² ὀφειλέται . . . τοῦ κατὰ σάρκα ζῆν, 1²⁴ τοῦ ἀτιμάζεσθαι (consec.), 11⁸ OT ὀφθαλμοὺς τοῦ μὴ βλέπειν *such as*, ¹⁰ OT σκοτισθήτωσαν οἱ ὀφθ. τοῦ μὴ βλέπειν, 1 Co 10¹³ τοῦ δύνασθαι, Ac 14⁹ πίστιν τοῦ σωθῆναι (consec.), 9¹⁵, 2 Co 8¹¹ ἡ προθυμία τοῦ θέλειν, Ph 3²¹ τὴν ἐνέργειαν τοῦ δύνασθαι αὐτόν *the power by which he can*, Ac 3¹² Ro 7³ Ph 3¹⁰ Heb 10⁷ OT 11⁵ Hom. Clem. 9²². Often the consec. sense is only weak: Lk 1⁷³ 4¹⁰ 5⁷, 24²⁵ βραδεῖς τῇ καρδίᾳ τοῦ πιστεῦσαι, Ac 7¹⁹ 18¹⁰, Ro 6⁶ 7⁸

---

¹ Schwyzer II 132. Birklein, *Entwicklungsgeschichte des substantivierten Infin.* (= Schenz, Beitr. III 1, Würzburg 1888) 55f. Moulton-Howard 448ff.

² But see Thuc. I 4, etc., and Tacitus *Ann.* II 59 Aegyptum proficiscitur cognoscendae antiquitatis.

³ Blass-Debr. § 400, 8.

Ph 3¹⁰, LXX 3 Km 17²⁶.—The mere infin. already has the same final sense, but for the purpose of clarity τοῦ may be added to a second final infin. (only in writings with pretence to style, viz. Mt Lk Ac, e.g. Mt 2¹³ μέλλει γὰρ Η. ζητεῖν τὸ παιδίον τοῦ ἀπολέσαι αὐτό, Lk 1⁷⁷ ἐτοιμάσαι ... τοῦ δοῦναι, ⁷⁸ᶠ ἐπιφᾶναι τοῖς ἐν σκότει ... τοῦ κατευθῦναι, 2²². ²⁴ παραστῆσαι ... καὶ τοῦ δοῦναι, Ac 26¹⁷ᶠ ἀποστέλλω σε, ἀνοῖξαι ..., τοῦ ἐπιστρέψαι ..., τοῦ λαβεῖν. For τοῦ after ἐγένετο, see Ac 10²⁵.— Τοῦ μή c. inf. after verbs of hindering, ceasing, etc. (Lk and LXX) has class. precedent (Xen. Anab. 3, 5, 11), but the use goes further in NT and LXX and τοῦ μή has a consecutive sense: Lk 4⁴² 17¹ 24¹⁶ Ac 10⁴⁷ 14¹⁸ 20²⁰· ²⁷, LXX Ge 16² συνέκλεισεν τοῦ μή, 20⁶, Ps 38² 68²⁴ (Ro 11¹⁰).—Another Septuagintism, especially in Lk-Ac and Jas, is τοῦ c. inf. after verbs which in class. Greek would take the simple infin., e.g. Lk 4¹⁰ ΟΤ ἐντέλλεσθαι (Ps 90 (91)¹¹), 5⁷ κατανεύειν, 9⁵¹ στηρίζειν τὸ πρόσωπον, Ac 3¹² ποιεῖν (BU II 625, 28 πᾶν ποιεῖν τοῦ: ii–iii/A.D.), Ac 2¹ D 10²⁵ (not D) Act. Barn. 7 ἐγένετο, 15²⁰ ἐπιστεῖλαι αὐτοῖς τοῦ ἀπέχεσθαι, 21¹² παρεκαλοῦμεν ... τοῦ μὴ ἀναβαίνειν αὐτόν, 23¹⁵ ἕτοιμος, ²⁰ συντίθεσθαι. 27¹ ἐκρίθη τοῦ *it was determined to*, 20³ ἐγένετο γνώμη τοῦ, Jas 5¹⁷ προσεύχεσθαι, Herm. V. III 7, 2 ἀνέβη ἐπὶ τὴν καρδίαν; LXX e.g. 3 Km 1³⁵ ἐνετειλάμην, Ezk 21¹¹ 1 Mac 5³⁹ ἕτοιμος.

3. Τῷ c. infin. is sometimes instrumental in the Koine but usually causal (Mayser II 1, 323f; II 3, 61¹⁰; Polyb.). Only once in NT and causal: 2 Co 2¹³ *had no rest because* τῷ μὴ εὑρεῖν με Τίτον (various corrections: DE ἐν τῷ μή; LP τὸ μή; S*C² τοῦ μή).

B. *With a Preposition or Prepositional Adverb* ¹.

The construction was frequent enough in class. Greek, but in Hellenistic (especially NT) its frequence is proportionately far higher, particularly εἰς τό and ἐν τῷ. The prepositions occur in the following order of frequence in NT (Burton § 407): εἰς (63–72), ἐν (52–56), διά (27–31), μετά 15, πρός 12, πρό (9), ἀντί, ἐκ, ἕνεκεν, ἕως 1. In the Ptol. pap. on the other hand it is: διά 112, περί 38, μεχρί 18, πρός 16, ἐπί 15, ἕως 14, πρό 11, εἰς 10, χάριν 10, ὑπό 10, παρά, ἕνεκα 8, πρός c. dat. 7, ἐν, μετά 5, ἅμα, ἐκ 4, πλήν 3, ἄνευ 2, ἀντί 1. Conspicuous is the frequence of διά in the Koine, and of εἰς and ἐν in Biblical Greek.

1. Διά τό c. infin. almost = ὅτι or διότι, denoting cause: Mt 13⁵· ⁶ 24¹² Mk 4⁵· ⁶ Lk 2⁴ 6⁴⁸ 8⁶ 9⁷ etc., in Jn 2²⁴ διὰ τὸ αὐτὸν γινώσκειν πάντας (om. Syrˢⁱⁿ) (the preposition with art. infin. is unusual in Jn),

---

¹ Mayser II 1, 324ff. Burton §§ 406–417. Goodwin §§ 800–803. Johannessohn DGPS *passim*.

§ 2] THE VERB: NOUN FORMS 143

Ac 4^2 8^{11} etc., Ph 1^7 (no other ex. in Paul), Heb 7^{23f} 10^2, Jas 4^2 (parallel with διότι in³). LXX Ge 39^9 Ex 16^8 17^7 19^{18} 33^3 Dt 1^{36} 1 Mac 6^{53} 10^{77} 11^2 14^{35} 2 Mac 2^{11} $3^{18.\ 38}$ 4^{30} 6^{11} 8^{36} 10^{13} 15^{17} 3 Mac 1^{11} 5^{30} 4 Mac 15^4. In Mk 5^4 it is evidential rather than causal (Burton § 408).

2. Εἰς τό c. inf. = ἵνα or ὥστε, expresses purpose or result in Xenophon and often in LXX and post-Christian Greek, and is difficult to distinguish from τοῦ c. inf.; it occurs in Heb, 1 Pt, and Jas, but especially in Paul where it expresses hardly anything but purpose (e.g. Ro 12^3 εἰς τὸ σωφρονεῖν, while Luke favours τοῦ c. inf. It may also express " tendency, measure of effect, or result " (Burton § 411). In LXX: = לְ Ge 30^{38} εἰς τὸ πιεῖν, 32^8 εἰς τὸ σώζεσθαι, 49^{15} εἰς τὸ πονεῖν, Ex 27^{20} εἰς φῶς καῦσαι, 1 Mac 12^{36} εἰς τὸ διαχωρίσαι, 2 Mac 1^3 εἰς τὸ σέβεσθαι, 2^{25} εἰς τὸ . . . ἀναλαβεῖν, 3 Mac 6^6 εἰς τὸ μὴ λατρεῦσαι, 7^3 εἰς τὸ . . . κολάζεσθαι: Johannessohn DGPS 300–2. See Mayser II 1, 331 and Moulton Proleg. 220 for papyrus exx.: here it is telic, but remoter purpose is in mind, which is just the position in NT according to Moulton. It is not strictly final.

These exx. seem to be final or very near it:
Mt 20^{19} εἰς τὸ ἐμπαῖξαι, 26^2 27^{31}.—Mk 14^{55} (D ἵνα θανατώσουσιν). —Lk 5^{17} (not D).—Lacking in Joh. writings.—Ac 7^{19}.—Ro $1^{11.\ 20}$ (but a causal clause follows, and so may this be; as the passage deals with divine action, however, it is better to retain the usual near-final meaning of εἰς τό, whatever theologians may say: i.e. RV text is correct against RSV and NEB), 3^{26} (parall. to ^{25} εἰς ἔνδειξιν), $4^{11.\ 11.\ 16.\ 18}$ 7^4 8^{29}, Eph 1^{12}, Ph 1^{10}, 1 Th 2^{16} εἰς τὸ ἀναπληρῶσαι the purpose of God (final), 3^5 *in order to know*, 1 Co 10^6 9^{18}.—Heb 2^{17} 8^3 (6 other exx. in Heb, all final).

These exx. may have a looser connection with what goes before. Here we are reminded of Westcott's distinction between εἰς τό and ἵνα, especially where they occur in close proximity; εἰς τό marks the remoter aim. Moulton (Proleg. 218ff) felt that in Heb. the use was uniformly telic, but Paul's use was not so uniform:—

Ro 12^3, φρονεῖν εἰς τὸ σωφρονεῖν, 1 Co 8^{10} εἰς τὸ ἐσθίειν expresses a measure of effect (*leading him to eat*), 11^{22} μὴ γὰρ οἰκίας οὐκ ἔχετε εἰς τὸ ἐσθίειν καὶ πίνειν *houses to eat and drink in*, 2 Co 8^6 εἰς τό *to such a degree that*, Ga 3^{17}, 1 Th 2^{12} either equivalent to simple infin. or to ἵνα after verbs of exhorting, etc., 3^{10} δεόμενοι εἰς τὸ ἰδεῖν = ἵνα ἰδῶμεν, 4^9 same (epexegetic).—Heb 11^3 *by faith we perceive that the universe was fashioned by the word of God* εἰς τὸ μὴ ἐκ φαινομένων τὸ βλεπόμενον γεγονέναι: perhaps consec. (NEB), but Westcott urged its final force because Heb always makes εἰς τό c. inf. final.—Jas 1^{19} ταχὺς εἰς τὸ ἀκοῦσαι the infin. simply limits an adj. as it limits a noun in Ph 1^{23}: τὴν ἐπιθυμίαν ἔχων εἰς τὸ ἀναλῦσαι (p⁴⁶ DEFG om εἰς in error).

3. Μετά τό c. inf. indicates time: *after*. Mt 26^{32}, Mk 1^{14} 14^{28} 16^{19}, Lk 12^5 22^{20}, Ac 1^3 7^4 10^{41} 15^{13} 19^{21} 20^1, 1 Co 11^{25}, Heb $10^{15.\ 26}$.— LXX Ge 5^4 etc., Ru 2^{11}, 1 Km 1^9 5^9, 1 Mac $1^{9.\ 20}$.—For Polyb. and Diod. Sic. see Krebs, *Die Präp. bei Polyb.* 61.

4. Πρός τό c. inf. indicates purpose but is sometimes weakened to *with reference to*, and is much rarer than εἰς τό. It may express tendency and ultimate goal, rather than purpose, as in papyri.

Mt 5²⁸ ὁ βλέπων γυναῖκα πρὸς τὸ ἐπιθυμῆσαι: there is hardly any telic force, but simple accompaniment (*and*); not even consecutive 6¹ πρὸς τὸ θεαθῆναι αὐτοῖς (final), 13³⁰ 23⁵ 26¹².—Mk 13²².—Lk 18¹ πρὸς τὸ δεῖν προσεύχεσθαι *with regard to*.—Ac 3¹⁹ SB (rest εἰς).—2 Co 3¹³ final, Eph 6¹¹ (DEFG εἰς), 1 Th 2⁹, 2 Th 3⁶.—Jas 3³ TR.

LXX: Je 34¹⁰, 1 Mac 10³⁸ 12¹⁰, 2 Mac 4⁴⁵ 5²⁷, 3 Mac 4¹¹ (all final). Polyb. 1, 48, 5.—Jos. Ant. 14, 170; 15, 148, etc.

No doubt the obvious correspondence with the Heb. לְ c. inf. assisted in the weakening of this expression in Bibl. Greek, till it means simply *in — ing* or is merely like a simple ptc, as in לֵאמֹר.

5. Παρά τό c. inf. is not NT, but 1 Clem 39⁵· ⁶ = LXX Jb 4²⁰· ²¹ *because*, Polybius, papyri. LXX: causal Ge 29²⁰ (A om) Ex 14¹¹ Dt 9²⁸ 4 Km 1³· ⁶· ¹⁶ A Ba 3²⁸ Ze 3⁶ 4 Mac 10¹⁹ Dit. Syll.³ 834¹⁰.

6. Ἀντί τοῦ *instead of* (original meaning): Jas 4¹⁵. But causal Ezk 29⁹ 34⁷⁻⁹ 36³, pap. 113 B.C.

7. Διὰ παντὸς τοῦ ζῆν Heb. 2¹⁵.

8. Ἐκ τοῦ 2 Co 8¹¹ ἔχειν *according to your means* (cp. καθὸ ἂν ἔχῃ ¹²).

9. Ἕνεκεν τοῦ 2 Co 7¹² φανερωθῆναι (ἕν. redundant, but analogy of ἕν. τοῦ ἀδικήσαντος just before. Ἕνεκα before τοῦ c. inf. in Joseph. Ant. 11, 293, and in papyri (Mayser II 1, 325), and LXX 1 Esd 8²¹ ἕνεκεν τοῦ μὴ γενέσθαι ὀργήν, Am 1⁶ 2⁴ etc., and Menander Fr. 425, 2.

10. Ἕως τοῦ Ac 8⁴⁰ ἐλθεῖν (founded on the analogy of πρίν, and post-class.); Polyb., Joseph., etc., pap. from iii/B.C.; LXX especially frequent with ἐλθεῖν Ge 10¹⁹ 19²² 43²⁵] Mac 7⁴⁵ (without τοῦ) 16⁹; Ge 3¹⁹ 8⁷ 13¹⁰ 24³³ 28¹⁵ 33³ 1 Mac 3³³ 5¹⁹· ⁵⁴ 14⁴¹ (Johannessohn DGPS 304).

11. Μέχρι (ἄχρι) τοῦ c. inf. (class.) not Bibl. Greek.

12. Πρὸ τοῦ *before*. In all parts of LXX (usually = בְּטֶרֶם) but only twice in Isa, twice in 2–4 Mac, and not in Wi or Si (these books prefer πρίν): Ge 17, Ex 2, Le 1, Dt 1, Jos 1, JgRu 2, 4 Km 2, Ch 2, To 5, Jdt 2, Jb 2, Ps 6, Pr 6, MP 5, Isa 2, Je 4, Ezk 1, 2 Mac 2. With pres., Jn 17⁵ εἶναι, D γενέσθαι). With aor. Mt 6⁸, Lk 2²¹ 22¹⁵ Ac 23¹⁵ Jn 1⁴⁹ 13¹⁹, Ga 2¹² πρὸ τοῦ γὰρ ἐλθεῖν τινας. 3²³. In Ptol. pap. only aor. inf. (Mayser II 1, 327).

Of other genitive prepositions, NT has no πλήν (class. *except*) or ὑπέρ (class. final; 2 Mac 4³⁶), and no ἀπό, ἐπί, μετά, περί, ἄνευ (Am 3⁵), χωρίς or χάριν.

13. Ἐν τῷ c. infin.[1] is a marked feature of the style of Luke; in a temporal sense it occurs about 30 times in Lk, but only 5 in Ac. In its temporal sense it is a Hebraism and non-classical: it is the usual LXX rendering of בְּ c. infin. (Heb) and it renders כְּ c. infin. (Aram. Dan

---

[1] Mayser II 1. 328; Moulton-Howard 451; and see above (Introduction p. 8).

§ 2] THE VERB: NOUN FORMS 145

6²¹ Θ). It is doubtful whether its temporal sense occurs in Soph. *Ajax* 554 ἐν τῷ φρονεῖν γὰρ μηδὲν ἥδιστος βίος; this is still the class. meaning of *consists in*. The total instances are: Lk 34, Ac 8, Paul 4, Heb 4, Mt 3, Mk 2. Thus in NT 55, LXX 500, Xenophon 16, Thucydides 6, Plato 26.

(a) The usual NT meaning is temporal (*while* or *after*) though in some instances it is not impossible to trace the element of cause too. There are few, if any, class. parallels for the meaning *while, during*, for which a gen. absol. or pres. ptc. would have been used. Probably the Heb. בְּ influenced the authors of Bibl. Greek, as in LXX Ge 28⁶ 1 Km 2¹⁹ Mal 1⁷·¹². Mk 4⁴ ἐν τῷ σπείρειν αὐτόν, Mt 13⁴·²⁵ 27¹² Lk 8⁵.— Lk 1⁸ 2⁶·⁴³ (might be causal: *because they were returning*), 5¹ etc. Clearly its frequence in Lk is due to LXX influence (Zerwick § 273). Very often in Lk it is combined with ἐγένετο-constructions as a subordinate clause = וַיְהִי בְּ, e.g. 1⁸ 2⁶; Luke's imitation of LXX is particularly plain here (Zerwick § 275), e.g. Ge 11² for בְּ ἐγένετο ἐν τῷ κινῆσαι αὐτούς, 35¹⁸; for כַּאֲשֶׁר 24⁵²; for וַיְהִי הֵם מְרִיקִים שַׂקֵּיהֶם 42³⁵.— Ac 2¹ (causal, explaining why they were gathered together), 9³, 19¹ ἐγένετο.—Ro 3⁴ OT, 15¹⁸ ἐν τῷ πιστεύειν (DEGF om) *because you believe*.—Ga 4¹⁸. Ptol. pap. (Mayser II 1, 328f). Johannessohn, *Das biblische ΚΑΙ ΕΓΕΝΕΤΟ und seine Geschichte*, Göttingen 1926, 199ff.

Though Luke uses the aor. infin. he is more fond of the pres.; there are but twelve exx. of aor. in NT. It is probably not true to say quite simply that pres. infin. = *while* and aor. inf. = *after*. Aor. is timeless while pres. is durative. The context must decide relative time. Thus in Heb 2⁸ we have aor.; but RSV, looking at the context, could be correct to render it *putting everything in subjection*, not *having put* (NEB *in subjecting all things*). It is, however, a rough and ready rule to suppose, as with pres. and aor. ptc., that temporal ἐν τῷ c. pres. inf. indicates contemporaneity, and ἐν τῷ c. aor. infin. indicates anterior action. This being so, we may compare Lk 10³⁵ with 19¹⁵: ἐν τῷ ἐπανέρχεσθαι (pres.) is *at my return*, but ἐν τῷ ἐπανελθεῖν αὐτόν is *after his return*. We may also compare Lk 9²⁹ with 14¹: ἐν τῷ προσεύχεσθαι αὐτόν (pres.) is *while he was praying*, but ἐγένετο ἐν τῷ ἐλθεῖν αὐτὸν εἰς οἶκον is *after he had gone into the house*. The following exx. of aor. infin. in Lk-Ac may or may not imply anterior action: Lk 2²⁷ ἐν τῷ εἰσαγαγεῖν *after they entered*, 3²¹ ἐν τῷ βαπτισθῆναι *after they were baptized*, but the context may require *while they were being baptized* (NEB *during a general baptism of the people*, because it goes on to state καὶ Ἰησοῦ βαπτισθέντος; 8⁴⁰ (SB pres), 9³⁴·³⁶ 11³⁷ 14¹ 19¹⁵ 24³⁰, Ac 11¹⁵.

LXX (= בְּ) Ge 28⁶ ἐν τῷ εὐλογεῖν αὐτόν (pres.) *while he blessed him*, Mal 1⁷·¹² ἐν τῷ λέγειν ὑμᾶς (pres.) *when you say*.—Ge 39¹⁵ = בְּ ἐν τῷ ἀκοῦσαι αὐτόν (aor.) *when he heard*, 44³¹ ἔσται ἐν ἰδεῖν αὐτόν (aor.) *when he sees*.

(b) It appears in the LXX in a causal sense (= בְּ): Ge 19¹⁶ ἐκράτησεν ... ἐν τῷ φείσασθαι κύριον αὐτοῦ *because the Lord was merciful to him*, 1 Mac 2⁵⁴·⁵⁸ ἐν τῷ ζηλῶσαι ζῆλον *because he was deeply zealous* RSV, 2⁵⁵ ἐν τῷ πληρῶσαι λόγον *because he fulfilled the command* RSV, 2⁵⁶ ἐν τῷ ἐπιμαρτύρασθαι τῇ ἐκκλησίᾳ *because he testified in the assembly* RSV.

NT: Lk 1²¹ ἐθαύμαζον ἐν τῷ *because he delayed*, Mk 6⁴⁸ βασανιζομένους ἐν τῷ ἐλαύνειν *by the rowing*, Ac 3²⁶ ἐν τῷ ἀποστρέφειν instr. (Je 11¹⁷), 4³⁰ similar, Heb 8¹³ ἐν τῷ λέγειν *because he says*, 2⁸ ἐν τῷ ὑποτάξαι causal, or like a ptc.

It appears also in LXX in a final sense, translating ל: 1 Km 1²⁶ ἐν τῷ προσεύξασθαι *here in order to pray*.

(c) Other uses include an epexegetical: He 3¹² ἐν τῷ ἀποστῆναι NEB (RSV consec.), 2 Co 2¹³ DE ἐν τῷ μὴ εὑρεῖν (see above p. 142) Preisigke Sammelbuch I 620, 6f (inscr. 97 B.C.) λείπεσθαι ἐν τῷ μὴ εἶναι ἄσυλον *is wanting in this, that it has no* ... ; 1 Clem 10¹ πιστὸς εὑρέθη ἐν τῷ αὐτὸν ὑπήκοον γενέσθαι *in this, that* ... , Lk 12¹⁵ οὐκ ἐν τῷ περισσεύειν τινὶ ἡ ζωὴ αὐτοῦ ἐστιν.

§ 3. Cases with the Infinitive [1]

1. (a) There are few exceptions in the Koine to the class. rule that the subject of a dependent infin. is not expressed again if it is the same as the subject of the independent verb; dependence of the infin. upon a preposition makes no difference. (b) If the infin. has a nominal predicate or is connected with an apposition which defines the subject of the main verb, the apposition is not a ground for altering the construction to that of accus. and infin.; however, a nominal predicate will do this sometimes. (c) Also, if the object of the infin. is identical with the object of the main verb, there need be no repetition of the object.

Examples:—

(a) Subject of infin. not expressed: Lk 24²³ λέγουσαι ... ἑωρακέναι, Ro 1²² φάσκοντες εἶναι σοφοί, 1 Jn 2⁶·⁹ ὁ λέγων ἐν αὐτῷ μένειν ... ἐν τῷ φωτὶ εἶναι, Ti 1¹⁶ θεὸν ὁμολογοῦσιν εἰδέναι, Jas 2¹⁴. Also for θέλω, βούλομαι, ζητέω, etc. there are abundant exx.

(b) Nom. with infin.: Mt 19²¹ θέλεις τέλειος εἶναι, Jn 7⁴ WH ζητεῖ αὐτὸς ἐν παρρησίᾳ εἶναι (p⁶⁶ BW*D have αὐτὸ accus.; syr^cur *b e* om αὐτός), Ac 18¹⁵ κριτὴς ἐγὼ τούτων οὐ βούλομαι εἶναι, Ro 9³ ηὐχόμην ἀνάθεμα εἶναι αὐτὸς ἐγώ, 1²² φάσκοντες εἶναι σοφοί *claiming to be wise*, Ph 4¹¹ ἔμαθον αὐτάρκης εἶναι *learnt how to be*, 2 Co 10² δέομαι τὸ μὴ παρὼν θαρρῆσαι *I beg that when I am present I may not be bold*, Heb 5¹² ὀφείλοντες εἶναι διδάσκαλοι, 11⁴ ἐμαρτυρήθη εἶναι δίκαιος *certified to be righteous*. The construction conflicts with that in Mk 14²⁸ (μετὰ τὸ

---

[1] K-G II § 475f. Schmid *Attizismus* II 57; III 81; IV 83. 620. Mayser II 1, 334ff.

ἐγερθῆναί με προάξω), Ac 5³⁶ (Θεῦδας λέγων εἶναί τινα ἑαυτόν), and Jas 4² (οὐκ ἔχετε διὰ τὸ μὴ αἰτεῖσθαι ὑμᾶς).

(c) Also if the obj. of the infin. is identical with that of the governing verb, there need be no repetition of the obj.: Ac 26²⁸ ἐν ὀλίγῳ με πείθεις Χριστιανὸν ποιῆσαι *you seek to convince me that you have made me in a moment a Christian*; a striking parallel is provided by Fridrichsen (*Coniectanea neot.* III, 1938) from Xen. Mem. I 2, 49 πείθων τοὺς συνόντας αὐτῷ σοφωτέρους ποιεῖν τῶν πατέρων (K–G II 32; Zerwick § 279ᵇ).

2. Although class. writers preferred a personal construction it was possible to make it impersonal, and on the whole the latter is preferred in NT and Koine. But δοκέω at least has personal construction in NT: Act 17¹⁸ δοκεῖ καταγγελεὺς εἶναι, 1 Co 3¹⁸ εἴ τις δοκεῖ σοφὸς εἶναι; 8² 14³⁷, Ga 2⁹ etc., Jas 1²⁶ (whereas there is impersonal δοκεῖ in Herm. M. IV 2, 2; S. IX 5, 1; Clem. Hom. 10²); and we find personal ἔδοξα ἐμαυτῷ δεῖν πρᾶξαι (Ac 26⁹) as well as impersonal ἔδοξέ μοι (Lk 1³ etc., Ac 15²⁸ etc.), and there is, even in the passive, δεδοκιμάσμεθα πιστευθῆναι (1 Th. 2⁴) *we have been approved to be entrusted with*. Adjectives like δυνατός and ἱκανός have a personal construction too. Moreover, there is the personal construction with πρέπει (Heb 7²⁶). However, there is nothing like the class. λέγομαι εἶναι.

3. Quite often in the Koine and NT, although the governing verb and the infin. have the same subject, the latter will be in the accus. This is distinct from class. Greek, which has either the nominative or no noun at all with the infin. It is a Latin construction and is reproduced in Greek inscriptional translations from the Latin but, as Moulton pointed out (Proleg. 213), this perfectly natural levelling process developed in regions untouched by Latin, and no outside influence was needed to increase the tendency towards uniformity. The reflexive pronoun, and sometimes the non-reflexive pronoun, in the accus. case, is added superfluously to the infin. In class. Greek they preferred to insert a non-reflexive referring to the subject of the main verb in the nominative; so they would probably have put αὐτὸς δέ for ἑαυτόν in Ac 25⁴ (ἀπεκρίθη τηρεῖσθαι τὸν Παῦλον, ἑαυτὸν δὲ μέλλειν . . .) where Luke may have deviated from class. usage into the accus. because he wished to co-ordinate the new subject with Παῦλον.

Reflexive pronoun:

Lk 23² λέγοντα ἑαυτὸν Χριστὸν βασιλέα εἶναι, 20²⁰ ὑποκρινομένους ἑαυτοὺς δικαίους εἶναι (D om εἶναι), Ac 5³⁶ λέγων εἶναί τινα ἑαυτόν,

8⁹ λέγων είναί τινα εαυτόν μέγαν, Ro 2¹⁹ πέποιθας σεαυτόν οδηγόν είναι *you are sure that you are* (αυτός would be class., as in fact in 9³), 6¹¹ λογίζεσθε εαυτούς είναι νεκρούς (hardly accus. in class. Greek), 2 Co 7¹¹ συνεστήσατε εαυτούς αγνούς είναι (non-reflexive with ptc. in class. Greek, Rev 2⁹ 3⁹ των λεγόντων 'Ιουδαίους είναι εαυτούς (gen. in class. Greek), Ph 3¹³ εγώ εμαυτόν ούπω λογίζομαι κατειληφέναι (superfluous εμαυτόν), Heb 10³⁴ γινώσκοντες έχειν εαυτούς κρείσσονα ύπαρξιν.

Non-reflexive pronouns:

Lk 20⁷ D απεκρίθησαν μη ειδέναι αυτούς πόθεν, Ac 25²¹ επικαλεσαμένου τηρηθήναι αυτόν, Eph 4²² απόθεσθαι υμάς (but a long way from governing verb εδιδάχθητε).

In the Ptol. pap., on the other hand, the non-refl. predominates over the reflexive (Mayser II 1, 335f).

4. The personal pronoun and not the reflexive, is added quite often when the articular infin. is introduced by a preposition: there is but one NT instance of this without a preposition (2 Co 2¹³ τω μη ευρείν με Τίτον). Mt 26³² Mk 14²⁸ μετά το εγερθήναί με προάξω (for αυτός), Mt 27¹² Lk 2⁴ ανέβη ... διά το είναι αυτόν (superfluous pronoun), 19¹¹ 9³⁴ 10³⁵ 22¹⁵, Ac 1³ παρέστησεν εαυτόν ζώντα μετά το παθείν αυτόν, 4³⁰ 8⁴⁰ 19²¹D, Ro 1²⁰ καθοράται ... εις το είναι αυτούς αναπολογήτους, 3⁴ OT, Heb 7²⁴ (superfl. αυτόν), Jas 4² ουκ έχετε διά το μη αιτείσθαι υμάς, Jn 2²⁴. Frequent in Hermas (V. II 1, 3; M. IV 1, 7; S. VI 1, 5; VIII 2, 5. 9; 6, 1; IX 6, 8; 18, 3). Papyri (Mayser II 1, 336).

5. The infin. is often used alone, where in class. Greek they would have employed the full accus. c. infin. construction.

Mt 23²³ έδει ποιήσαι (sc. υμάς), Lk 2²⁶ ην αυτώ κεχρηματισμένον μη ιδείν θάνατον (sc, αυτόν), Ac 12¹⁵ η δε διισχυρίζετο ούτως έχειν (sc. ταύτα, as in 24⁹), Ro 13⁵ ανάγκη υποτάσσεσθαι, Heb 13⁶ p⁴⁶ M ώστε θαρρούντας λέγειν (rest add ημάς), 1 Pt 2¹⁵ φιμούν (sc. υμάς?). Mayser II 1, 336f.

6. The accus. c. infin. is restricted in use in the Koine in comparison with class. Greek, the ότι periphrasis having taken its place in nearly all NT writers according to the tendency of later Greek. But there is still a place for accus. c. infin., after verbs of stating, showing, perceiving, making, allowing, and κελεύω (where the obj. is a different person from the subject). Then there is εγένετο and συνέβη and similar expressions like δεί and ανάγκη. Some anomalies occur, as when the accus. inadvertently remains (as sometimes in class. Greek) even

although the infin. is replaced by ἵνα or ὅτι: Mk 1²⁴ οἶδά σε τίς εἶ, Lk 13²⁵ οὐκ οἶδα ὑμᾶς πόθεν ἐστέ, Mk 11³² εἶχον τὸν Ἰωάννην ὅτι προφήτης ἦν, Jn 9²⁹ τοῦτον δὲ οὐκ οἴδαμεν πόθεν ἐστίν, Ac 3¹⁰ 4¹³ 16³ p⁴⁵DEH ᾔδεισαν τὸν πατέρα αὐτοῦ ὅτι "Ἕλλην ὑπῆρχεν, 27¹⁰, 2 Th 2⁴ ἀποδεικνύντα ἑαυτὸν ὅτι ἐστὶν θεός.

7. The accus. c. inf. occurs as well as gen. or dat. c. infin. (especially in Luke).

(a) with verbs of commanding: Mk 6²⁷ ἐπέταξεν ἐνεχθῆναι τὴν κεφαλὴν αὐτοῦ, Ac 15² ἔταξαν ἀναβαίνειν Παῦλον, 10⁴⁸ προσέταξεν αὐτοὺς βαπτισθῆναι. Dative:—Mk 6³⁹ etc. Ac 22¹⁰ 1 Co 5¹¹ ἔγραψα ὑμῖν μὴ συναναμίγνυσθαι, Rev 3¹⁸ συμβουλεύω σοι ἀγοράσαι παρ' ἐμοῦ. N.B. λέγω c. dat. Mt 5³⁴·³⁹ Lk 12¹³ Ac 21⁴, c. accus. Mk 5⁴³ Lk 19¹⁵ Ac 22²⁴.

(b) with impers. expressions: ἔξεστιν, ἔθος ἐστίν, ἀθέμιτον αἰσχρόν καλόν ἐστιν, συμφέρει. Accus.:—Jn 18¹⁴ συμφέρει ἕνα ἄνθρωπον ἀποθανεῖν, Mt 17⁴ Mk 9⁵ Lk 9³³ καλόν ἐστιν ἡμᾶς ὧδε εἶναι, Ro 13¹¹ ὥρα ἡμᾶς ἐγερθῆναι (ἡμῖν class.), Mk 9⁴⁵ καλόν ἐστίν σε εἰσελθεῖν ... χωλόν, Mk 9⁴³·⁴⁷ (vl. σοι and σε), Mt 18⁸·⁹ σοι. Dative:—Lk 2²⁶ ἦν αὐτῷ κεχρηματισμένον μὴ ἰδεῖν θάνατον, Ac 5⁹ συνεφωνήθη ὑμῖν πειράσαι. Wavering:— Mt 3¹⁵ πρέπον ἐστιν ἡμῖν πληρῶσαι (S* ἡμᾶς), Mk 2²⁶ ἔξεστιν c. accus. SBL (c. dat. ACDW), Lk 6⁴ ἔξεστιν c. accus. (D dat., like Mt 12⁴), 20²² ἔξεστιν c. accus. (CDW dat.), [Mk 10² ἔξεστιν dat.] [P. Lille 26⁶ (iii/B.C.) ἔξεστιν accus.], 1 Co 11¹³ πρέπον ἐστιν accus., papyri Mayser II 1, 338.

(c) With ἐγένετο ¹ often: e.g. Ac 9³ ἐγ. αὐτόν ἐγγίζειν, 16¹⁶ ἐγ. δὲ ... παιδίσκην τινὰ ὑπαντῆσαι ἡμῖν, and even after a dat.: 22⁶ ἐγένετο δέ μοι ... περιαστράψαι φῶς. This is sometimes so, even when the person in the dat. is the same as in the accus.: 22¹⁷ ἐγ. μοι ... γενέσθαι με, Ga 6¹⁴ p⁴⁶ ἐμοὶ δὲ μὴ γένοιτό με καυχᾶσθαι (rest om με).

(d) With verbs of asking, etc. (ἐρωτάω, παρακαλέω, αἰτέομαι, ἀξιόω, παραινέω) the accus. c. inf. may follow: Ac 13²⁸ ᾐτήσαντο Πειλᾶτον ἀναιρεθῆναι αὐτόν, 1 Th 5²⁷ ὁρκίζω ὑμᾶς ἀναγνωσθῆναι τὴν ἐπιστολήν, Ac 21¹² παρεκαλοῦμεν τοῦ μὴ ἀναβαίνειν αὐτόν. But with δέομαι the gen. follows: Lk 9³⁸ δέομαί σου ἐπιβλέψαι, Ac 26³ (δέομαι ἡμᾶς is class.).

(e) Often there is accus. c. inf., although it stands in apposition to a pronoun in the gen. or dat.: e.g. Lk 1⁷³ᶠ τοῦ δοῦναι ἡμῖν ... ῥυσθέντας λατρεύειν, Ac 15²²·²⁵ (ABL dat.) etc., Ga 6¹⁴ p⁴⁶, Heb 2¹⁰ [2 Pt 2²¹ κρεῖττον ἦν αὐτοῖς μὴ ἐπεγνωκέναι ... ἢ ἐπιγνοῦσιν ὑποστρέψαι is classically correct; Lk 9⁵⁹ (but accus. in DΘ), Ac 27³ SAB (but accus. in HLP)].

---

¹ But the dat. and infin. is more usual with ἐγένετο: Ac 11²⁶ ἐγένετο αὐτοῖς διδάξαι, 20¹⁶, Ga 6¹⁴, P. Par. 26 (163 B.C.) ὑμῖν γίνοιτο κρατεῖν.

CHAPTER ELEVEN

THE VERB: ADJECTIVE-FORMS: PARTICIPLE

THE USE OF the participle [1] is more lavish in Greek than in Latin. We are here discussing its substantival, adverbial, attributive, and predicative uses, leaving the genitive and accusative absolute for a later chapter. The predicative use (e.g. παύομαι λέγων), which supplements the main verbal idea, is on its way out. The adverbial use (e.g. 1 Ti 1¹³ ἀγνοῶν ἐποίησα) is still strong, and so are the attributive and substantival. As far as forms go, the fut. is in eclipse (see pp. 86f, 135). For *Aktionsart*, see above pp. 86f. For periphrastic conjugation, see above p. 89.

The participle is not so much a mood, as an adjective, and so its modal function will be apparent only from the context. The ptc. standing independently as a main verb may be like an indicative or an imperative, but the NT and papyri instances are not difficult to explain as true participles (see p. 343).

§ 1. Substantival Participle

The neuter ptc., usually with article (as class.), is often used in the Koine to designate an abstract or concrete noun, whether individually or collectively. It is also used with masc. or fem. article of a person. The neuter is not so frequent as in class. Greek. For papyri, Mayser II 1, 346ff.

(a) *Personal.* Articular: these have pres. tense where we expect aor., esp. Mk 5¹⁵, ¹⁶ ὁ δαιμονιζόμενος even after his healing; action (time or variety) *is* irrelevant and the ptc. has become a proper name,

---

[1] K-G I 197–200; II 46–113. Stahl 680–761. Schwyzer II 384ff. Moulton Einl. 284–288; 352–368. Mayser II 1, 339–357. Jannaris 489–506. Wackernagel I 281–294. Radermacher² 205–210. H. Balser, *De linguae Graecae participio in neutro genere substantive posito*², Leipzig 1878. C. B. Williams, *The Participle in the Book of Acts*, Diss. Chicago 1909. H. B. Robinson, *Syntax of the Participle in the Apostolic Fathers*, Chicago 1915. C. O. Gillis, *Greek Participles in the Doctrinal Epistles of Paul*, Diss. of S-W. Bapt. Sem., 1937. W. K. Pritchett, "Μή with the Participle," *AJP* 79, 1958, 392ff.

§ 1-2]   THE VERB: ADJECTIVE FORMS   151

it may be under Hebraic influence, insofar as the Heb. ptc. is also timeless and is equally applicable to past, pres. and fut. So also Heb 7⁹ ὁ δεκάτας λαμβάνων, Ph 3⁶ διώκων τὴν ἐκκλησίαν. Sometimes the pres. has its proper durative force, e.g. 1 Th 1¹⁰ ὁ ῥυόμενος ἡμᾶς (Jesus' work is durative), 2¹² (5²⁴) ὁ καλῶν ὑμᾶς, 4⁸ ὁ διδοὺς τὸ πν. αὐτοῦ. ... Virtually a proper name: ὁ ἐρχόμενος (fut), Mt 26⁴⁶ ὁ παραδιδούς με (my betrayer), Mk 1⁴ 6¹⁴. ²⁴ ὁ βαπτίζων (the Baptizer), Jn 8¹⁸ ἐγώ εἰμι ὁ μαρτυρῶν, 6⁶³, Ac 17¹⁷ τοὺς παρατυγχάνοντας (casual passers-by NEB), Ro 2¹ ὁ κρίνων (you the judge), Ro 8³⁴ τίς ὁ κατακρινῶν, Eph 4²⁸ ὁ κλέπτων (generic), LXX 1 Km 16⁴ ὁ βλέπων (gen.), Si 28¹ ὁ ἐκδικῶν (gen.).   This ptc. can have an obj. or complement: Jn 1²⁹ ὁ αἴρων (the sin-bearer), Ga 1²³ ὁ διώκων ἡμᾶς (our persecutor), Mt 27⁴⁰, BU 388 III 16 ὁ παρὰ Πτολεμαΐδος ἀργυρώματα λαβών.

Anarthrous: Mt 2⁶ OT ἡγούμενος prince, Mk 1³ OT φωνὴ βοῶντος voice of a herald, Lk 3¹⁴ στρατευόμενοι, Ro 3¹¹ᶠ OT BG(A) (rest art. LXX Ps 13 (14)¹ᶠᶠ usually anarth.), Rev 2¹⁴ ἔχεις ἐκεῖ κρατοῦντας.

With πᾶς, usually articular (unless it means every): Mt 5²² πᾶς ὁ ὀργιζόμενος, ²⁸·³² πᾶς ὁ ἀπολύων anyone who divorces, 7²⁶ πᾶς ὁ ἀκούων any hearer, ⁸ πᾶς ὁ αἰτῶν λαμβάνει every beggar receives, Lk 6³⁰ ADPR ⁴⁷ etc., Ac 1¹⁹ πᾶσι τοῖς κατοικοῦσιν, 10⁴³ 13³⁹, Ro 1¹⁶ 2¹ etc. Anarthrous: Mt 13¹⁹ παντὸς ἀκούοντος, Lk 11⁴ παντὶ ὀφείλοντι, 6³⁰ SBW, 2 Th 2⁴, Rev 22¹⁵.

(b) Neuter: Mt 1²⁰ τὸ ἐν αὐτῇ γεννηθέν her unborn baby, 2¹⁵ and often τὸ ῥηθέν, Lk 2²⁷ κατὰ τὸ εἰθισμένον (D ἔθος), 12³³·⁴⁴ τὰ ὑπάρχοντα property (8³), 3¹³ τὸ διατεταγμένον ὑμῖν your assessment, 4¹⁶ τὸ εἰωθὸς αὐτῷ his custom, 8⁵⁶ τὸ γεγονός the occurrence, 9⁷ τὰ γινόμενα happenings, Jn 16¹³ τὰ ἐρχόμενα the future, 1 Co 1²⁸ τὰ ἐξουθενημένα . . . τὰ μὴ ὄντα . . . τὰ ὄντα, 7³⁵ 10³³ Sᶜ τὸ . . . συμφέρον (but rest σύμφορον) your welfare, 10²⁷ πᾶν τὸ παρατιθέμενον, 14⁷·⁹ τὸ αὐλούμενον, etc., 2 Co 3¹⁰ᶠ τὸ δεδοξασμένον, τὸ καταργούμενον, 2 Th 2⁶ τὸ κατέχον, Heb 12¹⁰ κατὰ τὸ δοκοῦν αὐτοῖς . . . ἐπὶ τὸ συμφέρον, 12¹¹ πρὸς τὸ παρόν, P. Fay. 91, 28 κατὰ τὰ προγεγραμμένα, BU 362 V 9 τὰ κελευσθέντα; in Hell. Greek τὸ συνειδός = conscience (but a noun in Paul). Ambiguous is τὰ διαφέροντα (Ro 2¹⁸ Ph 1¹⁰; see ICC in loc.): either different values (= moral distinctions NEB) or superior things (RV, RSV, Lat. utiliora).

§ 2. Attributive Participle

Normally the ptc. ὤν is used with the predicate when further defining words are added to the predicate, e.g. Ac 14¹³ SB ὅ τε ἱερεὺς τοῦ Διὸς τοῦ ὄντος πρὸ τῆς πόλεως, 28¹⁷ τοὺς ὄντας τῶν Ἰουδαίων πρώτους, Ro 8²⁸ τοῖς κατὰ πρόθεσιν κλητοῖς οὖσιν, 2 Co 11³¹ ὁ ὢν εὐλογητὸς εἰς . . ., 1 Ti 1¹³ τὸν πρότερον ὄντα βλάσφημον. There is no need for ὤν where the predicate stands alone. The redundant use of ὤν is however characteristic of Ac and the Ptol. papyri: Ac 5¹⁷ ἡ οὖσα αἵρεσις τῶν Σαδδουκαίων, 13¹ τὴν οὖσαν ἐκκλησίαν, 14¹³ D τοῦ ὄντος Διὸς πρὸ πόλεως, Ro 13¹ αἱ δὲ οὖσαι, Eph 1¹ p⁴⁶ D τοῖς ἁγίοις οὖσιν καὶ πιστοῖς (which thus need not be rejected), P. Tebt. 309 (ii/A.D.) ἀπὸ τοῦ ὄντος ἐν κώμῃ [τοῦ ἱεροῦ] θεοῦ..., P. Lille 29, 11 (iii/B.C.) τοὺς νόμους τοὺς περὶ τῶν οἰκετῶν ὄντας. It is conclusive from the papyri that the ὤν is somewhat redundant and means little more than *current* or *existent*. Translate *the local Zeus* (14¹³D), *the local church* (13¹), *the local school of the Sadducees* (5¹⁷); see *Beginnings* IV 56, Schwyzer II 409, Mayser II 1, 347f, Moulton Einl. 360.

The attributive ptc. stands both with and without the article and is equivalent to a relative clause: Mt 17²⁷ τὸν ἀναβάντα πρῶτον ἰχθύν, 25³⁴ τὴν ἡτοιμασμένην ὑμῖν βασιλείαν *which has been prepared*, Mk 3²² οἱ γραμματεῖς οἱ ἀπὸ Ἱεροσολύμων καταβάντες, 5²⁵ γυνὴ οὖσα ἐν ῥύσει αἵματος, 14²⁴ τὸ αἷμα... τὸ ἐκχυννόμενον (pres.), Lk 6⁴⁸ ὅμοιός ἐστιν ἀνθρώπῳ οἰκοδομοῦντι οἰκίαν (= a rel. clause in the parallel Mt 7²⁴), 10³⁷ ὁ ποιήσας τὸ ἔλεος, 15¹² τὸ ἐπιβάλλον μέρος τῆς οὐσίας, Ro 3⁵ μὴ ἄδικος ὁ θεὸς ὁ ἐπιφέρων τὴν ὀργήν; Ga 3²¹ νόμος ὁ δυνάμενος ζωοποιῆσαι. Anarthrous: Ac 19²⁴ Δημήτριος... ποιῶν ναοὺς ἀργυροῦς *Demetrius, a maker of silver shrines* (attrib.) or *because he made* (adverbial), Heb 7⁸ ἀποθνῄσκοντες ἄνθρωποι *mortal men* (attrib.) not adverbial. We must distinguish the attributive ptc. from a simple apposition (e.g. οἱ δὲ Φαρισαῖοι ἀκούσαντες εἶπον Mt 12²⁴, not *the Pharisees who heard*).

Also equivalent to a relative clause is the very frequent apposition ὁ λεγόμενος, (ἐπι)καλούμενος, with proper name following, always with an article after the person or object named: Mt 1¹⁶ Ἰησοῦς ὁ λεγόμενος Χριστός, Jn 5² κολυμβήθρα ἡ ἐπιλεγομένη... Βηθεσδά (S* τὸ λεγόμενον; W τῇ ἐπιλεγομένῃ) [the omission of ἡ D is an atticistic correction [1] made by those who were oblivious of NT usage], Ac 1¹² ὄρους τοῦ καλουμένου ἐλαιῶνος, 10¹⁸ Σίμων ὁ ἐπικαλούμενος Πέτρος (rel. clause 10⁵. ³²), Rev 12⁹ ὁ ὄφις... ὁ καλούμενος Διάβολος.

Whereas in class. Greek a relative clause would have been more correct after an anarthrous noun, in NT we often find an articular ptc., especially if it imparts some information which is well known, perhaps because of misunderstanding of an underlying Semitic ptc. (Moule 103), although it is not quite peculiar

---

[1] In cl. Attic the art. was not placed before the ptc., but before the proper noun. BU 512, 2 παρὰ Σύρου Συρίωνος ἐπικαλουμένου Πετακᾶ is half-way between class. and NT usage.

to Biblical Greek, viz. BU 416³ καμήλους δύο θηλείας αἱ κεχαραγμέναι = who were....

Mk 15⁴¹ ἄλλαι πολλαὶ αἱ συναναβᾶσαι, Lk 7³² παιδίοις τοῖς ἐν ἀγορᾷ καθημένοις, Jn 12¹² ὄχλος πολύς (BL add art.) ὁ ἐλθών, Ac 4¹² οὐδὲ γὰρ ὄνομά ἐστιν ἕτερον τὸ δεδομένον = ᾧ ἐδόθη, 1 Co 2⁷ θεοῦ σοφίαν... τὴν κεκρυμμένην, 1 Pt 1⁷ χρυσίου τοῦ ἀπολλυμένου, 2 Jn⁷ ὅτι πολλοὶ πλάνοι... οἱ μὴ ὁμολογοῦντες, Jude⁴ τινες ἄνθρωποι οἱ πάλαι προγεγραμμένοι. Unclassical also is the ellipse of the art. in 1 Pt 3¹⁹·²⁰ with a ptc. which follows a definite antecedent: τοῖς... πνεύμασιν... ἀπειθήσασίν ποτε. But after τινες the articular ptc. is classical (Stahl 691, 694): Lk 18⁹ πρός τινας τοὺς πεποιθότας ἐφ' ἑαυτοῖς, Ga 1⁷ εἰ μή τινές εἰσιν οἱ ταράσσοντες ὑμᾶς, Col 2⁸. Mk 14⁴ is not an instance because here we have a periphrastic tense: ἦσάν τινες ἀγανακτοῦντες. Lysias 19, 57 (v–iv/B.C.) εἰσί τινες οἱ προαναλίσκοντες. Also cp. the class. Greek construction οὐδείς (ἐστιν) ὁ with fut. ptc.

We also find in the NT, as in class. Greek, the articular ptc. dependent on a personal pronoun: Jn 1¹² αὐτοῖς... τοῖς πιστεύουσιν, Ac 13¹⁶ (sc. ὑμεῖς), Ro 9²⁰ σὺ τίς εἶ ὁ ἀνταποκρινόμενος (Jas 4¹² σὺ τίς εἶ ὁ κρίνων [vl. ὃς κρίνεις]), 14⁴, 1 Co 8¹⁰ (p⁴⁶ B om σε). In some passages we must supply the pronoun, esp. with the imper.: Mt 7²³ OT 27⁴⁰, Lk 6²⁵, Heb 4³ 6¹⁸.

§ 3. Adverbial Participle [1]

This circumstantial ptc. differs from a supplementary ptc. in that the latter cannot without impairing the sense be detached from the main verbal idea, whereas the circumstantial is equivalent to a separate participial clause. Such clauses may be either syntactically "joined" to the construction of the sentence, or they may be "absolute". Normally the clause will have reference to some noun or pronoun in the sentence agreeing with it in gender and number and case, but it may be syntactically independent in an isolated construction (see below, p. 322).

The relationship of this ptc. to the predicate may be of time, manner, cause, purpose, condition, or concession. This is not expressed by the ptc. itself, unless fut., but it is learned from the context or else from some added particle like καίπερ, ἅμα, εὐθύς, ποτέ, νῦν. The Koine does not on the whole favour this

---
[1] K-G II 77ff. Stahl 681ff. Moulton Einl. 363ff. Mayser II 1, 384ff.

method but prefers a prepositional phrase, a true temporal (etc.) clause, or a further co-ordinate sentence; thus Luke prefers κατὰ ἄγνοιαν ἐπράξατε (Ac 3¹⁷) to ἀγνοῶν ἐποίησα (1 Ti 1¹³).

(a) *Modal-temporal* is the most frequent kind of adverbial participial phrase in NT and Koine, as well as elsewhere. Often there is no stress whatever on the temporal relationship.

Mt 19²² ἀπῆλθεν λυπούμενος *in sorrow*, Mk 11⁵ *what do you mean by loosing?* Mt 27⁴ *by betraying*, 2¹⁶ 13² 6¹⁷ 19²².—Mk 1⁷.—Jn 16⁸.—Ac 21³².—1 Ti 1¹³.—1 Pt 5¹⁰.—BU 467, 15 etc. With ἅμα:—Mk 12³⁸ D Ac 24²⁶ 27⁴⁰ Col 1¹² p⁴⁶B, 4³. With εὐθύς:—Mk 6²⁵. With οὕτως (modal), class., in NT in Ac only: 20¹¹·³⁵ 27¹⁷.

Under this head should be included the large number of pleonastic participles in Biblical Greek (for pleon. ptc. in Ptol. pap., see Mayser II 1, 349). Apart from verbs of speaking (see below) the ptcs are ἄγων (pap.), ἀρξάμενος, ἔχων (pap.), φέρων (pap.), and (most used in NT) λαβών. These often have the meaning of the preposition *with*: Mt 15³⁰ (BU 909, 8) ἔχοντες μεθ' ἑαυτῶν (double pleonasm), LXX Ge 24¹⁵ ἔχουσα τὴν ὑδρίαν ἐπὶ τῶν ὤμων αὐτῆς, 1 Mac 8⁶ ἔχοντα ἑκατὸν εἴκοσι ἐλέφαντας, Mt 25¹ παραλαβών, λαβών, Mk 14³ ἔχουσα ἀλάβαστρον μύρου, Lk 2⁴²D, Ac 21²³ εὐχὴν ἔχοντες ἀφ' ἑαυτῶν, Jn 18³ *with a detachment* = Mt 26⁴⁷ μετ' αὐτοῦ; much of this is paralleled in the Koine. But λαβών and some other merely descriptive ptcs. seem to owe their origin in Bibl. Greek to a Hebraic pattern. In Heb. such a ptc. indicates a movement or an attitude which precedes an action. Usually it is superfluous, but it can have its justification sometimes, perhaps very slightly temporal: Mt 13³¹·³³ 14¹⁹ 21³⁵·³⁹ etc. LXX Jdt 12¹⁹ καὶ λαβοῦσα ἔφαγε καὶ ἔπιε, Nu 7⁶ 1 Esd 3¹³. So ἀναστάς (קום) and verbs of "departure": Mt 2²⁰ ἐγερθείς; 26⁶² ἀναστάς, Mk 10¹, Lk 15¹⁸·²⁰ 24¹², Ac 5¹⁷ 8²⁷ 9⁶·¹¹·³⁴·³⁹ 10²⁰ 11⁷ 22¹⁰·¹⁶, LXX Ge 22³ Nu 22²⁰; Mt 13²⁸·⁴⁶ ἀπελθών, 25¹⁸·²⁵; Mt 2⁸ 25¹⁶ 21⁶ Lk 7²² 13³² 14¹⁰ πορευθείς; 15²⁵ ἐρχόμενος; LXX Ge 21¹⁴ Ex 12²¹ ἀπελθόντες; Ge 45²⁸ 1 Mac 7⁷ πορευθείς; all these verbs after Heb. הלך. After Heb. ישב is καθίσας: Mt 13⁴⁸ Lk 5³ 14³¹ 16⁶, LXX Nu 11⁴ Dt 1⁴⁵.

Reminiscent of the class. ἀρχόμενος *at the beginning*, ἀρξάμενος occurs with meaning *from ... onwards* (class., and Lucian *somn.* 15 ἀπὸ τῆς ἕω ἀρξάμενος ἀχρὶ πρὸς ἑσπέραν) and pleonastically (perhaps again, through Heb. influence)[1]: LXX Ge 44¹² ἀπὸ τοῦ πρεσβυτέρου ἀρξάμενος (+ ἕως ... unclass.), Mt 20⁸¹, Lk 23⁵, 24²⁷ ἀρξάμενος ἀπὸ Μωϋσεως, ⁴⁷ ἀπὸ Ἱερουσαλήμ, Jn 8⁹ ἀπὸ τῶν πρεσβυτέρων (+ ἕως τῶν ἐσχάτων unclass.), Ac 1²² + ἄχρι, 8³⁵ ἀπὸ τῆς γραφῆς ταύτης, 11⁴ ἀρξάμενος Πέτρος ἐξετίθετο αὐτοῖς καθεξῆς, only slightly pleonastic, as the emph. is on καθεξῆς; cp. LXX Jg 19⁶ ἀρξάμενος (B ἄγε δή) αὐλίσθητι, Jb 6⁹, Xen. of Eph. 5, 7, 9 ἀρξαμένη κατέχομαι. The Hebraism προσθεὶς ἔφη is similar (see below p. 227). But besides the pleonastic ptc., parataxis with καί is possible, also on the Heb. model; use of the participial phrase is reduced in Biblical Greek through this co-ordination. In LXX the ptc. has yielded to parataxis under Heb. influence: cp. Ge 32²² ἀναστὰς δὲ τὴν νύκτα ἐκείνην ἔλαβε τὰς δύο γυναῖκας ... καὶ διέβη with 32²³ καὶ ἔλαβεν αὐτοὺς καὶ διέβη. NT authors however usually have recourse to the ptc.; but exx. of parataxis are Lk 22¹⁷ λάβετε τοῦτο καὶ διαμερίσατε, Ac 8²⁶ ἀνάστηθι καὶ πορεύου (but D ἀναστὰς πορεύθητι), 9¹¹ B lat copt ἀνάστα πορεύθητι (rest ἀναστάς), 10²⁰ D* ἀνάστα κατάβηθι (rest ἀναστάς), 3 Km 19⁵·⁷ T. Abr B 110²⁰.

Very frequent also in NT are the pleonastic participles λέγων, εἰπών, ἀποκριθείς, etc. In both LXX and NT the λέγων which corresponds to לֵאמֹר appears repeatedly after ἀποκρίνομαι, λαλέω, κράζω, παρακαλέω, etc., and often we have the formula ἀποκριθεὶς εἶπεν[2] (but not in Jn): twice in second part of Ac (19¹⁵ 25⁹) LXX Ge 18⁹; it is the LXX tr. of ויאמר ויען, whereas the asyndetic ἀπεκρίθη λέγων in Jn may be Aramaic; there never occurs ἀποκρινόμενος εἶπεν (Plato) or ἀπεκρίθη εἰπών.

This was already in slight use in class. Greek (Hdt ἔφη λέγων, εἰρώτα λέγων, ἔλεγε φάς), and can with little effort be paralleled in the Ptol. pap. Although the ptc. here has an obj. it does occur without: UPZ I 6³⁰ (163 B.C.) ἀπεκρίθησαν ἡμῖν φήσαντες, P. Giss. 36¹⁰ (135 B.C.) τάδε λέγει 'Α. καὶ 'Α. καὶ ..., αἱ τέτταρες λέγουσαι ἐξ ἑνὸς στόματος (Mayser II 3, 63¹⁴). However, λέγων is not pleonastic if the preceding verb governs an obj.: BU 624¹⁵ πολλὰ γὰρ ἠρώτησε λέγων ὅτι δουλεύσω, P. Par. 51²³ καὶ πάλιν ἠξίωκα τὸν Σάραπιν καὶ τὴν Ἶσιν λέγων· Ἐλθέ ... Pleonastic for certain are:—BU 523⁶ καὶ ἀντέγραψας λέγων ... πέμψον, P. Par. 35³⁰ ἀπεκρίθησαν ἡμῖν φήσαντες. There is no doubt, however,

---

[1] On pleonastic ἄρχομαι see J. W. Hunkin, "Pleonastic ἄρχομαι in the NT", JThS, 25, 1924, 390–402; G. Delling in Kittel WB I 477; Lagrange S. Luc CVI.

[2] Mt 25⁹ (pl.),³⁷·⁴⁴ (fut.), Mk 15⁹ (D ἀποκριθεὶς λέγει), Jn 12²³ (pres.), Ac 15¹³ (not D). Ἀπεκρίνατο λέγων LXX Ezk 9¹¹B (rare). Note the difference between Synoptists and Jn. The Synoptists follow LXX but are more idiomatic in that they put the Heb. main verb in the ptc. (ἀποκριθείς); but Jn does not favour the ptc. and even prefers asyndeton. He also avoids the other redundant ptcs. of the Synoptists: ἐλθών, ἀφείς, ἀναστάς. He prefers co-ordination.

that such expressions when used on a large scale, as in Bibl. Greek, point away from the popular language to a specialized Semitic background. Cp. the concentration of ἀποκριθείς (ἀπεκρίθη καί) εἶπεν in Rec. B of T. Abr.: 106⁴· ¹¹· ¹⁸ 107¹B 108¹· ²¹· ²³ 110⁷· ¹⁶· ²¹ 111¹⁸ 112⁶· ⁹ 113⁹ 114⁶ 118¹⁵.

Λέγων occurs with other verbs too, especially in Luke, John and Paul. Thoroughly Septuagintal is Lk 1⁶³, ἔγραψεν λέγων (as follows), LXX 2 Km 11¹⁵ ἔγραψεν ἐν βιβλίῳ λέγων, 4 Km 10⁶, 1 Mac 11⁵⁷ (see Klostermann on the passage in Lk);

Also Lk 5²¹ ἤρξαντο διαλογίζεσθαι ... λέγοντες (12¹⁷); Mt 15²³ ἠρώτων λέγοντες, 26⁷⁰ ἠρνήσατο λέγων (cp. Ac 7³⁵ εἰπόντες), Lk 12¹⁶ 20² εἶπεν λέγων, Jn 1³² ἐμαρτύρησεν λέγων (S* e om λέγων), 4³¹ 9² (D om) etc. ἠρώτων (-τησαν) λέγοντες, 19¹² ἐκραύγαζον (vl. ἔκραζον) λέγοντες (S* ἔλεγον for ἐκρ. λ.), Mt 8²⁹ ἔκραξαν λέγοντες, 14³⁰ etc. Other participles of *saying* occur with these verbs: Lk 5¹³ ἥψατο εἰπών, 22⁸ ἀπέστειλεν εἰπών, Ac 7³⁵ ἠρνήσαντο εἰπόντες (prob. not pleon.), 21¹⁴ ἡσυχάσαμεν εἰπόντες, 22²⁴ ἐκέλευσεν ... εἴπας, Jn 11²⁸ ἐφώνησεν τὴν ἀδελφὴν εἰποῦσα (not pleon. = *with the words*); Mt 2⁸ πέμψας εἶπεν *sent with the words*, Mk 5⁷ κράξας λέγει (D εἶπε), 9²⁴ κράξας ἔλεγεν (DΘ λέγει; p⁴⁵ W εἶπεν), Ac 13²² εἶπεν μαρτυρήσας.

Moreover, in Heb. *answered* is followed by ויאמר and so, besides ἀπεκρίθη λέγων, the NT and LXX also have ἀπ. καὶ εἶπεν (often Jn, not Mt, rarely Mk Lk), the participial construction thus giving way in Bibl. Greek to the paratactic : ἀπεκρίθη καὶ εἶπεν Jn 14²³ 18³⁰ 20²⁸ etc. (Jn almost always so, unless ἀπ. stands without addition), Lk 17²⁰, LXX Je 11⁵ ἀπεκρίθην καὶ εἶπα, Mk 7²⁸ ἀπεκρίθη καὶ λέγει. With other verbs (in Jn especially): 1²⁵ ἠρώτησαν αὐτὸν καὶ εἶπαν αὐτῷ, 9²⁸ ἐλοιδόρησαν αὐτὸν καὶ εἶπαν, 13²¹ ἐμαρτύρησαν καὶ εἶπεν, 18²⁵ ἠρνήσατο καὶ εἶπεν, Lk 8²⁸D, Ro 10²⁰ ἀποτολμᾷ καὶ λέγει.

Thoroughly Septuagintal also is the addition of the ptc. of the same verb in order to strengthen the verbal idea. It renders the Hebrew Infinite Absolute [1], being the nearest approach to the infin., since the infin. itself would be too literal. It is very rare indeed in secular Greek; better Greek would render the Inf. Absol. idea by means of the dat. of the verbal substantive, and yet in the LXX it is rendered 171 times by the ptc. (against 123 by the dat., 23 by accus., and 5 through an adverb). E.g. Ge

---

[1] K-G II 99f. Moulton Einl. 118f. H. St. John Thackeray, "The Infinitive Absolute in the LXX," *JThS* 9, 1908, 597ff; *OT Grammar* 48f. Johannessohn DGKPS 57.

22¹⁷ εὐλογῶν εὐλογήσω σε, 26²⁸ ἰδόντες ἑωράκαμεν, Ex 3⁷ ἰδὼν ἴδον, Jb 6¹, 1 Km 20³. In NT, only in LXX-quotations: Mt 13¹⁴ βλέποντες βλέψετε, Ac 7³⁴ ἰδὼν εἶδον, Heb 6¹⁴ εὐλογῶν εὐλογήσω σε καὶ πληθύνων πληθύνω σε, Eph 5⁵ ἴστε γινώσκοντες (uncertain textually), 1 Clem 12⁵ γινώσκουσα γινώσκω, P. Tebt. II 421¹² (iii/A.D.) ἐρχόμενος δὲ ἔρχου (ε)ἰς Θεογονίδα (but this may not be an instance: simply *when you come, come to Th.*).

(b) *Causal use*. This follows the class. pattern in the Koine, except that in NT we do not find ἅτε, οἷον or οἷα (papyri). Mt 1¹⁹ δίκαιος ὤν (= ὅτι), Lk 10²⁹ θέλων δικαιῶσαι ἑαυτόν, Ac 19³⁶ ἀναντιρρήτων ... ὄντων τούτων, 23¹⁸ ἔχοντά τι λαλῆσαί σοι *because he has something to say*, 2 Co 12¹⁶ ὑπάρχων πανοῦργος, 1 Th 5⁸; Phm⁹ is ambiguous (causal or concessive), so also Ga 2³. The papyri show a hybrid construction, beginning with διὰ τό c. inf. and ending with the causal ptc.: P. Par. 12²¹ διὰ τὸ χωλὸν ὄντα, P. Leip. 108⁵ διὰ τὸ ἐμὲ μετρίως ἔχοντα.

(c) *Concessive use*. Not frequent. Koine has καίπερ, καίτοι, and καὶ ταῦτα, like NT. Mt 7¹¹ πονηροὶ ὄντες, Ac 19³⁷, 17²⁷ καί γε (D* καίτε; S καίτοιγε; A καίτοι), 1 Co 9¹⁹ ἐλεύθερος ὤν, 2 Co 10³ ἐν σαρκὶ... περιπατοῦντες, Ph 3⁴ καίπερ, Phm⁸ πολλὴν... παρρησίαν ἔχων, Heb 5⁸ καίπερ ὢν υἱός 4³ καίτοι c. gen. ptc., 11² καὶ ταῦτα, 7⁵ καίπερ, 12¹⁷ καίπερ (p⁴⁶ καίτοι), 2 Pt 1¹² καίπερ.—P. Par. 8, 16 νυνὶ πλεονάκις ἀπαιτούμενοι οὐκ ἀποδίδωσι *although they are often asked to do it*.

(d) *Conditional use*. Papyri (Mayser II 1, 351): BU 543¹³ εὐορκοῦντι ἔστω μοι εὖ, ἐφιορκοῦντι δὲ ἐναντία, 596¹¹ τοῦτο οὖν ποιήσας *if you do that* ἔσῃ μοι μεγάλην χάριταν κατατεθειμένος. Lk 9²⁵ κερδήσας (Mt 16²⁶ ἐὰν κερδήσῃ), Ac 15²⁹, Heb 11³², Jn 15² μὴ φέρον καρπόν *if it does not*, but (same verse) πᾶν τὸ καρπὸν φέρον (substantival ptc.) = *fruiting branch*; however, Jn's method is often to have variety of vocabulary and syntax in close proximity.

(e) *Final use*. Papyri (op. cit. 351f) esp. with ἀποστέλλω, πέμπω etc., with fut. ptc. (class.); only in Mt Lk. Mt 27⁴⁹ ἔρχεται σώσων (W σῴζων, S* σῶσαι, D καὶ σώσει), Ac 8²⁷ ἐληλύθει προσκυνήσων, 22⁵ ἐπορευόμην ἄξων, 24¹¹·¹⁷, 25¹³ ἀσπασόμενοι vl. Usually it is the pres. ptc.: Lk 7⁶ ἔπεμψεν φίλους ὁ ἑκατοντάρχης λέγων αὐτῷ, 10²⁵ ἀνέστη ἐκπειράζων αὐτόν.

The addition of ὡς (ὥσπερ, ὡσεί)[1] will express subjective motive: Ac 3¹² ἡμῖν τε ἀτενίζετε ὡς . . . πεποιηκόσιν, 28¹⁹, Lk 16¹ 23¹⁴ 1 Co 4¹⁸ ὡς μὴ ἐρχομένου δέ μου, 7²⁵ in the conviction that, Heb 13¹⁷ ἀγρυπνοῦσιν ὡς λόγον ἀποδώσοντες with the thought that they must (fut. ptc.), 12²⁷, 1 Pt 4¹², Rev 1¹⁵, Ac 23¹⁵, ²⁰ 27³⁰ under pretence of, 2 Co 5²⁰ gen. abs. (as well as comparison: Ac 2² Rev 1¹⁵).

N.B. class. Greek was fond of lengthening sentences by accumulating the circumstantial participles. The nearest approach to this form of ugliness in NT is 2 Pt 2¹²⁻¹⁵ βλασφημοῦντες ἀδικούμενοι ἡγούμενοι ἐντρυφῶντες. On the other hand, Luke introduces ptcs. quite effectively and thus presents a flowing style which is refreshing after the jerky epistolary style of Paul; Lk 4²⁰ καὶ πτύξας τὸ βιβλίον ἀποδοὺς τῷ ὑπηρέτῃ ἐκάθισεν; with καί connecting, Ac 14²⁷ παραγενόμενοι δὲ καὶ συναγαγόντες, 18²² κατελθὼν εἰς Καισάρειαν, ἀναβὰς καὶ ἀσπασάμενος τὴν ἐκκλησίαν, κατέβη εἰς Ἀντιόχειαν (asyndeton to avoid ugliness), ²³ ἐξῆλθεν, διερχόμενος τὴν Γαλατικὴν χώραν, στηρίζων τοὺς μαθητάς = ἐξῆλθεν καὶ διήρχετο στηρίζων, 19¹⁶ ἐφαλόμενος ὁ ἄνθρωπος ἐπ αὐτούς . . . , κατακυριεύσας ἀμφοτέρων ἴσχυσεν = ἐφήλετο καί . . . (the vl. καὶ κατακυριεύσας S*HLP gives the second ptc. a weaker connection with the first). Matthew, whose gospel is more stylistic than the others, has a little of the same tendency: 14¹⁹ κελεύσας (SZ ἐκέλευσεν) . . . λαβών . . . ἀναβλέψας, 27⁴⁸ δραμών . . . καὶ λαβών . . . πλήσας τε (τε om D) . . . καὶ περιθείς.

§ 4. Predicative Participle [2]

In the same way as the ordinary adj., the ptc. may fulfil the rôle of a predicate and answer either to the subject or the direct complement of the proposition. In this way, with εἶναι and γίνεσθαι the ptc. forms a periphrastic tense (see pp. 87–89).

As a predicate answering to the subject the ptc. is found with verbs expressing a manner of existence, like ὑπάρχω, but in NT this is restricted and is found almost only in Luke, Paul and Hebrews. In the Ptol. pap. (Mayser II 1, 352f) the predicating ptc. is apparently still very well attested, though not in comparison with class. Greek. When this kind of verb has an adj. or prepositional phrase as a predicate, strictly there should be introduced the ptc. ὤν, but not so inevitably in NT and Hell. Greek; thus Phrynichus designates φίλος σοι τυγχάνω as " Hellenistic ". The omission of ὤν is to be remarked in the

---

[1] With this ὡς there may be ellipse of the ptc. (class.): Ro 13¹³ ὡς ἐν ἡμέρᾳ, 1 Co 9²⁶ 2 Co 2¹⁷, Ga 3¹⁶ Eph 6⁷ Col 3²³ 2 Th 2², 1 Pt 4¹¹.

[2] K-G II §§ 481–484. Stahl 699ff. Mayser II 1, 352ff. Moulton Einl. 361ff. Radermacher² 208.

following NT passages (as also in Strabo, Appian, and Philostratus):
Mk 1²³, Lk 4¹ Ἰησοῦς δὲ πλήρης πνεύματος ἁγίου ὑπέστρεψεν, Ac 6⁸ πλήρης, 19³⁷ οὔτε ἱεροσύλους οὔτε βλασφημοῦντας (concessive), Heb 7²ᶠ.

(A) *The Participle in the Nominative*

As in class. Greek, and often in the Koine:—

MODIFYING VERBS:

	NT examples	Parallels, excl. class. Greek
ὑπάρχω	Ac 8¹⁶, Jas 2¹⁵ (Ac 19³⁶ ptc. prob. adjectival)	Koine i/B.C.
προϋπάρχω	Lk 23¹² (not D) (Ac 8⁹ ptc. prob. adverbial)	Josephus
παύομαι	Lk 5⁴, Ac 5⁴², 6¹³ etc., Eph 1¹⁶ Col 1⁹, Heb 10²	Hell., LXX Ge 11⁸, 18³³, Nu 16³¹ etc., Hermas
τελέω	Mt 11¹, Lk 7¹ D	Hermas Josephus
διατελέω	Ac 27³³	LXX 2 Mac 5²⁷, Hom. Clem 14⁸, Pap. Milligan p. 9 διατελῶ εὐχομένη *I pray continually*
ἐπιμένω	Jn 8⁷, Ac 12¹⁶	Koine 2 Cl. 10⁵
διαλείπω	Lk 7⁴⁵, Ac 8²⁴ D, 17¹³ D	LXX Je 17⁸, 51 (44)¹⁸ Lit. Hell. Koine
ἐγκακέω	Ga 6⁹, 2 Th 3¹³	
λανθάνω	Heb 13²	P. Hamb. I 27, 9 (250 B.C.)
φαίνομαι	Mt 6¹⁸	Koine
προφθάνω	Mt 17²⁵	Ep. Arist. 137
καλῶς ποιέω	Ac 10³³, Ph 4¹⁴, 2 Pt 1¹⁹, 3 Jn⁶	Koine

VERBS OF EMOTION:

ἀγαλλιάομαι	Ac 16³⁴	
τρέμω	2 Pt 2¹⁰	
χαίρω	Mt 2¹⁰ (*they were glad to see the star*), Jn 20²⁰, Ph 2²⁸	Koine
εὐχαριστῶ	1 Co 14¹⁸ KL (p⁴⁶ inf; SBD λαλῶ)	

VERBA SENTIENDI:

συνίημι	2 Co 10¹² SB p⁴⁶ αὐτοὶ ἐν ἑαυτοῖς ἑαυτοὺς μετροῦντες . . . οὐ συνιᾶσιν *they do not realise that they are measuring themselves by their own standards* (but D*G vulg. om οὐ συνιᾶσιν ἡμεῖς δέ)	Plut. 3. 231d Lucian D. Deor. 2, 1
μανθάνω	1 Ti 5¹³ ἅμα δὲ καὶ ἀργαὶ μανθάνουσιν περιερχόμεναι or sc. εἶναι?). Cp. class. μανθάνω διαβεβλήμενος. More often inf.: Ph 4¹¹, 1 Ti 5⁴, Ti 3¹⁴, 1 Cl. 8⁴ OT, 57²	

(*B*) *The Participle in Oblique Case*

(*a*) With verbs of sensual or spiritual perceiving and knowing: ἀκούω, βλέπω, γινώσκω, ἐπίσταμαι, εὑρίσκω, θεάομαι, θεωρέω, κατανοέω, οἶδα, ὁράω; all these are found in the Ptol. pap. (Mayser II 1, 354ff). Also in NT are: δοκιμάζω, ἔχω, μανθάνω. This ptc. is quite plentiful in NT, where it is almost always in an oblique case (Lk 8⁴⁶ ἔγνων δύναμιν ἐξεληλυθυῖαν ἀπ' ἐμοῦ *I felt that power had gone out*, not *I felt the power going*

§ 4]   THE VERB: ADJECTIVE FORMS   161

out), and we do not find parallels to the class. ὁρῶ ἡμαρτηκώς *I see that I have sinned* (NT has ὅτι, see Mk 5²⁹ 1 Jn 3¹⁴). Ἀγνοέω and αἰσθάνομαι are found with ptc. in the papyri, but not NT.

Ἀκούω: in NT, if the content of the hearing is given, usually the accus. c. infin. or else ὅτι or ὡς; it is no longer frequently the ptc. In class. Greek the ptc. tended to denote facts and the infin. mere hearsay; but this distinction has quite disappeared and all we can say is, that with the ptc. the accus. appears to denote what is learned (indirect speech), while the gen. is retained for direct audition or hearing with the ears.

Accus. with ptc.: Mk 5³⁶ παρακούσας τὸν λόγον λαλούμενον exceptional (this is direct audition and one would expect gen. B seeks a remedy by inserting the article: τὸν λόγον τὸν λαλούμενον, since without it the meaning should be *overhearing that the word was being spoken*); Lk 4²³ ὅσα ἠκούσαμεν γενόμενα; Ac 7¹² ἀκούσας ὄντα σιτία; 2 Th 3¹¹ ἀκούομεν γάρ τινας περιπατοῦντας *we hear that*; 3 Jn⁴ ἀκούω τὰ ἐμὰ τέκνα... περιπατοῦντα; P. Par. 48¹² ἀκούσαντες δὲ ἐν τῷ μεγάλῳ Σεραπείῳ ὄντα σε *that you were*. Even in Ac sometimes (9⁴ 26¹⁴) the accus. stands for class. gen.; indeed, the gen. is rare in NT outside Ac.

Gen. with ptc.: Mk 12²⁸ ἀκούσας αὐτῶν συνζητούντων, 14⁵⁸, Lk 18³⁶ ὄχλου διαπορευομένου, Jn 1³⁷ ἤκουσαν... αὐτοῦ λαλοῦντος, Ac 2⁶ 6¹¹ etc. Note in Ac 11⁷ 22⁷ ἤκουσα φωνῆς λεγούσης μοι (but accus. in 9⁴ 26¹⁴ [E gen]); if this pointless variation can occur in a writer like Luke, the class. distinction between accus. and gen. has now broken down.

Βλέπω, θεωρέω, θεάομαι, κατανοέω, ὁράω: ptc. Mt 24³⁰ ὄψονται τὸν υἱόν... ἐρχόμενον, 15³¹, Mk 5³¹ βλέπεις τὸν ὄχλον συνθλίβοντά σε, Jn 1³² τεθέαμαι τὸ Πν. καταβαῖνον, ³⁸. Papyri. LXX To 11¹⁶ Su³⁷. Use of ὄντα is class.: Heb 3¹ᶠ κατανοήσατε τὸν ἀπόστολον... πιστὸν ὄντα; Ac 8²³ ὁρῶ σε ὄντα. 17¹⁶ θεώρ. κατείδωλον οὖσαν τὴν πόλιν. But the ptc. of the verb *to be* may be omitted: Mt 25³⁸ᶠ σε εἴδομεν ξένον, ἀσθενῆ (BD corr. to ptc. ἀσθενοῦντα), Jn 1⁵⁰ εἶδόν σε ὑποκάτω τῆς συκῆς; the use of ὡς occurs instead in Ac 17²² ὡς δεισιδαιμονεστέρους ὑμᾶς θεωρῶ, of which the sense must be *from what I see, it appears as if*, when we compare 2 Th 3¹⁵ ὡς ἐχθρὸν ἡγεῖσθε *as if he were an enemy*.

Sometimes with *to see*, as with other verbs, this kind of ptc. (especially in the pf.) is more plainly separated from the obj. of the main verb, and becomes in effect a distinctive complement, leaving the obj. and its main verb still very closely linked together: Mt 22¹¹ εἶδεν ἄνθρωπον οὐκ ἐνδεδυμένον, etc. (relative clause) = *he saw a man and he had not on*, Mk 11¹³ ἰδὼν συκῆν ἀπὸ μακρόθεν ἔχουσαν φύλλα (*which had*), LXX To 1¹⁷ εἴ τινα... ἐθεώρουν τεθνηκότα *who was dead*, P. Leip. 40²⁰ καὶ εἶδεν τὰς θύρας χαμαὶ ἐρριμένας *which were*. On ὅτι after *to see*, (see pp. 136f). In Mark the accus. c. ptc. construction occurs after ἰδεῖν 15 times, and ὅτι occurs 6 times.

Γινώσκω: in the Ptol. pap. usually with accus. c. ptc., but quite often also with infin. or ὅτι, διότι or ὡς—without much difference of meaning (Mayser II 1, 354f). Infin. or ὅτι also in NT. Lk 8⁴⁶ (Luke has altered Mk 5³⁰ which is not a case in point, since Mk uses the ptc. attributively: ἐπιγνοὺς τὴν ἐξ αὐτοῦ δύναμιν ἐξελθοῦσαν), Ac 19³⁵, Heb 13²³, BU 1078² γείνωσκέ με (this stereotyped letter-formula is very common in Ptol. pap.) πεπρακότα πρὸς τὸν καιρόν, 1078¹⁰ γείνωσκε δὲ ἡγεμόνα εἰσεληλυθότα τῇ τρίτῃ καὶ εἰκάδι.

Δοκιμάζω: 2 Co 8²² ὃν ἐδοκιμάσαμεν *we have proved* σπουδαῖον ὄντα (for inf. see p. 147). With ptc., absent from LXX and papyri.

Ἐπίσταμαι: Ac 24¹⁰ ὄντα σε κριτὴν ἐπιστάμενος, 26³ γνώστην ὄντα σε ... ἐπιστάμενος AC 614 (S* BEH om ἐπιστ.), 1 Clem 55² ἐπιστάμεθα πολλοὺς παραδεδωκότας ἑαυτούς, Ptol. pap., but more often with ὅτι or διότι. With ὅτι Ac 15⁷ etc.

Εὑρίσκω as a rule with ptc. (class.). Very often in Ptol. pap.: P. Leip. 40¹⁰ εὑρήκασι τοῦτον ... τυπτόμενον ὑπὸ γαλλιαρίων. Mt 12⁴⁴ εὑρίσκει (sc. τὸν οἶκον) σχολάζοντα, 24⁴⁶ ὃν ... εὑρίσκει οὕτως ποιοῦντα etc., LXX Ge 26¹² καὶ εὗρεν ... ἑκατοστεύουσαν κριθήν. Away from the obj.: Ac 9² τινας εὕρῃ τῆς ὁδοῦ ὄντας *who were*. Passive with nom. of ptc. like class. φαίνομαι: Mt 1¹⁸ εὑρέθη ἐν γαστρὶ ἔχουσα.

Οἶδα: only 2 Co 12² οἶδα ... ἁρπαγέντα τὸν τοιοῦτον (but ὅτι in ³ᵗ). Ptol. pap. dates: 254 253 145. With adj. without ptc. Mk 6²⁰. Elsewhere infin. or (usually) ὅτι, as in LXX and often in papyri.

(b) With verba dicendi et putandi (Mayser II 1, 312ff, 356):

Ἔχω: Lk 14¹⁸ ἔχε με παρῃτημένον. P. Oxy. 292, 6 διὸ παρακαλῶ σε ... ἔχειν αὐτὸν συνεσταμένον.

Ἡγέομαι: Ph 3² ἀλλήλους ἡγούμενοι ὑπερέχοντας ἑαυτῶν. Ὁμολογέω: 1 Jn 4² Ἰ.Χ. ἐν σαρκὶ ἐληλυθότα (B inf.), ³ S, 2 Jn⁷. Without ὄντα: Jn 9²², Ro 10⁹.

(c) With verba declarandi (Mayser II 1, 355) never in NT, but Ign. Rom. 10² δηλώσατε ἐγγύς με ὄντα.

PART II

WORD-GROUPS DEFINING A NOUN OR ADJECTIVE

CHAPTER TWELVE

THE ADJECTIVAL AND PREDICATIVE DEFINITE ARTICLE

THE NEW TESTAMENT USE of the article comes well up to class. Attic standards on the whole [1]. In later papyri the art. is used as a relative pronoun, but never in NT; nor is it a demonstrative pronoun except in the poetic quotations in Ac 17²⁸ and except with μέν and δέ. In Ionic (Herodotus) and later vernacular Greek the art. is sometimes omitted between the preposition and infin., but never in NT.

We have already considered the art. in its substantival use (see pp. 36f). In its adjectival, it particularizes an individual member of a group or class.

§ 1. The Individual Article with Proper Nouns [2]

(a) Names of persons

In class. Greek, names of persons without attribute or apposition have no art. at their first mention. This appertains

---

[1] T. F. Middleton, *The Doctrine of the Greek Article*, 1808, rev. by H. J. Rose, 1858 last ed. K-G I 598–640. Schwyzer II 19–27. Jannaris, index. Mayser II 1, 56ff; II 2, 1–117, 171 (lit); III 3, index. Winer-Schmiedel §§ 17ff. Wackernagel II 125–152. Moulton Einl. 128ff. Radermacher² 112–118. Abel §§ 28–32. E. C. Colwell, "The Definite Article," *JBL* 52, 1933, 12–21. A. Svensson, *Der Gebrauch des bestimmen Artikel in d. nachklass. Epik.* 1937 Lund. Humbert §§ 59–77. D. M. Nelson, *The Articular and Anarthrous Predicate Nominative in the Greek NT*, unpubl. diss. of S. Baptist Theol. Seminary, Louisville, 1945. R. H. Poss, *The Articular and Anarthrous Construction in the Epistle of James*, diss. of S-W. Baptist Theol. Seminary, 1948. J. Gwyn Griffiths, "A Note on the Anarthrous Predicate in Hellenistic Greek," *Exp. T.* 62, July 1951, 314. B. M. Metzger, reply to Griffiths, *Exp. T.* 63, Jan. 1952, 125. H. G. Meecham, "The Anarthrous θεός in John i.1 and 1 Cor. iii.16 ", *Exp. T.* 63, Jan. 1952, 126. Moule 106–117. R. W. Funk, *The Syntax of the Greek Article: Its Importance for Critical Pauline Problems* (Diss., Vanderbilt Univ.) 1953.

[2] Carolus Schmidt, *De articulo in nominibus propriis apud Atticos scriptores pedestres*, Kiel 1890. H. Kallenberg, *Philologus* 49, 1890, 515–547; *Studien über den gr. Artikel*, Berlin 1891. F. Völker, *Syntax der griechischen Papyri*: I Der Artikel, Münster 1903. Gildersleeve II §§ 536ff. *AJP* 11, 1890, 483ff; 24, 1913, 482 (articles by Gildersleeve); 27, 1916, 333–340 (F. Eakin, for i–ii/A.D. pap.); 341ff (C. W. E. Miller). A. Deissmann, "Die Artikel bei Eigennamen in der späteren griech. Umgangssprache," *Berliner philol. Wochenschr.* 22, 1902, 1467f. B. Weiss, " Der Gebrauch des Artikel bei den Eigennamen ", *Th. Stud. u. Krit.* 86, 1913, 349–389.

also in Hellenistic: the art. is used after the person has already been pointed out (*anaphoric*, or pointing back) or when he is often referred to, as in letters in the papyri, giving a familiar tone proper to the colloquial language. A father's or a mother's name, appearing in the gen., usually has the art., although there are many exceptions. Moreover, names of slaves and animals have the art. even when mentioned for the first time, whereas the names of more important persons are anarthrous. The NT formula Σαῦλος ὁ καὶ Παῦλος has many parallels in the Koine. The final development of the popular tendency to use the art. is seen in MGr where proper names almost always have it. It is a mark of familiar style, like pointing with the finger, but despite the pundits it was largely a matter of individual caprice even in class. Greek, for some writers, like Plato, are extremely partial to articular personal names [1]. No rule will account for τὸν Ἰησοῦν ὃν Παῦλος κηρύσσει in Ac 19¹³ and τὸν Ἰησοῦν γινώσκω καὶ τὸν Παῦλον ἐπίσταμαι in ¹⁵. Moreover, the MSS are frequently divided. In other places, Luke abides by the rule: thus in Ac 8³ we are introduced to Σαῦλος (anarth.) but are referred back (anaphoric) in 9¹ to ὁ δὲ Σαῦλος, and meanwhile Δαμασκόν (anarth.) has been introduced, to be referred to anaphorically in 9³ as τῇ Δαμασκῷ.

Ἰησοῦς

In the Gospels, except perhaps Jn, Jesus takes the art. as a matter of course except where an articular appositional phrase is introduced (Mt 26⁶⁹· ⁷¹ μετὰ Ἰ. τοῦ Γαλιλαίου [Ναζωραίου], 27¹⁷· ²² Ἰ. τὸν λεγόμενον Χρ.—Lk 2⁴³ Ἰ. ὁ παῖς, 2⁴¹⁹ περὶ Ἰησοῦ τοῦ Ναζαρηνοῦ). The rule is almost invariable in Mk, even with the gen. (5²¹· ²⁷ 14⁵⁵· ⁶⁷ 15⁴³); the exceptions are Ἰησοῦ Χριστοῦ (1¹) and the vocative (1²⁴ 5⁷ 10⁴⁷). This would indicate that in 1⁹ the anarthrous Ἰησοῦς is to be taken closely with the phrase which follows, i.e. *Jesus of Nazareth in Galilee*. The

---

[1] As the following statistics for the art. with proper names will indicate:
In the first thousand verses of
Aesch. *Prom. V* the art. occurs 210 times
Soph. *Oed. T.*   „   „   „   303 „
Eurip. *Med.*   „   „   „   159 „
Aristoph. *Vespae* „   „   „   562 „
 (where the speech is much less elevated)
Plato *Phaed.*   „   „   „   768 „ .
 (Gildersleeve, *AJP* 11; 486n.).

article does not occur before the prepositional phrase, it is true, but in any case this is not usual in Mark (except for scribal insertions). If it were *Jesus came from N. in Galilee*, it would have to be ὁ Ἰησοῦς to accord with Mark's practice. In Mt there is rather more latitude (anarthrous in the gen.: 14¹ 26⁵¹, and nom. 20³⁰; Ἰησοῦ Χριστοῦ 1¹).

In view of this it is over subtle to explain the anarthrous Jesus in some MSS of Mt 28⁹ Lk 24¹⁵ on the ground that it is his first appearance as the risen Christ; rather accept the reading ὁ Ἰησοῦς of DL, which accords with Gospel usage.

Even in Ac, the first mention of Jesus is articular (1¹ SAE; but anarth. in BD).

Jn however normally follows the class. idiom by introducing proper names without the art., and adding it subsequently. This is usual also in the Koine and the rest of NT. E.g. the risen Christ is now τὸν Ἰησοῦν 20¹⁴ on his first appearance. However, ἀπεκρίθη Ἰησοῦς appears to be a set phrase (1⁴⁸·⁵⁰ etc.). The MSS are particularly divided in Jn 21.

In the Epistles and Rev., however, Jesus stands without the art., except for: 2 Co 4¹⁰ᶠ (D*FG om art.), Eph 4²¹, 1 Th 4¹⁴, 1 Jn 4³; and then there is strong anaphora. The Epistles also usually omit the article with Χριστός; it is here regarded as a proper name rather than = Messiah, probably reflecting a development in Christology. But in Col 2⁶ the author reverts to the earlier designation of Χριστός as a title = Messiah. See H. J. Rose's appendix to his ed. of Middleton, 486–496, for the art. with Ἰησοῦς, κύριος, Χριστός.

Indeclinables

The art. without its proper force has occasionally to serve to determine the case: Mt 1²ᶠᶠ ἐγέννησεν τὸν Ἰσαάκ ... τὸν Ἰακώβ etc. (But the same form is also used in the case of declinable nouns, such as τὸν Ἰούδαν² and τοῦ Οὐρίου.⁶) It is superfluous with names which have a clause in apposition. Mt 1⁶ τὸν Δαυὶδ τὸν βασιλέα (700 om τὸν β.), in ¹⁶ τὸν Ἰωσὴφ τὸν ἄνδρα Μαρίας (P. Oxy. I 2 B 6 prob. rightly om the first τόν), Jn 4⁵ Ἰωσὴφ τῷ υἱῷ αὐτοῦ (SB add τῷ), Lk 3²³⁻³⁸ ὢν υἱός, ὡς ἐνομίζετο, Ἰωσὴφ τοῦ Ἡλεὶ τοῦ Ματθὰτ ... τοῦ Ἀδὰμ τοῦ θεοῦ. N.B. no art. with the first in the list of genitives, as in the ii/A.D.

inscriptions (Moulton Proleg. 236), Ac 7⁸ ἐγέννησεν τὸν Ἰσαάκ, 13²¹ ἔδωκεν . . . τὸν Σαούλ.

THE DECLENSION OF Αβρααμ IN NT IS AS FOLLOWS:

Nom	Αβρααμ	—18 times
Voc	Αβρααμ	—Lk 16²⁴⁻³⁰
Acc	{ τὸν Αβρααμ	—Mt. 3⁹ Lk 3⁸ 16²³ Heb 7⁶·
	Αβρααμ	—Lk 13²⁸ Jn 8⁵⁷ᶠ Ro 4¹
Gen	{ τοῦ Αβρααμ	—rare (and then anaph.): Jn 8³⁹ Ga 3¹⁴, ²⁹
	Αβρααμ	—19 times
Dat	{ τῷ Αβρααμ	—11 times
	Αβρααμ	—Heb 7¹
with prepn.	Αβρααμ	—always, exc. Ga 3⁹

The genitive of proper nouns

In the papyri a parent's name is added in the gen. with the nominative art. normally. In the more official papyrus texts however the parental gen. has the nom. art. before it only when the name of the son or daughter is in the gen. Thus Mt 10² is thoroughly vernacular (Mayser II 2, 7. 22ff. 118): Ἰάκωβος ὁ τοῦ Ζεβεδαίου. Also in the accus. Δαυὶδ τὸν τοῦ Ἰεσσαί Ac 13²² OT, but sometimes as in class. Greek without the art.: Ἰούδαν Σίμωνος Ἰσκαριώτου Jn 6⁷¹ etc., Σώπατρος Πύρρου Βεροιαῖος Ac 20⁴ (pap. exx. in Abel § 44a). However, with the gen. case it is not usual to repeat the art., and τοῦ τοῦ (*of the son of*) is avoided (exc. 1 Clem 12² ὑπὸ Ἰησοῦ τοῦ τοῦ Ναυή): e.g. in class. Greek Περικλέους τοῦ Ξανθίππου, where τοῦ belongs to the first name since in the nom. we have Περικλ. ὁ Ξανθίππου; in NT Ἰωσὴφ τοῦ Ἡλὶ τοῦ . . . Lk 3²³ᶠᶠ (see Klostermann p. 419 on this passage for parallels); papyri Βερενίκης τῆς Νικάνορος (254 B.C.) Mayser II 2, 7f.

It is not clear whether we are to supply υἱός with the apostle Ἰούδας Ἰακώβου (Lk 6¹⁶ Ac 1¹³) or ἀδελφός following Jude¹.

To identify a mother by her son we have (as class.) Μαρία ἡ Ἰωσῆτος Mk 15⁴⁷ (mother, not wife, because this follows Μαρία ἡ Ἰακώβου τοῦ μικροῦ καὶ Ἰωσῆτος μήτηρ⁴⁰), Μαρία ἡ Ἰακώβου Mk 16¹ Lk 24¹⁰. The art. is omitted except for Mt 27⁵⁶ ἡ τοῦ Ἰακ. μήτηρ. And to identify a wife by her husband (class. also): P. Ryl. II 140[7] Ἀντωνίας Δρούσου *the estate of A., wife of D.*, Mt 1[6] τῆς τοῦ Οὐρίου, Jn 19[25] Μαριάμ ἡ τοῦ Κλωπᾶ. The possession of slaves by a family may be indicated by this construction: τοὺς (scil. brothers, Christians) ἐκ τῶν (scil. slaves) Ἀριστοβούλου, Ναρκίσσου Ro 16[10, 11], τῶν (scil. slaves?) Χλόης 1 Co 1[11].

(b) Geographical names

(1) *Names of peoples.* These do not require the art. any more than personal names. (a) Anarthrous Ἰουδαῖοι in Paul's defences against the Jews: Ac 26[2, 3, 4, 7, 21] 25[10]; πάντες Ἰουδαῖοι 26[4] BC*E* (+ οἱ SAC[2] therefore wrong), the exception being 25[8] (τὸν νόμον τῶν Ἰουδαίων). Anarthrous Ἰουδαῖοι also in Paul, exc. in 1 Co 9[20] (ἐγενόμην τοῖς Ἰουδαίοις ὡς Ἰουδαῖος) where he must have some special occasion in mind like Timothy's circumcision; τοῖς ἀνόμοις etc. (the Galatians?) in the following clauses, with τοῖς virtually demonstrative. (b) Anarthrous Ἕλληνες, although in class. Greek regularly with the art. (K-G I 599; Gildersleeve II § 538), and also in the Ptol. pap. (Mayser II 2, 13); the point with Paul is never the totality of a nation, but its characteristic (*the Greek way of life*); consequently Ro 1[14] (Ἕλλησίν τε καὶ βαρβάροις) is, like σοφοῖς τε καὶ ἀνοήτοις which follows it, quite class.[1]: Demosth. 8, 67 (πᾶσιν Ἕλλησι καὶ βαρβάροις = all, whether Greeks or barbarians). (c) Correctly class.: Ἀθηναῖοι πάντες Ac 17[21]. (d) But in the Gospel narrative (and to some extent in Ac) we usually find the art. with Ἰουδαῖοι and other names of nations: however, Mt 28[15] παρὰ Ἰουδαίοις (D adds τοῖς), 10[5] Lk 9[52] εἰς πόλιν (κώμην) Σαμαριτῶν, Jn 4[9] οὐ γὰρ συγχρῶνται Ἰουδαῖοι Σαμαρίταις (vl.). (e) An instance of a national name in masc. sing. is ὁ Ἰσραήλ (prob. because Jacob is thought of). The art. is wanting in Hebraic phrases like γῆ Ἰσραήλ, ὁ λαὸς Ἰσραήλ, etc. To conclude, class. Greek has art. only if it is anaphoric or the people is well known (K-G I 598f); there is no art. in the Attic inscriptions (Meisterhans-Schwyzer 225, 14); in the Ptol. pap. there is very little conformity with any rule (Mayser II 2, 12f).

---

[1] Blass-Debr. § 262, 1.

(2) *Lands and islands* [1]. Like personal names, place names have the art. only if there is some special reason. But ἡ 'Ασία and ἡ Εὐρώπη take the art. regularly from early times, and in the Ptol. papyri (ἡ 'Ασία only), as the two grand divisions of the earth that are naturally opposed to each other; [2] but 'Ασία is articular even when it is used to denote the Roman province (in Ac 2⁹ᶠ Μεσοποταμία, 'Ασία and ἡ Λιβύη ἡ κατὰ Κυρήνην are the only places with an art., because they seem like adjectives and one can supply γῆ). The only exceptions are Ac 6⁹ (ἀπὸ Κιλικίας καὶ 'Ασ.) and 1 Pt 1¹ (where the names of all the countries are without the art. and there is no art. at all in the whole address [3]. Beginnings of letters are formula-like: ἐκλεκτοῖς παρεπιδήμοις διασπορᾶς Πόντου etc.). Many other names of countries also, being originally adjectives (sc. γῆ, χώρα) are never anarthrous. Cp. ἡ 'Ιουδαία γῆ in Jn 3²² and also according to D in 4³. (The anarthrous 'Ιουδ. Ac 2⁹ therefore is corrupt; there are several emendations proposed). Ἡ Γαλιλαία (except Lk 17¹¹ μέσον Σαμαρείας καὶ Γαλιλαίας, where the omission with Σ. has caused omission with Γ. for balance). Ἡ Ἑλλάς Ac 20² (so MGr). Ἡ 'Ιουδαία (for which the Hebraic γῆ 'Ιούδα is also used Mt 2⁶). Ἡ Μεσοποταμία. Ἡ Μυσία (adj.). But names of countries in -ία that are identical with the feminines of related adjectives fluctuate (Gildersleeve II § 547): e.g. in one section of Xenophon (Anab. 1, 2, 21) we have εἰς τὴν Κιλικίαν and ἐν Κιλικίᾳ and εἰς Κιλικίαν; NT anarthrous Ac 6⁹. 'Αραβία also fluctuates in Xen. and Hdt. Φρυγία fluctuates in Dem., Isocr., Xen., and Hdt. NT Φρυγίαν καὶ Παμφυλίαν Ac 2¹⁰ (although strictly adjs.), but τῆς Παμφυλίας Ac 13¹³. The NT always has art. with 'Ιταλία, generally with 'Αχαΐα (exc. Ro 15²⁶ 2 Co 9²). If χώρα or γῆ accompany the proper names, as frequently in Hdt., then those proper names are frankly adjectival, and we find the art. Gildersleeve II § 548). The preposition makes a difference; thus εἰς Συρίαν (although

---

[1] K-G I 598f. Meisterhans-Schwyzer 225, 15 (anarthrous except for Attica, Greece, and Asia, in Attic inscriptions). Gildersleeve II § 547ff. Radermacher² 116 (articular, if the adjectival nature of the name is still obvious, i.e. scil. γῆ. Thus ἡ Μεσοποταμία, ἡ 'Ασία, but Αἴγυπτος). Mayser II 2, 13f.
[2] K-G I 599. Gildersleeve 239ff.
[3] See pp. 221f. Winer-Schmiedel § 18, 14. See also Mayser II 2, 14 for parallels in the abbreviated style of memorials, etc., where there is a long list as in 1 Pt 1¹.

strictly an adj.), Ac 21³, but Σ. does not have the art. in Isoc., Plato or Xen. (Gildersleeve II § 547); also εἰς 'Αραβίαν Ga 1¹⁷. Not being an adj., Αἴγυπτος never takes the art. in NT if we can except the reading of SBDAC p⁴⁵ in Ac 7¹¹ (where in any case the adj. ὅλος appears) and that of BC in 7³⁶. In the Ptol. pap. however, it has the art. always, except after a preposition and in the subordinate genitive (Mayser II 2, 13f). However, the geographical genitive does require the art. and so does the postpositive partitive genitive of the name of a country. This was in fact a rule of class. Greek, well observed by Thucydides (Gildersleeve II § 553). See Ac 13¹⁴ 'Αντιόχειαν τῆς Πισιδίας DEHLP (rest accus.), 21³⁹ Ταρσεύς, τῆς Κιλικίας, 22³ 27⁵.

(3) *Names of towns and cities.* In MGr they always have the art. unless the town is preceded by a preposition (e.g. ἐξ 'Αμβούργου εἰς Νέαν 'Υόρκην); there was always, even in class. Greek, a tendency to resist the art. with common or proper nouns in prepositional phrases. But in class. Greek names of towns do not require the art. and even the anaphoric use is sometimes merely a device to avoid a hiatus; NT follows the rule, and has the art. only for a special reason. The art. is present only because it is anaphoric in Ac 9³· ³⁸· ⁴² (τῆς 'Ιόππης), 17¹³ (ἐν τῇ Β, because εἰς Β. in ¹⁰), ¹⁶ (ἐν ταῖς 'Α., because ἕως 'Α. in ¹⁵); in 18² τῆς 'Ρώμης is due to attraction to τῆς 'Ιταλίας; in 28¹⁴ the art. denotes Rome as the goal of the journey (demonstrative). Even Τρῳάς, although subject to an art. because it is 'Αλεξάνδρεια ἡ Τρῳάς, is anarthrous in Ac 16⁸ 20⁵ 2 Ti 4¹³ (as in Xen. Hdt), and is articular only anaphorically in Ac 16¹¹ 20⁶ 2 Co 2¹² (referring to 1²³ where Troas was in mind). Yet there is no apparent reason for the art. with towns mentioned as halting-places: Ac 17¹ τὴν 'Αμφίπολιν καὶ τὴν 'Απολλωνίαν (εἰς Θεσσ. because of the preposition). Note further ἤλθομεν εἰς Μίλητον (Ac 20¹⁵), but on leaving and so anaphoric ἀπὸ δὲ τῆς Μιλήτου ⁽¹⁷⁾, both with preposition; also παραπλεῦσαι τὴν Ἔφεσον ⁽¹⁶⁾, but πέμψας εἰς Ἔφεσον (because preposition). Yet there is a preposition with articular place-names in 20¹³ 21¹ (in spite of εἰς Πάταρα, etc.), 23³¹. Thus there is a rule, but it is not unbroken.

Unless an adj. is present (Rev 3¹²) 'Ιεροσόλυμα, 'Ιερουσαλήμ rarely take the art. If they do, it is anaphoric: Jn 2²³ 5². In Jn 10²² the art. is absent (but added by ABWL). The exceptions to this rule are Jn 11¹⁸ Ac 5²⁸. Josephus usually observes it.

(4) *Names of rivers and seas* ¹. They are generally articular in NT and Ptol. pap. (except sometimes with a preposition). In class. Greek rivers usually take ὁ ποταμός, like Mk 1⁵ ὁ 'Ιορδάνης ποταμός (elsewhere ὁ 'Ιορδάνης) and Her. V. I 1, 2 τὸν ποταμὸν τὸν Τίβεριν. Cp. Jn 18¹ τοῦ χειμάρρου Κεδρών (SBCD corrupt). Ac 27²⁷ ὁ 'Αδρίας (class.).

(c) *Astronomical names and natural phenomena*

Winds. Always without art. in NT. Νότος *south wind* Lk 12⁵⁵ Ac 27¹³ 28¹³. With and without in the papyri (Mayser II 2, 18).

Points of the compass. With prepositions, they never have art. in NT: Mt 2¹ 8¹¹ etc. (ἀπὸ ἀνατολῶν), 12⁴² (βασίλισσα νότου), 24²⁷ (ἕως δυσμῶν), Lk 12⁵⁴ (ἀπὸ δυσμῶν), 13²⁹ (ἀπὸ βορρᾶ καὶ νότου), Rev 7² 16¹² (ἀπὸ ἀνατολῆς ἡλίου). The NT exception is Mt 2². ⁹ ἐν τῇ ἀνατολῇ; therefore perhaps not a compass-point but *in its rising*.

"Ηλιος and σελήνη. The art. prevails, as in papyri (Mayser II 2, 18f), but we do find Mt 13⁶ ἡλίου δὲ ἀνατείλαντος (D adds τοῦ), Lk 21²⁵ ἐν ἡλίῳ καὶ σελήνῃ καὶ ἄστροις (yet foll. by ἐπὶ τῆς γῆς), Ac 27²⁰ μήτε δὲ ἡλίου μήτε ἄστρων ἐπιφαινόντων, 1 Co 15⁴¹ ἄλλη δόξα ἡλίου ... σελήνης ... ἀστέρων, Rev 7² 16¹² ἀπὸ ἀνατολῆς ἡλίου, 22⁵ φωτὸς ἡλίου.

§ 2. The Individual Article with Common Nouns [2]

(a) *Individual anaphoric use: Introduction*

Used with nouns, the art. has the same double import in Hell. Greek as in class. Greek: it is either individualizing or generic. It either calls special attention to one definite member of a class so that ὁ = οὗτος ὁ (e.g. πλείονες = *more*, but οἱ πλείονες = *the majority*), or else it makes the contrast between the whole class, as such, and other classes, so that οἱ ἄνθρωποι = *mankind*, as opposed to οἱ θεοί. The generic use is considered below, pp. 180f. The necessity for using the art. is not dispensed

---

[1] K-G I 599f. Gildersleeve II §§ 558–561. Mayser II 2, 16.
[2] K-G I 589ff. Gildersleeve II §§ 565–567, 569, 571–572.

with by the addition of οὗτος or ἐκεῖνος, or a possessive. But the art. is often omitted where we expect it by the rules, especially in set phrases, titles, salutations, letter headings, pairs, lists (e.g. Ro 8³⁵· ³⁸f), definitions (e.g. Ro 1¹⁶f 8²⁴). The Heb. construct state had an influence here (see pp. 179f). Sometimes the absence is almost inexplicable: Jas 2⁸ νόμον τελεῖτε βασιλικόν; we must understand it predicatively *the law as a royal commandment* (Radermacher² 117). Codex Bezae will often omit the art. in an arbitrary way, perhaps through Latin influence.

The individualizing use of the art. was described by Apollonius Dyscolus, an early grammarian, as *anaphoric*, in that it refers back to what is already familiar. Thus ὁ ἀδελφὸς αὐτοῦ is anaphoric, *that brother of his*; while ἀδελφὸς αὐτοῦ is *a brother of his*. It means that the art. will not normally be used when a person or object is first introduced, or when only an undefined part of a group or class is referred to, or when a person or object is thought of only predicatively (and therefore not individually and definitely). In such cases there is no anaphora to particular or well-known specimens or to a class considered as a whole. So it is usual to express a predicate without the art. (see exceptions, pp. 182–184).

It is not difficult to find instances where NT writers conform to this rule; we have seen it already with the proper names. We see it again in Lk 4¹⁷ βιβλίον and afterwards τὸ βιβλίον; Ro 5³· ⁵ ὑπομονὴν κατεργάζεται, ἡ δὲ ὑπομονὴ δοκιμήν, ἡ δὲ δοκιμὴ ἐλπίδα· ἡ δὲ ἐλπίς ...,⁷ (although he is not previously mentioned, *your good man* τοῦ ἀγαθοῦ is very definite); Jas 2¹⁴ πίστιν and then ἡ πίστις; LXX Bel et Drac.³· ⁴ Βήλ and then τῷ Βήλ. Therefore when we find τῷ ἁμαρτωλῷ Lk 18¹³ it must mean the *sinner of sinners*; in Ro 12¹⁹ we must think of it as *the well-known wrath*; in 1 Co 10¹⁴ that *worship of idols which you know so well*; in Rev 3¹⁷ ὁ ταλαίπωρος is *that wretched man*; Mt 5¹ τὸ ὄρος = that great hill which stood like a throne behind the sea (Zerwick § 124), Lk 14¹⁷ τὸν δοῦλον is the servant whose particular task it was to do this; Mt 8¹² ὁ κλαυθμὸς καὶ ὁ βρυγμὸς τῶν ὀδόντων *that memorable* or *greatest of all*.

The art. was commonly used in class. Attic prose to mark a proper or usual connection of an obj. with its subject: τὴν χεῖρα is *his hand* Jn 7³⁰, τὸν ἀδελφόν *his brother* 2 Co 12¹⁸, just as in the papyri ἡ γυνὴ καὶ οἱ υἱοί is *his wife and children* (Mayser II 2,

23), and Ac 21⁵ σὺν γ. καὶ τέκνοις = *with their wives and children* (art. omitted because a formula, like Ac 1¹⁴ σὺν γυναιξίν, Ro 1⁷ ἀπὸ θεοῦ πατρὸς ἡμῶν), Heb 12⁷ τίς γάρ υἱός, ὃν οὐ παιδεύει πχτήρ (not ὁ πατήρ *his father*) *a father*.

(b) *Articular Use with certain nouns*

1. θεός and κύριος ¹.

Since these words come near to being proper nouns in NT, it is not surprising that the art. is so often omitted. Κύριος even more than θεός seems to have assumed this rôle, for we have Mt 21⁹ ὀνόματι κυρίου, Ac 2²⁰ vl. τὴν ἡμέραν κυρίου, 5⁹ τὸ πνεῦμα κυρίου, 2 Co 3¹⁷¹ τὸ πνεῦμα κυρίου, τὴν δόξαν κυρίου, Jas 5¹¹ τὸ τέλος κυρίου ². These names are especially anarthrous after a preposition, e.g. ἐν κυρίῳ *passim*, ἀπὸ θεοῦ Jn 3², or when they depend in the gen. on another anarthrous noun: Mt 27⁴³ θεοῦ εἰμι υἱός, Lk 3² ἐγένετο ῥῆμα θεοῦ. Another near-proper name is θεὸς πατήρ 2 Pt 1¹⁷ Jude ¹. In the LXX the anarthrous יהוה is rendered by the more slavish translators by means of anarthrous κύριος; but the addition of ל, אל, and את causes the art. to be used, hence: τῷ κυρίῳ, τὸν κύριον. But in NT we have both ἄγγελος κυρίου and ἐν κυρίῳ. Like the LXX is κύριος ὁ θεός, with and without gen.: Lk 1⁶⁸ OT κύριος ὁ θεὸς τοῦ Ἰσραήλ, Rev 1⁸ etc. κύριος ὁ θεός. As a general rule it may be said that for Paul ὁ κύριος = Christ, and κύριος = Yahweh (Zerwick § 125ª); in which case, we must understand ὁ δὲ Κύριος τὸ πν. ἐστιν (2 Co 3¹⁷) as = Yahweh but anaphoric.

2. οὐρανός, γῆ, θάλασσα, κόσμος.

These words are frequently anarthrous, especially after a preposition. But οὐρανός is anarthrous where there is no preposition: Ac 3²¹ 17²⁴ 2 Pt 3¹⁰ (ABC add οἱ). Papyri: Mayser II 2, 29. Γῆ prefers the art., even sometimes with a

---

¹ B. Weiss, *Theol. Stud. u. Krit.* 84, 1911, 319-392, 503-538. Baucr s.v. κύριος II 2. W. W. Graf Baudissin, *Kyrios als Gottesname im Judentum* ..., I Teil, Giessen 1929; *Der Gebrauch des Gottesnamens Kyrios in Sept.*

² This flatly contravenes the canon of Apollonius to the effect that an anarthrous noun may not be governed by a noun having the art.; but κύριος must be taken as a proper name = Yahweh.

preposition; however, we have it anarthrous: Mk 13²⁷ ἀπὸ ἄκρου γῆς ἕως ἄκρου οὐρανοῦ, Ac 17²⁴ οὐρανοῦ καὶ γῆς κύριος, 2 Pt 3⁵ οὐρανοί... καὶ γῆ, ¹⁰ οὐρανοί (ABC add οἱ)... στοιχεῖα... γῆ (CP add ἡ). With the preposition, anarthrous: Mt 28¹⁸ (BD add τῆς), Lk 2¹⁵ 1 Co 8⁵ 15⁴⁷ Eph 3¹⁵ Heb 12²⁵ 8¹. Θάλασσα too is anarthrous after a preposition or in gen. after another noun: Mt 4¹⁵ OT ὁδὸν θαλάσσης, Lk 21²⁵ ἤχους θαλάσσης, Jas 1⁶ κλύδωνι θαλάσσης, Jude¹³ κύματα ἄγρια θαλ. The same is true of κόσμος: anarthr. predicate Ro 4¹³ 11¹². ¹⁵, and in prepositional formulae: ἐν κόσμῳ 1 Co 8⁴ 14¹⁰ Ph 2¹⁵ etc. 2 Pt 1⁴ vl., ἀπὸ [καταβολῆς] κόσμου Mt 25³⁴ etc. Also anarthrous: 2 Co 5¹⁹ Ga 6¹⁴.

3. θάνατος.

It frequently appears without an art., especially in certain phrases like ἕως θανάτου (Mt 26³⁸), ἔνοχος θανάτου, ἄξιον θανάτου, παραδιδόναι εἰς θάνατον, γεύεσθαι θανάτου. Apart from the anaphoric use (e.g. ἡ πληγὴ τοῦ θ. Rev 13³· ¹²), the art. is used (a) either of the actual death of a definite person (1 Co 11²⁶), or (b) of death in the abstract: Jn 5²⁴ καταβέβηκεν ἐκ τοῦ θ. εἰς τὴν ζωήν, or (c) where Death is half personified (Rev 13³· ¹²), or (d) where assimilation to a noun in connection with it causes a borrowing of the art.: τὸ ἀπόκριμα τοῦ θ. (2 Co 1⁹).

4. πνεῦμα.

It is urged sometimes (e.g. A. M. Perry, *JBL* 68, 1949, 329ff) that the omission of the art. is important theologically, but the usage is often arbitrary. Τὸ ἅγιον πνεῦμα (rather more often τὸ πν. τὸ ἅγ.) is sometimes personal. When it is anarthrous it is a divine spirit inspiring man (1 Th 1⁵), but the matter is complicated threefold by the question of the non-use of the art. with proper nouns, and in prepositional expressions (increased in Hell. Greek), and even (in Biblical Greek through influence of the Heb. construct state) before a genitive. In none of these situations need the lack of the art. indicate any indefiniteness of reference, and with πνεῦμα the reference could still be to the Pentecostal Spirit. Nevertheless in Luke τὸ πν. τὸ ἅγ. tends to be the Pentecostal Spirit while ἅγιον πνεῦμα is an unknown power, God's spirit as opposed to that of men or demons (Procksch in Kittel WB I 105). Doubtless also anaphora complicates the matter, as in Luke $2^{26.\ 27}$ Ac 2^4 8^{18}. In 10^{44} ἔπεσεν τὸ πν. τὸ ἅγ. ἐπὶ πάντας, there is reference to the well-known fact of the out-pouring. Omission, even when the reference is the Holy Spirit, is also occasioned by the presence of a preposition or by assimilation to an anarthrous noun : Ro 14^{17} after a list of anarthrous abstract nouns and after ἐν, Mt 1^{18} ἐκ πνεύματος ἁγίου. Without a preposition (Lk $1^{15.\ 35.\ 41.\ 67}$ 2^{25} 3^{16} 4^1 11^{13} Ac 1^2 4^{25} 6^5 7^{55} $8^{15.\ 17.\ 19}$ 10^{38} 11^{24} 19^2) it is not the personal Holy Spirit, but the influence of a divine spirit which is intended, if St. Luke omits the article.

5. γράμματα :

2 Ti 3^{15} ἱερὰ γράμματα SC^bD*FG 33 Clem Epiph (AC* corr. to τά) is a technical formula (see Schrenk in Kittel WB I 765^{11ff}), Est 6^1, Jos. Ant. 16, 168.

6. ἐκκλησία :

1 Co 14^4 ἐκκλησίαν οἰκοδομεῖ, 3 Jn^6 ἐνώπιον ἐκκλησίας. Is it a *congregation* or *the Church?* (see K. L. Schmidt in Kittel WB III 508^{18ff}).

7. *Abstract nouns* [1].

They may be articular or anarthrous in all periods down to MGr. They tend to be anarthrous if there is greater emphasis on the abstract quality, but no vital difference was felt in class. Greek; the passage is too easy from articular to anarthrous. Thus Plato *Meno* 99A ἡ ἀρετή, 99E ἀρετή, 100B ἡ ἀρετή ... ἀρετή. So Paul, Ro 3^{30} ὃς δικαιώσει περιτομὴν ἐκ πίστεως καὶ ἀκροβυστίαν διὰ τῆς πίστεως (prob. no significance for exegesis, but the art. is anaphoric : *by that same faith*). Translators do not trouble to distinguish τῇ χάριτι in Eph 2^8 from χάριτι in 2^5 (NEB *by his grace* both times); it may be that τῇ is merely anaphoric, looking back to ^{5}, but there is another point of view : omission of the art. tends to emphasize the inherent qualities of abstract nouns while the art. makes them more concrete, unified and individual. In 2^8 then the reference is to God's historical act of saving grace; in 2^5, to grace as such, in contrast to other means of redemption (Zerwick § 131). The difficulty therefore is to account for the presence of the art.,

---

[1] K-G I 606 i. Gildersleeve II §§ 565–567. Mayser II 2, 30f.

just as with concrete nouns the problem is rather to account for its absence.

E.g. Mt 5⁶ τὴν δικαιοσύνην (contrast 5¹⁰), 7²³ τὴν ἀνομίαν (difficult), Ro 12⁷ εἴτε διακονίαν, ἐν τῇ διακονίᾳ· εἴτε ὁ διδάσκων, ἐν τῇ διδασκαλίᾳ; Ro 12⁹ᶠ ἡ ἀγάπη ἀνυπόκριτος, τῇ φιλαδελφίᾳ φιλόστοργοι, τῇ τιμῇ ἀλλήλους προηγούμενοι, τῇ σπουδῇ μὴ ὀκνηροί, because they are virtues assumed to be well known; 1 Co 13¹³ νυνὶ δὲ μένει πίστις ἐλπὶς ἀγάπη ... μείζων δὲ τούτων ἡ ἀγάπη (anaph.), 14²⁰ μὴ παιδία γίνεσθε ταῖς φρεσίν, ἀλλὰ τῇ κακίᾳ νηπιάζετε (art. by attraction to the concrete ταῖς φρεσίν *your* mind), Col 3⁵ πορνείαν ἀκαθαρσίαν πάθος ἐπιθυμίαν ... καὶ τὴν πλεονεξίαν, ἥτις ἐστὶν εἰδωλολατρία *and that principal vice, covetousness* (the added clause individualizes the noun, as in Ac 19³ 26²⁷ 2 Co 8¹⁸), Heb 1¹⁴ εἰς διακονίαν, κληρονομεῖν σωτηρίαν (2³ 5⁹ 6⁹ 9²⁸ 11⁷), but τῆς σωτηρίας 2¹⁰.

Νόμος.

Paul is fond of anarthrous νόμος, but on no easily intelligible principle. Thus, in Ga, ὁ νόμος 10 times, νόμος 21. Ro 2¹³ is especially difficult: οὐ γὰρ οἱ ἀκροαταὶ νόμου (+ τοῦ KLP) δίκαιοι παρὰ τῷ (BD* om) θεῷ, ἀλλ' οἱ ποιηταὶ νόμου (+ τοῦ DᶜEKL) δικαιωθήσονται; it may not be the total Mosaic Law which Paul has in mind, but law as such (yet we still expect anaphoric τοῦ on the second mention). See also anarthr. νόμος in Jas 1²⁵ 4¹¹ 2¹¹ (but artic. in ¹⁰), ¹² νόμος ἐλευθερίας (not Mosaic). Attempts have been made, from Origen onwards, to establish a principle [1] that the articular form indicates the Mosaic Law, but the context is a surer guide. See also Ro 3²⁰ διὰ γὰρ νόμου ἐπίγνωσις ἁμαρτίας (epigrammatic: *to know any sin there must be some law*), 5¹³ ἄχρι γὰρ νόμου (*till a law came*), 6¹⁴ ἁμαρτία (not *no sin*, but "sin as power", as usual in Paul; see Lohmeyer *Zschr. f. nt. Wiss.* 29, 1930, 2ff; J. Jeremias, *Die Abendmahlsworte Jesu*, 1935, 72f) ὑμῶν οὐ κυριεύσει· οὐ γάρ ἐστε ὑπὸ νόμον (*under any law*).

Σάρξ being virtually an abstract noun is anarthrous: *the natural state of man*; frequent ἐν σαρκί and κατὰ σάρκα (+ τήν as vl. 2 Co 11¹⁸ Jn 8¹⁵).

ἀλήθεια.

Altogether inexplicable by the rules of anaphora are Jn 8⁴⁴ (καὶ ἐν τῇ ἀληθείᾳ οὐκ ἔστηκεν, ὅτι οὐκ ἔστιν ἀλήθεια ἐν αὐτῷ), 17¹⁷ (ἁγίασον αὐτοὺς ἐν τῇ ἀληθείᾳ· ὁ λόγος ὁ σὸς ἀλήθειά ἐστιν),

---

[1] Sanday-Headlam *ICC Ro* on 2¹³ᶠ, p. 58; Burton *ICC Ga* 447–460.

3 Jn³ (μαρτυρούντων σου τῇ ἀληθείᾳ, καθὼς σὺ ἐν ἀληθείᾳ περιπατεῖς). But Colwell's rule (see below, pp. 183f) may be relevant (Moule 112). Zerwick's suggestion is (§ 132) that the definite reference with the art. is to Christ as the real truth, life, light, etc.; all other truths, lives, lights, being transitory. So he explains the repeated art. in Jn 14⁶ ἡ ὁδὸς καὶ ἡ ἀλήθεια καὶ ἡ ζωή, which otherwise is inexplicable, not being anaphoric. Therefore 2 Jn¹ (οὓς ἐγὼ ἀγαπῶ ἐν ἀληθείᾳ, καὶ οὐκ ἐγὼ μόνος ἀλλὰ καὶ πάντες οἱ ἐγνωκότες τὴν ἀλήθειαν) *whom I sincerely love, and ... all who have sincere standards* (anaphora?), ⁴ (περιπατοῦντες ἐν ἀληθείᾳ) *behaving with sincerity*, ³ *sincerity*, 3 Jn¹ *whom I sincerely love*, 2 Ti 2²⁵ 3⁷ Ti 1¹ ἐπίγνωσις ἀληθείας, Heb 10²⁶ ἡ ἐπίγνωσις τῆς ἀληθείας (not Christ, but articular by attraction), Eph 4²¹ (καθώς ἐστιν ἀλήθεια ἐν τῷ Ἰησοῦ), 2 Co 11¹⁰ (ἐστιν ἀλήθεια Χριστοῦ ἐν ἐμοί), 3 Jn⁴ (cp. above) ἵνα ἀκούω τὰ ἐμὰ τέκνα ἐν τῇ ἀληθείᾳ περιπατοῦντα *in the Truth* (Christ), ⁸ ἵνα συνεργοὶ γινώμεθα τῇ ἀληθείᾳ (Christ), ¹² Δημητρίῳ μεμαρτύρηται ὑπὸ πάντων καὶ ὑπὸ αὐτῆς τῆς ἀληθείας *Christ himself*. This distinction is a peculiarity of Biblical Greek; the papyri have the art. each time, P. Par 46; 47 (152 B.C.); 63. 16 (165 B.C.).

In the Ptol. pap. the following other abstract nouns are articular: φιλοτιμία, ἀηδία, τολμηρία, μέγεθος, ὕψος, πλῆθος, λογεία. The following are anarthrous: φιλανθρωπία, ἀντίλημψις, ἐπισημασία, εὐγνωμοσύνη, ἀμνησία, ἡγεμονία μέγεθος (usually), φύσις, βάθος, μῆκος (usually), κρίσις, ἀναμέτρησις. These vary: πλάτος, γνῶσις (Mayser II 2, 31).

8. *Numerals*.

Usually with cardinal numerals there is no art., but if the art. stands it indicates (as in class. Greek) a certain fraction, as in the scribal correction of Mt 25² αἱ (Z) πέντε ... αἱ (E fam¹³ 543 28) πέντε, after δέκα, *the first five of them ... the other five of them*; Lk 17¹⁷ οἱ ἐννέα *the nine of them*; Rev. 17¹⁰ ἑπτά ... οἱ πέντε ... ὁ εἷς ... ὁ ἄλλος. Or else the art. marks a contrast of one fraction from another. Thus in Mt 20²⁴ = Mk 10⁴¹ *the ten* are the *remaining* ten disciples, not a fixed group of disciples (Wackernagel II 318).

The ordinary numeral also commonly lacks the art. as in class. Greek (e.g. ὀγδόῳ ἔτει), especially after a preposition, and specially with ὥρα.. Mt 27⁴⁵ ἀπὸ ἕκτης ὥρας, Mk 15³³, Ac 12¹⁰ 16¹² (vl. -τη prob. corrupt), 2 Co 12². But there is anaphora with ὥρα in Mt 20⁹ 27⁴⁶. In Mt 20⁶ there is the art. because of ellipse of ὥρα, and in Ac 3¹ because further defining words are introduced (τὴν ὥραν τῆς προσευχῆς τὴν ἐνάτην). Cp. papyri: P. Petr. II 10 (2) 5 (240 B.C.), P. Hib. 110, 65. 100 (253 B.C.) ὥρας πρώτης; P. Hib. 75, 79 (255 B.C.) ὥρα ιᾱ; 106 (255 B.C.) ὥρας ιβ̄. With ἡμέρα the art. tends to be used, e.g. τῇ τρίτῃ ἡμέρᾳ always, and Jn 6³⁹ff ἐν τῇ ἐσχάτῃ ἡμέρᾳ (but 2 Ti 3¹ Jas 5³ ἐν ἐσχάταις ἡμέραις); but a preposition may cause its omission: Ac 20¹⁸ Ph 1⁵ (+ τῆς p⁴⁶ SBAP) ἀπὸ πρώτης ἡμέρας, like 1 Pt. 1⁵ ἐν καιρῷ ἐσχάτῳ.

(c) *Absence of Article after Prepositions* [1]

Such phrases may be formulae inherited from a pre-articular age of Greek. In class. Greek they are often anarthrous, like proverbs and enumerations, although anaphora or contrast may restore the art.: e.g. Lys. 12, 16 εἰς ἄστυ *to town*, but 54 εἰς τὸ ἄστυ; Demosth. 19, 30 ἐν ἀγορᾷ but 27, 58 ἐν τῇ ἀγορᾷ. In NT: Mk 7⁴ ἀπ' ἀγορᾶς, 15²⁷ ἐκ δεξιῶν ... ἐξ εὐωνύμων, Mt 24³³ ἐπὶ θύραις, Lk 7³² ἐν ἀγορᾷ (but in Mt 11¹⁶ etc. ἐν ταῖς ἀγοραῖς [CEFW om ταῖς]), Jn 6¹⁷ εἰς πλοῖον *aboard*; papyri ἐπὶ πόταμον *riverwards*, κατὰ πόλιν *in town*, κατὰ γῆν καὶ θάλασσαν *by land and sea* (class.), ἐν δεξιᾷ *on the right* (class.). The omission in time-designation is class.: e.g. πρὸς ἑσπέραν Lk 24²⁹ (Ac 28²³), πρὸ καιροῦ Mt 8²⁹ (24⁴⁵ Lk 4¹³ 8¹³ Ac 13¹¹ Ro 5⁶ Heb 11¹¹), διὰ νυκτός Ac 5¹⁹ (vl. art.), μεχρὶ μεσονυκτίου Ac 20⁷ (but κατὰ τὸ μεσονύκτιον 16²⁵). For personal anatomy one might expect the individualizing art., but ἐπὶ πρόσωπον Lk 5¹² etc. (2 Co 10⁷), and the omission occurs also in profane authors like Polybius; class. similar κατ' ὀφθαλμούς, ἐν ὀφθαλμοῖς.

Formulae like ἀπ' ἀγροῦ understandably have no art. because no individual field is in mind; but referring to a definite field in Mt 13²⁴ ἐν τῷ ἀγρῷ αὐτοῦ. But also ἐν τῷ ἀγρῷ (D Chrys om τῷ) without indiv. reference (Mt 13⁴⁴) like τὰ κρίνα τοῦ ἀγροῦ (6²⁸). The excuse for the art. must then be that it is generic, *the country* (like τὸ ὄρος *the highlands* Mk 3¹³ etc.).

(d) *Absence of Article before a noun which governs a genitive* [2]

A noun is sometimes made definite by a defining gen. or adj. In Heb. a noun may be in the construct state or have a suffix

---
[1] K-G I 605f. Gildersleeve II § 569. Eakin 333. Mayser II 2, 14ff.
[2] Radermacher² 116. Zerwick §§ 136–137.

attached to it, and in either case it would be anarthrous. This influenced the LXX and in turn the NT writers in varying degrees. Thus ἄγγελος κυρίου is not *an angel* but *the angel*, δόξα λαοῦ σου is *the glory*. It usually happens that the second noun is also anarthrous; this balance is a Greek characteristic, not Heb. The canon of Apollonius Dyscolus asserts that, of nouns in regimen, either both have the art. (like ἐν τῷ λόγῳ τῆς ἀληθείας Col 1[5]), or neither (like ἐν λόγῳ ἀληθείας 2 Co 6[7]). Philo tends to violate the canon, Plato to keep it (exx. in Radermacher[2] 116). But the canon must be modified to this extent, that the governing noun may be anarthrous while the governed is articular (Ro 3[25] εἰς ἔνδειξιν τῆς δικαιοσύνης αὐτοῦ; Eph 1[6] εἰς ἔπαινον δόξης τῆς χάριτος αὐτοῦ); this through Heb. influence. It is obvious that this omission occurs chiefly in prepositional phrases, to which secular writers normally do not add a gen. after the Semitic way: ἀπὸ προσώπου, διὰ χειρός, διὰ στόματος, ἀπὸ ὀφθαλμῶν σου Lk 19[42]; ἐκ κοιλίας μητρός (Mt 19[12] Lk 1[15] Ac 3[2] 14[8]), ἐν βίβλῳ ζωῆς Ph 4[3] (cp. Rev, Mk 12[26]), ἐν δακτύλῳ θεοῦ (Lk 11[20]). A further complication is that proper nouns and geogr. names in the gen. may be anarthrous even when subordinate to an articular noun: ἡ Ἄρτεμις Ἐφεσίων, τὴν Ἐφεσίων πόλιν, ἐν τῷ βίβλῳ Μωϋσέως.

(e) *Generic Article* [1]

The principle of the generic art. is to select a normal or representative individual. When all is said, the whole question is affected by personal taste; we have in one sentence both ὑπὲρ δικαίου and ὑπὲρ τοῦ ἀγαθοῦ Ro 5[7] (*ICC Ro* 128). Almost all the exx. in poetry have been explained on other principles, sometimes by anaphora, sometimes on the principle of contrast (Gildersleeve II § 563). Contrary to our own usage, the art. is put before nouns denoting a species, family or class of any of the kingdoms of nature; and before abstract nouns of virtues, vices, sciences, etc. (Jannaris § 1201), e.g. ὁ ἄνθρωπος *mankind*, ὁ σῖτος *corn*, ἡ ἀρετή *virtue*, ὁ κλέπτης (Jn 10[10]) *thieves*.

A generic art. also accompanies plurals like ἄνθρωποι, ἔθνη, νεκροί (exc. after a preposition): Mt 14[2] ἠγέρθη ἀπὸ τῶν νεκρῶν, 22[31], 1 Co 15[42] τῆς ἀναστάσεως τῶν νεκρῶν, Eph 5[14] OT ἐκ τῶν νεκρῶν, Col 2[12] BDEFG (rest om τῶν), 1 Th 1[10] (ACK om τῶν). But Mt 17[9] etc. ἐκ νεκρῶν

---

[1] K-G I 589, 1. Mayser II 2, 41ff. Gildersleeve II §§ 563f.

ἐγερθῇ, Ac 17³² 23⁶ etc. ἀνάστασιν νεκρῶν (construct state and Apoll. canon), 1 Pt 4⁵ κρῖναι ζῶντας καὶ νεκρούς, Heb 1⁴ B p⁴⁶ Chrys ἀγγέλων. Double art.: τὰ ἔθνη τοῦ κόσμου Lk 12³⁰ (Apoll. canon); but ἔθνη is especially liable to be anarthrous: Ac 4²⁵ OT Ro 11¹²ᶠ 15¹² OT; οὐχὶ καὶ ἐθνῶν Ro 3²⁹ᶠ; esp. with prepositions Ac 4²⁷ 15¹⁴ 2 Co 11²⁶ Ga 2¹⁵.

(*f*) *Repetition of Article with several nouns connected by* καί [1]

The art. may be carried over from the first noun to the other(s), especially if they are regarded as a unified whole and the gender and number are the same: Col 1² τοῖς ἐν Κ. ἁγίοις καὶ (sc. τοῖς) πιστοῖς ἀδελφοῖς ἐν Χ. *the saints and the faithful brethren*; Eph 2²⁰ τῶν ἀποστόλων καὶ προφητῶν; Lk 22⁴ τοῖς ἀρχιερεῦσιν καὶ στρατηγοῖς; Ac 15² πρὸς τοὺς ἀποστόλους καὶ πρεσβυτέρους. This is so even occasionally when the gender is different but the number the same, as in P. Tebt. I 14¹⁰ (114 B.C.); Lk 1⁶ ἐν πάσαις ταῖς ἐντολαῖς καὶ δικαιώμασιν τοῦ κυρίου, 14²³ εἰς τοὺς ὁδοὺς καὶ φραγμούς, Mk 12³³ vl. Ac 15²⁰·²⁹ 21²⁵ Col 2²² κατὰ τὰ ἐντάλματα καὶ διδασκαλίας τῶν ἀνθρώπων, unless κατὰ τά is due to dittography (but in LXX Isa 29¹³, to which this is an allusion, there is no κατά as well as no τά).

One must look critically at the common view that in Ti 2¹³ we have two clauses in apposition: τοῦ μεγάλου θεοῦ καὶ [sc. τοῦ] σωτῆρος ἡμῶν 'Ι.Χ. The same is true of 2 Pt 1¹ τοῦ θεοῦ ἡμῶν καὶ [sc. τοῦ] 'Ι.Χ. (S κυρίου for θεοῦ) [2]. In Hell., and indeed for practical purposes in class. Greek the repetition of the art. was not strictly necessary to ensure that the items be considered separately. The relevant consideration on the other side is that the phrase *God and Saviour* in contemporary language referred to only one person, c. A.D. 100. Moreover, the art. could have been repeated to avoid misunderstanding if separate individuals had been intended [3].

Often the repetition, even with nouns of the same gender, does indeed indicate that two distinct subjects are involved. Οἱ Φαρισαῖοι καὶ Σαδδουκαῖοι involves no misunderstanding, but

---

[1] K-G I 611, 2. Gildersleeve II §§ 603–605. Mayser II 2, 47ff. Radermacher² 115. Zerwick §§ 138, 139.

[2] See Lock in *ICC* on Ti 2¹³, Hort on Jas 2¹, Moulton Proleg. 84, A. T. Robertson, " The Greek Article and the Deity of Christ ", *Expositor* VIII, 21 (1921) 182–188, Stauffer in Kittel WB III 107²⁶⁸, Moule 109. Stauffer's plea, based on position of ἡμῶν, is grammatically weak.

[3] *NEB* (text) is probably correct, following previous standard versions except AV which follows Vulgate (comma between, in Sixtine and Clementine).

the repetition of the art. prevents misunderstanding in Lk 11⁵¹ μεταξὺ τοῦ θυσιαστηρίου καὶ τοῦ οἴκου, Jn 19⁶ οἱ ἀρχιερεῖς καὶ οἱ ὑπηρέται (not a unified whole like the chief-priests, elders and scribes of Mt 16²¹ etc.), Ac 26³⁰ ὁ βασιλεὺς καὶ ὁ ἡγεμών, 1 Co 3⁸ ὁ φυτεύων καὶ ὁ ποτίζων ἕν εἰσιν (cp. Jn 4³⁶), 1 Th 1⁷· ⁸ ἐν τῇ Μακεδονίᾳ καὶ ἐν τῇ 'Αχαίᾳ (two separate provinces), then they are grouped together (ἐν τῇ Μακεδονίᾳ καὶ 'Αχαίᾳ) and contrasted with ἀλλ' ἐν παντὶ τόπῳ. Repetition generally takes place with τε καί, and that is probably why D adds τῶν in Ac 14⁶ τῶν ἐθνῶν τε καὶ 'Ιουδαίων. There is frequently a variety of readings, e.g. Ro 4¹² τοῖς οὐκ ἐκ περιτομῆς μόνον ἀλλὰ καὶ τοῖς στοιχοῦσιν (*ICC Ro* in loc.)

(g) *Article with Quotations* [1]

As in class. Greek the neuter art. may be prefixed to quoted words : Mt 19¹⁸ τὸ Οὐ φονεύσεις (DM om τό), Mk 9²³ *so far as the* εἰ δύνῃ *is concerned*, Ro 13⁹, 1 Co 4⁶ τὸ Μὴ ὑπὲρ ἃ γέγραπται ; unless we emend, it is best taken as a quotation of a slogan (Howard in *Exp. T* 33, 479), Ga 4²⁵ vl., 5¹⁴, 6⁹ τὸ δὲ Καλὸν ποιοῦντες μὴ ἐνκακῶμεν (τό introduces a proverbial phrase; or τὸ καλόν is generic), Eph 4⁹, Heb 12²⁷.

(h) *Article with Indirect Interrogatives* [2]

Class., but in NT this usage is rarely represented except in Lk-Ac. The meaning is not affected by the addition of the art. : Lk 1⁶² ἐνένευον ... τὸ τί ἂν θέλοι, 9⁴⁶ 19⁴⁸, Ac 4²¹ 22³⁰, 1 Th 4¹, Ro 8²⁶ (ICC in loc; Moule 200); Mk 9¹⁰ τί ἐστιν τὸ ἐκ νεκρῶν ἀναστῆναι (unless τό ... is articular infin.).

In conclusion, almost anything in Greek can by the addition of the art. be made substantival, whether adj., ptc., infin., adv., prepositional expression, numeral, or any phrase whatever.

A characteristic of Hell. Greek is an anarthrous noun followed by an articular attribute (Zerwick § 145). See below pp. 185, 206, 221.

§ 3. The Article with a Predicate

An adj. or ptc. or a second noun may refer to a noun either as an attribute or as a predicate. As an attribute it usually

---
[1] K-G I 596f. Gildersleeve I 265.
[2] Mayser II 1, 80; II 3, 52f.

occurs between art. and noun. As a predicate it occurs either before the art. or after the noun, and the connection between them will be supplied by a copula, either stated or understood. Although predicate nouns are usually anarthrous, the art. thus distinguishing the subject from the complement, the art. may be inserted if the predicate noun is supposed to be a unique or notable instance (e.g. Mt 6²² *the eye* alone *is the light of the body*). A predicate adj. or ptc. and the pronoun ὁ αὐτός (*the same*) will also have the art.

E. C. Colwell (*JBL*, 52, 1933, 12–21) formulates rules for the art. with predicate nouns in NT in sentences in which the verb occurs. He finds that (a) definite predicate nouns take the art., if (as is usual) they follow the verb; (b) otherwise they usually lack it; (c) proper nouns lack it; (d) in relative clauses it does not apply since nouns always follow the verb, anarthrous or not. Obviously if such a rule stands the test, it is valuable for textual decisions and translation.[1]

Examples : (a) Mt 5¹³ ὑμεῖς ἐστε τὸ ἅλας τῆς γῆς, 13³⁷, 16¹⁶ σὺ εἶ ὁ χριστός, 24⁴⁵, 26⁶³, 27¹¹. ³⁷, Mk 3¹¹, 6³ οὐχ οὗτός ἐστιν ὁ τέκτων, 15². ¹² ὃν λέγετε τὸν βασιλέα τῶν Ἰουδ. (not AD), ³⁹, Lk 4⁴¹, 22⁷⁰, 23³. ³⁷, Jn 1⁴. ⁸. ³⁹. ⁴⁹, 5³⁵ ἐκεῖνος ἦν ὁ λύχνος, 8¹² ἐγώ εἰμι τὸ φῶς (cp. 9⁵ φῶς εἰμί), ⁴⁴, 11²⁷, 18³³, 20³¹, Ac 9²⁰, 21³⁸, Jas 3⁶ ὁ κόσμος predicate (M. Dibelius, *Der Brief des Jakobus*, Gött. 1921, in loc.), 1 Jn. 3⁴ καὶ ἡ ἁμαρτία ἐστιν ἡ ἀνομία 4¹⁵ 5⁵. With an adj. usually the predicate adj. is anarthrous, but Mt 19¹⁷ εἷς ἐστιν ὁ ἀγαθός, Rev 3¹⁷.

(b) Mt 4³· ⁶ 14³³ 27⁴⁰· ⁵⁴ *Son of God* precedes the verb and so anarthr., ⁴² *King of Israel* precedes, 13³⁹.—Mk 15³⁹ Lk 4³· ⁹ Jn 10³⁶ *Son of God* precedes.—Jn 5³⁷ *Son of man* precedes.—Jn 1¹ θεὸς ἦν ὁ λόγος (there need be no doctrinal significance in the dropping of the art., for it is simply a matter of word-order), 9⁵ φῶς εἰμι, 14⁹ βασιλεύς εἶ τοῦ Ἰσρ. 19²¹ βασιλεὺς τῶν Ἰουδ. εἰμί.

There are three passages in Mt where the author, striving for variety, has fallen into a definite pattern.

(1) 12⁴⁸ *my mother* (artic.) follows verb, ⁵⁰ *my mother* (anarth.) precedes verb. (2) 13³⁷· ³⁹ ὁ σπείρων ... ἐστιν ὁ υἱός (artic. following) ὁ δὲ ἀγρός ἐστιν ὁ κόσμος ... οὗτοί εἰσιν οἱ υἱοί ... τὰ δὲ ζιζάνιά εἰσιν οἱ υἱοί ..., ὁ δὲ ἐχθρός ... ἐστιν ὁ διάβολος, ὁ δὲ θερισμὸς συντέλεια αἰῶνός ἐστιν (anarthr. preceding), οἱ δὲ θερισταὶ ἄγγελοί εἰσιν. (3) 23⁸· ¹⁰ εἷς γάρ ἐστιν ὑμῶν ὁ διδάσκαλος (artic. following) ... εἷς γάρ ἐστιν ὑμῶν ὁ πατήρ (idem) ... ὅτι καθηγητὴς ὑμῶν ἐστιν εἷς ὁ Χριστός (anarth. preceding). See also Mt 18¹· ⁴.

---

[1] Thus Colwell's rule tends to prove WH wrong in 2 Pt 1¹⁷ ὁ υἱός μου ὁ ἀγαπητός μου οὗτός ἐστιν. Then Tischendorf rightly places the predicate after the verb. (SA, etc.).

Colwell notes that variants in the MSS, as well as the undoubted text, also obey his canon, and from this he infers that not only among the NT authors but also among the scribes of a much later period this articular rule applied. For instance, it is true of S and B which, though they differ, differ according to rule in these passages: Mt 23¹⁰ B καθηγητης υμων εστιν εις (anarthr. preceding), S εις γαρ υμων εστιν ο καθηγητης (artic. following).—Jn 1⁴⁹ B συ βασιλευς ει του Ισραηλ (anarthr. preceding), S συ ει ο βασιλευς του I (artic. following).—Jas 2¹⁹ B εις θεος εστιν (anarthr. preceding), S εις εστιν ο θεος (articular following).

In Colwell's count, which is somewhat arbitrary, only 15 articular predicate nouns precede the verb [1], while 239 follow it, and only 40 anarthrous predicate nouns follow the verb [2] while 99 precede it. Judicious selection among the MS variants may remove some of the exceptions to Colwell's canon but cannot remove all. So that while the canon may reflect a general tendency it is not absolute by any means; after all, it takes no account of relative clauses or proper nouns, and he has also omitted a considerable class of "qualitative" nouns like that in ὁ θεὸς ἀγάπη ἐστίν. Moreover, he is the first to admit the lack of objectivity in his method of counting: he professes to include only *definite* nouns among his anarthrous predicates, and the degree of definiteness is extremely difficult to assess.

---

[1] Lk 4⁴¹, Jn 1²¹ 6⁵¹ 15¹, Ro 4¹³ 1 Co 9¹· ² 11³· ²⁵ 2 Co 1¹² 3²· ¹⁷, 2 Pt 1¹⁷, Rev 19⁸ 20¹⁴.

[2] E.g. Mt 20¹⁶, 27⁴³ *Son of God* (anarthr. following; but θεοῦ precedes), Mk 4³² 9³⁵ 12³⁸, Lk 20³³ 22²⁴, Jn 4¹⁸ 18¹³· ³⁷, Ac 10³⁶, Ro 4¹¹· ¹⁸ 7¹³ 8¹⁶· ²⁹ 11⁶, 1 Co 12²⁷ 16¹⁵ 2 Co 5²¹ 6¹⁶, Ga 4³¹, 1 Th 4³, 1 Pt 5¹², Heb 11¹. Paul is the most significant breaker of Colwell's rule.

CHAPTER THIRTEEN

ATTRIBUTIVE RELATIONSHIP: ADJECTIVES AND NUMERALS

§ 1. The Adjectival Attribute[1]

As in class. Greek, nouns appear instead of adjs. in an attributive sense: ἀνήρ Lk 24^{19} Ac 1^{16} 3^{14} ἄνδρα φονέα, 22^3; ἄνθρωπος Mt 18^{23}; πύθων Ac 16^{16} SBAC*D* (gen., not adjectival, in p^{45} C^3 D^2 E). Sometimes a noun will assume the form of an adj. by coining a fem. or neuter: δούλη Lk 1$^{38.\ 48}$ Ac 2^{18}, δοῦλα neut. pl. Ro 6^{19}, ὄμηρα neut. pl. LXX 1 Mac 13^{16}; Rev 4^3 λίθῳ ἰάσπιδι καὶ σαρδίῳ.

Three relative positions are possible for the art. and noun with attributive adjs., ptcs., or numerals: I. Classical ὁ ἀγαθὸς ἀνήρ. II. ὁ ἀνὴρ ὁ ἀγαθός (the ptc., especially with additional adjuncts, is liable to be placed in this position). III. Hellenistic ἀνὴρ ὁ ἀγαθός: much more frequent in the pap. than in class. Greek (Mayser II 2, 57f); the adj. is a kind of limiting afterthought[2] to a noun which originally was more vague. E.g. Lk 23^{49} γυναῖκες αἱ συνακολουθοῦσαι women, viz. those who..., Jn 14^{27} εἰρήνην ἀφίημι ὑμῖν, εἰρήνην τὴν ἐμὴν δίδωμι ὑμῖν, 2 Ti 1^{13} ἐν πίστει καὶ ἀγάπῃ τῇ ἐν Χ.Ι. This happens especially with the ptc.: Ac 7^{35} ἐν χειρὶ ἀγγέλου τοῦ ὀφθέντος αὐτῷ, Ro 2^{14} ἔθνη τὰ μὴ νόμον ἔχοντα[3].

Thus the attribute participates in the force of the art. either by taking an intermediate position or, if placed in the post-position, by assuming its own art. There are occasions however when the adj. is not in the intermediate position and has has no art. of its own. In these circumstances, it is predicative[4] (see last ch. for *nouns* used predicatively); Mk 7^5 κοιναῖς ταῖς χερσίν DW (rest om. art.) *with hands unwashed*, 8^{17} πεπωρωμένην

---

[1] K-G I §§ 404–405. Gildersleeve II §§ 608–613. Mayser II 2, 51–59.
[2] K-G I 613f. Radermacher^2 115. Zerwick § 145.
[3] For the further significance of this word-order, see above (Introduction, p. 8). Cp. BU 46 (A.D. 193) ὄνους τέσσαρες τοὺς καλλίστους, Mk 15^{41} Ac 10^{41} 19$^{11.\ 17}$ 26^{22} 1 Pt 1^7.
[4] But the odd variant τὸ γὰρ πνεῦμα ἅγιον Lk 12^{12} must be a slip; also 1 Jn 5^{20}.

ἔχετε τὴν καρδίαν ὑμῶν, Jn 5³⁶ ἔχω τὴν μαρτυρίαν μείζω *I have a witness which is greater*, Ac 14¹⁰ εἶπεν μεγάλῃ τῇ φωνῇ, Lk 6⁸ τῷ ξηρὰν ἔχοντι τὴν χεῖρα, 1 Co 11⁵ ἀκατακαλύπτῳ τῇ κεφαλῇ, Heb 7²⁴ ἀπαράβατον ἔχει τὴν ἱερωσύνην *has a priesthood which is inalienable*, 9¹ τὸ ἅγιον κοσμικόν. More difficult to translate is ὁ ὄχλος πολύς Jn 12⁹ (as scribes found : AB³D om ὁ; W adds ὁ to πολύς),¹². It ought to mean *the crowd is great*, but evidently = ὁ πολὺς ὄχλος (Mk 12³⁷); it is probably done on the analogy of πᾶς and ὅλος. Cp. πολλῇ τῇ ἐμφερείᾳ Plut. etc. in Radermacher² 112; ὁ φόνος πολύς Arr. An. I 9, 6. Also Isocr. *Philipp.* 56 τὸ σῶμα θνητὸν ἅπαντες ἔχομεν (Jn 5³⁶).

§ 2. The Article with Several Attributes

Where in class. Greek there are several attributes, the art. may or may not be repeated (Gildersleeve II § 669). Moreover, it often becomes clumsy to insert all the attributes between the art. and noun (as in 1 Pt 3³ ὁ ἔξωθεν ἐμπλοκῆς τριχῶν καὶ περιθέσεως χρυσίων ἢ ἐνδύσεως ἱμάτιον κόσμος), and there is a tendency to divide them so that some stand before the noun and some after it. Clauses placed after the noun do not always require repetition of the art. (e.g. Plato *Rpb* 532c πρὸς δὲ τὰ ἐν ὕδασι φαντάσματα θεῖα) and may be translated predicatively. The art. is repeated where the defining clause implies a contrast or if the meaning would be ambiguous, and also where the defining words are emphatic, as in Rev. 2¹² τὴν ῥομφαίαν τὴν δίστομον τὴν ὀξεῖαν Heb 11¹² ἡ ἄμμος ἡ παρὰ τὸ χεῖλος . . . ἡ ἀναρίθμητος.

There is nothing particularly emphatic about the following, but the numeral is thought of as part of the noun and there is but one real attribute: Jn 6¹³ Jas 1¹ Rev 21⁹. Predicative additions of an adj. etc. in NT:—Mt 24⁴⁵ ὁ πιστὸς δοῦλος καὶ φρόνιμος, 1 Co 10³ τὸ αὐτὸ βρῶμα πνευματικόν S°DEFG (p⁴⁶ A om αὐτό; S*BA πν. βρ.), 16²¹ τῇ ἐμῇ χειρὶ Παύλου, Ga 1⁴ τοῦ ἐνεστῶτος αἰῶνος πονηροῦ S°DEFG (p⁴⁶ S*BA τοῦ αἰῶνος τοῦ ἐνεστῶτος πονηροῦ), 1¹³ τὴν ἐμὴν ἀναστροφήν ποτε ἐν τῷ Ἰουδαϊσμῷ, Col 1⁸ τὴν ὑμῶν ἀγάπην ἐν πνεύματι, 1 Pt 1¹⁸ τῆς ματαίας ὑμῶν ἀναστροφῆς πατροπαραδότου (not C).

Moreover, an adj. or ptc. which follows a gen. always takes the art., unless it be understood predicatively: Mt 3¹⁷ ὁ υἱός μου ὁ ἀγαπητός, 2 Co 6⁷ τῶν ὅπλων τῆς δικαιοσύνης τῶν δεξιῶν καὶ ἀριστερῶν, Eph 6¹⁶ τὰ βέλη τοῦ πονηροῦ τὰ (om BD*FG) πεπυρωμένα, Heb 13²⁰ 1 Pt 5¹⁰; predicatively Ti 2¹¹ ἐπεφάνη ἡ χάρις

§ 2-3]   ADJECTIVES AND NUMERALS   187

τοῦ θεοῦ (ἡ add C^c) σωτήριος πᾶσιν ἀνθρώποις : see Radermacher[2] 117.   Also Ac 23²⁷ Ro 2²⁷ 8¹ A 16¹ 2 Co 11⁹ Ga 3¹.

It is possible for all the attributes to occur after the noun and yet for the art. not to be repeated: 1 Co 8⁷ τῇ συνηθείᾳ ἕως ἄρτι τοῦ εἰδώλου, Eph 3⁴ τὴν σύνεσίν μου ἐν τῷ μυστηρίῳ τοῦ Χ. (the art. would contrast this particular σύνεσις of Paul with another), 2 Th 3¹⁴ τῷ λόγῳ ἡμῶν διὰ τῆς ἐπιστολῆς, Col. 1⁴, Ph 1⁵. But if there is danger of ambiguity or confusion, the art. occurs, as in the following: Ro 7⁵ 8³⁹ 2 Co 9³ 1 Th 1⁸ ἡ πίστις ὑμῶν ἡ πρὸς τὸν θεὸν ἐξελήλυθεν.

Instead of additional attributes being placed after the noun they may, sometimes (but not usually) with the art., be placed before, as in class. Greek: Lk 1⁷⁰ τῶν ἁγίων τῶν ἀπ' αἰῶνος . . . προφητῶν AC, 1 Pt 4¹⁴ τὸ τῆς δόξης καὶ τὸ τοῦ θεοῦ πνεῦμα (but meaning is: *and therefore* the Spirit of God). In NT this position is usually found with the adjs. ὁ ἄλλος, οἱ λοιποί, as in the papyri (Mayser II 2, 60): Jn 19³² τοῦ ἄλλου τοῦ συσταυρωθέντος, Rev 2²⁴ τοῖς λοιποῖς τοῖς ἐν Θυατείροις.

§ 3. Numerals

It is not a class. idiom to use εἷς for *first*, but Heb. (אֶחָד) and Aram., by way of LXX (Ps 23 (24) tit. τῇ μιᾷ σαββάτου, Ge 8¹³ etc. μιᾷ τοῦ μηνός, Ex 40² Nu 1¹·¹⁸ Ezra 10¹⁶ᶠ 2 Mac 15³⁶), Mt 28¹ εἰς μίαν σαββάτων, Lk 24¹, Jn 20¹·¹⁹ Ac 20⁷ 1 Co 16², Rev 6¹ μίαν *first*, 9¹² ἡ οὐαὶ ἡ μία. Mk 16² τῆς μιᾶς σαββάτων. But Mk 16⁹ (later ending) is exceptional: πρώτῃ σαββάτου. Jos. Ant. 1, 1, 1 αὕτη μὲν ἂν εἴη πρώτη ἡμέρα, Μωϋσῆς δ' αὐτὴν μίαν εἶπεν.   Ga 4²⁴ δύο διαθῆκαι, μία μέν . . . *the first*.

Also Aramaic is the use of reciprocal εἷς τὸν ἕνα, 1 Th 5¹¹. But cf. Hdt. 4. 50 ἓν πρὸς ἕν, συμβάλλειν, Lucian *Conscr. Hist.* 2 ἕν . . . ἑνί.

Distributive ἀνά and κατά with a numeral are class. (Mk 6⁷D, 40 Lk 9¹⁴ 10¹ Herm. S. IX 2, 3), but the following are less so, censured by the Atticists and rather Semitic and colloquial Koine: δυὸ δυό (Mk 6⁷, LXX Ge 7⁹, Si 36¹⁵), συμπόσια συμπόσια, πρασιαὶ πρασιαί (6³⁹¹), δεσμὰς δεσμάς (Mt 13³⁰ Epiph. Orig.; see Lagrange *S. Matth.* 268), τάγματα τάγματα (Herm. S. VIII 2, 8; 4, 2), ἑπτὰ ἑπτά Ge 7³, τρία τρία (P. Oxy. I p. 188 iii/A.D.), ἀνὰ δύο δύο (Gosp. Pet. 35, Lk 10¹ BK II), ἀνὰ ἓν ἕν (P. Columb. no. 318 c. A.D. 100), κατὰ δύο δύο (P. Oxy. VI 886¹⁹ iii/A.D.), κατὰ ἕνα ἕνα Isa 27¹². Heb אחד אחד, לאחד, etc.

The multiplicative ἑβδομηκοντάκις ἑπτά, as in LXX Ge 4²⁴, for שִׁבְעִים וְשִׁבְעָה (77), is 77 *times* (Moulton Proleg. 98), i.e. *70 times* (*and*) *seven*, not *70 times seven* (an error still perpetrated by NEB, without so much as a footnote) Mt 18²². D* rightly interprets it as ἑβδομηκοντάκις ἑπτάκις, and Vulg. as *septuagies septies*. The same principle applies with ἑπτάκις ἑπτα *14 times* (not *seven times seven*) T. Benj. 7⁴. So δώδεκα for δωδεκάκις in Rev 22², δύο for δίς in 9¹². Semitic speech has ambiguous numerals.

In Mk 4⁸·²⁰ B reads εἰς . . . ἐν . . . ἐν, S reads εἰς . . . εἰς . . . εἰς (a correction), ADWQ εν . . . εν . . . εν (= ἓν . . . ἓν . . . ἓν) correct. Ἕν is a sign of multiplication = ἑκατονταπλασίονα (an Aramaism).

CHAPTER FOURTEEN

ATTRIBUTIVE RELATIONSHIP: PRONOUNS AND PRONOMINAL ADJECTIVES

§ 1. Attributive Pronouns

1. *Possessive pronouns: unemphatic* [1]

It was a tendency of the NT as well as the Koine to prefer the gen. of the pers. pronoun (μου) to the nom. possessive pronoun (ἐμός). The rule for word-order in the Koine generally seems fairly close to the class. model. The genitives of the pers. pronouns μου, σου, ἡμῶν, ὑμῶν, αὐτοῦ, αὐτῆς, αὐτῶν stand without an art. of their own with an articular noun, either (a) after the noun, or (b) before its art., in the LXX, NT and Hell. generally; (c) where the noun has an attribute the gen. pers. pronoun follows the attribute. But if they are very emphatic, we may expect to find the 1st and 2nd pres. pronouns between the art. and the noun, even without this attribute [2]. (d) The 3rd pers. pronoun in this position is not necessarily emphatic in Hell. Greek. With anarthrous nouns it is immaterial whether the gen. pronoun precedes or follows the noun (Mayser II 2, 66).

Exx.:—

(a) Very commonly, e.g. ὁ πατήρ μου Jn 15¹ etc., and abundantly frequent esp. with 3rd p. in the pap.[3]

(b) Less commonly, and special attention should be paid to the variant readings: Mt 2² αὐτοῦ τὸν ἀστέρα, 7²⁴, 8⁸ ἵνα μου ὑπὸ τὴν στέγην, 16¹⁸ 17¹⁵ 23⁸.—Mk 5³⁰ 9²⁴.—Lk 6⁴⁷ 12¹⁸ 15³⁰ 16⁶ 19³⁵ etc.—Jn 1²⁷ 2²³ 3¹⁹. ²¹. ³³ 4⁴⁷ 9¹¹. ²¹. ²⁶ 11³². ⁴⁸ 12⁴⁰ 13¹ etc.—Ro 14¹⁶ 1 Co 8¹² Ph 2² 4¹⁴ Col 2⁵ 4¹⁸ 1 Th 2¹⁶ 3¹⁰. ¹³ 2 Th 2¹⁷ 3⁵ Phm ⁵ 1 Ti 4¹⁵ 2 Ti 1⁴.—1 Jn 3²⁰.—Rev 3¹. ². ⁸. ¹⁵ 10⁹ 14¹⁸ 18⁵ etc.—PSI IV 372. 12 (250 B.C.)

---

[1] K-G I 619, 4; 627, 3. Schwyzer II 202ff. Mayser II 2, 64ff. Winer-Schmiedel § 22, 14–17. Radermacher² 72f, 111. A. Wifstrand, *A Problem concerning Word Order in the NT*, Studia theol., Lund 1951. *Internat. Zeitschriftenschau f. Bibelwiss.*, 1951–2, 180f. Helbing Kasussyntax 178.
[2] K-G I 619, 2. UPZ 113. 12 (156 B.C.) τῆς ὑμῶν ἀγωγῆς. Moulton Einl. 59, 1. In NT, apparently only Pauline, and almost confined to ὑμῶν.
[3] NT uses ἐμοῦ and σοῦ only in connection with another gen., e.g. Ro 1¹² ὑμῶν τε καὶ ἐμοῦ, 16¹³ αὐτοῦ καὶ ἐμοῦ.

ἅ καταβεβόσκηκέ σου τὰ πρόβατα. Before two nouns to save repetition: Lk 12^{35} ὑμῶν αἱ ὀσφύες ... καὶ οἱ λύχνοι, Jn 11^{48} ἡμῶν καὶ τὸν τόπον καὶ τὸ ἔθος.—Ac 21^{11}.—1 Th 1^3 2^{19} 2 Ti 3^{10} Ti 1^{15}.—Rev 2^{19}.—Diod. Sic. 11. 16. The above are unemphatic pronouns, but they may be inserted in this pre-position for special emphasis: Lk 12^{30} 22^{53}, 1 Co 9^{11} εἰ ἡμεῖς ὑμῶν τὰ σαρκικὰ θερίσομεν, Eph 2^{10} αὐτοῦ γάρ ἐσμεν ποίημα, Ph 3^{20}.

(c) Mt 27^{60} ἐν τῷ καινῷ αὐτοῦ μνημείῳ, 2 Co 4^{16} ὁ ἔξω ἡμῶν ἄνθρωπος, 5^1 ἡ ἐπίγειος ἡμῶν οἰκία, 1 Pt 1^3 2^9 5^{10} etc.

(d) The 3rd p. αὐτοῦ = *his* is found in the middle position of the attributive, not merely when emphatic, as in class. Greek, but in NT and Koine also when unemphatic (Mayser II 2, 66): Ro 11^{11} τῷ αὐτῶν παραπτώματι ἡ σωτηρία τοῖς ἔθνεσιν, 3^{24} τῇ αὐτοῦ χάριτι, 1 Th 2^{19}, Ti 3^5 κατὰ τὸ αὐτοῦ ἔλεος emph. (D*EFG τὸ ἐλ. αὐτοῦ), Heb 2^4 τὴν αὐτοῦ θέλησιν, 7^{18} διὰ τὸ αὐτῆς ἀσθενὲς καὶ ἀνωφελές (no emph.), 1 Pt 1^3 τὸ πολὺ αὐτοῦ ἔλεος, 5^{10} τὴν αἰώνιον αὐτοῦ δόξαν, 2 Pt 1^9 τῶν πάλαι αὐτοῦ ἁμαρτιῶν, LXX 2 Mac 7^9, Herm. M. VI 2, 2, Clem. Hom. 17. 11 3^8 and often. But emphatic: Ro 3^{25} τῷ αὐτοῦ αἵματι. For 3rd p. ἐκείνου, see Jn 5^{47} 2 Co $8^{9.14}$ 2 Ti 2^{26} etc. (but Ro 6^{21} τὸ τέλος ἐκείνων). For 3rd p. τούτου: Ro 11^{30} 2 Pt 1^{15} (but contrary to rule: Ac 13^{23} Heb 13^{11} Rev 18^{15})

Possessive pronouns: *emphatic*.

On the other hand, the genitives ἐμαυτοῦ, σεαυτοῦ, ἑαυτοῦ, τούτου, ἐκείνου usually have the position of an attribute, not a predicate, both in class. and in Hell. Greek (Mayser II 2, 65). As a possess. gen. with a noun, ἐμαυτοῦ is found in NT only at 1 Co 10^{33} τὸ ἐμαυτοῦ συμφέρον, while σεαυτοῦ is never found like this. In NT also, esp. in Paul, the emph. ὑμῶν is found in attributive position (cp. Soph. Oed. Rex 1458 ἡ μὲν ἡμῶν μοῖρα) thus making ὑμέτερος almost superfluous in all NT writings (not ten instances, and none in Mt-Mk). The attributive ὑμῶν: 1 Co 16^{17} τὸ ὑμῶν ὑστέρημα (BCD ὑμέτερον), 2 Co 1^6 9^2 (vl. ἐξ ὑμῶν), 12^{19} 13^9, 1 Th 3^7, Clem. Hom. 10^{15} (but the predicative position in Ph 3^{20} ἡμῶν γὰρ τὸ πολίτευμα for greater emphasis; and Heb 10^{25} τὴν ἐπισυναγωγὴν ἑαυτῶν, for ὑμῶν αὐτῶν; reflexives: Lk 19^{13} δέκα δούλους ἑαυτοῦ *of his*, Ac 21^{11} δήσας ἑαυτοῦ τοὺς πόδας, Ga $6^{4.8}$ (D*FG αὐτοῦ), Eph 4^{16} (SD*G αὐτοῦ), Herm. S. II 5; S. IV 5 (P. Mich. αὐτῶν); V 4, 3A (P. Mich. αὐτοῦ) (Mayser II 2, 70). Where the emphatic pronoun occurs in predicative position, there is often a variant reading created by scribes who correct it to unemph. pronoun, for which this position would be normal.

Possessive adjectives [1].

Ἐμός, σός, ἡμέτερος, ὑμέτερος had been used in class. Greek as emph. possessives, but they are out of vogue now, being replaced by the gen. (or dat.: σοι ἦσαν Jn 17⁶) of the pers. pronoun or by ἴδιος. Still ἐμός is frequent in Jn, and occurs in 1 Co ten times (e.g. 11²⁴ τὴν ἐμὴν ἀνάμνησιν 16¹⁸), but often there is no emphasis: Lk 22¹⁹ Ro 10¹ Ga 1¹³ Ph 1²⁶; it = μοῦ. But ἐμός and σός may be reflexive, as occasionally in class. Greek (K-G I 568f): Mt 7³ 2 Co 1²³ Phm¹⁹ (ἔγραψα τῇ ἐμῇ χειρί), 3 Jn⁴ τὰ ἐμὰ τέκνα, Herm. S I 11 τὸ σὸν ἔργον ἐργάζου. Ἡμέτερος and ὑμέτερος are rarer: Ro 11³¹ 15⁴ 1 Co 15³¹ 16¹⁷ (ὑμῶν p⁴⁶ SA).

Word-order: in Jn about 30 times in post-position (unemphatic): ἐμός 3²⁹ (ἡ χαρὰ ἡ ἐμή), 5³⁰, ³⁰ 6³⁸ 7⁶, ⁸ 8¹⁶, ³¹, ³⁷, ⁴³, ⁵¹, ⁵⁶ 10²⁶, ²⁷ 12²⁶ 14¹⁵, ²⁷ 15⁹, ¹¹, ¹² 17¹³, ²⁴ 18³⁶ (4); σός 17¹⁷ (ὁ λόγος ὁ σός), 18³⁵; ὑμέτερος 7⁶ 8¹⁷. In pre-position, only three times (emphatic): 4⁴² τὴν σὴν λαλίαν, 5⁴⁷ τοῖς ἐμοῖς ῥήμασιν, 7¹⁶ ἡ ἐμὴ διδαχή.—In Mt Mk Lk only emphatic; therefore pre-position (e.g. Mt 7²² τῷ σῷ ὀνόματι bis).—With no art. Ph 3⁹ μὴ ἔχων ἐμὴν δικαιοσύνην τὴν ἐκ νόμου (predicatively: *which is my own*. In Jn 4³⁴ ἐμὸν βρῶμα, 13³⁵ 15⁸ (attrib.); predicative 14²⁴ 16¹⁵ 17⁶, ⁹, ¹⁰, ¹⁰, also Mt 20²³ Mk 10⁴⁰ οὐκ ἔστιν ἐμὸν τοῦτο δοῦναι.

Ἴδιος as *simple, possess. pronoun, or reflex. adjective* [2].

With the old class. meaning *peculiar, private*: Mk 15²⁰ τὰ ἴδια ἱμάτια αὐτοῦ (Θ om αὐτοῦ; BD om ἴδια), Ac 1¹⁹ τῇ ἰδίᾳ διαλέκτῳ αὐτῶν (B*SD lat om ἰδίᾳ), 4³², 1 Co 3⁸ 7² (ἕκαστος τὴν ἑαυτοῦ γυναῖκα ἐχέτω, καὶ ἑκάστη τὸν ἴδιον ἄνδρα ἐχέτω. Is this simply variety in style? Or is ἴδιος class.?), 7⁷ (certainly the class. use: *his own private gift*), 12¹¹ ἰδίᾳ ἑκάστῳ, 15³⁸ (*its own peculiar body*), Ti 1¹² ἴδιος αὐτῶν *their own poet* (i.e. not another nationality), Heb 7²⁷ (individual sins, as oppos. to the people's; cp. 4¹⁰). However, in the post-class. period there enters the meaning = ἑαυτοῦ (class. οἰκεῖος): Pap. Rev. Laws 52, 13, 23 (258 B.C.) εἰς τὴν ἰδίαν χρείαν. Moreover, the LXX, NT, Josephus, Plutarch, etc. use it not only as a reflexive, but even as a mere possessive, differing little if at all from αὐτοῦ. Reflexive: Mt 14¹³ etc. κατ' ἰδίαν = class. καθ' ἑαυτόν, Lk 2³ (vl. ἑαυτοῦ), Jn 1¹¹ εἰς τὰ ἴδια ἦλθεν, ⁴² τὸν ἀδελφὸν τὸν ἴδιον, Ac 24²³

---

[1] Mayser II 2, 67f, 68, 71ff. Moulton Einl. 59. G. D. Kilpatrick, "The Possessive Pronoun in the NT." *JThS* 42, 1941, 184–186 (for Mk and Lk). Cuendet 40 (for word-order).

[2] Mayser I² 2, 65; II 2, 73f. Meisterhans-Schwyzer 235. E. L. Green, "Ἴδιος as a possessive in Polybius," *Proc. Amer. Philol. Assoc.* 34, 4. Schwyzer II 205⁵.

τῶν ἰδίων, 2 Co 5¹⁰ p⁴⁶ lat τὰ ἴδια, 2 Pt 3³. ¹⁶ Wi 19¹³ P. Oxy. I 37 τὸ ἴδιόν μου τέκνον. Possessive: Mt 22⁵ τὸν ἴδιον ἀγρόν, 25¹⁴, Ti 2⁹ ἰδίοις δεσπόταις, 1 Pt 3¹· ⁵ τοῖς ἰδίοις ἀνδράσιν, 2 Pt 2¹⁶ ἰδίας παρανομίας. *Word-order* (Cuendet 41): in Syn. Gosp. pre-position (e.g. Lk 6⁴¹ ἐν τῷ ἰδίῳ ὀφθαλμῷ, emph.), in Jn usually post-position.

2. *Attributive demonstrative pronouns*

"Ὅδε ¹.

It no longer forms part of the living language; it is rare in NT and papyri but occurs attributively in Jas 4¹³ εἰς τήνδε τὴν πόλιν, and hardly correctly even here ² as it appears to mean τὴν καὶ τήν *such and such*, as in popular Attic and Hell.: LXX Ru 1¹⁷. MGr ὁ τάδε(ς) = ὁ δεῖνα: *Mr So-and-so*; Wackernagel II 107f., and literature.

Οὗτος and ἐκεῖνος ³.

Whereas in the Ptol. pap. we hardly ever find them used attributively but only predicatively, on the the other hand in both the LXX and NT the attributive is by far the greater use. It is only in books like 2–4 Mac and Wi, and the writings of John and Paul that there is any approach to normal contemporary usage in this respect.

The omission of the art.⁴ is possible where conceivably the noun is regarded as a predicate of the pronoun, which is quite in accord with class. Greek. In the Ptol. pap. it is frequently omitted where ordinal numerals are concerned: Zen. pap. (258 B.C.) ἤδη δ' ἐστὶν ἔτος τοῦτο δεύτερον, UPZ (163 B.C.) ἔτος τοῦτο δέκατον *this is the tenth year*; cp. Lk 1³⁶ *this is the sixth month*, 2² *this was the first census*, ¹² *this shall be a sign to you*, Jn 2¹¹ ταύτην ἐποίησεν ἀρχὴν τῶν σημείων *he did this as a beginning of the miracles*, 2 Pt 3¹ *this is the second letter*. So also Achilles Tatius 7. 11. 2 (iv/A.D.) τρίτην ταύτην ἡμέραν, Menander *Epitr.* 26f (iv/B.C.), Lucian *dial. mort.* 13. 3. But even Hdt 5, 76

---

¹ See above, p. 44. K-G I § 467 pp. 641ff. Gildersleeve II § 665. Meisterhans-Schwyzer 231–232. Τοιᾶσδε only in 2 Pt 1¹⁷.

² It is correctly used in 1 Clem 50³ 63².

³ K-G I 627ff, 645ff. Mayser II 2, 79–82. N. Turner, "The Unique Character of Biblical Greek," *Vet. Test.* 5, 1955, 2, pp. 208–213.

⁴ J. E. Harry, "The omission of the article with substantives after οὗτος, ὅδε, ἐκεῖνος in prose," *Trans. Amer. Phil. Assoc.* 29, 1898, 48–64. Bauer⁴ col. 1087. Winer-Schmiedel § 23, 12. L.S.s.v. οὗτος B I 4. Mayser II 2, 81.

τέταρτον δὴ τοῦτο, and LXX Ge 27³⁶ δεύτερον τοῦτο. Nu 14²² Jg 16¹⁵. However, the real difficulty occurs where there is no copula, real or understood, but a main verb which excludes the possibility of supplying the verb *to be* and taking the noun as a predicate of the demonstrative pronoun. The difficulty is that in an attributive sense the art. is always present in earlier Greek (with the negligible exception of the Epic poets and sometimes in the tragedians). Yet in NT there are clear instances of omission: Mk 16¹⁷ σημεῖα δὲ τοῖς πιστεύσασιν ταῦτα παρακολουθήσει *these miracles* (but ταῦτα may be construed as obj. of the ptc.), Ac 1⁵ οὐ μετὰ πολλὰς ταύτας ἡμέρας (οὐ reverses the meaning of πολλάς: thus *after these few days*), 24²¹ περὶ μιᾶς ταύτης φωνῆς ἧς ἐκέκραξα (*this single utterance*). The def. art. was being carelessly used, as time went on, in these connections. Radermacher notes its absence, where it would have been inevitable at an earlier period (πᾶς βίοτος *the whole life* on a Galatian inscription, and Dionysius of Halicarnassus has καθ' ἕκαστον ἐνιαυτόν) and there is little doubt of the attributive sense in the phrases τούτου πράγματος, ταῦτα ἀδικήματα, τοῦτο μνῆμα, ὀνόματα ταῦτα, τούτῳ δικαίῳ, τόδε σῆμα (p. 113). In the imperial period therefore the usage was already established and we should not strive to render the anarthrous demonstrative in NT in a predicative way unless the copula (actual or understood) makes this necessary.

The position of the attributive pronoun, like that of the adj., is either before the art. or after the noun. The post-positive position may in part be due to Hebrew influence, for in LXX Ge 7¹ (and thus in Syn. Gosp. and Heb 3¹⁰) בַּדּוֹר הַזֶּה becomes ἡ γενεὰ αὕτη, and it was probably the later Hebrew עוֹלָם הַזֶּה (*this world-time*) that produced ὁ καιρὸς οὗτος (Mk 10³⁰ Lk 12⁵⁶ 18³⁰) and ὁ κόσμος οὗτος (Jn, Paul), which Paul more correctly terms ὁ νῦν καιρός, and עוֹלָם הַבָּא accounts for ὁ αἰὼν ἐκεῖνος Lk 20³⁵ (in Pastorals ὁ νῦν αἰών 1 Ti 6¹⁷ Ti 2¹²). There are a few examples of pre-positive position in NT (Mt 12³² 11²⁵ 12¹ 14¹ Ac 12¹) but not usually in the Heb. sense of *world-time*.

Τοιοῦτος and τοσοῦτος [1].

Τοιοῦτος is occasionally preceded by the art. (when referring

---

[1] K-G I 630, 5. Meisterhans-Schwyzer 232. Gildersleeve II § 586. Mayser II 2, 82ff.

to individuals or individualizing a class): e.g. Mk 9^{37} ABDLNW τῶν τοιούτων παιδίων (SC παιδ. τούτων), 2 Co 12^3 τὸν τοιοῦτον ἄνθρωπον, Jn 4^{23} τοιούτους ζητεῖ τοὺς προσκυνοῦντας (predicative). Τοσοῦτος has the art. only Rev 18^{17} ὁ τοσοῦτος πλοῦτος.

Αὐτός = *self* as attributive [1].

It is in general agreement with class. and Koine usage. It is found in the predicative position, e.g. αὐτὸ τὸ πνεῦμα Ro 8^{26} = *the Spirit himself*; but attributive τὸ αὐτὸ πνεῦμα 2 Co 4^{13} = *the self-same Spirit*. The art. however does not belong to αὐτός but to the noun, and is therefore sometimes omitted, as in Jn 2^{24} αὐτὸς Ἰησοῦς. It is found in connection with the pers. pronoun (αὐτὸς ἐγώ *I myself*) where it is to be distinguished from the reflexive (*I do this to myself*): Ac 20^{30} ἐξ ὑμῶν αὐτῶν, 1 Co 5^{13} ἐξάρατε τὸν πονηρὸν ἐξ ὑμῶν αὐτῶν *yourselves* (not reflexive), Ga 4^{17} ἵνα αὐτοὺς ζηλοῦτε = αὐτοὺς αὐτούς (in 3rd p. αὐτός is not repeated) *the men themselves*.

It is a debatable point whether in the Ptol. papyri αὐτός can stand in demonstrative sense for οὗτος or ἐκεῖνος [2]; it is any way almost restricted to the official style of writing. If so, it appears again abundantly in NT in Luke, especially in certain phrases (and even where Semitic sources are not in question, e.g. Ac 16^{18} 22^{13}) [3]. This significantly affects the exegesis of certain passages, where the translation is *this* or *that*, but not *the same*, or even *that very*, e.g. Lk 10^7 ἐν αὐτῇ τῇ οἰκίᾳ, Lk 13^1 ἐν αὐτῷ τῷ καιρῷ (ἐν ἐκείνῳ τῷ κ. Mt 11^{25}) LXX To 3^{17}; (ἐν) αὐτῇ τῇ ὥρᾳ, ἡμέρᾳ Lk 2^{38} (= ἐκείνῳ in 7^{21}) 10^{21} 12^{12} (ἐκεῖνος Mk 13^{11}) 13^{31} 20^{19} 24^{13} etc., P. Teb. I 411^3 (ii/A.D.) αὐτῇ ὥρᾳ, P. Oxy III 528. 14 (ii/A.D.) αὐτῇ τῇ ὥρᾳ, inscr. Ditt. Syll.^{2} 1173^1 (ii/A.D.) αὐταῖς ταῖς ἡμέραις, T. Abr. 113^{29} 116^{27} (αὐτῇ τῇ ὥρᾳ); αὐτῇ τῇ νυκτί Herm. V. III 1, 2 S; 10, 7; ἐν αὐτῇ τῇ νυκτί LXX To 2^9. It appears to be synonymous with ἐκεῖνος in the otherwise puzzling sentence, 2 Ti 2^{26} ἐζωγρημένοι ὑπ' αὐτοῦ εἰς τὸ ἐκείνου θέλημα.

---

[1] K-G I 627, 4. Gildersleeve II §§ 654–655. Ljungvik BSSV 8f. Mayser II 2, 75ff.

[2] Moulton says it can (Proleg. 91), but Black doubts this (AAGA^2 72); the latter prefers the hypothesis of the influence of Aramaic proleptic pronoun (see p. 41).

[3] Moulton-Howard, App. p. 432.

3 Indefinite pronouns in attributive use [1]

τις.

As to word-order, though they are enclitics, τις and τι occasionally, when used adjectivally, stand before their noun, as long as they are not first word in the sentence (and even first word in Soph. *Trach.* 865, *Oed. Rex* 1471 Plato *Theaet.* 147c., Plutarch *Tranqu.* c. 13): Ac 3², καί τις ἀνήρ, Ro 1¹¹. But τινές [2] may now stand first in the sentence: Mt 27⁴⁷ τινὲς δὲ τῶν, Lk 6² idem, Jn 13²⁹ τινὲς γάρ, 1 Ti 5²⁴ τινῶν ἀνθρώπων. Attributive τις, often with adjs. and numerals (*about*) in class. Greek, is now largely used in the sense of *quidam* = *so to speak*: Jas 1¹⁸ ἀπαρχήν τινα, Heb 10²⁷ φοβερά τις ἐκδοχή; but τινα in Ac 8⁹ (εἶναί τινα ἑαυτὸν μέγαν) is not an instance, but is *a person of imporance* (like Ga 2⁶ 6³), with μέγαν inserted for emphasis. With numerals also in Lk 7¹⁸ δύο τινάς, Ac 23²³ τινας δύο: not *about two* but *a certain pair*; so also Lk 22⁵⁰ Jn 11⁴⁹ εἷς τις *a certain one*.

As substitutes for τις there are ἄνθρωπος: Mt 12¹⁰, 13²⁸ ἐχθρὸς ἄνθρωπος, ⁴⁵ ἀνθρώπῳ (BS* om) ἐμπόρῳ CDΘ, ⁵² 18²³. Mk 1²³ etc. and ἀνήρ (in Lk, e.g. 9³⁸ Ac 3¹⁴) like Aram. אֲנָשׁ³ but also = Heb אִישׁ *each, anyone* (Thackeray OT Gr. 45). We find ἀνήρ and ἄνθρωπος = τις in Homer and class. Greek (K-G I 272; Svensson op. cit. 136–140). Also γυνή: Mt 15²².

εἷς.

Another post-class. substitute for τις is the numeral εἷς [4], as also in the Ptol. papyri, in the sense of *aliquis* or *quidam*, with analogies in modern languages (*one, ein, un*). In Luke it does not seem to be a Semitism; he always follows εἷς with a gen. (e.g. 15¹⁵ ἑνὶ τῶν πολιτῶν; same phrase in Hyperides *Lycophr.* 13 (iv/B.C.), which makes it conform closely to Greek usage: pap. Mayser II 2, 86 ἀποστείλας τῶν οἰκοδόμων ἕνα. In Mk also in three places (5²² 14¹⁰· ⁶⁶) we have gen.; whereas in Mt 9¹⁸ 26⁶⁹

---

[1] K-G I 662, 663. Mayser II 2, 84ff. On confusion of relative and interrogative pronouns. including their attributive form (i.e. τις and ὅστις, πόσος and ὅσος, πῶς and ὡς) see pp. 4, 49f.

[2] Also τινές (substantivally) stands at the beginning of the sentence Ac 17¹⁸ τινὲς δέ, 19³¹, Jn 7⁴⁴ etc., especially where there is a contrasted clause Ph 1¹⁵ τινὲς μέν . . . τινὲς δέ (classical).

[3] Wellhausen Einl.² 20. Moulton-Howard 433 (Epict. 3, 23, 15). Black AAGA² 248–52.

[4] Schwyzer II 27. Mayser II 2, 85. Lagrange *S. Matth.* XCVIII. Winer-Schmiedel § 26, 5. Radermacher² 76. Moulton Einl. 154.

there is no gen. after εἷς or μία. Mt (e.g. εἷς γραμματεύς 8¹⁹) thus comes closer to Semitic than do Mk or Lk, and is probably influenced by Heb. אֶחָד or Aram. חַד. In 21¹⁹ he has συκῆν μίαν, where Mk 11¹³ has no μίαν (except SKM for harm.). Mt 18²⁴ 19¹⁶ Mk 10¹⁷ have εἷς for τις, where Lk has τις. Εἷς is more likely to reflect Semitic influence on the rare occasions when it is in post-position Mt 9¹⁸ ἄρχων εἷς SᵇB lat syrᵖᵉ. ʰˡ (S*ᶜ C* DWΘ fam¹ 700 copt om εἷς), Jn 6⁹ παιδάριον ἕν AΓ, LXX Da 7⁸ ἄλλο ἕν κέρας ἀνέφυη, 1 Esd 4¹⁸ γυναῖκα μίαν, but even here we have papyrus precedent (PSI IV 571, 15 ἄλλον ἕνα *a further one* παρατρέφω, 252 B.C.). The use with τις is class.: Lk 22⁵⁰ εἷς τις, Mk 14⁴⁷ (SA om τις), Jn 11⁴⁹ (Schwyzer II 215 b. 1).

-ουν and -ποτε [1].

These additions form an indef. pronoun, e.g. ὁστισοῦν, ὅστις δήποτε, but rarely if at all in NT. There is Ga 2⁶ ὁποῖοί ποτε ἦσαν *whatever kind of persons they were* (ποτε is not a separate word, *at one time*.) Ac 19²⁶ D ὁ Παῦλος οὗτος τίς ποτε (not τοτε): gig *hic Paulus nescio quem*.

οὐ... πᾶς.

This peculiarly Biblical Greek [2] phenomenon should be included among negative indef. pronouns. The Hebraistic οὐ (μὴ)... πᾶς = לֹא... כֹּל, as also πᾶς... οὐ = כֹּל... לֹא [3]. Mt 24²² Mk 13³⁰ οὐκ ἂν ἐσώθη πᾶσα σάρξ, Lk 1³⁷ οὐκ... πᾶν ῥῆμα (*nothing*), Jn 12⁴⁶ πᾶς ὁ πιστεύων... μὴ μείνῃ, Ac 10¹⁴ οὐδέποτε ἔφαγον πᾶν κοινόν, Ro 3²⁰, 1 Co 1²⁹, Eph 4²⁹ 5⁵ πᾶς πόρνος... οὐκ ἔχει, 2 Pt 1²⁰, 1 Jn 2²¹ 3¹⁵, Rev 7¹· ¹⁶ 9⁴ 18²² 21²⁷ 22³, LXX Ps 142 (143) ² etc., DaO' θ 2¹⁰ πᾶς βασιλεὺς... οὐκ ἐπερωτᾷ, 2¹¹, O' 5⁹ 6⁵ etc., θ 4⁶ etc., Acta Pionii 11⁴ μὴ σύμπασαν for μηδεμίαν. As in class. Greek, οὐ πᾶς with nothing intervening: Mt 7²¹ 1 Co 15³⁹ *not everyone*. The harshness is mitigated where a positive

---

[1] K-G II 410, 3. Schmid Attiz. I 184, 426; IV 553. Wackernagel II 116, 121f, 317. Mayser I² 2, 70; II 2, 86f. Rademacher² 76f.

[2] Extra-biblical exx. are rare: Dion. Halic. (*de Plat. ad Pomp.*) 756 οὐκ ἀπὸ τοῦ βελτίστου πάντα περὶ αὐτῶν γράφων. P. Ryl. II 113¹²ᶠ (A.D. 133) μὴ ἔχοντας πᾶν πρᾶγμα πρὸς ἐμέ. Apoll. Disc. *de Synt*. I 14 πᾶς λόγος ἄνευ τούτων οὐ συγκλείεται (where however one could join οὐ closely with συγκλ., as in the French *toute autre doctrine ne leur plaît pas* = all other... displeases.

[3] Wackernagel II 273f. Ljungvik BZSSV 18ff. Moulton Einl. 126f. Rademacher² 219f.

clause with ἀλλά follows, containing the main point of the sentence: Jn 3^16 ἵνα πᾶς ὁ πιστεύων μὴ ἀπόληται, ἀλλὰ ἔχῃ that every believer may have . . . , and not perish, 6^39.

§ 2. Attributive Pronominal Adjectives

ἄλλος and ἕτερος [1].

For the position of ἄλλος with another attribute see p. 187 and Cuendet 112f.

Ἕτερος is not in wide use in the NT and does not occur in Mk (16^12 only), Jn (19^37 only), Peter, Rev. It is chiefly found in Lk, and to some extent in Mt and Paul. It is correctly used in 1 Co 10^24 τὸ ἑαυτοῦ . . . τὸ τοῦ ἑτέρου, Ph 2^4 τὰ τῶν ἑτέρων D*FG. In Lk 19^20 ὁ ἕτερος apparently = the third (A om ὁ). But in all writers it has largely lost its sense of duality by this time [2]. Mt 16^14 οἱ μὲν . . . ἄλλοι δέ . . . ἕτεροι δέ (in the last two clauses Mk 8^28 Lk 9^19 have ἄλλοι twice). Lk 8^6ff καὶ ἕτερον three times (D ἄλλο, as in Mt 13^5ff Mk 4^5ff). 9^59 πρὸς ἕτερον to another. 61 εἶπεν δὲ καὶ ἕτερος another said. 1 Co 12^81 ᾧ μὲν . . . ἄλλῳ δέ . . . ἑτέρῳ—then four times ἄλλῳ δὲ . . . ἑτέρῳ . . . ἄλλῳ δέ. Ἄλλος and ἕτερος are found together for variety, showing there is little difference between them: 2 Co 11^4 ἄλλον Ἰησοῦν . . . πνεῦμα ἕτερον . . . εὐαγγέλιον ἕτερον, Ga 1^6. 7 εἰς ἕτερον εὐαγγέλιον, ὃ οὐκ ἔστιν ἄλλο εἰ μή . . . (but ἄλλο probably serves to introduce the εἰ μή- clause. Papyri, e.g. UPZ I 42^32. 33 (162 B.C.) καὶ ἄλλοι . . . καὶ ἕτεροι. Heb 11^36 ἕτεροι = others. Mt 15^30 καὶ ἑτέρους πόλλους. So also Lk 3^18 πόλλα μὲν οὖν καὶ ἕτερα, Ro 8^39 οὔτε τις κτίσις ἑτέρα, 13^9 εἴ τις ἑτέρα ἐντολή, 1 Ti 1^10 εἴ τι ἕτερον. In class. Greek ὁ ἕτερος is never used for anything but a definite division into two parts, as it is in e.g. Mt 10^23 ἐν τῇ πόλει ταύτῃ . . . εἰς τὴν ἑτέραν SBW (DCE corr. to ἄλλην, leaving the incongrous art.), Lk 4^43 ταῖς ἑτέραις πόλεσιν—the remaining cities. But ἄλλος too appears to mean the next, as in Hom. Clem. 15^4 19^1 τῆς ἄλλης ἡμέρας. Thus ὁ ἄλλος will usurp the province of ὁ ἕτερος and denote a division into only two parts: Mt 5^39 (Lk 6^29) τὴν ἄλλην (of a cheek), 12^13 ἡ ἄλλη (of a hand), Jn 18^16 19^32 20^3f etc. There

---

[1] K-G I 635, 275n. Meisterhans-Schwyzer 250, 5. 6. Gildersleeve II 587–593 (ἕτερος); 594–599 (ἄλλος). Mayser II 2, 87ff. Radermacher² 77. Moulton Einl. 125. 128. Winer-Schmiedel § 26, 6.
[2] Hom. Clem. 19^9 a striking alternation: πολλούς . . . ἄλλους δὲ . . . ἑτέρους δὲ . . . ἄλλους δέ (ἄλλους = ἑτέρους).

were isolated examples of this in class. Greek¹. Papyri: Mayser II 1, 57; Corp. Pap. Rain. 22¹⁵ (ii/A.D.) τὸ ἄλλο ἥμισυ. The concentrated phrasing ἄλλοι ἄλλο is class. (*one one thing* . . . *one another*): Ac 19³² 21³⁴.

ἕκαστος ².

In Attic inscriptions until 318 B.C. without exception, ἕκαστος with a noun and art. is in the predicative position; the rule is observed also in Attic writers except in prepositional expressions and genitive expressions of time. However, popular speech dispenses with the art., and the proportions in the Ptol. papyri are (with: without) 1 : 3 in iii/B.C. and 1 : 4 in ii–i/ B.C.; and in popular speech ἕκαστος is used only rarely in an attributive position; we have intensive εἷς ἕκαστος, and (Heb 3¹³) ἕνα ἑκάστην ἡμέραν, (Rev 22²) μῆνα ἕκαστον. It is added to a plural subject without affecting the construction (class. and Koine): Winer § 58, 4, K-G I 286ff, Mayser II 2, 115, II 3, 37³⁷ff. Jn 16³² (εἷς in same way : 1 Co 4⁶) ἵνα σκορπισθῆτε ἕκαστος . . . κἀμὲ μόνον ἀφῆτε.

Καθ' εἷς is a colloquialism which does not occur widely in NT: Mk 14¹⁹ εἷς κατὰ εἷς (C εἷς ἕκαστος, harm. with Mt 26²²), Jn 8⁹, Ro 12⁵ τὸ δὲ καθ' εἷς (pap. Mayser I² 3, 205³⁸ff τὸ καθ' ἕν; LXX 3 Mac 5³⁴ ὁ καθεὶς τῶν φίλων), Rev 21²¹ ἀνὰ εἷς ἕκαστος. Its origin lies in the compression of καθ' ἕνα ἕκαστον *each one by one* into καθένα ἕκαστον and the next step was to invent καθ' εἷς when a nominative was needed (ἀνὰ εἷς appears by the same principle: distributive ἀνά). A further step was an addition to produce the pleonastic *one one by one* εἷς κατὰ εἷς.

In the NT ἑκάτερος does not survive.

ἀμφότεροι.

This is substantival ³ in the NT, as in the papyri, except for Lk 5⁷ ἀμφότερα τὰ πλοῖα.

---

¹ Eurip. Iph T. 962f: θάτερον . . . τὸ δ' ἄλλο. Plato Leg. 629D τὸ μὲν . . . τὸ δ' ἄλλο, but probably corrupt.
² K-G I 634. 7. Meisterhans-Schwyzer 232. 38. Gildersleeve II 660, 661, 662. Mayser II 2, 90ff. Rademacher² 113, 117.
³ Ac 23⁸ Eph 2¹⁴ τὰ ἀμφότερα. Eph 2¹⁶ τοὺς ἀμφοτέρους, 2¹⁸ οἱ ἀμφότεροι. See Mayser II 2, 94.

ὅλος [1].

Whole. Usually anarthrous in NT, whereas always articular in Ptol. papyri: Mt 22³⁷ BS*Θ (vl. +art.), Mk 12³⁰·³³ BD* (vl. + art.), Lk 5⁵ δι' ὅλης νυκτός SABWL (CD + τῆς), 10²⁷ B* (vl. + art.), Jn 7²³ ὅλον ἄνθρωπον *a whole man,* Ac 11²⁶ ἐνιαυτὸν ὅλον. With anarthrous city-names: Ac 21³¹ ὅλη 'Ιερουσαλήμ (=πᾶσα 'Ιεροσόλυμα Mt 2³). With art., always predicative: Mt 16²⁶ τὸν κόσμον ὅλον, 26¹³ ἐν ὅλῳ τῷ κόσμῳ.

ἅπας.

Only found in Lk-Ac with any frequency, and σύμπας is lacking altogether. Outside Lk: Mt 6³² 24³⁹ (D πάντες) 28¹¹ (A πάντα), Mk 8²⁵ (DW πάντα) 11³² 16¹⁵ (D om), Ga 3²⁸ ASB³; Eph 6¹³, Jas 3². Even Luke does not always observe the not invariable class. rule of πᾶς after a vowel and ἅπας after a consonant (1³ ἄνωθεν πᾶσιν); but ἅπας generally occurs after a consonant, as in papyri (see Mayser I¹ 161f; II 2, 96 n. 3). The MSS vary with πᾶς. Word order, like πᾶς.

πᾶς [2].

(1) In the interests of exegesis it is important to ask how much is involved in the Hellenistic deviation from class. standards as to the def. art. with πᾶς. First of all, πᾶς before an anarthrous noun means *every* in the sense of *any*; not every individual, like ἕκαστος, but any you please [3]. Similarly, the negative is *none, no,* as in Mt 24²² οὐκ ἂν ἐσώθη πᾶσα σάρξ (Semitic, see pp. 7, 196f).

Mt 3¹⁰ πᾶν δένδρον *any tree,* Lk 3⁹ *any tree,* not *every tree,* 2 Ti 3¹⁶ πᾶσα γραφή *whatever is Scripture.*

On the other hand, this anarthrous πᾶς also means *all, the whole of,* just as it does when it has the art. It may be that is

---

[1] K-G I 631. 6. Mayser II 2, 95f, 568. Meisterhans-Schwyzer 234, 45. Winer-Schmiedel § 20, 12.

[2] K-G I 631, 6. Gildersleeve II 642-52. Meisterhans-Schwyzer 233ff. Mayser II 2, 96f. Winer-Schmiedel § 20, 11. Radermacher² 112, 113, 117.

[3] This is important for the correct interpretation of Mt 19³ κατὰ πᾶσαν αἰτίαν, which is not *for every cause,* but *for any cause* you like to single out among those in the Law, i.e. *for any cause at all.* Jesus was not being asked for his opinion on the varying merits of each Mosaic ground for divorce, but whether he rejected all grounds.

due to Hebraic influence: for כָּל־בָּשָׂר becomes πᾶσα σάρξ *all flesh, everything fleshly* (Mt 24²² Lk 3⁶ Ro 3²⁰ 1 Co 1²⁹). Mt 3¹⁵ πᾶσα δικαιοσύνη *the whole of*; Ac 2³⁶ πᾶσα οἶκος Ἰσραήλ *whole*, 4²⁹ μετὰ πάσης παρρησίας *complete*, 23¹ πάσῃ συνειδήσει ἀγαθῇ; Ro 11²⁶ πᾶς Ἰσραήλ *the whole of Israel*; Col 1²³ (S°D° add τῇ), 1¹⁵ πρωτότοκος πάσης κτίσεως; Eph 2²¹ πᾶσα οἰκοδομή (but S^aACP have art.) prob. not here as class. *whatever is built*, but (under Semitic infl.) *the whole building*; 1 Pt 2¹³ πᾶσα κτίσις *the whole creation.*

It is more likely, however, that πᾶς with this meaning will have the art: Ac 12¹¹ πάσης τῆς προσδοκίας *the whole*, Ro 8²² πᾶσα ἡ κτίσις (cp. 1 Pt 2¹³), 1 Co 13² πᾶσαν τὴν γνῶσιν and πᾶσαν τὴν πίστιν *all that exists*; Eph 2²¹; 4¹⁶ πᾶν τὸ σῶμα; Ph 1³ ἐπὶ πάσῃ τῇ μνείᾳ (DE om τῇ) *the whole.*

But sometimes a distinction can be traced between πᾶς with and without the art. in the same passage: 2 Co 1⁴ ὁ παρακαλῶν ἡμᾶς ἐπὶ πάσῃ τῇ θλίψει ἡμῶν *in all our affliction*, εἰς τὸ δύνασθαι ἡμᾶς παρακαλεῖν τοὺς ἐν πάσῃ θλίψει *in any affliction.*

If πᾶς is placed after a noun with the art., special stress is laid upon the noun, e.g. 1 Co 15⁷ ἔπειτα Ἰακώβῳ, ἔπειτα τοῖς ἀποστόλοις πᾶσιν. A frequent use is that of πᾶς with ptc., even without the art., e.g. Mt 3¹⁰ πᾶν δένδρον μὴ ποιοῦν, 13¹⁹ παντὸς ἀκούοντος, Lk 11⁴.

Nevertheless the distinction of an anarthrous and articular noun with πᾶς is not very clear in NT, even to the extent that πᾶς with an articular noun can approach the meaning of *any*: Mk 4¹³ πάσας τὰς παραβολάς *any parables*, not *all the parables*.

(2) The plural (*all*) does not require the art., any more than οὗτος does at this period, and much depends on the noun itself which accompanies πάντες: Ac 17²¹ πάντες Ἀθηναῖοι and 26⁴ πάντες Ἰουδαῖοι are class., for people-names do not require the art. (see p. 169). With πάντες ἄνθρωποι *everybody* (Ac 22¹⁵ Ro 5¹². ¹⁸ 12¹⁷. ¹⁸ etc.) and πάντες ἄγγελοι (Heb 1⁶ OT) the meaning is weakened and the art. is omitted because no totality is really involved: so also Ga 6⁶ πᾶσιν ἀγαθοῖς, 1 Pt 2¹ πάσας καταλαλιάς (S* sing.). When however totality is involved the art. is still needed: Eph 3⁸ πάντων ἁγίων (P + τῶν; p⁴⁶ om τῶν ἁγίων). Its omission in Lk 4²⁰ is unclassical (πάντων ἐν τῇ συναγωγῇ) and that may have caused the MSS to change the position of ἐν τῇ σ. in various ways.

(3) Sometimes, however, the art. occurs before πᾶς, and then ὁ πᾶς and οἱ πάντες contrast the whole with the part:[1] Ac 19[7] οἱ πάντες ἄνδρες *the sum total of the men* (which is different from the predicative *men as a whole* πάντες οἱ ἄνδρες, see Zerwick § 142), 20[18] τὸν πάντα χρόνον *all that time*, 27[37] αἱ πᾶσαι ψυχαί *we were in all* . . . , Ga 5[14] ὁ πᾶς νόμος = " universa lex " as opposed to πᾶς ὁ νόμος = " integra lex nullo praecepto excepto " (Zerwick § 142), 2 Co 5[10] τοὺς πάντας ἡμᾶς the sum total of us.

The non-attributive substantival use of οἱ πάντες is frequent in Paul: Ro 11[32] 1 Co 9[22] 10[17] 2 Co 5[15] Eph 4[13] Ph 2[21]; and τὰ πάντα Mk 4[11] vl., Ac 17[25] Ro 8[32] 11[36] 1 Co 12[6. 19] 15[27]! (pap. Mayser II 2, 101f).

(4) In relation to its noun, various positions are possible for πᾶς [2]: 1. πᾶς ἄνθρωπος, 2(a) πᾶς ὁ ἄνθρωπος, 2(b) ὁ ἄνθρωπος πᾶς, 3. ὁ πᾶς ἄνθρωπος, and the plurals respectively. Mayser (II 2, 102) shows that the Koine has developed the emphatic form 2(b), at the expense of 2(a) which incidentally is extremely popular in Biblical Greek (LXX NT). Hebrew influence has brought this about. The entry of a demonstrative pronoun may be between πᾶς and its noun or outside: 2(a) πάντα ταῦτα τὰ πονηρά Mk 7[23], πάντα τὰ ῥήματα ταῦτα Lk 1[65], 2(b) τὴν ἐξουσίαν ταύτην ἅπασαν Lk 4[6]. Only Lk has the order ταῦτα πάντα.

The following tables prove the essential unity of Biblical Greek against that of the Ptolemaic papyri, especially when the second table (percentage proportion) is examined. Types 2(b) and 3 occur scarcely at all in Biblical Greek, but occur strongly in secular. Type 2(a) is very strong in Biblical Greek, but only average in the papyri.

---

[1] Class. exx. e.g. Thuc. 1, 60, in K-G I 632f, Gildersleeve II 309ff. Papyri: Mayser II 2, 100f.
[2] See N. Turner op. cit. 211f; Cuendet 131f).

ACTUAL OCCURRENCES

	Type 1 s.	Type 1 pl.	Type 2(a) s.	Type 2(a) pl.	Type 2(b) s.	Type 2(b) pl.	Type 3 s.	Type 3 pl.
Papyrus iii/B.C.	17	2	14	40	18	56	22	5
Papyrus ii–i/B.C.	23	11	11	20	5	90	19	13
LXX								
Ge	58	12	69	160	2	1	1	–
Ex	99	1	64	105	1	1	–	–
Le	109	6	57	56	–	–	5	–
Nu	93	21	83	113	–	2	1	–
Dt	80	15	64	154	–	–	2	–
Pentateuch	439	55	337	588	3	4	9	–
Jo 1–12	28	3	43	33	1	–	1	1
Jo 13–24	9	3	16	38	–	–	–	–
Joshua	37	6	59	71	1	–	1	1
Jg Ru B	31	6	36	36	–	1	1	3
Jg Ru A	25	8	42	41	–	–	–	1
E. Kms	104	24	102	162	–	–	3	1
L. Kms	73	18	91	124	–	–	–	–
1 Chr	53	21	24	43	–	1	7	3
2 Chr	79	13	62	100	1	2	1	3
Chronicles	132	34	86	143	1	3	8	6
1 Esd (paraphrase)	18	5	19	46	–	4	1	1
2 Esd-Ne	32	9	33	31	–	–	2	4
Ps 1–77	17	4	22	105	–	–	–	–
Ps 77–151	23	8	20	120	–	–	–	–
Psalms	40	12	42	225	–	–	–	–
Pr	33	10	4	20	–	–	–	–
Eccl	20	2	9	12	–	–	2	–
Ca	–	7	–	1	–	–	1	2
Jb	31	2	3	16	–	2	–	1
Wi	11	2	2	1	–	3	1	–
Si	112	10	11	24	–	2	–	–

§ 2] PRONOUNS AND PRONOMINAL ADJECTIVES

	Type 1 s. pl.	Type 2(a) s. pl.	Type 2(b) s. pl.	Type 3 s. pl.
Est	26 1	10 28	– 1	– 2
Jdt	38 7	57 68	2 –	– –
To S	12 6	11 50	1 2	1 –
To B	16 2	4 37	– –	– –
Min. Proph.	20 9	36 110	– –	– –
Isa	67 9	26 75	1 6	– 1
Je α	38 4	35 73	– –	1 –
Je β	28 5	44 102	– 1	1 –
Je γ	2 –	1 6	– –	– 2
Ezk α	50 10	20 86	– –	– –
Ezk β	21 6	23 59	1 1	– –
Da O′	35 3	19 56	– 1	– –
Da θ	32 4	21 43	– –	– –
1 Mac	39 30	2 86	3 5	– –
2–4 Mac	44 12	17 38	3 2	16 2
NT				
Mt. Mk	29 3	21 46	2 5	– –
Lk	18 2	28 47	– 3	– –
Ac	26 6	24 45	– 4	1 2
Jn	4 –	15 3	2 2	– –
Jn. Epp	8 –	16 1	– –	– –
Rev	29 1	2 18	1 1	– –
Ro. Co.	39 8	20 20	– 9	– 1
Ga. Th	12 2	3 9	– 1	1 1
Eph. Col. Ph	45 2	9 13	– 1	– 1
Past	21 5	1 7	– 2	– –
Heb	13 1	2 7	– –	– –
1 Pt	9 –	2 1	– –	– –
Jas	7 –	– 1	– –	– –
2 Pt	2 1	– –	– –	– –
Jude	1 –	1 3	– –	– –
T. Abr. A	17 1	13 18	– 2	– –
B	4 3	3 3	– 2	– –
Ps. Sol.	11 2	7 3	– –	– –

PERCENTAGE OF TYPE WITHIN EACH BOOK

	Type 1 s.	*Type* 1 pl.	*Type* 2(a) s.	*Type* 2(a) pl.	*Type* 2(b) s.	*Type* 2(b) pl.	*Type* 3 s.	*Type* 3 pl.
Papyrus iii/B.C.	10	1	8	23	10	32	13	3
Pap. ii–i/B.C.	12	6	6	10	2	46	10	7
LXX								
Ge	20	4	22	55	½	¼	¼	–
Ex	33	¼	23	39	¼	¼	–	–
Le	46	2	24	24	–	–	2	–
Nu	30	7	26	36	–	¾	¼	–
Dt	25	5	20	49	–	–	1	–
Pentateuch	30	4	25	40	¼	¼	¾	–
Jo 1–12	25	2	39	30	1	–	1	1
Jo 13–24	13	5	24	57	–	–	–	–
Joshua	22	3	33	40	1	–	½	½
Jg. Ru B	27	5	32	32	–	1	1	2
Jg. Ru A	21	7	36	36	–	–	–	1
E. Kms	26	6	26	41	–	–	¾	¼
L. Kms	24	6	30	40	–	–	–	–
1 Chr	35	14	15	28	–	–	5	2
2 Chr	30	5	23	40	½	¾	½	1¼
Chronicles	32	8	21	35	¼	¾	2	1
1 Esd (paraphrase)	19	6	20	47	–	5	1½	1½
2 Esd–Ne	29	8	30	28	–	–	2	4
Ps 1–77	11	3	15	71	–	–	–	–
Ps 77–151	13	5	12	70	–	–	–	–
Psalms	13	3	13	70	–	–	–	–
Pr	49	15	6	30	–	–	–	–
Eccl	44	4	20	27	–	–	4	1
Ca	–	70	–	10	–	–	10	20
Jb	56	4	5	29	–	4	–	2
Wi	55	10	10	5	–	15	5	–

§ 2] PRONOUNS AND PRONOMINAL ADJECTIVES

	Type 1 s.	Type 1 pl.	Type 2(a) s.	Type 2(a) pl.	Type 2(b) s.	Type 2(b) pl.	Type 3 s.	Type 3 pl.
Si	70	6	7	15	–	1	–	–
Est	38	1	15	41	1	1	–	3
Jdt	22	4	33	40	1	–	–	–
To S	14	8	13	60	1	3	1	–
To B	27	4	6	63	–	–	–	–
Min. Proph.	11	5	21	63	–	–	–	–
Isa	37	5	14	40	½	3	–	½
Je α	26	3	22	48	–	–	1	–
Je β	15	2½	24	56	–	½	½	–
Je γ	20	–	10	60	–	–	–	20
Ezk α	30	6	12	51	–	–	–	–
Ezk β	20	5½	21	54	1	1	–	–
Da O'	30	2½	17	49	–	1	–	–
Da θ	32	4	21	43	–	–	–	–
1 Mac	23	1	18	52	2	3	–	–
2–4 Mac	33	9	13	28	2	2	12	2
NT								
Mt. Mk	27	3	20	43	2	5	–	–
Lk	18	2	28	47	–	3	–	–
Ac	25	5	23	44	–	3	1	1
Jn	15	–	59	11	7	7	–	–
Jn. Epp	32	–	64	4	–	–	–	–
Rev	57	2	3	35	2	2	–	–
Ro. Co	40	8	21	21	–	9	–	1
Ga. Th	41	7	10	31	–	3¾	3¾	3¾
Eph. Col. Ph	63	3	13	18	–	1	–	1
Past	58	14	3	16	–	6	–	–
Heb	56	4	9	30	–	–	–	–
1 Pt	75	–	17	8	–	–	–	–
Jas	87	–	–	12	–	–	–	–
2 Pt. Jude	37½	12½	12½	37½	–	–	–	–
T. Abr. A	33½	2	25½	34	–	4	–	–
B	25	19	19	19	6	12	–	–
Ps. Sol.	48	9	30	13	–	–	–	–

CHAPTER FIFTEEN

ATTRIBUTIVE RELATIONSHIP: SUBSTANTIVES

§ 1. In the same case: Apposition [1]

A substantival attribute placed either before or after another noun, or a pers. pronoun, is said to be in apposition. This will occur with a proper noun, and the apposition then has the art. to distinguish that person from others of the same name: Ἰωάννης ὁ βαπτιστής, Σίμων ὁ Καναναῖος, Ἰάκωβος ὁ τοῦ Ἀλφαίου, Σαῦλος ὁ καὶ Παῦλος, ὁ βασιλεὺς Ἡρῴδης (or Ἡρῴδης ὁ βασιλεύς), Φίλιππος ὁ εὐαγγελιστής, Τιμόθεος ὁ συνεργός μου. The proper noun itself is generally anarthrous; and so the readings τῆς (SABD) Μαρίας τῆς μητρός (Ac 12¹²) and τὸν Ἰωάννην (D*) τὸν ἐπικληθέντα Μάρκον (12²⁵) are probably incorrect. There are some exceptions to the use of the art. with the apposition: Ac 7¹⁰ Φαραὼ βασιλέως Αἰγύπτου, 10⁶ Σίμωνι βυρσεῖ, 13¹ Μαναὴν Ἡρῴδου τοῦ τετραάρχου σύντροφος, 21¹⁶ Μνάσωνί τινι Κυπρίῳ. Col 1³ vl. ¹² vl. 2² 3¹⁷ ὁ θεὸς πατήρ [2], 1 Pt 5⁸ ὁ ἀντίδικος ὑμῶν διάβολος (ἀντιδ. adjectival?). The proper noun usually comes first; hence D corrects ἡ Μαγδαληνὴ Μαρία to Μαρία ἡ Μαγδ. Lk 24¹⁰. Sometimes ὁ (ἐπι)καλούμενος or ὁ καί c. gen. precedes the surname. The latter is rare in the nominative in pre-Christian papyri (Mayser I² 2, 69; II 1, 60ff; II 3, 56); instead ὃς καί. In rather formal wording, as in the opening of an epistle, κύριος or θεός will occur without art., followed by an anarthrous appositional phrase: Ro 1⁷ ἀπὸ θεοῦ πατρὸς ἡμῶν καὶ κύριος..., Ph 3²⁰ κύριον Ἰησοῦν Χριστόν 1 Th 1¹ ἐν θεῷ πατρὶ καὶ κυρίῳ Ἰ. Χ., 1 Ti 1¹ θεοῦ σωτῆρος ἡμῶν. On Jn 8⁴⁴, see above p. 40, but note that to be predicative (*the devil is your father*) πατρός ought not to have the art.; τοῦ διαβόλου is therefore in apposition or else possessive genitive. A phrase in apposition with a pers. pronoun requires the art. in class. Greek: so Mk 7⁶ ὑμῶν τῶν ὑποκριτῶν, Lk 6²⁴ ὑμῖν τοῖς πλουσίοις, Ac 13³³ C² EHLP τοῖς τέκνοις αὐτῶν ἡμῶν.

---

[1] K-G I § 406, pp. 281ff. Mayser II 2, 103ff. Radermacher² 116.
[2] But variants make. it easier; e.g. in Col 1³: τῷ πατρὶ D*G Chrys, καὶ πατρὶ SA.

§ 2. In a different case:

1. Adjectival Genitive[1]

I. *True Genitive*

This is a large subject, as the genitive is so hard worked a case in Greek. The adjectival is the commonest way the case is used, and Luke is particularly fond of it. The relationship expressed by the gen. is so vague that it is only by means of the context and wider considerations that it can be made definite. For practical purposes perhaps the only real division among the genitives is that between subjective and objective (Zerwick § 25). The sole question which the translator and exegete need ask is whether the relationship is directed outwards from the noun in the genitive to some other person or from some other person to the noun in the genitive; or, to put it differently, whether or not the action implied by the independent noun is carried out by the noun in the genitive. Obviously, ἡ πτῶσις αὐτῆς Mt 7^{27} is subjective: the house *falls*; so is Ac 6^1 γογγυσμὸς τῶν Ἑλληνιστῶν: the Hellenists *murmur*; so also 2 Co 6^7 *the armour of righteousness* is probably that which the divine righteousness provides.[2] Clearly οἱ εὐλογημένοι τοῦ πατρός μου and τὸν ἀγαπητόν μου, like the LXX ἐκλεκτοὺς κυρίου, are subjective. But Ph 1^3 is quite ambiguous: ἐπὶ πάσῃ τῇ μνείᾳ ὑμῶν may be (a) subjective: *whenever you remember me*, or (b) objective: *whenever I think of you*.

(a) *Possessive Genitive.* In class. and Koine Greek the relationship of parents to children is expressed in this way, with or without υἱός (see above, pp. 168f): but in the latter case the phrase is ὁ τοῦ δεῖνος, contrary to class. usage which omits the second art. The frequent addition of υἱός is Semitic rather than typically Greek, and even in the papyri this and θυγάτηρ are added only for clarity (Mayser II 2, 9): Lk 3^2 Ἰωάννην τὸν Ζαχαρίου υἱόν. The only exception to the use of υἱοί with the sons of Zebedee (Mt 26^{37} 27^{56} Mk 10^{35} Lk 5^{10}) is Jn 21^2 οἱ τοῦ Z. ABL (SD οἱ υἱοὶ Z.). Figuratively υἱός is used with a noun in the genitive in order to express a certain quality. It

---

[1] K-G I § 414-421. Schwyzer II 89-137. Mayser II 2, 118ff. Eakin 335ff.
[2] Kittel WB, English translation, *Righteousness*, 1951, 53.

would seem to be a Semitism; it is rare in pre-Biblical Greek and is there confined to such phrases as υἱὸς Ἑλλάδος *a son of Greece*. It is very common in LXX: Ps 88²³ 2 Km 7¹⁰ 1 Mac 2⁴⁷ 4², and Hebrew uses the words *man, son, daughter, mother, father, lord*, in this sense.¹ In the NT: Mk 3¹⁷ υἱοὶ βροντῆς *thunderbolts*, Mt 5⁹· ⁴⁵ *sons of God*, 9¹⁵ בְּנֵי הַחֻפָּה *bridegroom's friends*, 13³⁸ *men of the kingdom* ... *of evil*, Lk 10⁶ *man of peace*, 16⁸ *men of this age*, 20³⁶ *of the resurrection* (= those who will rise), Jn 17¹² 2 Th 2³ Ap. Pet. 2 τῆς ἀπωλείας, Jn 8³⁹· ⁴⁴ Ga 3⁷ *children of Abraham*, Ac 13¹⁰ *of the Devil*, Eph 2² Col 3⁶ TR *of disobedience* (= disobedient), 1 Th 5⁵ υἱοὶ φωτός ἐστε καὶ υἱοὶ ἡμέρας (and then without υἱοί), Ap. Pet. 3 Herm V. III 6, 1 υἱοὶ τῆς ἀνομίας, Ac 3²⁵ Ps. Sol. 17¹⁵ τῆς διαθήκης, Ac 4³⁶ υἱὸς παρακλήσεως (Bauer s.v. υἱός 1 c.δ). Vulg. inserts *filii* in Heb 10³⁹ where Greek has simple gen. In the same sense as υἱός we have τέκνον in Lk 7³⁵ Ga 4²⁸ Eph 2³ 1 Pt 1¹⁴ 2 Pt 2¹⁴ etc. In ecclesiastical Greek, e.g. Epiph. Haer. 43, 2.

(*b*) *Partitive Genitive*². This is the gen. of a whole which is divided. It is still in use in the Koine, but since class. times it has been more and more displaced by the use of the prepositions ἀπό, ἐκ, ἐν ³. This ἐν is rare in the papyri (Mayser II 2, 352f), and ἀπό is more frequent than ἐκ. This ἐκ is not common in class. Greek but we do find μόνος ἐξ ἁπάντων. Partitive ἀπό is even rarer there; it abounds in LXX and prevails in MGr (Mayser II 2, 348f.; Johannessohn DGKPS 17).

There is a construction which is not widely acknowledged in NT: the partitive ἀπό and ἐκ introducing a phrase which can stand independently of a noun as subject or object of a verb, with something like τινές suppressed, a substantival phrase in fact.⁴ It may be either subj. or obj.:—(a) subject: Mt 27⁹ ὃν ἐτιμήσαντο ἀπὸ υἱῶν Ἰσραήλ OT, Lk 8³⁵ D παραγενομένων ἐκ τῆς πόλεως (sc. *some people from*), Jn 3²⁵ ἐγένετο ζήτησις (sc. ἐν τοῖς) ἐκ τῶν μαθητῶν, 7⁴⁰ ἐκ τοῦ ὄχλου ... ἔλεγον (vl.

---

¹ Thackeray OT Gr. 41f. Deissmann *Bibelstudien*, 1895, 162–166. Johannessohn DGKPS 32. Lagrange *S. Matth.* 166.
² K-G I § 414, 5. Mayser II 2, 121ff.
³ Esp. in LXX, through Heb. מִן partitive. E.g. Ex 9⁴· ⁶· ⁷ (οὐκ ἐτελεύτησεν ἀπὸ πάντων τῶν κτηνῶν οὐδέν), 1 Mac 4¹⁵ ἔπεσαν ἐξ αὐτῶν εἰς ἄνδρας τρισχιλίους.
⁴ K-G I 345. Mayser II 2, 351f, 195f. Johannessohn DGKPS 18f. Schwyzer II 102.

πολλοί, to improve), 16¹⁷ εἶπον ἐκ τῶν μαθητῶν *some of his disciples*, Ac 19³³ ἐκ δὲ τοῦ ὄχλου συνεβίβασαν (*some of the crowd*), 21¹⁶ συνῆλθον δὲ καὶ τῶν μαθητῶν (*some disciples*), Rev 11⁹ 15⁷ p⁴⁷ ἐκ τῶν τεσσάρων ἔδωκαν (*some of the four*). LXX 1 Km 14⁴⁵ 2 Km 14¹¹ τῆς τριχός, 4 Km 10²³ τῶν δούλων, 1 Mac 7³³ ἐξῆλθον ἀπὸ τῶν ἱερέων, 10³⁷ καταστα θήσεται ἐξ αὐτῶν (*let some of them be stationed*). (b) object: Mt 23³⁴, Mk 2²¹ *some of it*[1], 6⁴³ ἀπὸ τῶν ἰχθύων *some fish*, 12² ἀπὸ τῶν καρπῶν *some fruit*, 14²³ ἐξ αὐτοῦ (drink) *some of it*, Lk 11⁴⁹, 2 Jn⁴, Rev 2¹⁰, Herm. S. VIII 6, 5 ἐξ αὐτῶν, Mk 9³⁷ WΘ ἐκ τῶν τοιούτων παιδίων Lk 21¹⁶ θανατώσουσιν ἐξ ὑμῶν (*some of them*). LXX Ge 27²⁸ δῴη σοι ὁ θεὸς ἀπὸ τῆς δρόσου τοῦ (*may God give you some dew from heaven*), 2 Km 11¹⁷ ἔπεσαν ἐκ τοῦ λαοῦ (*some of the people fell*). This is a Bibl. Greek construction, not unknown but rare in class. Greek, really originating in LXX, and is parallel to similar constructions in Heb., Syriac and Arabic. Scribes felt the need to correct the construction in 1 Mac 6⁴⁸ καὶ ἐκ τῆς παρεμβολῆς τοῦ βασιλέως ἀνέβαινον A (SV οἱ δέ) *some soldiers of the king's army went up*. There is much further evidence: Ge 3¹² 44 33¹⁵ 45²³ Ex 17⁵ 1 Mac 8⁸.

With τις it is usually the simple genitive; but Ac 7⁵² Heb 1⁵, ¹³ are interrogative τίς. Thus Mt 9³ τινες τῶν γραμματέων, Lk 7³⁶ τις τῶν Φαρισαίων. The exceptions are John's Gospel and the LXX (e.g. Ex 16²⁷ τινες ἐκ τοῦ λαοῦ). Partitive gen. without preposition appears to be the rule with ἕκαστος (e.g. Ro 14¹²), and usually so with εἷς (e.g. Mt 5²⁹, ³⁰ 10⁴²) ². Other exx. are: Mk 2¹⁶ οἱ γραμματεῖς τῶν Φαρισαίων (vl) *among*?, Lk 18¹¹ Rev 9²⁰ οἱ λοιποὶ τῶν ἀνθρώπων, Ro 15²⁶ τοὺς πτωχοὺς τῶν ἁγίων *among*. However, ἐκ is usually found with πᾶς (Lk 14³³, Le 21²¹ πᾶς ἐξ ὑμῶν) in spite of the class. πᾶς Ἑλλήνων, and with τίς ³: Mt 6²⁷ τίς ἐξ ὑμῶν, 27²¹ τίνα ἀπὸ τῶν δύο (syr^sin only τίνα),

---

[1] The best reading from a syntax point of view in Mk 2²¹ is εἰ δὲ μή, αἴρει ἀπ' αὐτοῦ (*some of it*) τὸ πλήρωμα τὸ καινὸν (*the new fulness*) ἀπὸ τοῦ παλαιοῦ (*namely, some of the old*). The prepositional phrase immediately follows the verb, which is good Bibl. Greek word-order. The MS variants are probably afterthoughts to remove the Aramaic construction of a proleptic pronoun followed by a noun. (For Proleptic Pronouns, see p. 41. See also Black AAGA² 37, 251; Moulton-Howard 461.) The suggestion is given to me verbally by Dr. G. D. Kilpatrick, and adopted by him in the (privately circulated) *Mark: a Greek-English Diglot for the use of Translators*, B. and F.B.S., 1958, 6.
[2] But ἐκ in LXX Ge 3²² εἷς ἐξ ἡμῶν, etc., Mt 10²⁹ 18¹² etc.
[3] But gen. only in Ac 7⁵² Heb 1⁵, ¹³. Some texts are uncertain: Mt 22²⁸ τίνος τῶν ἑπτά, Mk 12²³ τίνος αὐτῶν (Δ c k om αὐτῶν), Lk 7⁴² τίς αὐτῶν (D om αὐτῶν), 14⁵ τίνος ὑμῶν (D ἐξ ὑμῶν), 20³³ τίνος αὐτῶν (S* e ff² om αὐτῶν).

Lk 11¹⁵ Jas 2¹⁶. Against the apparent Semitism (בְּ or לְ, as in Le 11³· ²⁶) we must set the class. precedent for a partitive ἐν, as in Ac 5³⁴ τις ἐν τῷ συνεδρίῳ (D ἐκ), 1 Co 15¹², Jas 5¹³· ¹⁴· ¹⁹ τις (τινες) ἐν ὑμῖν. Probably we have a true Semitism from the Hebrew superlative in Rev 5¹¹ μυριάδες μυριάδων καὶ χιλιάδες χιλιάδων (from 1 Enoch: Rev ICC in loc.). The partitive gen. may be used predicatively as well as attributively: Lk 22⁵⁸ Jn 18¹⁷ 1 Co 12¹⁵· ¹⁶ ἐκ, Ac 21¹⁶ 1 Ti 1²⁰ (ὧν ἐστιν 'Υμέναιος). It is debatable whether we have partitive gen. in Col 1¹⁵ (πρωτότοκος πάσης κτίσεως) and Rev 3¹⁴ (ἡ ἀρχὴ τῆς κτίσεως) = among, or whether the idea is not rather that of rule and supremacy.

We have πάντων in Mk 12²⁸ without preposition: ποία ἐστὶν ἐντολὴ πρώτη πάντων (only πασῶν M*; om πάντων DW lat etc.); πάντων however may belong to the next verse: πάντων πρῶτον. "Ακουε 'Ισραήλ (Euseb. minusc.). Without preposition are also the Hebraic superlative constructions τὰ ἅγια τῶν ἁγίων and εἰς τοὺς αἰῶνας τῶν αἰώνων.

After an indication of quality we have one NT example of a phenomenon which has class. precedent, namely the assimilation of gender and number of a neuter substantival adj. to that of its dependent gen.; this occurs in Lk 19⁸ τὰ ἡμίσεια τῶν ὑπαρχόντων (for ἥμισυ, sc. μέρος), which reminds us of the class. ἡ ἡμίσεια τῆς γῆς (K-G I 279; Mayser II 2, 123; Abel § 44 d). Otherwise the neuter adj. is properly used: Mk 6²³ ἕως ἡμίσους τῆς βασιλείας, LXX Est 5³, Rev 11¹³ τὸ δέκατον τῆς πόλεως, 12¹⁴ ἥμισυ καιροῦ.

The geographic gen. is partitive. It indicates the country within which a town lies and is class. and Koine. We may translate *in*. Mt 21¹¹ Mk 1⁹ Ναζαρὲθ τῆς Γαλιλαίας, Jn 2¹ Κανᾶ τῆς Γαλιλαίας, Ac 16¹² ἥτις ἐστὶν πρώτη μερίδος τῆς Μακεδονίας πόλις = *a city in*, Ac 22³, ἐν Ταρσῷ τῆς Κιλικίας (Mayser II 2, 126; K-G I, 334).

(c) *Objective and subjective genitive*.[1] A noun in the gen. may be the object of the action implied in the noun on which it depends. There is much ambiguity here in NT interpretation. Often a gen. might equally well be subjective or objective: it is moreover important not to sacrifice fullness of interpretation to an over precise analysis of syntax. There is no reason why a gen. in the author's mind may not have been both subjective and objective. *The love of Christ constrains us* is not to be so strictly analysed, if the author thought of Christ's love to us and our love to him as a compelling force.[2] But it is always an

---

[1] K-G I 335ff. Mayser II 129.   [2] Zerwick § 25.

objective gen. which depends on *gospel* in the following instances: the good news *about* τῆς βασιλείας Mt 4²³ etc. (which is the same thing as the dir. obj. in Lk 8¹ εὐαγγελίζεσθαι τὴν βασιλείαν), *about* Ἰησοῦ Χριστοῦ Mk 1¹, *about* τοῦ Χριστοῦ 1 Co 9¹² (= dir. obj. in Ac 5⁴²). It may be indirect object: Ga 2⁷ τὸ εὐαγγέλιον τῆς ἀκροβυστίας, *good news for the uncircumcised* (like the indir. obj. in Ac 14²¹ εὐαγγελίζεσθαι τὴν πόλιν). Also indirectly objective are the following expressions: Ro 3²² Jas 2¹ etc. πίστις Ἰησοῦ Χ. (but πίστις εἰς τὸν κύριον Ἰ. Χ. Ac 20²¹ 24²⁴ etc., and ἐν Χ. Ἰ Col 1⁴, especially where there is close proximity with a subjective genitive, e.g. 1 Th 1⁸ ἡ πίστις ὑμῶν ἡ πρὸς τὸν θεόν, Col 2⁵ ἡ εἰς Χριστὸν πίστις ὑμῶν), ὑπακοὴ τοῦ Χριστοῦ or τῆς πίστεως or τῆς ἀληθείας (Ro 1⁵ 2 Co 10⁵ 1 Pt 1²² etc.), which are parallel to the indir. obj. with the verb in Ac 6⁷ ὑπήκοον τῇ πίστει. But 2 Co 7¹⁵ πάντων ὑμῶν is subjective. Lk 4¹⁹ LXX ἐνιαυτὸν κυρίου δεκτόν possessive? But Moule, 40, suggests that it is tinged with the subjective idea: *the year when the Lord will accept* (man).

Either subjective or objective or both may be phrases like πίστις Ἰησοῦ Χριστοῦ Ro 3²², ἀγάπη τοῦ θεοῦ (Χριστοῦ) Ro 8³⁵ 2 Co 5¹⁴ (subj.) Lk 11⁴² 2 Th 3⁵ (obj.). But δικαιοσύνη τοῦ θεοῦ Ro 1¹⁷ 3²², τῆς πίστεως 4¹¹·¹³, indicates the source, and is therefore subjective, as shown by the phrases ἡ ἐκ θεοῦ δικαιοσύνη Ph 3⁹, ἡ ἐκ πίστεως Ro 9³⁰ and ἡ διὰ πίστεως δικαιοσύνη Ph 3⁹. Actually Ro 3⁵ (Ps 97 (98)²) is more like a possessive gen.: *the justice which God dispenses*. Other instances of a subjective gen. of origin or cause are Ro 1¹ 15¹⁶ εὐαγγέλιον τοῦ θεοῦ (since the obj. is said to be περὶ τοῦ υἱοῦ αὐτοῦ ³), and the phrase τὸ εὐαγγέλιόν μου (ἡμῶν) where the gen. is the preacher, although κατά also occurs for this in the titles (Ro 2¹⁶ 16²⁵ 2 Co 4³ 1 Th 1⁵ 2 Th 2¹⁴ 2 Ti 2⁸). That is doubtless the way to regard Mk 1⁴ βάπτισμα μετανοίας; it does not lead to, but springs from, repentance. So also Col 2² πληροφορία τῆς συνέσεως: *conviction which is the result of insight* (or *intelligence*); 1 Th 1³ τῆς ὑπομονῆς τῆς ἐλπίδος: *the sustaining patience which hope brings*; it is parallel to τοῦ ἔργου τῆς πίστεως and τοῦ κόπου τῆς ἀγάπης, *work done from faith and love*.

It is not easy to decide in 2 Co 13¹³ (ἡ κοινωνία τοῦ ἁγίου πνεύματος) between subjective and objective (Hauck in Kittel WB, s.v. κοινωνία). In 1 Co 2¹³ οὐκ ἐν διδακτοῖς ἀνθρωπίνης σοφίας λόγοις ἀλλ' ἐν διδακτοῖς πνεύματος the context requires subjective genitive: *which human wisdom teaches* (cp. Jn 6⁴⁵ Isa 54¹³); but in 1 Mac 4⁷ διδακτοὶ πολέμου is the very reverse, *masters of warfare*, unless it means *taught by war*.

The following are objective genitive: Mt 13¹⁸·³⁶ *the parable about*, 24⁶ ἀκοὰς πολέμων *about wars* (Lk 21⁹ ἀκούσητε πολέμους), Mk 6⁷ etc. ἐξουσία c. gen. = *authority over* (Foerster in Kittel WB II 563), Jn 7¹³

20¹⁹ *for fear of*, Ac 4⁹ εὐεργεσία ἀνθρώπου *help given to a sick man* (NEB), Ro 2⁷ ὑπομονὴ ἔργου ἀγαθοῦ *pereverence in* (2 Th 3⁵ ὑπομονὴ τοῦ Χριστοῦ *steadfast loyalty to Christ*? or subjective?), 7² νόμος τοῦ ἀνδρός *the law about the husband* (Le 14² ὁ νόμος τοῦ λεπροῦ *the law about the leper*; class. ὁ νόμος τῆς βλαπῆς; Abel § 44 g), 1 Co 1¹⁸ ὁ λόγος τοῦ σταύρου, 1 Pt 3¹⁴ φόβον αὐτῶν (context decides for objective: *fear of them*), Col. 3¹⁴ σύνδεσμος τῆς τελειότητος *the bond producing perfection*, Heb 9⁸ τὴν τῶν ἁγίων ὁδόν, 10¹⁹ εἰς τὴν εἴσοδον τῶν ἁγίων *for entering the Holy Place* (Michaelis in Kittel WB V 109. 54ff.) This is perhaps the explanation of ὁδὸς ἐθνῶν (*a way leading to*) Mt 10⁵; ὁδὸν θαλάσσης Mt 4¹⁵; ἡ θύρα τῶν προβάτων Jn 10⁷ (or subjective: *where the sheep enter*?); ἡ θύρα πίστεως Ac 14²⁷ (*leading to faith*? obj., or *where faith enters*? subj.); ἡ θύρα τοῦ λόγου Col 4³ (same); μετοικεσία Βαβυλῶνος Mt 1¹¹·¹² *leading to*; ἡ διασπορὰ τῶν Ἑλλήνων Jn 7³⁵; κῶμαι Καισαρίας Mk 8²⁷ (or possessive). The question of Semitism may be raised in view of LXX Ge 3²⁴ ἡ ὁδὸς τοῦ ξύλου τῆς ζωῆς *leading to*, Ps 44 (43)²² πρόβατα σφαγῆς = צֹאן טִבְחָה *destined for* (Ro 8³⁶), Am 8¹⁰ πένθος ἀγαπητοῦ אֵבֶל יָחִיד *towards, concerning*. Moreover, there seems to be a gen. of place—where: Col 1²⁰ αἵματος σταυροῦ (blood) *shed on the cross*, 2 Co 11²⁶ κινδύνοις ποταμῶν, λῃστῶν *in rivers, among robbers*; and a gen. of time duration: Lk 2⁴⁴ ἦλθον ἡμέρας ὁδόν *a day's journey* (class.).

(d) *Genitive of relationship*. Often θεοῦ and Χριστοῦ in Paul are used to express an ill-defined relationship which may be called " mystical " (Deissmann *Paulus*, 1925, 126f), especially after ἐκκλησία, since it seems to be interchangeable with Deissmann's " in "-formula: see especially 1 Th 2¹⁴ *the churches OF God which are in Judea IN Christ Jesus*, Ga 1²² *IN Christ*, Ro 16¹⁶ αἱ ἐκκλησίαι πᾶσαι τοῦ Χριστοῦ *OF Christ*. Indeed, so rich is Paul's compression of language with genitives that the attempt to define too narrowly the various types of genitive is vain; they all denote a relationship which is amplified by the context. We might even be tempted to borrow Paul's own comprehensive way of speech and render δικαιοσύνη θεοῦ simply *divine grace*.[1] Perhaps some genitives which we have taken as subjective or objective may come under this " mystical" genitive: 2 Th 3⁵ τὴν ὑπομονὴν τοῦ Χριστοῦ *steadfast loyalty in the Body of Christ*; Ro 3²²·²⁶ *faith exercised within the Body*.

(e) *Genitive of quality*.[2] This is a feature of Biblical Greek which has been handed down to MGr, e.g. χαράβι τοῦ πολέμου

---

[1] Zerwick § 28: genetivus " generaliter " determinans.
[2] Schwyzer II 122. Mayser II 2, 135f; II 3, 168. Johannessohn DGKPS 27f. Radermacher² 108f. Nachmanson, Eranos 9, 63ff. Wackernagel, *Mélanges de Saussure* 135.

§ 2] ATTRIBUTIVE RELATIONSHIP: SUBSTANTIVES 213

battleship. With the help of Heb. influence the Bibl. Greek gen. often provides an attribute which normally would be supplied by an adj. The adj. was nearly non-existent in Heb., and so the LXX introduces such phenomena as πύργος ἰσχύος Ps 60 (61)[4] (from מִגְדַּל־עֹז) and ἡ στολὴ τοῦ ἁγίου Ex 29²⁹ (from בִּגְדֵי הַקֹּדֶשׁ). There may be class. parallels, but they are poetic (Eurip. *Bacch*. 389 ὁ τᾶς ἡσυχίας βίοτος = ἥσυχος βίοτος: Jebb's note. Soph. *Ajax* 464f. K–G I 264). There may be Koine parallels, but they are few.[1]

Combinations with σῶμα are especially common in Paul: Ro 6⁶ 7²⁴ τοῦ θανάτου (= adj. θνητός in 6¹² 8¹¹), Ph 3²¹ Col 1²² 2¹¹; with ἡμέρα Ro 2⁵ 2 Co 6² 1 Pt 2¹². Other exx. Mt 5²² etc. γέεννα τοῦ πυρός, Mk 1⁴ etc. βάπτισμα μετανοίας (?), Lk 2¹⁴ ἐν ἀνθρώποις εὐδοκίας S*AB*DW *among approval-men* (i.e. "among men of whom God approves"); the Heb. would be בְּנֵי רְצוֹנוֹ (εὐδοκία = רָצוֹן, as in Si 15¹⁵ 39¹⁸); supply αὐτοῦ as in the opposite instance in Eph. 2³ (τέκνα ὀργῆς).[2] Lk 4²² οἱ λόγοι τῆς χάριτος, 16⁸ οἰκονόμος τῆς ἀδικίας, ⁹ ὁ μαμωνᾶς τῆς ἀδικίας (= ὁ ἄδικος μαμωνᾶς 16¹¹), 18⁶ κριτὴς τῆς ἀδικίας, Ac 1¹⁸ 2 Pt 2¹⁵ μισθός (τῆς) ἀδικίας, Ac 6¹¹ ῥήματα βλασφημίας S*D (Rev 13¹ 17³ ὀνόματα βλασφημίας), 7³⁰ ἐν φλογὶ πυρός (2 Th 1⁸ ἐν πυρὶ φλογός) = LXX Ex 3² ἐν πυρὶ φλογός, 8²³ χολὴ πικρίας, 9¹⁵ σκεῦος ἐκλογῆς (Ro 9²². ²³ σκεύη ὀργῆς ... ἐλέους), Ro 1²⁶ πάθη ἀτιμίας, 6⁴ ἐν καινότητι ζωῆς *new life*, 7⁶ ἐν καινότητι πνεύματος καὶ οὐ παλαιότητι γράμματος *in a new spirit and not according to an out-of-date literalness*, 8²¹ δουλείας τῆς φθορᾶς, Col 1⁵ λόγῳ τῆς ἀληθείας τοῦ εὐαγγελίου *of the true Gospel* (or apposition: *the Truth which is the Gospel*?), 2 Ti 4⁸ ὁ τῆς δικαιοσύνης στέφανος (or apposition?), 1 Pt 1⁴ τέκνα ὑπακοῆς, 5⁴ τῆς δόξης στέφανον, Heb 3¹² καρδία πονηρὰ ἀπιστίας, 5¹³ ἄπειρος λόγου δικαιοσύνης *incapable of understanding correct speech* (Schrenk in Kittel WB II 200⁵ᶠ), 12¹⁵ ῥίζα πικρίας, Jas 1¹² Rev 2¹⁰ στέφανον τῆς ζωῆς (or appositive: *that crown which is life*), Jas 1²⁵ ἀκροατὴς ἐπιλησμονῆς, 2⁴ κριταὶ διαλογισμῶν πονηρῶν *judge by false standards* (*NEB*) (better than Schrenk op. cit. II 98; Büchsel in Kittel WB III 944 n. 3), 1 Jn 2¹⁶ ἡ ἐπιθυμία τῆς σαρκός (or subjective?), Rev 14¹⁰ etc. ὁ οἶνος τοῦ θυμοῦ LXX Ezk 14⁴ 44¹² κόλασις (τῆς) ἀδικίας. On the Heb. pattern, ἡμέρα is used in this connection: Mt 10¹⁵ κρίσεως, Lk 1⁸⁰ ἀναδείξεως, Ro 2⁵ ὀργῆς, 1 Pt 2¹² ἐπισκοπῆς, LXX Ezk 22²⁴ (= בְּיוֹם זַעַם), Soph. 2³.

---

[1] P. Tebt. 105 (ii/B.C.) ἀκίνδυνος παντὸς κινδύνου ἀνυπόλογον πάσης φθορᾶς, and ἀνυπεύθυνοι παντὸς ἐπιτίμου. Etc. See Moulton Einl. 113 n. 1. The gen. of quality may be used predicatively however, as in normal Greek: ἦν ἐτῶν δώδεκα Mk 5⁴² Lk 2⁴² (not D). See Preisigke, s.v. ἔτος.

[2] See the discussion by Schrenk in Kittel WB II 245–8; C. H. Huntzinger, *ZNW* 44, 85ff.

A further Semitism [1] is the addition of the personal (or demonstrative) pronoun to the gen. of quality when properly it belongs to the first noun, e.g. his throne of glory (= *his glorious throne*) becomes " the throne of his glory " (Mt 19²⁸); this body of death (= *this dead body*) becomes " the body of this death " (Ro 7²⁴), our body of humiliation (= *our humble body*) becomes " the body of our humiliation " (Ph 3²¹); his son of love (= *his beloved son*) becomes ὁ υἱὸς τῆς ἀγάπης αὐτοῦ (Col 1¹³);[2] his word of power (= *his powerful word*) becomes " the word of his power " (Heb 1³); his plague of death (= *his mortal wound*) becomes " the plague of his death " (Rev 13³). This is because the Semitic rule adds the suffix in composite expressions to the second member, although the suffix pertains to the whole phrase.

(*f*) *Genitivus materiae, and epexegeticus.*[3] The appositive genitive. This gen. represents more than an adj.; it represents a second noun in apposition to the first, or indicates the material of which the first noun consists. It conforms to class. and Koine usage but is incidentally Hebraic: cp. class. πλοῖα σίτου, papyri οἴνου κεράμια and Heb. נֵבֶל־יַיִן (ἀσκὸς οἴνου) Ge 40¹⁶ 1 Sam 10³.

Mt 12³⁹ Lk 11²⁹ τὸ σημεῖον Ἰωνᾶ *the sign which was Jonah*, Mt 24³⁰ ambiguous, either *the sign which is the S.M.* (appos.), or *the sign which the S.M. will give* (possess.), see Feuillet in Rev. Bibl. 56, 1946, 354; very prevalent in Mark:—1⁴ *baptism involving repentance?*, ²⁸ *the region Galilee*, 4³¹ *a grain consisting of mustard seed*, ³⁷ *a storm involving wind*, 5¹¹ *a herd consisting of swine*, ²⁵. ²⁹ *a fount containing blood*, 8⁸. ²⁰ *an abundance consisting of broken pieces*, ¹⁵ *leaven consisting of the Pharisees*, 9⁴¹ *a cup containing water*, 10¹⁴ τῶν γὰρ τοιούτων ἐστὶν ἡ βασιλεία τοῦ θεοῦ not necessarily possessive (as Mt 18³ and Jn 3³. ⁵ understood it); but *consists of such*; children are the very nature of the kingdom. 14³ ἀλάβαστρον μύρου, ¹³ κεράμιον ὕδατος, 15²⁶ *an inscription consisting of his accusation*, Jn 2²¹ τοῦ ναοῦ τοῦ σώματος αὐτοῦ, Ac 2³⁸ *the gift which is the Spirit*, Ro 4¹¹ σημεῖον περιτομῆς (-μὴν is a correction by AC*) *which is circumcision*, 5¹⁸ *justification which is life* (Zerwick § 33), 2 Co 3³ ἐν πλαξὶν καρδίας σαρκίναις FK lat syrᵖ arm Iren Orig Eus (rest καρδίαις), 5¹ ἡ οἰκία τοῦ σκήνους, ⁵ τὸν ἀρραβῶνα τοῦ πνεύματος *the guarantee consisting of the Spirit* (cp. 1²²), Ga 5⁵ either (appos.) *the*

---

[1] Zerwick § 30.
[2] Which makes it more likely that ὁ υἱὸς ὁ ἀγαπητός is *beloved son*, not *only son*, being a parallel phrase.
[3] K-G I 333. Mayser II 2, 122f. NT examples in U. Holzmeister, *Verb. Dom.* 25, 1947, 112–117.

thing hoped for, which is righteousness (as ICC Ga p. 279) or (subj. gen.) *the thing which the righteous hope for*, Eph 1¹⁴ εἰς ἀπολύτρωσιν τῆς περιποιήσεως: either (appos.) *till our redemption which is our purchase by God* (or *which is our possession*, if active), or (obj. gen.) *till the redemption of those whom God has acquired* (interpreting abstract noun by concrete), 2¹⁴ τὸ μεσότοιχον τοῦ φραγμοῦ, 4⁹ τὰ κατώτερα τῆς γῆς: may be partitive, or appositive (Zerwick § 33) *the lower regions, that is, the earth* (it might also be comparative gen.: regions lower *than* the earth; Büchsel in Kittel WB III 641f), Col 2² πλοῦτος τῆς πληροφορίας *a wealth consisting of conviction*, Heb 6¹ θεμέλιον ... μετανοίας, Jas 3¹⁸ καρπὸς δικαιοσύνης *the harvest of a life devoted to the will of God* (Kittel WB II 203, ET), cp. Pr 3⁹ 11³⁰ Am 6¹², Rev 14¹⁸ the grapes *which are the earth* (Zerwick § 33). LXX Isa 38¹⁴ τὸ ὕψος τοῦ οὐρανοῦ.

The gen. with πόλις, of city-names, which is like Latin, occurs almost only in poetry in class. Greek; it has one example in Ptol. papyri (Mayser II 2, 117) but appears more frequently in later Greek, and is attested only at 2 Pt 2⁶ for certain: πόλεις Σοδόμων καὶ Γομόρρας, because πόλεως Θυατείρων may be gen. of πόλις Θυάτειρα (Ac 16¹⁴). However, names of festivals with gen.: Jn 13¹ (Ex 34²⁵) τῆς ἑορτῆς τοῦ πάσχα, 7² (Dt 31¹¹) τῆς σκηνοπηγίας, Lk 22¹ (Dt 16¹⁶) τῶν ἀζύμων, class. Greek.

II. *Ablatival Genitive* (" Genitivus separationis ").

For replacing of this by means of ἀπό and ἐκ, see below pp. 235f.

(*a*) *With adjectives and adverbs* (much rarer now than in class. Greek, and κοινός and ἴδιος are never used with gen.):

(i) with adjectives having the idea of sharing: Mt 23³⁰ 1 Co 10¹⁸, ²⁰ Heb 10³³ substantival κοινωνός c. gen. of person (*an associate of*). 1 Pt 5¹ 2 Pt 1⁴ Paul: (συγ-)κοινωνός c. gen. of thing. Eph 3⁶ συνκληρονόμα ... συμμέτοχα τῆς εὐαγγελίας. Ro 8²⁹ σύμμορφος τῆς εἰκόνος. Heb 1⁹ OT μέτοχος.

(ii) adjectives of fullness and emptiness: Mt 23²⁸ etc. μεστός, Lk 4¹ etc. πλήρης (κενός and ἐνδεής c. gen. never, although κένος ἀπό in Herm.) LXX Johannessohn DGKPS 43.

(iii) adjectives of worthiness and guilt: Mt 3⁸ 1 Co 6² etc. (ἀν-)ἄξιος. With ἔνοχος LXX has gen. and dat. (Johannessohn DGKPS 43). Mt 26⁶⁶ etc. Ge 26¹¹ Isa 54¹⁷ Si prol⁹ (dat. Jb 15⁵).

(iv) adjectives of strangeness (class.): Eph 2¹² ξένος. Jas 1¹³ ἀπείραστος *inexperienced in* (class. ἀπείρατος; for pap. Moulton Einl. 113 n.); but this may not be its meaning here. 2 Pt 2¹⁴ ἀκατάπαυστος ἁμαρτίας *not ceasing from sin* (but vl.-παστος perhaps *unfed*). Paul has created the phrase ἄνομος θεοῦ—ἔννομος Χριστοῦ (1 Co 9²¹)¹. The following always have ἀπό: Mt 27²⁴ ἀθῷος, Ac 20²⁶ καθαρός (Bauer s.v., Mayser II 2, 353, 570), Ro 7³ ἐλεύθερος *independent of* (pap. in Preisigke Arch. f. P. III 419³¹ vi/A.D. (ἐκ in 1 Co 9¹⁹), Jas 1²⁷ (CP ἐκ)

---

¹ The nearest parallels are Soph. Ant. 369, Eurip. Med. 737, and MGr ἄφοβος τοῦ θεοῦ (Thumb² § 45, 3).

άσπιλος. For LXX see Johannessohn DGPS 282. Very rare is όμοιος ύμών Jn 8⁵⁵ SCLX (ύμῖν ABDW); it is invariably the dat. (9⁹, 1 Jn 3² etc.); Barn 10³ όμοιοι χοίρων, Did. 3¹ ομοίους εκείνου, Aelian Hist. An VIII 1 (K-G I 413). Latin infl?. The gen. with όμοιος in LXX Isa 13⁴ may not be an instance: φωνή ... όμοία εθνών πολλών *a voice like [the voice] of a great multitude*.

(v) adverbs. Unlike LXX (Ge 45¹⁰ and often), εγγύς¹ never has gen. (Johann. DGKPS 43): dat. Ac 9³⁸ 27⁸? Mt 4²⁵ etc. πέραν, 5⁴³ etc. ό πλησίον, 21³⁹ etc. έξω, 23²⁵ τὸ έξωθεν τοῦ ποτηρίου, Mk 15¹⁶ έσω τῆς αύλῆς *further into the palace* (DP έσω εἰς τὴν αὐλήν), Lk 7⁶ SD μακράν (ABCL μ. ἀπό), 8²⁶ ἀντιπέρα, 17²¹ ἐντός, Jn 4⁵ πλησίον, 1 Co 6¹⁸ etc. ἐκτός, 2 Co 10¹⁶ ὑπερέκεινα, Ph 2²⁷ παραπλήσιον (vl. dat.). Also see pp. 276ff.

(b) *Genitive of comparison.* In the latter part of the class. period it was still being used much more often then ή. But as in class. Greek and pap. (Mayser II 2, 140ff), ή is used chiefly in instances where the gen. would not have been sufficiently clear: Mt 10¹⁵ 19²⁴ Ac 4¹⁹ ύμῶν μᾶλλον ή τοῦ θεοῦ, 5²⁹ 20³⁵ Ro 13¹¹ 1 Ti 1⁴ ἐκζητήσεις παρέχουσιν μᾶλλον ή οίκοδομίαν θεοῦ, 2 Ti 3⁴ φιλήδονοι μᾶλλον ή φιλόθεοι. But sometimes there is ή without such good reason: Jn 3¹⁹ 4¹ 1 Co 14⁵ 1 Jn 4⁴.

The class. gen. of comparison² occurs still in e.g. Mt 3¹¹ ἰσχυρότερός μου, Lk 12⁷ πολλῶν στρουθίων διαφέρετε, Ac 23¹³· ²¹ 24¹¹ 25⁶ πλείων c. gen., Mk 14⁵ 1 Co 15⁶ επάνω (= πλείων in colloqu. Greek) c. gen., 1 Ti 5⁹ έλαττον c. gen. There is an abbreviated comparison, omitting a gen. art (Mt 5²⁰ ἐὰν μὴ περισσεύσῃ ἡ δικαιοσύνη ὑμῶν πλεῖον τῶν γραμματέων, Ac 4²² ἐτῶν ... ἦν πλειόνων τεσσεράκοντα: *of more years* (gen. of definition) *than forty* (gen. of comp., indeclinable), see Moule 42), which can cause ambiguity at times: Jn 5³⁶ ἐγὼ ἔχω τὴν μαρτυρίαν μείζω τοῦ 'Ιωάννου (*greater than John had* or *greater than John*), 21¹⁵ ἀγαπᾷς με πλέον τούτων (*more than these* or *more than these do*). The NT uses παρά and ὑπέρ in place of both gen. and ή. There are a few class. exx. (ὑπέρ rarer than παρά), and in MGr παρά or ἀπό is the regular substitute for gen. of comp. Lk 3¹³ πλέον παρὰ τὸ διατεταγμένον, 16⁸ φρονιμώτερον ύπέρ, 18¹⁴ D μᾶλλον παρ' ἐκεῖνον (SBL om μ.; W ή ἐκεῖνος), Jn 12⁴³ μᾶλλον ὑπέρ (ABD ἤπερ), Heb 4¹² Barn 5⁹ ὑπέρ. LXX Ge 49¹² ὑπέρ and ή together (Johannessohn DGKPS 45).

---

¹ K-G I 352, 5. Meisterhans-Schwyzer 213, 11. Mayser II 2, 528. Radermacher² 144.

² What is not class. is πρῶτός μου, πρῶτον ὑμῶν Jn 1¹⁵· ³⁰, because πρότερος would occur here.

III. Position of Attributive and Partitive Genitive.[1]

The attributive gen. very rarely stands first either in class. or Koine Greek, but it does so, e.g. in Mt 1^{18} τοῦ 'Ιησοῦ X. ἡ γένεσις, obviously for emphasis on Jesus. The usual order in class. Greek was either (a) οἱ τῆς χώρας νόμοι, or (b) οἱ νόμοι οἱ τῆς χώρας. But increasingly more common in Hell. Greek, especially in NT, was (c) οἱ νόμοι τῆς χώρας. Mayser's figures for the pre-Christian papyri [2] are:

	(a)	(c)	Proportion		(a)	(c)	Proportion
iii/B.C.	32	44	3 : 4	ii–i/B.C.	45	94	1 : 2

It is doubtful whether any LXX books have a large proportion of (a) and (b), whereas in the first two chapters of Ge (c) occurs at $1^{10.\ 14.\ 17.\ 26.\ 28.\ 30}$ $2^{9.\ 12.\ 18.\ 18.\ 19.\ 19.\ 20}$. In the pap. (b) is extremely rare except in the attribute of proper nouns (e.g. Μαρία ἡ τοῦ 'Ιακώβου in NT). In Mk the relative position of the articular noun and its gen. is striking: it is almost invariably position (c), never (a) as is regular in the papyri; and (b) occurs twice with personal relationship and once (11^{30}) τὸ βάπτισμα τὸ 'Ιωάννου. Thus, possessive: 2 (b) : 35 (c), objective 0 (b) : 5 (c), subjective 1 (b) : 4 (c), content 0 (b) : 5 (c), partitive 0 (b) : 7 (c). In any case, the partitive gen. (as in class. Greek) must take this position, outside the art. and noun, either before or after, without repetition of the art. In the rest of NT, although (b) is still infrequent, (a) is more common than in Mark: e.g.

(a)	Jn 18^{10} BAC 2 Co $8^{6.\ 19}$ (ten in Paul), 1 Pt 3^1 4^{17} $5^{1.\ 1}$ 2 Pt 1^8 2^7 3^2
(b)	Jn 6^{33} SD ὁ ἄρτος ὁ τοῦ θεοῦ, 7^{28} S ὁ νόμος ὁ M., Ac 15^1 τῷ ἔθει τῷ Μωϋσέως (DEHLP om 2nd τῷ)[3], 1 Co 1^{18} ὁ λόγος ὁ τοῦ σταυροῦ, 2 Co 4^{11} ἡ ζωὴ ἡ (p⁴⁶) τοῦ (but 4^{10} ἡ ζ. τοῦ), Ti 2^{10} τὴν διδασκαλίαν τὴν τοῦ σωτῆρος ...

---

[1] K-G I 617. 3. Mayser II 2, 143ff.
[2] This is based on the following for iii/B.C.: P. Hib. nos. 27–121; Zen. P. I and II, nos. 59001–59297; ii–i/B.C. UPZ I; P. Teb. nos. 5–124.
[3] But with Μωϋσέως the position is that of (c), i.e. anarthrous: Mk 12^{26} Lk 2^{22} 24^{44} Ac 13^{39} 15^5 28^{23}.

A frequent construction is the appearance, as a kind of afterthought, of the art. with an attribute after an anarthrous noun: Ac 1¹² ἀπὸ ὅρους τοῦ καλουμένου ἐλαιῶνος, 26¹² καὶ ἐπιτροπῆς τῶν ἀρχιερέων, Jas 1²⁵ εἰς νόμον τέλειον τὸν τῆς ἐλευθερίας.

IV. The Joining together of several different Genitives

Characteristic of Paul and often ambiguous or obscure. Rather rarely two genitives depend on the same noun, which then usually stands between them: Ac 5³² αὐτοῦ μάρτυρες τῶν ῥημάτων τούτων *his witnesses for these things*, 2 Co 5¹ ἡ ἐπίγειος ἡμῶν οἰκία τοῦ σκήνους (possess. and appos.), Ph 2³⁰ τὸ ὑμῶν (subj.) ὑστέρημα τῆς πρός με λειτουργίας (obj.), 2 Pt 3² τῆς τῶν ἀποστόλων ὑμῶν ἐντολῆς τοῦ κυρίου καὶ σωτῆρος perhaps *of the commandment of the Lord and Saviour transmitted by the apostles to you*, Rev 7¹⁷ ἐπὶ ζωῆς πηγὰς ὑδάτων (scribes attempted to remove the obscurity: ζώσας).

More commonly, especially in Paul, but also in the papyri [1] one gen. is dependent on the other, the result being sometimes a clumsy accumulation. We can usually assume in such circumstances that the governing gen. will precede the dependent one [2]:

LXX Wi 13⁵ ἐκ γὰρ μεγέθους καλλονῆς κτισμάτων, 2 Co 4⁴ τὸν φωτισμὸν τοῦ εὐαγγελίου (gen. of origin: *light from the Gospel*) τῆς δόξης τοῦ Χριστοῦ (obj.). Note that the last of the genitives is usually a possessive. Eph 1⁶ εἰς ἔπαινον δόξης [3] τῆς χάριτος αὐτοῦ *for the praise of his grace* (DE τῆς δόξης, which would be *praise of the glory of his grace*; cp. Eph 1¹². ¹⁴), 1¹⁸ ὁ πλοῦτος τῆς δόξης τῆς κληρονομίας αὐτοῦ, 1¹⁹ κατὰ τὴν ἐνέργειαν τοῦ κράτους τῆς ἰσχύος αὐτοῦ, 4¹³ εἰς μέτρον ἡλικίας τοῦ πληρώματος τοῦ Χριστοῦ, Col 2¹² διὰ τῆς πίστεως τῆς ἐνεργείας τοῦ θεοῦ, 1 Th 1³, Rev 14⁸ 16¹⁹ 19¹⁵. Note the order of words in 1 Pt 3³ ὁ ... ἐμπλοκῆς τριχῶν ... κόσμος.

---

[1] Abel § 44, Mayser II 2, 143, 144.
[2] There are exceptions: Mt 24³¹B μετὰ σάλπιγγος φωνῆς μεγάλης, 2 Co 3¹⁸ ἀπὸ κυρίου πνεύματος (assuming it = *the Sp. of the Lord*), Heb 6² βαπτισμῶν διδαχῆς (p⁴⁶B prob. rightly: διδαχήν) *teaching concerning baptisms*.
[3] To be taken very closely together, as in Ph 1¹¹ εἰς δόξαν καὶ ἔπαινον.

V. Attributive and Partitive Genitives in Mark

True Genitive

Possessive	Partitive	Objective Subjective	Quality	Content	Price
1$6.7.15.16.16$	1$9.28$ 2$6$	1$1.4.14.17$	1$4$ 2$29$	1$4.28$ 4$11$	6$37$ 8$37$
1$9.24.29.30$	1$6.21$ 3$22$	2$28$ 4$19$ 6$7.$	4$4.19$	3$1.37$ 5$11$	
2$10.18.26.28$	5$1.22$ 6$15$	4$3$ 7$4.35$	5$1.42$	2$5.29$ 7$24.$	
3$5.17.27.28.34$	2$3$ 7$1.2$	9$35$ 1$0$$44$	6$21.48$	3$1$ 8$8.15.$	
5$37.38.40.41$	8$10.27.28$	1$13.22$ 1$29.$	8$33$ 1$1$$13$	2$0$ 9$41$ 1$0$$1.$	
6$3.17.24.56$	9$1.37$ 1$1$$1.$	2$7$ 1$37.8$	1$5$$38$	1$4$ 1$2$$16$	
7$3.5.27.28.31$	5 1$2$$13.28$	1$44.9$ 1$5$$2.9$		1$4$$2.3.13$	
8$23.38$ 9$24.31.41$	1$4$$10.12.$			1$5$$26$	
1$0$$25.35.46.47.48$	4$3.47.66$	subj.			
1$1$$10.15$	1$5$$35$	7$8.9.13$			
1$2$$14.17.26.35.40$		1$1$$30$ 1$2$$24$			
1$3$$35$ 1$4$$3.47.54$					
1$5$$21.40.43.46$					

Ablatival Genitive

With adjectives	Comparison
3$29$ 6$47$ 8$19$ 9$36$ 1$4$$64$	1$7$ 4$31$ 9$35$ 1$2$$22.28.31.33.43$ 1$4$$5.12$ 1$6$$2$

One gospel has been chosen in order to illustrate the variety and difficulty f interpreting the genitive.

2. Adjectival Dative [1]

(a) *With nouns.* It occurs in class. and Koine Greek with a verbal noun, but in NT only 2 Co 9$11.12$ εὐχαριστία τῷ θεῷ. With other nouns: 1 Co 7$28$ θλίψις τῇ σαρκί, 2 Co 2$13$ ἄνεσις τῷ πνεύματι, 12$7$ σκόλοψ τῇ σαρκί. Many apparent instances display not an attributive, but a predicative, use of the dat. (ATR, 536f). However, Col 2$14$ may be an example of a noun with a dat. attribute: τὸ ... χειρόγραφον τοῖς δόγμασιν *subscription to the ordinances.*

---

[1] K-G I § 424. Meisterhans-Schwyzer 209ff. 26–31. Schwyzer II 137–173. Radermacher[2] 110. J. Humbert, *La Disparition du Datif (du Ier au Xe siècle)*, Paris 1930. Mayser II 2, 145–151.

(b) *With adjectives.* Mk 6⁴⁸ etc. ἐναντίος (πρός Ac 26⁹) Ac 4¹⁶ 7¹³ 1 Ti 4¹⁵ (vl. ἐν) ἀρκετός, ἱκανός, φανερός, Ac 7³⁹ ὑπήκοος, 10⁴⁰ Ro 10²⁰ ἐμφανής, Ac 16¹⁵ πιστός, 26¹⁹ etc. ἀπειθής, Ti 2¹¹ σωτήριος, 3⁸ ὠφέλιμος. These correspond to a cognate verb which has the dat. Then there are adjectives of likeness: ὅμοιος frequent (in the "abbreviated" construction: Rev 9¹⁰ ἔχουσιν οὐρὰς ὁμοίας σκορπίοις, 13¹¹ εἶχεν κέρατα δύο ὅμοια ἀρνίῳ), Mt 20¹² ἴσους ... ἡμῖν, 1 Co 11⁵ ἓν καὶ τὸ αὐτὸ τῇ ἐξυρημένῃ, Ph 3²¹ σύμμορφος, Ro 6⁵ σύμφυτοι τῷ ὁμοιώματι τοῦ θανάτου αὐτοῦ (unless instr. dat., in which case the gen. goes with συμφ., but this is unnatural), 2 Pt 1¹ (Jude 7) τοῖς ἰσότιμον ἡμῖν λαχοῦσιν πίστιν ("abbreviated"), Heb 11¹¹ αὐτῇ Σάρρᾳ = class. *together with Sarah* (better sense than αὐτὴ Σάρρα).

(c) *Dative of respect.* The dat. of respect (e.g. ὀνόματι by name) in NT has almost displaced the class. accus. of respect, and as in the papyri (Mayser II 2, 149f, 285) it becomes almost an adverb, and is especially used when contrast is involved, e.g. φύσει ... νόμῳ, λόγῳ μὲν ... ἔργῳ δέ.

Mt 5³ πτωχὸς τῷ πνεύματι, ⁸ καθαρὸς τῇ καρδίᾳ, 11²⁹ ταπεινὸς τῇ καρδίᾳ, Ac 4³⁶ etc. τῷ γένει *by birth* (and pap.), 7⁵¹, 14⁸, 16⁵ τῷ ἀριθμῷ (BU II 388 III⁸ ii–iii/A.D.), 18⁵·²⁵, Ro 5¹⁷ πολλῷ μᾶλλον, 12¹⁰⁻²² (several), 1 Co 7³⁴, 14²⁰, 2 Co 7¹¹ difficult: συνεστήσατε ἑαυτοὺς ἁγνοὺς εἶναι τῷ πράγματι (ἐν would make better sense than εἶναι; DᵇEKLP read εἶναι ἐν), Ga 2⁵ εἴξαμεν τῇ ὑποταγῇ *yield submissively*, ¹⁵ Ph 2⁷ (Philo Byz. σχήματι or σχήμασι 69¹²), 3⁵ *with respect to circumcision*, Heb 5¹¹ νωθροὶ γεγόνατε ταῖς ἀκοαῖς, 10²⁹ πόσῳ ... χείρονος *by how much ... worse*. Diod. 12¹⁸ 13⁸⁹ προβεβηκὼς τῇ ἡλικίᾳ, UPZ II 161⁶¹ (119 B.C.), 162 VII 29 (117 B.C.) τοῖς ἔτεσιν. With this dat., ἐν is often used: Lk 1⁷ προβεβηκότες ἐν ταῖς ἡμέραις αὐτῶν (1¹⁸ 2³⁶), but προβεβηκὼς (ταῖς) ἡμέραις LXX Jo 23¹·² 3 Km 1¹ (accus. τὴν ἡλικίαν is atticistic 2 Mac 4⁴⁰ 6¹⁸), Ditt. Syll³ 647¹⁷ (ii/B.C.). There is both dat. and accus. of respect in LXX: 2 Mac 5¹¹ τεθηριωμένος τῇ ψυχῇ (accus. in Lucian: atticistic), Johannessohn DGKPS 69–71.

3. Adjectival Accusative.[1]

During the Hell. period the accus. of respect (or specification, or general reference) yields to the dat. of respect, as we have just seen, or to a prepositional phrase, as in the pre-Christian papyri and LXX, as well as in NT. Sometimes the two cases appear side by side: Mt 27³² (τῷ) ὀνόματι, 27⁵⁷ τοὔνομα.

---

[1] K-G I 315ff. Mayser II 2, 151. Schwyzer II 67–88 (part).

§ 2-3] ATTRIBUTIVE RELATIONSHIP: SUBSTANTIVES 221

But NT uses τῷ γένει for the class. τὸ γένος (Mk 7²⁶ Ac 4³⁶), and where Diod. Sic. (20, 1) has τὴν ψυχήν, Heb 12³ has τῇ ψυχῇ.

Jn 6¹⁰ τὸν ἀριθμὸν *as to number*. But in Ac 17²⁸ ἐκ τοῦ γὰρ γένος ἐσμέν the translation is *we are his offspring* (because of v. 29), although in Aratus Phaenom. 5 γένος is an accus. of general reference. Ac 18⁸ vl. σκηνοποιὸς τὴν τέχνην (but better reading is τῇ τέχνῃ), cp. P. Oxy. I 40 (ii–iii/A.D.) ἰατρὸς ὑπάρχων τὴν τέχνην, Heb 2¹⁷ 5¹ πιστὸς ἀρχιερεὺς τὰ πρὸς τὸν θεόν (same phrase is adv. accus. in Ro 15¹⁷). For δεδεμένος τοὺς πόδας see p. 247. For τὸ λοιπόν see p. 336.

§ 3. Attributive Prepositional Phrases [1]

In the same way that adjectives, pronouns, pronominal adjectives, and nouns in gen. or dat. or accus., may be employed as attributive phrases defining a noun, so also may a prepositional expression be used. The class. arrangement is still found: Ac 26³ τῶν κατὰ Ἰουδαίους ἐθῶν, Ro 11²¹ τῶν κατὰ φύσιν κλάδων, ²⁷ ἡ παρ' ἐμοῦ διαθήκη, 16¹⁵. If this prepositional expression stands in post-position, the repetition of the art. is necessary for the sake of clarity, e.g. Ac 3¹⁶ ἡ πίστις ἡ δι' αὐτοῦ, Ro 3²⁴ τῆς ἀπολυτρώσεως τῆς ἐν Χριστῷ Ἰησοῦ, Ga 1²² ταῖς ἐκκλησίαις ταῖς Ἰουδαίαις ταῖς ἐν Χριστῷ, Ph 3¹¹ τὴν ἐξανάστασιν τὴν ἐκ νεκρῶν, 1 Th 1⁸ ἡ πίστις ὑμῶν ἡ πρὸς τὸν θεόν. For this very reason we hardly ever find a prepositional clause used as attribute to an anarthrous noun: in 1 Co 12³¹ εἴ τι for ἔτι is read by p⁴⁶ D*F, making καθ' ὑπερβολήν no longer an attribute of the anarthrous ὁδόν. The only real exceptions appear to be: Mk 1²³ ἄνθρωπος ἐν πνεύματι ἀκαθάρτῳ, Ro 14¹⁷ χαρὰ ἐν πνεύματι ἁγίῳ, 2 Co 12² ἄνθρωπον ἐν Χριστῷ, and with the art. before the attribute: Ac 16²³ ἀδελφοῖς τοῖς κατὰ τὴν Ἀντιόχειαν (an address), 26¹⁸ πίστει τῇ εἰς ἐμέ, ²² ἐπικουρίας ... τῆς ἀπὸ τοῦ θεοῦ, Ro 9³⁰, Ph 3⁹, 1 Ti 1⁴, 2 Ti 1¹³.

In NT, as opposed to class. Greek, a considerable number of instances of omission of the second art. appear to exist, apart from those cases where the noun has additional defining clauses: Mk 6⁶ τὰς κώμας κύκλῳ (but κύκλῳ may define the verb περιῆγεν; it is used with a verb in Ro 15¹⁹; Swete takes it so), Lk 16¹⁰ ὁ πιστὸς ἐν ἐλαχίστῳ = ὁ ὤν ..., Ro 6⁴ διὰ τοῦ βαπτίσματος

---

[1] K-G I 594. 6. Schwyzer II 417ff. Mayser II 2, 152ff. Winer-Schmiedel § 20, 1–6. Radermacher² 112. 117. Johannessohn DGPS 365.

εἰς τὸν θάνατον, 10¹, 1 Co 10¹⁸, 11²⁴ 12¹², 2 Co 1¹¹, 9¹³ Ph 1¹⁴ (unless ἐν κυρίῳ is taken with πεποιθότας), Col 1², 1 Th 4¹⁶, Eph 2¹¹, 4¹, 6⁵ SAB, Col 3²² p⁴⁶ S, 1 Ti 6¹⁷.

It is not surprising that we find the types δικαιοσύνη ἡ ἐκ πίστεως and τὸ χάρισμα διὰ πολλῶν fairly frequently in NT, and there is no need to explain away the construction or adopt a more orthodox variant reading, for these types appear (less regularly than the other two) in the Koine. Thus, for pre-Christian papyri:—

	iii/B.C.	ii–i/B.C.
1. ἡ ἐκ πίστεως δικαιοσύνη	98	210
2. ἡ δικαιοσύνη ἡ ἐκ πίστεως	74	6
3. δικαιοσύνη ἡ ἐκ πίστεως	16	66
4. ἡ δικαιοσύνη ἐκ πίστεως	10	5

See Mayser II 2, 161.

In conclusion we may note that attributive adverbs[1], though found already in class. Greek, occur much less frequently in NT than other attributives. Nevertheless they do occur sometimes, e.g. Ro 3²⁶ ἐν τῷ νῦν καιρῷ, cp. PSI IV 402, 7, ἐν τῶι νῦν καιρῶι (iii/B.C.); Ac 20²⁶ ἡ σήμερον ἡμέρα (Ro 11⁸ 2 Co 3¹⁴); 2 Pt 3⁶ ὁ τότε κόσμος.

---

[1] K-G I 594, 6; 609.   Mayser II 2, 168–171.   Winer-Schmiedel § 20, 7.

PART III

WORD-MATERIAL WHICH DEFINES A VERB

CHAPTER SIXTEEN

PREDICATIVE USE OF ADJECTIVES AND ADVERBS

§ 1. Adjectives

The predicative use of adjectives, participles and pronouns has already been discussed in connection with the definite article. When the predicate occurs before the articular noun it tends to be emphatic. For papyrus examples, see Mayser II 2, 172f. For class. Greek, K–G I 273, 2.

Μέσος and ἄκρος were used in this predicative way in class. Greek, but more rarely now: Mt 25⁶ μέσης δὲ νυκτός Lk 23⁴⁵ ἐσχίσθη δὲ τὸ καταπέτασμα τοῦ ναοῦ μέσον, Jn 19¹⁸ μέσον δὲ τὸν Ἰησοῦν, Ac 26¹³ ἡμέρας μέσης. But elsewhere τὸ μέσον with partitive gen. We never have the class. περὶ μέσας νύκτας, but κατὰ μέσον τῆς νυκτός (Ac 27²⁷) or κατὰ τὸ μεσονύκτιον (16²⁵); for class. τὸ δάκτυλον ἄκρον we have τὸ ἄκρον τοῦ δακτύλου (Lk 16²⁴), like τὸ ἄκρον τῆς ῥάβδου αὐτοῦ (Heb 11²¹). We may take Mt 24³¹ (ἀπ' ἄκρων οὐρανῶν) and Mk 13²⁷ (ἀπ' ἄκρου γῆς) in the class. predicative sense, but they may equally well be intended for the gen. of τὰ ἄκρα and τὸ ἄκρον.

In class. Greek a predicative adj., especially a temporal numeral ending in -αῖος, may correspond to an adverb, since it defines a verb. Although this idiom is rare in NT, yet in the neuter gender it became increasingly popular in post-classical Greek and eventually became the regular way of forming adverbs in MGr.

Mk 4²⁸ αὐτομάτη ἡ γῆ καρποφορεῖ, Lk 21³⁴ αἰφνίδιος, 24²² γενόμεναι ὀρθριναὶ ἐπὶ τὸ μνημεῖον (cp. Herm. S.V 1, 1 ὀρθρινὸς ἐλήλυθας), Jn 4¹⁸ τοῦτο ἀληθὲς εἴρηκας (SE ἀληθῶς) class., 13³⁴ καινὴν δίδωμι *I give you it anew*, Ac 12¹⁰ αὐτομάτη, 14¹⁰, 20⁶ D πεμπταῖοι, 28¹³ δευτεραῖοι ἤλθομεν *on the second day*, Ro 10¹⁹, 1 Co 9¹⁷, Heb 11²³ p⁴⁶ ἐκρύβη τρίμηνος, 2 Mac 10³³ V ἄσμενοι περιεκάθισαν.

There is therefore not surprisingly some confusion of μόνος with the adv. μόνον: Mk 6⁸ μηδὲν εἰ μὴ ῥάβδον μόνον (D μόνην), Ac 11¹⁹ μηδενὶ εἰ μὴ μόνον (D μόνοις) Ἰουδαίοις, Heb 12²⁶ OT σείσω ού μόνον τήν γῆν, άλλα καί ..., 2 Ti 4⁸, 1 Jn 5⁶ ούκ έν τῷ ὕδατι μόνον (B μόνῳ). In Jn 5⁴⁴ μόνου is best taken adverbial; not *from him who alone is God*, but *only from God* (Jewish monotheism was unimpeachable; Jesus was referring to their love of human praise), in spite of the word order. Lk 5²¹ adv. μόνος.

§ 2. Adverbs[1]

Already in class. Greek adverbs are used predicatively, e.g. έγγύς, πόρρω: Eph 2¹³ οἵ ποτε ὄντες μακράν έγενήθητε έγγύς, Ph 2⁶ τὸ εἶναι ἴσα (adv) θεῷ, 4⁵ ὁ κύριος έγγύς. But ούτως is not good class.: Mt 1¹⁸ ἡ γένεσις ούτως ἦν (class. = τοιαύτη ἦν or ούτως ἔσχεν, as Ac 7¹ etc.), 19¹⁰, Mk 2¹², Ro 4¹⁸, 9²⁰, 1 Pt 2¹⁵, LXX Ge 1⁶. ⁹. ¹¹. In spite of PSI IV 442, 14f (iii/B.C.) ού δίκαιον οὖν έστιν ούτως εἶναι *so to behave oneself*, the construction may correspond to Aramaic כדין (Lagrange, *S. Matth.* XCVIII). More class. are Mk 11¹⁹ όψὲ έγένετο, Jn 18²⁸ ἦν δὲ πρωΐ. Fairly frequent in NT is ἔχω with predicative adv.: Jn 4⁵² κομψότερον, Ac 21¹³ 2 Co 12¹⁴ 1 Pt 4⁵ έτοίμως. Also γίνομαι: Ac 20¹⁸ πῶς ... έγενόμην (D ποταπῶς ἦν), 1 Th 2¹⁰ ὡς ὁσίως καὶ δικαίως καὶ άμέμπτως ὑμῖν τοῖς πιστεύουσιν έγενήθημεν.

Proleptic attraction (*whither* for *where*) is found once in NT: Lk 16²⁶ μηδὲ οἱ (S*BD om οἱ) έκεῖθεν πρὸς ἡμᾶς διαπερῶσιν (unless we supply θέλοντες διαβῆναι from the foregoing); *whence* for *where* Mt 25²⁴. ²⁶ συνάγων ὅθεν; *thither* for *thence* Mt 2²² έφοβήθη έκεῖ άπελθεῖν (reverse Ac 22⁵); ποῦ for ποῖ Jn 7³⁵.

Very rarely έκεῖ may be temporal: Mt 24⁵¹ Lk 13²⁸.

§ 3. Adverbial Verbs

Some verbs came to express certain adverbial ideas; they were used as main verbs, but the main verbal idea was transferred to an infin. or ptc. E.g. λανθάνω c. ptc. *unconsciously, secretly* Heb 13² (elsewhere adv. λάθρᾳ, Mt 1¹⁹ etc.), LXX To 12¹³ B, Jos. BJ 3, 7, 3; διατελέω, έπιμένω, ού διαλείπω c. ptc. = *permanently, incessantly* Jn 8⁷ (έπέμενον έρωτῶντες), Ac 12¹⁶ (*he knocked persistently*), 27³⁴ (ἄσιτοι διατελεῖτε), Lk 7⁴⁵ ού διέλειπεν καταφιλοῦσα, P. Oxy. 658⁸ θύων καὶ σπένδων τοῖς θεοῖς διετέλεσα; φιλέω c. infin. Mt 6⁵ *gladly*, Ael. 14, 37

---

[1] K-G I 38, 4; 43 n. 1. Schwyzer II 414. Mayser II 2, 175ff.

§ 3–4] PREDICATIVE USE OF ADJECTIVES AND ADVERBS 227

(φιλῶ τὰ ἀγάλματα ... ὁρᾶν). We mention here [1] the Hebraistic προστίθεμαι c. infin.: in Hebrew the verb which represents the adv. may be joined syntactically with the verb which represents the main verbal idea (וַיֹּסֶף לִשְׁלֹחַ *he sent again*) but sometimes both verbs are finite (Ge 25[1]); the first method is more common and is imitated in Lk 20[11f] (not D) προσέθετο πέμψαι, Mk 14[25] D οὐ μὴ προσθῶ πεῖν. The question for the translator is whether the meaning is *he did something AGAIN* or *he ALSO did something*. Lk 20[11f], by the parallel Mk 12[4, 5] (πάλιν), would mean *he sent again*. But Ac 12[3] appears to mean *he also arrested Peter*. It is one of the very few Hebraisms in the atticistic Josephus (Ant. 6, 287; 19, 48), but here the meaning must be *to attach oneself to, acquiesce in* (Thackeray *JThS* 30, 1929, 161–370). 1 Clem 12[7] καὶ προσέθεντο αὐτῇ δοῦναι σημεῖα *also gave*, P. Grenf. I 53[29] (iv/A.D.) (see Moulton-Howard 445). LXX Ge 4[2] προσέθηκεν τεκεῖν *also bore*, Ex 10[28] προσθεῖναι ἰδεῖν *see again* 14[13] Dt 3[26] 18[16] Jo 7[12] etc. Similarly there is προσθεὶς εἶπεν: LXX Ge 25[1] προσθέμενος Ἀβραὰμ ἔλαβε γυναῖκα *took another*, 38[5] προσθεῖσα ἔτι ἔτεκεν *bore again*, Jb 27[1] 29[1] 36[1] προσθεὶς εἶπεν *again spoke*, Lk 19[11] προσθεὶς εἶπεν παραβολήν *another parable*? or *he also told a parable*? Polyc. 31, 7, 4, Apoc. Pet. 4, Acta Phil. 10.

For *beforehand*, προλαμβάνω c. inf. Mk 14[8], προϋπάρχω c. ptc. Lk 23[12]. For *willingly* θέλω (fin. and ptc.), unless it involves a definite act of will, Mk 12[38] Lk 20[46] τῶν θελόντων περιπατεῖν *who love to*, Jn 6[21] ἤθελον οὖν λαβεῖν αὐτὸν εἰς τὸ πλοῖον, 8[44] *you gladly do his will* (so in class. Greek with ἐθέλω; Origen contra Marc., ed. Wetst. 35, with βούλομαι). For *from the beginning* ἄρχομαι Ac 1[1] ὧν ἤρξατο (= ἃ ἐποίησεν ἀπ' ἀρχῆς). So also the adverbial use of τυγχάνω, φθάνω, φανερός εἰμι.

§ 4. Position of the Adverb

An adverb usually follows the adj. or verb which it determines, in NT. Mt 2[16] ἐθυμώθη λίαν, 4[8] ὑψηλὸν λίαν, Lk 12[28] ἐν τῷ ἀγρῷ τὸν χόρτον ὄντα σήμερον *which exists to-day* not *which is in the field to-day*. Exceptions: Mk 16[2] λίαν πρωΐ (D om λίαν), 2 Ti 4[15] λίαν γὰρ ἀντέστη, P. Par. 42[3] λίαν σοι χάριν μεγάλην

---

[1] W-M § 54, 5. Thackeray OT Gr. 52f. Lightfoot on Clem. 1 Co. 12. Moulton Proleg. 67, 233. Deissmann BS 67. MM Vocab. s.v. Moulton-Howard 445.

ἐσχήκαμεν. Therefore, in Col 1³ it will be more natural to take πάντοτε with the former verb εὐχαριστοῦμεν than with the subsequent ptc. προσευχόμενοι. Occasionally the adv. is given great emphasis by its divorce from its verb: e.g. Lk 7⁶ at the beginning of the clause. But in Lk 1⁵¹ the adverbial phrase διανοίᾳ καρδίας goes closely with ὑπερηφάνους (i.e. *haughty in heart*) and not with διεσκόρπισεν which is furthest from it.

To what does μόνον refer in 1 Co 15¹⁹ εἰ ἐν τῇ ζωῇ ταύτῃ ἐν Χριστῷ ἠλπικότες ἐσμὲν μόνον? Not to *this life*, but *we have done no more than hope in Christ*.

Mt has the peculiar habit, in the imperative, of giving second place to adverbs which in other moods he puts first:

Imperative	Other moods
3¹⁵ ἄφες ἄρτι	9¹⁸ ἄρτι ἐτελεύτησεν 26⁵³ ἄρτι παρακαλέσαι ADCW
18¹⁶ παράλαβε ... ἔτι	19²⁰ ἔτι ὑστερῶ 26⁶⁵ τί ἔτι χρείαν ἔχομεν;
27⁴² καταβάτω νῦν, ⁴³ ῥυσάσθω νῦν	26⁶⁵ νῦν ἠκούσατε

In the exception, 5¹³ ἰσχύει ἔτι, it should be observed that DW omit ἔτι.

However, in the Ptol. pap. the normal position of adverbs in the simple sentence increasingly tends to be before the verb to which they belong. Even in the class. period a considerable flexibility obtained, under the influence of rhythm or emphasis, and the conversational style differed markedly from the rhetorical.

	Conversational style		Rhetorical		Ptol. pap.	
	Plato: Apol	Xen. Hell. I	Thuc. II	Demosth. I	iii/ B.C.	ii–i/ B.C.
Pre	171 (5)	77 (3·5)	2·5	2·1	30	40
Post	35 (1)	22 (1)	1	1	28	25

(Mayser II 2, 181f.)

§ 4]   PREDICATIVE USE OF ADJECTIVES AND ADVERBS   229

In the language of Ptol. documents the normal pre-positive adverbs and those which for a rhetorical purpose are post-positive are fairly evenly distributed. In many documents, such as official acts, the tendency to emphasize the adverb in post-position is very strong. Conversely certain adverbs are always pre-positive, others always post-positive; others again are both.

In Mark πάλιν is used both as an adv. and as a conjunction. When, like εὐθύς, it occurs at the beginning of its phrase, it may be reasonable to take it as a mere conjunction.[1] Usually, however, it occurs either just before or just after its verb: i.e. 23 out of 29 instances. This close proximity with the verb suggests that here we should treat it as a true adverb (before verb 4^1, 7^{31} 8^{25} $10^{1.\ 24}$ 12^4 $14^{39.\ 40}$ vl. 70 $15^{4.\ 12.\ 13}$; after verb $2^{1.\ 13}$ $3^{1.\ 20}$ 7^{14} vl. 8^{13} $10^{1.\ 32}$ 11^{27} 14^{69}). But the text is doubtful at 5^{21} where we have both πάλιν εἰς τὸ πέραν and εἰς τὸ πέραν πάλιν, and perhaps the fact that Mark usually has πάλιν near its verb sways the balance in favour of the latter.

Nevertheless Mark uses εὐθύς only five times near the verb, i.e. as an adverb (viz. 1^{28} 5^{13} vl. $^{36.\ 42}$ 6^{25} 7^{25} 1^{31} vl. 3^6 vl.); elsewhere it is probably merely a connective conjunction, occurring at the beginning of its clause (viz. $1^{10.\ 12.\ 18.\ 20.\ 21.\ 23.\ 29.\ 30.\ 31}$ vl. $^{42.\ 43}$ 2^{2} vl. $^{8.\ 12}$ 3^6 $4^{5.\ 15.\ 16.\ 17.\ 29}$ $5^{2.\ 29.\ 30.\ 42}$ $6^{25.\ 27.\ 45.\ 50.\ 54}$ $7^{25.\ 35}$ 8^{10} 9^8 vl. $^{15.\ 20.\ 24}$ 10^{52} $11^{2.\ 3}$ $14^{43.\ 45.\ 72}$ 15^1). Some thirty of these instances are καὶ εὐθύς: *and so* (consecutive, like the Heb.), like καὶ ἰδού in Matthew. But it must be said that sometimes, as at 6^{25}, εὐθύς has rather stronger adverbial force: *she went in immediately*.[2]

---

[1] 5^{21} 8^1 vl. 10^{10} 11^3 vl. 12^5 vl. 14^{61}.
[2] For πάλιν and εὐθύς I owe much to private communications from Dr. G. D. Kilpatrick.

CHAPTER SEVENTEEN

CASE ADDITIONS TO THE VERB: WITHOUT A PREPOSITION [1]

§ 1. Nominative [2]

(a) *The nominative "ad sensum"*: Eph 3¹⁷ κατοικῆσαι τὸν Χριστὸν ... ἐν ταῖς καρδίαις ὑμῶν, ἐν ἀγάπῃ ἐρριζωμένοι, 4¹·² παρακαλῶ οὖν ὑμᾶς ... ἀξίως περιπατῆσαι ..., ἀνεχόμενοι, Col 2² ἵνα παρακληθῶσιν αἱ καρδίαι αὐτῶν, συνβιβασθέντες, 3¹⁶ ὁ λόγος τοῦ Χριστοῦ ἐνοικείτω ..., διδάσκοντες.

(b) *Proper nouns without syntax* [3]. Proper nouns usually fit syntactically into the construction (e.g. Mt 1²¹·²⁵ τὸ ὄνομα αὐτοῦ Ἰησοῦν, Mk 3¹⁶ Πέτρον, vl. Πέτρος, Ac 18² εὑρών τινα ... ὀνόματι Ἀκύλαν, 27¹ ἑκατοντάρχῃ ὀνόματι Ἰουλίῳ), but sometimes they are introduced independently in the nominative: Lk 19²⁹ 21³⁷ τὸ ὄρος τὸ καλούμενον Ἐλαιῶν (unless this is ἐλαιῶν, like 19³⁷), Jn 13¹³ φωνεῖτέ με ὁ κύριος ... Rev 9¹¹ ὄνομα ἔχει Ἀπολλύων, P. Par. 18. 3 (Abel § 42 (a)).

The divine name (ὁ ὢν καὶ ὁ ἦν καὶ ὁ ἐρχόμενος Rev 1⁸) is used in nom. after ἀπό: Rev 1⁴. There is some LXX history behind this name, which is based on Ex 3¹⁴ ἐγώ εἰμι ὁ ὤν ... ὁ ὢν ἀπέσταλκέ με. Jeremiah has ὁ ὢν δέσποτα κύριε (4) and Hos 1⁹ οὐκ εἰμί ὑμῶν (Ziegler *Duodecim Prophetae*, Göttingen 1943, in loc., and *Beitr. z. Ieremias-LXX*, 1958, 40). It may have been regarded as indeclinable in Greek.

(c) *Nom. is found in parenthesis (class.)*: ὄνομα αὐτῷ (=שְׁמוֹ), LXX Jg 13², Jn 1⁶ (but S*D*W add ἦν); 3¹ (but S* ὀνόματι) adds ἦν, however. More common are the phrases ᾧ (ἦ, οὗ) ὄνομα, and ὀνόματι. Zen. pap. 59037, 7 (258 B.C.) ὄνομα δ' ἐστί αὐτῶι Ἡδύλος, 59148, 2 (256 B.C.) ὧι ὄνομα Ὀνήσιμος.

---

[1] K-G I 44–51 (nom. voc.), 250–448 (acc. gen. dat.). Schwyzer II 52ff. Gildersleeve I §§ 3–25 (nom. voc.). Johannessohn DGKPS. R. Helbing, *Die Kasussyntax der Verba bei den LXX*, Göttingen 1928. A. Jannaris § 1242ff (MGr). L. D. Brown, *A Study of the Case Construction of Words of Time*, New York, 1904. Wackernagel I 14f, 17–20, 294–312.

[2] K-G I 44ff. Meisterhans-Schwyzer § 84, 1–5. Gildersleeve I §§ 3–13. Radermacher² 21, 111, 219, 223. Mayser II 2, 185–197.

[3] Thackeray OT Gr 23. Johannessohn DGKPS 7. Abel § 42 a. Mayser II 2, 185ff. Moulton-Howard 154. Kittel WB II 342f.

(d) *The nom. with time-designation.* Here we expect accus. It may be an instance of ellipse and we are to supply a main verb(e.g. εἰσιν) with καί. Class.: ὅσαι ἡμέραι *daily.* LXX Jo 1¹¹ Α ἔτι τρεῖς ἡμέραι ὑμεῖς διαβήσεσθε (true text has καί before ὑμεῖς), Eccl. 2¹⁶ ἤδη αἱ ἡμέραι ἐρχόμεναι τὰ πάντα ἐπελήσθη, Mt 15³² ὅτι ἤδη ἡμέραι (S accus.) τρεῖς (D adds εἰσιν καί) προσμένουσίν μοι, Lk 9²⁸ 13¹⁶(?), Ac 5⁷ Acta Paul. Thecl. 8 (P. Oxy. I 6. 3) ἡμέραι γὰρ ἤδη τρεῖς καὶ νύκτες Θέκλα καὶ ἐγήγερται, and fairly often in post-Ptolemaic papyri. Adverbial nom.: Mk 6³⁹f συμπόσια συμπόσια, πρασιαὶ πρασιαί.

Nom. pendens is a nom. standing at the head of a clause without construction. See p. 316.

Ἴδε with nom. as object is explained by the fact that, like ἰδού, ἴδε has become a stereotyped particle of exclamation. So have ἄγε and φέρε: Jn 1²⁹ ἴδε ὁ ἀμνὸς τοῦ θεοῦ, 19²⁶· ²⁷ ἴδε ὁ υἱός σου ... ἴδε ἡ μήτηρ σου.

§ 2. Genitive [1]

(a) *True Genitive*

1. *A possessive* [2] *gen.* may be used predicatively with εἶναι *to belong to,* e.g. Jn 17⁶ W σοῦ ἦσαν (rest dat.), Ac 27²³, 1 Co 1¹² 3⁴ 6¹⁹, 3⁹ *fellow-workers belonging to* (not *with*) *God,* 3²¹, 14³⁷ DFG κυρίου ἐστιν (but p⁴⁶ S*BA add ˙ἐντολή), Heb 5¹⁴ 12¹¹. With γίνεσθαι, e.g. Ac 20⁹ ἐγένετο γνώμης.

2. *With verbs and verbal adjectives.* The gen. with verbs like *accuse* denotes the ground of accusation: only Ac 19⁴⁰ ἐγκαλεῖσθαι στάσεως. The construction is so rare [3] that one is tempted to take the gen. closely with σήμερον, and thus construe in the usual way περὶ τῆς σήμερον στάσεως. Elsewhere in Ac we have the class. περί after ἐγκαλεῖσθαι and κρίνεσθαι, 23⁶· ²⁹ 26⁷.

Gen. with μεταδίδωμι (Helbing 252, Mayser II 2, 197) is not found in the NT; instead we have accus. (Ro 1¹¹ 1 Th 2⁸) and elsewhere the dative. With μεταλαμβάνω (Helbing 136, Mayser II 2, 197f) *to receive a share of* always the gen., e.g. Ac 2⁴⁶ 27³³ Heb 6⁷. With μετέχω (Helbing 136, Mayser II 2, 198) ἐκ is found only 1 Co 10¹⁷, elsewhere gen. (1 Co 9¹² Heb 2¹⁴). But

---

[1] Schwyzer II 89-137. Mayser II 2, 118-145, 187-240.
[2] K-G I 372, 1 b. Mayser II 2, 188f. Radermacher² 124.
[3] But see Dio Cass. 58. 4. 5. ἀσεβείας.

with the last two verbs, the gen. is limited to Luke, Paul and Hebrews. With κοινωνέω gen. occurs only [1] at Heb 2¹⁴.

To *touch* still has gen., never accus. in NT (Mayser II 2, 199, Helbing 123), but ψηλαφάω has accus. (Lk 24³⁹ Ac 17²⁷ 1 Jn 1¹) and in passive Heb 12¹⁸. To *take hold of* (ἐπι-) λαμβάνομαι regularly has gen., especially the part grasped, in LXX, NT and papyri (Mayser II 2, 202, Helbing 127): in Lk 14⁴ Ac 9²⁷ 16¹⁹ 18¹⁷ ἐπιλαβόμενος ἰάσατο αὐτόν the accus. goes with the main verb (but see Delling in Kittel WB IV 9, n. 3), in Lk 23²⁶ SBCDL have accus. but WA have gen., Mk 8²³ D λαβόμενος τὴν χεῖρα τοῦ τυφλοῦ (unusual Greek), in LXX Ezk 16⁴⁹ χεῖρα . . . οὐκ ἀντελαμβάνοντο (but accus. is rare in class. and Hell. Greek). But κρατέω has surrendered to the accus., as in Hell. Greek, only the part grasped being in the gen.: Mt 9²⁵ Mk 1³¹ 5⁴¹ Lk 8⁵⁴ Mk 9²⁷ SBD. But if it means *to hold fast to* (Ac 27¹³ Heb 4¹⁴ 6¹⁸), or like ἔχομαι *hold sway over*, more literary works have gen. (Ac 27¹³ Heb 4¹⁴ 6¹⁸) but Rev 2¹⁴, ¹⁵ accus. If it means *to arrest*, NT has accus. (but Luke avoids). Gen. with αἴρω Mt 22¹³ D lat syr, and with the figurative uses of (ἀντ-) ἔχομαι (Helbing 128f, Mayser II 2, 200, Nägeli 54).

Gen. (class.) is still used with *desire, reach, obtain* (Helbing 136–144, Mayser II 2, 203ff), but there is a tendency towards the accus. in Hell. Greek. Thus ἐπιθυμέω c. gen. Ac 20³³ 1 Ti 3¹ LXX Ex 34²⁴ Pr 21²⁶; c. accus. often in LXX (Helbing 138; Johannessohn 40) Ex 20¹⁷ Dt 5²¹, Mt 5²⁸ BDWE (S* gen.). Accus. δικαιοσύνην after πεινάω and διψάω Mt 5⁶ (class. gen.; LXX Ex 17³ διψάω ὕδατι). But with the following verbs of *reaching, obtaining*, there are relics of the gen. in the more cultured authors: τυγχάνω Lk 20³⁵ Ac 24³ 2 Ti 2¹⁰ Heb 8⁶, ἐπιτυγχάνω Heb 6¹⁵ 11³³ (but accus. Ro 11⁷, and pap. 161 B.C. UPZ I 41²⁵). Phrynichus protests against the Hell. accus. with κληρονομέω *inherit*, but it occurs Mt 5⁵ 19²⁹ Lk 10²⁵ Heb 6¹² LXX Si 4¹³ 6¹.

While the gen. with *to fill, be full of*, is still apparent, the accus. is encroaching on the gen. already in LXX (Ex 31³; Johannessohn DGKPS 37, Helbing 144–150) and Koine (K-G I 354, Mayser II 2, 205, Völker *Pap. gr. synt. spec.* 14): Ph 1¹¹

---

[1] Dative: Ro 12¹³ 15²⁷·1 Ti 5²² 1 Pt 4¹³ 2 Jn ¹¹; ἐν Ga 6⁶ Barn 19⁸ and papyri; εἰς Ph 4¹⁵.

πεπληρωμένοι καρπὸν δικαιοσύνης, Rev 17³ γέμοντα ὀνόματα βλασφημίας.

We may include here the difficult gen. in 2 Pt 2¹⁴ καρδίαν γεγυμνασμένην πλεονεξίας (vl. dat.) *trained in extortion*? (it may be gen. of quality, giving further definition: *a heart trained and greedy*).

Although *to eat, drink, of* (= מן LXX) have partitive preposition or the accus.¹, nevertheless gen. is found in NT with the meaning *satiate, eat one's fill*, chiefly where we may suspect the influence of literary style (class. authors would have used the gen. often where accus. is found in NT): Ac 27³⁸. With γεύομαι occurs θανάτου and other genitives, on the Aram. model: Mt 16²⁸ Mk 9¹ Lk 9²⁷ 14²⁴ Jn 8⁵² Ac 23¹⁴ Heb 6⁴ᶠ; the accus. is not class. (e.g. Jn 2⁹ τὸ ὕδωρ, Heb 6⁵ ²) and is a Hebraism ³, perhaps influenced by the construction with טָעַם (sifre Num. on 11⁴ אֹותָם עָצְמָה), and it is fairly common in LXX: 1 Km 14⁴³ 2 Km 19³⁵ Jb 12¹¹ 34³ Si 36²⁴ To BA 7¹¹ Jon 3⁷.

The partitive gen. occurs in NT with verbs of perception ⁴, especially with a personal object. For ἀκούω, the class. rule is that the person whose words are heard is in the gen. (sometimes with παρά) but the thing (or person) about which one hears is in the accus., and ἀκούω c. accus. may mean *to understand*. In NT, ἀπό is also found with the person (Ac 9¹³ 1 Jn 1⁵) as in Heb. (see especially ἀπὸ τοῦ στόματός τινος Lk 22⁷¹ Ac 1⁴D 22¹⁴). NT breaks the class. rule with τὴν βλασφημίαν Mt 26⁶⁵ Mk 14⁶⁴ DWAG, τὸν ἀσπασμόν Lk 1⁴¹, λαλοῦντας Ac 2⁶D. We have to ask whether the class. distinction between gen. and accus. has significance for exegesis in NT. There may be something in the difference between the gen. in Ac 9⁷ (the men with Paul heard *the sound*) and the accus. in Ac 22⁹ (they did not *understand* the *voice*): Zerwick § 50. On the whole, the accus. is used of the hearing of speech in NT (except Lk 6⁴⁷, which corrects Mt 7²⁴,

---

¹ ἀπό Mt 15²⁷ Mk 7²⁸ Lk 22¹⁸ LXX Le 11⁸ 22⁶; ἐκ Jn 4¹⁴ 6²⁶ 1 Co 11²⁸ Rev 14¹⁰ LXX Ge 9²¹. Accus.: Mt 15² Mk 1⁶ 1 Co 8¹⁰ 10¹⁸. ²⁵. ²⁷.

² But Moule (36) suggests that καλὸν θεοῦ ῥῆμα is virtually a substantival clause = καλὸν εἶναι θεοῦ ῥῆμα (cp. the ὅτι-clause 1 Pt 2³). Moulton (Proleg. 66) however had found the variation from gen. in 6⁴ to accus. in 6⁵ " subtle and suggestive."

³ Behm in Kittel WB I 675 n. 7. There are one or two secular parallels: see Mayser II 2, 206 (οἱ συμπόσιον γευόμενοι) but the Aristotelian instance to which Mayser refers is conjectural.

⁴ Helbing 150–159. Mayser II 2, 207ff.

Jn 7⁴⁰ 12⁴⁷ 19¹³ vl.), whereas the gen. would be class. (unless it means *understand*). In Jn it seems possible to trace a distinction between the gen. (*obey* 5²⁵· ²⁸ 10³· ¹⁶ etc.) and accus. (mere perception 3⁸ 5³⁷) with ἀκούω and φωνή, but there is no such discrimination in Ac or Rev or LXX (Ac 9⁴· ¹¹ 11⁷ (p⁴⁵ D accus.) 22⁷· ⁹· ¹⁴ (E gen.) Rev 1¹⁰ 4¹ 10⁴ (p⁴⁷ SCP) 14¹³ 16¹ 21³ : Johannessohn DGKPS 36, Mayser II 2, 207). In class. Greek αἰσθάνομαι = *understand* if it has accus. as Lk 9⁴⁵ (NT = συνίημι elsewhere).

So also with *remember* and *forget* the accus. is now encroaching on the gen. Gen. with μιμνῄσκω Heb 2⁶ 13³ (as usually LXX: Johannessohn DGKPS 37, Helbing 108). But gen. (usually e.g. Lk 17³²) and accus. (e.g. Mt 16⁹, Jn 15²⁰ SD (rest gen.), 1 Th 2⁵, 2 Th 2⁸, 2 Ti 2⁸, Rev 18⁵) with μνημονεύω. Gen. with ἐπιλανθάνομαι, only Heb 6¹⁰ 13²· ¹⁶, accus. Ph 3¹³ Heb 13² S*, and papyri. Gen. with ὑπομιμνῄσκω Lk 22⁶¹, accus. Jn 14²⁶ 3 Jn¹⁰, but he may have had ὄζω in mind, and Hom. Clem. 13¹⁶ has μύρου δὲ πνέει, τῆς ἀγαθῆς φήμης, and Stobaeus (v/A.D.) ἐμπνεῖν Ἀραβίης ὀδμῆς (Schwyzer II 2, 128).

The verbs of emotion ὀργίζομαι, θαυμάζω, ἐλεέω, no longer have gen. of cause, but ἀνέχομαι *bear with* retains it: Mt 17¹⁷ Col 3¹³ (not gen. in Mt 18²⁷ with σπλαγχνίζομαι, but with δοῦλος). The gen. has survived in LXX and NT with verbs meaning *to care for*, but ἐντρέπομαι has only accus. in NT and nothing of the former gen. survives. Verbs meaning *to rule* or *surpass* also still have gen., but καταβραβεύω has accus.

The gen. of price occurs with *to buy*, *sell*, and *agree on* (συμφωνέω), in addition to ἐκ. Moule (39) suggests classifying Jude¹¹ here: μισθοῦ ἐξεχύθησαν *they went headlong for a reward*.

The substantivized verbal adjective, as a passive, has the gen. to designate the agent, e.g. Mt 11¹¹ Lk 7²⁸ γεννητοὶ γυναικῶν, Mt 24³¹ ἐκλεκτοὶ θεοῦ *chosen by God*, Ro 1⁷ ἀγαπητοὶ θεοῦ *beloved of God*, Jn 6⁴⁵ διδακτοὶ θεοῦ, 1 Co 2¹³ οὐκ ἐν διδακτοῖς ἀνθρωπίνης σοφίας λόγοις *words dictated by wordly wisdom*. Hebrew influence is apparent here. The θεο- in θεοστυγεῖς (Ro 1³⁰) may be a gen. (= θεοῦ), and so we should take the word passively in a subjective, not an objective sense: *out of favour with God*. With a passive ptc.: Mt 25³⁴ οἱ εὐλογημένοι τοῦ πατρός, Lk 2²⁷ τὸ εἰθισμένον τοῦ νόμου (D ἔθος).

§ 2] CASE ADDITIONS WITHOUT PREPOSITION 235

3. *Local and temporal.* Very little trace of local gen. remains, and it was rare and poetical in Attic [1]. It survives in ποῦ, αὐτοῦ, etc. LXX To B 10⁷ οἴας ἀπῆλθεν, Lk 5¹⁹ ποίας εἰσενέγκωσι, 19⁴, Ac 19²⁶?, 1 Pt 1¹ *sojourners in the Diaspora* (E. G. Selwyn, *The First Epistle of St. Peter*, London 1955, 118). The class. gen. of time-within-which still occurs: Mt 2¹⁴ νυκτός *during the night*, Mk 5⁵ Lk 18⁷ Ac 9²⁴ ἡμέρας καὶ νυκτός, Mt 24²⁰ Mk 13¹⁸ χειμῶνος, Mt 24²⁰ D σαββάτου, Lk 2⁸ 9³⁷ p⁴⁵ Rev 21²⁵. Class. is τοῦ λοιποῦ (like τὸ λοιπόν) *henceforth*: Ga 6¹⁷ Eph 6¹⁰ p⁴⁶ S*BA. A distributive gen. occurs with numerals, e.g. class. δὶς τῆς ἡμέρας *twice a day*, Lk 18 ¹² δὶς τοῦ σαββάτου, Heb 9⁷ ἅπαξ τοῦ ἐνιαυτοῦ. But the gen. of point of time is not class.: Mt 25⁶ μέσης νυκτός *at midnight*, Mk 13³⁵ μεσονυκτίου and ἀλεκτοροφωνίας (SBC μεσονύκτιον), Lk 24¹ ὄρθου βαθέως, Jn 11⁴⁹. ⁵¹ 18¹³ τοῦ ἐνιαυτοῦ ἐκείνου *that year*, Ac 26¹³ ἡμέρας μέσης; it occurs in the Ptol. pap. ὥρας ἑωθινῆς and the like (Mayser II 2, 225), and in MGr τοῦ χρόνου *next year*.

(b) Ablatival Genitive [2]

The gen. (or ablative) of separation has been largely replaced by ἀπό or ἐκ which, in addition to the regular gen., were both found in class. Greek; LXX and Koine also often use ἀπό (Johannessohn DGKPS 38f, Helbing 159–181, Mayser II 2, 227ff, 234ff), as well as later Greek. The verbs concerned are ἐλευθερόω, καθαρίζω, λούω, λυτρόω, λύω, ῥύομαι, σῴζω, χωρίζω. In NT, also with gen. ἀπαλλοτριόω *separate* Eph 2¹² 4¹⁸, ἀποστερέομαι 1 Ti 6⁵, μεθίστημι Lk 16⁴ AW (SBD ἐκ; L ἀπό), καθαιρέομαι Ac 19²⁷ SBAE (HLP accus.), κωλύω τινά τινος Ac 27⁴³ (as normally), but τι ἀπό τινος *to refuse someone something* (Semitism, LXX Ge 23⁶) Lk 6²⁹, φείδομαι (class. always gen.: as in Ac 20²⁹ Ro 8³² 2 Pt 2⁴· ⁵) LXX has prepositions (Abel § 44k); also ἀπέχομαι, ὑστερέω, βραδύνω, παύομαι(ἀνα-, κατα-), ἀφίσταμαι, λείπομαι, ἀστοχέω 1 Ti 1⁶ (but περί τι, 1 Ti 6²¹ 2 Ti 2¹⁸).

The gen. may also depend to some extent on prepositions in compounds; here it is mainly κατά (*against* or *down upon*) which concerns

---

[1] K-G I 384. 2. Meisterhans-Schwyzer 205. 14. Mayser II 2, 223ff.
[2] K-G I §§ 420f. Meisterhans-Schwyzer 207, 18. 19. Mayser II 2, 227ff. Radermacher² 123ff. Helbing 159–178.

us, and the more usual compounds, which in class. Greek had gen., have now tended to go over to accus. (e.g. καταδικάζω Mt 12⁷ Jas 5⁶; κατακρίνω): Helbing 182ff., Mayser II 2, 237ff.

§ 3. Dative[1]

The case tended to disappear in later Greek, but the process has scarcely begun yet; in the NT there is not much to choose between the comparative frequency of accus., gen., or dat., but the special popularity of ἐν makes the dat. more frequent than it would normally be. Besides this encroachment of ἐν, there is the growth of διά, σύν and μετά in the post-classical period at the expense of the simple dat. There are in NT already traces of the process which ended in the complete disappearance of the simple dat. in MGr; Zerwick (§ 36) points to Mk 8¹⁹ (εἰς = for), Ac 24¹⁷ (εἰς = for the benefit of), 1 Pt 1⁴ (εἰς = for). It is the more remarkable, therefore, that in Hell. Greek the dat. does sometimes oust the class. accus. (e.g. Rev 2¹⁴ ἐδίδασκεν c. dat.), and in NT the dat. is still retained in a large range of meanings, notwithstanding the constant tendency to add ἐν (even with instrumental dat.).

The dat. indicates the person more remotely concerned:

(a) *As indirect object.*

To give: dat. as well as εἰς c. acc., (ἐπι-)χορηγέω, ἐπαγγέλλομαι *promise* Jas 2⁵ dat. *To serve*: διακονέω, δουλεύω, λατρεύω, ὑπηρετέω always dat., but προσκυνέω has dat., accus., and (Hebraistic) ἐνώπιον c. gen.; and ἀρέσκω has dat. and (Ac 6⁵) ἐνώπιον c. gen. *To show, reveal, appear*: always dat. (verb *to be* in this sense 1 Co 14¹¹ ἔσομαι τῷ λαλοῦντι βάρβαρος).

Verbs of *speaking, writing*, etc. The following have dat.: ᾄδω and ψάλλω Eph 5¹⁹ Col 3¹⁶ (LXX Je 20¹³), αἰνέω Rev 19⁵, ἀπολογέομαι *make a defence before* Ac 19³³ 2 Co 12¹⁹ Hell., ἀποτάσσομαι *say farewell to* Mk 6⁴⁶ etc. Hell., ἐξ-, ἀνθ- ὁμολογέομαι Mt 11²⁵ Lk 2³⁸ 10²¹ Ro 14¹¹ 15⁹, εὔχομαι Ac 26²⁹ (but πρός 2 Co 13⁷), καυχάομαι *boast to* 2 Co 7¹⁴ 9², ὁμολογέω *praise* Heb 13¹⁵, *confess before* Mt 7²³ Ac 24¹⁴ (+ ἐν also), *promise* Mt 14⁷ Ac 7¹⁷ vl., προσεύχομαι dat. only, ψεύδομαι c. accus. Ac 5³ *deceive by lying* (class.), 5⁴ c. dat. *lie to.* In class. Greek κελεύω usually has accus., as in NT (but dat. Mt 15³⁵ EFG); class. dat. = *summon*. Other verbs for *censure and command*: dat. (but ἐγκαλέω κατά c. gen. Ro 8³³).

---

[1] K-G I 406–448. Meisterhans-Schwyzer 208ff. 23–40. Mayser II 2, 240–297. Radermacher² 126ff. Helbing 191–319. Schwyzer II 137–173 (part). J. Humbert, *La Disparition du Datif en Grec*, Paris 1930. A. Green, *The Dative of Agency. A Chapter of Indo-European Case-Syntax*, Diss. New York, 1913.

Λέγω πρός, which is common in Luke (Gosp. 99, Ac 52), absent in Mt, Mk 5, Jn 19 times, Paul twice, is part of the Hellenistic tendency to use prepositions in place of the simple case.

	λέγω	εἶπον	κατηγορέω	ἀποκρίνομαι	λαλέω
John	2⁸, 3⁴ 4¹⁵, ³³, ⁴⁹ 6⁵, 7⁵⁰	4⁴⁸, 6²⁸ vl. ³⁴ 7³, ³⁵, 8⁵⁷ vl. 11²¹, 12¹⁹ 16¹⁷, 19²⁴	5⁴⁵	8³³ vl. Otherwise always dative	Always dative

It is mainly with the reflexive that πρός occurs after verbs of *saying* in Mk and Jn. Representative figures from other books written in Biblical Greek show a large proportion of πρός c. accus.

	πρός or dat. after verbs of speaking: λαλέω, λέγω, εἶπον								
	Lk	Ac	Heb	Rev	Gen. 1-25	Gen. 26-50	4 Mac	T. Abr. A	T. Abr. B	Ep. Barn
πρός	99	45	4	–	27	31	–	31	32	10
dat.	187	48	4	28	75	154	4	30	36	15
μετά				6						

But the reversal of technique half way through LXX Genesis is remarkable; either different translators divided the LXX books between them, or the books were subsequently revised piecemeal.

Besides the dat., πέποιθα and πιστεύω have also ἐν, ἐπί (dat., acc), εἰς; and πειθάρχω has accus. (class.). Dat. occurs with πείθομαι, ὑπακούω, ἀπιστέω, ἀπειθέω. When πιστεύω has dat., it may mean *believe in*: Ac 5¹⁴ 16³⁴ (D ἐπί c. accus.) 18⁸ (D εἰς); same meaning with εἰς (e.g. εἰς τὸ ὄνομα) and ἐπί c. accus. (Mt 27⁴² SBL Ac 9⁴² 11¹⁷ 16³¹ 22¹⁹ Ro 4²⁴), ἐπί c. dat. only with ref. to LXX (according to J. Jeremias in Kittel WB IV 275f): Ro 9³³ 10¹¹ 1 Pt 2⁶ ὁ πιστεύων ἐπ' αὐτῷ, but this is not true, because of 1 Ti 1¹⁶ and Lk 24²⁵ *slow of heart* τοῦ πιστεύειν ἐπὶ πᾶσιν οἷς ἐλάλησαν (but this might mean *on the basis of*, not *in* [1]), and Mt 27⁴² WEF (SBL ἐπί c. accus.; DΘ αὐτῷ). When πιστεύω is followed by ἐν, the meaning may be *believe* absolute, and the prepositional phrase taken separately, viz. in Mk 1¹⁵ *believe, in the sphere of the Gospel*, in Jn 3¹⁵ B ἐν αὐτῷ to be taken closely with ἔχῃ ζωήν (Bauer s.v.).

---

[1] A. Schlatter, *Der Glaube im NT*⁴, 1927, 591f.

But LXX has ἐν: Ps 77²², 105¹².²⁴ Si 35²¹.²³ Je 12⁶, Johannessohn DGKPS 60f. According to Bultmann in Kittel WB VI 204, πιστεύω εἰς = to believe that Jesus is the Christ, or that J. died and rose, etc.
The dat. with ἐλπίζω to hope in (instead of ἐπί c. gen. or dat., or εἰς) occurs only in Mt 12²¹ (D + ἐν) = Isa 42⁴ (ἐπί c. dat). Jude¹¹ τῇ πλάνῃ τοῦ Βαλαάμ . . . ἐξεχύθησαν abandon themselves to?

(b) The dat. of advantage and disadvantage¹ (or "dativus commodi") marks out a person whose interests are much less remotely concerned than in the previous section.

Mt 13¹⁴ ἀναπληροῦνται αὐτοῖς (D + ἐπί) ἡ προφητεία, 23³¹ Lk 4²² Jn 3²⁶ Ro 10² etc. μαρτυρέω bear witness to someone, Mt 27⁷ εἰς ταφὴν τοῖς ξένοις, Lk 18³¹ τελεσθήσεται πάντα τὰ γράμματα . . . τῷ υἱῷ (D περί c. gen), 1 Pt 5⁹ τῇ ἀδελφότητι ἐπιτελεῖσθαι, 2 Co 2¹ ἔκρινα ἐμαυτῷ τοῦτο, also Mt 6²⁵ Lk 12²² μεριμνάω, Lk 1⁵⁵ ἐλάλησεν πρὸς τοὺς πατέρας ἡμῶν, τῷ Ἀβραὰμ καὶ τῷ σπέρματι . . . (dat. can hardly be in appos. to accus., and may be dat. commodi: he spoke to our fathers in favour of Abraham; Zerwick § 40), LXX 1 Esd 4⁴⁹ ἔγραψεν πᾶσι τοῖς Ἰουδαίοις. The dat. commodi is probably "the curious dative" (Moule, 43) in Rev 8⁴ ἀνέβη ὁ καπνὸς ταῖς προσευχαῖς in favour of their prayers, although it may be temporal dat. (BGU 69, A.D. 120, ἃς καὶ ἀποδώσω σοι τῷ ἔγγιστα δοθησομένῳ ὀψωνίῳ which I will pay you with the next wages that are paid). For dat. of disadvantage see Rev 2⁵.¹⁶ ἔρχομαί σοι; advantage 21² κεκοσμημένην τῷ ἀνδρὶ αὐτῆς. See also: Mk 10¹² 1 Co 7³⁹ γαμέομαι, Ro 14⁴ τῷ ἰδίῳ κυρίῳ στήκει ἢ πίπτει, 14⁶ κυρίῳ φρονεῖ . . . κυρίῳ ἐσθίει in honour of, 11²⁵ ἑαυτοῖς φρόνιμοι p⁴⁶ FG (AB + ἐν, SCD + παρ'), 6²⁰ ἐλεύθεροι . . . τῇ δικαιοσύνῃ, 8¹² ὀφειλέται . . . τῇ σαρκί, 1 Co 7²⁸ θλῖψιν τῇ σαρκί (D*FG + ἐν), 2 Co 10⁴ δυνατὰ τῷ θεῷ, 2¹³ ἄνεσιν τῷ πνεύματί μου, Jas 3¹⁸ καρπὸς . . . σπείρεται τοῖς ποιοῦσιν εἰρήνην.

(c) *Reference.* Paul has various loose combinations: Ro 6¹⁰ τῇ ἁμαρτίᾳ ἀπέθανεν . . . ζῇ τῷ θεῷ, 2 Co 5¹³ εἴτε γὰρ ἐξέστημεν, θεῷ· εἴτε σωφρονοῦμεν, ὑμῖν, *for God's sake . . . in your interest.* This is aptly named a dat. of reference, in so far as the idea of personal interest is so diminished as to be no more than a vague reference. Jas 2⁵ τοὺς πτωχοὺς τῷ κόσμῳ, Jude¹⁴ ἐπροφήτευσεν . . . τούτοις (J. B. Mayor in loc. *he prophesied for these*, but better sense in the context is provided if this is the dat. of vaguer reference: *as to these*, although περί c. gen. would be more natural, like Mt 15⁷ Mk 7⁶).

(d) "Dativus relationis" is very similar (see p. 220). Where class. Greek tended to have accus. (even in NT at Mt 27⁵⁷

---

¹ K-G I 417, 17. Mayser II 2, 270ff.

άνθρωπος... τούνομα Ἰωσήφ), the dat. now occurs in an adverbial sense:

Mt 5³·⁸ πτωχὸς τῷ πνεύματι, καθαρὸς τῇ καρδίᾳ, Mk 5²² Lk 1⁶¹ Ac 18²⁴ etc. ὀνόματι, Mk 7²⁶ Ac 4³⁶ 18²⁴ τῷ γένει, Ac 16⁵ στερεοῦσθαι τῇ πίστει περισσεύειν τῷ ἀριθμῷ, Ro 12¹⁰ τῇ φιλαδελφίᾳ ... φιλόστοργοι, 1 Co 14²⁰ νηπιάζειν τῇ κακίᾳ, 2 Co 7¹¹ ἁγνὸς τῷ πράγματι (if text is sound), Ph 2³⁰ παραβολευσάμενος τῇ ψυχῇ, 3³ οἱ πνεύματι θεοῦ λατρεύοντες, Col 2⁵ τῇ σαρκί *physically*.

(*e*) *Ethical dative.* Perhaps Mt 21⁵ OT ἔρχεταί σοι and Rev 2⁵·¹⁶ (Hebraisms) (see under (b)), 2 Pt 3¹⁴ ἄσπιλοι καὶ ἀμώμητοι αὐτῷ (God) εὑρεθῆναι. The ethical dat. in Ac 7²⁰ ἀστεῖος τῷ θεῷ (*in God's eyes*) is a Hebraism, reminding us of LXX Jon 3³ πόλις μεγάλη τῷ θεῷ לֵאלֹהִים (an elative; i.e. *very big* according to D. W. Thomas in *Vet. Test.* III, 1953, 15ff, as the LXX fail to appreciate that אלהים or אל sometimes express a superlative). The dat. in Lk 2¹¹ ἐτέχθη ὑμῖν σήμερον σωτήρ may be described as "sympatheticus"; see SIG 1240. 25 (ii/A.D.) πληθύοι αὐτῷ οἶκος παίδων γοναῖς (Schwyzer II 147f; J. Weber, *Der sympathetische Dativ bei Herodot*, diss. Münster 1915).

(*f*) Where εἶναι with dat. forms part of the predicate it usually carries the idea of credit (or discredit) in the person's eyes:

Mt 18¹⁷ ἔστω σοι ὥσπερ ὁ ἐθνικός, Lk 5¹⁰ κοινωνοὶ τῷ Σίμωνι (D gen.) *Simon had in them partners,* Ac 9¹⁵ σκεῦος ἐκλογῆς ἐστίν μοι οὗτος *I have in him,* 19³¹ ὄντες αὐτῷ φίλοι (but gen. Jn 19¹² etc.), Ro 1¹⁴ ἀνοήτοις ὀφειλέτης εἰμί, 8¹² (but 15²⁷ gen.), 1 Co 1¹⁸ τοῖς μὲν ἀπολλυμένοις μωρία ἐστίν *serves as folly,* 2¹⁴, 11¹⁴·¹⁵ ἀτιμία αὐτῷ, 15³² τί (μοι) τὸ ὄφελος, 2 Co 2¹⁵ Χριστοῦ εὐωδία ἐσμὲν τῷ θεῷ, Ga 5¹³ μὴ τὴν ἐλευθερίαν εἰς ἀφορμὴν τῇ σαρκί (ellipse of verb), 1 Th 2¹⁰ ὁσίως ... ὑμῖν ἐγενήθημεν (but adverbs are rare in this construction), LXX To 3¹⁵ μονογενής εἰμι τῷ πατρί μου.

(*g*) There is also more obviously a dat. of possession (K-G I 416, 15; Mayser II 2, 269f), in which the personal interest, which is always latent in the dat. is strengthened to the point of ownership, and the class. distinction between the gen. for emphasis on the possessor and dat. for emphasis on the object possessed is often preserved: Mt 19²⁷ 18¹² Ac 21²³. Exceptions: Lk 12²⁰ ἃ ἡτοίμασας, τίνι ἔσται; (D corrects to τίνος), Ac 2³⁹ ὑμῖν ἐστιν ἡ ἐπαγγελία, Ro 7³, 7⁴ (cp. Heb. הָיָה לְאִישׁ). Besides εἰμί and γίνομαι, ὑπάρχω is used like this (Lk 8³ Ac 28⁷ 2 Pt 1⁸).

(*h*) In addition, εἰμί c. dat. occurs with the meaning to *happen to*: Mt 16²² οὐ μὴ ἔσται σοι τοῦτο, and with ellipse of the verb: Mk 1²⁴ τί ἡμῖν καὶ σοί, Lk 1⁴³ πόθεν μοι τοῦτο; 1 Co 5¹² etc. τί γάρ μοι; Epict. 1, 22, 15 τί μοι καὶ αὐτῷ, εἰ οὐ δύναταί μοι βοηθῆσαι (see 1, 27, 13).

(*i*) *Dat. of Agent* [1]. In NT there are very few exx. of dat. with passive = ὑπό c. gen. Lk 23¹⁵ ἐστὶν πεπραγμένον αὐτῷ (D + ἐν, *c* in); however, it could be taken as *in his case*, Ro 8¹⁴ πνεύματι θεοῦ ἄγονται, Ga 5¹⁸ πνεύματι ἄγεσθε, LXX Ge 14¹⁹, Jos. Ant. 11, 206 ἡμῖν δεδήλωται, Gosp. Pet. 11 τοῖς ἀγαπωμένοις αὐταῖς, Clem. Hom. (atticistic) 3⁶⁸ 9²¹ 19²³.

(*j*) *Instrumental dat.* Jas 3⁷ δαμάζεται καὶ δεδάμασται τῇ φύσει τῇ ἀνθρωπίνῃ, 2 Pt 2¹⁹ ᾧ τις ἥττηται, Jude ¹ τοῖς ... Ἰησοῦ Χριστῷ τετηρημένοις κλητοῖς. It is the instrumental ἐν which is more used than plain dat. in Biblical Greek; it occurs only occasionally in secular Greek (see pp. 252f). Without the preposition: Lk 21²⁴ στόματι μαχαίρης, Ac 12² μαχαίρῃ. There are phrases like *to season with* Mk 9⁴⁹ Col 4⁶, *to burn with* Mt 3¹² Lk 3¹⁷ Rev 8⁸ 17¹⁶ (SBP) 21⁸ (with ἐν 14¹⁰ 16⁸ 17¹⁶ vl. 18⁸), LXX with and without ἐν, *to baptise with* usually ἐν but ὕδατι Lk 3¹⁶ (D + ἐν) Ac 1⁵ 11¹⁶, χρίω πνεύματι 10³⁸, *to vindicate by* Ro 3²⁸ (also ἐν and ἐκ), *to mix with* Rev 15² (also ἐν and μετά), *to measure with* Lk 6³⁸ Rev 21¹⁶ (also ἐν).

This instrumental dat. is sometimes used where the class. rule expects the gen. construction: Eph 5¹⁸ LXX Pr 4¹⁷ μεθύσκομαι οἴνῳ, Mt 20¹⁸ Mk 10³³ κατακρινοῦσιν αὐτοῦ θανάτῳ, (Hellenistic: Büchsel in Kittel WB III 953 n. 1) 2 Pt 2⁶ καταστροφῇ κατέκρινεν.

Other exx. of instrumental dat. are probably: Ro 1²⁰ τοῖς ποιήμασιν νοούμενα *perceived by means of his works*, 5¹⁵, ¹⁷ τῷ ... παραπτώματι *by the transgression*, 8¹³ πνεύματι ... θανατοῦτε *by the Spirit*, 8¹⁴, Ga 5⁵, ¹⁶, ¹⁸, ²⁵, Ro 12² μεταμορφοῦσθε τῇ ἀνακαινώσει τοῦ νοός *transformed by*, Eph 2⁵ χάριτί ἐστε σεσωσμένοι *by grace*.

(*k*) *Associative dat.* which, when used with verbs is often known as " dativus sociativus " or " comitativus ", expresses the " means by which ", but with strong emphasis on physical

---
[1] Moulton-Howard 459.

§ 3] CASE ADDITIONS WITHOUT PREPOSITION 241

accompaniment or nearness. E.g. ἀκολουθέω often has dat., but also μετά and the Biblical ὀπίσω; συνέπομαι Ac 20⁴; ἐγγίζω Lk 7¹²; κολλάομαι Lk 15¹⁵ etc.; κοινωνέω Ro 12¹³ etc.; ὁμιλέω Ac 24²⁶; and other verbs of this kind. However, μάχομαι (class. dat.) has only πρός (Jn 6⁵²), πολεμέω (class. dat.) only μετά (Rev 2¹⁶ 12⁷ 13⁴ 17¹⁴).

But this dat. may be more loosely connected with the verb to describe accompanying circumstances or manner, and it is then often designated " dativus modi ". NT adds ἐν with the former:

Mt 16²⁸ ἐρχόμενον ἐν τῇ βασιλείᾳ αὐτοῦ, Mk 1²³ 7²⁵ p⁴⁵ ἐν πνεύματι ἀκαθάρτῳ, Lk 14³¹ ἐν δέκα χιλιάσιν ὑπαντᾶν, 23⁴² ὅταν ἔλθῃς ἐν τῇ βασιλείᾳ σου (BL correct to εἰς), Ac 7¹⁴ πᾶσαν τὴν συγγένειαν ἐν ψυχαῖς ἑβδ. πέντε, 1 Co 4²¹ ἐν ῥάβδῳ ἔλθω, Heb 9²⁵ εἰσέρχομαι ἐν αἵματι, Jude¹⁴ ἦλθεν ... ἐν ἁγίαις μυριάσιν αὐτοῦ. Of clothing: Lk 4³² 24⁴, Ac 1¹⁰ ἐν ἐσθήσεσι λευκαῖς, Col 2¹⁵, LXX 1 Mac 11⁵⁸ 3 Mac 1¹⁶. Of manner (dat. alone): Mt 8¹⁶ ἐξέβαλεν τὰ πνεύματα λόγῳ, Mk 5⁴ πέδαις καὶ ἁλύσεσιν δεδέσθαι, 14⁶⁵ ῥαπίσμασιν αὐτὸν ἔλαβον (a Latinism? see Cicero Tusc. 2, 34 verberibus accipere. But Acta Joan. 90 τί εἰ ῥαπίσμασίν με ἔλαβες; pap. c. A.D. 100, Blass-Debr. § 198 κονδύλοις ἔλαβεν), Lk 2³⁷ νηστείαις καὶ δεήσεσιν λατρεύουσα, Ac 2⁸·¹¹·⁴⁰ τῇ ἰδίᾳ διαλέκτῳ, 16³⁷ δημοσίᾳ, 24⁴ ἀκοῦσαι ... τῇ σῇ ἐπιεικείᾳ *with your clemency*, Ro 8²⁴ τῇ ἐλπίδι ... ἐσώθημεν *in hope* but not actually, 1 Co 10³⁰ χάριτι *with thankfulness*, 11⁵, 14¹⁵ προσεύξομαι τῷ πνεύματι ... τῷ νοΐ (or local dat.?), Ph 4⁶ τῇ προσευχῇ καὶ τῇ δεήσει μετὰ εὐχαριστίας (NB. both dat. and μετά), Col 3¹⁶ ψαλμοῖς etc., Heb 6¹⁷ ἐμεσίτευσεν ὅρκῳ (but μετά in Mt 26⁷² and pap.).

Then there are various stereotyped phrases (e.g. παρρησίᾳ): Ph 1¹⁸ παντὶ τρόπῳ. But μετά and ἐν are found in such phrases in both LXX (Johannessohn DGPS 209ff) and NT, and papyri (e.g. μετὰ βίας). Some are almost peculiar to Biblical Greek, e.g. ὁδῷ, ἴχνεσιν, with πορεύομαι, περιπατέω, στοιχέω: Lk 10³¹ B, Jas 2²⁵ ἑτέρᾳ ὁδῷ ἐκβαλοῦσα, but usually figuratively in NT: Ac 9³¹ πορεύομαι τῷ φόβῳ τοῦ κυρίου, 14¹⁶ ταῖς ὁδοῖς αὐτῶν, 21²¹ τοῖς ἔθεσιν περιπατέω, Ro 4¹², 13¹³ Ga 5¹⁶ Jude¹¹ Hom. Clem. 10¹⁵ τῷ ὑμῶν στοιχεῖτε παραδείγματι.

(*l*) The Hebrew infinite absolute shows its influence in the use of the cognate dat. of verbal nouns in LXX and NT (Thackeray OT Gr 48f, Johannessohn DGKPS 56f), e.g. Ge 2¹⁷ Mt 15⁴. There was already some class. precedent (Schwyzer II 166), but Biblical Greek has a wealth of exx: Lk 22¹⁵ ἐπιθυμίᾳ ἐπεθύμησα, Ac 2¹⁷ ἐνυπνίοις ἐνυπνιάζεσθαι, 4¹⁷ ἀπειλῇ ἀπειλησώμεθα vl., 5²⁸

παραγγελία παρηγγείλαμεν, 23¹⁴, 28²⁶ LXX, Ga 5¹ τῇ ἐλευθερίᾳ...
ἠλευθέρωσεν, Jas 5¹⁷. However, the addition of an attribute
almost always results in the substitution of the accus. of content:
so Jn 3²⁹ χαρᾷ χαίρει becomes Mt 2¹⁰ ἐχάρησεν χαρὰν μεγάλην;
but not always, because we find Mk 5⁴² ἐξέστησαν ἐκστάσει
μεγάλῃ 1 Mac 14²⁹ δόξῃ μεγάλῃ ἐδόξασαν.

(m) *Cause*. This dat. is extraordinary ¹. Ac 15¹ περιτμη-
θῆτε τῷ ἔθει τῷ Μωϋσέως (not D) may be *because of the Law* (for
according to we would expect κατά). Most exx. are in Paul:
Ro 4²⁰ οὐ διεκρίθη τῇ ἀπιστίᾳ, ἀλλ' ἐνεδυναμώθη τῇ πίστει, 11²⁰
τῇ ἀπιστίᾳ ἐξεκλάσθησαν, ³⁰. ³¹, 14¹⁵ μὴ τῷ βρώματί σου ἐκεῖνον
ἀπόλλυε, 2 Co 2⁷ τῇ περισσοτέρᾳ λύπῃ καταποθῇ (or local?), 2¹³
τῷ μὴ εὑρεῖν με *because I did not find*, Ga 6¹² ἵνα τῷ σταυρῷ τοῦ Χρ.
μὴ διώκωνται, Col 2¹⁴ (transposing τοῖς δόγμασιν after ὃ ἦν)
which was against us because of the decrees (but Eph 2¹⁴ adds ἐν,
suggesting that this is a dat. of attendant circumstances, even
instrumental; i.e. take the phrase closely with the verb implied
in χειρόγραφον *written in*...), Ph 1¹⁴ πεποιθότας τοῖς δεσμοῖς μου
confident because of my imprisonment, Heb 13¹⁶ τοιαύταις
εὐαρεστεῖται, 1 Pt 4¹² μὴ ξενίζεσθε τῇ, Jude¹¹ τῇ ἀντιλογίᾳ τοῦ
Κόρε ἀπώλοντο *because of the contradicting of*. More commonly
a preposition takes the place of dat. at this period.

(n) *With compound verbs* ². Here the dat. is frequent, but is
often supplemented by a preposition, and increasingly so in
Hell. Greek. The construction with the dat. is often figurative
e.g. ἀνατίθεμαι Ac 25¹⁴ etc. The dat. predominates with verbs
compounded with ἀντι-, and πρός is rare. But compounds with
εἰσ- always take a preposition. Compounds with ἐν- in a
literal sense always have a preposition; but these figurative
meanings always have a plain dat.: ἐγκαλέω, ἐμμαίνομαι, ἐμπαίζω,
ἐνέχω, ἐντυγχάνω (Ro 11², Wi 8²¹, BUI 246¹² ii–iii/A.D.). With
ἐπι- the practice fluctuates, but usually the plain dat. is
figurative. With παρα- it is almost only the dat., and Ac 15¹⁹
has dat. where Hell. Greek has usually accus. (Mayser II 2,
299f); the same is true of περι- and προσ- and συν-.

(o) *Locative* ³. This is the " in- " case, the case of position.
The predominant use is now with prepositions, e.g. ἐν ᾽Αθήναις, not

---
¹ K-G I 438, 11. Mayser II 2, 284.
² K-G I 431 n. 1; 443 n. 1. Helbing 268–319. Mayser II 2, 285ff.
³ K-G I 441ff. Schwyzer II 154ff. Mayser II 2, 295f.

§ 3] CASE ADDITIONS WITHOUT PREPOSITION 243

'Αθήναζε, and even in the class. period the plain dat. was extremely limited. It is doubtful whether there are any more than these exx. in NT: πάντῃ, πανταχῇ; Jn 21⁸ οἱ μαθηταὶ τῷ πλοιαρίῳ ἦλθον; Ac 2³³ 5³¹ τῇ δεξιᾷ τοῦ θεοῦ ὑψωθείς. For pap. see Mayser, and also Vettius Valens 181, 22, and Herm. V. IV 3, 7.

(*p*) *Temporal.* (i) Of time-when [1]. Still in NT, but ἐν often enters to clarify the meaning, as class. The dat. is used for only point of time, strictly speaking, but p⁴⁶ in Ro 13¹³ has ἡμέρᾳ for *in the day* (the rest add ἐν). Normally, the dat. alone (or with ἐν) indicates a specific day or night, e.g. Mk 14³⁰ ταύτῃ τῇ νυκτί; it is useless to multiply examples. There is the Hebraism ἡμέρᾳ καὶ ἡμέρᾳ *every day* 2 Co 4¹⁶. It is usual to add ἐν when ἐκείνῃ and ταύτῃ are used. Φυλακή *night watch* and ὥρα are used like ἡμέρᾳ, but ἔτει only has ἐν (Lk 3¹). The temporal dat. is still used with names of festivals: Mt 14⁶ γενεσίοις δὲ γενομένοις SBDL is apparently a dat. absolute [2], Mk 6²¹ (p⁴⁵ + ἐν), Mt 12¹ etc. τοῖς σάββασιν *on the sabbath*, Lk 2⁴¹ τῇ ἑορτῇ τοῦ πάσχα (D + ἐν). Other instances: Ac 13³⁶ ἰδίᾳ γενεᾷ, Ro 11³⁰ᶠ τῇ τούτων ἀπειθείᾳ *at the time of their disbelief*, Eph 2¹² τῷ καιρῷ ἐκείνῳ p⁴⁶ (2nd hand) SBAD*FG (p⁴⁶ DᶜEKLP + ἐν), 3⁵ ἑτέραις γενεαῖς *in other generations*, 1 Ti 6¹⁵ καιροῖς ἰδίοις.

(ii) Of duration of time. Class. usage has accus.; Hell. Greek uses dat. (even Josephus) mainly with transitive verbs: Lk 1⁷⁵ πάσαις ταῖς ἡμέραις ἡμῶν (cp. Mt 28²⁰ πάσας τὰς ἡμέρας), 8²⁹ πολλοῖς χρόνοις συνηρπάκει αὐτόν (unless it means *on many occasions*), Ac 8¹¹ ἱκανῷ χρόνῳ, 13²⁰ ὡς ἔτεσιν . . . ἔδωκεν *for 450 years*, Ro 16²⁵ χρ. αἰωνίοις σεσιγημένου. Examples abound in Hellenistic sources; and since they are usually with transitive verbs, it may be that there was some reticence felt at placing a second accus. alongside a verb which already had an accus. of dir. object. Textual variants in NT illustrate the uneasiness of scribes about the use of the dat.: Mk 8² ἤδη ἡμέραις τρισίν B

---

[1] K-G I 445, 2. Schwyzer II 158f. Moulton Einl. 116f. Mayser II 2, 296f.
[2] There may be instances in Greek of dat. absolute. See C. C. Tarelli on Plutarch (Moule 45). In the NT: Mk 9²⁸ p⁴⁵ (SBCDLWΘ fam¹ fam¹³ 700 have gen. absol) εἰσελθόντι αὐτῷ, Ac 28¹¹ παρασήμῳ Διοσκούροις *with the Dioscuri as ship's insignia* (inscriptional precedent, W. M. Ramsay, *St. Luke the Physician*, London 1908, 36f).

(some have nom.; some accus.), Lk 8²⁷ χρόνῳ ἱκανῷ (some have gen.), Jn 14⁹ τοσούτῳ χρόνῳ SDLWQ (BA corr. to accus.), Ac 28¹² B ἡμέραις τρισίν (some nom.; some accus., as Mk 8²).

§ 4. Accusative [1]

(a) *The simple accus.* of external object occurs also with verbs which were originally intransitive, as a characteristic of Hell. Greek. The absol. ἐνεργέω *to be at work* is increased to *to be at work at something* in literary Koine (1 Co 12⁶ Ph 2¹³ etc.), by the simple addition of an accusative.[2]

Similar words in NT are: ἐμπορεύομαι *defraud* 2 Pt 2³ (Bauer s.v.), ἐνεδρεύω Lk 11⁵⁴ Ac 23²¹, εὐσεβέω Ac 17²³ 1 Ti 5⁴, θριαμβεύω 2 Co 2¹⁴ Col 2¹⁵ (Kittel WB III 160, n. 2), ἱερουργέω Ro 15¹⁶, καρτερέω Heb 11²⁷ (Bauer s.v.), πλεονεκτέω Paul, συνεργέω Ro 8²⁸ BA, τρίζω Mk 9¹⁸, ὑβρίζω, χορηγέω 2 Co 9¹⁰ 1 Pt 4¹¹. The same process has occurred with verbs of emotion: ἀπορέομαι Ac 25²⁰ SBAHP; ἐλεέω Mt 9²⁷ etc. Ptol. pap. (Mayser II 2, 308); εὐδοκέω Mt 12¹⁸ (OT) S*B, Heb 10⁶·⁸, LXX Ps 50¹⁸ etc.; θέλω with same meaning Mt 27⁴³ ῥυσάσθω νῦν εἰ θέλει αὐτόν, LXX Ps 21⁹ 40¹² To 13⁸; θαυμάζω Lk 7⁹ (D om αὐτόν) Jn 5²⁸ Ac 7³¹ Jude¹⁶; ἱλάσκομαι *propitiate* Lk 18¹³ (pass.), *expiate* Heb 2¹⁷, LXX, Philo; κλαίω Mt 2¹⁸ (not LXX) Lk 23²⁸ D; κόπτομαι class. Lk 8⁵²; πενθέω 2 Co 12²¹, LXX (only dat. in Ptol. pap.). The same tendency to accus. in Hell. Greek appears with verbs which (in class. Greek) would have governed the (partit.) gen.: Mt 5⁵ κληρονομέω τὴν γῆν, ⁶ πεινάω διψάω, ²⁸ ἐπιθυμέω γυναῖκα, Jn 6⁵³ ἐσθίω πίνω; if the writer wishes to emphasize the *part* he often uses prepositions (Mt 15²⁷ 1 Co 11²⁸). Hellenistic addition of an object sometimes changes the entire meaning, as appears in μαθητεύω: cp. Mt 27⁵⁷ B with 28¹⁹ Ac 14²¹.

The accus. also accompanies verbs of fearing, fleeing, swearing, guarding from; but NT does have ἀπό c. gen. in addition, under strong Semitic influence (occasionally class.). Thus φοβέομαι has accus. except at Mt 10²⁸ = Lk 12⁴ (ἀπό), LXX has accus. and ἀπό c. gen., whereas Ptol. pap. has only accus. Jas 5¹² ὄμνυμι c. accus., while elsewhere there is a preposition as in LXX; but (ἐν-) ὁρκίζω *adjure* still has accus. Φεύγω ἀπό *shun* 1 Co 10¹⁴, *flee from* Mt 3⁷ = Lk 3⁷, Mt 23³³, Rev 9⁶ (in class. Greek ἀπό was only local, as in Jn 10⁵ᶠ Jas 4⁷), ἀπὸ προσώπου

---

[1] K-G I 293-331. Schwyzer II 67ff. Meisterhans-Schwyzer 204-6-12. Mayser II 2, 151, 297-336. Johannessohn DGKPS 67. Radermacher² 120-122.

[2] F, Krebs *Zur Rection der Kasus*, 1887-90, *passim*. Moulton Proleg. 63ff.

(שֵׁם לְפִי) Rev 20¹¹. Before Plutarch, ἐντρέπομαι usually has gen., but accus. in Mt 21³⁷ Lk 18² Heb 12⁹.

On the other hand, the dat. is sometimes used instead of, or besides, the class. accus.: καλῶς ποιέω (class. accus.) has the Hellenistic dat. Lk 6²⁷, and so does εὖ ποιέω Mk 14⁷ (A corrects to accus.), but accus. still in LXX (Schwyzer II 144; Mayser II 2, 263f). In addition to class. accus. προσκυνέω has dat. about 150 times in LXX (against about ten times with accus.), also in Dio Cassius, Jos., Aristeas, Lucian, 2 Clem. 3¹; so NT e.g. Mt 2². ¹¹ Jn 4²¹ Ac 7⁴³ 1 Co 14²⁵ Heb 1⁶ Rev 4¹⁰ 7¹¹ 13⁴. ¹⁵ 14⁷ 16² 19⁴. ¹⁰. ²⁰ 22⁸. ⁹; with acc., only Mt 4¹⁰ = Lk 4⁸, Lk24⁵² (D om), Jn 4²². ²². ²³ (S* dat.) ²⁴ 9³⁸ D. Rev several times (9²⁰ 13⁴. ⁸. ¹² 14⁹. ¹¹ 20⁴) in addition to dat. The dat. in LXX is due to influence of לְ, and in order to avoid the interpretation kiss¹. Of human superiors: c. dat. Mt 2². ⁸ 8² 9¹⁸ 14³³ 15²⁵ 18²⁶ 28⁹ Mk 15¹⁹ Jn 9³⁸: c. accus. Mk 5⁶ vl.

The accus. has usurped the place of class. dat. with verbs meaning *censure, revile, blaspheme, curse* (Helbing 1–23): ἐπηρεάζω (Lk 6²⁸ 1 Pt 3¹⁶; not in LXX); ὀνειδίζω (Wi 2¹² is only ex. of dat. in LXX); καταράομαι (the dat. in Mt 5⁴⁴ D* and Lk 6²⁸ EHL is an atticistic correction; the rare dat. in LXX is also probably atticistic: 4 Km 2²⁴ Ep. Je⁶⁵); φθονέω Ga 5²⁶ p⁴⁶ BG (SACD dat.). As well as class. εἰς NT (Hell. Greek) has plain accus. with βλασφημέω like LXX (4 Km 19⁴. ⁶. ²²), Jos., Vett. Val., Babrius (ii/A.D.): Lk 23³⁹ Ac 19³⁷ Rev 13⁶. Whereas class. Greek has dat. of person with εὐαγγελίζομαι, NT has accus. as well. With ἐγκόπτω *hinder* (class. dat.), NT has accus.: Ac 24⁴ Ga 5⁷ 1 Th 2¹⁸ (Stählin in Kittel WB III 855). Some NT exx. of accus. gaining over gen.: Mt 1²⁰ 9⁴ ἐνθυμέομαι (gen. in P. Par. 63 vii 9, ii/B.C.), Mt 12⁷ Jas 5⁶ καταδικάζω, Ro 2¹⁰ προηγέομαι Ph 1¹¹ πληρόομαι.

(b) *Content, or internal object* ("cognate accusative"). This follows a Semitic principle, and may consist of a noun with an attribute: Mt 2¹⁰, 2 Co 6¹³ τὴν δὲ αὐτὴν ἀντιμισθίαν πλατύνθητε, perhaps pregnant for τὸν αὐτὸν πλατυσμὸν ὡς ἀντιμισθίαν (or adverbial: *with the same reward*, or accus. in apposition to a sentence, Moule 35f), 1 Pt 3¹⁴ τὸν φόβον αὐτῶν (*of them*) μὴ φοβηθῆτε, Rev 16⁹ ἐκαυματίσθησαν καῦμα μέγα, Jn 7²⁴ κρίνω with τὴν δικαίαν κρίσιν, Mk 10³⁸ τὸ βάπτισμα, ὃ ἐγὼ βαπτίζομαι, βαπτισθῆναι, Jn 17²⁶ ἡ ἀγάπη ἣν ἠγάπησάς με (D ᾗ), Eph 2⁴. No attribute: Lk 2⁸ φυλάσσω φυλακάς, Jas 5¹⁸. It may consist of

---
¹ Kittel WB VI 762f.

an adj. or pronoun: Lk 12⁴⁷ᵗ δαρήσεται πολλάς, ὀλίγας; the neuters of certain pronouns (τοῦτο, τί, οὐδέν, πάντα) are less frequent than in class. Greek but they still appear: Lk 4³⁵ μηδὲν βλάψας (or accus. of respect?), Mt 19²⁰ τί ὑστερῶ, Mk 7³⁶ ὅσον *as much as* (W 700 dat.), Ac 10²⁰, Ro 6¹⁰, 1 Co 9²⁵, 10³³, 11², 2 Co 12¹¹, 12¹³, 12¹⁴·¹³¹ τρίτον, Ga 2²⁰ ὃ νῦν ζῶ, 5² ὑμᾶς οὐδὲν ὠφελήσει, Ph 1⁶ πεποιθὼς αὐτὸ τοῦτο *in just this confidence* (= *I am sure*), 2¹⁸ Mt 27⁴⁴ τὸ δ' αὐτό *in the same way*. We might take ἅ like this in Col 2¹⁸ ἃ ἑώρακεν ἐμβατεύων, εἰκῇ φυσιούμενος *upon what he vainly imagined in the vision of his initiation* (making the conjectural emendations unnecessary). Papyri of 145 and 118 B.C.: πολλὰ χαῖρε and χαίρειν (Mayser II 2, 319).

(c) *Double accusative*[1]. The NT conforms mainly to class. usage, with certain verbs: e.g. *teach* and *remind* Mk 6³⁴, Jn 14²⁶, Ac 21²¹, 1 Co 4¹⁷, Heb 5¹² τοῦ διδάσκειν ὑμᾶς τινα τὰ στοιχεῖα (but διδάσκω c. dat. Rev 2¹⁴); *enquire* and *entreat* Mk 6²². ²³ Lk 12⁴⁸ Mt 21²⁴ Mk 4¹⁰, LXX has both single and double accus.; *dress* and *undress* Mt 27³¹ Mk 15¹⁷. ²⁰ (ἐγδύω τινά τι in pap.), Lk 19⁴³, LXX περιβάλλω τινά τι, τί τινι, ἕν τινι. Causatives are more popular than in class. Greek and have double accus.: ποτίζω Mk 9⁴¹ 1 Co 3², φορτίζω Lk 11⁴⁶ τοὺς ἀνθρώπους φορτία. We find the double accus. of both external and internal object: Lk 4³⁵, Jn 17²⁶, Ac 13³² ἡμεῖς ὑμᾶς εὐαγγελιζόμεθα τὴν ... ἐπαγγελίαν, Ga 4¹², 5², Eph 2⁴, Rev 14⁷ p⁴⁷ δοξάσατε αὐτὸν δόξαν An accus. of object and a predicative accus. (without the help of a ptc. or a particle like ὡς, such as would be needed with other cases) occurs in the class. manner: *to reckon as* Ac 13⁵ (but with ὡς Mt 21²⁶, with εἰς 21⁴⁶ vl.); *to receive as* Jas 5¹⁰; *to make to be* Lk 19⁴⁶ ὑμεῖς δὲ αὐτὸν ἐποιήσατε σπηλαῖον, Jn 6¹⁵, Ro 4¹⁷ LXX πατέρα ... τέθεικά σε, Lk 12¹⁴ Heb 1²; *to do something to* Mt 27²² τί οὖν ποιήσω Ἰησοῦν, Herm. S. I 4 τί ποιήσεις τὸν ἀγρόν, LXX Nu 24¹⁴ τί ποιήσεις ... τὸν λαόν σου; *to designate as*, Mk 10¹⁸, Lk 1⁵⁹, Jn 9²² (D + εἶναι), 10³⁵, Ro 10⁹, 1 Jn 4² (B accus. c. inf.), 2 Jn⁷, and Semitism καλέσεις τὸ ὄνομα αὐτοῦ Ἰωάννην etc. Mt 1²¹. ²³. ²⁵ Lk 1¹³. ³¹ 2²¹; *to consider as* Lk 14¹⁸. ¹⁹ ἔχω, Ac 20²⁴ ποιοῦμαι, Ro 6¹¹ p⁴⁶ DAEFG λογίζομαι, Ph 3⁷ ἥγημαι (cp. Lat. *habeo*); *to prove to be* 2 Co 6⁴ Ga 2¹⁸. To this predicative accus. we may add 1 Co 9⁵ ἀδελφὴν γυναῖκα after περιάγω (it is not attributive:

---

[1] K-G I 318ff. Mayser II 2, 320–323. Helbing 38–68. Rademacher² 121.

a wife who is a sister, but predicative : *a sister as a wife*) ; Lk 11¹¹ *which of you shall the son ask as the father* (τὸν πατέρα predicative of τίνα) ; 1 Pt 1¹⁷ *if you invoke as father the one who judges* (πατέρα a predicate of τὸν . . . κρίνοντα). In a Semitic way, εἰς (like normal Greek ὡς) may be added to this predicate : Mt 21⁴⁶ εἰς προφήτην (vl. ὡς), Ac 13²² εἰς βασιλέα, ⁴⁷ (= Isa. 49⁶), 7²¹, 1 Clem. 42⁴ εἰς ἐπισκόπους, BGU 1103¹¹ (13 B.C.) ὃ εἶχεν εἰς φερνάριον *which he has received for dowry*.

(d) *Accus. with passive.* This occurs with the passive of verbs which have double accus. in the active, and is classical : e.g. μουσικὴν διδαχθείς. 1 Co 12¹³ ἓν πνεῦμα ἐποτίσθημεν, 2 Th 2¹⁵, Heb 6⁹, Lk 16¹⁹ ἐνεδιδύσκετο πορφύραν. In the Koine, and actually already in LXX, occurs accus. instead of gen. with *fill, be full* : Ph 1¹¹ πεπληρωμένοι καρπὸν δικαιοσύνης, Col 1⁹ πληρωθῆτε τὴν ἐπίγνωσιν *filled with knowledge*. The person which appears in dat. with active voice may become the subject with the passive, and therefore such a passive will have accus. of the thing (as in English : " I am given a book ") : Lk 12⁴⁷ δαρήσεται πολλάς, Ga 2⁷ πεπίστευμαι τὸ εὐαγγέλιον, 1 Th 2⁴, 1 Co 9¹⁷.

(e) *Adverbial accus.* (i) Manner : for τὸ λοιπόν see p. 336. Also δωρεάν *gratuitously* and μακράν have become simple adverbs. Mt 15¹⁶, Heb 5¹³ D* E* ἀκμήν (Hellenistic, not LXX). This accus. is often formed by a superfluous article : Lk 11³ 19⁴⁷ Ac 17¹¹. ²⁸ D 19⁹ D τὸ καθ᾽ ἡμέραν *daily* (class.) ; Ac 5²¹ D τὸ πρωΐ, Ro 1¹⁵ τὸ κατ᾽ ἐμέ, 9⁵, 12⁵. ¹⁸, 15²², 16¹⁹, 1 Co 14²⁷, 1 Pt 3⁸. For Jn 8²⁵ τὴν ἀρχήν see pp. 49f. Lk 11⁴¹ τὰ ἐνόντα may be attributive accus. (*alms relating to what is within*) or accus. of respect (*as for what is inside, give alms*), but neither makes as good sense as adverbial accus. (*give alms from the heart*). Other instances : ὃν τρόπον Mt 23³⁷ 2 Ti 3⁸ etc. (LXX often) (pap. Mayser II 2, 329), τὸν ὅμοιον τρόπον Jude⁷, Mt 13³⁰ LXΔ δήσατε αὐτὰ δεσμάς (SBCEF add εἰς ; D om αὐτά), Lk 9¹⁴ κατακλίνατε αὐτοὺς κλισίας. Cp. adverbial nom., p. 231.

(ii) Extent. In Mt 4¹⁵ ὁδὸν θαλάσσης (in LXX Isa 8²³ perhaps a harmonization with the NT) is a literal translation of Heb. יָם דֶּרֶךְ = *seawards*, rather than a ref. to some road leading to the sea. Lk 22⁴¹ ὡσεὶ λίθου βολήν, 2³⁶ ζήσασα . . . ἔτη ἑπτά, Mt 28²⁰, Mk 4²⁷ Ac 26⁷ 2 Th 3⁸ ADE (SB gen.). Distributive : Mt 20² τὴν ἡμέραν *per day* (Mayser II 2. 333), Mk 9²⁶ πολλὰ σπαράξας *fit after fit*. There is a Hell. Greek idiom for indicating duration of time by placing the preposition with the inappropriate noun: e.g. instead of *six days before the passover* Jn 12¹ reads *before six days of the passover* ¹.

(iii) Point of time. This is not unclass. (e.g. Demosth. 54, 10 ἐκείνην τὴν ἑσπέραν *on that evening*), and is found in the Koine (Moulton Proleg. 63), LXX (e.g. Ge 43¹⁶ Ex 9¹⁸), and Church writers (e.g. Justin M. Apol. 1, 67, 8 τὴν δὲ τοῦ ἡλίου ἡμέραν; but 67, 3 dative). In NT Jn 4⁵² ἐχθὲς ὥραν ἑβδόμην, Ac 10³ ὥραν ἐνάτην, 10³⁰ (unless τὴν ἐνάτην = *the ninth-hour prayer*, cogn. accus.), 20¹⁶ τὴν ἡμέραν τῆς πεντηκοστῆς (D + εἰς), Rev 3³ ποίαν ὥραν.

(iv) For the accus. in apposition to a clause, see pp. 220f.

---

¹ Moulton Proleg. 100f.

CHAPTER EIGHTEEN

CASE ADDITIONS TO THE VERB: WITH A PREPOSITION [1]

§ 1 Preparatory Note on Prepositions in NT

This study is important for the exegete, provided he is aware that class. niceties must not be pressed too far. In the search for a theology of prepositions it is straining credulity for instance to adopt a distinction between ἐκ and διά in Ro 3³⁰ (ICC Ro in loc.; Moule 195). In Hell. Greek there is a strong preference for the preposition against the simple case, and also a growing laxity which entails closer examination of the context. Thus the meanings of εἰς and ἐν tend to approximate to each other in Hell. Greek.

Although the NT has kept most of the old "proper" prepositions the number was decreasing until only seven were left in MGr, and ἀμφί and ὡς have been discarded as in LXX and pap.[2], while ἀνά and ἀντί have been much curtailed. The variety in the use of each preposition has also diminished. On the other hand, ἐν εἰς ἐκ are much more widely used. The dat. is beginning to wane at this period with all prepositions (except ἐν in NT) and has disappeared entirely with ἀνά μετά περί ὑπό, bringing to a close a development already present in the class.

---

[1] K-G I 448–555. Schwyzer II 417ff. Jannaris 365–399. Wackernagel II 153–248. Mayser II 2, 337–543. F. Krebs, *Die Präpositionen bei Polybius*, Würzburg 1882; *Die Präpositionsadverbia in der späteren historischen Gräcitat*, 2 Teile, Munich 1884–5; *Zur Rection der Kasus in der späteren histor. Gräcitat*, 1887–90. R. Helbing, *Die Präpositionen bei Herodot und andern Historiken* (B.z.h.S.dgr.Spr. 16), 1904. W. Kuhring. *De praepositionum Graecarum in chartis Aegypt. usu quaestiones selectae*, Bonn 1906. C. Rossberg, *De praepositionum Graecarum in chartis Aegypt. Ptolemaeum aetate usu*, Jena 1909. P. F. Regard, *Contributions à l'étude des prépositions dans la langue du NT*, Paris 1919. J. Waldis, *Die Präpositions-Adverbien mit der Bedeutung "vor" in der Septuaginta*, Lucerne 1921-2. M. Johannessohn, DGPS, Berlin 1926. R. F. Rickelson, *The Ablative after διά*, Diss. S.W. Bapt. Sem., 1944. P. Southern, *The NT Use of the Preposition KATA*, ibid. 1949. B. Blackwelder, *Causal Use of Prepositions in the Greek NT*, ibid. 1951. Kittel WB VI 11, 1958, 683ff. (πρό); VI 12, 1958, 720–725 (πρός).

[2] Rossberg 11. Regard Prép. 683f. Mayser II 2, 338.

period. There is now a preference for the accus. In the LXX the dative is used with περί four times only, and with ὑπό in Job 12⁵ A only. In NT the only prepositions which still have all three cases are ἐπί and παρά [1]. In MGr only the accus. is used with prepositions.

The niceties of class. Greek in the precise use of cases after prepositions are obliterated in Hellenistic; the distinctions in the cases after διά ἐπί πρός, for example, are becoming less clear.

Because of the tendency of the language towards fuller forms, the "improper" prepositions begin to gain ground in Hell. Greek: in the NT there are 42, against 18 "proper". These are adverbs or nouns in various cases which assumed the character of prepositions, but are not compounded with verbs. They now supplement the old stock of prepositions.

No distinct line of demarcation between adverbs and prepositions can easily be drawn and the combination of a preposition and adverb is common in the Koine; [2] e.g. in NT ἀπὸ τότε for ἀφ' οὗ Mk 8² D (popular), ἐκ πάλαι etc. [3]

The old adverbial meaning of the prepositions is not well attested in Hell. Greek, except of course when compounded with verbs, and it is doubtful whether all the instances suggested for the NT can be accepted, viz. ὑπέρ (accent?) 2 Co 11²³ ὑπὲρ ἐγώ *I more* (Wackernagel II 167), 11⁵ 12¹¹ ὑπὲρ λίαν (but perhaps a compound ὑπερλίαν, like ὑπερεκπερισσοῦ Eph 3²⁰ 1 Th 3¹⁰ 5¹³), Lk 16⁸ φρονιμώτεροι ὑπέρ; ἐν Mk 1²³ ἐν πνεύματι ἀκαθάρτῳ *with an unclean spirit in him*; Ph 3¹³ ἐν δέ *but thereby*, for ἐν δέ. The Ptol. pap. have παρά thus apparently only once (Mayser II 2, 339) and ἐπὶ δέ *moreover*, ἐξ καὶ πρός *six and more* (Pap. Oxy. I 68²⁴ A.D. 131). The LXX has τὸ πρὸς πρωΐ *right early* Ps. 45⁶, πρὸς ἐπὶ τούτοις *moreover besides this* Sir 29²⁵, and Cant 1¹⁶ has πρός *moreover*, and Aquila Deut 33³ has the same; Aquila Eccles. 1¹⁷ 7²³ ⁽²²⁾ πρός (adv.). Symmachus in Eccles 9² has πρός τε (adv.).

In brief, the LXX and NT share the following innovations of the Hellenistic period in the use of prepositions: (a) the tendency to discard one of the cases where formerly a preposition was used with more than one. (b) Adverbs and adverbial prepositions now supplement the old stock of prepositions: thus

---

[1] On the other hand. the accus. is declining with ὑπό ὑπέρ περί, while μετά περί ὑπό have ceased to take the dat., and κατά has lost its hold of the gen.

[2] Schmid, *Der Attizismus* IV 625. Hatzid. 213.

[3] See also ἀφ' ὅτε Hermas, and μέχρι ὅτε (Blass-Debr. §§ 241, 2; 455, 3).

ἐναντίον, ἐνώπιον etc. for πρό; ἐπάνω for ἐπί; ἀπάνωθεν, ἐπάνωθεν, ὑπεράνω for ὑπέρ; ὑποκάτω for ὑπό; ἀνὰ μέσον for μεταξύ; κύκλῳ, περικύκλῳ for περί; ἐχόμενος etc. for παρά. (c) There is a new use of ὑπέρ and περί. (d) εἰς and ἐν are now confused in two ways: 1. ἐν is used after verbs of motion (= ב), 2. εἰς is used for ἐν after expressions denoting rest. (e) There is a change in the relative frequence of prepositions: e.g. ἀπό encroaches on ἐκ and ὑπό.

§ 2. Prepositional Periphrases for the simple cases

This usage is greatly extended in Hell. Greek; e.g. εἰς and πρός c. accus. serve for the simple dat., ἐν c. dat. for the simple dat., and παρά is used after a comparative in place of the simple gen. In place of the simple gen., Polybius can write ἡ κατὰ τὸν ἥλιον πορεία.

(a) *For Genitive*: see pp. 207ff, 231ff. For partitive ἀπό, see pp. 208f; for gen. of separation, see pp. 258f; for ἀπό instead of accus. after verbs of fleeing, fearing, etc., see p. 244. Besides these, there is the Pauline use of ἀπό in the sense of alienation, where older Greek would have the simple case, e.g. Ro 9³ ἀνάθεμα ... ἀπὸ τοῦ Χ., Col 2²⁰ ἀποθνήσκω ἀπό (for dat.). The following verbs are followed by ἀπό in the same way: παρέρχομαι Mt 26³⁹ = Mk 14³⁵, παραφέρω Mk 14³⁶ = Lk 22⁴² (cp. MGr θὰ περάσω ἀπὸ τὴ Σμύρνη; we must not interpret ἀπό as *far from*), μετανοέω Ac 8²² (ἐκ in Rev 2²¹ etc.; noun in Heb 6¹), ἄφαντος γίνομαι Semitism Lk 24³¹, καταργέομαι Ro 7⁶ Ga 5⁴, φθείρω 2 Co 11³, εἰσακούω Heb 5⁷ (but the meaning is difficult; perhaps *on account of*).

(b) *For Dative*[1]. For διά c. gen. in instrumental or modal use see p. 267. As a circumlocution for the simple case ἐνώπιον c. gen. Ac 6⁵ appears to render לִפְנֵי, בְּעֵינֵי, or נֶגֶד; to a less extent also ἔμπροσθεν, ἐναντίον (Heb 13²¹ 1 Jn 3²²). Lk 15¹⁸·²¹ ἁμαρτάνω ἐνώπιον, Mt 7⁶ βάλλω ἔμπροσθεν, Heb 4¹³ ἐμφανὴς ἐνώπιον.

The preposition ἐν, too, takes the place of plain dat. in instances where *in* is quite unsuitable as a translation.

---

[1] K-G I 436, n. 7; 483. Mayser II 2, 354ff. Johannessohn DGPS 239f. Radermacher² 127.

(i) In an adverbial sense, quite briefly stated. Thus in Ro we have: *powerfully* 1⁴, *openly* 2²⁸, *secretly* ²⁹, *patiently* 9²², *in this way* 14¹⁸, *in carnal things* 15²⁷, *joyfully* ³², *quickly* 16²⁰. Perhaps we may also include the six exx. in 12⁷·⁸: *liberally, zealously, cheerfully*, etc. In 1 Co we have *weakly, fearfully, tremblingly* 2³, 15⁴²·⁴²·⁴³ quat., ἐν πρώτοις 15³, *peacefully* 16¹¹, and perhaps *in love* 16¹⁴. Other NT exx. come to mind: the class. ἐν τάχει *quickly* Lk 18⁸, ἐν δικαιοσύνῃ = δικαίως Ac 17³¹ Rev 19¹¹, ἐν πάσῃ ἀσφαλείᾳ = ἀσφαλέστατα (Ac 5²³), *boldly* (Col 2¹⁵). The ἐν δόλῳ of Mk 14¹ shows how close we are to the instrumental sense: *by means of guile* or *guilefully*.

(ii) An ἐν of accompaniment is apparently the equivalent of μετά or σύν or simple dat. (= *with*), as in class. Greek. The idea of manner is often implied. There is in Mk 1²³ 5² the man *with* the unclean spirit, unless we may take this as *in the power of*; but in 5²⁵ the woman must be *with*, not *in the power of*, a flow of blood. *With* is also the way to translate Lk 14³¹ *with ten thousand* (especially as μετά occurs in the adjacent parallel phrase), Ro 1²⁷ relations *with* women, 15²⁹ to come *with* a blessing, 1 Co 4²¹·²¹ come *with* a rod ... *with* love (but this may be instrumental rather than of accompaniment), Heb 9²²·²⁵ *with* blood, Jude¹⁴ *with* his saints. The method is classical enough and belongs to the Koine, but its use in the LXX to render בְּ seems to have suggested an increase of use in NT. Col 1⁵ ἐν τῷ λόγῳ τῆς ἀληθείας τοῦ εὐαγγελίου *by means of the Gospel* (or perhaps temporal ἐν: *when the true Gospel was preached*.

(iii) There is the relatively frequent instrumental use,[1] in the stricter sense : e.g. nineteen times in Mt 1-14, twenty-five in Ro, twenty-eight in 1 Co, and very common in Rev. It is least common in the second part of Ac. It is as old as Homer, who uses this preposition for seeing *with* the eyes, but it is comparatively rare before the LXX,[2] in which it is extremely common (on the model of בְּ)—much more so proportionately than in the NT. Moreover, it is not very common in the Koine,[3] where many apparent instances, as in NT, may be accepted satisfactorily in the strictly locative sense. We cannot rule out the possibility [4] of *in water* Mt 3¹¹, nor of *in one mouth* Ro 15⁶, since words are certainly formed here, as thoughts were considered to be formed in the heart. Our own idiom is often *in* in these phrases: *in* God's will (Ro 1¹⁰), *in* the likeness (8³), to sum up *in* one word (13⁹), but usually we shall employ *with*. Semitic influence may be behind *swear by* (Mt 5³⁴),

---

[1] K-G I § 431, 3a. Kuhring § 30. Rossberg 28, 2. Mayser II 2, 357f. Deissmann BS 115f (against Hebraism). Johannessohn DGKPS 52ff. N. Turner, "The Preposition EN in the NT," *Bible Translator*, vol. 10, no. 3, 1959. Lagrange *S. Matth.* XCIX.
[2] K-G I 464f. Helbing 146f. Radermacher² 130, n. 4.
[3] ἐν μαχαίρῃ in the pap., but not combined with *kill*, etc. (Moulton Einl. 15f., Kuhring 43f, Rossberg 28, Mayser II 2, 358, 393). NT has ἐν μαχαίρῃ. ἐν ῥομφαίᾳ Mt 26⁵² Lk 22⁴⁹ Rev 2¹⁶ 6⁸ 13¹⁰ 19²¹.
[4] Many readers will prefer a stronger word, even " certainty ". But I hesitate because of the imminent parallel ἐν πνεύματι ἁγίῳ καὶ πυρί.

§ 2] CASE ADDITIONS WITH PREPOSITION

with his arm (Lk 1⁵¹), *ransom by* (Rev 5⁹), *call with a loud voice* (14¹⁵); and Semitic influence was probably at work in Mt 7² ἐν τῷ μέτρῳ (because Lk 6³⁸ avoids it), 7⁶ ἐν τοῖς ποσὶν αὐτῶν, 22¹⁶ ἐν ἀληθείᾳ (because Mk 12¹⁴ Lk 20²¹ have ἐπ' ἀληθείας), 24⁴¹ ἐν τῷ μύλῳ (Lk 17³⁵ ἐπὶ τὸ αὐτό). But Greek usage sufficiently accounts for *salted with* (Mt 5¹³), *to be known by means of* (Lk 24³⁵), *mingle with* (Rev 8³), *burn with fire* (18⁸). So also Mt 9³⁴ Ac 17³¹ Col 1¹⁶.

A causal sense is probably best included here. We must render *because of* at Mt 6⁷ 11⁶ 13⁵⁷ Jn 16³⁰ (= *propterea*) Ac 7²⁹ 24¹⁶ Ro 2¹⁷·²³ 5³·¹¹ 14²¹ 1 Co 2⁵·⁵ 4⁴ 10⁵ Col 1¹⁶, and *because* (ἐν ᾧ) at Ro 2¹ 8³ Heb 2¹⁸ 6¹⁷.

A curious instrumental dat. of price is found with ἐν, a distinctly Semitic construction literally rendering the *beth pretii* ¹: Ro 3²⁵ 5⁹ Rev 5⁹ (*at the cost of his blood*).

Then there is a semi-forensic sense, suggested by 1 Co 6² 11¹³ and found in the Koine: *in your judgment*.

Probably εἰς, as in MGr, also occurs as a substitute for the dat. (or gen.): Ga 3¹⁴ ἵνα εἰς τὰ ἔθνη ἡ εὐλογία τοῦ Ἀβραὰμ γένηται, unless we understand εἰς = *among*. Cp. γίνομαι εἰς in papyri (Mayser II 2, 406) *to fall to someone as a possession*.

(c) *The accus.* occasionally appears in place of the predicative nominative owing to the Hellenistic tendency towards greater expressiveness and this is assisted by the Semitic εἰς (= ל) ², although there are occasionally parallels outside Biblical Greek (Jannaris § 1552, Radermacher² 20f). (i) with γίνομαι and εἰμί: Mt 19⁵ = Ge 2²⁴, 1 Co 6¹⁶ ἔσονται εἰς σάρκα μίαν (but Mt 19⁶ has truer Greek predicative nom.), Mt 21⁴² = Ps 118²² ἐγενήθη εἰς κεφαλήν, Lk 3⁵, 1 Co 15⁴⁵ = Ge 2⁷ ἐγένετο... εἰς ψυχὴν ζῶσαν, 2 Co 6¹⁸ Heb 8¹⁰ LXX, and (outside of quotations) Lk 13¹⁹ ἐγένετο εἰς δένδρον, Jn 16²⁰ ἡ λύπη ὑμῶν εἰς χαρὰν γενήσεται, Ac 5³⁶ ἐγένετο εἰς οὐδέν, 8²³ εἰς γὰρ χολὴν ... ὁρῶ σε ὄντα, 1 Th 3⁵, 1 Jn 5⁸, Rev 8¹¹, 16¹⁹. (ii) with λογίζομαι: ³ Ac 19²⁷, Ro 4³ = Ge 15⁶, 9⁸, 2²⁶, LXX Isa 40¹⁷ 1 Mac 2⁵² (A corrects to nom.).

(d) *For Accusative*: on εἰς for predicative accus. see pp. 246f.

---

¹ *Hebrew and English Lexicon*, ed. Brown, Driver, Briggs, Oxford 1906, s.v. ב, III. 3.
² Zerwick § 20. Johannessohn DGKPS 4f. Psichari 201f. Jannaris § 1552. Helbing 60–67. Moulton Proleg. 71f. Moulton-Howard 462f.
³ Helbing 66f. Bonaccorsi 603f. Mayser II 2, 362ff; 416ff. Heidland in Kittel WB IV 287, 288 n. 4.

§ 3. Anomalies in the use of Prepositions

(a) For ἀπό with nom. see p. 230.

(b) Εἰς for local ἐν [1].

Etymologically these two prepositions are related, and at this period, from c. 150 B.C., εἰς is used instead of ἐν in a local sense, for the distinction between motion and rest becomes obscured in Hell. Greek. The same approximation occurs between πρός c. accus. and παρά c. dat. In the Koine εἰς and ἐν are freely interchanged, until in MGr εἰς has absorbed ἐν completely, consistently with the disappearance of the dat. However, under Hebraic influence ἐν appears almost twice as often as εἰς in NT, and confusion between the two prepositions has already begun, εἰς often appearing for ἐν and more rarely ἐν for εἰς (see p. 257).

Even in the class. period we sometimes find εἰς for ἐν in a compressed or pregnant construction,[2] but no NT writer except Mt [3] is entirely innocent of the replacing of ἐν by εἰς in a local sense; in Lk–Ac most of the exx. are found. Mk 1[9] ἐβαπτίσθη εἰς τὸν Ἰορδάνην (possibly pregnant, implying the notion of *coming*), Lk 9[61] τοῖς εἰς τὸν οἶκόν μου (no idea of motion), 11[7] (D ἐν), Jn 1[18] εἰς τὸν κόλπον (Syr[cur] gen.): there is therefore nothing very profound here concerning mutual motion between Father and Son; nevertheless John (including Rev) does not usually blur the distinction between εἰς and ἐν, and except for Mt he has fewer exx. of εἰς = ἐν than any NT author. Mk 1[39] (EF ἐν) 2[1] (SBD ἐν), 8[26] μηδενὶ εἴπῃς εἰς τὴν κώμην, 10[10] (AC ἐν), 13[3. 9] εἰς συναγωγὰς δαρήσεσθε (= Mt 10[17] ἐν, D εἰς), [16] (= Mt 24[18] Lk 17[31] ἐν), Lk 4[23] (vl. ἐν), 9[61], Jn 20[7] τὸ σουδάριον... ἐντετυλιγμένον εἰς ἕνα τόπον (pregn?), Ac 2[5] (S°BDCE ἐν) [27] OT (motion impossible), [39] τοῖς εἰς μακράν (a Semitism; not in LXX of Isa 57[19]), 4[5] S (pregn?), 7[4] (but perhaps by attraction), [12] (but LXX Ge 42[2], which is cited, has ἐν), 8[23] (or *destined for the gall of bitterness*), 9[21] SA (rest ἐν), 9[28], 11[25] D, 12[25] SB (pregn.?), 14[25] (BCD ἐν), 17[13] D, 18[21] D, 19[22] (D ἐν), 21[13], 23[11. 11], 25[4], 26[20], 1 Pt 5[12] (a post-script?) τὴν χάριν... εἰς ἣν ἑστήκατε KLP. Especially Semitic are the following: Lk 1[44] ἐγένετο ἡ φωνὴ εἰς τὰ ὦτά μου, Ac 20[16] 21[17] 25[15], Jn 17[23] 1 Jn 5[8] εἰς (τὸ) ἕν. But εἰς = ἐν occurs in the secular Koine: P. Oxy VI 929[12] ταῦτα δὲ πάντα συνενῆι εἰς τὸν χιτῶνα καροῖνον *inside the brown tunic*, see also Bauer s.v. εἰς.

---

[1] Mayser II 2, 371ff. Moulton Einl. 93. Rossberg 54. Radermacher[2] 140, 145. Johannessohn DGPS 330ff.

[2] As in NT Jn 9[7] ὕπαγε νίψαι εἰς τὴν κολυμβήθραν, 20[19]. 26 ἔστη εἰς τὸ μέσον, 1 Pt 3[20] εἰς ἣν ὀλίγοι διεσώθησαν *by entering which* (pregn.).

[3] C. H. Turner examined the use of εἰς for ἐν in Mk and pointed out that Matthew and Luke disliked the confusion, especially Matthew. See *JThS* 26, p. 14.

The Pauline and Johannine epistles and Rev (in spite of its Semitic character) do not often confuse local ἐν and εἰς. This is important for the exegete, because in Mt, the epistles, and Rev we can always presume that εἰς has its full sense even where one might suspect that it stood for ἐν (e.g. Mt 28^{19} baptism *into* the name, i.e. a relationship as the goal of baptism; also Mt 10^{41} receiving a righteous man εἰς ὄνομα of a righteous man, which is not the same as ἐν ὀνόματι, for it has the Semitic causal sense, εἰς being לְ. See לְשֵׁם Jo 9^9 Ezk 36^{22}: *because of* or *for the sake of* a righteous man's name. Cp. Mt 12^{41} they repented *because of* the preaching of Jonah. See Zerwick § 70a, 76. But in Mt 5^{35} μὴ ὀμόσαι ... εἰς Ἱεροσόλυμα, *by*).

In the LXX (e.g. Ge 31^{33} Nu 35^{33}), Diodorus (e.g. 3, 44), and in Hermas (e.g. V, I 2, 2; II 4, 3; S. I 2), εἰς = ἐν is common. Note especially κρύπτω εἰς Jb 40^8 $^{(13)}$, Pr 1^{11} Isa 2^{10} Je 4^{29} Ps 88^{40} (Johannessohn DGPS 331f, Jannaris § 1548, Oepke in Kittel WB II 418f. n). There do not seem to be any papyrus exx. earlier than the Imperial period, e.g. P. Fay. 111^{11} b (A.D. 95–100) ἐνετιλάμην συ εἰς Διονυσιάδα μῖναι *I have bid you remain at Dionysias*. The earlier examples are pregnant with the idea of motion (Mayser II 2, 371ff), but while it is true that some of the instances in NT (especially Lk 21^{37} Jn 19^{13}) may be the "pregnant" construction, the real explanation at this date lies not so much here as in the inevitable progress of the absorption of ἐν by εἰς [1].

(c) Interchange of εἰς and ἐν in a metaphorical (non-local) sense.

Polyb. V 13, 8 εἰς δὲ τὴν ὑστέραιον *on the next day*, Lk 1^{20} εἰς τὸν καιρὸν αὐτῶν *at their proper time* (ἐν correctly Mt 21^{41} 2 Th 2^6), 13^9 εἰς τὸ μέλλον *in the future* (P. Oxy. I 36, iii 3), class. ἐς αὔριον, Ac 13^{42} εἰς τὸ μεταξὺ σάββατον *on the next Sabbath*, 2 Co 13^2 Ph 1^{10} εἰς ἡμέραν Χριστοῦ, 1 Th 4^{15} εἰς τὴν παρουσίαν (P. Oxy. XIV. 1764. 9). In Ac 7^{53} εἰς διαταγὰς ἀγγέλων may be a Hebraism (A. T. Robertson 482) or an Aramaism (*Beginnings* II 148). Also εἰς varies with ἐν in the formula which renders לְךָ לְשָׁלוֹם (1 Km 1^{17} etc., Mk 5^{34} Lk 7^{50} 8^{48} εἰς; LXX Jg 18^{6}B Jas 2^{16} Lk 7^{50}D 8^{48}D ἐν). We have εἰς in the baptismal formula Ac 19^3 εἰς τὸ Ἰωάννου βάπτισμα. Corresponding to Heb בְּ, εἰς or ἐν occurs where the dat. would suffice, with πιστεύω, ὄμνυμι, εὐδοκέω (e.g. with βαπτίζω: Ac 8^{16} 19^5 εἰς τὸ ὄνομα, as well

---

[1] For this reason alone the argument of J. H. Greenlee seems mistaken in his article in *The Bible Translator*, vol. 3, Jan. 1952.

as Ac 10⁴⁸ ἐν τῷ ὀνόματι). Variation occurs too with ποιέω and ἐργάζομαι (see pp. 236f.). In Jn 15²¹ ποιήσουσιν εἰς ὑμᾶς and Mt 26¹⁰ ἠργάσατο εἰς ἐμέ, εἰς occurs where one expects ἐν. With ἴστημι: Ro 5² ἐν ᾗ ἐστήκαμεν, but 1 Pt 5¹² εἰς ἥν στῆτε. But variation was possible in class. Greek also with verbs of public speaking; so in NT κηρύσσω Mk 13¹⁰ εἰς (D ἐν), 14⁹ εἰς (Mt has ἐν), Lk 24⁴⁷ 1 Th 2⁹ (S* dat.), and εὐαγγελίζομαι Ga 1¹⁶ ἐν, 1 Pt 1²⁵ εἰς; Ac 17¹⁵ D; "it is an Aramaic construction" (Black AAGA² 71).

But a distinction between the two prepositions may sometimes, especially in Paul, be intended. Ph 1⁵ κοινωνία εἰς τὸ εὐαγγέλιον: Jerome (Vulg.) and other translators may have failed to appreciate that Paul is not prone to confuse εἰς and ἐν. A process may be envisaged therefore (Zerwick § 77). The Vulg. etc. may also be wrong at Ph 2¹¹: not *confiteatur quia dominus Iesus Christus in gloria est Dei Patris*, but *in gloriam* (confess *to* the glory of . . .), Zerwick § 78. Even more important theologically, the distinction between εἰς and ἐν has been missed in Col 1¹⁶: *omnia per ipsum et ipso* (εἰς αὐτόν) *creata sunt*; but to Paul Christ is the *efficient and the final* cause (§ 79). Probably the only instance where Paul does confuse them is Eph 3¹⁶ κραταιωθῆναι . . . εἰς τὸν ἔσω ἄνθρωπον (strangely, Vulg. has *in* c. accus.: §80).

(*d*) Sometimes also εἰς appears to stand for ἐπί and πρός. Except for mere stylistic variation there *is* no point in the change in Phm⁵ πρὸς τὸν κύριον 'Ι. καὶ εἰς πάντας τοὺς ἁγίους (so also 2 Ti 2²¹ 3¹⁷). In Mk 5³⁸ καὶ ἔρχονται εἰς τὸν οἶκον, the sequel εἰσελθὼν λέγει αὐτοῖς makes it clear that εἰς = πρός. In Mk the instances of πρός are limited and εἰς assumes much of the sphere of πρός and ἐν; the full meaning of εἰς and ἐν cannot be insisted on. So also Mt 12⁴¹ *repent* c. εἰς (class. πρός), 21¹, Mk 11¹, ⁸ (= ἐπί), Lk 9¹⁰ 18³⁵ 19²⁹, Jn 4⁵ εἰς πόλιν *to*, not *into*, 11³¹, ³⁸ ὑπάγει (ἔρχεται) εἰς (D in ³⁸ corrects to ἐπί) τὸ μνημεῖον *towards*, and in 20³ εἰς cannot be *into* (from the context). Ἁμαρτάνω c. εἰς: Mt 18²¹ Lk 15¹⁸ (cp. P. Eleph. 1, 9 κακοτεχνεῖν μηδὲν . . . εἰς Δημητρίαν); βλασφημέω εἰς Lk 12¹⁰. There is the Hebraism (or Aramaism) in Lk 15²² δότε δακτύλιον εἰς τὴν χεῖρα (for class. περί), and εἰς often directs to a part of the body *to*, or *on*, which an act is done: Mk 8²³ Mt 27³⁰ ἔτυπτον εἰς τὴν κεφαλήν, 2 Co 11²⁰, cp. P. Tebt. III 798¹⁶ λακτίσαντες εἰς τὴν κοιλίαν, Acta Petr. et Paul. 187¹ δραμὼν τῇ ἐξῆς ἡμέρᾳ 'Ιουβενάλιος ἔρριψεν ἑαυτὸν εἰς τὰ ἴχνη τοῦ Πέτρου. With verbs of seeing:

Mt 22¹⁶ βλέπω εἰς, cp. P. Oxy XIV 1680¹¹ βλέπων εἰς τὸ ἀσύστατον. With verbs of speaking: Jn 8²⁶ λαλῶ εἰς τὸν κόσμον.

It may be that πρός tends to be used with a personal object, εἰς with an impersonal: 2 Co 1¹⁵ᶠ πρὸς ὑμᾶς, then εἰς Μακεδονίαν, εἰς τὴν Ἰουδαίαν; Mk 2¹³ πρὸς αὐτόν but 3⁷ a vl. gives εἰς τὴν θάλασσαν. Nevertheless εἰς αὐτόν Ro 11³⁶.

(e) Confusion of διά τινος and τινα. See pp. 267f.

(f) Confusion of παρά τινος and τινι. See p. 273.

(g) Use of ἐν for εἰς. This occurs often enough in the LXX and even in Imperial and later papyri (Johannessohn DGPS 330ff; Mayser II 2, 372f).

Since there are 2,698 exx. of ἐν in NT it is not surprising that sometimes it bears the meaning of *into* or *into a state of* (especially ἐν μέσῳ). Mt 26²³ after *dip* (but Mk 14²⁰ εἰς), Lk 1¹⁷ ἐπιστρέψαι ... ἐν φρονήσει δικαίων (or instrumental ἐν?), 4¹ (SBDLW have ἐν after *was led*) but the parallel has εἰς (Mt 4¹); Ro 1²³·²⁵ have ἐν after *change*, but 1⁶ has εἰς. After ἱστάναι (tr.) and τιθέναι the use of ἐν is class. : Ac 5²⁷; Mt 27⁶⁰ (Mk 4³⁰ is instrumental), Mk 6²⁹·⁵⁶ 15⁴⁶ Lk 1⁶⁶ 21¹⁴ 23⁵³ Jn 19⁴¹ Ac 1⁷ 5⁴·¹⁸·²⁵ 7¹⁶ 9³⁷ Ro 9³³ 1 Co 12²⁸ 2 Co 5¹⁹ 1 Pt 2⁶. Sometimes after δίδωμαι the preposition is pleonastic and means no more than *to*, but not always: Lk 12⁵¹ (*bring into*), Jn 3⁵³ (*committed into*), 2 Co 1²², 8¹⁶ (*put into the heart*). After other verbs of motion of course the usage is more extensive in later Greek than in class., especially so in LXX. The usage is not class. after verbs of coming and going (e.g. Rev 11¹¹ A), but it is literary and non-literary Hellenistic.

However, ἐν, is not likely to be *to* or *into* after ἔρχομαι in Mk. Except for ἐπί c. accus. in two instances, Mark's rule is invariable for expressing motion after this verb: εἰς (22 times) or πρός (12 times); and so in 5²⁷ 8³⁸ 13²⁶ the prepositional phrase will not express motion from place to place, but rather the accompanying circumstances or the sphere in which motion occurs. Nor is there any support at all for the rendering *into* after πίπτω in Heb 4¹¹; never, except in the compound ἐν μέσῳ, does ἐν occur in NT in a pregnant sense after this verb, even in the more Semitic parts. In a work like Hebrews it is even less likely to occur in the LXX sense of a literal rendering of ב. Nor is Lk 7¹⁷ a case of constructio praegnans: the Word spread abroad *in* .... (Nain is certainly away from Judaea, but the addition of "surrounding districts" makes *in* more natural than *to*.)

§ 4. True Prepositions[1]

I. WITH ONE CASE

Hellenistic Greek tends to limit prepositions to one case each, preferably accus.

(a) Genitive

'Αντί is represented by 318 exx. in LXX, but only 22 in NT. The class. ἀνθ' ὧν remains, and coincides with Heb. תַּחַת אֲשֶׁר etc.: *because* Lk 1²⁰ 19⁴⁴ Ac 12²³ 2 Th 2¹⁰; *therefore* Lk 12³. It alternates with ὅτι and διότι in Biblical Greek, and sometimes the two are combined: ἀνθ' ὧν ὅτι. For *therefore* there is also ἀντὶ τούτου. The class. ἀντί with a kind of gen. of price also remains: Mt 17²⁷ δὸς αὐτοῖς ἀντὶ ἐμοῦ καὶ σοῦ (class. ὑπέρ), 20²⁸ = Mk 10⁴⁵ λύτρον ἀντὶ πολλῶν (1 Ti 2⁶ ἀντίλυτρον ὑπέρ), Ro 12¹⁷ κακὸν ἀντὶ κακοῦ. Clearly in a substitutionary sense: Lk 11¹¹ ἀντὶ ἰχθύος ὄφιν, 1 Co 11¹⁵ κόμη ἀντὶ περιβολαίου (*instead of a wrap*), Jas 4¹⁵ ἀντὶ τοῦ λέγειν ὑμᾶς (*instead of saying*). It is more difficult to decide in the case of the atonement passages and of Jn 1¹⁶ χάριν ἀντὶ χάριτος ἐλάβομεν (substitutionary? i.e. the Spirit *in place of* Jesus' presence; or does it imply *a succession of* graces?)[2].

'Από takes the place of ὑπό in a causal sense[3]. Mt 13⁴⁴ etc. ἀπὸ τῆς χαρᾶς, Lk 12⁵⁷ ἀφ' ἑαυτῶν κρίνετε *because of yourselves? for your own sake?*, 22⁴⁵ *for grief* (class. ὑπό), Ac 20⁹ κατενεχθεὶς ἀπὸ τοῦ ὕπνου, 2 Pt 1²¹ ὑπὸ πνεύματος ἁγίου φερόμενοι ἐλάλησαν ἀπὸ θεοῦ ἄνθρωποι (or perhaps for τὰ ἀπὸ θεοῦ?). The MSS vary greatly between ἀπό and ὑπό with the agent after passive verbs: Lk 1²⁶ angel sent ἀπὸ τοῦ θεοῦ, Lk 6¹⁸ 7³⁵ 8⁴³ Ac 10³³ 15⁴. 2 Co 7¹³ Jas 1¹³ 5⁴ Rev 12⁶ (all pregnant: *prepared and derived from?*). Note the variants: Mt 11¹⁹ B² CDEF ἀπὸ τῶν τέκνων, 16²¹ (D ὑπό), Mk 8³¹ AXW (1st hand), Ac 4⁹D ³⁶B (D ὑπό) 15⁴ BC (yet ὑπό in previous verse) 1 Pt 2⁴ C. Variants for ὑπό in LXX: Isa 11¹¹ (AQ ἀπό) etc.

'Από stands for παρά c. gen. (rare in class. Greek): after ἀκούω

---

[1] K-G I § 428ff. Krebs, D. P. Polyb. Radermacher² 137ff. Moulton Einl. 158ff. Johannessohn DGKPS; DGPS. Mayser II 2, 373ff.
[2] J. M. Bover, "Χάριν ἀντὶ χάριτος", *Biblica* 6, 1925, 454–460. M. Black, *JThS* 42, 1941, 69f (*grace instead of disgrace*).
[3] Imperial papyri, see Kuhring 35. See also Johannessohn DGPS 281f. Also MGr.

(see pp. 233f), μανθάνω (Ga 3² Col 1⁷), παραλαμβάνω (1 Co 11²³ etc.). After *coming* from a person: Jn 3² 16³⁰ ἀπὸ θεοῦ (Jn 8⁴² ἐκ, 16²⁷ παρά, ²⁸ ἐκ), Ga 2¹².

The confusion of ἀπό and ἐκ is common enough in Hell. Greek, and the process of incorporating ἐκ in ἀπό has begun already in NT; nevertheless ἐκ still outnumbers ἀπό: thus Rev has proportion 100 : 20. In a local sense the usage is still fairly accurate, except e.g. in Mk 16⁹ (C*DWL correct to παρά), Ac 13⁵⁰ 16³⁹ (E corrects to ἐκ, since they went *out of*, not *from*, the city), Heb 11¹⁵. But particularly in Lk, ἀπό is used with ἐξέρχομαι (going *out of*): 13 times, and never with ἐκ, in contrast to Mk who only once has ἀπό with ἐξέρχομαι (11¹²), but ἐκ 10 times (Zerwick § 62a). Nevertheless ἐξέρχομαι does have the sense of going *away from* in Lk 5⁸ (ἔξελθε ἀπ' ἐμοῦ). Similarly Ac 12⁷ has ἐκ where one expects ἀπό (ἐξέπεσαν αὐτοῦ αἱ ἁλύσεις ἐκ τῶν χειρῶν).

But to mark the place of origin, ἀπό appears as well as ἐκ: Mt 21¹¹, Jn 1⁴⁴ has both (ἦν ὁ Φ. ἀπὸ Βηθσαϊδά, ἐκ τῆς πόλεως 'Ανδρέου), ⁴⁵ (but ⁴⁶ 4²² ἐκ), 11¹ has both (ἀπὸ Βηθανίας, ἐκ τῆς κώμης Μαρίας), Ac 10³⁸; ἀπό apparently occurs where πόλις or κώμη is not included. Always ἀπό for the country of origin (except in Jn): Ac 6⁹ 21²⁷ 23⁸⁴ 24¹⁶, papyri (Mayser II 1, 14ff; II 2, 377, 383.).

In the sense of *after* (class. ἐκ): Mk 7⁴ ἀπ' ἀγορᾶς *on return from market*, Heb 11³⁴ ἀπὸ ἀσθενείας *after weakness*. Temporal sense: ἀπὸ τότε Mt 16²¹ 26¹⁶ Lk 16¹⁶ (never ἐκ), ἀπ' ἄρτι Jn 13¹⁹ etc. (never ἐξ), but ἐκ τούτου Jn 6⁶⁶ 19¹² etc. (unless causal), ἀπὸ δὲ τῶν ἡμερῶν 'Ἰωάνου Mt 11¹², ἀπὸ καταβολῆς κόσμου Mt 25³⁴ Lk 11⁵⁰ Heb 4³ 9²⁶ Rev 13⁸ 17⁸, ἀπὸ κτίσεως κόσμου Ro 1²⁰; but ἐκ παιδιόθεν Mk 9²¹, ἐκ γενετῆς Jn 9¹, ἐκ κοιλίας μητρός μου Ga 1¹⁵ (cp. LXX Isa 49¹), ἐκ πολλῶν ἐτῶν Ac 24¹⁰, ἐκ τοῦ αἰῶνος Jn 9³².

There cannot be much significance in the change in 1 Th 2⁶ οὔτε ζητοῦντες ἐξ ἀνθρώπων οὔτε ἀφ' ὑμῶν οὔτε ἀπ' ἄλλων. Vulg. ignores the distinction; in Mt 3¹⁶ ἀνέβη ἀπὸ τοῦ ὕδατος (after standing on the bank?) surely nothing different is intended from Mk's ἀναβαίνων ἐκ τοῦ ὕδατος (Mk 1¹⁰).

'Ἐκ: for partitive use, see pp. 208ff. As subjective gen. 2 Co 8⁷ τῇ ἐξ ὑμῶν ἐν ἡμῖν ἀγάπῃ, 9² (p⁴⁶ SBCP om ἐξ). One or two peculiarities confront us: it is used in a causal sense ¹ (= ὑπό):

---

¹ Mayser II 2, 388f. Abel § 46 b. MGr: Thumb² § 161, 5.

Mt 23²⁵ *they are full because of greed*, but perhaps *full of greed*, Jn 4⁶ *because of the journey*, 2 Co 7⁹ ζημιωθῆτε ἐξ ἡμῶν, 13⁴ ἐξ ἀσθενείας, 1 Pt 2¹² *because of good deeds*, 1 Jn 4⁶ ἐκ τούτου γινώσκομεν (or instr.), Rev 8¹³ οὐαί . . . ἐκ, 16¹⁰·¹¹·¹² *because of*. The instrumental use is similar: class. σωτηρία ἔκ τινος, θνήσκω ἔκ τινος, and τὰ ἐξ Ἑλλήνων τείχεα; Lk 16⁹ *make friends* ἐκ τοῦ μαμωνᾶ, Jn 6⁶⁵ Rev 2¹¹ (like the class. δωρηθὲν ἐκ θεῶν, Ac 26²³ (or local?), Ga 3⁸ ἐκ πίστεως *by means of?*, 1 Jn 4⁶ (see causal), Rev 18³ ἐκ . . . ἐπλούτησαν; papyri in Abel § 46 b. Rev 15² τοὺς νικῶντας ἐκ τοῦ θηρίου is probably a compressed phrase (sc. *by separating themselves from* or *and delivered themselves from*). It is difficult to decide in Ro 1⁴ ὁρισθέντος υἱοῦ θεοῦ . . . ἐξ ἀναστάσεως whether ἐκ is causal or temporal. A frequent use in Paul is the sense *belonging to* (*-ists*, of a sect or school): ὁ ἐκ or οἱ ἐκ Ro 3²⁶ οἱ ἐκ πίστεως Ἰησοῦ *believers in Jesus* (the noun after ἐκ expresses the character or standards of these men), 4¹⁴ οἱ ἐκ νόμου *nomistae*, ¹⁶ *who share Abraham's faith*, Ga 3⁷·⁹, 3¹⁰ *believers in justification by works*. Outside Paul (without def. art.): Jn 8²³ etc. 1 Jn 3¹⁹ *God-ists, devil-ists, world-ists*, also Jn 8⁴⁴·⁴⁷ 15¹⁹ 17¹⁴ 1 Jn 3⁸·¹⁰·¹². Indeed ἐκ in general is very common in the Johannine writings.

Πρό has 48 instances, mainly temporal, e.g. Mt 5¹² 8²⁹ Lk 2²¹ Jn 11⁵⁵ (D has πρὶν τὸ πάσχα in accordance with the general preference for accus. with prepositions in Hell. Greek), 1 Co 2⁷. It is local: Ac 5²³ vl., 12⁶ (vl. πρός c. dat.),¹⁴, Jas 5⁹. Preference: Jas 5¹² 1 Pt 4⁸, perhaps Col 1¹⁷ (or temporal). For the Hellenistic construction πρὸ ἐξ ἡμερῶν τοῦ πάσχα (Jn 12¹), πρὸ ἐτῶν δεκατεσσάρων (2 Co 12²) etc., see Wackernagel II 194f: like the Latin means of dating with *ante*, e.g. *ante diem tertium Nonas Maias* (the second day before the nones of May). But the earliest exx. are before the date of Latin influence: LXX Am 1¹ πρὸ δύο ἐτῶν τοῦ σεισμοῦ, Herm S. VI 5, 3, Hom. Clem. 9¹, 13¹¹, Did. 7⁴ (see also Jannaris § 1651, K-G I 391, Johannessohn DGPS 188f, Moulton Proleg. 100ff. See previous chapter, p. 248).

(b) *Dative*

Ἐν. See pp. 254–7 for εἰς and ἐν confused. In spite of the substitution of εἰς by some authors, ἐν is the most popular preposition in NT. J. H. Moulton described it as "a maid of all work" in late Greek and thought the increasing vagueness of its meaning contributed to its ultimate disappearance; in MGr it no longer survives in the spoken language. In the Koine all the prepositions become increasingly elastic and their sense has to be determined more often by the context than was earlier the case. This is notably so with εἰς, ἐν and ἐκ. Such elasticity makes it dangerous to press doctrinal distinctions as though our authors were writing class. Greek. For idiomatic translation, either the immediate context or else parallel usage of the prepositional expression in other contexts will be decisive. But *in* or *among* is still the primary meaning in Hell. Greek, even NT Greek.

Three factors contributed to the popularity and extension of usage in NT: first, the growing lack of clarity in the dat. case; then, the influence of the LXX, wherein ἐν had been widely employed to render the much-used ב; but equally important is the influence of Christian ideas, especially in phrases peculiar and vital to the Christian religion, like *in Christ*.

The meanings in NT may be classified: (1) Local: (a) *in* etc., actual and metaphorical, (b) *into* etc. (praegnans); see p. 257. (2) Temporal: *in, at, within, during*. (3) Peculiarly Christian usages, especially *in the Lord, in Christ*. After this we reach controversial meanings, where the idea of *within* is seldom satisfactory, and these together represent about one-third of all the NT instances: (4) Circumstance and instrument. (5) As a dat. of advantage or disadvantage. (6) Various occasional uses: reference, rate, etc.

(1) *Local*: (a) The meaning which still predominates in NT is *within, inside, on, at, among*, but a distinction must be made between those in a material sense and those in a metaphorical sense. Among the former are quotation-formulae: *in the book* (ἐν τῷ Ὡσηέ Ro 9²⁵), *in the Law, in David* (Heb 4⁷), ἐν Ἠλίᾳ *in the story of Elijah* Ro 11², of which there are class. exx. (K-G I 431, 462–6): as well as *among* and *in the house of* (ἐν τοῖς τοῦ Lk 2⁴⁹), and *at home* (Mk 2¹ 1 Co 11³⁴ 14³⁵), and the class. ἐν μέσῳ; there is also the notion of being *inside* clothing or equipment (Mk 12³⁸ Jn 20¹² Jas 2²) which is class. Among the metaphorical are phrases like *in the heart, in secret, in prayers, in thoughts, in the mortal body, on the right hand, in the mouth, in*

glory, in the vine, in a race, in the church. There are some borderline cases: 1 Co 7¹⁷ may be *in* or *to* the churches. Ac 17³¹ ἐν ἀνδρί may be *in the person of* or may be instrumental. There may be a causal ἐν in Ro 1²⁴ (*because of the lusts of their hearts*); [1] so also 1²¹.

The local sense is slightly extended to denote *in the sphere of*, especially of God, Christ, and the gospel, and probably also of the Spirit's sanctification (1 Pt 1²) and the Name. The following are some spheres *in* which individuals, Christians or not, are mentioned: the gospel, the Law, darkness, circumcision, uncircumcision, grace (but in Ro 5² it may be instrum.), new life, death, sin, the flesh, the spirit, a calling, Adam (for in 1 Co 15²² it is not instrumental; Adam is a representative man *in* whom all mankind is viewed), the Christian wife or husband (1 Co 7¹⁴ also representative). 1 Co 7¹⁵ might be *in the sphere of* (Christian) peace, or probably *into* peace. Ro has 23 exx. of this use, and 1 Co has 14.

(b) *into*: see p. 257.

(2) *Temporal meanings*: ἐν often reinforces the dat. of time, both point of time and duration. The first may be rendered *in*, *at*, or *on*; the second by *within* or *during*, e.g. *in one day* (1 Co 10⁸), and this may be the way to take ἐν ὀλίγῳ in Ac 26²⁸ (*in a short time*), although *by a short argument* (scil. λόγῳ) is not impossible. Note here also ἐν with the articular infin., especially with Luke; most NT exx. have the temporal significance, and sometimes it is the class. meaning: e.g. *in rowing* Mk 6⁴⁸, *in the abounding* Lk 12¹⁵, *in turning* Ac 3²⁶, and also Mt 13⁴ Mk 6⁴⁸ Ro 3⁴ 15¹³ Ga 4¹⁸. All these are present infin. and the meaning is usually *while*, but with aor. infin. *when* or *after* (e.g. Lk 9³⁶). However, this is not invariable, because the aor. construction in 1 Co 11²¹ must mean *while you are eating* or *in eating*.

(3) *Peculiarly Christian usages*: the phrases *in Christ, in the Lord*, difficult to define, occur in Ro, for instance, 21 times and in 1 Co 21 times. The inventiveness of Christian usage is seen also in their frequent resort to similar expressions, such as *in the truth, in the Spirit, in the Name*. Sometimes Paul says we are in Christ (or the Spirit), and sometimes that Christ (or the Spirit) is in us: once indeed he says both in the same sentence,

---

[1] H. A. A. Kennedy, *Exp. T.* xxviii, 322, argues for this.

Ro 8⁹ *you are not in the flesh but in the Spirit, if the Spirit of God dwells in you*. Such ideas seem to be mutually exclusive and it is tempting in view of contemporary Greek to translate the preposition simply *belongs to* or *with*. However, full weight must be given to the mystical conception of being *in Christ*[1], inside a new sphere of experience and spiritual existence, so that the early Christian could define it illogically and experientially as Christ being *in me*. In no other way is the ἐν of the Johannine epistle to be explained: *in* (not *with*) God is no darkness; men walk *in the sphere of* either darkness or light, truth or lies, love or hate; his word is *in* us, his love is made perfect *in* us, we abide *in* God and he abides *in* us (*with* is inadequate). It would be misleading to explain this as God *with* us or *for* us, and we *with* him; it is more profound. This applies to all other Christian experiences: hope, consecration, peace. It would not be safe to ignore the primary force of the preposition in any of these. They are states in which the believer moves. It is legitimate to take Eph 4⁴ 1 Th 4⁷ 1 Co 7¹⁵ as instances of *constructio praegnans*; but then the translation is *into*, not simply *to*. Paul carefully distinguishes ἐπί from ἐν in 1 Th 4⁷ and has a reason for the change from one preposition to the other. It is misleading in Col 3²⁰ to render *pleasing TO the Lord*; Paul means that obedience to parents is fit and proper *in that state* of grace in which the Christian now lives. In Paul, *to* after εὐάρεστος is simple dat., not ἐν, and we would expect only the dat. here if *to* is meant; moreover, the parallel with ἐν κυρίῳ, in the command to women just above, would be lost; for just above it can only mean *in the Lord*. We perceive then that it is from theology and Biblical syntax, and not from comparative syntax, that light is shed on this peculiar relationship expressed by ἐν; to compare non-Biblical parallels is largely irrelevant. Internal syntax-study reveals for the NT that πιστεύω is followed by εἰς or ἐπί or simple dat. when it means *believe in* someone or something; when the meaning is *believe* someone, it has the simple dat. The instances with ἐν are predicated of Christ or the gospel and mean *in the sphere of* Mk 1¹⁵ Jn 3¹⁵ vl. [2].

---

[1] A. Deissmann, *Die nt. Formel " in Christo Jesu "*, Marburg, 1892. Oepke in Kittel WB II 534 n. Zerwick § 88.

[2] The same is probably true of πίστις ἐν: Ro 3²⁵ Col 1². ⁴ Eph 1¹. ¹⁵ 1 Ti 3¹³ 2 Ti 3¹⁵ either *the belief of those who are in Christ*, or *Christ's personal faith*. (In Eph 3¹² the object after πίστις is expressed by a gen.)

With καλέω in 1 Co 7¹⁸ the phrase does not mean *to un-circumcision* but *while he was uncircumcised*; and 7²⁴ *let each remain in the state he was in when he was called*. Therefore in 7²² (ἐν κυρίῳ κληθείς) it is the less likely that the meaning is *called to* or *by* the Lord. Moreover, the presence of another preposition besides ἐν in Col 3¹⁵ indicates that here ἐν cannot mean *to* but must denote membership *within* the Body. Elsewhere in NT εἰς is used with καλέω for inviting *to* weddings, fellowship, eternal life, and glory; and ἐπί with dat. for inviting to liberty and impurity (nine times in all). In Ro 6¹¹ there is the simple dat. as well as ἐν: ζῶντας δὲ τῷ θεῷ ἐν Χριστῷ Ἰησοῦ. When Paul means *to live to*, and not *in the sphere of*, he uses the simple dat.: Ga 2¹⁹, Ro 6¹⁰, 14⁷·⁸, 2 Co 5¹⁵; and when he means *to live by* he uses ἐκ: 1 Co 9¹⁴ 2 Co 13⁴·⁴ and OT quotations. There can be no question about the meaning of ἐν with ζάω in Ga 2²⁰ Ph 1²² *in the flesh*, Col 2²⁰ *in this world*, Ti 2¹² *in the present age*. For *to* with φανερόω the dat. is used; ἐν means *in, in the sphere of*. So with παρρησιάζομαι.

(4) *Circumstance and instrument*: see pp. 241, 252f.

(5) *Advantage or disadvantage*. No doubt occasionally ἐν c. dat. stands pleonastically for the normal dat., *to* or *for*[1] (sometimes in Attic poetry): *did to him* Mt 17¹², *done to me* Mk 14⁶, *speak to the perfect* 1 Co 2⁶, *veiled to those* 2 Co 4³, *to me* (perhaps *through me*) Ga 1¹⁶. *To the churches* is possible in 1 Co 7¹⁷ 2 Co 8¹ 2 Th 1⁴, but *within* is not impossible; *among* is possible Lk 2¹⁴ Ac 4¹² (the sphere of activity is emphasized). *Among* is possible Ro 10²⁰, where the presence of the preposition depends on the variant readings; 1st time p⁴⁷ BDFG; 2nd time BD). It may well be that in 1 Co 14¹¹ ἐν (SBA) was inserted by Paul in order to prevent λαλῶν being taken closely with ἐμοί, but it is omitted by some good authorities (p⁴⁶ DFG Clem. Alx. Chrys.). Jas 5³·⁵ ἐν not equivalent to a plain dat. (*treasure for the last days, for a day of slaughter*) but εἰς of Greek OT is deliberately altered to ἐν, since we are now *in* the last days. Jude ¹ (difficult): the preposition may be displaced, but *beloved in God* in the Christian mystical sense is reasonable. Ac 20³² not simply a general statement that God's grace gives an inheritance *to* those who are sanctified, but that he will give to these

---

[1] Zerwick § 90.

particular saints at Ephesus, whose pastors Paul is addressing, an inheritance *among* all the sanctified, emphasizing the corporate nature of the Church *within* which these believers have their place [1].

(6) *Various occasional usages.* There are still a few phrases which elude classification. There is the ἐν which, as in the papyri, seems to mean *amounting to, at the rate of*, in the parable of the Sower: *sixtyfold, a hundredfold* Mk $4^{8.\ 20}$, and the quotation at Ac 7^{14}. A meaning *consisting in ordinances* Eph 2^{15} can be supported from the papyri, and this seems right at 1 Co 4^{20}; RSV *the kingdom ... does not consist in talk*. For ἐν = occupied in (1 Ti 4^{15} Col 4^2) we have papyrus support. It is permissible to classify a number of phrases as dat. of reference: *concerning* or *with reference to*. In Ro 8^{37} we are said to be conquerors *with regard to* all these things: 11^2 *about Elijah*. So also 14^{22} 15^{13} 16^2 1 Co $1^{5.\ 5.\ 7.\ 10}$ 3^{21} 4^2 7^{15} 9^{15} 12^6 $15^{28.\ 41.\ 58}$. A variety of interpretations is possible at Col 2^{15} (1) local *in him*, or *on it* (the cross), (2) instrum. *by means of him* or *by means of it* (the cross; cp. Eph 2^{16}).

Σύν: *including* in Attic Greek (μετά *with*). Ionic and Hellenistic *with*, synom. for μετά. In NT, most frequent in Lk-Ac (but Ac 14^4 οἱ μὲν ἦσαν σὺν τοῖς Ἰουδαίοις, οἱ δὲ σὺν τοῖς ἀποστόλοις has something of the inclusive meaning of *on the side of*). It is absent from Heb, 1 Pt, 2 Th, Phm, Past, Johann. Epistles, Rev [2], and almost absent from Jn (12^2 18^1; without vl. only 21^3; μετά very common). Only in Col does Paul make much use of it. It appears to be a synonym of μετά, e.g. Mt 26^{35} σὺν σοὶ ἀποθνήσκω *in your company*, Lk 9^{32} Πέτρος καὶ οἱ σὺν αὐτῷ, 1 Th 4^{17} 5^{10} Ph 1^{23} Jas 1^{11}.

(c) *Accusative*

This becomes the popular case with prepositions in Hellenistic Greek.

Ἀνά: [3] rare in class. Greek, only 13 times in NT and only in ἀνὰ μέσον, ἀνὰ μέρος *in turn*, and in distributive sense as a

---

[1] Luke does not in fact use δίδωμι with ἐν for *give to*. Out of 81 occasions when he uses this verb with a possible indirect object, 74 have simple dat., and of the seven others it is very doubtful whether the preposition means *to* in any instance: it more naturally introduces an adverbial expression and is not an indirect object.

[2] See Wackernagel II 154, who notes the fact that the "stylistic" Hebrews and the "vulgar" Rev. shares this aversion to σύν.

[3] K-G I 473f. Tycho Mommsen, *Beitr. z. Lehre von den griech. Präp.*, Berlin 1895, 381. Mayser II 2, 401ff. Krebs Polyb. 33f. Preisigke s.v. Moulton Einl. 170. Radermacher² 20, 72, 138, 140, 143, 145.

particle, each: ἔχων ἀνὰ πτέρυγας ἕξ Rev 4⁸, and as a distributive preposition: Mk 6⁴⁰ AL (but SBD κατά) Lk 9¹⁴ 10¹ Jn 2⁶ (Hellenistic).

Εἰς:[1] "une des prépositions les plus riches en surprises" (Psichari 178). See pp. 253–256.

Its use is very extensive and it is encroaching on the functions of other prepositions, especially ἐν.

(1) In its normal local sense it is used with a variety of verbs of *coming, going*, etc., when the verb indicates direction, and so is used of motion into a place or state. Mk 14⁵⁴ ἕως ἔσω εἰς τὴν αὐλήν. It occurs also with verbs like πέμπω ἀποστέλλω παραβάλλω ἀποδημέω καταλύω ἄγω (and compounds): so Lk 21¹² παραδιδόντες εἰς τὰς συναγωγάς, 2 Ti 4¹⁸ σώσει εἰς τὴν βασιλείαν αὐτοῦ, 1 Pt 3²⁰ εἰς ἣν ὀλίγοι... διεσώθησαν.

(2) Distributive εἰς with numbers = *-fold, up to*: Mk 4⁸ εἰς τριάκοντα (vl. ἐν or τὸ ἕν).

(3) Purposive εἰς, with τέλος [2] (*with a view to the end, fully*) Lk 18⁵ Jn 13¹ LXX Barn Herm, P. Tebt. III 793 xi 8 τὸν (sic) Δωρίωνος δεξιὸν εἰς τέλος ἐξέτεμεν; with τὸ παντελές Lk 13¹¹; with κενόν Paul (class. διὰ κενῆς, as in LXX Jb and Ps) 1 Th 3⁵ Diodorus, LXX Pr; with μάτην (on analogy of εἰς κενόν). Otherwise purposive εἰς Mt 8³⁴ (εἰς ὑπάντησιν), 27⁷, Mk 1⁴ Ac 2³⁸ etc. εἰς ἄφεσιν ἁμαρτιῶν, Mk 14⁸, Lk 2³² LXX, 21¹³, Jn 9³⁹ εἰς κρίμα, Ro 5¹⁸ εἰς κατάκριμα... εἰς δικαίωσιν, 10¹, ⁴,¹⁰, 13⁴ εἰς τὸ ἀγαθόν *for your good*, 1 Co 14²², Ph 1¹⁹ εἰς σωτηρίαν (LXX Jb 13¹⁶), Col 3¹⁰ εἰς ἐπίγνωσιν, ¹⁵ εἰρήνην... εἰς ἥν, Ti 3¹⁴, Heb 6⁶ εἰς μετανοίαν, 9²⁶, Jas 5³ εἰς μαρτύριον ὑμῖν, 1 Pt 1⁵, 2²¹, 3⁹; P. Ryl. II 174¹⁵ εἰς ἀθέτησιν καὶ ἀκύρωσιν *to be annulled and cancelled*; NB εἰς τοῦτο completed by ἵνα or ὅπως, or infin. clause: Jn 18³⁷ Ac 26¹⁶ Ro 9¹⁷.

(4) εἰς for Heb. לְ Mt 21⁴⁶, εἰς τί = לָמָה Mt 14³¹.

(5) Some contexts would certainly suit a causal sense:[3] Mt 3¹¹ *because of repentance* (so some modern translators); 10⁴¹; 12⁴¹ = Lk 11³² μετενόησαν εἰς τὸ κήρυγμα Ἰωνᾶ: they repented *because of* the preaching of Jonah (but *at* is sufficient); Ac 2³⁸ *be baptized* εἰς ἄφεσιν τῶν ἁμαρτιῶν *on the basis of* (but *with a view to* is sufficient, if your theology is satisfied), Ac 7⁵³; Ro 4²⁰ *on account of* the promises of God, Abraham did not waver (but *looking to* is sufficient); 11³² God has imprisoned all *because of disobedience*; 2 Ti 2²⁶ God gave them repentance *because they knew the truth* (but purposive εἰς is better); Ti 3¹⁴ to maintain good works,

---

[1] K-G I 468ff. Krebs Polyb. 106. Rossberg 30ff. Johannessohn DGPS 293–305. Moulton Einl. 93ff. Radermacher² 20f, 122, 128, 135f, 140, 145.

[2] Bauer s.v. εἰς 3. Mayser II 2, 419, 570. Preisigke s.v. τέλος.

[3] On the possibility of causal εἰς in NT, see J. R. Mantey in *JBL* 70, 1951, 45ff, 309ff, and Zorell's Lexicon s.v.

because of the compelling need of them; Heb 12⁷ you are enduring *because of discipline* (but *as a discipline* is sufficient); 1 Jn 5¹⁰. Mantey brought forward examples from Hellenistic Greek in support of a *causal* sense for εἰς, but some of them can be taken in a purposive way. By way of reply, R. Marcus observed that if Mantey is right to interpret these NT passages causally his support must come from theology rather than linguistics.[1] In Mt 14³¹ Mk 15³⁴ εἰς τί is not strictly = διά τί (Mt 9¹⁴ Mk 2¹⁸) but is *in order to what* rather than *because of what.* Hardly any of the Hellenistic parallels brought forward by Mantey are convincing, as Marcus has shown.

II. WITH TWO CASES: GEN. AND ACCUS.

Διά:[2] c. gen.

Through, place Mk 9³⁰ διὰ τῆς Γαλιλαίας, time Lk 5⁵ δι' ὅλης νυκτός, Heb 2¹⁵ διὰ παντὸς τοῦ ζῆν, 1 Mac 12²⁷ 2 Mac 13¹⁰ 4 Mac· 3⁷; unclass. is the meaning the period of time within which something takes place: Mt 26⁶¹ Mk 14⁵⁸ διὰ τριῶν ἡμερῶν *within three days,* Lk 9³⁷ D διὰ τῆς ἡμέρας *in the course of the day,* Ac 1³ *during forty days* (not continuously, but *now and then*). Of agency:[3] Ro 11³⁶ δι' αὐτοῦ (creation), 1 Co 1⁹ 12⁸ Ga 1¹ Phm⁷ Heb 2¹⁰ 13¹¹ 1 Pt 2¹⁴. Of manner: 1 Ti 2¹⁵ σωθήσεται δὲ διὰ τῆς τεκνογονίας *shall be kept safe throughout childbirth* (temp.) or *shall be saved by means of* (Moule 56), 1 Pt 3²⁰ διεσώθησαν δι' ὕδατος (attendant circumstances or environment), Heb 3¹⁶ οἱ ἐξελθόντες ἐξ Αἰγύπτου διὰ Μωϋσέως, Ac 15²⁷ διὰ λόγου *openly* (as opp. to *by letter,* ³² διὰ λόγου πολλοῦ *at length, with much talk,* Ro 2²⁷ *with all your scripture and circumcision,* 4¹¹ (Schrenk in Kittel WB I 765) *believers for all their uncircumcision,* 14²⁰ *with offence,* Ac 24², Ro 8²⁵, 1 Co 16³, 2 Co 2⁴, 3¹¹, 5⁷, 6⁸, 10⁹, Ga 3¹⁹, but not 4¹³ (not as vulg. *per,* but *propter*), Col 1²², Eph 6¹⁸ *with all possible,* 1 Ti 2¹⁰ 4⁵·¹¹ 2 Ti 2² *in the presence of,* Heb 9¹², 13²², 1 Jn 5⁶ 2 Jn ¹², 1 Th 4¹⁴ τοὺς κοιμηθέντας διὰ τοῦ Ἰησοῦ *with Jesus.* In an urgent petition = *by* (Latin *per,* Attic πρός c. gen.): Ro 12¹ παρακαλῶ ὑμᾶς διὰ τῶν οἰκτιρμῶν τοῦ θεοῦ, 15³⁰, 1 Co 1¹⁰ 2 Co 10¹ διὰ τῆς πραΰτητος καὶ ἐπιεικείας τοῦ Χριστοῦ. Uncertain meaning: Ac 3¹⁶ ἡ πίστις ἡ δι' αὐτοῦ *faith which is caused by him* (author) or *faith in him* (circumstantial), 2 Pt 3⁵.

c. accus.

Through (local), only poetical in class. Greek, but Hellenistic prose: Lk 17¹¹ only, SBL, διήρχετο διὰ μέσον...: never Polyb. (Krebs 68f) or LXX (Johannessohn DGPS 241, n. 1). Elsewhere consecutive *on account of,* e.g. Mk 6²⁶ Ac 18² 28² Rev 12¹¹ 13¹⁴; but sometimes there

---

[1] *JBL* 71, 1952, 44.
[2] K-G I 480ff. Krebs Polyb. 65. Rossberg 37f. Mayser II 2, 419ff. Johannessohn DGPS 235. Radermacher² 135 (instrum.), 138 (διά ~ ἕνεκα), 142 (accus. instrum.). 145 (διά ~ ἐν). Moulton Einl. 169ff. Moule 54–58.
[3] Mayser II 2, 421ff. Ljungvik BSSVS 29ff. Johannessohn 237.

are indications of a later final sense, denoting purpose (ἕνεκα in class. Greek)[1] = γιά MGr *for*: Mt 24[22], Mk 2[27] τὸ σάββατον διὰ τὸν ἄνθρωπον ἐγένετο, Jn 11[42] 12[30], Ro 3[25] διὰ τὴν πάρεσιν τῶν προγεγονότων ἁμαρτημάτων *with a view to*, 4[25] ὃς παρεδόθη διὰ τὰ παραπτώματα ἡμῶν (*because of*) καὶ ἠγέρθη διὰ τὴν δικαίωσιν ἡμῶν (*with a view to*), 11[28] etc.

Κατά:[2] more frequent c. accus. than gen.

c. gen.

Against (hostile) Mt 12[30], Mk 9[40], 14[55] κατὰ τοῦ Ἰησοῦ, Lk 11[23] Ro 8[31]. Local, *down from* Mt 8[32], Ac 27[14] ἔβαλεν κατ' αὐτῆς ἄνεμος τυφωνικός (*down from Crete?* or *against the ship?* The first may be better topographically), 1 Co 11[4] etc.; *throughout* (Hellenistic) Lk 4[14] καθ' ὅλης τῆς περιχώρου, 23[5], Ac 9[31. 42] 10[37]. Special uses: 2 Co 8[2] ἡ κατὰ βάθους πτωχεία *profound poverty* (*from the depths* or *down to the depths*) Mt 26[63] Heb 6[13. 16] with ὄμνυμι.

c. accus., various senses (generally as class.):

1. For possessive or subjective gen. (from local sense *spectans ad* to metaph. *pertinans ad*), frequ. in Hell. Greek: Ac 17[28] οἱ καθ' ὑμᾶς ποιηταί *your poets*, 18[15] νόμου τοῦ καθ' ὑμᾶς *your law*, 16[39] D, 25[14] τὰ κατὰ Παῦλον *Paul's case*, Ro 1[15] τὸ κατ' ἐμὲ πρόθυμον *as far as I am concerned*), 9[11] ἡ κατ' ἐκλογὴν πρόθεσις τοῦ θεοῦ *God's purpose of choosing*. Perhaps the Gospel headings come under this category: i.e. *of Matthew*; this is found with the authorship of books (2 Mac 2[13] κατὰ Νεεμίαν). 2. But more probably *in accordance with*: Ro 8[26. 27] 2 Co 7[9. 11] κατὰ θεόν *in a godly way*, 11[21] κατὰ φύσιν *in accordance with nature*, 1 Co 15[3] κατὰ τὰς γραφάς 2 Co 10[3] κατὰ σάρκα *in accordance with material standards*, Ga 3[15] *in human fashion*, Eph 4[24] *in God's image*, Heb 9[9]. 3. Distributive: Mt 27[15] Mk 15[6] καθ' ἑορτήν *at each feast*, Heb 7[27] *daily*, 9[25] *yearly*, Mk 6[40] κατὰ ἑκατὸν καὶ κατὰ πεντήκοντα SBD *one hundred each*, 1 Co 14[31] καθ' ἕνα *one by one*, Eph 5[33] οἱ καθ' ἕνα *individually*, Heb 9[5] κατὰ μέρος *in detail*. The phrase κατὰ εἷς or καθεῖς (Mk 14[19] Jn 8[9] Ro 12[5]) has now become stereotyped as an adverb. More difficult to assess are: Mt 19[3] κατὰ πᾶσαν αἰτίαν (causal), Mk 13[8] κατὰ τόπους *in places*, Lk 1[18] κατὰ τί *in view of what?* whereby (or causal?), 15[14] κατὰ τὴν χώραν ἐκείνην *throughout that land*, Ac 12[1] *at* (temporal), 25[23] τοῖς κατ' ἐξοχήν *eminent men* (a stock phrase for *par excellence*), 1 Co 7[6] *as a concession*, 2 Co 8[3] κατὰ δύναμιν *according to their power*, 8[12] *in proportion to what one has*, 10[7] τὰ κατὰ πρόσωπον *what is in front of you*, Heb 7[16] κατὰ νόμον ... κατὰ δύναμιν *by virtue of*.

Μετά:[3] c. gen.:

Its frequence relative to that of σύν:

---

[1] H. G. Meecham, *Exp. T. L.* no. 12, Sept. 1939, 564.
[2] K-G I 475ff. Krebs Polyb. 128. Mayser II 2, 427ff. Johannessohn DGPS 245ff. Radermacher[2] 139ff. Moulton Einl. 158 (frequence), 169f.
[3] K-G I 505ff. Tycho Mommsen, *Beitr. z. Lehre von d. griech. Pap.* 256f. Krebs 58ff. Rossberg 8f. (frequence), 49–50 (use). Mayser II 2, 440ff. Johannessohn DGPS 202–216. Moulton Einl. 158 (frequence), 170. 172. Radermacher[2] 128, 138, 140f 145, 146.

	Ptol. texts (Rossberg)	Polyb. (Krebs)	Lucian	NT (Moulton)
μετά	1·5	6·7	7	3·5
σύν	1	1	1	1

Ionic influence accounts for the greater relative frequence of σύν in Ptol. pap. and NT. On the whole, μετά far outweighs σύν in NT, but in some individual books σύν holds its own (e.g. Ac). The accus. is on the decline: thus in Ptol. pap. gen.: accus. is 2·5:1 (iii/B.C.), 3:1 (ii/B.C.), 10+:1 (i/B.C.). The NT has 3·6:1 (361:100), LXX Ezek β 14·5:1, Ps 16:1.

(1) *amongst* Mk 1¹³ ἦν μετά τῶν θηρίων, 10³⁰ μετά διωγμῶν, Lk 22³⁷ μετά ἀνόμων ἐλογίσθη, 24⁵ μετά τῶν νεκρῶν, Jn 11⁵⁶, 1 Ti 4¹⁴ μετά ἐπιθέσεως τῶν χειρῶν (impersonal for person: *among those who laid on their hands*), but perhaps (2), Heb 12¹⁴ 2 Ti 2²² εἰρήνην διώκεω μετά not *peace with*, but *in company with* (Foerster in Kittel WB II 412, 415), 1 Jn 4¹⁷ τετελείωται ἡ ἀγάπη μεθ' ἡμῶν.

(2) *with*, of mutual participation (e.g. κρίνομαι 1 Co 6⁶, λαλέω Jn 4²⁷; also πολεμέω, εἰρηνεύω, συμφωνέω, etc.) or accompanying circumstances (e.g. μεθ' ὅρκου Mt 14⁷) or instrument (e.g. Lk 22⁵² ἐξήλθατε μετά μαχαιρῶν). In contrast to σύν, the meaning of μετά is never *in addition to*. In composition with a verb, when the meaning is *with*, συν- or ὁμο- is used, and not μετα- (except with μετέχω, μεταδίδωμι and μεταλαμβάνω).

c. accus., only *after* (temporal): an exception may be Heb 9³ μετά τό δεύτερον καταπέτασμα. Ac 1⁵ etc.

Περί:[1]—*about*, literal or metaph.
c. gen. extremely common.

Esp. metaph. with such verbs as *think, care*, etc.: Mt 9³⁶ ἐσπλαγχνίσθη περί αὐτῶν, Mt 20²⁴ Mk 10⁴¹ ἠγανάκτησαν περί, Lk 2¹⁸ θαυμάζω, Jn 7¹³, 9¹⁷, 1 Th 5²⁵ προσεύχεσθε περί ἡμῶν, 1 Pt 5⁷ αὐτῷ μέλει περί ὑμῶν, Lk 24²⁷ τά περί ἑαυτοῦ, Ac 18²⁵ Ph 2²⁰. Absolutely, at the beginning of the sentence: 1 Co 7¹·²⁵ 8¹ 12¹ 16¹. Also *on behalf of, on account of* (= ὑπέρ) class. and Hell., in the debatable phrase Mt 26²⁸ τό αἷμά μου τῆς διαθήκης τό περί (D ὑπέρ) πολλῶν ἐκχυννόμενον (ὑπέρ in parallels of Mk, Lk, Paul), Heb 10²⁶ περί ἁμαρτιῶν (same sense 10¹²

---

[1] K-G I 491ff. Krebs 98ff. Rossberg 8f (frequ.), 41ff (use). Kuhring 15. Mayser II 2, 445ff. Johannessohn DGPS 219ff. Radermacher² 118, 125, 135, 139, 140, 141, 143, 145, 146. Moulton Einl. 158. 170. Moule 62f.

ὑπὲρ ἁμαρτιῶν); Heb 5^{1. 3} ὑπέρ... ὑπέρ...: then περί... περί... περί..., Jn 17⁹, Ac 26¹ (B ὑπέρ), 1 Co 1¹³ D*B p⁴⁶ ἐσταυρώθη περὶ ὑμῶν, Ga 1⁴ (S°B ὑπέρ). Perhaps with περισσός in mind, AV has *above all things* in 3 Jn² περὶ πάντων... εὐοδοῦσθαι (*in every respect*), but it may correspond to the salutation which occurs in papyrus letters: πρὸ μὲν πάντων εὔχομαί σε ὑγιαίνειν *before all*.

c. accus. rarer:

About literally (local and temporal), Mk 4¹⁰ Lk 22⁴⁹ οἱ περὶ αὐτόν *his disciples* or *those who were round him*, but οἱ περὶ Παῦλον (Ac 13¹³) includes Paul, as in class. idiom. But πρὸς τὰς περὶ Μάρθαν καὶ Μαρίαν (Jn 11¹⁹ p⁴⁵ Θ AC² Γ) denotes Martha and Mary only (as in later Greek; see Bauer s.v. 2 δ). Temporal: Mt 20³ etc. περὶ τρίτην ὥραν *about the third hour*. Also *concerning* with ἐπιθυμίαι (Mk 4¹⁹), περισπάομαι, θορυβάζομαι (Lk 10⁴⁰ᶠ), τοὺς περὶ τοιαῦτα ἐργάτας (Ac 19²⁵); the general tendency, culminating in MGr, was for the prepositions to be followed only by the accus., and already in Aristotle there are instances where περί c. accus. is used for the Attic περί c. gen. (Wackernagel II 215); so Paul, Ph 2²³ τὰ περὶ ἐμέ *my affairs*, exactly as 2²⁰ τὰ περὶ ὑμῶν *your affairs*, 1 Ti 1¹⁹ περὶ τὴν πίστιν ἐναυάγησαν, 6^{4. 21}, 2 Ti 2¹⁸ 3⁸, Ti 2⁷ περὶ πάντα *in all respects*.

Πρίν:

= πρό, c. acc. Mk 15⁴² D πρὶν σάββατον, Jn 11⁵⁵ D πρὶν τὸ πάσχα; c. gen. (as Hell. Greek) Mt 26³⁴ p^{37. 45} L fam¹ πρίν (ἤ) ἀλεκτοροφωνίας; acc. or gen.? Jn 8⁵⁸ D lat πρὶν Ἀβραάμ.

Ὑπέρ : ¹ = *over*, but not locally in NT (except Heb 9⁵ D* E* for ὑπεράνω); locally in papyri (Mayser II 2, 461). Comparatively rare in Ptol. pap. (13th place among true prepositions) and Herodotus (16th place) and NT (12th place). The accus. is comparatively rare: Ptol. 20:1, LXX 239:211 (1:1), NT 6:1.

c. gen.

For, on behalf of (Mk 9⁴⁰ 1 Co 4⁶), often oppos. to κατά in the same passages; περί is often substituted, but there is also the reverse change of περί to ὑπέρ for *concerning* (e.g. λέγω ὑπέρ)², which is almost confined to Paul in NT: Jn 1³⁰ ὑπὲρ οὗ ἐγὼ εἶπον (corrected to περὶ S°AC³L), Ac 8²⁴ *pray* ὑπὲρ ἐμοῦ, 2 Co 1⁸ ἀγνοεῖν... ὑπὲρ τῆς θλίψεως, 8²³ ὑπὲρ Τίτου *as for Titus*, 12⁸ *about this*, 1 Th 3² παρακαλέσαι ὑπὲρ τῆς πίστεως ὑμῶν *to encourage you concerning your faith*, 2 Th 2¹ ἐρωτάω ὑπέρ, Ph 4¹⁰ φρονέω ὑπέρ *think upon*; note the two prepositions together in the same sense Eph 6¹⁸ᶠ προσευχόμενοι περὶ πάντων τῶν ἁγίων καὶ ὑπὲρ ἐμοῦ. Etc.

---

¹ K.-G I 486ff. Schwyzer II 518f. Krebs 40ff. Rossberg 8f, 40f. Kuhring §§ 19. 20. Johannessohn DGPS 216ff. Radermacher² 139 (ὑπέρ = ἀντί), 140, 143 (frequence). Moulton Einl. 158 (relative frequ.) 170f. Mayser II 2, 456ff.
² Mayser II 2, 457ff. Johannessohn DGPS 217f.

§ 4]   CASE ADDITIONS WITH PREPOSITION   271

in Paul. The boundary between ἀντί and ὑπέρ c. gen. is very narrow (substitution), necessarily so because what is done *on behalf of one* is often done *in one's stead*; the compound of ἀντί occurs closely with ὑπέρ in 1 Ti 2⁶ ἀντίλυτρον ὑπέρ πάντων; Mk 14²⁴ *blood is shed* ὑπέρ (but ἀντί in 10⁴⁵), Jn 11⁵⁰, Ac 21²⁶, Ro 5⁷·⁸, 1 Co 15²⁹, 2 Co 5¹⁴·¹⁵·²¹, Ga 3¹³, Phm¹³, 1 Ti 2⁶, Ti 2¹⁴. Adverbial ὑπέρ: 1 Co 4⁶(?) 2 Co 11²³.

III. WITH THREE CASES

'Επί:[1]

	Polyb.	Ptol. pap.	NT	LXX Pent.	Isa.	LXX total	
gen.	1·5	4·5	1·2	2·5	1	1730	1·4
dat.	1	1	1	1	1	1219	1
acc.	3	2·5	2	3·7	2	4629	3·8

Even in class. Greek the distinctions between the cases with this preposition are difficult to define; all attempts to be dogmatic in Biblical Greek are doomed. Although all cases are largely represented, there is a tendency for the accus. to prevail, as is seen in Mk 4³⁸ (Wackernagel II 215) where D has an atticistic correction to the gen. ἐπί προσκεφαλαίου.

c. gen.

(1) Local, usually = *upon*: Mk 2¹⁰ etc. ἐπί τῆς γῆς; but also place to which: Mk 4²⁶ βάλῃ τὸν σπορόν ἐπί τῆς γῆς; Rev 14¹⁹ S (p⁴⁷ ἐπί c. acc.; ACP εἰς) etc.; *at, by* Mt 21¹⁹ ἐπί τῆς ὁδοῦ, etc.; *in the presence of* Mt 28¹⁴, Mk 13⁹ etc. (2) Metaph., *over* (authority, oversight), with καθίστημι and βασιλεύω, but ἐξουσία ἐπί c. gen. is exclusively Biblical. (3) Temporal:[2] Mk 2²⁶ ἐπί 'Αβιάθαρ ἀρχιερέως, Mt 1¹¹, Ac 11¹⁹ ΑΕ τῆς θλίψεως τῆς γενομένης ἐπί Στεφάνου *at the time of Stephen's death* (but vl. ἐπί c. dat. *on account of*), Heb 1² etc. ἐπ' ἐσχάτου τῶν ἡμέρων (Semitism). Mk 12²⁶ Lk 20³⁷ *in the passage where.*

c. dat.

(1) Local, not easy to distinguish from ἐπί c. accus. or gen.: *before, upon* Eph 1¹⁰ τὰ ἐπί τοῖς οὐρανοῖς καὶ τὰ ἐπί τῆς γῆς (interchangeable;

---

[1] K-G I 495ff. Meisterhans-Schwyzer 211, 36; 217, 29. Krebs 76. Rossberg 44f. Kuhring § 29. Johannessohn DGPS 305ff. Radermacher² 125, 126, 128, 136. Moulton Einl. 173f. Moule 49f. Mayser II 2, 462ff.

[2] C. H. Turner, "'Επί Ποντίου Πειλάτου (1 Tim. vi. 12, 13)", *JThS* 28, 1927, 270ff.

as also Ac 27⁴⁴ ἐπὶ σανίσιν and ἐπί τινων τῶν ἀπὸ τοῦ πλοίου), Mt 24³³, Jn 4⁶, Mt 16¹⁸ (D acc.), Ac 8¹⁶ (D* acc.) etc. (2) More often to denote cause, especially with verbs expressing motion, and also Mt 4⁴ Lk 1⁵⁹ etc.; Ro 5¹² 2 Co 5⁴ ἐφ' ᾧ *because*,¹ Lk 5⁵ ἐπὶ δὲ τῷ ῥήματί σου. (3) Addition, Lk 3²⁰ 16²⁶ (SBL ἐν), Col 3¹⁴, Heb 8¹. (4) Condition Ro 8²⁰, 1 Co 9¹⁰, Ga 5¹³, 1 Th 4⁷, Ti 1². (5) Final Ga 5¹³ ἐπ' ἐλευθερίᾳ ἐκλήθητε, Eph 2¹⁰, Ph 3¹², 1 Th 4⁷. (6) Consecutive 2 Ti 2¹⁴. (7) Temporal Jn 4²⁷ ἐπὶ τούτῳ (S*D ἐν) *at this juncture*, 1 Co 14¹⁶, Ph 1³ ἐπὶ πάσῃ τῇ μνείᾳ ὑμῶν, 2¹⁷, 4¹⁰ ἐφ' ᾧ *whereon*, Eph 4²⁶, 1 Th 3⁷, Heb 9²⁶ *at the close of the ages*, 11⁴.

c. accus.:

(1) In class. Greek it answers to question "whither", but also in Hellenistic it is interchangeable with gen. and dat.: Mk 4³⁸ (DW gen.), Mt 14²⁵ περιπατῶν ἐπὶ τὴν θάλασσαν SBW (CD gen.), but gen. in Mk 6⁴⁸ Jn 6¹⁹; Mt 14²⁶ WEFG (SBDC gen.); Rev 13¹ ἐπὶ τῶν κεράτων ... καὶ ἐπὶ τὰς κεφαλάς; 13¹⁶, 14⁹ ἐπὶ τοῦ μετώπου ... ἢ ἐπὶ τὴν χεῖρα (p⁴⁷ corrects to gen). Κάθημαι ἐπί c. accus. Rev 4², c. dat. 21⁵, c. gen 14¹⁶. (2) In metaph. sense: Lk 1³³ βασιλεύσει ἐπί; same interchange, e.g. Mt 25²¹ ἐπὶ ὀλίγα ἧς πιστός, ἐπὶ πολλῶν σε καταστήσω; it is used with σπλαγχνίζομαι *upon* (Mt 15³²), μοιχάομαι *with* (Mk 10¹¹, cp. LXX Je 5⁸ χρεμετίζω ἐπί) etc. (3) Temporal: Ac 16¹⁸ ἐπὶ πολλὰς ἡμέρας *for many days*; Mt 25⁴⁰? ἐφ' ὅσον ἐποιήσατε (vulg. *quamdiu*), etc.; Ac 4⁵ ἐπὶ τὴν αὔριον (Hell. Greek: Krebs 17, Mayser II 2, 540).

Παρά ²

The most frequent after ἐν, εἰς, ἐπί in Ptol. pap. but in 12th place in NT.

The relative frequency of the cases reveals a sharp contrast between the NT and contemporary Koine.

	Hdt.	Ptol. pap.	Mk	Lk-Ac	Ro Co Ga	NT	Pent	Isa	Ps.	LXX
gen.	1·8	22·5	6	1·6	0·2	1·6	2	8	1·6	501	2·
dat.	1	1	1	1	1	1	1	1	1·	191	
acc.	3·5	2·5	7	1·5	1·3	1·2	2	1·3	1	293	1·

¹ ICC Ro.⁵ p. 349. But cf. S. Lyonnet, "Le sens de ἐφ' ᾧ en Rom 5: 12 et l'exégèse des pères grecs", *Biblica* 36, 1955, 436-456.
² K-G I 509ff. Meisterhans-Schwyzer 207, 17; 219, 40. Krebs 51ff. Rossberg 51ff. Mayser II 2, 482ff. Radermacher² 126, 136, 139, 141f, 225. Moulton Einl. 158, 173. Johannessohn DGPS 226-35.

c. gen.:

In class. Greek *from the side of* (so Lk 1⁴⁵); unclass. with κατηγορέομαι Ac 22³⁰ HLP (rest ὑπό), and Mk 3²¹ οἱ παρ' αὐτοῦ *his kinsfolk*.

c. dat.:

In all NT writers except Heb and Jude (but Mt 13⁵⁶ has αἱ ἀδελφαὶ πρὸς ἡμᾶς εἰσι, instead of class. Attic παρ' ἡμῖν, marking the Hellenistic preference for accus.: Wackernagel II 215); rarest of the cases: *by, beside* (nearly always personal), not of immediate neighbourhood: Jn 19²⁵; *in the house of* Lk 19⁷ Jn 1⁴⁰ Ac 10⁶, *amongst* Rev 2¹³. Figurative: Lk 1³⁰ *with*, etc. The local παρά c. dat. has almost disappeared in NT.

c. accus. (never occurs in Johannine writings, incl. Rev, or in Cath. epistles):

Beside, in answer to questions where? and whither? But not, as frequently in class. Greek, with personal names (πρός instead), oppos. of κατά (metaph.) *contrary to, beyond* Ro 1²⁶ 11²⁴ 1 Co 3¹¹ 2 Co 8³; *more than* Lk 13². ⁴ παρὰ πάντας, Ro 1²⁵ 12³ 14⁵; *minus* or *except* Lk 5⁷ D παρά τι *almost*, 2 Co 11²⁴ *40 minus one*, Herm. S VIII 1, 14; IX 19, 3; *because* 1 Co 12¹⁵ᶠ οὐ παρὰ τοῦτο οὐκ ἔστιν ἐκ τοῦ σώματος *that is no reason for its not being*. Mt Mk have παρά c. accus. only in local sense.

Πρός [1]

In 8th place of frequency in the Ptol. papyri. With regard to the use of the cases, NT and LXX are decidedly *sui generis*.

	Hdt.	Polyb.	Ptol. pap.	NT	LXX
gen.	2	0·2	0·02	0·16	23 (0·2)
dat.	1	1	1	1	104 (1)
acc.	6	15	4	116	*passim*

c. gen.:

In class. Attic πρός, like ὑπό, was used with all three oblique cases. But πρός c. gen. is found only three times in Polyb., rarely in inscriptions and in the Ptol. pap. (Mayser II 2, 493f). It occurs only 23 times in LXX

---

[1] K-G I 515ff. Meisterhans-Schwyzer 220. 43; 45. Wackernagel II 208. Mayser II 2, 492ff. Krebs 113ff. Rossberg 54ff. Kuhring 17, 29, 31. Johannessohn DGPS 259–71. Radermacher² 135, 136, 141, 145, 146. Moulton Einl. 173.

(Moulton Proleg. 106); in NT, only at Ac 27³⁴ τοῦτο πρὸς τῆς ὑμετερας σωτηρίας ὑπάρχει *advantageous to* (very close to Thuc. 3, 59, 1 οὐ πρὸς τῆς ὑμετέρας δόξης τάδε).

c. dat.:

By, at (class.). Six times in NT (accus. instead): Mk 5¹¹ πρὸς τῷ ὄρει, Lk 19³⁷ (D acc.), Jn 18¹⁶ 20¹¹ (vl. acc.) ¹² Rev 1¹³.

c. accus.: abundantly used.

In accordance with (class.): Mt 19⁸ Mk 10⁵ Lk 12⁴⁷ 1 Co 12⁷ 2 Co 5¹⁰. With verbs of saying, it illustrates the Hellenistic tendency to use prepositions in place of the simple case (pp. 236f, 251). So with verbs of coming, sending, etc. Also taking the place of παρά after εἰμι etc.: e.g. Mt 13⁵⁶ πρὸς ὑμᾶς εἰσιν, 26¹⁸· ⁵⁵ vl, Mk 6³ Jn 1¹, especially Mk 9¹⁰ ἐκράτησαν πρὸς ἑαυτούς, 11³¹ διελογίζοντο πρὸς ἑαυτούς (cp. Mt 21²⁵ παρ' ἑαυτοῖς), Mt 21¹ πρὸς τὸ ὄρος (vl. εἰς), Mk 1³³, 2², 11¹· ⁴. Temporal: *about*, such phrases as πρὸς ἑσπέραν, καιρόν, ὥραν, ὀλίγας ἡμέρας, Lk 8¹³ 24²⁹ Jn 5³⁵ Heb 12¹⁰ᶠ etc. Relationship, hostile or friendly: Mt 27⁴ Jn 21²²· ²³ Mk 12¹² Lk 20¹⁹, Ac 28²⁵ ἀσύμφωνος, 1 Co 6¹ πρᾶγμα ἔχω πρός, Heb 4¹³. Purpose, result: 2 Co 10⁴ Eph 4²⁹ 1 Ti 4⁸.

Ὑπό ¹

In the Ptol. papyri, 12th place: in NT 10th place.

PROPORTIONS:

	Hdt.	Polyb.	Ptol. pap.	NT	Pent	Mi. Pr.	2–4 Mac	1 Mac	Isa	LXX
gen.	10·8	61	60·4	3·3	0·5	4	5	3	6	(291) 1·4
dat.	1	1	1	0	0	0	0	0	0	*
acc.	1	25	10·6	1	1	1	1	1	1	(203) 1

* Only Jb 12⁵ A.

Whereas ὑπό still occurs with dat. about eleven times in Polyb., it never (ex. Jb 12⁵ A) occurs so in LXX or NT and there is the same tendency as with πρός.

¹ K-G I 521ff. Meisterhans-Schwyzer 222, 50. Mayser II 2, 509ff. Krebs 47ff. Rössberg 58ff. Kuhring § 25. Johannessohn DGPS 174ff. Radermacher² 139, 142, 145. Moulton Einl. 170.

§ 4–6]   CASE ADDITIONS WITH PREPOSITION   275

c. gen.: *by* (agent), after passive and virtually passive verbs.
c. accus.:

Under (combining the old local use of ὑπό c. gen. and dat.: Mayser II 2, 371); never in Jn (except 1⁴⁸ ὑπὸ τὴν συκῆν) or Rev (which has ὑποκάτω). In class. temporal sense (*circa*), only Ac 5²¹ ὑπὸ τὸν ὄρθρον.

§ 5. Repetition or Omission of the Preposition [1]

Both repetition and omission of the preposition before two or more phrases connected by καί is found in Ptol. pap. and NT. Polyb. is fond of repeating the preposition, especially in quotations, sometimes three or four times. The omission can sometimes be rather harsh in NT: Mt 4²⁵ ἀπὸ τῆς Γαλιλαίας . . . καὶ Ἰουδαίας καὶ πέραν τοῦ Ἰορδάνου.

Actually, repetition is more usual when each of the united ideas has to be brought into emphatic prominence; but in by far the greater majority of instances in the Ptol. papyri, especially in the unofficial style of writing, the preposition is not repeated. Repetition in any large degree is a peculiar feature of Biblical Greek [2]. In Thucyd. book 1 there are only six instances of repetition, out of 25 opportunities for its occurrence, and in these six instances there is an emphasis which makes repetition necessary. Let us compare this with Biblical Greek.

	Ezek. (B-text) *	Mk	Mt	Lk	Ac	Jn	Ro 1 Co	Eph	Past	Rev
opportunities	93	26	35	55	56	15	24	16	24	38
repetitions	78	10	11	9	16	8	14	6	4	24

* The result is even more remarkable, assuming the AQ readings.

§ 6. Improper Prepositions

"Ἄνευ [3]

Only three examples in NT: Mt 10²⁹ ἄνευ τοῦ πατρὸς ὑμῶν

---

[1] K-G I 548. Mayser II 2, 515f. Krebs 10f. Black AAGA² 83. See also above, Introduction, p. 4, n. 7.
[2] See N. Turner, "An Alleged Semitism", *Exp. T.* LXVI 8, 1955, 252–254.
[3] K-G I 402, 4. Kuhring 46f. Mayser II 2, 518ff. Johannessohn DGPS 337–339. Radermacher² 140.

without the knowledge of or *without the permission of*, like ἄνευ θεῶν in Ptol. pap. (Mayser II 2, 519f) 1 Pt 3¹ 4⁹. Usually ἄνευ has post-positive position only after interrog. and rel. pronouns, but 3 Mac 4⁵ and Aristot. *Metaph.* 1071ᵃ 2 are among the exceptions (Wackernagel II 199).

"Ενεκα, ἕνεκεν [1]
= *propter* and διά c. accus. Position nearly always pre-positive in NT, following Semitic model; but post-positive in Ptol. pap. and Polyb. more than twice as often as pre-positive.

"Εως and μέχρι (ἄχρι) [2].
In the Ptol. pap., although these prepositions will appear with the same meaning in the same phrase, ἕως is much more frequent than μέχρι both in its temporal and local meaning. Whereas the relationship in the Ptol. papyri is 1:8, in Polyb. it is only 1:1·7. Originally ἕως was a conjunction (see pp. 110f), becoming a preposition in the Hell. period. It is often combined with an adverb: πότε, κάτω, ἄρτι, σήμερον; and sometimes it receives strengthening from another preposition: ἕως πρός Lk 24⁵⁰, ἕως ἐπί Ac 17¹⁴, ἕως ἔξω Ac 21⁵, ἕως καὶ εἰς 26¹¹, ἕως ἔσω εἰς τὴν αὐλήν Mk 14⁵⁴.

"Αχρι(ς) occurs in Mt 24³⁸, and Lk-Ac, Paul, Heb, Rev; μέχρι(ς) in Mt, and occasionally in Lk, Ac, Paul, Heb; they are also conjunctions (e.g. ἄχρις οὗ Ro 11²⁵, μέχρις οὗ Mk 13³⁰). All absent in Jn, except 8⁹ S.

§ 7. Prepositional Adverbs

"Αμα [3]
This adv. has the dat. only at Mt 13²⁹ ἅμα αὐτοῖς τὸν σῖτον (D ἅμα καὶ τ.σ. σὺν αὐτοῖς); elsewhere ἅμα σύν 1 Th 4¹⁷ 5¹⁰. Cp. ἅμα μετ' αὐτῶν Ditt. Syll.³·705 ⁵⁷ (112 B.C.).

Ἐγγύς
Very frequent in NT. See p. 216.

Ἔσω [4]
Mk 15¹⁶ ἔσω τῆς αὐλῆς (vl. ἔσω εἰς τὴν αὐλήν). Only used as an adv. in the Ptol. papyri (Mayser II 2, 528).

---

[1] K-G I 462c. Meisterhans-Schwyzer 213, 12; 215, 23–27. Mayser II 2, 520ff. N. Turner, *Vet. Test.* 5, 1955, 210f.
[2] K-G I 346, 2. Meisterhans-Schwyzer 217, 30. Schwyzer II 549f. Mayser II 2, 522ff. Johannessohn DGPS 304f. Radermacher² 140.
[3] K-G I 432, 2; II 82 n. 3. Mayser II 2. 526ff. Johannessohn DGPS 212, 322. Radermacher² 142.
[4] Radermacher² 66, 224.

Ἐκτός [1]
Except: as a preposition in Ptol. pap. 30, in NT 9 (e.g. Ac 26²² 1 Co 15²⁷), in LXX 20, in Polyb. 43. See p. 216.

Ἐνάντιον [2]
In NT the meaning is weakened from *opposite* (class.) to *before* (a mere substitute for πρό). Never as adv. in NT. Mk 2¹² ACD (vl. ἔμπροσθεν), Lk 1⁸ SAC, 20²⁶, 24¹⁹ (D ἐνώπιον), Ac 7¹⁰ 8³² OT. Ἀντικρύς *opposite:* Ac 20¹⁵ ἀντικρὺς Χίου. ἀπ- and κατ- ἀντικρύ(ς) do not appear at all. The β-text has κατὰ Χίον at Ac 20¹⁵.

Ἐντός [3]
See p. 216. Rare in LXX, only twice in NT, but 37 times in Polyb., and about 20 times in Ptol. pap. (Mayser II 2, 530).

Ἐνώπιον [4]
Hellenistic, earliest in LXX. Frequent in Lk and 1st part of Ac and Rev. In Jn, only at 20³⁰ 1 Jn 3²² 3 Jn⁶. Never in Mt Mk. κατενώπιον Eph 1⁴ Col 1²² Jude ²⁴ (Biblical Greek word).

Ἔξω [5]
See p. 216. In class., Polyb., Ptol. pap. and NT, used as a preposition.

Κυκλόθεν
LXX Je 17²⁶, NT (Rev), Ptol. pap. (Mayser II 2, 532).

Λάθρα
K-G I 402, 4. Mt, Mk, Jn, Ac.

Μεταξύ [6]
Rare in NT and LXX (only Ge² Jg¹, Km⁴, Wi³), which prefer ἀνὰ μέσον and ἐν μέσῳ. Μεταξύ is the literary and even atticizing form, and occurs in three insertions from Aquila: Jg 5²⁷ (in same verse ἀνὰ μέσον), 3 Km 15⁶· ³². NT: Mt 18¹⁵ etc. Adverbial: Jn 4³¹ Ac 13⁴².

Ὄπισθεν
As a preposition only at Mt 15²³ Lk 23²⁶. But ὀπίσω occurs 26 times (300 in LXX); twice as an adv. The prepositional use belongs to Bibl. Greek and arises from LXX rendering of אַחֲרֵי. It does occur, but extremely rarely, in the Koine (Mayser II 2, 533: "lässt sich als Präposition nur im Kanop. Dekr. 62 und in post postiver Form nachweissen." But see also P. Oxy. 43B IV 3 (iii/A.D.) ὀπίσω Καπιτολείου). Ac 5³⁷ Rev 13³.

---

[1] K-G I 402, 4. Mayser II 2, 529. Kurhing § 51. Johannessohn DGPS 336. Rademacher² 140, 144.
[2] K-G I 353. Meisterhans-Schwyzer 215, 22. Mayser II 2, 529f. Johannessohn DGPS 190 (365 times in LXX). Rademacher² 144.
[3] K-G I 385 n. 3. Meisterhans-Schwyzer 205, 14. Johnnessohn DGPS 336.
[4] Mayser I² 3, 120; II 2, 530ff. Johannessohn DGPS 194-196, 359-361. Rademacher² 140, 143, 145. Moulton Einl. 159 n. 2.
[5] K-G I 402, 4. Mayser II 2, 531ff. Rademacher² 144.
[6] K-G I 348 n. 4. Mayser II 2, 532f. Johannessohn DGPS 173f. Rademacher² 138, 144. P. Katz, *Vetus Test.* 8, 1958, 267.

Ὀψέ
Literature in Bauer s.v. Mt 28¹ Mk 16¹ ὀψὲ σαββάτων. A Latinism? *Just after.*

Πέραν¹
In pap. of 258 B.C. πέρα Μέμφεως. See p. 216.

Πλήν
Except: Mk 12³² Jn 8¹⁰ EGHK Ac 8¹ 15²⁸ 27²²; also as adv. and conjunction.

Χάριν²
Lk, Jn, Past. Cp. ἕνεκα. With one exception, post-positive. Hell. Greek favours the pre-positive position (but οὗ χάριν etc. in pap.).

	Polyb.	Ptol. pap.	LXX	NT
post-positive	76	18	8	8
pre-positive	100	32	13	1

Χωρίς³
Without. Hellenistic.

§ 8. Proper Prepositions combined with Adverbs

The tendency of the later language is towards fuller forms, and these are Hellenistic⁴. Ἔναντι Lk 1⁸ BD Ac 7¹⁰ S 8²¹ (vl. ἐνώπιον). Ἀπέναντι occurs three times only in Polyb., four or five times only in all the Ptol. pap. examined by Mayser (II 2, 538), but six times in NT alone and 80–90 in LXX: Mt 27²⁴ (vl. κατέναντι) 6¹ Mk 12⁴¹ (vl. κατέναντι) Ac 3¹⁶ 17⁷ Ro 3¹⁸ OT. Κατέναντι occurs only once in the Ptol. papyri as a preposition, but 83 in LXX, 9 in NT (e.g. Mt 27²⁴ κατέναντι τοῦ ὄχλου *in the sight of*); see Mayser II 2, 541.

Ἔμπροσθεν⁵ is in NT the normal word for *before* in the spatial sense, as alternative to πρό which is seldom used in a local sense. In class. Greek and Ptol. pap. (Mayser II 2, 539) it is used more often as an adv. than with the gen. It is extremely rare outside

---

[1] K-G I 402, 4. Mayser II 2, 533.
[2] K-G I 461 n. Meisterhans-Schwyzer 222, 52. Mayser II 2, 535. Johannessohn DGPS 244. Radermacher² 144.
[3] K-G I 402, 4. Mayser II 2, 536ff. Kuhring § 34. Johannessohn DGPS 337, 339. Radermacher² 140–144.
[4] Mayser II 2, 538. Johannessohn DGPS 193, d. Radermacher² 140, 143, 144.
[5] Johannessohn DGPS 189–198. Radermacher² 144, 145.

Bibl. Greek, and Semitic influence is obvious. Mt Mk Lk Jn Ac Past Rev; more frequent in Mt (e.g. 10^{32} 27^{11}). Rev 19^{10} (B ἐνώπιον) 22^8 (A πρό). Temporal = πρό (also class.) perhaps Jn $1^{15, 30}$ (or = *ranks before me*). Adverbial: only Lk $19^{4, 28}$ Ph 3^{13} Rev 4^6. Adjectivally: ἔμπροσθέν μου γέγονεν Jn $1^{15, 30}$.

Ἐπάνω [1]. *On top of.* In place of simple ἐπί. Hell. Greek also uses ὑπεράνω: only Eph 1^{21} 4^{10} Heb 9^5. Such compounds are already found in Attic, but the meaning is weakened by this time. The later language prefers the longer forms. Ἄνω and κάτω are always adverbs. Βάλλω ἔξω and βάλλω κάτω are always preferred to ἐκβάλλω and καταβάλλω (Mt 4^6 5^{13}). Mt 5^{14} ἐπάνω ὄρους (for older ἐπ' ὄρους), 21^7 ἐπάνω αὐτῶν. Adverbial: Mt 2^9.

Ὑποκάτω: an adv. and preposition from Plato on; still more frequent in Koine (Diodorus, Plutarch); only twice in Polyb. About 90 times in LXX as substitute for ὑπό (Johannessohn DGPS 183): very prevalent in Kms (19 against 17 ὑπό c. acc.) and MiPr (8 against 4) and Ezek (13 against 6), Isa (8:4); but Pent only 16 against 42. Never in Est, 1 Esd, To, Wisdom literature or Mac (exc. Si once). In NT eleven times and only as a preposition. Lk 8^{16} ὑποκάτω κλίνης (for older ὑπὸ κλίνην). Rarely as adv. in Ptol. papyri.

§ 9. Biblical Circumlocutions by means of Nouns with Gen.

Πρόσωπον:[2] for Heb. מִפְּנֵי the LXX bequeathes ἀπὸ προσώπου c. gen. to Bibl. Greek (Thackeray OT Gr. 44) in place of the normal ἀπό or παρά. It occurs in Ac 3^{20} 5^{41} (with *come, go*), 7^{45} Rev 6^{16} 12^{14} 20^{11} (with *drive, hide, flee*). So from לִפְנֵי πρὸ προσώπου Mt 11^{10} Lk 1^{76} (SB ἐνώπιον) Ac 13^{24}. So κατὰ πρόσωπον: Lk 2^{31} Ac 3^{13} 25^{16} 2 Co 10^1 (= בִּפְנֵי). So εἰς πρ. 2 Co 8^{24} and Aquila Ge 17^1. Prepositional compounds of πρόσωπον are undoubtedly a Semitism in spite of their occurrence in the papyri of ii/A.D. and one of iv/A.D. (MM Vocab. 553).

---

[1] Mayser II 2, 539ff. Radermacher[2] 144. G. D. Kilpatrick, "Mark xiv. 5 'Ἐπάνω,'" *JThS* 42, 1941, 181ff.

[2] Johannessohn DGPS, 184–186, etc. Cf. also 1 Clem $4^{8, 10}$ 18^{11} 28^3 Barn. 6^9 11^7 ἀπὸ προσώπου. Ign Pol 2^2 εἰς πρόσωπον. 1 Clem 35^{10} κατὰ πρόσωπον. 1 Clem 34^3 Ign Eph 15^3 πρὸ προσώπου. Aqu. 1 Km 22^4 2 Km 6^{14} πρὸ προσώπου, Aqu. Isa 7^2 ἀπὸ (ἐκ Q) προσώπου.

Χείρ : Heb. בְּיַד becomes εἰς χεῖρας *in the power of* Mt 26⁴⁵ Lk 23⁴⁶ Jn 13³ Heb 10³¹ etc., or ἐν (τῇ) χειρί Jn 3³⁵ Ac 7³⁵ (vl. σύν), or διὰ χειρός, χειρῶν (Ge 39⁴ etc.) Mk 6² Ac 2²³ 5¹² and oft. Heb. מִיַד becomes ἐκ χειρός Lk 1⁷¹ Ac 12¹¹. (Johannessohn DGPS *passim*.)

Στόμα although Heb. influence has increased the usage, στόμα is used in many similar ways in class. Greek: διά (Lk 1⁷⁰ Ac 1¹⁶ etc.), ἐκ, ἐπί. (Johannessohn DGPS *passim*.)

CHAPTER NINETEEN

NEGATIVES

(especially the encroachment of MH upon the province of OY)

§ 1. General[1]

The distinction between οὐ and μή is now far less subtle than in class. Greek. Broadly, in the LXX οὐ renders לֹא and μή אַל, and οὐχί הֲלֹא (e.g. Ge 40⁸).

In his examination of the Ptol. pap., Mayser observes that the use of the two negative particles (οὐ as objective, μή as subjective), as handed down from the classical period, managed to hold its own in the Koine of the Hellenistic period as far as finite verbs are concerned. There are of course many deviations from classical standards. The infin. and ptc. play a special role in so far as here μή has won from οὐ the major part of its use (Mayser II 2, 543).

In post-classical prose, appreciation of the nice differences between οὐ and μή, which broadly speaking are like those between *non* and *ne*, has partially disappeared. It is not good to bring the difference between οὐ and μή under a definite rule, but doubtless there is a large increase in the use of μή in the later language. The same observations apply to the NT. There is sometimes no valid reason in favour of one particle against the other, and either may be used according to the author's own way of looking at things. There can be no difference between ἁμαρτίαν μὴ πρὸς θάνατον and ἁμαρτία οὐ πρὸς θάνατον 1 Jn 5¹⁶. Blass[2] made the rule that, in the NT, οὐ negatives the indicative (facts) and μή the remaining moods (ideas): this applies also to οὐδείς μηδείς, οὐδέ μηδέ, οὔτε μήτε,

---

[1] K-G II 178–223. Gildersleeve *AJP* 3, 202. O. Birke, *De particularum μή et οὐ usu Polybiano, Dionysiaeo, Diodoreo, Straboneo*, Diss. Leipzig 1897. E. L. Greene, "Μή and οὐ before Lucian," in *Studies in Honor of Gildersleeve*, 1902. Mayser II 2, 543–567. Radermacher² 210 (with literature).

[2] Blass-Debr. § 426.

ούπω μήπω, ούκέτι μηκέτι, ούδαμώς μηδαμώς, ούδέποτε μηδέποτε. There are exceptions where μή negatives the indic., and ού is used with infin. and ptc. With a few exceptions, Blass's rule applies to the Ptol. papyri (Mayser II 2, 552) for the infin., but with the ptc. ού maintains its position fairly constantly, although even here also μή finally prevailed.

In general it seems that ού stands its ground where a clause with άλλά follows it, and for the major part where the negative expressions form a single idea, like ούκ ολίγοι, ού πολλοί, etc. (Mayser II 2, 550). Mt 9¹³ ού θυσίαν, Mk 9³⁷ ούκ έμέ, Ro 9²⁵ τόν ού λαόν μου, 10¹⁹ (LXX Dt 32²¹) έπ' ούκ έθνει עַם לֹא. Like ού βούλομαι (*refuse to*) in Ptol. pap., we find in NT ού θέλω Mk 9³⁰ (*I am averse to*), ούκ έχω Mt 13¹², ούκ έάω Ac 16⁷ (*forbid*), ούκ άγνοέω 2 Co 2¹¹ (*know well*). So also Lk 15¹³ Ac 1⁵ μετ' ού πολλάς ήμέρας, Jn 3³⁴ ούκ έκ μέτρου, Ac 17⁴ ούκ ολίγα, 20¹² ού μετρίως, 21³⁹ ούκ άσήμου, 27¹⁴ μετ' ού πολύ, 1 Co 1²⁶ ού πολλοί, Eph 5⁴ τά ούκ άνήκοντα. In LXX: 2 Mac 4¹³ ούκ άρχιερεύς. In the Ptol. pap. ούκ ολίγοι = πολλοί, ούκ εύ ών = κάκος, and ούχ ό τυχών = *unusual*. It should be observed that ού πᾶς is capable of two meanings, limiting and denying: (1) *not all*, i.e. *some*,¹ and (2) *not any*, i.e. *none at all* (ούδείς).² Both senses appear in Jn. The similar use of μή in class. Greek ³ does not appear in NT; in each instance the μή has another explanation.

§ 2. Main clauses

The prohibitive future has μή in NT (and ού μή Mt 16²²), whereas class. Greek sometimes has μή (as in Hom. Clem. 3⁶⁹ μηδένα μισήσετε). Mt 5²¹ 6⁵ 20²⁶ ούχ ούτως έσται έν ύμιν.

Both ού and μή are both found in questions: ⁴ ού or ούχί or ούδέ or ούκοῦν ⁵ if a positive answer is expected (= *nonne*)

---

[1] E.g. Mt 7²¹ 19¹¹ 1 Co 15³⁹.
[2] E.g. Mt 24²² ού... πᾶσα σάρξ = Heb, כֹּל לֹא or לֹא כֹּל; Ac 10¹⁴ ούδέποτε έφαγον πᾶν κοινόν.
[3] Plato *Gorg.* 459, 6 ό μή ιατρός, *Ant.* 5, 82 οί μή καθαροί, Thuc. 2, 45, 1 τό μή έμποδών.
[4] K-G II 524. F. C. Babbitt, "Questions with μή," *Proc. Amer. Philol. Assocn.* 32, 43.
[5] Jn 18³⁷ is difficult, because a neg. answer is expected; ούκοῦν appears to be merely inferential (the stress on the οὖν). In Ac 2⁷ ούχί ιδού is a Koine idiom, like the class. ἆρ' ού; *Beg.* in loc.

Mt 7^{22} $13^{27.55}$ Mk 14^{60} Lk 12^6 17^{17} Ac 13^{10} 21^{38} Ro 2^{26} 1 Co 9^1 (οὐχί alongside οὐ) 14^{23}; μή or μήτι if a negative answer (*num, surely not*): Mt 7^{16} 26^{25} (Judas's μήτι ἐγώ εἰμι expects a negative answer but receives a positive), Jn 5^{38} (may be a question: *do you marvel at this?*), 7^{51} (Nicodemus is rather subtle in using μή), 21^5, 6^{67}, $7^{31.47}$, Ro 11^1 (μή ἀπώσατο is expressly answered in 11^2 with οὐκ ἀπώσατο), 1 Co 6^3 (elliptical μήτιγε, as Demosth. 2, 23). Sometimes the difference is illustrated in a single verse: Lk 6^{39} μήτι δύναται τυφλὸς τυφλὸν ὁδηγεῖν (answer no); οὐχὶ ἀμφότεροι εἰς βόθυνον ἐμπεσοῦνται (answer yes); 1 Co 9^8 μή κατὰ ἄνθρωπον ταῦτα λαλῶ, ἤ καὶ ὁ νόμος ταῦτα οὐ λέγει; 2 Co 12^{18} μήτι ἐπλεονέκτησεν ὑμᾶς Τίτος (no); οὐ τῷ αὐτῷ πνεύματι περιεπατήσαμεν (yes); Jn 4^{33-35}, Ro 9^{20f}.

A positive answer will be expected if οὐ μή (= *nonne*) is found in questions: Lk 18^7 Jn 18^{11} Rev 15^4.

Where μή negatives the whole sentence the verb alone may already be negatived by οὐ (Paul, as class.), and so μή ... οὐ stands with a sentence which expects a positive answer: Ro 10^{17ff} μή οὐκ ἤκουσαν *surely you haven't not-heard it* (missed hearing it), 1 Co 9^{4f} μή οὐκ ἔχομεν: 11^{22}, 2 Co 12^{20} μήπως ... οὐχ ... εὕρω.

In some passages the strength of μή is somewhat modified: Jn 4^{29} μήτι οὗτός ἐστιν ὁ Χριστός *he must be* (or *perhaps he is*) *the Messiah*; hardly *num* here; it is more like οὐ; the distinction is sometimes difficult to draw for much depends on the tone of the speaker; it is here rather hesitant, as in 4^{33}. On the later μήτι = *perhaps*, see Abbott Joh. Gr. 2702 b 1. See also A. T. Robertson, " The NT Use of μή with hesitant question in the Indicative Mood," Expos. Series VIII No. 152, 1923.

In main clauses μή occurs with subjunctive (Mk 12^{14} Ga 6^9), optative (only wish-opt. in NT., viz. Mk 11^{14} Ro $3^{4.6.31}$ Ga 6^{14} etc.), and imperative (Mt 6^3 μή γνώτω, 24^{18} μή ἐπιστρεψάτω ὀπίσω, LXX Ex 34^3 Ps 6^2). But see 1 Co 5^{10}, 1 Pt 2^{18} (οὐ μόνον), 3^3 (ὧν ἔστω οὐχ ὁ ... κόσμος), and we find οὐ and ἔστω in Ptol. pap. and οὐδενὶ ἐξέστω in inscr. cited by Radermacher (171).

§ 3. Dependent Clauses

The indicative with εἰ has οὐ in the NT and Koine, if the condition is " real ", seldom the μή which was normal in classical;[1] sometimes even class. Greek had οὐ if εἰ = ἐπεί or = *if, as you hope* (K-G II 189f), in which case always οὐ in NT and Koine. Lk 11⁸ εἰ καὶ οὐ δώσει, 16³¹ εἰ Μωϋσέως... οὐκ ἀκούουσιν, Jn 10³⁷ εἰ οὐ ποιῶ τὰ ἔργα... εἰ δὲ ποιῶ. So also Lk 14²⁶ 16¹¹ Jn 1²⁵ 3¹² Ro 11²¹ 1 Co 7¹¹ 15¹³ 1 Ti 3⁵ 5⁸ Jas 2¹¹ Rev 20¹⁵. Contrary to normal Greek usage, οὐ enters once with " unreal " indicative : Mt 26²⁴ Mk 14²¹ καλὸν αὐτῷ εἰ οὐκ ἐγενήθη. But μή is always found when εἰ = *nisi* (e.g. Mt 5¹³ Ac 26³² Ga 1⁷).

Relative clauses regularly have οὐ with indic., and μή on very rare occasions : Lk 8¹⁸ ὃς ἂν μὴ ἔχῃ (conditional), Ac 15²⁹ D, Col 2¹⁸ ἃ μὴ ἑώρακεν C vulg syr^p (p⁴⁶ S*ABD om μή), Ti 1¹¹ διδάσκοντες ἃ μὴ δεῖ (= 1 Ti 5¹³ τὰ μὴ δέοντα), 2 Pt 1⁹ ᾧ γὰρ μὴ πάρεστιν ταῦτα (correct according to literary style, as the speech is not about definite things : K-G II 185f), 1 Jn 4³ ὃ μὴ ὁμολογεῖ, Rev 14⁴ p⁴⁷ οἳ μὴ μετὰ γυναικῶν ἐμολύνθησαν (rest : οὐκ). See also Ac 3²³ Rev 13¹⁵, LXX Le 23²⁹ (πᾶσα ψυχὴ ἥτις μὴ ταπεινωθήσεται), Si 13²⁴.

In statement clauses with ὅτι and ὡς, and temporal and causal clauses with indic., although οὐ largely remains, μή is encroaching in the Koine.[2] Jn 3¹⁸ ὅτι μὴ πεπίστευκεν *because (such a person) would not have believed* (but οὐ in 1 Jn 5¹⁰), Heb 9¹⁷ ἐπεὶ μή ποτε ἰσχύει, B.U. 530³⁵ ἐπὶ μὴ ἀντέγραψας αὐτῇ (i/A.D.), Jos. c. Ap. 1, 217, Hom. Clem. 8¹⁴ etc. Blass-Debr. § 428, 5.

§ 4. Participles [3]

The post-classical language strongly tends towards μή (MGr only μή) with participles, whereas in class. Attic the decision to use μή depended on the meaning of the ptc. in each instance. NT follows the Hellenistic tendency and μή is the rule, especially with articular ptc., and even where the ptc. has

---

[1] Classical μή: Lk 6⁴D εἰ δὲ μὴ οἶδας; 1 Ti 6³ εἴ τις ἑτεροδιδασκαλεῖ καὶ μὴ προσέχεται (yet οὐ in 3⁵ 5⁸).
[2] K-G II 188. Jannaris § 1818. Mayser II 2, 551. Moulton Einl. 271n. Radermacher² 211.
[3] K-G II 198ff. Jannaris §§ 1815f. Mayser II 2, 556ff. G. E. Howes, " The Use of μή with the Participle, where the negation is influenced by the construction upon which the Participle depends," *Harvard Studies* 12, 1901, 277ff, A. G. Laird, " When is generic μή particular? " *AJP* 43, 1922, 124–45.

§ 4–5] NEGATIVES 285

an "indicative" sense: 2 Co 6³ μηδεμίαν ἐν μηδενὶ διδόντες προσκοπήν, Ti 1⁶· ⁷ τέκνα ἔχων πιστά, μὴ ἐν κατηγορίᾳ ἀσωτίας. Indeed the use of μή in NT is wider than in the Ptol. papyri. The proportions for the latter are: iii/B.C. οὐ: μή = 4 : 1, ii–i/B.C. οὐ: μή = 2 : 3 (Mayser II 2, 556, 562). However, the use of individual NT authors does vary to some extent. Thus in Mt and Jn οὐ is scarcely found at all apart from Mt 22¹¹ εἶδεν ἄνθρωπον οὐκ ἐνδεδυμένον ἔνδυμα γάμου (C³D μή), Jn 10¹² ὁ μισθωτὸς καὶ οὐκ ὢν ποιμήν (μή more correct as it refers to no definite person; but καὶ μή is not liked in the Koine). But Lk–Ac is more classical in this respect: Lk 6⁴² αὐτὸς... οὐ βλέπων (not D), Ac 7⁵ οὐκ ὄντος αὐτῷ τέκνου, 19¹¹ 28² οὐχ ὁ τυχών (*no ordinary*; in Ptol. pap. with same meaning: BU 436⁹ καὶ ὕβριν οὐ τὴν τυχοῦσαν συνετελέσαντο *committed a more than ordinary outrage* ¹), 26²² οὐδὲν ἐκτὸς λέγων, 28¹⁷ οὐδὲν... ποιήσας, ¹⁹ οὐχ ὡς ἔχων.

But Paul, Heb. and 1 Pt (with few exceptions) prefer the Hellenistic μή. The exceptions are Ro 9²⁵, 1 Co 9²⁶ ὡς οὐκ (but 2 Co 10¹⁴ ὡς μή where it is a conception only and not a fact), 2 Co 4⁸ᶠ (p⁴⁶ μή), 5¹² CDEFG (p⁴⁶ SB μή). The fact that Paul almost invariably uses μή with participles does lead to ambiguity ²: Ga 6⁹ μὴ ἐκλυόμενοι (which in class. Greek must be *if we do not faint*; but by Paul it is intended as a fact), Ro 8⁴ ἐν ἡμῖν τοῖς μὴ κατὰ σάρκα περιπατοῦσιν (it would be *IF we do not walk*... in class. Greek, but Paul probably means *us who DO not*...).

§ 5. Infinitive ³

Here in general is μή, but there are traces of an older use of οὐ. It is simplifying too much to say that μή stands throughout; it occurs indeed even after verbs of feeling (Ac 25²⁵ 2 Co 11⁵), but there is Ac 19²⁷ εἰς οὐθὲν λογισθῆναι and 2 Ti 2¹⁴ μὴ λογομαχεῖν ἐπ' οὐδὲν χρήσιμον, even if with Blass in Mk 7²⁴ Jn 21²⁵ Ac 26²⁶ we rather perversely take the οὐ more closely with the main verb than with the infin. (Blass-Debr. § 429). A redundant μή appears with infin. sometimes depending on a

---
[1] Mayser II 2, 518, 546. Preisigke s.v. τυγχάνω 4. Bauer s.v. 2d.
[2] Zerwick § 307a.
[3] Mayser II 2, 552ff, 564f. Jannaris § 1815. Moulton Einl. 271 n.

negative main verb (class. and Hell.), e.g. Lk 4⁴², 17¹ ἀνένδεκτόν ἐστιν τοῦ τὰ σκάνδαλα μὴ ἐλθεῖν, 20²⁷ WA (SBD etc. avoid it by harmonizing with Mt Mk), 22³⁴ (SB om μή), Ac 4²⁰ οὐ δυνάμεθα ... μὴ λαλεῖν, Ga 5⁷, 1 Pt 3¹⁰, 1 Jn 2²².

§ 6. Double Negatives

These are of two types, self-cancelling and pleonastic. The self-cancelling is classical and appears rarely in NT: Lk 8¹⁷ οὐ γάρ ἐστιν κρυπτὸν ὃ οὐ φανερὸν γενήσεται; also Mt 24² Ac 4²⁰ 1 Co 9⁶ 12¹⁵. Sometimes however it is not so much that the negatives are self-cancelling as that both have their full force: Mt 10²⁶ Lk 12² οὐδὲν δὲ συγκεκαλυμμένον ἐστὶν ὃ οὐκ ἀποκαλυφθήσεται, Mt 24² etc. οὐ ... ὃς οὐ, Ac 19³⁵ τίς ἐστιν ... ὃς οὐ.

Pleonastic negatives, which were frequent in class. Attic and well suited to the lively Greek temperament, are not as plentiful now. The negative was strengthened by sequences like οὐ (μή) ... οὐδείς (μηδείς), e.g. Mk 5³ καὶ οὐδὲ ἁλύσει οὐκέτι οὐδεὶς ἐδύνατο αὐτὸν δῆσαι, 11² vl. οὐδείς ... οὔπω, ¹⁴ μηκέτι ... μηδείς, 15⁴·⁵ (οὐ ... οὐδέν often in Ptol. pap.), Lk 4² 23⁵³ Jn 15⁵ 19⁴¹Ac 8³⁹ (οὐκ ... οὐκέτι in Ptol. pap.) Ro 13⁸ 2 Co 11⁹ 1 Ti 1⁷ μή ... μηδέ ... μηδέ is frequent in Ptol. pap.) Heb 13⁵. But two constructions are not classical: (1) the use of τις with the negative in the Koine (for οὐδείς), e.g. Mt 11²⁷ οὐδὲ τὸν πατέρα τις ἐπιγνώσκει, 12¹⁹, Jn 10²⁸ οὐχ ἁρπάσει τις, 1 Co 6¹², 1 Th 1⁸ μή ... τι (in Ptol. pap. μηθὲν ... τι, οὔτε ... τι, and μηδὲ ... τινάς (Mayser II 2, 567); (2) the amalgam of οὐδέ and οὐ μή to form a very strong but pleonastic οὐδ' οὐ μή, e.g. Mt 24²¹ (D οὐδὲ μή), Mk 14²⁵ οὐκέτι οὐ μὴ πίω (SDWCL om οὐκέτι), Heb 13⁵ from LXX Dt 31⁶ where only A has οὐδ' οὐ μή (p⁴⁶ οὐδὲ μή), Mt 25⁹BDC Did 4¹⁰ μήποτε οὐ μή, LXX Am 2¹⁵ Jb 32²¹, pap. Wilcken Chr. no. 122⁴ (A.D. 6) οὐδ' οὐ μὴ γένηται. On μὴ οὐ see p. 98. On οὐ μή see pp. 95–98.

§ 7. Yes and No

Yes ναί Mt 5³⁷ Lk 7²⁶ 2 Co 1¹⁷ Jas 5¹² and no οὔ or οὐχί (MGr ὄχι) Mt 13²⁹ Lk 1⁶⁰ etc. Note the contrast of objective and subjective negative in Mk 12¹⁴ ἔξεστι ... δοῦναι ἢ οὔ; δῶμεν ἢ μὴ δῶμεν;

§ 8. Position of the Negative

As a rule the negative precedes what is negatived, except that it may also (as in class. Greek) precede the preposition or ὡς if such occurs before a ptc. or adj.: Ac 1⁵ Lk 15¹³ D οὐ μετὰ πολλὰς ἡμέρας, 2 Co 10¹⁴ p⁴⁶ μὴ ὡς (the rest correct to ὡς μή), Heb 11³ τὸ μὴ ἐκ φαινομένων. Often negative and verb are blended in one idea: οὐκ ἐάω (and more popular οὐκ ἀφίω) *prevent* Ac 19³⁰ etc. This may be altered to achieve emphasis, and in Ac 7⁴⁸ the position of οὐχ puts *the Most High* in relief, as μή in Jas 3¹ puts πολλοί in relief (also οὐδέν emphatic, away from λανθάνειν in Ac 26²⁶, and οὐ before the inappropriate verb in 1 Co 2²). So LXX Nu 16²⁹ᵇ. But a negative which is separated from its verb may affect the complement: Mk 9³⁷ οὐκ ἐμὲ δέχεται *it is not me that he receives*, 2 Co 3³ ἐνγεγραμμένη οὐ μέλανι *written not with ink*. The rule is several times broken with πᾶς: Ro 3²⁰ πᾶσα σάρξ . . . οὐ, Eph 5⁵ 1 Jn 2²¹ πᾶς . . . οὐ, Eph 4²⁹ πᾶς . . . μή, 1 Co 15⁵¹ πάντες οὐ κοιμηθησόμεθα (*must*=οὐ πάντες). On the other hand, οὐ πάντως (Ro 3⁹) must be reversed or taken separately: *no! absolutely* or *certainly not* (*not in all cases* is scarcely possible); scribes felt the difficulty, too.

BOOK TWO
THE SENTENCE COMPLETE: SYNTHETIC SYNTAX

PART I
THE ORDINARY SIMPLE SENTENCE

CHAPTER TWENTY

SUBJECT AND PREDICATE: APPARENT ABSENCE OF SUBJECT [1]

§ 1. Impersonal Verbs [2]

Hellenistic (Polyb.) βρέχει Jas 5¹⁷ for class. ὕει (Mayser II 3, 2; Abel § 39a); but personal at Mt 5⁴⁵ (as class., and LXX Ge 19²⁴). For βροντῆσαι Jn 12²⁹ has βροντὴν γεγονέναι. The problematic ἀπέχει Mk 14⁴¹ may be impersonal, for class. ἀρκεῖ: *it is receipted, the account is settled* (consistent with the meaning of the variant in DW ἀπέχει τὸ τέλος *it has its end, the matter is settled*); so in P. Lond. IV 1343³⁸ (709 A.D.), etc.[3] Lk 24²¹ may not be impers., τρίτην ταύτην ἡμέραν ἄγει, but the subject is Jesus: *he has already allowed three days to pass* (see Bauer s.v., ἄγω, 4). In Mk 2² ὥστε μηκέτι χωρεῖν μηδὲ τὰ πρὸς τὴν θύραν, the last four words may be the subject of χωρεῖν (Moule 27). Impers. μέλει Mt 22¹⁶ Mk 12¹⁴ Jn 10¹³ 1 Co 9⁹ 1 Pt 5⁷. But in Mk 4³⁸ Lk 10⁴⁰ 1 Co 7²¹ a clause is the subject.

The impers. passive, quite common in Latin, is fairly so in NT but on the whole is very rare in Greek apart from some exx. of the perfect παρεσκεύασται *preparations are made*. The desire to avoid God's name enters into the picture in NT. Mt 7² μετρηθήσεται ὑμῖν (but a cognate noun μέτρον may be understood), Lk 6³⁸ δίδοτε καὶ δοθήσεται ὑμῖν (but further on μέτρον ... δώσουσιν), 1 Pt 4⁶ νεκροῖς εὐηγγελίσθη; a cognate noun may be supplied here, but not in Ro 10¹⁰ πιστεύεται ... ὁμολογεῖται, 1 Co 15⁴²ᶠ σπείρεται ... ἐγείρεται.

Certain verbs are only apparently impersonal, since the clause which follows can be taken as subject, e.g. ἐρρέθη in Mt 5³¹ Ro 9¹²; and so also δεῖ, ἔξεστιν, ἐξόν, ἐγένετο, ἐνδέχεται,

---

[1] K-G I § 352, pp. 32ff. Gildersleeve I 68–82. Meisterhans-Schwyzer 195. Wackernagel I 113f. Mayser II 3, 1ff. Zerwick §§ 1–4.
[2] For δέον, χρή, ἔδει see pp. 88, 90, 148, 322; for δοκεῖ p. 147.
[3] Alternative suggestions: A. Pallis, *Notes on St. Mark*, new ed., Oxford 1932, 47ff; G. H. Boobyer *NTS* 2, 1955–6, 44ff.

γέγραπται, πρέπει, ὠφελεῖ, which have a following infin. as subject (e.g. Ac 7²³ ἀνέβη ἐπὶ τὴν καρδίαν, Semitic). Lk 17¹ has as subject τοῦ τὰ σκάνδαλα μὴ ἐλθεῖν (Moule 27); so with λυσιτελεῖ (only Lk 17²), πρέπον ἐστιν, συμφέρει, συνέβη. In 1 Pt 2⁶ περιέχει ἐν γραφῇ, the quotation may be the subject. But in Mt 13¹² περισσευθήσεται is probably passive and impers., because of the parallel (not *he shall be made to abound*).

§ 2. Impersonal "they"

Much more usual than the impers. passive, and a characteristic feature of Mk's style, is the 3rd plural without subject, meaning *one* or *they*. Languages which lack any special indeterminate subject like *man* (German) or *on* (French) tend to display this finite plural in verbs of speaking and narrating. The tendency of Aramaic to avoid the passive has exercised an influence extending to other verbs in NT, e.g. Lk 12²⁰ (ἀπαιτοῦσιν), and the same Aramaic tendency appears in words like ἀναβαίνω, said of the fish which *is taken up* Mt 17²⁷, or ἐξέρχομαι in place of ἐκβάλλομαι Lk 4⁴¹ 8²; see also ἀπελθεῖν εἰς τὴν γέενναν in place of βληθῆναι Mk 9⁴⁴; so Mt 5¹⁵ οὐδὲ καίουσιν λύχνον, 9² ἰδοὺ προσέφερον αὐτῷ παραλυτικόν, ¹⁷ οὐδὲ βάλλουσιν οἶνον. Dan 4²² O' and θ, 4²⁸ σοί λέγουσιν (O' λέγεται), 4²⁹ ἀπὸ τῶν ἀνθρώπων σε ἐκδιώκουσιν ... χόρτον ὡς βοῦν ψωμιοῦσίν σε. In Mk 2¹⁸ the undefined plural may be impers. or it may refer to the subject of the preceding sentence; but ἔλεγον in 3²¹ is an example of the impers. pl. which C. H. Turner showed to be a special feature of Mark (*JThS* 25, 1924, 377-386). In at least two places this is of some importance to the exegete, for (1) at Mk 3²¹ we read *when his own people heard, they went out to take him, for THEY said* ... ἔλεγον γὰρ ὅτι ἐξέστη. It is wrong to assume that his mother and brothers think that Jesus is mad, for the verb ἔλεγον can be considered an indef. plural: *rumour had it*, that he was mad. (2) Also Mk 14² becomes more intelligible if ἔλεγον is taken as an indefinite plural: the chief priests and scribes were plotting the death of Jesus with subtilty, *for* (true text of Mark) *THEY said, Not during the feast* .... This γάρ gives a reason for their decision, and *they* is therefore someone else, not the chief priests and scribes (C. H. Turner, op. cit. 384f).

Aramaic influence has enlarged the class of verbs which may be so used, since Aramaic avoids the passive, but Moulton and Milligan (Vocab. 52) cite a iii/A.D. papyrus with ἀπαιτοῦσιν, like Lk 12²⁰; so also P. Fay. III 14 λέγουσιν, P. Hib. 27. 167 κάουσιν. In class. Greek the construction was used primarily with verbs of saying, φασί, λέγουσι, καλοῦσι, ἔρχονται, but in NT we have also τεθνήκασιν (Mt 2²⁰), συλλέγουσιν (Mt 7¹⁶ Lk 6⁴⁴), προσέφερον (Mk 10¹³). In Heb 10¹ προσφέρουσιν and δύνανται may be in this class. The subject οἱ ἄνθρωποι is actually present in Mk 8²⁷ Lk 6³¹, and this may be the intermediate stage towards the impers. verb. The suppression of the subject seems to bring emphasis on the action. At times the 3rd pl. may be used circumspectly for God's own action, and so his name rather than οἱ ἄνθρωποι is to be understood: Lk 6³⁸ δώσουσιν, 12²⁰·⁴⁸ (ἀπ-)αἰτοῦσιν, 16⁹ (*that God may receive you into eternal dwellings*), 23³¹ (?). See Moulton-Howard 447.

§ 3. Scil. "the Scripture"

In the quotation formula λέγει, etc. a subject θεός or γραφή is understood: Ro 10⁸ λέγει p⁴⁶ SAB (DFG insert ἡ γραφή); λέγει also in 2 Co 6² Ga 3¹⁶ etc., φησίν in 1 Co 6¹⁶ Heb 8⁵, εἴρηκε Heb 4⁴. We have something like a diatribe in 2 Co 10¹⁰ φησίν *says my opponent*. See also Wackernagel I 113.

CHAPTER TWENTY-ONE

SUBJECT AND PREDICATE:
ABSENCE OF THE VERB "TO BE"

§ 1. The Copula[1]

From the standpoint of class. Attic there is nothing remarkable about the extensive absence of the copula in NT, for this was the most common form of ellipse and, except where ambiguity threatened, was almost the rule. The NT is indeed nearer to Ionic Greek where " en dehors de quelques expressions consacrées, [Herodotus] n'exprime plus, dans la langue courante, un jugement en juxtaposant simplement le sujet et l'attribut. Il ajoute une copule." (Barbelenet 103). The pure nominal phrase is still a living thing in Herodotus, but very seriously limited (ibid. 18); it is commoner in the Ionic poets (ibid. 19). In NT the ellipse is not so general as in the earlier Attic Greek and is almost confined to ἐστιν and to these " expressions consacrées ", viz. dead phrases of either an impersonal or stereotyped and epigrammatic character (incl. ὄνομα) or else very live phrases of a rhetorical and dramatic sort. It was the post-classical tendency to view the pure nominal phrase as an ellipse and to reserve it for poetic archaism, stylistic expressions and set formulae (Schwyzer II 623). The NT has gone further than class. Attic or contemporary literary Hellenistic in inserting the copula, but not so far as Herodotus, except in Mk and Jn. Semitic influence may have assisted the NT, but more probably

---

[1] K-G I § 354, pp. 40ff. Gildersleeve I 83–86. Meisterhans-Schwyzer § 80, pp. 195ff. Mayser II 3, 16ff. J. E. Harry, " On the omission of the copula in certain combinations in Greek," *Proc. Amer. Philol. Assocn.* 34, p. viii ff. J. Kinzel, *Die Kopula bei Homer und Hesiod*, Progr. Mährisch-Ostrau 1908, 1909. C. G. Wilke, *De ellipsi copulae verbi* εἶναι *in fabulis Euripideis*, Breslau 1877. D. Barbelenet, *De la Phrase à Verbe être dans l'Ionien d'Hérodote*, Paris 1913. E. Ekman, *Der reine Nominalsatze bei Xenophon*, 1938. P. F. Regard, *La Phrase nominale dans la Langue du NT*, Paris 1919. A. W. Milden, " The possessive in the predicate in Greek ", *Proc. Amer. Philol. Assocn.* 37, 24; " The article in the predicate in Greek," ibid. 40, 63.

it is a matter of literary standards.[1] Luke and Paul resort much less to the copula than Mark or John. In MGr it is not usual to omit the appropriate part of εἶναι unless oratorical effect is deliberately sought.

So side by side in Biblical Greek there are the Attic pure nominal phrase and the Ionic nominal phrase with the copula, both used by each Biblical writer with equal spontaneity; but the writers vary considerably in their preferences. In common with the Indo-Germanic languages in general, Greek was tending to replace the pure nominal phrase by the phrase with a copula, and some writers have taken the process further than others.

(a) *Fixed phrases*

In detail, the part of the verb which most usually is to be supplied is 3rd sing. pres. ind., as in class. Greek. This is seen in certain impers. phrases introduced by the neuter of an adj. (αἰσχρόν, ἀρκετόν, ἀδύνατον, δῶρον, δῆλον, εἰ δέον, εἰ δυνατόν, ἐξόν, κακόν, καλόν, μέγα, ὄφελον, (ἔτι) μικρόν (καί), οὐ μόνον, οὐχ οἷον, πρόδηλον, συμφέρον, φανερόν), or by a noun expressing possibility or necessity (ἀνάγκη, χρή, ὥρα). This is so occasionally, even in Ionic (Hdt). It is true that πρέπον is never found without ἐστιν in NT (unlike 1 Mac 12[11]; but ἦν in 3 Mac 7[13]), and neither are the impers. ἄξιον or δίκαιον found without ἐστιν, as they are in contemporary Hellenistic writers. But ellipse is frequent with the other words. There is however no regular pattern within the NT.

A similar archaic usage is the Ionic ἔνι (= ἐν) as a kind of adverbial predicate without the copula. It is always negative in NT, not in Hdt. (Barbelenet 13).

A more frequent NT example of the survival of a lifeless formula is the pure nominal phrase containing ὄνομα, whether as a parenthesis or as a main or subordinate clause. The formula may be Hebraistic, through the influence of שֵׁם and וּשְׁמָהּ (LXX 1 Km 1[1] etc.), but it is not absent from class. and Hell. Greek and the papyri. The papyri and NT even here

---

[1] In the nearly exhaustive references at the close of this chapter not enough notice or discussion of text variants could be given. The student of the text will, however, gather the general principles behind each author's usage, and the exceptions, and ought thereby to be able to come nearer to a decision between the text variants.

sometimes insert a copula: Jn 18¹⁰ Lk 8³⁰, Zen. pap. 59037, 7 (258 B.C.).

Another antique survival of the pure nominal phrase is the stereotyped phrase at the beginning and end of letters. We may supply either the optative or imperative or fut. indic. (Mayser II 3, 19). The formulae are less stereotyped at the end than at the beginning of letters. No doubt Semitic influence assisted their survival in NT (cf. שָׁלוֹם לָכֶם Ge 43²³). See Büchsel in Kittel WB III 300f.

The survival of the pure nominal phrase is seen above all, as in class. Greek (even in Hdt.), in proverbial saws which abound in the NT. When we do occasionally find the copula it may be that special emphasis is intended.

(b) *Spontaneous or live expressions*

These on the contrary are not verbally the same phrases as in earlier Greek, which testifies to the originality and spontaneity of the method of using the pure nominal phrase in NT. Attic influence may explain it, since the corresponding phrase in Ionic Greek usually has the copula (Regard 45).

On the Semitic model, and occurring in an OT atmosphere, is ἰδού (scil. pres. or impf. or even aor. or fut. of εἰμί and of πάρειμι and (παρα)γίνομαι), although there are secular parallels. Besides, interjections do not need a verbal predicate in normal Greek, as οὐά in Mk 15²⁹. Yet the copula does occur with ἰδού in NT. On the Semitic model is οὐαί (אוֹי הוּא, etc.) and yet the copula appears here too.

Free of any suspicion of archaism are pure nominal phrases in the form of exclamations. They are very common in NT, even when we exclude direct LXX quotations, e.g. ἅγιον τὸ ὄνομα αὐτοῦ Lk 1⁴⁹, εὐλογημένος ὁ ἐρχόμενος Mt 21⁹ 23³⁹ = Lk 13³⁵ 19³⁸ = Jn 12¹³, εὐλογητὸς κύριος Lk 1⁶⁸, εὐλογητὸς ὁ θεός 2 Co 1³, and μακάριοι ὧν, μακάριος ἀνὴρ ὅς Ro 4⁷ᶠ Jas 1¹². Usually the order is attribute-subject. Again we are reminded of Semitic influence, but we should remember the class. and Hell. parallels. Moreover, there are many instances where the copula creeps in, even in the μακάριος phrase. In the doxologies, indic., imper., or optative might equally well be supplied. However, in spite of LXX precedent,[1] it is not the optative

---

[1] 3 Km 10⁸ γένοιτο εὐλ., Jb 1²¹ εἴη εὐλ.

idea which is in mind, for God is thought of as being *already* blessed and glorious. Since there is no need to pray for it, the phrase is simply an exclamation.

Akin to this is the pure nominal phrase in a series of graphic clauses. The most outstanding instance is the series of exclamations in 1 Co 15$^{39-56}$ and Ph 1$^{21-24}$. It is typically Pauline but it is found in the LXX and in contemporary Hell. authors. The statements are usually brief and vivid and abound in passages which rise to heights of oratory. One frequently finds it in the apodosis and protasis of conditional sentences. Yet sometimes in NT the copula is found in this kind of phrase, especially if the identity of the subject would otherwise be obscure. This literary tendency also appears when there is a striving after rhetoric in epigrammatic phrases and those which express general or abstract truths, especially in connection with the demonstrative pronoun; again there are exceptions. Some of these questions are stereotyped, but the majority are spontaneous. In the NT it is equally common to find the copula as the pure nominal phrase in questions.

The pure nominal phrase is found sometimes in indirect questions in Lk and Paul, as in literary Hell. Greek; also after ὅπου, ὡς, ὥσπερ, καθώς. Pernot (p. 53) notes the rather frequent absence of the copula in Jn after ὅτι (although it is far more often inserted) and we find this ellipse all over the NT (Mt Mk Lk 1 2 Co Ph Ro Rev), as well as in class. and Hell. writers, and papyri.

(c) *Ellipse of other parts besides ἐστιν*

This is more rare, and the pers. pronoun is usually added to avoid ambiguity—though not always in Paul. Almost universally in NT, εἰμι is inserted. If there is ellipse of εἶ, there is usually a pronoun, but ellipse is rare. Only in Paul is both pronoun and ἐσμεν absent. The ellipse of ἐστε is also rare: Lk 6^{20} has neither pronoun nor copula. Ellipse of εἰσιν is much more frequent, especially when it closely follows that of ἐστιν. The fut. indic. never suffers ellipse in NT except for rare instances of ἔσται. Almost the only kind of phrase in which ἦν might be supplied is that with ὄνομα; there are a few other instances, especially in vivid and interrogative phrases and the stereotyped εἰ δυνατόν. It is all but impossible to decide whether ἦν is a copula or something stronger. Other persons of impf. indic. are to be supplied very occasionally: ἦσαν or ἐγένοντο, and ἤμην.

There are but two or three places in NT (nearly all in Paul) where subjunctive ᾖ and ὦσιν may be supplied. The ellipse after ὅς ἄν etc. is classical (K–G § 354e, n. 2c; Gildersleeve I § 86). As well as epistolary formulae and formal wishes, there is the spontaneous use of the pure nominal phrase where optative is expected, as with εἰρήνη (Hebraic). There is no ellipse of ἔστω except in χάρις τῷ θεῷ (class. and early papyri). There are some further exx. in NT and Koine vernacular. Imper. ἐστέ may be supplied with some participles in Peter and Paul. But the ptc. is perhaps in itself imperatival; the phenomenon, which may be a peculiarity of the " eastern " Koine, is frequent in the vernacular and in Malalas. Something like ἴσθι is presumably to be supplied with δεῦρο. There is never need to supply ἔσεσθε.

Some phrases have only an apparent ellipse, because they follow immediately upon a previous clause which has the copula, and the copula is to be understood of both phrases: Mt 22[14] 25[351] 28[3] Lk 19[2] Jn 15[5] 20[26] 1 Co 14[10, 22] 11[3] 2 Co 10[11] 1 Jn 3[12] Rev 10[1] etc.

§ 2. Stronger or Essential meaning of ἐστιν or εἰσιν

On occasion, when emphasis or feeling is more than normal, there is even ellipse where the meaning is *there is (are)* or *it is*, and stronger than a mere copula. This happens also in both class. and literary Hell. Greek, and even sometimes in the papyri. Something like ἐστιν is to be supplied *before* ἵνα at times in Jn, and to some extent in Mk, Lk, and Paul. We may compare the ellipse before οὐχ ὅτι in Jn and Paul.

§ 3. Individual writers

The books of Biblical and certain secular writers may be laid side by side and in a general way the relative tendency to introduce or omit the copula will be discovered. It will be seen that in the Gospels there is some considerable difference from secular usage. (The copula infin. and ptc. have been excluded.)

§ 3] ABSENCE OF THE VERB "TO BE"

	Mt	Mk	Lk	Ac	Jn
Verb *to be*	257	174	318	213	395
Ellipse	81	37	91	27	47
Proportion	3:1	5:1	3:1	8:1	8:1

	Ro	1 Co	2 Co	Ga	Eph	Ph	Col	1 Th	2 Th	1 Ti	2 Ti	Ti	Ph
To be	67	133	48	48	38	11	24	9	6	20	13	8	2
Ellipse	105	90	72	19	19	29	5	10	7	16	7	5	2
Propn.	$\frac{3}{4}$:1	1:1	$\frac{3}{4}$:1	$2\frac{1}{2}$:1	2:1	$\frac{1}{2}$:1	5:1	1:1	1:1	1:1	2:1	$1\frac{1}{2}$:1	1:1

	Paul (non-Past)	Past	Heb	Jas	2 Pt Jude	Joh. Epp.	Rev 1–4, 21f	Rev 5–20	Rev tot	1 Pt
To be	386	41	35	27	15	105	48	44	92	8
Ellipse	358	28	60	16	4	2	39	52	91	28
Propn.	1:1	$1\frac{1}{2}$:1	$\frac{1}{2}$:1	2:1	5:1	50:1			1:1	$\frac{1}{4}$:1

	Strabo I 1 64 B.C.–A.D. 21	Diod. Sic. pt. 1 (c. 50 B.C.)	Dio Chrys. *Kingship* I, II (A.D. 40–120)	Philostr. *Vit. Apoll.* I (ii–iii/A.D.)	Hdt I–IV approx.*
To be	37	48 (some are essential)	51	70	381
Ellipse	54	27	55	83	70
Propn.	$\frac{3}{4}$:1	2:1	1:1	1:1	5:1

* For Hdt, the figures are based on Barbelenet; I take responsibility for the others.

Individual writers: Paul [1].

(a) *Fixed phrases:* δῆλον ὅτι 1 Co 15²⁷ 1 Ti 6⁷ DᶜKLP; αἰσχρόν c. infin. 1 Co 11⁶ (but 14³⁵ Eph 5¹² copula), δίκαιον 2 Th 1⁶, εἰ δυνατόν Ro 12¹⁸ Ga 4¹⁵, ἐξόν c. infin. 2 Co 12⁴, μέγα εἰ 1 Co 9¹¹ 2 Co 11¹⁵, συμφέρον 2 Co 12¹, ὄφελον c. ind. 1 Co 4⁸ 2 Co 11¹ Ga 5¹², ἀνάγκη c. inf. Ro 13⁵ SBA (but p⁴⁶ᶜ DEFG Irenˡˢᵗ have imper. without ἀνάγκη; p⁴⁶* imper. and καί without ἀνάγκη), ὥρα c. infin. Ro 13¹¹, οὐχ οἷον 9⁶, etc. (Exceptions: Ph 1⁷ καθώς ἐστιν δίκαιον, 1 Co 4³ 7⁹ 11²⁰ etc.). Epistolary formulae: χάρις (ὑμῖν) καὶ εἰρήνη Ro 1⁷ etc., χάρις ἔλεος εἰρήνη 1 Ti 1² 2 Ti 1², ἡ χάρις ... μετά Ro 16²⁰; and Ro 15³³ 1 Co 16²¹ Eph 6²³ Col 4¹⁸ 2 Th 3¹⁶ 2 Ti 4²² (Exception: with ἔσται 2 Co 13¹¹). Proverbial expressions: 1 Ti 2⁵ εἷς γὰρ ὁ θεός, Ti 1¹⁵ πάντα καθαρὰ τοῖς καθαροῖς; 1 Co 6¹³ τὰ βρώματα τῇ κοιλίᾳ ...; note πιστὸς ὁ θεός 1 Co 1⁹ etc., with the exception πιστὸς δέ ἐστιν ὁ κύριος 2 Th 3³. Strangely, the copula does appear with οὐαί 1 Co 9¹⁷ (unlike Syn. Gospels).

(b) *Spontaneous phrases:* exclamations (we are reminded of Heb. infl. in the Semitism μακάριος ὁ Ro 14²², but there are Greek parallels; another Hebraism, not from the LXX, is ὡς ὡραῖοι Ro 10¹⁵). Ro 11³³ ὡς ἀνεξεραύνητα, 1 Co 12³ ἀνάθεμα Ἰησοῦς, κύριος Ἰησοῦς, 15¹⁴ κενὸν ἄρα τὸ κήρυγμα ἡμῶν, ¹⁷· ²⁴· ⁵⁷, 2 Co 2¹⁴, χάρις τῷ θεῷ Ro 6¹⁷ etc., Ro 7²⁴ ταλαίπωρος ἐγὼ ἄνθρωπος, Ph 4⁵ ὁ κύριος ἐγγύς, etc. There are phrases with μάρτυς, as 1 Th 2⁵· ¹⁰ Ph 1⁸ (but ἐστιν is retained Ro 1⁹). Then there is the negative phrase οὐ θαῦμα 2 Co 11¹⁴ (see Bertram in Kittel WB III 40). Doxologies: εὐλογητὸς ὁ θεός (בָּרוּךְ אֱלֹהִים); 2 Co 1³ Eph 1³, ᾧ ἡ δόξα Ga 1⁵ etc. (but ἐστιν added 1 Pt 4¹¹). (Exceptions: ὅς ἐστιν εὐλ. Ro 1²⁵, ὁ ὢν εὐλ. 2 Co 11³¹.) Graphic sentences (typical of Pauline style): ἄρα ἡ πίστις ἐξ ἀκοῆς, ἡ δὲ ἀκοὴ διὰ ῥήματος Χριστοῦ Ro 10¹⁷, οὗ δὲ τὸ πνεῦμα κυρίου, ἐλευθερία (sc. essential ἐστιν) 2 Co 3¹⁷, τὰ γὰρ βλεπόμενα πρόσκαιρα, τὰ δὲ μὴ βλεπόμενα αἰώνια 4¹⁸; 7⁴· ⁵ (sc. essential ἐστιν), Ph 3¹, Ga 3¹⁸, Ro 2²⁸ᶠ, 5¹⁶· ¹⁸, 6²³ 7¹² 8⁶· ¹⁰ 1 Co 1²⁶ 3²²ᶠ 4¹⁰ 2 Co 10¹⁰ Ph 1²¹· ²²· ²⁴ 3¹⁹, 4⁸,

Conditional sentences: with ellipse in both apodosis and protasis Ro 11⁶· ¹²· ¹⁵ᶠ. (Exceptions: the copula is sometimes found in these graphic sentences, especially if the identity of the subject would otherwise be obscure: ὁ γὰρ ἐν κυρίῳ κληθεὶς δοῦλος ἀπελεύθερος κυρίου ἐστίν· ὁμοίως ὁ ἐλεύθερος κληθεὶς δοῦλός ἐστιν Χριστοῦ 1 Co 7²².)

Other expressions, mainly rhetorical or epigrammatic: 1 Co 5⁶ οὐ καλὸν τὸ καύχημα ὑμῶν, Ro 9⁷ (οὐδὲ) πάντες τέκνα, 13¹⁰ πλήρωμα οὖν νόμου (ἡ) ἀγάπη, 1 Co 1²⁴ p⁴⁶ Clem Alx Χριστὸς θεοῦ δύναμις καὶ θεοῦ σοφία ² ; Ro 3²⁰· ²² 4¹³ 5¹⁶ 6²¹ 7⁹ 8⁷ 10⁴ 13¹¹ 14¹⁸ 2 Co 4¹⁵ 5¹⁷· ¹⁸ 8²³· ²⁴ Ro 10¹· ¹² 12¹⁹ Ga 5⁸ 1 Co 11¹¹· ¹² 13¹³ 15²¹· ³⁹ (and so throughout

---

[1] I have drawn up a complete list of every occurrence in the NT, but there is room only for representative instances in this volume, and the rest must be left over for a separate monograph. The word "etc." indicates that there are further examples. See also footnote above, p. 295.

[2] The source from which Paul may have derived the phrase, i.e. Danθ 2²⁰, has the copula: ἡ σοφία καὶ ἡ δύναμις αὐτοῦ ἐστι.

§ 3] ABSENCE OF THE VERB "TO BE" 301

this eloquent chapter: 40. 41. 46. 47. 48. 56. 56) 2 Co 1⁷. ²¹ 2⁶ 5⁵ 10⁴ Eph 5⁹. ²³ Col 2¹⁷ 1 Th 2³ 4⁶ 2 Th 3² 1 Ti 4⁴ 5²⁵ 2 Ti 3¹⁶ Ti 1¹⁵ (Exceptions: Ro 1¹⁹ 1 Co 6¹⁸ 7²⁹ (periph. pf.) 1¹⁸ 2¹⁴ 3¹⁹ 4⁴ 6¹⁷. ¹⁹ 9¹⁶ 11⁷. ⁸. ¹⁵. ²⁵ (Lk's parallel 22²⁰ omits the copula; Cadbury remarks on the strangeness of this ¹, in view of Luke's regular practice of inserting the copula, esp. if he found it in his sources. It is probably not a Pauline phrase, but one which he inherited) 12¹⁴. ²² 3⁷ 6⁷ 7¹⁴. ¹⁴ 14¹⁵, Col 1¹⁸ καὶ αὐτός ἐστιν ἡ κεφαλὴ τοῦ σώματος, 1 Ti 1⁵ τὸ δὲ τέλος τῆς παραγγελίας ἐστιν ἀγάπη.)

Much emphasis (= *is certainly*) appears to be achieved by the insertion of ἐστιν in πιστὸς δέ ἐστιν ὁ κύριος 2 Th 3³ (better text); so also Ro 1¹⁶ 2²⁸ 11²³ 1 Co 1²⁵ 3¹⁷. ²¹ 11⁷ᶠ 14³³ 2 Co 3¹⁷ Ga 3¹² 4². ²⁶ 5¹⁹ Eph 5¹³. ³² 6¹² 1 Ti 3¹⁶ 4⁸. ⁸ 6¹⁰ 2 Ti 4¹¹. ¹¹ Ti 1¹⁰. There is no subject expressed in ἐστιν ἀπίστου χείρων 1 Ti 5⁸, ἐλευθέρα ἐστιν Ro 7³ 1 Co 7³⁹, Ro 13⁴. ⁶ 1 Co 7⁴⁰ Ga 5³, and therefore the verb *to be* is inserted for clarity's sake.

Demonstratives: there is sometimes ellipse when the attribute is a demonstrative adj. or adv. (οὕτως καὶ τὸ χάρισμα, etc.) Ro 5¹⁵ 9⁶. ⁸. ⁹ 1 Co 12¹² 14¹² 2 Co 10⁷ Eph 2⁸ 1 Th 5¹⁸ 1 Ti 2³. (Exceptions: Ro 8⁹. ¹⁴ 1 Co 9³ 10²⁸ 11²⁴ 2 Co 1¹² 10¹⁸, Ga 3⁷ (emphatic however), 4²⁴ (εἰσιν = *represent*), Eph 4¹⁰ 6¹ Col 3²⁰ 1 Ti 5⁴ Ti 3⁸; and τοῦτ' ἔστιν is a frequent idiom: Ro 1¹² 7¹⁸ 9⁸ 10⁶. ⁸ Phm¹².)

Interrogatives: τί γάρ μοι; 1 Co 5¹² etc., τί (μοι) τὸ ὄφελος 15³², τί οὖν; Ro 3⁹ 6¹⁵ 11⁷, τί γάρ; Ro 3³ Ph 1¹⁸. Questions introduced by τίς or τί: Ro 3¹ 8³¹ 1 Co 5¹² 2 Co 2². ¹⁶ 6¹⁴ (sc. essential ἐστιν) ¹⁴. ¹⁵. ¹⁶ Ga 3¹⁹ 1 Th 2¹⁹. By ποῦ: Ro 3²⁷ 1 Co 1²⁰ ter 12¹⁷. ¹⁷ 15⁵⁵. ⁵⁵ OT, 12¹⁹ (sc. ἦν), Ga 4¹⁵. By πόθεν: 1 Co 13⁵⁴. ⁵⁶ 15³³. Simple interrogative: ἦ 'Ιουδαίων ὁ θεὸς μόνον; ... Ro 3²⁹; also 4⁹ 7⁷ Ga 3²¹ 1 Th 2¹⁹ (sc. ἐστε). By μή: Ro 3⁵ 9¹⁴, in a series of five rhetorical questions 1 Co 12²⁹. ³⁰. (Exceptions: τί οὖν ἐστιν 'Απολλῶς; 1 Co 3⁵ 9¹⁸ 14¹⁵ Ro 9²⁰ 14⁴ 2 Co 3⁸, 1 Co 10¹⁶. ¹⁶ (but = *represent*; stronger than copula), 2 Co 12¹³.)

Subordinate clauses: indir. questions: τί Ro 8²⁷ 12², τίς, τί Eph 1¹⁸ (but after ἐστιν in the previous clause), τί τὸ πλοῦτος Col 1²⁷. (Exceptions: ὁποῖόν ἐστιν 1 Co 3¹³, τίς ἐστιν Eph 1¹⁸, τί ἐστιν 5¹⁰.) After ὅπου sc. ἐστιν 1 Co 3³. In protasis of conditions: sc. ἐστιν 1 Co 11⁶; sc. ἦν 1 Co 12¹⁷. ¹⁷; sc. essential ἐστιν, *there is* Ro 3³⁰ 13⁹; sc. ἐστιν or ἦν Ro 4¹⁴; sc. ἐστιν 8³¹ 11⁶ 2 Co 3⁹ 5¹⁷ Eph 4²⁹; sc. ἦν? 2 Co 3¹¹. This is Lukan and Pauline practice, which accords with class. and Hell. usage. (Exceptions: ἐὰν ᾖς Ro 2²⁵, εἴπερ εἰσιν 1 Co 8⁵, ἦν 1 Co 12¹⁹, ἐστε 2 Co 2⁹, ἐστιν (periph. pf.) 4³, εἰμι 2 Co 12¹¹, εἴ τις ἐστιν Ti 1⁶.) In relative clauses (see under Graphic, above): also Ro 9⁴ ὧν ἡ υἱοθεσία (sc. essential ἐστιν), 14²³, 1 Co 5¹ (sc. ess. ἐστιν), 8⁶ (do.), 2 Co 1²⁰, 8¹⁸ (do.); Ph 3¹⁵ 4³; confined to Luke, Paul, Heb. in NT, but more general in class. and Hell. (Exceptions: ἐστιν Ro 1²⁵ 3⁸ 4¹⁶ 5¹⁴ 8³⁴ 16⁵ 1 Co 3¹¹ 4¹⁷ 2 Co 4⁴ Ga 1⁷ 4¹ 4²⁴ *constitutes* ... *represents*, 4²⁶ difficult, as ἐστιν is merely copula, 5¹⁹ *consists of*, Eph 1¹⁴. ²³ 3¹³; 4¹⁶ 5⁵ *constitutes*; 6². ¹⁷,

---

¹ *Style and Literary Methods of Luke*, 149.

Ph 4^8, Col $1^{7.\ 15.\ 18.\ 24.\ 27}$ $2^{10.\ 17.\ 22.\ 23}$ $3^{5.\ 14}$ 4^9 2 Th 2^9 3^{17}; 1 Ti 1^{20} 2 Ti 1^{15} 2^{17} *se trouve*; 1 Ti 3^{15} 4^{10} 2 Ti 1^6 ess. ἐστιν; Ro 9^4 16^7 1 Ti 6^1 εἰσι; Ga 3^{10} εἰσι *se trouvent*; Ro 1^6 ἐστε, 2 Co 11^{15} ἔσται.) After ὡς: Ro 5^{15} ὡς τὸ παράπτωμα, 2 Co 10^7, Col 1^6 (but ἐστιν in previous clause), Eph 5^{23}. (Exceptions: copula after ὥσπερ 1 Co 8^5; after καθώς Eph 4^{21} (essential) Ph 1^7 Col 1^6 (periphr. pres.) 1 Th 2^{13} (ess. ἐστιν).) After καθάπερ: sc. essential ἦν 2 Co 8^{11} (exception: 1 Co 12^{12}). After ὅτι: Ro 7^{16} 8^{18} 11^{36} $14^{14.\ 23}$ 1 Co $8^{4.\ 4}$ 2 Co 10^7 13^5 Ph 2^{11} (ὅτι κύριος Ἰησοῦς Χριστός). Regard (p. 55) thinks that this emphasizes κύριος, since this type of phrase has the copula elsewhere, e.g. 1 Jn 4^{15}. 1 Ti 1^8 Eph 2^{11} (sc. ἐστε). (Exceptions: Ro 1^{32} εἰσιν, 2^2 4^{21} 7^{14} 8^{16} ἐσμεν 15^{14} ἐστε 1 Co 1^{11} $6^{15.\ 16}$ $10^{19.\ 19}$ 11^3 15^{58} (but emph.) 14^{37} 16^{15} 2 Co 1^{18} 2^3 9^{12} 13^6 ἐσμεν Eph 4^{25} ἐσμεν 5^{30} (do.) 5^{16} εἰσιν ^{23} ἐστιν 2 Th 2^4 (do.) 2 Ti 1^{12} (do.).)

(c) *Ellipse of other parts besides* ἐστιν: Scil. εἰμι: Ro 7^{24} (exclam.), κἀγώ 2 Co 11^{22} ter. Not even the pronoun is present with πρόθυμος Ro 1^{15} *d e* vulg (2) Orig. Ambst. Ambr., and εἰ δὲ καὶ ἰδιώτης τῷ λόγῳ 2 Co 11^6 (D*E add εἰμι), ἀλλ' οὐ τῇ γνώσει 11^6, ὃς κατὰ πρόσωπον μὲν ταπεινός 10^1. (Exceptions: more often εἰμι, whether essential or copula, is present: Ro 1^{14} 7^{14} $11^{1.\ 13}$ 1 Co 1^{12} 3^4 $9^{1.\ 2}$ $12^{15.\ 15.\ 16.\ 16}$ 13^2 $15^{9.\ 9.\ 10}$ 2 Co 12^{10} Ph 4^{11} Col 2^5 1 Ti 1^{15}.)

Scil. εἶ even without pronoun: εἰ δὲ υἱός, καὶ κληρόνομος Ga 4^7 (but the sense is made clear by εἶ in previous clause). See further under Interrogatives. (Exception: Ga 4^7.)

Scil. ἐσμεν: with pronoun 2 Co 10^7. No pronoun: εἰ δὲ τέκνα, καὶ κληρονόμοι Ro 8^{17} (but ἐσμεν in previous sentence), Ph 3^{15} 2 Co 4^8 7^5 11^6; see also Graphic. (Exceptions: Ro 6^{15} 8^{12} 14^8 12^5 vl. etc.)

Scil. ἐστε: see Graphic. 2 Co 1^{14} Eph 2^{11} (after ὅτι) 2^{13} (= *vous trouvez*). (Exceptions: Ro $6^{14.\ 16}$ 8^9 1 Co 1^{30} 3^3 1 Th 2^{20} 4^9 $5^{4.\ 5}$ etc.)

Scil. εἰσιν: in connection with ellipse of ἐστιν 2 Co 8^{23}. But not always: Ro 2^{13} 4^{14} $11^{16.\ 28.\ 28}$ 1 Co 16^9 2 Co 8^4 (ptc. as main verb) 10^{10}. (Exceptions: Ro 2^{14} (cp. previous verse) 13^1 (periphr. pf.)^3 15^{27} 1 Co $14^{10.\ 22}$ 10^{18} 3^8 2 Co 11^{22} (question: Ἑβραῖοί εἰσιν; essential εἰσιν) Eph 5^{16} (ὅτι) 1 Ti 5^{24} $6^{2.\ 2}$ (ὅτι) 2 Ti 3^6 (ess.) Ti 1^{10} (ess.) 3^{10} (ess.).)

Scil. fut. indic.: doubtful are 1 Co 15^{21} 2 Co 3^{11}. Apart from these possible instances of ἔσται the fut. never suffers ellipse in Paul (or indeed in NT). Scil. imperf. indic.: very rare; there is the stereotyped εἰ δυνατόν Ga 4^{15}, also 1 Co 2^4 Ph 2^5 Ro 4^{13}. There is ellipse of ἦσαν in καθώς τινες αὐτῶν 1 Co 10^7. Otherwise the impf. is always expressed.

Scil. subjunctive: this ellipse occurs only in Paul (and Heb 12^{16}?). 2 Co 8^{11} ὅπως . . . καὶ τὸ ἐπιτελέσθαι, ^{13} οὐ γὰρ ἵνα ἄλλοις ἄνεσις, ὑμῖν θλίψις (sc. ess. ᾖ), 12^{20} μή πως ἔρις (do.). It is probably subjunctive which has to be supplied in 2 Co 5^{10} (εἴτε . . . εἴτε . . .), and we may supply ὦσιν before ἐν τῇ διακονίᾳ Ro 12^7; another instance is 2 Co 12^{20} where ὦσιν is preferable to εὑρεθῶσιν. Also scil. the essential verb Ro 4^{16}. In this respect Paul is nearer to class. practice than any other NT writer. However, the insertion of subjunctive is much more regular.

§ 3]   ABSENCE OF THE VERB "TO BE"   303

. Scil. optative: see epistolary formulae, above. Other wishes are: ἐπικατάρατος πᾶς ὅς ... (ὁ ...) Ga 3[10. 13], εἰρήνη ἐπ' αὐτοὺς καὶ ἔλεος 6[16]. Paul does not use opt. of εἰμί.

Scil. imperative: ἔστω is rarely omitted except in the formula χάρις τῷ θεῷ (see Exclamations), which is class. too (K-G § 354 n. 2e; Abel § 157) and occurs in the early papyri. There are also ἡ ἀγάπη ἀνυπόκριτος Ro 12[9], ὁ λόγος ὑμῶν πάντοτε ἐν χάριτι Col 4[6], and perhaps before κατὰ τὴν ἀναλογίαν Ro 12[6]. (Exceptions: ἤτω 1 Co 16[22], ἔστω 2 Co 12[16] Ga 1[8].) 'Εστέ may be supplied with the ptcs. in Ro 12[9f. 16ter] Col 3[16] 2 Co 9[11. 13] 8[24] BD*G (against S) Eph 4[2], and Regard includes the ptcs. at Eph 5[15-23] 6[16. 18. 18] (pp. 211f). But the ptc. itself may be imperatival; in fact, ἐστέ imper. does not occur at all in NT (but there is ἴστε with γινώσκοντες Eph 5[5], which may be intended for ἐστέ), 1 Ti 4[15] ἴσθι.

(d) *Stronger meanings of* ἐστιν *and* εἰσιν: even here there is ellipse in Paul, which is not confined to the copula; there is the meaning *there is* (*are*), or *it is*; e.g. 1 Th 5[3] εἰρήνη καὶ ἀσφάλεια, 2 Ti 1[5] ὅτι καὶ ἐν σοί, Ro 2[8. 9. 10] 4[16. 16] 8[1] 9[16. 32] 11[11] 1 Co 8[6] 11[30] 13[8] 15[40] 2 Co 1[20] 3[17] 4[6] 6[2] Ga 2[21] 3[4. 5] Eph 2[8. 9] 4[4. 5. 9], a series of four in the vehement passage Ph 2[1], 1 Ti 2[5]. Something like ἐστιν is to be supplied before ἴνα 1 Co 7[29] 1 Ti 3[15], and οὐχ ὅτι 2 Co 1[24] 3[5] Ph 4[11. 17] 2 Th 3[9]. Normally of course the verb *to be* is not absent.

It may be that we are to supply ἐστιν in 1 Co 10[17] ὅτι εἷς ἄρτος (sc. ἐστιν), ἕν σῶμα οἱ πολλοί ἔσμεν: *because there is one bread, we the many are one body*, instead of the usual interpretation which is less intelligible.

Individual writers: the Fourth Gospel.

We find here almost the very opposite of Pauline usage: the pure nominal phrase and ellipse of the copula is the exception rather than the rule.

(a) *Fixed phrases:* (ἔτι) μικρὸν καί 14[19] 16[16. 17. 19]. (Exceptions: (τὸ) θαυμαστόν ἐστιν ὅτι 9[30].) Parenthetical ὄνομα αὐτῷ 1[6] (ἦν S*D*W), 3[1] (ὀνόματι S*). (Exception: ἦν δὲ ὄνομα 18[10].) Proverbial: πνεῦμα ὁ θεός 4[24]. (Exc. 13[16] 15[20].)

(b) *Spontaneous phrases:* ἰδού 19[5], ἴδε 1[29. 36. 48] 19[14. 26f], μακάριοι οἱ 20[29] (Hebr. infl.?), but ἔστε 13[17]. In Jn even exclamations may retain ἐστιν: as σκληρός ἐστιν ὁ λόγος 6[60]. Οὕτως with ἐστιν 3[8], οὗτος with ἐστιν 1[19. 30] etc. (22 times), ἐκεῖνος 5[39] etc. (5 times). But the copula is absent in the interrogative idiom τί ἐμοὶ (ἡμῖν) καὶ σοί Jn 2[4] which has a parallel in Hebrew besides affinities with class. speech (K-G I 417). Another idiomatic phrase is τί πρός σε (ἡμᾶς) Jn 21[22f]; there is the Latin *quid hoc ad te*, which has a class. Greek parallel in the proverb-like οὐδέν πρὸς Διόνυσον, although normally there is ἐστι (cf. οὐδέν ἐστι δήπου πρὸς ἐμέ Demosth. 18, 21) and parallels later in Epictetus (see Schenkl's Index, under πρός): τί (οὐδὲν) πρός ἐμέ (σέ) and in a papyrus of 9 B.C. (BU IV 1158[17]). There is also the conversational formula τί οὖν 1[21] (sc. εἶ) and the interrogatives οὗτος δὲ τί 21[21] (note the ch.) and τί πρός σε 21[22f] (do.). But much more, frequently ἐστιν appears in questions: 21[20] 6[9] 7[36] etc.; this is true also of indir. questions 2[9] 9[29, 30] 7[27] etc., of the protasis of a condition 9[25], of relative clauses 1[41] etc., after καθώς 19[40] etc., after ἕως 9[4]. Ellipse is rather frequent after ὅτι: 4[53] (sc. ἦν), 10[38] (sc. ἐστιν and εἰμί) 14[10] (sc. εἰμί), 11 (sc. εἰμί and ἐστιν), 20 (sc. εἰμί bis and ἐστε). But this is only nine instances, compared with sixty where the copula is inserted: 2[17] 3[21] etc. including ὅτι = *because* 1[30] 3[23, 33] etc.

(c) *Ellipse of other parts besides* ἐστιν: see above. There is also ellipse of εἰμί at 1[23] ἐγὼ φωνὴ βοῶντος, and of εἶ at 17[21] (but σύ appears), and of ἐσμεν at 17[11] (καθὼς ἡμεῖς), and of ἐστέ 15[5] (ὑμεῖς τὰ κλάσματα), and of ἦν 19[41] (καὶ ἐν τῷ κήπῳ μνημεῖον καινόν). The subjunctive ὦ may be understood at 17[26], but the ellipse occurs immediately after the insertion of ᾖ. The opt. probably has to be supplied in the formal wish εἰρήνη (σοι) at 20[19, 21, 26]. Presumably ἴσθι is to be supplied with δεῦρο ἔξω 11[43]. Against these ten instances of ellipse there are some 202 instances without it.

(d) *Stronger meanings*: there is no instance of ellipse here, but something like ἐστιν is to be supplied *before* ἵνα at 12[38] 18[9, 32] 19[24] and ἀλλ' ἵνα 9[3] 13[18] 15[25], and before οὐχ ὅτι 6[46] 7[22]. With ἵνα this may be a kind of imperative, as in the phrases which begin with γιὰ νά in good MGr. (Pernot 69). The presence of ἐστιν or εἰσιν is the rule with stronger meanings: 1[47] 4[35] etc. (12 times).

Individual writers: the Johannine Epistles.

(a) *Fixed phrases:* εἰρήνη σοι 3 Jn 15. But an exception to the NT practice is the presence of ἔσται in the formula at 2 Jn³. Regard ascribes this to inherited Ionic influence (p. 42). Proverbial expressions: ὁ θεὸς ἀγάπη ἐστιν 4[8, 16] is an instance which in other parts of NT would be a pure nominal phrase, even in Jn, e.g. πνεῦμα ὁ θεός. So also ὁ θεὸς φῶς ἐστιν 1⁵, καὶ ἡ ἁμαρτία ἐστὶν ἡ ἀνομία 3⁴, πᾶσα ἀδικία ἁμαρτία ἐστιν 5[17].

(b) *Spontaneous:* ellipse 1³ καὶ ἡ κοινωνία δὲ ἡ ἡμετέρα μετὰ τοῦ πατρός. (Exceptions: copula ἐστιν 42 times, other parts 26 times.)

Individual writers: Luke–Acts.

Luke prefers the copula on every possible occasion, apart from set phrases, titles, and a few exclamations and questions.

(a) *Set phrases:* φάνερον ὅτι Ac 4[16], ἐξόν 2[29], σκληρόν 26[14]. Proverbial: Lk 10² (= Mt 9[37]) ὁ μὲν θερισμὸς πολύς, οἱ δὲ ἐργάται ὀλίγοι, 14[34] (= Mk 9[50]) καλὸν τὸ ἅλας, 10⁷ (= Mt 10[10] 1 Ti 5[18]), 18[19] (= Mk 10[18], as opp. to Mt 19[17]), 16[15, 16]. Also Lk 1[26f] 2[25] 8[41] 24[13] ᾧ (ᾗ) ὄνομα (D

§ 3]   ABSENCE OF THE VERB "TO BE"   305

ὀνόματι, as elsewhere in Lk and almost always in Ac and class.) 24[18] (SB ὀνόματι) Ac 13[6] (p[45] ὀνόματι, D ὀνόματι καλούμενον). Lk 1[5. 27] καὶ τὸ ὄνομα. Epistolary formulae: χαίρειν Ac 15[23] 23[26]. (Exceptions: δέον with ἐστιν Ac 19[36], ὄνομα with ἐστιν Lk 1[63] 8[30] (as opp. to Mk 5[9]), εἰ δυνατόν with εἴη Ac 20[16]; also ἐστιν with μακάριον Ac 20[35], καλόν Lk 9[33], ἀνενδεκτόν 17[1], ἱκανόν 22[38], εὐκοπώτερον 16[17] 18[25] (= Mk 10[25] Mt 19[24]), and so on Ac 2[24] 4[19] 6[2] 12[3] 10[28] 13[46] 25[16] 28[22]. Proverbial: τὰ ἀδύνατα παρὰ ἀνθρώποις δυνατὰ παρὰ τῷ θεῷ ἐστιν Lk 18[27] (as opp. to Mt Mk).)

(b) *Spontaneous*: (καὶ) ἰδού Lk 1[38] 5[18] etc. (Exceptions Lk 2[25] 17[21] etc.) οὐαί Lk 6[24f] 10[13] etc. Exclamations: εὐλογημένος ὁ ἐρχόμενος Lk 13[35] 19[38] (= Mt Jn); so also Lk 10[23] 12[43] (as Mt) etc., μακάριος 1[45] 11[27] 14[15], ὑμεῖς μάρτυρες Lk 24[48], οὐκ εὐθέως τὸ τέλος 21[9] (sc. ἔσται?), ὑμεῖς δὲ οὐχ οὕτως 22[26] (sc. ἐστε), εὐλογημένη σύ 1[42. 48], τὸ σκότος πόσον 11[38] D, μεγάλη ἡ Ἄρτεμις Ac 19[28. 34]. Doxology: δόξα ἐν ὑψίστοις (sc. ἔστω or εἴη) Lk 2[14]. Verbal adj.: οἶνον νέον εἰς ἀσκοὺς καινοὺς βλητέον Lk 5[38] (only instance in NT, but class. and Hell.). Other phrases (esp. rhetorical or declarative), e.g. οὗ τὸ πτύον ἐν τῇ χειρὶ αὐτοῦ Lk 3[17]; also 11[34] 22[20]. Demonstrative: ὁ βασιλεὺς τῶν Ἰουδαίων οὗτος Lk 23[38] (Mt-parall. has copula), οὕτως 12[21], οὗτοι 24[44]. Interrogatives: Lk 4[34] (Mk Mt Jn), 36[,]8[28, 45], 21[7], 22[27], 24[17], Ac 10[21] etc. Indir. questions: Lk 7[39] 13[23] Ac 26[23] 17[19]. After ὅπου Lk 17[37] (but parall. Mt 24[28] adds ἐὰν ᾖ). In protasis of conditional (Lucan and Pauline habit): Lk 11[35]D [36]. In a rel. clause there is ellipse after καθότι Lk 19[9] S*. After ὅτι Lk 16[15] (Lk sometimes avoids Mk's ellipse, by adding ἀνέστη 9[8. 19]). But under this heading there are a very great many exceptions, and with spontaneous phrases in Lk–Ac the copula is the general rule.

(c) *Other parts besides ἐστιν.*

See above. Scil. ptc. ὄντα in WH of Ac 26[21] (rest have it). Scil. εἰμι Ac 7[32] OT (but not LXX, which adds εἰμι: Ex 3[6]) 10[39] 18[6]. But εἰμι inserted 28 times. Sc. ptc. ὄντες in WH of Lk 6[3] (rest have it). Sc. εἶ: see Exclamations (usually inserted). Ἐσμεν always inserted (ten times). Sc. ἐστε indic.: ὑμεῖς μάρτυρες τούτων Lk 24[28], and see above (otherwise inserted). Sc. εἰσιν Lk 24[17] and see above (but usually inserted). Sc. ἔσται: Lk 21[7] καὶ τί τὸ σημεῖον (no other ellipse of fut. indic.: inserted 48 times). Sc. ἦν Lk 1[5] (*there was*) γυνὴ αὐτῷ 2[25. 36. 37]; see also above. (But ἦν inserted 113 times; ἦσαν 43 times; ἤμην 5; ἦμεν 2; ἤμεθα Ac 27[37]). Scil. optative: Lk 10[5] 24[36] εἰρήνη τῷ οἴκῳ τούτῳ, 1[28] ὁ κύριος μετὰ σοῦ; see also Subordinate Clauses. There is ellipse of either opt. or imper. in ἐν οὐρανῷ εἰρήνη καὶ δόξα ἐν ὑψίστοις Lk 19[38], τὸ αἷμα ὑμῶν ἐπὶ τὴν κεφαλὴν ὑμῶν Ac 18[6]. Sc. ἔστε imper. Lk 12[36] ὑμεῖς ὅμοιοι, 24[47] with ptc. Sc ἴσθι: Ac 7[3] δεῦρο εἰς ....

(d) *Stronger meanings.*

Ellipse before ἵνα: Lk 18[41] (but prob. imperatival ἵνα). Ellipse of ἐστιν *it is*: Ac 12[22] θεοῦ φωνὴ καὶ οὐκ ἀνθρώπου (inserted 37 times).

Individual writers: Mark.

The ellipse here is usually confined to fixed phrases.

(a) *Fixed phrases:* ὄνομα 14³², 5⁹ (parall. Lk 8³⁰ adds ἐστιν). εἰ δὲ μή 2²¹ᶠ. ἀδύνατον 10²⁷ (Mt adds ἐστιν). εἰ δυνατόν 13²² = Mt 24²⁴ (but ἐστιν is retained at Mk 14³⁵ Mt 26³⁹). καλόν 14²¹ BWL (others add ἦν; Mt's parall. has ἦν, also Lk 9³³; even in Mk the copula is retained at 7²⁷ 9⁵· ⁴²· ⁴³· ⁴⁵· ⁴⁷). (Exceptions 2⁹ 10²⁵· ⁴⁰.) Proverbial expressions: καλὸν τὸ ἅλας Mk 9⁵⁰ = Lk 14³⁴, τὸ μὲν πνεῦμα πρόθυμον, ἡ δὲ σάρξ ἀσθενής 14³⁸ = Mt 26⁴¹, οὐδεὶς ἀγαθός 10¹⁸ = Lk 18¹⁹ (Mt. 19¹⁷ adds the copula in εἷς ἐστιν ὁ ἀγαθός), παρὰ θεῷ πάντα δυνατά 10²⁷ = Mt 19²⁶.

(b) *Spontaneous expressions:* ellipse with ἴδε 3³⁴ 13¹· ²¹, οὐαί 13¹⁷ 14²¹, τί ἐμοί (ἡμῖν) καὶ σοί 1²⁴ 5⁷. In other less stereotyped forms of questions, the copula has also to be supplied: τίς ἡ σοφία 6², τίνος ἡ εἰκὼν αὕτη 12¹⁶ (parall. Lk 20²⁴ avoids the ellipse), πόθεν τούτῳ ταῦτα 6², simple interr. οὐ 4²¹. But there are exceptions: τί ἐστιν τοῦτο 1²⁷, τί ἐστιν εὐκοπώτερον 2⁹ = Lk 5²³, τίς ἐστιν ἡ μήτηρ μου 3³³, τίς ἄρα οὗτός ἐστιν 4⁴¹, ποῦ 14¹⁴ = Lk 22¹¹, πόθεν 12³⁷, ποῖος 12²⁸, πόσος 9²¹. Exclamations or simple declarations: 13⁷ (where Mt 24⁶ adds ἐστιν) οὔπω τὸ τέλος, 14³⁶ πάντα δυνατά σοι. But even these have ἐστιν: οὐχ οὕτως δέ ἐστιν ἐν ὑμῖν 10⁴³ = Mt 20²⁶, even when impersonal: πῶς δύσκολόν ἐστιν 10²⁴. Other non-ellipses: ἔνοχός ἐστιν = 3²⁹, but here we have no subject expressed and the verb must be there to supply it (*he is*). The same applies to οὐκ ἔστιν θεὸς νεκρῶν 12²⁷ = Lk 20³⁸ (*he is*), and to οὐκ ἔστιν ὧδε 16⁶ = Mt 28⁶ = Lk 24⁶. Ἔρημός ἐστιν ὁ τόπος 6³⁵ = Mt 14¹⁵ (emph.?). Κύριός ἐστιν ὁ Υἱὸς ... καὶ τοῦ σαββάτου 2²⁸ = Lk 6⁵ = Mt 12⁸. In οὐ γάρ ἐστίν τι κρυπτὸν ἐάν 4²², it is the essential ἐστιν *there is*, as also most probably in 6⁴ = Mt 13⁵⁷, 9⁴⁰ = Mt 12³⁰ = Lk 9⁵⁰, 12³³. The copula is not omitted with οὕτως 4²⁶ 10⁴², nor with demonstratives 3³⁵ etc. (13 times). The copula is inserted in indir. questions: 5¹⁴ 9¹⁰ 13³³, and after ὅπου 5⁴⁰ (ἦν); in relat. clauses 2¹⁹ etc. (10 times). With two exceptions (6¹⁵) where the parall. Lk 9⁸ inserts ἀνέστη, 8²⁸ where the parall. Lk 9¹⁹ adds ἀνέστη), the copula occurs in clauses beginning with ὅτι: 2¹ 6⁴⁹· ⁵⁵ 12³⁵ 13²⁸ᶠ; of these exceptions, it looks as if προφήτης is direct speech, with ὅτι introducing a mere exclamation of the people, in 6¹⁵, and in the same way there is no need for ἐστιν in 8²⁸ if ὅτι is thought of as introducing the dir. speech εἷς τῶν προφητῶν. When Mark intends ὅτι to introduce indir. speech he has the copula, as ἀκούσας ὅτι Ἰησοῦς ὁ Ν. ἐστιν 10⁴⁷ (parall. Lk 18³⁷ has παρέρχεται). Thus the proportion in this section is striking: ellipse 15 or less, copula 56.

(c) *Other parts.*

Strangely enough there is sometimes the ellipse of εἰμι in Mk: ἐγὼ ὁ θεὸς Ἀβραάμ 12²⁶ = Ac 7³² (the LXX of Ex 3⁶ adds εἰμι), μήτι ἐγώ 14¹⁹. There is ellipse of ἦν with καλόν 14²¹ and at 1¹¹ (καὶ φωνὴ ἐκ τῶν οὐρανῶν), although BWA add ἐγένετο (and Lk's parall. 3²² adds γενέσθαι), and 1⁴⁵ vi. The apparent ellipse of ἦν in καὶ αὐτὸς μόνος 6⁴⁷ is covered by ἦν in the previous clause. There is one instance of ellipse of ἦσαν, 15⁴⁰ ἐν αἷς καὶ Μαρία ... There is ellipse of ἔστω at 14³⁶ = Mt 26⁴⁰ (οὐ τί ἐγὼ θέλω), where the parallel Lk 22⁴² avoids it, and perhaps at 14² (μὴ ἐν τῇ ἑορτῇ). Elsewhere the appropriate part of εἶναι fails to be inserted: again the proportion is striking, ellipse 7, verb 88.

(d) Stronger meanings.

Even here, when drama is present, there is ellipse: εἷς τῶν δώδεκα *(it is)* 14²⁰. It is probably also so before ἀλλ' ἵνα 14⁴⁹ (imperatival) 2¹⁰. Some read the opening of the gospel like this: scil. ἐστιν before καθώς *(the beginning of the gospel is as it is written ...)*. But Mark's fondness for the verb *to be* is against this interpretation. The insertion of ἐστιν = *consists in* 7¹⁵ 10¹⁴ (or *belongs to*) 12²⁹, 1²⁷ *means*.

Individual writers: Hebrews.

In avoidance of the copula Heb. is even more class. and literary in tendency than Paul; there is always good reason for the insertion of ἐστιν where it occurs.

(a) Fixed phrases. Ellipse with πρόδηλον 7¹⁴ (but κατάδηλον has ἐστιν 7¹⁵, emphatic), ἀδύνατον 6⁴· ¹⁸ 10⁴ 11⁶, λόγος 5¹¹, ἔτι μικρὸν ὅσον ὅσον 10³⁷ (but LXX Isa 26²⁰ has ἀποκρύβηθι μικρὸν ὅσον ὅσον), ὡς ἔπος εἰπεῖν 7⁹, ἀναγκαῖον 8³, ἀνάγκη 9¹⁶· ²³, ἔθος 10²⁵, φοβερόν 10³¹, καλόν 13⁹. Epistolary formula ἡ χάρις μετά 13²⁵.

(b) Spontaneous phrases. Ellipse: 13⁸ 'Ιησοῦς Χ. ... ὁ αὐτός, 5¹³ 8¹ 9¹⁶ᶠ 4¹². ¹³. ¹³ 5⁴ 2¹⁰. ¹¹ 6⁸. ⁸. ¹⁰ 9¹⁷ 10²³. ³⁰. Ellipse after ὡς 3² (sc. ἦν), πηλίκος 7⁴ (do.), τίς 7¹¹ (sc. ἐστιν), in relative sentences (unlike Paul) 9⁹ 11¹⁰, after ὅτι 11¹⁹, with demonstratives 9²⁰ (τοῦτο τὸ αἷμα, where LXX has ἰδοὺ τὸ αἷμα) 13¹⁷. In doxology ᾧ ἡ δόξα 13²¹. (Presence of εἰσιν in a question 1¹⁴, ἐστιν with demonstratives 2¹⁴ 7⁵ 9¹¹ 10²⁰ 11¹⁶ 13¹⁵, ἐστιν = *he is* 5¹³ 8⁶ 9¹⁵, = *belongs to* 5¹⁴, after relative 7²; presence of εἰσιν in periphr. pf. 7²⁰· ²³. Therefore the presence of ἐστιν at 11¹ (ἔστιν δὲ πίστις ἐλπιζομένων ὑπόστασις) is either very exceptional or is not a copula (= *represents*)).

(c) Other parts.

Th. Nissen (in *Philologus* 92, 1937, 248) conjectures at 12¹⁶ μή τις πόρνος ⟨ἢ⟩ ἢ βέβηλος. Otherwise ellipse of subjunctive in 12¹⁵ (the only other place in NT is Paul). 13⁴ τίμιος ὁ γάμος (sc. ἔστω), ⁵ ἀφιλάργυρος ὁ τρόπος Scil. ἔστε imperatival with ptc. 13⁵ (as Paul, Peter, Luke). Ellipse of ἦν 3⁵· ⁶ (and see stronger meanings); of εἰ 7²¹ (σὺ ἱερεύς, even when LXX inserts εἰ). (Exceptions: insertion of ἦσαν 2¹⁵, of ἐσμεν 3⁶ 4² 10¹⁰· ³⁹, of ἔσται (after μήποτε) 3¹², of ἦν 7¹⁰· ¹¹ 8⁴· ⁴· ⁷ 11³⁸ 12²¹, of εἰσιν 11¹³ (but = *they are*), of ἔστε 12⁸· ⁸.)

(d) *Stronger meanings.*

Ellipse of ἐστιν *there is* or ἦν *there was* 9². ⁴. ⁵. Scil. ἐστιν before οὐχ ἵνα 9²⁵; scil. ἐστιν *there is* 9¹⁶ ὅπου γὰρ διαθήκη, ²⁷ μετὰ δὲ τοῦτο κρίσις, 10³, 10¹⁸ ὅπου δὲ ἄφεσις τούτων, ¹⁸, 12⁷. (No ellipse: 4¹³ 9⁵ (οὐκ ἐστιν *it is impossible*), 11⁶ *exists*.)

Individual writers: James.

On the contrary, Jas is not very fond of the pure nominal phrase, outside stereotyped expressions.

(a) *Fixed phrases.* χρή 3¹⁰, ἔνι 1¹⁷. Epistol. formulae χαίρειν 1¹. Proverbial ἡ γὰρ κρίσις ἀνέλεος τῷ μὴ ποιήσαντι ἔλεος 2¹³.

(b) *Spontaneous.* Proportion of ellipse 9 : copula 15. The idiomatic question τί τὸ ὄφελος 2¹⁴. ¹⁶, ἰδού 3⁴. Exclamations 1¹². ²⁶ 3². ⁶. Interrogative 3¹³ 4¹, 4¹⁴ ποία ἡ ζωή AKLP lat copt. Indir. question 4¹⁴ S*B 614 syrʰ arm. (No ellipse 15 times.)

(c) *Other parts.* No ellipse (12 times).

(d) *Stronger meanings.* Ellipse *it is* 3⁸ ἀκατάστατον κακόν, *there is* 3¹⁶ ὅπου γὰρ ζῆλος καὶ ἐριθεία, ἐκεῖ ἀκαταστασία, *it is* 4¹ οὐκ ἐντεῦθεν. (No ellipse 4¹². ¹⁴ L vulg ¹⁷.)

Individual writers: 1 Peter.

He tends towards the ellipse.

(a) *Fixed phrases.* εἰ δέον 1⁶, κρεῖττον 3¹⁷. Epistol. formula εἰρήνη ὑμῖν 5¹⁴.

(b) *Spontaneous.* Doxology εὐλογητὸς ὁ θεός 1³, αὐτῷ τὸ κράτος 5¹¹ (but ᾧ ἐστιν [A om. ἐστιν] ἡ δόξα 4¹¹). Demonstrative 2¹⁹ᶠ. Interrog. 2²⁰ 3¹³. (Exceptions : 1²⁵ 2¹⁵ 3⁴. ²⁰. ²².)

(c) *Other parts.* We may supply the imper. (2nd pl.) with adjs. and ptcs. : 1¹⁴. ²² 2¹⁸ 3¹. ⁷. ⁸ᶠ 4⁸ᶠᶠ (but Moulton Proleg. 182f); ἐστε (pres. ind.) is absent: ὑμεῖς δὲ γένος ἐκλεκτόν 2⁹, οἵ ποτε οὐ λαός ¹⁰, μακάριοι 3¹⁴ 4¹⁴. Impf. ἦν (perhaps ἐστιν) is to be understood in ἀρκετὸς γὰρ ὁ παρεληλυθὼς χρόνος 4³; scil. εἰμι in ὅτι ἐγὼ ἅγιος 1¹⁶ (LXX inserts εἰμι). (Exceptions: ἦτε inserted 2²⁵, ἔστω 3³.)

(d) *Stronger meanings.* Ellipse 4¹⁷ ὅτι ὁ καιρὸς τοῦ ἄρξασθαι, ¹⁷ εἰ δὲ πρῶτον ἀφ' ἡμῶν, τί τὸ τέλος.

Individual writers: 2 Pt. and Jude.

Strangely the ellipse is never found except in the stereotyped doxology and with the Hebraic οὐαί. The ptc. is probably imperatival in itself, without the need to supply ἐστε. There is thus no instance of a spontaneous phrase containing the ellipse. Doxology 2 Pt 3¹⁸ Jude ²⁵; οὐαί Jude ¹¹.

Individual writers: Matthew.

It is almost only in stereotyped phrases, proverbs, and exclamations that Matthew omits the copula, and even here (as with πρέπον, ἀδύνατον, ἐξόν, καλόν) he inserts the copula sometimes. The only exceptions are the Semitic ἰδοῦ and οὐαί, and the interesting case of ὅτι (ellipse with which is characteristic of Mt.).

(a) *Fixed phrases.* With ἀρκετόν 6³⁴ 10²⁵, εἰ δυνατόν 24²⁴ (= Mk 13²²), although ἐστιν is inserted at 26³⁹ (= Mk 14³⁵), ἀνάγκη 18⁷ BL 33 (but SDW insert ἐστιν). Semitic influence may explain δῶρον 15⁵, ἵλεώς σοι (scil. ὁ θεὸς εἴη or more prob. a homonym for חָלִילָה) 16²². Proverbial expressions: ὁ μὲν θερισμὸς πολύς 9³⁷ = Lk 10², so also 10¹⁰ = Lk 10⁷, 11⁸ (parall. Lk 7²⁵ has εἰσιν), 19²⁶ = Mk 10²⁷ (Lk 18²⁷ adds ἐστιν), 26⁴¹ = Mk 14³⁸. No ellipse: Mt adds ἐστιν in εἷς ἐστιν ὁ ἀγαθός 19¹⁷ (against Mk 10¹⁸ Lk 18¹⁹). (Exceptions: πρέπον has ἐστιν 3¹⁵, and so has ἀδύνατον 19²⁶ (against the parall. Mk 10²⁷); ἦν is inserted with ἐξόν 12⁴ and with καλόν 26²⁴ (against Mk 14²¹), ἐστιν with καλόν 15²⁶ 17⁴ 18⁸·⁹, with οὐδέν 23¹⁶·¹⁸, εὐκοπώτερον 19²⁴ = Mk 10²⁵ Lk 16¹⁷ 18²⁵; also οὐκ ἔστιν θέλημα ἵνα 18¹⁴.)

(b) *Spontaneous.* With ἰδού 3¹⁷ 7⁴ 9¹⁰ 11¹⁹ 12¹⁰·¹⁸·⁴²·⁴⁹ 17⁵ 24²³·²⁶ 25⁶ (but copula 24²⁶). With οὐαί 18⁷·⁷ 23¹³·¹⁶·²³·²⁵·²⁷·²⁹ 24¹⁹ 26²⁴. Exclamations: μακάριοι οἱ 5³⁻¹⁰ 13¹⁶ = Lk 10²³, 24⁴⁶ (sing.) = Lk 12⁴³ (but the copula does occur in the same formula 5¹¹, 11⁶ = Lk 7²³, 16¹⁷), τὸ σκότος πόσον 6²³ = Lk 11³⁶ D, μεγάλη σου ἡ πίστις 15²⁸, εὐδία 16², σήμερον χειμών 16³, δευτέρα ὁμοία αὐτῇ 22³⁹ (but Mt adds ἐστιν to οὔπω τὸ τέλος 24⁶, against Mk 13⁷, and retains ἐστιν in οὐχ οὕτως δέ ἐστιν ἐν ὑμῖν 20²⁶ = Mk 10⁴³, οὐχὶ ἡ ψυχὴ πλεῖόν ἐστι 6²⁵). Graphic sentences: οἱ ταῦροί μου καὶ τὰ σιτιστὰ τεθυμένα καὶ πάντα ἕτοιμα 22⁴ (the only place where there is ellipse with ἕτοιμος in NT[1]). Rhetorical: ἐχθροὶ τοῦ ἀνθρώπου οἱ οἰκιακοὶ αὐτοῦ 10³⁶. Demonstrative: 24⁷ (but the copula is not normally omitted with demonstratives: 33 times). Interrogatives: the idiom τί ἐμοί (ἡμῖν) καὶ σοί 8²⁹, and τί πρός σε (ἡμᾶς) 27⁴; questions with τίς or τί 23¹⁹ 24³ 26⁸, ποῖος 22³⁶ (but more often the copula is inserted: 16 times). After ὅτι Mt often prefers the ellipse: 5¹² 7¹³·¹⁴ 24³² (but ³³ and the Mk-parall. insert ἐστιν). Relative: 3¹². There is no ellipse where ἐστιν = *he is* (i.e. no subject expressed): 28⁶ = Mk 16⁶ = Lk 26⁶, 27⁴², 26⁶⁶. The verb is also inserted in emphatic phrases beginning with οὐκ ἔστιν: 13⁵⁷ = Mk 6⁴, 10²⁴ = Lk 6⁴⁰ = Jn 13¹⁶ 15²⁰. The position of the predicate and insertion of ἐστιν add emphasis in κύριός ἐστιν ὁ υἱός ... καὶ τοῦ σαββάτου 12⁸ = Mk 2²⁸ = Lk 6⁵, εἷς γάρ ἐστιν ὑμῶν ὁ διδάσκαλος 23⁸·⁹·¹⁰, ἐρημός ἐστιν ὁ τόπος 14¹⁵. But this does not explain ὁ καιρός μου ἐγγύς ἐστιν 26¹⁸, and there are 30 other instances where the copula is inserted for no apparent reason.

---

[1] In class. Greek also it is only in elevated language that there is an ellipse with this word.—J. E. Harry, *Proc. Amer. Philol. Assocn.*, 1903, xxxiv, pp. viiiff.

310   A GRAMMAR OF NEW TESTAMENT GREEK   [§ 3

(c) *Other parts* (*except as included above*). Ellipse of εἰμί 22³² (but inserted 13 times); of εἰσιν 1¹⁷ 10⁸⁶ (but inserted 12 times); of ἔσονται 24⁴¹ (but added in parall. Lk 17³⁵) (but fut. indic. is inserted 35 times); of ἦσαν or ἐγένετο in 24³⁷ ὥσπερ γὰρ αἱ ἡμέραι (but impf. indic. is inserted 26 times, subjunctive 6 times, imperat. 4 times). Ellipse of imperative: 27¹⁹·²⁵ 26⁵·³⁹.

(d) *Stronger meanings.* No ellipse (10 times).

Individual writers: Revelation.

The occurrence of the copula is about half and half, the apparent lack of preference being due perhaps largely to the use of various sources.

(a) *Fixed phrases.* Ellipse in epistolary formulae: χάρις ὑμῖν καὶ εἰρήνη 1⁴, ἡ χάρις μετὰ πάντων 22²¹; ὄφελον with finite verb 3¹⁵; εἰ δὲ μή 2⁵·¹⁶; ὄνομα αὐτῷ 6⁸ 9¹¹.

(b) *Spontaneous phrases.* Ellipse in exclamations: μακάριος 1³ 16¹⁵ 20⁶ 22⁷, plur. 14¹³ 19⁹ 22¹⁴; ὁ γὰρ καιρὸς ἐγγύς 1³ (but cp. 22¹¹), ἅγιος κύριος 4⁸ (not LXX), μεγάλα καὶ θαυμαστὰ τὰ ἔργα σου 15³, δίκαιαι καὶ ἀληθιναὶ αἱ ὁδοί σου 15³, ὅτι ἰσχυρὸς κύριος 18⁸, ὅτι ἀληθιναὶ καὶ δίκαιαι αἱ κρίσεις αὐτοῦ 19², οὗτοι οἱ λόγοι πιστοὶ καὶ ἀληθινοί 22⁶, καὶ ὁ μισθός μου μετ' ἐμοῦ ¹² (Exceptions 5¹² 16²¹ 22¹¹). Doxologies: αὐτῷ ἡ δόξα 1⁶, τῷ ἀρνίῳ ἡ εὐλογία 5¹³, similarly 7¹², ἡ σωτηρία τῷ θεῷ 7¹⁰, similarly 19¹. Relative: 1⁴ 20¹⁰ (exceptions 2⁷ 5¹³ 20²·¹² 21⁸·¹⁷ 22¹²). Demonstratives: 17⁹ 20⁵ (exceptions 13¹⁰·¹⁵ 14¹² 17¹¹ 20¹⁴). Interrog. 5² 13⁴ 18¹⁸. Indir. quest. 2¹³. Καὶ ἰδού 4¹ 6²·⁵·⁸ 7⁹ 12³ 14¹·¹⁴ 19¹¹, ἰδοὺ 21³, οὐαί 8¹³ 18¹⁰·¹⁶·¹⁹. Other ellipses: 2¹⁹ 19¹² 21¹⁶·¹⁹·²¹·²³. Other copulae 21¹⁶·²² (but cp. next verse).

(c) *Other parts.* Scil. εἰσιν 1¹⁴·¹⁵ff 14⁴ 16⁷ 17¹⁴ 21¹⁹. Scil. ἦν 1¹⁶ 4⁷ 10¹·²·⁸ 9⁵·⁹·¹⁶ 13¹⁸ 14² 20⁸ 21¹¹·¹⁴. Scil. ἦσαν 7⁵ 9⁷·¹⁷·¹⁹. Scil. εἰμί 21⁶ (A adds εἰμί) 22¹³, εἰ 15⁴, ἔσται 22⁴. (No ellipse: εἰμί 1⁸·¹⁷ 3¹⁷ 2²³ 18⁷ 19¹⁰ 22⁹·¹⁶, εἰ 2⁹ 3¹·¹⁵·¹⁶·¹⁷ 4¹¹ 5⁹, εἰσιν 1¹⁹·²⁰ 2²·⁹ 3⁴·⁹ 4⁵ 5⁶·⁹ 7¹³·¹⁴·¹⁵ 11⁴ 14⁴·⁵ 16⁶ 17⁹·⁹·¹²·¹⁵ 19¹⁰ 21⁵, ἔσομαι 21⁷, ἔσται 10⁶·⁹ 21³·⁴·⁷, ἔσονται 20⁶ 21³, ἦν 3¹⁵ 4⁶·¹¹ 5¹¹ 10¹⁰ 13² 21²¹, ἦσαν 9⁸ 18²³.

(d) *Stronger meanings.* Sc. ἦν *there was* 4⁶ 9¹⁰ 10¹, *se trouve* 11⁸; ἦσαν *there were* 9⁷; εἰσιν *there are* 22¹⁵ (No ellipse 9¹⁹ 13¹⁸ 16¹⁴ 17⁸·⁸·¹⁰·¹¹·¹⁴·¹⁸ 19⁸·¹⁰ 21¹·¹²·²⁵ 22²·³·⁵·¹⁴.)

CHAPTER TWENTY-TWO

CONGRUENCE OF GENDER AND NUMBER

§ 1. Incongruence in Gender

Whereas in class. Greek a discordant neuter of the *pronominal* predicate (τί, οὐδέν, ὅ, ἕν, πλεῖον, etc.) will appear (e.g. Plato *Civ.* 341e), as in Mt 6²⁵ Lk 12²³ (ἡ ψυχὴ πλεῖον ἐστι), Ac 12¹⁸ 1 Co 6¹¹ 11⁵ 13² 15¹⁰ Ga 6³, Hell. Greek exceeds classical usage by extending the practice to neuter *adjectival* predicates even where the subject is not abstract and does not represent a class, e.g. P. Rei. 11. 25 ἡ χεὶρ ἥδε κύριον ἔστω, Mt 6³⁴ ἀρκετὸν ... ἡ κακία, Ac 12³ D ἀρεστὸν ... ἡ ἐπιχείρησις, 2 Co 2⁶ ἱκανὸν ... ἡ ἐπιτιμία. Like the Koine, NT follows Latin (quod est, id est, hoc est) with the discordant explanatory neuter pronoun in ὅ ἐστιν and τουτ' ἔστιν (Mayser shows that ὅ ἐστιν is vernacular, τουτέστιν literary: II 1, 75, 77): e.g. Mt 27³³ (exc. A) ⁴⁶ Mk 3¹⁷ 12⁴² 15¹⁶· ²² Jn 1⁴¹ Eph 5⁵ 6¹⁷ Col 1²⁷ p⁴⁶ BAFGIP 2¹⁰ p⁴⁶ BDEFG 2¹⁷ BFG 3¹⁴ vl. Heb 2¹⁴ 7⁵ 9¹¹ 1 Pt 2¹⁹ (exceptions: Ac 16¹² 1 Co 3¹⁷ Eph 3¹³ Ph 1²⁸ Col 2¹⁰ vl. ¹⁷ vl.). We find assimilation of the gender of the pronoun to that of the antecedent, and not to that of the subject, in Col 3⁵ Rev 4⁵ 5⁶· ⁸. When an adj. agrees with two or more nouns differing in gender it is usually repeated, or else, if it precedes the first noun, it agrees with it (Lk 10¹ εἰς πᾶσαν πόλιν καὶ τόπον) and, if it follows, it takes the gender of the nearer noun (Heb 9⁹ δῶρά τε καὶ θυσίαι ... μὴ δυνάμεναι); in Heb 3⁶ βεβαίαν (om. p¹³ p⁴⁶ B) is interpolated from 3¹⁴.

§ 2. "Constructio ad sensum" [1]

These good Greek constructions [2] take the form of:—

(*a*) Collective noun with plural verb. In the Ptol. papyri, LXX, and NT, especially with ὄχλος, λαός, στρατία, οἰκία,

---

[1] K-G I § 359, pp. 52ff. Gildersleeve I 119–122. Wackernagel I 103. Mayser II 3, 25.

[2] There is in the NT nothing so blatant as LXX Ex 9⁷ where a subordinate clause is not syntactically connected with its main clause: ἰδὼν δὲ Φαραώ ... ἐβαρύνθη ἡ καρδία Φαραώ.

πλῆθος, σπέρμα. This is not too harsh if the verb occurs in a fresh clause (Jn 6² 1 Co 16¹⁵) but more noticeable when the collective noun is followed by a plural circumstantial ptc. (Lk 2¹³, Ac 21³⁶ where DHLP have corrected the ptc. to sing.) and when the plural verb follows in the same clause: Mt 21⁸ Jn 7⁴⁹ Ac 6⁷ (AE corr. to sing.) 25²⁴ (BHΨ corr. to sing.) Rev 8⁹ 9¹⁸ (p⁴⁷ corr. to sing.), Herm. S IX 1. 8 (pap. Mich. corr. to sing.), Evang. Thom. 15² ὄχλος δὲ πολὺς παρειστήκεισαν ἀκούοντες. In Mk at any rate the tendency is that if ὄχλος comes first the verb is plur.: if the verb comes first it is sing. The same tendency occurs in the Koine: PSI IV 402. 4 (mid. iii/B.C.) ὁ λαὸς ὁ ἐν τῆι πόλι τὰς κολυκύνθας ὀπτῶσιν, IV 380. 4 (249 B.C.) ἐπέθετο (sing. verb. first) ἡμῖν ὁ λαὸς καὶ τὰς χεῖρας ἐπενηνόχασιν (plur. verb follows) τοῖς ποιμέσιν.

(b) A masc. ptc. may follow a fem. or neut. personal collective noun like ἐκκλησία, ἔθνος or πλῆθος: Lk 10¹³ (p⁴⁵ DEG corr. to fem.), Ac 5¹⁶, Ga 1²³, Eph 4¹⁷ᶠ. In the same way a masc. pronoun may follow a noun in another gender: Mt 28¹⁹ ἔθνη... αὐτούς, Jn 6⁹ παιδάριον ὅς (vl. ὅ), Ga 4¹⁹ τέκνα οὕς, Ph 2¹⁵ γενεᾶς... ἐν οἷς, Co 2¹⁵ ἀρχαί... αὐτούς, ¹⁹ κεφαλή ... ἐξ οὗ.

(c) A masc. ptc. may follow a neut. personal noun like πνεῦμα, βδέλυγμα: Mt 9²⁶ (AC³NX corr. to neut.), Mk 1²⁶ D, 9²⁰ 13¹⁴ (DAEF corr. to neut.), Lk 9⁴⁰ p⁴⁵, 11²⁴ p⁴⁵ minusc.

(d) ἕκαστος with plur. verb occurs eleven times in NT (Mt 2, Lk 1, Jn 2, Ac 2, Eph 1, Heb 1, Rev 2), the correct sing. 25 times (Lk 1, Jn 1, Ac 2, Ro 3, 1 & 2 Co 13, Ga 1, Eph 2, Jas 1, 1 Pt 1), which presents a contrast to the LXX where the plur. verb occurs 89 times (sing. 56). See Mayser II 3, 37.

§ 3. The "Schema Atticum "[1]

On many occasions the NT (and Hermas), LXX, and Koine break the classical rule of the "schema Atticum", whereby a neut. plur. subject has a sing. verb. MGr does not follow it at all. However, it is not quite true to say with Jannaris (§ 1171) that among the post-classical authors only Atticists keep the sing. verb, because like Biblical Greek the Ptol. papyri hold a middle course between the Attic and the later use (Mayser II 3, § 151).

---

[1] K-G I § 364, p. 64. Gildersleeve I 97-102. Mayser II 3, 28ff.

§ 3–4] CONGRUENCE OF GENDER AND NUMBER 313

The NT usually keeps the rule when the subject is used in a non-personal sense (πρόβατα, σώματα), especially with abstracts, or unless the subject is a pronoun: Mt 10^2 18^{12} Lk 12^{27} Jn $10^{3.\ 4.\ 8}$ p^{45} L $^{10.\ 12}$ p^{45} SBA ^{27} vl. ^{28} vl. 17^7 vl. 19^{31} Ac 5^{12} 1 Ti 5^{25} vl. Rev 15^4 p^{47}. But the following exceptions break the class. rule and conform to Koine standards : Mt 6^{28} (as opp. to Lk 12^{27}), Lk 24^{11}, Jn 19^{31} (sing. immediately before), Rev 1^{19}; there has been an attempt sometimes on the part of scribes to atticize, e.g. Jn 10^8 $p^{45,\ 12.\ 27.\ 28}$ 17^7, Ac 5^{12} (note the parchment fragment of iv/A.D. init.: ZNW 26, 1927, 118), 1 Ti 5^{25}, Rev 15^4 p^{47}. The NT usually breaks the class. rule with words used in a personal sense (ἔθνη, τέκνα, δαιμόνια) but there is a good deal of fluctuation with πνεύματα, and the Atticists have been at work on the MSS :– τέκνα Mt 10^{21} (exc. BΔ) = Mk 13^{12} (exc. B); ἔθνη Mt 6^{32} (exc. EG) 12^{21} 25^{32} (exc. AE), Lk 12^{30} (exc. p^{45} AD), Ac 4^{25} 11^1 (exc. D*) 13^{48}, Ro 2^{14} (exc. D cE) $15^{12.\ 27}$, 1 Co 10^{20} vl., Ga 3^8, 2 Ti 4^{17} (exc. KL), Rev 11^{18} p^{47} S* 15^4 $18^{3.\ 23}$ 21^{24} δαιμόνια Lk 4^{41} SC 8^{30} CF ^{35}S c ^{33}(exc. SU), Jas 2^{19}; πνεύματα Mk 1^{27} 3^{11} vl. 5^{13} (exc. B), Ac 8^7, Rev 4^5 16^{14} vl. The following instances thus approach more nearly the class. style, and the variants may well be scribal atticisms, except perhaps in Paul :— τέκνα Mt 10^{21} BΔ = Mk 13^{12} B, 1 Jn 3^{10}, 2 Jn^{13}, Ro 9^8, 1 Co 7^{14}; ἔθνη Mt 6^{32}EG 25^{32}AE, Lk 12^{30} p^{45}AD, Ac 11^1 D*, Ro 2^{14} D cE 9^{30}, 1 Co 10^{20} KL, Eph 4^{17}, 2 Ti 4^{17} KL, Rev 11^{18} vl.; δαιμόνια Lk 4^{41} vl. $8^{2.\ 30}$ vl. ^{35} vl. ^{38} ^{33} SU 10^{17}; πνεύματα Mk 3^{11} vl. 5^{13} B, Lk 11^{26} 10^{20} vl., 1 Co 14^{32} (vl. πνεῦμα), Rev 16^{13} S ^{14} vl.

§ 4. Number of the Verb when there are several subjects [1]

The rules as to sing. or plur. verb where several co-ordinate words form the subject were as lax in class. Greek as they are in the NT.

(i) The verb, if it stands first, usually agrees with the first subject: Mt 5^{18} Mk 2^{25} Jn 2^2 18^{15} 20^3 Ac 11^{14} $16^{30.\ 31}$ Ro 16^{21} 1 Co 13^{13} 2 Ti 1^{15} (variants: Lk 8^{19} Ac 17^{14} Ro 15^{26} p^{46} B). The exception is when the group which forms the subject has already been conceived as a whole (i.e. when all the subjects partake in the action expressed by the verb): Mk 10^{35} Lk 23^{12} Ac 5^{24}.

---

[1] K-G I § 370, pp. 77f.   Gildersleeve II 468ff.   Mayser II 3, 30ff.

(ii) The verb, if it stands between the subjects, agrees with the first subject: Lk 8²² Jn 4³⁶ etc.

(iii) If there are verbs on either side of the subject, the rule seems to be that the first verb (finite or ptc.) agrees with the first noun and the second verb with both (i.e. it is plural): Mt 17⁸ ὤφθη (SBD plur.) ... Μωϋσῆς καὶ Ἡλίας συλλαλοῦντες, Lk 2³³, Jn 12²², Ac 5²¹·²⁹ 13⁴⁶D 14¹⁴D.

(iv) If one of the subjects is 1st pers., the verb is 1st pers. plur. and modifying ptcs. are masc. plur.: Lk 2⁴⁸ Jn 10³⁰ 1 Co 9⁶.

(v) Attributive adjectives and ptcs. agree with the noun which is nearer: Lk 10¹ 1 Th 5²³ Heb 9⁹ (in Heb 3⁶ the adj. is interpolated from 3¹⁴).

(vi) When sing. words in the subject are connected by ἤ or οὔτε the verb, or an attribute, is usually sing.: Mt 5¹⁸ 12²⁵ 18⁸ 1 Co 14²⁴ Ga 1⁸ Eph 5⁵ (Jas 2¹⁵ is an understandable exception).

(vii) When the verb comes last, after two subjects Mk has plural verb (13³¹), which is altered by Mt to sing. (24³⁵); cf. LXX Da 3³³. But Mk has sing. verb. in 4⁴¹. Jn also (1¹⁷), and Mt (6¹⁹), and Paul (1 Co 15⁵⁰), have sing. verb.

§ 5. Solecisms in the New Testament

There are two varieties: those found only in Rev, which are severe, and those in the Johannine books and the rest of NT, which are largely excusable.

(a) Revelation

(i) Circumstantial ptcs. and appositional phrases tend to be in the nom. instead of the necessary oblique case (see Allo, *Apocalypse* p. cxlv f): 1⁵ (but the nom. phrase is probably intended as a quotation or else as an indecl. divine title; in the next verse the appositional τῷ ἀγαπῶντι agrees with its antecedent αὐτῷ), 2¹³ ἐν ταῖς ἡμέραις Ἀντιπᾶς ὁ μάρτυς μου ὁ πιστός μου, ²⁰, 3¹², 7⁴, 8⁹, 9¹⁴, 14¹², 20². 17⁴ is extraordinary: ποτήριον ... γέμων βδελυγμάτων καὶ τὰ ἀκάθαρτα. Some of the OT translators also do this: 3 Km 1²⁰ καί συ, ... οἱ ὀφθαλμοὶ πάντος Ἰσραὴλ πρός σε; for papyri examples see Abel § 40 m.

(ii) Less often it is the accus. or gen. which is *pendens*: 1¹¹? 1¹⁵ ὅμοιοι χαλκολιβάνῳ ὡς ἐν καμίνῳ πεπυρωμένης (why fem. and why gen.? There are scribal corrections), 7⁹ (accus. following nom.), 21⁹ (gen. following accus.).

(iii) Quite often masc. is found mistakenly for fem. or neut.: 4⁸A (but S has indic., and 046 neut.), 5⁶S (BAP have neut.), 5⁶ (P neut.), 11⁴ (SccP have fem.), 14¹⁹ (S has fem),

§ 5] CONGRUENCE OF GENDER AND NUMBER 315

17^3 γυναῖκα ... γέμοντα, ^{4} γέμων S*, 13^{14} (S neut.), ^{11} p^{47}, 14^1, 9^{14} SA. On the reading ἄρσεν or ἄρρενα 12^5, see Blass-Debr. § 136, 3. Examples of this solecism from late Greek in Jannaris § 1181 b; from a papyrus, Abel § 40 m.

(iv) λέγων, λέγοντες, appear as if they were indeclinable: 4^1 5^{12} 11^{1} vl. ^{15} (p^{47} SCP have fem.) 14^7 (exc. p^{47}) 19^6 vl. This results from a literal rendering of לֵאמֹר in the LXX, and appears also Ac 6^{11} SD*A ^{13} S. Extended to ἔχων: 10^2 21^{14}.

(v) Plur. (not neut.) subject with sing. verb: 9^{12} ἔρχεται ἔτι δύο Οὐαί (but it may be a Semitic solecism of gender, and therefore neut. plur. Alternatively, δύο = second).

(vi) τέσσαρες for τέσσαρας Rev 4^4 vl.; frequent in MSS of LXX and the papyri.

In all these types of solecism it is usually the ptc. which is involved (esp. the ptc. of λέγω), and this is interesting because in later Greek the use of ptcs. developed along the same lines; the masc., especially in the nom. sing., is preferred—until in MGr the ptc. has but one indecl. form. An uneducated writer, like the author of Rev, is foreshadowing the language of the future. The tendency, reflected in the least educated writers of the NT, to neglect congruence of gender and case in appositions, is seen in the Koine: P. Ryl. II 112^{13} (A.D. 250) εὕδαμέν σε θυσιάζοντα (of a woman) and BU 10785^5 (A.D. 39) εἰδότος σοῦ (a woman)—gender; P. Par. 51^{25} (Milligan p. 21) ἐμὲ λέλυκας πολιὰς ἔχων—case; P. Amh. II 111-113 (A.D. 128) ἀπέχω παρ' αὐτοῦ τὸν ὁμολογοῦντα—case. Moulton (Proleg. 60) gives instances from the papyri of breach of concord in gender and case, usually the ptc. being concerned.

(b) *Rest of NT*

For papyri, see Mayser II 3, 22.

(i) The indecl. πλήρης,[1] which is indecl. only when followed by the gen., appears several times, but always with variants. It was commonly used in the Koine from i/A.D. onwards, and is found also in LXX (e.g. Jb 21^{24}): Jn 1^{14} (declinable in D) is important for exegesis because, if πλ is indecl. we may take it either with δόξαν or with αὐτοῦ; Ac 6^5 (decl. in BC^2) 6^3 (decl. in

---

[1] Mayser I^1 63f; I^2 2, 58. Thackeray *OT Gr*. 177. Moulton-Howard 162. Deissmann *LO*^{4}, 99f.

SBCD) 19²⁸ AEL (decl. in the rest), Mk 8¹⁹ (decl. in SBCL). When πλήρης is not followed by the gen. it is declinable, but there are indecl. variants to Mk 4²⁸.

(ii) No doubt εἴ τι might have been written throughout in Ph 2¹, instead of εἴ τις σπλάγχνα καὶ οἰκτιρμοί (Moulton Proleg. 59). In the papyri we find indecl. τι, and it is no cause for surprise if we find also indecl. τις (Zerwick § 5).

(iii) As in Rev, sometimes appositional phrases and circumstantial ptcs. are found in the nom. instead of oblique cases: Mt 10¹¹ D, Lk 20²⁷ 21⁶ Jas 3⁸ (unless we punctuate with a semicolon before ἀκατάσχετον), Lk 24⁴⁷ (corr. in D), Ac 10³⁷ (p⁴⁵ LP corr. to ἀρξάμενον), Ac 7⁴⁰, 2 Th 1⁸ D*FG. Sometimes the nom. ptc. is without construction: Mt 4¹⁶D 5⁴⁰D 17²D ⁹D ¹⁴D Mk 7¹⁹ (D indic.). This is the only instance which is important for exegesis: πᾶν τὸ ἔξωθεν εἰσπορευόμενον ... εἰς τὸν ἀφεδρῶνα ἐκπορεύεται, καθαρίζων πάντα τὰ βρώματα. Some refer καθ. to Jesus, of course (Origen, Jülicher, A. Schlatter: see Zerwick § 8). Others however take it as false concord, meant to agree with ἀφεδρῶνα, and translate: *the latrine which removes filth* (Zorell, Knabenbauer, Klostermann, Blass-Debr. §§ 126, 3; 137, 3.). Mk 9²⁰ 16¹⁴ W ὁ μὴ ἐῶν, Jn 7³⁸ (or place a stop after ἐμέ; see p. 320n), Ac 19³⁴. An accus. ptc. without construction: Ac 26³ (SᶜAC corr. it)—which shows that lack of congruence in ptcs. is not confined to the least educated writers of the NT. For frequent papyri examples, see Mayser II 3, 190ff, and for i and ii/A.D. see Blass-Debr. § 137, 3; § 466; Radermacher² 219; Ljungvik BSSVS 6ff. The use of πᾶς with art. and ptc. which in itself is normal popular Greek is so frequent in Mt that it raises the question of Semitic influence (the phrase beginning with כל or, as in Da 6⁸, כל די) in a legislative kind of style: 3¹⁰ 5²². ²⁸. ³² 7¹⁹. The same observation holds good of πᾶς ὅς and ὅστις: 7²⁴ 10³² 12³⁶ 19²⁹ 21²² 23³ (Lagrange *S. Matth.* XCVIIf). Luke is guilty too: Lk 12⁴⁸ παντὶ δὲ ᾧ ..., παρ' αὐτοῦ, and John: 6³⁹ 15².

(iv) Masc. πάντων for fem. πασῶν: Mk 12²⁸, P. Giss. 23, 4 (early ii/A.D.). But Abel (§ 41 a) quotes Thucyd. 4, 52, 2. Acta Thomae 41³⁹ πάντων τῶν ἐπιθυμιῶν, 66¹⁷ πάντων γυναικῶν, 70³⁰ πάντων τῶν ἡδονῶν.

(v) Nom. for accus. (a slip): Ro 2⁸ ὀργὴ καὶ θυμός, obj. of ἀποδώσει! Cp. LXX 3 Km 5¹⁴ ⁽²⁸⁾ καὶ ἀπέστειλεν αὐτοὺς εἰς τὸν Λίβανον, δέκα χιλιάδες, ἐν τῷ μηνί, ἀλλασσόμενοι.

(vi) Remarkable changes in person and number, in: Lk 13³⁴ 'Ιερουσαλήμ... ἡ... λιθοβολοῦσα τοὺς ἀπεσταλμένους πρὸς αὐτήν, ποσάκις ἠθέλησα ἐπισυνάξαι τὰ τέκνα σου... καὶ οὐκ ἠθελήσατε Semitic? Cf. Moule 180.

(vii) Since, of the numerals 1–100, only the first four are declinable, it is not surprising to find a tendency even for these to be indecl., e.g. Mk 14¹⁹ Jn 8⁹ εἷς καθ' εἷς.

(viii) πᾶσα indecl. at Mt 2³; and πᾶν also seems to be indecl., as it is used of persons in Jn 17² πᾶν ὃ δέδωκας αὐτῷ, δώσει αὐτοῖς...

(ix) Grammatically we expect the nom., instead of ὑποδεδεμένους Mk 6⁹ and at 12⁴⁰ οἱ κατεσθίοντες... καὶ... προσευχόμενοι refers perhaps to the distant genitive ἀπὸ τῶν γραμματέων (12³⁸).

(x) πᾶς πόρνος... ὅ ἐστιν Eph 5⁵, τὴν ἀγάπην, ὅ ἐστιν Col 3¹⁴ (vl. ἥτις ἐστίν). Such a solecism appears nowhere else in the Paulines. Is this important for authorship? See Moffatt *ILNT* 153ff.

CHAPTER TWENTY-THREE

THE SUBORDINATION OF CLAUSES

§ 1. Substantival Clauses [1]

They include clauses with infinitive, participle, ὅτι, ὡς, etc., and indirect questions. See pp. 134–149 (for verb and infin.), and pp. 325f (for problems of the Relative).

§ 2. Adjectival Clauses

See under Relative Pronouns, pp. 47f, 106–110.

§ 3. Adverbial Clauses

(a) Causal clauses [2]

Subordination by ὅτι and διότι is often so loose that only the feeble translation *for* is possible (e.g. Ac 18¹⁰ διότι ἐγώ εἰμι μετὰ σοῦ, Ro 1¹⁹. ²¹ 3²⁰ 8⁷ 1 Co 1²⁵ 4⁹ 10¹⁷ 2 Co 4⁶ 8⁸. ¹⁴). Strictly the meaning is *because, quoniam*, and διότι = διὰ τοῦτο ὅτι : e.g. Mt 5³⁻¹² Ac 22¹⁸ Jas 4³ 1 Pt 1²⁴. Correspondence with כִּי has influenced the meaning of ὅτι somewhat in Biblical Greek, to an almost consecutive sense, *so that*: Mt 8²⁷ ποταπός ἐστιν οὗτος ὅτι . . ., Mk 4⁴¹ Lk 4³⁶ 8²⁵ Jn 2¹⁸, Heb 2⁶ τί ἐστιν ἄνθρωπος ὅτι. So in Hebrew 1 Sam 11⁵ מַה־לָּעָם כִּי יִבְכּוּ.

Ἐπεί has a causal sense, but it too is weakened in Biblical Greek to *for otherwise*: Ro 3⁶ 11⁶. ²² 1 Co 5¹⁰ 7¹⁴ Heb 10². Purely causal Jn 13²⁹ ἐπεὶ τὸ γλωσσόκομον εἶχεν, Lk 1¹ ἐπειδήπερ. Ἐπειδή appears in the Ptol. papyri (BU 844¹⁵ ἐπιδὴ χρίαν αὐτοῦ ἔχω *because I need it*) but it is retreating gradually before ἐπεί (Mayser II 3, 82). Καθότι too in Hell. Greek may be little more than *for* (e.g. Lk 1⁷ καθότι ἦν Ἐλισαβὲτ στεῖρα, 19⁹ Ac 2²⁴ 17³¹, P. Par. 27, 23). Δι' ἣν αἰτίαν 2 Ti

---

[1] See also K-G II pp. 354ff. Mayser II 1, 306ff. Moulton Einl. 335f.
[2] K-G II, § 569, pp. 460–463. Mayser II 3, 82ff. Martin P. Nilsson, " Die Kausalsätze im Griechischen bis Aristoteles," (*Beiträge zur historischen Syntax der griechischen Sprache*, 18, ed. M. v. Schanz, Würzburg), 1907. Zerwick §§ 297–299.

1⁶, ¹² etc., ἐφ' ᾧ (see p. 272), ἀνθ' ὧν (see p. 258), ὡς, καθώς (see pp. 158, 320(2)), οὗ χάριν Lk 7⁴⁷—are also causal conjunctions.

(b) *Conditional Clauses*

There are four chief kinds of conditional clauses, and we have discussed them all under various heads in the chapters on the Mood of Verbs. For (i) εἰ with indic., representing the simple assumption, see pp. 92, 115. For (ii) εἰ with opt., representing the "potential" conception, see pp. 125ff. For (ii) εἰ with aor. or impf. indic., representing an assumption as not corresponding with reality, see pp. 91f. For (iv) ἐάν with subjunctive, indicating an expected result based on the present general or particular circumstances, see pp. 113f.

This is the class. norm. but in fact the opt. is now greatly reduced and in NT scarcely occurs at all in conditions, and never (as in class.) to express repetitions in past time. Moreover there is, according to classical standards, a misuse of εἰ with indic., and there is a liberal mixing in the various categories of conditional sentences. Whereas class. Greek had μή for negative in all conditions, the NT often has εἰ οὐ (but always ἐὰν μή).

Besides the more orthodox method of a subordinate clause with εἰ or ἐάν, a plain statement in the form of a ptc. (see p. 157) or independent clause will serve as the protasis of a condition. Thus in Mt 12⁴⁴ καὶ ἐλθὸν εὑρίσκει is *if he comes and finds*; it has always been obscure why the spirit necessarily returns. In 24⁴⁰ᶠ τότε ἔσονται δύο ἐν τῷ ἀγρῷ ... δύο ἀλήθουσαι is *if there are two in the field ..., if there are two women grinding*. In Ro 13³ θέλεις δὲ μὴ φοβεῖσθαι τὴν ἐξουσίαν is *if you wish to be fearless of*. Such interpretation lends point to the context and is good Greek.

Under this head note the strong Hebraism, εἰ in oaths and protestations.[1]

(c) *Comparative Clauses* [2]

The atticistic καθάπερ is found in Paul and Hebrews, but often as a possible scribal correction, e.g. Ro 10¹⁵ B (rest καθώς),

---

[1] Also in questions, in the Pauline εἴπερ *if indeed* and εἴγε *si tamen*, in εἴτε ... εἴτε (LXX for אם ... אם) *whether ... or*. See ch. 25.
[2] K-G II 490ff. Mayser II 2, 440; II 3, 92ff. See also, for ὡς, Index.

11⁸ SB (rest καθώς), 12⁴ p⁴⁶ SBA (D*EFG ὥσπερ). Phrynichus (425) condemns the Hellenistic καθώς, which occurs frequently in the ii/B.C. papyri (Mayser II 2, 440; II 3, 92, n. 4), and prefers καθό (Ro 8²⁶ 2 Co 8¹² 1 Pt 4¹³) or καθά (Mt 27¹⁰ Lk 1² D Eus).

1. As correlatives we find ὡς, ὥσπερ, καθώς, καθάπερ, alongside οὕτως or καί or οὕτως καί. Some authors prefer ὥσπερ (Mt 10 ὥσπερ: 4 καθώς, Jas, Rev), some καθώς (Mk, Eph, Past, 1 & 2 Pt, 1, 2, 3 Jn; Lk 17:1, Jn 32:1, Ac 12:3, Paul 81:15, Heb 9:3). Some authors make the ὥσπερ-clause follow the main clause (Ac 2² 3¹⁷ 11¹⁵ Heb 4¹⁰ 7²⁷ 9²⁵ Rev 10³); but in Paul it nearly always precedes (Ro 5¹². ¹⁹. ²¹ 6⁴. ¹⁹ 11³⁰ 12⁴ vl. 1 Co 11¹² 15²² 16¹ Ga 4²⁹; ὥσπερ ... ἀλλά 1 Co 8⁵, ὥσπερ ἵνα 2 Co 8⁷), the two exceptions being 1 Th 5³ and the introduction to a quotation in 1 Co 10⁷ (where however ὡς, in CD*KP 81 181 Marcion, is prob. correct as it accounts for the omission by haplography of τινες αὐτῶν ὥσπερ (ὡς) in FG *f g*, the eye travelling from ως to ως in καθως τινες αυτων ως γεγραπται). The ὥσπερ-clause precedes also in Lk 17²⁴ 18¹¹ (vl. ὡς) Jn 5²¹ (S ὡς) ²⁶ (S*DW Eus½ ὡς), whereas Mt has both orders: ὥσπερ ... οὕτως 12⁴⁰ 13⁴⁰ 24²⁷. ³⁷, ὥσπερ following 6². ⁷ 18¹⁷ 20²⁸ 25¹⁴. ³². Where καθώς introduces a following quotation in NT it almost invariably follows its main clause. Mk 1² would seem to be an exception, as it is usual to take ἐγένετο in 1⁴ as the main verb; however, the exception can be negatived if the καθώς-clause be taken with the preceding verse and the verb ἐστιν is supplied, although it is not at all like Mark to omit the copula in such circumstances. If we accept the necessary variants, the καθώς-clause introducing a quotation does precede in all other instances: Lk 2²³ Jn 6³¹ 12¹⁴ Ac 7⁴² Ro 1¹⁷ 3⁴ AD (but SB καθάπερ) ¹⁰ 4⁸ DG (rest καθάπερ) ¹⁷ 8³⁶ 9¹³ (B corr. to καθάπερ) ²⁹. ³³ 10¹⁵ vl. 11⁸ vl. ²⁶ 15³. ⁹. ²¹ 1 Co 1³¹ 2⁹ 2 Co 6¹⁶ 8¹⁵ Ga 3⁶ Heb 4³. ⁷ 5⁶. ¹

2. As *quandoquidem = even so as*, especially καθώς: Ro 1²⁸ 1 Co 1⁶ 5⁷ Eph 1⁴ Ph 1⁷, Mt 6¹² ὡς.

3. In Mk 4²⁶ ὡς = *as if* (ὡς ἄνθρωπος βάλῃ) SBD (others add ἐάν or ὅταν; so LXX Isa 7² 17¹¹ 31⁴); similar Lk 11⁵. ⁶, where ἐάν appears to be omitted before εἴπῃ.

4. In Bibl. Greek, through influence of כְּ, ὡς may serve to soften a statement: *as it were, perhaps, approximately*, Mk 6¹⁵ Lk 15¹⁹, T. Abr. 82¹¹ 118²⁶ ὡς ἐν ὀνείροις *in a sort of dream*, 118²² τινες ἐν ῥομφαίᾳ τελευτῶσιν ὡς (*or perhaps*) ἐπὶ τόξοις, 107⁵ ἤγγισεν τῇ πόλει ὡς (*approx.*) ἀπὸ σταδίων τριῶν. Perhaps Heb. 11²⁷.

---

[1] On the strength of this evidence of clause-order, G. D. Kilpatrick argues in *JThS* XI, 2, 1960, 340ff., that at Jn 7³⁸ the main clause ends with εἰς ἐμέ, and the dependent clause begins at καθώς (so *he that believes* is subject of *let him drink*). Among other things, this depends on whether it is feasible for τις to be resumed in the same sentence by such a phrase as ὁ πιστεύων εἰς ἐμέ. Besides the note in *JThS*, I owe much to Dr Kilpatrick for private communications on this point of word order.

5. The predicative use of ὡς is very common: Mt 22³⁰ ὡς ἄγγελοι θεοῦ εἰσιν, 18³ Lk 15¹⁹ 1 Co 7⁸. Class. writers would have preferred the adj. ἴσος.

6. Sometimes ὡς may be confused with ἕως, e.g. Ac 17¹⁴ ὡς ἐπί (SBAE corr. to ἕως), for in Hell. Greek ὡς ἐπί = *against, versus* (Polyb. 1, 29, 1), as also do ἕως ἐπί and ἕως εἰς (cp. 1 Mac 5²⁹ ἕως ἐπὶ τὸ ὀχύρωμα, where V reads ὡς).

7. ὡσεί (and rarely ὥσπερεί or ὡσάν) may stand for ὡς: Lk 3²³ ὡσεὶ ἐτῶν τριάκοντα (but 8⁴² ὡς ἐτῶν δώδεκα), Mt 14²¹ (D ὡς), etc. Ὡσάν 2 Co 10⁹ (Hellenistic), ὥσπερεί 1 Co 4¹³ vl. 15⁸ vl. (Mayser II 3, 167. Radermacher² 203. Moulton Einl. 261, n. 2).

(d) *Concessive Clauses*

For καίπερ and καίτοι see pp. 153, 157.

When one cannot render the particles κἄν and εἰ καί by *although*, they keep their proper sense as conditional, e.g. 2 Co 11¹⁵ οὐ μέγα οὖν εἰ καὶ οἱ διάκονοι αὐτοῦ μετασχηματίζονται ὡς διάκονοι δικαιοσύνης, Jn 8⁵⁵ κἂν εἴπω ὅτι, Lk 12³⁸. Concessive clauses with εἰ or ἐάν are essentially conditional clauses and follow the rules of class. Greek. When it does not mean *even if* or *and if* (καὶ ἐάν), κἄν is equivalent to ἐὰν καί (e.g. Mk 5²⁸ *if only*, 6⁵⁶, Heb 10² p⁴⁶, etc.). See Harsing 46, Jannaris § 598.

In the sense of *except if* Hell. Greek places ἐκτός (1 Co 14⁵ 15², 1 Ti 5¹⁹) before the class. εἰ μή (Mk 6⁵ 2 Co 13⁵ Ga 1⁷ etc.). Hell. Greek, from i/A.D. onwards, is also fond of considering εἴ τις as equivalent of ὅστις ὅ τι (as Mt 18²⁸ ἀπόδος εἴ τι ὀφείλῃς) and of adding ἄν (as 1 Co 7⁵ εἰ μή τι ἂν ἐκ συμφώνου, Hist. Lausiaca p. 70, 14 Butl. εἴ τι ἄν με διδάξῃς, ἐκεῖνο ποιῶ). See Radermacher ² 199, Ljungvik BSSVS 9ff.

(e) *Temporal Clauses*

There is a preference in Biblical Greek for temporal conjunctions, as against the genitive absolute, which is due perhaps to the frequency with which temporal clauses are introduced by כְּדִי or כַּד in Aramaic. For ὅταν, etc., see pp. 112f, 124f. There are also ὅτε (indic.), ἡνίκα (Paul), ὁπότε (only Lk 6³ AEHK; rest ὅτε), ἐπειδή (temporal only Lk 7¹ vl.), ἵνα (Jn 16²), ὡς (Ionic influence: Lk 1²³ 12⁵⁸ 24³² Jn 2⁹ Ga 6¹⁰; Mk 4³⁶ either *when he was in the boat* or *as he was, in the boat*), ὡς ἄν (see pp. 112f), ἕως *while* (Jn 9⁴), *until* (Mk 6⁴⁵ Jn 21²²ᶠ 1 Ti 4¹³), πρίν and πρὸ τοῦ (see pp. 78, 113, 140, 144).

(f) *Participle Absolute: accusative.*

'Εξόν occurs in NT only as a predicate to a missing ἐστιν, and altogether lacking are ὑπάρχον (PSI IV 340, 9, 257 B.C.), πρέπον, etc., which are also very rare indeed in the Ptol. papyri. The obscure τυχόν (*perhaps, without doubt*) occurs Lk 20[13] D Ac 12[15]D 1 Co 16[6]; δέον Ac 19[36] 1 Ti 5[13] 1 Pt 1[6].

Participle Absolute: genitive

The correct use is becoming rarer in Hell. Greek and it is misused more often; that is to say, the gen. is not truly absolute but is used even where the ptc. might have agreed with the subject or object of the sentence. This is one of the marks of the Koine (Mayser II 3, 66ff. Moulton Einl. 114. Radermacher[2] 208f) and of Biblical Greek (Johannessohn DGKPS 46).

Mark's usage is fairly regular: it is only a temporal use and always precedes the main clause, except for ὀψίας γενομένης 4[35] (unless we take this closely with the next sentence) and ἀνατείλαντος τοῦ ἡλίου 16[2]. Nevertheless there are falls from class. grace in Mark, as in many NT authors, which scribes have often corrected: he should have placed the ptc. in the dat. at 13[1] (so also Mt at 1[20] 5[1] (B corr) 8[1] (S* corr) 8[5] vl. 28 vl. 9[10, 18] 17[9] 18[24] 21[23] vl. 24[3] 27[17]; Lk at 12[36] 14[29] (p[45] corr.) 17[12] (BL corr.) 22[10]; Jn 4[51] vl. Ac 4[1], LXX Gen 18[1]). But Mayser quotes the same thing in papyri of 255, 249, 218, 221, iii/B.C. ter, 161, 156, ii/B.C. (II 3, 67f), and Thucyd. 1, 114, 1 has διαβεβηκότος ἤδη Περικλέους στρατιᾷ Ἀθηναίων ἠγγέλθη αὐτῷ, ὅτι (and Xen. Anab. 5, 2, 24). Mark should have made the ptc. agree with the accus. at 5[18] ἐμβαίνοντος αὐτοῦ εἰς τὸ πλοῖον παρεκάλει αὐτὸν ὁ δαιμονισθείς, 9[28] vl., 10[17], 13[3]; so should Luke at 9[42] 15[20] 18[40] and Ac 7[21] 19[30] 21[17] vl. 25[7]; and Mt 18[25] Jn 8[30] and Paul at 2 Co 12[21] vl.; papyri of 258, 254, iii/B.C., 168, 176, 114, 51. More irregular still, Mark has a gen. absol. agreeing with the subject at 6[22] SBC* (corr. by p[45] C[3]DWΘ), and so has Mt at 1[18] (but a clause lies in between), Luke at Ac 21[34], and the LXX at Ex 4[21], 1 Km 3[11] παντὸς ἀκούοντος αὐτά, ἠχήσει ἀμφότερα τὰ ὦτα αὐτοῦ. Instances in the Ptol. pap. are so plentiful that Mayser gives only a selection (II 3, 68ff). When these "mistakes" are made in the NT it is very rarely that the gen. absol. takes up a word which has preceded (but 2 Co 4¹⁸). There is no instance of gen. absol. without a finite verb, as often occurs in the Ptol. pap., e.g. βασιλέως προστάξαντος (= *in the King's name*) followed by a command.

(g) *Final Clauses.* See pp. 95, 100–6, 111, 128f 141–6.

(h) *Consecutive Clauses.* See pp. 102, 106, 136, 141f, 272.

CHAPTER TWENTY-FOUR

INCONSISTENCIES BETWEEN MAIN AND DEPENDENT CLAUSES

§ 1. Attraction of Relative Pronoun to case of antecedent [1]

Little need be noted, as this phenomenon is well known to students of class. Greek, the LXX, and the papyri (Mayser II 3, 102). It may not occur if the relative clause is sharply divided from the rest, as in Heb 8², but often the scribes have corrected by bringing in the relative attraction, e.g. Mk 13¹⁹ (ἧς AWC²), Jn 4⁵ (οὗ DWC*) ⁵⁰ (ᾧ AW) 7³⁹ (οὗ SDW) Ti 3⁵ (ὧν Dᶜ Cᵇ) Rev 1²⁰ (ὧν 046).

The Greek relative, unlike the English, includes in itself the demonstrative idea, so that we find compressions like Mk 10⁴⁰ ἀλλ' οἷς ἑτοίμασται (= τούτοις οἷς) and Lk 9³⁶ οὐδὲν ὧν (= οὐδὲν τούτων ἅ).

Equally classical is the attraction of the noun into the relative clause sometimes (the art. omitted), e.g. Jn 9¹⁴ ἐν ᾗ ἡμέρᾳ (for papyri, Mayser II 3, 98ff), and not necessarily immediately after the relative, e.g. Jn 11⁶ ἐν ᾧ ἦν τόπῳ, 17³ ὃν ἀπέστειλας Ἰησοῦν, 2 Co 10¹³ κατὰ τὸ μέτρον τοῦ κανόνος, οὗ ἐμέρισεν ἡμῖν ὁ θεὸς μέτρου (οὗ incidentally attracted to κανόνος).

§ 2. Inverse attraction of the antecedent to the relative [2]

This attraction of the case of the antecedent to that of the relative pronoun may occur even when the antecedent is not drawn into the relative clause, and even when it precedes the relative (as class.): Mk 6¹¹·¹⁶ 12¹⁰ OT (= Mt 21⁴²) λίθον ὃν ἀπεδοκίμασαν . . . , οὗτος ἐγενήθη, Lk 1⁷³ 12⁴⁸ Ac 10³⁶ 1 Co 10¹⁶ LXX Ge 31¹⁶ etc.

---

[1] K-G II 406ff. Meisterhans-Schwyzer 237ff 18–30. Mayser II 3, 98ff. Moulton Einl. 148. Radermacher² 220, 222.
[2] K-G II 413. Meisterhans-Schwyzer 239, 25. Mayser II 3, 107ff. Radermacher² 222. Wackernagel I 49f.

§ 3. Pleonastic insertion of Personal Pronoun [1]

It is a Semitism in the sense that the Heb. אֲשֶׁר לוֹ is reflected through LXX usage, helped by a parallel Aramaic idiom; but non-Biblical Greek, and indeed many languages, reveal the same pleonasm. LXX Gen 41¹⁹ βόες οἵας οὐκ εἶδον τοιαύτας, cp. Mk 13¹⁹ οἵα οὐ γέγονεν τοιαύτη, Mt 3¹² (= Lk 3¹⁷) οὗ τὸ πτύον ἐν τῇ χειρὶ αὐτοῦ, Mt 3¹¹ corrects Mk 1⁷ by omitting αὐτοῦ. Other exx.: Jn 1³³ ἐφ' ὄν ... ἐπ' αὐτοῦ, 18⁹, Ac 15¹⁷ OT 1 Co 8⁶ 2 Pt 2³ Rev 2². ¹⁷ 3⁸ 7². ⁹ 13⁸ 17² 20⁸. Nevertheless scribes have endeavoured to remove the feature: e.g. Mk 7²⁵ (SDW om αὐτῆς). Papyri: e.g. PSI IV 433, 7 ὅσα ποτὲ ὑπῆρχεν ἐν ταμιείωι (ἦν δ' ὀλίγα), ἐγὼ αὐτὰ ἐφύτευσα (261 B.C.).

§ 4. Prolepsis [2]

Prolepsis (anticipation) occurs when the subject (object) of the dependent clause is brought forward into the main clause. Such interlacing was frequent in class. Greek but is relatively rare in the Koine. In the NT the subject is brought forward in Mt 6²⁸ Mk 1²⁴ 7² 11³² 12³⁴ Lk 13²⁵ Ac 9²⁰ 19⁴ 1 Co 16¹⁵ Rev 3⁹; and the object (less often) in Lk 24⁷ Ac 13³² Ga 4¹¹ 5²¹.

§ 5. Anacoloutha after relative clauses [3]

In class. Greek there sometimes occurred a false grammatical connection when to a relative clause a second relative clause was joined by καί, to which clause the rel. pronoun was not appropriate in its existing form: e.g. Rev 17² μεθ' ἧς ἐπόρνευσαν ..., καὶ ἐμεθύσθησαν, Mk 6¹¹ (scribes have corrected), Lk 17³¹ 1 Co 7¹³ (p⁴⁶ SD* εἴ τις) Ti 1²ᶠ. But Semitic rather than class. is the anacolouthon in Mt 7⁹¹ τίς ἐστιν ἐξ ὑμῶν, ὃν αἰτήσει ὁ υἱὸς αὐτοῦ ἄρτον, μὴ λίθον ἐπιδώσει αὐτῷ; ἢ καὶ ἰχθὺν αἰτήσει, μὴ ὄφιν ἐπιδώσει αὐτῷ.

§ 6. Mingling of direct and indirect speech: recitative ὅτι [4]

The Koine found it much more difficult than the class. Greek and Latin languages to sustain indirect speech for very

---

[1] K-G II 432f, 443f. Jannaris § 1439. Ljungvik SSAA, 27f. Psichari 182f. Abel § 134. Pernot *Études* 152. Winer-Schmiedel § 22, 7. Thackeray *OT Gr* 46. Moulton-Howard 434f.
[2] K-G II 577f. Jannaris § 1937. Mayser II 3, 111.
[3] K-G II 431ff. Mayser II 3, 112.
[4] K-G II 431ff, 557. Mayser II 3, 46f, 112ff. P. Winter, "Hoti recitativum in Lc 1, 25. 61, 2, 23," *HTR* 48, 1955, 213–216.

long, and in the NT direct speech is preferred in narrative wherever possible, especially in Mk and Jn (but not so much in Lk, and even less in Mt [1]). The equivalent of inverted commas is "ὅτι recitativum". The lattter, and even the mingling of direct and indirect speech, is not unknown in class. Greek. The Hebrew כִּי and Aramaic דְּי helped to commend such an idiom to NT writers. It is the regular usage in Coptic. Note the peculiar positions of ὅτι in Jn 3^{28} and the way some writers will attempt *oratio obliqua*, reverting to *recta* in a very short time (Mk 6^{8f} Lk 5^{14} Ac 1^4 23^{22} 25^{4f}), although sometimes they will repent also of direct speech in mid-stream and change to indirect (Mk 11^{31f}, but D^2 W and Mt 21^{26} keep this in *oratio recta*), Jn 13^{29} Ac 23^{23f}.

---

[1] See C. H. Turner, *JThS* 28, 1927, 9–15.

PART II
CONNECTIONS BETWEEN SENTENCES

CHAPTER TWENTY-FIVE

CO-ORDINATING PARTICLES [1]

IN THE widest sense, prepositions and adverbs as well as conjunctions may be classed as particles, but in this chapter the study is confined to co-ordinating conjunctions. Nothing like a complete thesaurus will be attempted, attention being restricted to correct classification and observation of new tendencies, unusual instances, and instances with an interest for exegesis or textual criticism. The Koine and NT are more careless than the older Greek regarding the position of particles and, as in syntax generally, display the popular love of over-emphasis. The use of post-positive particles is declining and emphasis is achieved by forming more compound particles.

The double influence of later Greek usage and Jewish background worked upon NT writers and combined to achieve a considerable reduction in the number of particles as compared with more refined Greek; thus τοι and μήν (by themselves) and γοῦν are too subtle to be needed in the NT. Fascinating problems arise for the meticulous student. Why does οὖν occur so often in the fourth Gospel and what does it signify? Why is Paul so fond of οὐχί? Has Mark, who loves καί, any reason for changing to δέ at times? What NT writers use τε . . . καί, and is καί . . . καί the same thing?

§ 1. Simple Particles [2]

’Αλλά.

Paul is particularly fond of it [3]. It is a stronger adversative particle than δέ but is often weakened in the clause where it most frequently occurs, that is, after a preceding οὐ or οὐ μόνον:

---

[1] K-G II 116–339. Jannaris §§ 1700–1728. Mayser II 3, 114–174. J. D. Denniston, *The Greek Particles*², Oxford 1954.
[2] K-G II §§ 515ff. Mayser II 3, 116ff.
[3] Ro 67, 1 Co 71, 2 Co 66, Ga 23; cp. with Lk only 32, Ac 29, Mt 37, Heb 16, Rev 13, LXX Ge 20, Ex 13.

thus in Mt 10^{20} Mk 5^{39} 9^{37} 14^{36} Jn 12^{44} 1 Co 15^{10} etc. the meaning is simply *not so much . . . as*. The preceding negative may easily be supplied in Mt 11^{7-9} Ac 19^2 Ga 2^3, or an interrogative may be the equivalent of a negative in Jn 7^{48} Ac 15^{11}. Thus the meaning is *sed etiam*. It also occurs simply as *however, nevertheless*, at the beginning of a sentence, but stronger than δέ, e.g. Ro 5^{14} *sin is not imputed when there is no law; nevertheless* . . . . In Mk 14^{36} it reverses a previous command. Sometimes before a command it is not so much adversative as consecutive, and is best translated as an interjection, *Well!*: Mk 16^7 *See the place where they laid him. Well, go to his disciples* . . . . Ac 9^6 *I am Jesus* . . . *Well, rise and* . . . , Mt 9^{18} Mk 9^{22} Ac 10^{20} 26^{16}. After a conditional protasis, we must translate *at least*, e.g. Mk 14^{29} 1 Co 4^{15}. Introducing a strong addition, ἀλλά or ἀλλὰ καί may be *yes, indeed*, as in Jn 16^2 1 Co 3^2 2 Co 7^{11} 11^1 Ph 1^{18}. There is an ellipse (e.g. scil. *this has happened*) with ἀλλ' ἵνα in Mk 14^{49} Jn 1^8 9^3 13^{18} 15^{25} 1 Jn 2^{19}. It is clear from Mk 4^{22} that ἀλλά must sometimes have the meaning of εἰ μή *except* (so Mt 20^{23}, and ἀλλ' ἤ in Lk 12^{51} 2 Co 1^{13}), just as εἰ μή serves for ἀλλά (Lk $4^{26, 27}$)—a confusion which may be traceable to Aramaic influence.

Ἄρα [1]

Even Paul, who makes good use of it, sometimes breaks the classical rule by giving it first position (Ro 10^{17} 1 Co 15^{18} etc.). It is often combined with other particles: οὖν, γε, εἴπερ, ἐπεί, μήτι. Its use in the Ptol. papyri is rare and literary. It is not in itself an interrogative particle, like ἆρα, although it may be introduced into an interrog. sentence.

Ἆρα and ἆραγε.

Also particles of literary style, = οὖν, *num igitur, ergone*. Interrogative. Luke and Paul. There are four exx. in LXX, three of them in Ge (e.g. 18^{13}), but it is more frequent in Symmachus. Lk 18^8 Ac 8^{30} Ga 2^{17} (it would be ἄρα here, since μὴ γένοιτο in Paul always answers a question; it may however be ἆρα. if the clause is not interrogative but an argumentative statement posed for an imaginary opponent to answer).

---

[1] K-G II 317ff. Mayser II 3, 119ff.

§ 1] CO-ORDINATING PARTICLES 331

Γάρ [1].

The usage is classical. Paul uses it even more than he does ἀλλά, and Matthew and Luke are fond of it [2]. It is very rare in the Johannine writings, which makes the οὖν of D more likely than γάρ at Jn 9^{30}.

Γε [3].

A modal particle which lends emphasis to another word. It is very elusive in NT and is almost always merged with another particle as a meaningless appendage: with ἀλλά, αρα, εἰ, εἰ δὲ μή, καίτοι, μήτι. Nevertheless it may have some significance in καί γε since, through the LXX, we can trace the influence of the Heb. גַּם: Ac 2^{18} 1 Co 4^8 (D*FG om γε) *and indeed*, Lk 19^{42} *at least*. Occasionally without another particle: Lk 11^8 διά γε *at least because of*, 18^5, Ro 8^{32} (DFG om) ὅς γε *he who even*.

Δέ and μὲν . . . δέ [4].

Sometimes δέ will have the strong adversative force of ἀλλά after a foregoing negative (Ac 12$^{9.\ 14}$ Heb 4^{13} 6^{12}) but usually it is weaker and indistinguishable from καί. Indeed the proportion of this δέ to καί raises interesting problems in Biblical Greek since it varies considerably in and between different books; in the NT the proportion of δέ : καί varies from 1 : 0·6 in Paul to 1 : 73 in Rev (4-21). The variety is still greater in the LXX, from 1 : 1 in 4 Mac to 1 : 188 in Jer β.

At times δέ will introduce a parenthesis (Ac 1^{15} (SBA τε) 4^{13}D 12^3) and that is how νυνὶ δέ is best explained in the middle of a sentence (Col 1^{22}). One of the most characteristic departures from class. style is the rarity of the correlation of μέν and δέ in Biblical Greek; it occurs with any frequency only in some Paulines, Ac and Heb. Matthew has 20 instances, and this, together with his comparatively wide use of δέ (491 against Mk's 150), make the translation hypothesis for his gospel the less certain. Mark has only two or three instances, and Luke only

---

[1] K-G II 330ff. Mayser II 3, 121ff.
[2] Mt 125, Lk 96, Ac 80, Heb 91, Rev 16, Ro 143, 1 Co 108, 2 Co 74, Ga 35. LXX Ge 107, Ex (1–24) 70, Ex (25–40) 21, Isa 181, MiPr 3, 4 Mac 87. Didache 31, Ep. Barn. 47.
[3] K-G II 171–178. Mayser II 3. 123ff. T. K. Abbott, *ICC* on Eph and Col, pp. ivf.
[4] K-G II 261–278. Meisterhans-Schwyzer 250. 6. Mayser II 3, 125ff.

Proportion of δέ : καί

LXX	NT	Apost. Fathers, etc.
4 Macc 123:141 (1:1)	Paul	Didache 66:31
Ex (1–24) 369:800	Ga 58:21 (1:0·4)	(1:0·5)
(1:2·1)	Ro 145:77 (1:0·5)	Ep. Barn. 66:84
Ge 840:2023 (1:2·4)	1 Co 208:129 (1:0·6)	(1:1·3)
Isa (40–66) 81:672	2 Co 74:58 (1:0·8)	T. Abr. A 157:305
(1:8·3)	Ac 556:522 (1:1)	(1:2)
Isa (1–39) 82:882	Mt. 491:762 (1:1·5)	T. Abr. B 43:210
(1:10·7)	Lk (3–24) 511:853	(1:5)
Ex (25–40) 35:605	(1:1·6)	
(1:17)	Lk (1–2) 26:132	
Mi Pr 59:1548 (1:26)	(1:5)	
Jer α 22:917 (1:42)	Mk. 150:785 (1:5)	
Ezk α 26:1642 (1:63)	Rev (1–3) 4:69 (1:17)	
Jg A 17:1588 (1:93)	Rev (4–21) 8:586	
Ezk β 6:592 (1:99)	(1:73)	
Jer β 4:754 (1:188)		

The books are arranged in reverse order of Semitic style.

seven (to Luke, asyndeton often seems more effective, e.g. 7^{22}); the whole of the Pent. (LXX) has only about 20 exx. of μέν ... δέ, Dan O' has μέν 8 times, but the more slavish θ has none. Mt's exx. are all in the part usually assigned to Q, which fact, unless a translator took great liberties, is against Q having been originally Aramaic.

	Mt	Mk	Lk	Jn	Ac	Past	Heb	Jas	1 Pt	Jude
μέν only	–	2	3	4	34	–	5	1	–	–
μέν .. δέ	20	3	7	4	14	3	14	–	4	3

	Ro	Cor	Ga	Eph	Ph	Col	Thes	Tot Paul	NT	Pap. iii/B.C.	ii–i/ B.C.
μέν only	7	10	1	–	2	1	1	22	71	4	8
μέν ... δέ	12	19	2	1	4	–	–	38	110	18	47

The MSS differ considerably over the omission of μέν.

Δή [1].

An invitatory particle (class.), as Lk 2¹⁵ *come, let us go*, Ac 13² 15³⁶ 1 Co 6²⁰ 15⁴⁹ p⁴⁶. But ὃς δή *who ever*, in Mt 13²³.

Διό, διόπερ [2].

Properly subordinating, but not necessarily so in NT. Διό occurs most often in Ac and Paul, and is confused with διότι by scribes (e.g. A*W in Lk 1³⁵). The context favours διό (*and so*) in Ac 20²⁶, but the MSS appear to favour διότι.

Εἰ.

For conditions, see pp. 113ff. In direct questions, as opposed to indirect, it is a Bibl. Greek usage (Mt 12¹⁰ 19³ Lk 13²³ Ac 1⁶, LXX Ge 17¹⁷ 1 Km 10²⁴ 2 Mac 7⁷ 15³, nineteen times in Luke), probably a Hebraism from ־ֲה or אִם, which also may stand in both direct and indirect questions. In the Vulgate *si* renders this εἰ and as a result *si* in later Latin became a direct interrogative. Note that the interrog. ἦ is absent from Bibl. Greek (exc. in Jb 25⁵ B); like ἄρα, it is a mark of literary style.

In oaths [3], εἰ renders Heb. אִם (Mk 8¹² Heb 3¹¹ 4³, ⁵ LXX) and is the equivalent of a strong negative. Conversely, εἰ μή is a strong positive in Ro 14¹¹ D*FG (LXX Isa 45²³ S*B) ζῶ ἐγω, ..., εἰ μὴ κάμψει πᾶν γόνυ.

Ἔτι [4].

In NT = *still* Mt 12⁴⁶ 17⁵ (and parall.) 26⁴⁷; not *further*.

Εἴτε ... εἴτε.

Properly with subordinate clauses, but also with ellipse of the verb, either disjunctive or copulative: Ro 12⁶⁻⁸ 2 Co 5¹⁰ Eph 6⁸ Ph 1¹⁸.

---

[1] K-G II 122–131. Mayser II 3, 133f.
[2] K-G II 462. Meisterhans-Schwyzer 253, 25. Mayser II 3, 134f.
[3] Moulton-Howard 469. N. D. Coleman, "Some noteworthy uses of εἰ or εἶ in Hellenistic Greek—with a note on Mark viii. 12" *JThS* 28, 1927, 159ff. F. C. Burkitt, "Εἶ in Hellenistic Greek. Mark viii. 12" (reply to Coleman), *JThS* ib. 274ff.
[4] Mayser II 3, 136f. Radermacher² 69.

Ἤ and ἤ καί [1].

Disjunctive particles (*or*), especially when introducing a question: Mt 12²⁹ Ro 3²⁹ 9²¹ 1 Co 10²²; but (esp. in questions or negative sentences and with synonyms) almost copulative: Mt 5¹⁷ Jn 8¹⁴ (S corr. to καί) Ac 1⁷ 11⁸ Ro 9¹¹ FG Ga 3²⁸ D* 1 Co 11²⁷ 1 Th 2¹⁹. As a correlation, ἤ . . . ἤ *either* . . . *or* (ἤτοι . . . ἤ Ro 6¹⁶).

Καί [2].

1. *The copula*: a. καί. b. καὶ . . . καί.

2. *The adverb* (*also, even*).

1. (*a*) Καί joins together nouns, adjs., numerals, adverbs, or joins a part with the whole (Ac 5²⁹). Its excessive use in the narrative of many NT writers, esp. Mark, would appear vulgar to the normal reader; Luke and John to some extent mitigate this fault by the use occasionally of asyndeton, and of δέ, οὖν, or τε. The nuance may really be *and yet* (*et tamen*), as in Mt 3¹⁴ *and yet you come to me!* where we expect καὶ μήν or καίτοι. Or the nuance may be consecutive (Mt 5¹⁵ 2 Co 11⁹ Heb 3¹⁹ 2 Pt 1¹⁹) and even final (Mt 8²¹ ἀπελθεῖν καὶ θάψαι, 26¹⁵ Jn 14³ Rev 14¹⁵). This admittedly belongs to the uncultivated Koine, but note also the possibility of Aramaic influence [3], by which the waw of apodosis might well be rendered by καί: Dan θ 4² ἐνύπνιον ἴδον καὶ ἐφοβέρισέν με (καί = rel. pronoun [4]), θ' 7¹⁶ (καί purposive). The same appears in Mt: 6⁴ καὶ ὁ πατήρ (*for*, cp. Dan 10¹⁷) 18²¹ 21²³ etc. Καί in place of temporal subordination: Mt 26⁴⁵ Mk 15²⁵ Lk 19⁴³ 23⁴⁴ Jn 2¹³ Ac 5⁷ Heb 8⁸. Καί with fut. may also resume a final clause to express further result (Mt 26⁵³ Heb 12⁹). Although the papyri provide ample evidence that popular speech favours parataxis, we must remember as a

---

[1] K-G II 296ff. Mayser II 3, 138ff. Radermacher² 33f, 201, 207. H. Margolis in *Amer. Journ. Sem. Lang.*, 25, 1908–9, 257–275 (for LXX).
[2] K-G II § 521ff. Meisterhans-Schwyzer 161. 16; 162. 2; 249; 250. Mayser II 3, 140ff. S. Trenkner, *Le Style KAI dans le recit oral attique* (Institut d'Études Polonaises en Belgique) Brussels 1948. Abel § 78. Radermacher² 28, 37, 218, 222. Ljungvik BSSVS 55ff.
[3] Lagrange *S. Matth.* XCI.
[4] Cp. Lk 1⁴⁹ καὶ ἅγιον τὸ ὄνομα αὐτοῦ, for οὗ τὸ ὄνομα ἅγιον ἐστιν; esp. in Rev.

contributory influence that the Heb. waw introduced propositions of a temporal, conditional, causal and consecutive kind. Obviously Hebraic (not Aramaic) is the use of καί after (καί) ἐγένετο(δέ) in place of accus. and infin.[1]: Lk 5^1 9^{28} 19^{15} Ac 5^7. The translation of καὶ ἰδού constitutes a problem: R. A. Knox renders it in Lk with a variety of English. It is often as redundant as the ἐγένετο construction (Lk 7^{12} D implies that it is equivalent); at least the καί, if not the ἰδού, is often pleonastic, which is why p^{45} SBA omit καί in Ac 10^{17} (CD καὶ ἰδού): Lk 7^{12} Ac 1^{10} Rev 3^{20} (AP om καί).

(b) καὶ ... καί. The probability is that this is the Bibl. Greek equivalent of τε ... καί, which is there extremely rare. Thus Mk 4^{41} ὅτι καὶ ὁ ἄνεμος καὶ ἡ θάλασσα ὑπακούει αὐτῷ = *both wind and sea* (but RSV, NEB, etc. take the first καί as *even*); so Mk 9^{13} Lk 5^{36} Jn 6^{36} 7^{28} 11^{48} 12^{28} 15^{24} 17^{25} (*both the world and these*) Ac 26^{29} Ro 14^9 11^{33} etc., LXX Nu 9^{14b}, Pap. BU 417^{17} ὅτι καὶ σοὶ τοῦτο ἀνήκει καὶ συμφέρει. The scribes have corrected this in Mt 10^{28} and Jn 4^{36}.

2. The adverbial or epexegetical καί (*that is, even*): Mk 1^{19} Lk 3^{18} Jn 1^{16} (*that is, to receive grace upon grace*) 20^{30}, Ac 22^{25}, καὶ ἀκατάκριτον *and uncondemned at that*), Ro 1^5 (*that is, apostleship*, or hendiadys?: *grace of apostleship*), 13^{11} *idque*, 1 Co 2^2 *et quidem*, 6^{6-8}, Eph 2^8. It is pleonastic before a second adj., esp. after πολύς: Lk 3^{18} Jn 20^{30} Ac 25^7 Ti 1^{10} vl. The original meaning of καί, before it became also merely a coordinating particle, was *also*, as in Ro 8^{17} εἰ δὲ τέκνα, καὶ κληρόνομοι, Ph 4^3. This appears with pronouns frequently: Mt 2^8 κἀγώ *I too*, Lk 14^{12} Jn 7^{47}; Ro 8^{24} S ὃ γὰρ βλέπει, τίς καὶ ὑπομένει *who needs also to wait for that which he sees?* (p^{46} B*DFG misunderstood and omitted καί). And with adverbs of comparison: Ac 11^{17} ὡς καί, Ro 15^7 καθὼς καί. And after other particles: Lk 24^{22} ἀλλὰ καί *sed etiam*.

The idoms καὶ νῦν (אַתָּה) and καὶ τίς (classical) are fairly common, where καί is best rendered emphatically *well, then*: Mk 10^{26} Lk 10^{29} Jn 9^{36} 14^{22} SW Ac 3^{17} 7^{34} 10^5 13^{11} $20^{22, 25}$ 22^{16} Ro 3^7 2 Co 2^2 Ph 1^{22} 2 Th 2^6 1 Jn 2^{28}.

A chain of dependent genitives, which is not liked by NT writers, is avoided by the use of hendiadys: Mk 6^{26} (not *oaths*

---

[1] Thackeray *OT Gr* 50ff. Pernot *Études* 189–199. M. Johannessohn, *Das biblische* ΚΑΙ ΕΓΕΝΕΤΟ *und seine Geschichte*, Göttingen, 1926.

and guests, but *oaths sworn before the guests*), Lk 2⁴⁷ (not *his intelligence and answers*, but *the intelligence of his answers*), 21¹⁵ Ac 1²⁵ 14¹⁷ 23⁶ (*hope of the resurrection*), Ro 1⁵ 2 Ti 4¹ Ti 2¹³ Jas 5¹⁰ 1 Pt 4¹⁴ 2 Pt 1¹⁶.

(Τὸ) λοιπόν ¹.

Essentially the meaning is *from now, henceforth,* as Eph 6¹⁰ DG (τοῦ λοιποῦ p⁴⁶ S*AB), and λοιπόν 1 Th 4¹ (cp. BGU IV 1079. 6, A.D. 41). Although it is weakened in Hell. Greek to a mere *so*, it cannot mean its opposite, *still*, as in so many modern translations of Mk 14⁴¹ (Moffatt, Goodspeed, RSV, NEB), for *still* means *until now*. Jesus means *from now*. He says, "Are you going to *continue* sleeping?" To introduce *still* is to throw emphasis on the past, but the point is that they must not be asleep when the betrayer arrives (future). Ἀπέχει will then have a direct ref. to Judas. He has been paid; he is here. *Henceforth*, it is no time for sleep.

Μήν and ναί ².

Particles of solemn affirmation or corroboration. In class. Greek ἦ μήν, but Hell. Greek (esp. LXX and pap.) since ii/B.C. substitutes εἶ μήν: Heb 6¹⁴ εἶ μὴν εὐλογῶ εὐλογήσω σε (KL* corr. to ἦ) *yes, certainly I will bless*. But elsewhere in NT the corroborating and recapitulating particle is ναί (still current in MGr): Mt 11⁹. ²⁵ᶠ 15²⁷ Lk 11⁵¹ 12⁵ Jn 11²⁷ Ro 3²⁹ Ph 4³ Phm²⁰ Rev 1⁷ 14¹³ 16⁷, LXX Ge 17¹⁹ Jdt 9¹².

Νή.

With accus., (scil. ὄμνυμι) 1 Co 15³¹ LXX Ge 42¹⁵ᶠ *I swear by* (class.). K-G. II 147, 2. Mayser II 3, 147f.

Ὅθεν.

Consecutive co-ordinating particle (class.): Mt 14⁷ Ac 26¹⁹ Heb 2¹⁷ and often. Mayser II 3, 148. Meisterhans-Schwyzer 253, 25 (i/B.C. inscr.).

---

¹ K-G I 315 n. 15. Mayser II 3, 145f. Moule 161f. A. Cavallin, " (Τὸ) λοιπόν: Eine bedeutungsgeschichtliche Untersuchung," *Eranos* 39, 1941 (21-144.
² R.G II 135ff; 147, 2. Mayser II 3, 146f.

Ὅμως.

K-G II 85 n. 1; 95f. Mayser II 3, 148. Jn 12⁴² ὅμως μέντοι *but yet*. Displaced by hyperbaton in 1 Co 14⁷ *lifeless things may give a sound, nevertheless if* . . . (transfer ὅμως after διδόντα), Ga 3¹⁵ *it may be only a man's will, nevertheless no one* . . . (transfer before οὐδείς). Conceivably in these two passages we could accent it perispomenon, as adv. from ὁμός (Homer, class. poet.), and translate *likewise*. But ὅμως (sic) is much more frequent in Bibl. Greek (Wi 13⁶ 2 Mac 2²⁷ 14¹⁸ 15⁵ 4 Mac 13²⁷ SR 15¹¹ SR).

Οὖν.

The interrogative οὐκοῦν (only Jn 18³⁷) may be Pilate's ipsissimum verbum.

This interesting particle is the most widely used of the consecutive co-ordinating conjunctions and its use enters widely into the idiosyncratic style of the various Bibl. authors [1]. John is very fond of it (but not in the epistles); in Rev it occurs only in 1-3 (one of several distinguishing features in the syntax of this part of Rev). It occurs most frequently in narrative. It is characteristic of Luke to place it after a ptc.: Lk 5⁷ D 23¹⁶. ²² Ac 10²³ 15² vl. 16¹¹ 25¹⁷. He also invariably adds μέν if the opening word is a noun or pronoun. Its use sharply divides the work of the translators in LXX Ge and Ex; in Ge it occurs almost only in the second half, in Ex almost only in the first half: Ge (1-25) 3, (26-50) 27, Ex (1-24) 26, (25-40) 3.

It is not always strictly causative, but sometimes temporal (= *then*), esp. in Jn. Moreover μὲν οὖν (μενοῦν) is no longer the class. affirmation *indeed* (παντάπασι μὲν οὖν), but is usually resumptive (= *so then*); it occurs most frequently in Ac (merely resumptive: 1⁶. ¹⁸ 2⁴¹ 5⁴¹ 8⁴. ²⁵ 9³¹ 13⁴ 15³. ³⁰ 17¹². ³⁰ 19³⁸ 23¹⁸. ³¹ 26⁴, 26⁹ ἐγὼ μὲν οὖν ἔδοξα *why, I myself thought*, Moule 163). Also resumptive: Lk 3¹⁸ (μὲν οὖν nowhere else in Lk) Jn 19²⁴ Ph 2²³. Nevertheless μὲν οὖν has the class. use of modifying a previous statement by introducing a new one: *nay rather* Jn 20³⁰ Ac 12⁵ 14³ (see *Beg.* in loc., where it is suggested

---

[1] K-G 154; 163ff; 336. Mayser II 3, 148ff, W. Nauck, "Das οὖν Paräneticum," *ZNW* 49, 1958, 134. J. R. Mantey, "Newly discovered meanings for οὖν," *Expositor* ser. VIII 22, 1921, 205-214: contending that in Lk 14³⁴ Ac 8²⁵ Jn 20³⁰ (and papyri) οὖν = *nevertheless*.

to transpose [2] and [3], to give οὖν its usual meaning in Ac) 17[17] 25[4] 28[5] Heb 7[11] 9[1]. What is not classical is the use of μεν οὖν (γε) to open a sentence: Lk 11[28] Ro 9[20] (p[46] corrects) 10[18] (corr. by FG), Ph 3[8]: *much more, in fact.*

Οὐ, etc.

For negative particles, see ch. 19. For οὐ, μή, and οὐ μή in questions, see ch. 19 § 2; for οὐ μή otherwise, see ch. 8 § 2.2.

Πλήν [1].

In class. Greek, a preposition (as in Mk, Ac) or a conjunction in πλὴν ὅτι *except* (as Lk 22[22] Ac 20[23] Ph 1[18]). In Hell. Greek it becomes an adversative particle. D corrects to δέ in Lk 12[31] and to ἀλλά in 23[28]. Lk 17[1] corrects Mt 18[7] to οὐαὶ δέ (but SBDL harmonize it back again to πλὴν οὐαί). Matthew is fond of it; he changes Mk 14[36] ἀλλ' οὐχ into πλὴν οὐχ (26[39]). Paul's use is peculiar and like that of LXX, a pleonastic *only* 1 Co 11[11] Eph 5[33] Ph 1[18] (om B) 3[16] 4[14], LXX e.g. Ge 41[40] Ex 9[9, 11] 9[26] 4 Km 14[4] 15[35] (= Heb. רק).

Πότερον ... ἤ.

Only Jn 7[17] in NT and rarely in LXX (e.g. Jb 7[1, 2]).

Τε [2].

This copulative enclitic particle, declining in use in the Koine and later revived as an atticism, occurs in NT in all forms and compounds, but not very frequently (except in Ac), and it is an indication of stylistic pretension, its place being taken by καί or οὐδέ. In their use of τε we may group the books as follows: (1) Mk Jn Rev: 14 times, (2) Johannines: 1, (3) Mt: 9, (4) Pastorals: 1, (5) Lk: 11, (6) Paul: 32, (7) Heb: 23, (8) Ac: approx. 170. It is not surprising that in textual transmission scribes and editors were unable to resist introducing τε, sometimes at the expense of δέ: Ac 1[15] (SAB ἦν τε, wrongly in parenthesis) Lk 4[35] D 23[36] D 24[20] Mt 28[12] Ro 7[7]. Although the

---

[1] Mayser II 2, 534. Schmid Attizismus I 133.
[2] K.-G II §§ 517–520; 522. 2. Meisterhans—Schwyzer 249f. Mayser II 3, 155ff. Radermacher[2] 5f. J. A. Brown, *An Exegetical Study of* τε (Diss of Southern Baptist Theol. Sem.) 1948.

simple form almost disappeared οὔτε and μήτε lingered on awhile. But the single τε (without καί) occurs in Ac 2³³ 1 Co 4²¹ Heb 6⁵ 9¹ (only poet. in class. Greek). At times τε before γάρ appears to be a superfluous affectation: Ro 7⁷ 2 Co 10⁸ (see K-G II 245, Radermacher² 5).

The correlation τε ... τε (class. especially in poetry) occurs only in Ac 26¹⁶ and elsewhere in οὔτε ... οὔτε, εἴτε ... εἴτε, etc. In Ro 1²⁶ᶠ (τε ... ὁμοίως τε καί) the variant which reads δέ for the second τε has support from BU 417¹⁶ (ὁμοίως δὲ καὶ περὶ τῶν τοῦ ... Abel § 78). Ac 2⁴⁶ is not an instance of correlation.

The distribution of the correlation τε . . καί is instructive (* τε καί):—Mt 22¹⁰* 27⁴⁸ Lk 2¹⁶ 12⁴⁵ 15² 21¹¹·¹¹ 22⁶⁶* 23¹² 24²⁰, Ac 60 times, Ro 1¹²* ¹⁴·¹⁴·¹⁶ vl. ²⁰·²⁷ v. 2⁹·¹⁰ 3⁹ 10¹² vl. 1 Co 1² vl. ²⁴·³⁰ Ph 1⁷ Heb 2⁴·¹¹ 4¹² vl. 5⁷·¹⁴ 6²·⁴¹⁹* 8³ 9²·⁹·¹⁹ 10³³ 11³²·³² Jas 3⁷·⁷ Rev 19⁸ vl. It joins more closely than simple καί and joins words which have between themselves a close or logical affinity (*non solum ... sed etiam*). "Jews and Greeks" is the kind of phrase which demands τε ... καί or τε καί (Ac 14¹ 19¹⁰ vl. ¹⁷ vl. 20²¹ etc.). Other combinations occur: τε ... καί ... τε (Ac 9¹⁵ vl. 26¹⁰ᶠ ²⁰ vl.), τε ... τε ... καί (Heb 6² 11³²), τε καί ... καί ... καί (Ac 5²⁴ 21³⁰ Heb 2⁴). The correlative τε will usually stand after the first word of the phrase in correlation, but τε is misplaced in Ac 26²²: it should follow and not precede οἱ. When a preposition (or article) joins two ideas together, τε may be placed after the preposition (Ac 10³⁹ 25²³ 28²³).

In ascertaining the true text we should remember the strong tendency of atticizing editors and scribes to add τε, but this may not always be so in the case of Ac where τε occurs so often that it must be a stylistic feature of the author.

§ 2. Compound Particles

Δήπου [1].

An ironical particle (class. and literary Hell.), partly confirmatory and partly hesitant, appealing to mutual knowledge: Heb 2¹⁶ οὐ γὰρ δήπου.

Καί(τοιγε).

Parenthetical particle, *although*: Jn 4² Ac 14¹⁷ 17²⁷ᶠ.

---

[1] K-G II 131. Mayser II 3, 169.

Μέντοι.

A rare adversative particle, and very weak (*but*) in Jas 2[8] Jude[8]. Stronger in 2 Ti 2[19] and in Jn where it is most found: οὐ(δεὶς) μέντοι 4[27] 7[13] 20[5] 21[4] ὅμως μέντοι 12[42].

Οὐδέ, μηδέ.

See ch. 19. Besides beginning a sentence (Mk 8[26] Lk 7[9]), it may resume and emphasize a previous negative: Mt 6[15] Mk 3[20] Lk 16[31] Ro 4[15].

Οὔτε and μήτε.

Fairly evenly distributed in all parts of the NT, but in many of these instances the endings -δε and -τε are confused in the MSS (op. δέ and τε): e.g. Lk 20[36] οὐδὲ γάρ (corr. to οὔτε γάρ by SW), Mk 5[3] 12[25] 14[68] Lk 7[33] Ac 2[31] 23[8] (SBACE corr. to μήτε) 1 Co 6[9. 10] Ga 1[12] Jas 3[12]. This is not surprising in view of the general confusion, e.g. Pap. Rei. 13[10t] καὶ μήτ' αὐτὸν Ἄνδρωνα μηδ' ἄλλον ... μηδ' ... μηδέ ..., BU 388 II 36f πῶς οὔτε ὁ αὐτὸς χρόνος ἐν αὐταῖς πρόσκειται, ἀλλ' οὐδέ ....

In class. Greek οὔτε ... καί is very rare. In NT Jn 4[11] (D syr[iew] corr. to οὐδέ), 3 Jn[10]. See Jn 5[37t] οὔτε ... οὔτε ... καί ... οὐ.

Τοιγαροῦν.

Class. but not Thucyd. Not Koine, and only 13 times in Polyb. I Th 4[8] Heb 12[1] (p[46] τοίγαρ). First word.

Τοίνυν.

Only 5 times in Thucyd. Not Koine, and only 3 times Polyb. Second word (class.): Lk 20[25] ACW 1 Co 9[26]. First word (Hell.): Lk 20[25] SBL Heb 13[13].

§ 3. Unconnected words and sentences: Asyndeton [1]

Except occasionally for effect, this is contrary to the genius of Greek, but Paul and Hebrews are full of it (e.g. 1 Co 7[27] Heb 11[32ff]). It increases in the Ptol. pap. between iii and i/B.C. Yet in NT scribes frequently introduced connecting particles (see Jn, for variants between asyndeton, δέ, καί and οὖν). Matthew is fond of asyndeton with ἔφη and λέγει (see Lagrange *S. Matth.* XCII) and John has λέγει, λέγουσιν 70 times

---

[1] K-G II § 546. Meisterhans-Schwyzer 161; 250, 4. Schwyzer II 632ff. ; Mayser II 3, 179–183.

with asyndeton (against 31 with particle—but there are variants); Aramaic influence is probable (Lagrange *S. Jean* CIVf). On Mark see Zerwick, *Untersuchungen* 22f.

The use of τότε [1] to link sentences is not class. Mt has it 90 times, Mk 6, Lk 15, Ac 21, Jn 10, rest 18; LXX canonical books 156, Dan O' 43, θ' 30. Its extreme use in Mt must be explained ultimately as a rendering of Aramaic אדין or באדין, so frequent in Daniel, and rendered by τότε 30 times in LXX. The Heb. אז is less frequent. It is significant that LXX has τότε five or six times in 2 Esd 5, against only four times in the whole of Genesis (Lagrange *S. Matth.* CX). Scribes have sought to reduce the exuberance of τότε in Mt.

Because of his elementary knowledge of popular Greek, the author of Rev confines his transition-formulae to the very simplest kind, most often μετὰ ταῦτα (εἶδον), varying with καὶ (εἶδον) καὶ ἰδού. There is a poverty of particles and continual parataxis (Allo, *Apoc.* CLI).

Asyndeton makes the beginning of new long sections conspicuous, e.g. Ro 9^1 10^1 13^1 1 Pt 5^1 2 Pt 3^1.

---

[1] A. H. McNeile, "Τότε in St. Matthew," *JThS* 12, 1911, 127ff.

CHAPTER TWENTY-SIX

IRREGULARITY OF SUBORDINATION

§ 1. Parataxis instead of hypotaxis [1]

We have seen how prevalent parataxis is in popular speech (ch. 25, καί), and it goes even further in MGr. We find direct in place of indirect speech (Lk 14¹⁸ 1 Co 7⁴⁰ FG), and καί is often used in place of subordination (Mt 18²¹ 26⁵³ Lk 14⁵) on the Semitic model which happens to coincide with popular Greek, and even without καί there is parataxis where we expect conditional hypotaxis (Jn 7³⁴ 10¹² Ro 13³). Parataxis is too much for D in Mk 2¹⁵ (οἵ for καί). The imperatives ὁρᾶτε and βλέπετε are common in NT, as in the Koine (Mt 9³⁰ 24⁶ Mk 13³³) and are probably asyndetic additions to the normal imperative; so also ὕπαγε, ἔγειρε, θέλεις. Again, popular Greek coincides with a strong Hebraic idiom: e.g. LXX Ex 19²⁴ βάδιζε κατάβηθι (לֶךְ־רֵד), 3 Km 19⁷ ἀνάστα φάγε (קוּם אֱכֹל). For ἐγένετο with finite verb see p. 335; Moulton-Howard 425–428.

§ 2. Interpolation of sentences: Parenthesis [2]

The NT parentheses are harsher than would be permitted to a Greek stylist, especially those in Paul (Ro 1¹³ 2¹⁵ᶠ), which may be due to dictation of the letters, but also those in Ac (1¹⁵ 4¹³ 5¹⁴ 12³ᶠ). Short parentheses, such as those with οἶδα, μαρτυρῶ, ὁρᾷς, are found in class. Greek. Punctuation in Mark is often clarified if more parentheses than usual are recognized (Zerwick, *Untersuchungen* 130–138. C. H. Turner in *JThS* 26, 145). E.g. transpose 12¹², as ᵃ ᶜ ᵇ.

§ 3. Anacoloutha

(a) For *casus pendens* see ch. 22 § 5.
(b) For gen. absol. improperly used, see pp. 322f.

---

[1] K-G II § 516. Wackernagel I 62f. Mayser II 3, 184ff. Ljungvik BSSVS 76ff, 87ff. Radermacher² 213, 222.
[2] K-G II § 548. Schwyzer II 705. Mayser II 3, 186ff. Radermacher² 221. C. Grünewald, *Die Satzparenthese bei den zehn attischen Rednern* (B.z.h.Sd.gr.Spr.19) 1912.

(c) Chiefly in Paul's letters there occurs the anacolouthon whereby the original sentence construction is forgotten after an insertion: Ro 2^{17} (but read ἴδε for εἰ δέ?), 16^{27} (B improves by omitting ᾧ), Ga 2^{4f} (D* improves by omitting οἷς), 2^{6}, 1 Ti 1^{3ff}.

(d) Paul also tends to make a ptc. co-ordinate with a finite verb: 2 Co 5^{12} 6^{3} 7^{5} 8^{18ff} (χειροτονηθείς and also στελλόμενοι. But if ^{19} is a parenthesis, the ptc. depends on συνεπέμψαμεν and there is no anacolouthon), $9^{11.\ 13}$ $10^{4.\ 15.\ 15}$ 11^{6}.

(e) The imperatival ptc. is a well known phenomenon [1] in Peter and Paul, and it is common in the Koine. However, as ἐστέ (imperat.) never occurs in NT we must presume that it is understood as a copula with all these ptcs., which therefore do not constitute an anacolouthon. Note the durative sense of the ptcs.: *always* Ro 12^{9ff} 2 Co 6^{3-10} (the ptcs. skip over ^{2} and carry on the construction of ^{1}, which is resumed in ^{9}) 8^{24} B δ-text (SC correct to imperat.) Eph $3^{17.\ 18}$ 4^{1} (the ptc. may depend on the verb immediately before it) 5^{15-22} Ph 1^{29f} (but WH. make a long parenthesis and try to connect ἔχοντες with στήκετε) Col 2^{2} 3^{16f} 4^{11} 1 Pt $2^{12.\ 18}$ $3^{1.\ 7}$ 4^{8ff} 2 Pt 3^{3}.

The only example outside Peter and Paul is Heb 13^{5} (but Moulton would add Lk 24^{47}: Proleg. 182).

(f) Very frequent is the use of a finite verb co-ordinate with a ptc. and strengthening it unnecessarily. This is class., but not in the same profusion as in NT. It may be that there is ellipse of the verb *to be* with the ptcs. (Regard, *Phrase nom.* 186–216): Mt $13^{22.\ 23}$ Lk $8^{12.\ 14}$ Jn 1^{32} (for emphasis) 5^{44} (vl. corrects to ptc.) 15^{5} 2 Co 5^{6ff} 6^{9} Eph 1^{20} (not WH.) Col 1^{26} (D corr. to ptc.) 2 Jn ^{2} Rev 15^{f} $2^{2.\ 9}$ $3^{7.\ 9}$. LXX Ps 17^{33-35}.

---

[1] Moulton Einl. 284–288, 353f. Joüon, *Grammaire de l'Hébreu Biblique* § 121 e, n. 2. Zerwick § 265f. H. G. Meecham, "The Use of the Participle for the Imperative in the New Testament," *Exp. T.* 58, 1947, 207ff. C. K. Barrett, "The Imperatival Participle," *Exp. T.* 59, 1948, 165ff. Mayser II 1, 340f.

CHAPTER TWENTY-SEVEN

WORD ORDER

The details of clause order and of word order within the clause ought to be more closely examined than is possible in the strict compass of this syntax volume and will be reserved for a separate publication on style as distinct from syntax. Certain ways in which the study may benefit textual and exegetical research will however be indicated. The matter has also been separately discussed in part at various points in this volume: the position of adverbs (pp. 227ff), of demonstratives (pp. 193f), the combinations with πᾶς (pp. 201–5), the position of adjs. relative to their noun with special reference to πολύς (pp. 185f), the position of the dependent genitive (pp. 217f), of comparative clauses (p. 320), and the difference between εἰ καί and καὶ εἰ (or κἄν) (p. 321).

§ 1. Clause Order

(a) Normally the dependent clause follows the main clause.

1. FINAL clauses with ἵνα precede in a very few instances, and mainly in the gospels: Mt 9[6] (and parallels) 17[27] (Jn 14[21]?) Jn 19[28, 31] Ac 24[4] (Ro 7[13]?) Eph 6[21] Ὅπως-clauses never precede.

2. LOCAL clauses: ὅθεν-clauses (15 times in post-position) never precede. Οὗ-clauses (21 post-position) precede only at Mt 18[20] (2[9] 28[16] post-position) Ro 4[15] 5[20] (9[26] post-position) 2 Co 3[17] (1 Co 16[6] post).

3. TEMPORAL clauses: here alone the pre-position is as much in favour as the post-position. But as ἕως-clauses are invariably post-positive, we must alter our punctuation of 1 Ti 4[13] and take the clause with what precedes [1]. We find however that ὅτι-, ὅταν-, and ὡς (temp.)-clauses precede much more often than they follow, especially in the gospels; while ἐπεί(δη)-, ἐπάν-, and ἡνίκα-clauses invariably precede, and

---

[1] "Make yourself an example, until I come."

ὁπότε-, ἄχρι (οὗ)-, μέχρις οὗ-, and μέχρι-clauses invariably follow. But πρίν- and πρὸ τοῦ-clauses are about equally divided.

4. CAUSAL clauses: the majority have post-position, but ἐπεί and ἐπειδή are equally divided, and ἐπεὶ ἄν (1 Co 14¹⁶) has only pre-position. Ὅτι (causal) is post-positive 397 times, and the only exceptions are as follows: Lk 19¹⁷ Jn 1⁵⁰ (a question) 8⁴⁵ (14¹⁹?) 15¹⁹ 16⁶ 20²⁹ (a question) Ro 9⁷ Ga 4⁶ Rev 3¹⁰, ¹⁶ 18⁷. Invariably post-positive are ἀνθ' ὧν, ἐφ' ᾧ, καθότι, διότι. But διὰ τό c. infin. (post-positive 23 times) has pre-position in Mt 13⁶ 24¹² Mk 4⁶ Ac 18³ 27⁹.

5. COMPARATIVE clauses: see also ch. 23 § 3. c. 1. Καθώς (with καθάπερ and καθά as variants)—clauses follow the main clause invariably in Mt, in Mk (except for Mk 1²ᶠ, which is not an exception if punctuated with a stop after 1³), in Lk (except for 6³¹ 11³⁰ 17²⁶, ²⁸). But in Jn the distribution is more even (19 post: 13 pre), like the Joh. epp. (8:5). In Ac there are 10 post: 2 pre. In Ro 15 (+5 vl.) post: 1 pre. 1 and 2 Co 24 (+2 vl.): 7. Ga 3:0. Ph 2:1. Eph 10:0. Col 4:1. 1 and 2 Th 12:3. Past 0:1. Heb 7:2. 1 Pt 0:1. 2 Pt 2:0.

(b) Chiasmus [1].

Lund argues that chiasmus is largely Semitic: hence, in the material common to Mt and Lk, it occurs rather in Mt. The instances outside Biblical Greek are not extensive chiastic systems but usually the simpler kind of chiasmus of four terms only. The chiasmus in the MT of Ps 7¹⁶ 58⁶ is well preserved in LXX, but the remarkable ten-fold instance in Ps 3⁷ᶠ is not preserved quite so obviously, and in Ps 6³⁽⁴⁾ the LXX spoils the chiasmus by using ἐταράχθη in both members. Before Lund, a chiasmus of four or six members had already been pointed out by J. Weiss in Ro 14⁷ᶠᶠ 1 Co 7¹⁻⁷ 9¹⁹⁻²² Ph 4¹¹⁻¹³, but most writers had applied class. standards to the NT and failed to appreciate any influence of ancient Semitic culture or of contemporary Aramaic literature. Greek rhetorical forms do not explain everything in NT style, where the writers were Jews accustomed to the sound of a Hebrew liturgy. Lund

---

[1] N. W. Lund, *Chiasmus in the New Testament*, N. Carolina 1942. W. Milligan, *Lectures on the Apocalypse*³, 1892, pp. 94f, noticed chiasmus in Rev, using it to counter the source hypotheses of Vischer and Völter. J. Jeremias, *ZNW* 49, 1958, 145–156.

argues that although J. Weiss may correctly contend that the Paulines were written for the *ear*, the influence of the OT and the synagogue was paramount. Of this literary influence, Lund is concerned with one particular expression, chiasmus or inverted order. Discovering certain laws governing these structures in the OT, he makes tests for their occurrence in the NT. A point to which he might have given more attention is the important question whether the Semitic influence was direct from the Hebrew OT or whether it was by way of the LXX.

Instances of chiasmus are as follows—
(*a*) Mt 9^{17} old—burst—skins—skins—lost—new (ABC CBA)
(*b*) 1 Co 7^3 to woman—man—woman—to man (AB—BA)
(*c*) 1 Co 11^{8-12}

A	man A woman B woman B man A	B	man A woman B woman B man A	C	angels	B	woman B man A man A woman B	A	woman B man A man A woman B

Ps 89^{30-34} may have been the (unconscious?) model for Paul here, if he knew the psalms in Hebrew form.

(*d*) Col 3^{3f} death—life—hidden—Christ—Christ—manifested—life—glory.

(*e*) 1 Co 5^{2-6} is the kind of sentence which seems interminable to the Greek student and on which Semitic culture throws light, with a ABCBA arrangement and chiasmus within chiasmus:

A	puffed up	B	misconduct A presence B presence B misconduct A	C	Lord Jesus A you B me B Lord Jesus A	B	Satan A destruction B flesh C spirit C salvation B Day of Lord A	A	boast- ing

In this instance the study of chiasmus helps the textual critic. The first reference to "Lord Jesus" in member C has the addition ἡμῶν in p^{46} BKL 0142 DG lat syr^{pesh}, and as this addition balances the fourth member of the chiasmus-within-chiasmus, there is a good reason for accepting it.

(*f*) Not only does this study help with the text, but also in interpretation, e.g.: Mt 7^6

" Give not what is holy to the *dogs* (A),
Neither cast your pearls before *swine* (B),
Lest they [B must be *swine*] trample them under foot (B),
And they [A must be the *dogs*, not swine] turn and rend you (A)."
The last line is different from the usual interpretation.

Probably much longer passages than these, even whole epistles, among Paul's writings, may be planned (unconsciously?) on the chiasmic pattern.

§ 2. Word Order within the Clause [1]

(a) Idiosyncrasies of Biblical Greek through Semitic influence.

1. Co-ordinating particles as first word. Semitic languages avoid second-place conjunctions, and this tendency was inherited by Biblical Greek, which either placed the conjunction first or else avoided altogether the second-place conjunctions like γάρ, γε, μέν, δέ, οὖν, τε. Thus ἄρα is first word in Mt 12²⁸, τοίνυν in Lk 20²⁵ Heb 13¹³, μενοῦνγε in Ro 10¹⁸, τοιγαροῦν in Heb 12¹.

2. The verb (contrary to contemporary secular Greek, where mainly it has middle position) occurs as near the beginning as possible [2], followed by pers. pronoun, subject, obj., supplementary

---

[1] T. D. Goodell, " The Order of Words in Greek," *Trans. and Proc. Amer. Phil. Assn.* XXI. 5 (21. 24). W. Rhys Roberts, "A Point of Greek and Latin Word-Order," *Class. Rev.*, 1912, 177–9. G. Cuendet, *L'ordre des mots dans le texte grec et dans les versions gotique . . . des Évangiles, I. Les groupes nominaux*, Paris 1929. M. Frisk, *Studien zur griechische Worstellung*, Göteborg 1932. J. M. Rife, " The Mechanics of Translation Greek," *JBL* 52, 1933, 244ff. D. J. Wieand, *Subject-Verb-Object Relationship in Independent Clauses in the Gospels and Acts* (Diss. Univ. Chicago) 1946. Moulton-Howard 416–418. E. Norden, *Agnostos Theos*, Leipzig 1913, 365f " Stellung des Verbums in NT Griechischen." He makes the prominence of the verb in first-place a sign of Semitism, and on this he quotes Wellhausen with approval.

[2] The normal order in the ancient Greek was Subj.-Obj.-Verb (SOV) and the nearest books to this ideal in Bibl. Greek literature are 2–4 Mac.

	VSO	SVO	SOV	VOS	OSV	OVS
2 Mac	1	4	4	–	–	–
3 Mac	1	2	5	–	2	–
4 Mac	–	2	5	2	1	–
Plato	–	1	7	1	1	–

ptc. E.g. Lk 1^{11} ὤφθη δὲ αὐτῷ ἄγγελος κυρίου ἕστως ἐκ δεξιῶν. In Mk the copula occurs in this position in 24 out of 29 instances (the exceptions: 5^5 7^{15} 13^{25} 14^{49}). The predicative ptc. immediately follows the subject in Bibl. Greek: Mk 1^6 καὶ ἦν ὁ Ἰωάννης ἐνδεδυμένος, $14^{4.\ 40}$ Lk 2^{32} Ac 12^6. This is Hebraic word-order, for in Aramaic the verb tends to end the clause. In periphrastic tenses the subject comes between the copula and the ptc., e.g. Mk $1^{6,\ 33}$ $2^{4,\ 6.\ 18}$ 3_1 4_{38} $5_{11.\ 40}$ 6_{52} $14^{4.\ 40}$ $15^{7.\ 26.\ 40.\ 43}$ (exceptions 7^{15} 10^{32} 13^{25}). In Hebrew the subject follows the verb directly, but occasionally the object intervenes between the verb and subject (e.g. Ge 1^{17}), and the personal pronoun always does so (see 8 below).[1]

3. Article and noun adhere closely together, and in Hebrew they are actually one. That is why in LXX only 4 per cent of the def. articles stand apart from their nouns in books translated from the canonical literature, whereas in the books having no MT as *Vorlage* the percentage is as high as 11 per cent. For the NT epistles the figure is 18 per cent. It is still higher (25 per cent) when seven non-Biblical works of class., Koine, and MGr are chosen for a count (Rife, *JBL* 52, 248).

Some NT books approach this standard, but on the whole NT is closer to the Hebraic order (VSO) and towards the subsequent tendency of MGr (SVO)

	VSO	SVO	SOV	VOS	OSV	OVS
Synoptic parallels:						
Mk	3	9	4	–	1	1
Mt	1	5	1	–	–	1
Lk	1	4	2	–	–	1
Luke entire	9	19	8	2	–	1
John	–	4	3	1	2	–
Acts	6	31	1	1	1	5
Ro	–	4	5	–	–	1

The figures are those of Rife who restricted himself to main declarative clauses where both subj. and obj. were nouns, his method being to read from the beginning of each book until ten exx. were collected (*JBL* 52, 250f). But requirements of emphasis will everywhere upset rules of word-order. See also Zerwick *Untersuchungen* 75–108; P.-L. Couchoud, "La Place du Verbe dans Marc," *JThS* 30, 1929, 47ff.

[1] Therefore in Mk 2^{15f} punctuate (not as NEB, etc.): "For they were many. There followed him some scribes of the Pharisees. They noticed him eating . . . ."

§ 2] WORD ORDER 349

4. Again, Hebrew word-order supports the after-position of the adj., because nothing can come between art. and noun. Although the NT epistles display a very high proportion of non-Semitic word-order in this respect, the gospels more closely conform. The tendency in the Koine is for the adj. to precede the noun. A significant comparison is that between the papyri of ii–i/B.C. examined by Mayser and the first nineteen chapters of the LXX. The papyri have 140 exx. of the type ὁ ἀγαθὸς ἀνήρ and only four or five of ὁ ἀνὴρ ὁ ἀγαθός; whereas the Biblical chapters have ὁ ἀγαθὸς ἀνήρ 17 times, but ὁ ἀνὴρ ὁ ἀγαθός 56 times (the proportion in 1 Km 1–6 is 1 : 16). See Mayser II 2, 52ff and see also, pp. 189f.

5. As in the Heb. construct state, the genitive in translation Greek follows immediately upon its governing noun. The tendency in the literary style was, however, for the gen. to precede, and we find this much more frequently in the free Greek books of the LXX. In the NT it is consciously stylistic, as 2 Co 1¹⁹ ὁ τοῦ θεοῦ... υἱός, 2 Pt 3² τῆς τῶν ἀποστόλων ὑμῶν ἐντολῆς. The need to follow the Hebrew construction closely may result in the dissociation of analogous nouns, as in Ge 41⁸ *the magicians of Egypt and their wise men*.

6. Unemphatic direct or indirect personal pronouns (αὐτῷ, αὐτῇ, αὐτοῖς) come closely after the verb in Bibl. Greek on the model of the Heb. pronominal suffix which is one with the verb: Lk 1¹¹ ὤφθη δὲ αὐτῷ, Ac 27² ὄντος σὺν ἡμῖν Ἀριστάρχου. There are exceptions, e.g.: the pronoun αὐτῷ precedes the verb in Jn 7²⁶ 10⁴ 12²⁹ (but it follows the verb 145 times in Jn), and αὐτοῖς has an intruding word (other than δέ or οὖν) between it and the verb in 2²⁴ (ἑαυτόν p⁶⁶ WΘ), 8²¹ (οὖν πάλιν, but S omits πάλιν, and some minusc. have πάλιν *after* αὐτοῖς), 10⁷ (οὖν πάλιν, but p⁴⁵ p⁶⁶ SW om πάλιν, and SB om αὐτοῖς).

7. In Semitic word-order the demonstrative adj. always follows the noun, and this is usual in Bibl. Greek. See p. 193. Some displacements are difficult to understand, e.g. Lk 24³¹ αὐτῶν δὲ διηνοίχθησαν οἱ ὀφθαλμοί.

8. (i) As in Hebrew the prepositional phrase comes immediately after the verb if the Heb. preposition would have a pronominal suffix (e.g. Ge 24⁶), but the prepositional phrase comes after the subject (which itself is after the verb) if the Hebrew preposition would have a noun after it (e.g. Ge 24²).

This makes it certain that, against RSV, NEB, etc., in Mk 6²⁶ we interpret *he was grieved because of his oaths and guests* (not *he was unwilling . . . because of his oaths and guests*); and in Lk 11¹³ it is *your heavenly Father*, not *your Father will give from heaven*.

(ii) So also the prepositional phrase occurs immediately after its noun, following the Heb. phrase with אשר or the Heb. genitive of quality. The LXX books written in free Greek, especially 2–4 Mac, tend to place the prepositional phrase between article and noun (Johannessohn DGPS 362ff). The translation books tend to place the prep. phrase after the noun, usually with repetition of the article.

(*b*) Oratory and word-order. Interruption of the normal order to give oratorical effect may result in ambiguity : Ac 4³³ ΑΕ μεγάλη δυνάμει ἀπεδίδουν οἱ ἀπόστολοι τὸ μαρτύριον τῆς ἀναστάσεως Ἰησοῦ Χρ. τοῦ κυρίου (p⁴⁵ SB τὸ μαρτύριον οἱ ἀπόστολοι ; B τοῦ κυρίου 'Ι. τῆς ἀναστάσεως); either *the apostles of the Lord Jesus witnessed to the resurrection*, or *the apostles witnessed to the resurrection of the Lord Jesus*; the order is rather unnatural, whatever reading we adopt (see *Beg.* III, cclix n. 2). Ac 19²⁰ οὕτως κατὰ κράτος τοῦ κυρίου ὁ λόγος ηὔξανεν (τοῦ κυρίου must refer to ὁ λόγος). Ac 1² ἐντειλάμενος τοῖς ἀποστόλοις διὰ πνεύματος ἁγίου οὓς ἐξελέξατο (unnatural order). Heb 12²³ κριτῇ θεῷ πάντων *God of all* or *judge of all*? All this reveals a weakness inherent in the flexibility of the Greek language.

(*c*) Stereotyped phrases. A customary word-order is observed, e.g. ἄνδρες καὶ γυναῖκες, γυν. καὶ παιδία (but παιδία first in Mt 14²¹ D), ἐσθίειν καὶ πίνειν, βρῶσις καὶ πόσις, πόδες καὶ χεῖρες (reversed at Lk 24³⁹ but not in S), ζῶντες καὶ νεκροί, νυκτὸς καὶ ἡμέρας, etc. The suggestion that there is a stereotyped phrase may account for the peculiar order in Ro 8¹⁸ πρὸς τὴν μέλλουσαν δόξαν ἀποκαλυφθῆναι, and Ga 3²³ εἰς τὴν μέλλουσαν πίστιν ἀποκαλυφθῆναι (ἡ μέλλουσα δόξα being a set phrase).

INDEX TO REFERENCES

(a) NEW TESTAMENT.

Thick type represents more important discussion.

MATTHEW	PAGE	MATTHEW—continued	PAGE	MATTHEW—continued	PAGE
1. 1	. 167	4. 3	. 183	5. 4⁸	. 86
1. 2 f.	**167, 345**	4. 6	. 183	6. 1	. **144**
1. 6	. 167, 169	4. 8	. 227	6. 2	. 42, 77, 112
1. 11 f.	. 212	4. 11	. 67	6. 3	. 17, 39
1. 16	. 152, 167	4. 15	175, **212**, 247	6. 4	. 39, 334
1. 18	**78**, 140, 162,	4. 16	. 39, 316	6. 5.	86, 112, **226**
	176, **226**, 322	4. 23	. 51, 211	6. 6	. 77, 112
1. 19	. **157**	4. 25	. **275**	6. 7	. 253
1. 20	77, 151, 322	5. 1	. 173, 322	6. 8	. 49, **144**
1. 21	. **40**, 40, 246	5. 3	. 220, 239	6. 9	. 35
1. 22	. 70	5. 5	. **232**	6. 10	. **75**, 77
2. 1	. 26, 172	5. 6	. 177, **232**	6. 12	. 37
2. 2	26, 134, 172, 189	5. 8	. 220, 239	6. 13	. **14**, 77
2. 3	. 317	5. 9	. 208	6. 16	. 76, 112
2. 4	. 63, 65	5. 10	. 85	6. 17	37, 54, 154
2. 6	31, **48**, 151, 170	5. 12	. 76	6. 18	. 106, 159
2. 8	112, 154, 156, 335	5. 13	. 183	6. 19	. 42, **76**
2. 9	. 26, 172, 279	5. 14	. 279	6. 22	. 183
2. 10	. 160, 242	5. 15	150, **292**	6. 24	. 36
2. 12	. 52	5. 16	72, **150**	6. 25	24, 76, 99, 117
2. 13	. 141, 142	5. 17	. 77, **134**	6. 27	. 209
2. 14	. 235	5. 18	. 96	6. 28	76, 179, 313, 325
2. 15	. 151	5. 19	. 31, 45, **107**	6. 30	. **115**
2. 16	72, 154, 227	5. 20	. 96, 216	6. 32	. 313
2. 20	25, 75, 81, 154,	5. 21	. 86	6. 34	72, 76, 77, 311
	293	5. 22	. 151	7. 2	. **291**
2. 22	. 26, **64**, **226**	5. 24	. 75	7. 3	. 191
2. 23	. 7, 26	5. 25	. 88, 89, 110	7. 4	. 94
3. 3	. 44	5. 25	. 96	7. 5	. 139
3. 4	. **41**, **66**	5. 28	73, **144**, 151, **232**	7. 6	. 77, **346**
3. 5	. **16**, **66**	5. 29 f.	32, 42, 115,	7. 8	. 151
3. 6	. **66**		139	7. 9	. 55, 325
3. 7	. **66**	5. 32	. 107, 151	7. 11	. **157**
3. 9	. 42, 168	5. 34	. 149	7. 12	107, 108, **138**
3. 10	62, **199**, **200**	5. 35	. 255	7. 15	. 48
3. 11	. **252**, **266**	5. 36	. 75	7. 16	. 293
3. 12	. 325	5. 39	48, 77, 149, 197	7. 17	. 63
3. 13	. 141	5. 40	. 39, 316	7. 21	. 196
3. 14	39, 65, 139, **334**	5. 41	. 48	7. 23	. 153, 177
3. 15	88, 149, **200**	5. 42	. 76	7. 24	48, 189, **233**, 316
3. 16	. 25, **259**	5. 43	. 86	7. 26	. 151, 221
3. 17	. 25, 44, 186	5. 44	. **86**	7. 27	. 207
4. 1	. 134	5. 45	52, 53, 208, **291**	7. 28	. 66

351

INDEX TO REFERENCES

MATTHEW—continued		MATTHEW—continued		MATTHEW—continued	
	PAGE		PAGE		PAGE
8. 1	39, 322	11. 8	17	13. 53	52
8. 2	65	11. 10	37, 45	13. 56	273
8. 4	40, 78	11. 11	29	13. 57	253
8. 5	322	11. 12	58	14. 1	167
8. 8	139, 189	11. 16	86, 179	14. 2	180
8. 9	75	11. 19	258	14. 6	27, 243
8. 11	26	11. 20	31	14. 7	135
8. 12	29, 173	11. 21	91	14. 8	64
8. 16	241	11. 23	17, 37	14. 9	26
8. 17	40	11. 27	107, 108, 110, 286	14. 11	40
8. 21	334			14. 13	18
8. 24	66	11. 29	42, 220	14. 14	40
8. 27	318	12. 1	27	14. 19	158
8. 28	322	12. 4	137	14. 20	316
8. 29	156, 179	12. 5	27	14. 23	28
8. 34	65, 106	12. 6	21	14. 28 f.	27
9. 2	64, 292	12. 10	100, 195, 333	14. 29	75
9. 3	43, 209	12. 13	197	14. 31	266, 267
9. 4	23	12. 18	43	14. 33	183
9. 5	32	12. 21	238	15. 2	38, 112
9. 6	344	12. 24	152	15. 5	91, 309
9. 10	322	12. 25	43	15. 6	96, 97
9. 13	282	12. 28	347	15. 8	23
9. 15	208	12. 35	14, 22	15. 13	48
9. 16	65	12. 36	48, 316	15. 19	28
9. 17	292	12. 39	214	15. 20	140
9. 18	65, 196, 322, 330	12. 41	21, 255, 266	15. 22	195
9. 21	43	12. 42	172	15. 23	156
9. 22	35, 69	12. 44	162, 319	15. 25	65
9. 26	312	12. 45	41, 43	15. 28	33
9. 27	51	12. 48	183	15. 30	43, 154, 197
9. 38	106	12. 50	41	15. 31	161
10. 1	136, 139	13. 2	154	15. 32	49, 135, 231
10. 2	168	13. 3	141	15. 35	236
10. 4	80	13. 4	36, 145	15. 37	316
10. 5	169, 212	13. 5	142	16. 3	27
10. 11	316	13. 6	142, 172, 345	16. 7	49
10. 13	86	13. 8	36, 67	16. 14	36, 197
10. 14	48	13. 11	45, 135	16. 16	183
10. 15	213, 216	13. 12	110, 282, 292	16. 18	22, 27, 189
10. 16	38	13. 14	97, 157, 238	16. 19	89
10. 19	49, 117	13. 15	23	16. 21	258
10. 21	313, 313	13. 19	151, 200	16. 22	97, 240, 282, 309
10. 22	45, 89	13. 23	36, 333		
10. 23	112, 197	13. 24	179	16. 25	43, 107, 108
10. 25	139	13. 25	145	16. 26	98, 199
10. 26	77, 286	13. 26	72	16. 28	96, 233, 241
10. 28	335	13. 28	99, 154, 195	17. 1	18
10. 30	24	13. 29	276	17. 2	316
10. 32	48, 110, 316	13. 30	144, 187	17. 4	115, 149
10. 33	108, 110	13. 37	183	17. 9	316, 322
10. 41	266	13. 38	208	17. 11	63
10. 42	18	13. 39	183	17. 12	53, 264
11. 1	141, 159	13. 44	73, 179	17. 14	316
11. 3	63	13. 45	195	17. 15	189
11. 5	58	13. 46	70, 73, 154	17. 17	33, 35, 234
11. 6	253	13. 48	14, 73, 154	17. 19	18, 37
11. 7	134	13. 52	195	17. 22	24

INDEX TO REFERENCES 353

MATTHEW—continued		MATTHEW—continued		MATTHEW—continued	
	PAGE		PAGE		PAGE
17. 25	159	20. 33	94	23. 34	209
17. 27	42, 43, 53, 152, 258, 292, 344	21. 1	72	23. 37	42
		21. 3	86	24. 2	96
18. 1	29, 183	21. 4	70	24. 3	18, 322
18. 2	65	21. 5	239	24. 9	89
18. 3	321	21. 6	154	24. 12	142, 345
18. 4	29	21. 7	26	24. 13	45
18. 8	149	21. 8	31, 312	24. 20	235
18. 8 f.	31, 42	21. 9	174	24. 21	14, 70, 96, 286
18. 9	149	21. 11	210, 259	24. 22	196, 199, 268, 282
18. 10	78	21. 13	86		
18. 12	63	21. 18	51	24. 27	26, 172
18. 14	139	21. 19	96	24. 30	161, 214
18. 15	42, 43, 73	21. 21	16	24. 31	25, 218, 225, 234
18. 16	42, 57	21. 22	316		
18. 17	239	21. 23	322	24. 33	27, 179
18. 18	89	21. 26	246	24. 34	96
18. 20	344	21. 28	32	24. 35	96, 97
18. 21	342	21. 31	32	24. 40	36, 319
18. 22	188	21. 32	136, 141	24. 41	36
18. 23	47, 56, 185, 195	21. 33	55	24. 43	46, 63
18. 24	322	21. 34	135	24. 45	141, 183, 186
18. 25	64, 138, 322	21. 35	36	24. 46	162
18. 26	65	21. 41	27, 55	24. 51	226
18. 27	234	21. 42	21, 45, 253	25. 1	154
18. 28	321	21. 45	64	25. 2	178
18. 33	90	21. 46	246, 247, 266	25. 4	13
18. 35	23	22. 2	27	25. 5	67
19. 1	52	22. 4	309	25. 6	225, 235
19. 3	268, 333	22. 5	36, 192	25. 9	42, 75, 98, 99, 155
19. 5	253	22. 7	26, 72		
19. 10	115, 226	22. 8	27	25. 10	27
19. 17	183	22. 11	161, 285	25. 14	87, 192
19. 18	182	22. 13	232	25. 15	36
19. 20	246	22. 16	87, 257	25. 16	154
19. 21	146	22. 21	47	25. 18	154
19. 22	154	22. 27	316	25. 19	56
19. 24	216	22. 28	209	25. 20	69
19. 28	214	22. 30	57, 321	25. 24	226
19. 29	48, 232, 316	22. 31	180	25. 25	154
20. 4	107, 108	22. 36	31	25. 26	38, 226
20. 6	179	22. 37	39, 199	25. 27	90
20. 8	155	22. 39	42	25. 32	313
20. 9	179	23. 2	72	25. 34	152, 234
20. 10	14	23. 3	316	25. 35	135
20. 12	220	23. 5	144	25. 36	39
20. 17	18	23. 8	183, 189	25. 37	155
20. 18	63, 240	23. 10	184	25. 38 f.	161
20. 19	143	23. 13	81	25. 40	31
20. 20	87	23. 15	16	25. 44	155
20. 21	36	23. 16	48, 51	25. 45	31
20. 23	140	23. 18	48, 51	26. 2	63, 135, 143
20. 24	178	23. 23	90, 148	26. 4	54
20. 26	86, 107	23. 25	216, 260	26. 9	90
20. 27	108	23. 26	14	26. 10	256
20. 28	31, 43, 51, 57, 134, 258	23. 30	215	26. 12	144
		23. 31	42	26. 13	199
20. 30	167	23. 33	99	26. 15	27, 334

354 INDEX TO REFERENCES

Matthew—continued		Matthew—continued		Mark—continued	
	PAGE		PAGE		PAGE
26. 17	27, 135	27. 43	174	3. 5	23
26. 18	27, 63	27. 44	26, 246	3. 6	56
26. 24	90, 91, 284	27. 45	178	3. 11	93, 125, 183, 313
26. 25	87, 283	27. 46	45, 72, 179	3. 13	179
26. 28	269	27. 47	195	3. 14	78, 135
26. 29	96, 112	27. 49	87, 94, 157	3. 17	208
26. 32	143, 148	27. 54	183	3. 21	16, 273, 292
26. 33	115	27. 55	134	3. 22	152
26. 34	78, 140	27. 56	168	3. 28	110
26. 35	96, 97, 265	27. 57	44, 53, 220	3. 31	82
26. 38	75, 77, 175	27. 60	190	4. 1	31
26. 39	338	27. 62	17	4. 2	292
26. 45	24, 334	27. 63	63	4. 4	36, 145
26. 46	51, 151	27. 64	32	4. 5	142
26. 48	77	28. 1	27, 135, 187, 278	4. 6	142, 345
26. 50	50	28. 9	26, 167	4. 8	188, 265, 266
26. 51	55, 56, 167	28. 12	27	4. 10	16, 18, 21, 26, 270
26. 53	65, 334, 342	28. 15	72, 169		
26. 54	99	28. 17	37	4. 11	45
26. 56	70	28. 18	175	4. 12	102
26. 58	66	28. 19	40, 255	4. 13	200
26. 60	66			4. 17	63
26. 61	267	Mark		4. 20	188
26. 62	49, 154	1. 1	166, 211, 307	4. 22	330
26. 63	64, 66, 183, 268	1. 3	151	4. 25	110
26. 64	37	1. 4	87, 151, 211, 214	4. 26	320
26. 65	56, 233	1. 5	172	4. 28	225, 316
26. 67	37	1. 7	67, 154, 325	4. 30	28, 257
26. 69	166	1. 8	41	4. 34	18
26. 70	156	1. 9	166, 210, 254	4. 35	322
26. 71	39	1. 10	25	4. 36	321
26. 74	137	1. 11	25, 72	4. 37	52
26. 75	140	1. 14	143	4. 38	271
27. 1	136	1. 15	75, 82, 237, 263	4. 39	85
27. 4	80, 86, 154	1. 21	27	4. 41	318, 335
27. 5	27, 54	1. 23	159, 221, 241, 250, 252	5. 2	39, 252
27. 7	238			5. 4	143, 241
27. 8	71	1. 24	149, 166, 240, 325	5. 5	235
27. 9	208			5. 7	156, 166
27. 10	320	1. 26	312	5. 10	65
27. 11	37, 183	1. 31	67, 79	5. 11	274
27. 12	58, 145, 148	1. 44	40, 78	5. 12	65
27. 13	50	2. 1	261	5. 13	67, 313
27. 15	268	2. 2	291	5. 15 f.	41
27. 17	166, 322	2. 5	64	5. 15	21, 70, 83
27. 20	72	2. 6	23	5. 18	322
27. 21	209	2. 8	23	5. 19	69, 83
27. 22	166, 246	2. 12	226	5. 21	166, 229
27. 24	38, 86, 215	2. 15	342, 348	5. 23	40, 95
27. 26	135	2. 16	49, 209	5. 25	152
27. 29	24	2. 18	292	5. 26	15, 43
27. 30	256	2. 20	27	5. 27	15, 166, 257
27. 31	143	2. 21	41, 209	5. 28	321
27. 32	220	2. 23	56	5. 29	58, 161
27. 37	183	2. 25	41, 49	5. 30	27, 189
27. 40	81, 151, 153, 183	2. 26	137, 149	5. 31	161
		2. 27	268	5. 32	66, 139
27. 42	183, 237	3. 4	32	5. 33	70, 83

INDEX TO REFERENCES

MARK—continued		MARK—continued		MARK—continued	
	PAGE		PAGE		PAGE
5. 34	35, 83	8. 3	82	10. 33	240
5. 36	75, 161	8. 5	65	10. 37	36
5. 42	242	8. 7	138	10. 38	245
5. 43	138, 149	8. 12	127, 333	10. 40	324
6. 2	31	8. 16	64	10. 41	178, 255
6. 3	183	8. 17	23, 185	10. 43 f.	108
6. 4	306	8. 19	236, 316	10. 45	57, 258
6. 5	39, 321	8. 23	65, 232, 256	10. 47	166
6. 6	221	8. 27	65, 212, 293	10. 49	138
6. 7	187	8. 28	306	10. 51	95
6. 8	225, 326	8. 29	65, 80	10. 52	83
6. 9	317	8. 31	258	11. 2	70
6. 11	324, 325	8. 35	43, 108, 110	11. 5	82, 154
6. 15	306, 320	8. 38	257	11. 8	115
6. 16	324	9. 1	82, 96, 233	11. 11	17
6. 17	41, 41	9. 2	18	11. 13	87, 116, 161
6. 18	41, 41, 67	9. 3	46, 88, 89	11. 14	121, 122
6. 19	52	9. 5	149	11. 16	138
6. 20	162	9. 6	67, 117	11. 17	83
6. 21	27	9. 7	88	11. 19	93, 226
6. 22	41, 41, 55, 108, 322	9. 10	140, 182	11. 23	63
		9. 11	49	11. 24	73
6. 23	55, 210	9. 19	33, 35, 39	11. 25	112
6. 24	55, 151	9. 20	66, 312, 316	11. 30	217
6. 25	55, 154, 229	9. 21	70	11. 31 f.	326
6. 26	26, 335, 350	9. 22	69, 330	11. 32	67, 149, 325
6. 27	149	9. 23	182	12. 1	55
6. 28	40	9. 24	156, 189	12. 2	128, 129, 209
6. 31	18	9. 26	31	12. 4	135
6. 36	117	9. 28	18, 39, 49, 243, 322	12. 5	36
6. 37	37, 98			12. 7	94
6. 39	138, 231	9. 30	129, 282	12. 10	324
6. 40	187, 266, 268	9. 31	24, 63	12. 11	21
6. 41	67	9. 34	30	12. 12	64, 342
6. 43	209	9. 35	86	12. 14	99, 286
6. 45	40, 321	9. 37	107, 209, 282, 287	12. 23	209
6. 48	146			12. 26	137, 217
6. 52	23	9. 38	65	12. 28	31, 161, 210, 316
6. 55	116	9. 41	96, 246		
6. 56	93, 100, 125	9. 42	31, 92	12. 30	199
7. 2	45, 325	9. 43	31, 149	12. 31	42
7. 4	135, 179, 259	9. 44	292	12. 33	140, 181, 199
7. 5	185	9. 45, 47	31, 149	12. 34	325
7. 6	23, 206	9. 50	43, 44	12. 36, 37	41
7. 11	91	10. 1	82, 154	12. 38	154, 227
7. 19	316	10. 11	272	12. 40	45, 317
7. 20	46	10. 13	293	12. 41	67, 137
7. 21	23	10. 14	214	13. 1	322
7. 21 f.	28	10. 16	39	13. 2	96
7. 24	285	10. 17	322	13. 3	18, 322
7. 25	241, 325	10. 19	51	13. 4	89, 112
7. 26	67	10. 20	55	13. 8	268
7. 28	156	10. 21	72	13. 9	37
7. 33	18	10. 23	137	13. 11	112
7. 36	29, 246	10. 24	82, 137	13. 12	313
7. 37	26, 83	10. 25	31	13. 13	45
8. 1 f.	117	10. 30	193	13. 14	15, 82, 312
8. 2	243	10. 32	37	13. 15, 16	15

356 INDEX TO REFERENCES

MARK—continued		MARK—continued		LUKE—continued	
	PAGE		PAGE		PAGE
13. 17	51	15. 7	83	1. 49	296
13. 18	235	15. 9	155	1. 51	23, 228
13. 19	46, 70, 96, 324, 325	15. 10	83	1. 51–3	74
		15. 12	183	1. 54	136
13. 20	55	15. 15	135	1. 55	238
13. 22	144	15. 16	216	1. 59	65
13. 23	37	15. 20	191	1. 62	39, 123, 130, 182
13. 25	89	15. 22	102	1. 63	156
13. 26	257	15. 23	37, 65, 178	1. 65	16
13. 27	25, 175, 225	15. 27	179	1. 66	23, 23
13. 29	27	15. 29	24	1. 68	174
13. 30	96, 196	15. 34	72, 267	1. 70	25, 187
13. 31	97	15. 36	94	1. 71	24
13. 34	75, 77	15. 39	16, 183	1. 72	56, 136
13. 35	235	15. 41	153	1. 73	141, 324
13. 36	99	15. 43	166	1. 74	24
14. 1	27, 252	15. 44	5	1. 75	243
14. 3	154	15. 44 f.	69	1. 77, 78 f.	142
14. 4	70, 153	15. 47	168	1. 79	52
14. 6	264	16. 1	168, 278	1. 80	213
14. 7	112	16. 2	187, 227, 322	2. 1	57, 139
14. 8	138, 227	16. 4	135	2. 2	32, 192
14. 10 f.	129	16. 5	17	2. 3	57
14. 14	109	16. 6	57	2. 4	47, 142, 148
14. 19	198, 268	16. 7	330	2. 5	57
14. 20	55	16. 9	187, 259	2. 8	235, 245
14. 21	92, 284	16. 14	316	2. 11	239
14. 23	209	16. 17	193	2. 12	192
14. 24	152, 271	16. 18	52, 96	2. 13	312
14. 25	96, 112, 227, 286	16. 19	143	2. 14	213, 264
				2. 15	94, 175
14. 28	57, 143, 146, 148	LUKE		2. 21	40, 141, 144
		1. 1	33, 318	2. 22	142, 217
14. 29	37, 115, 330	1. 2	320	2. 24	142
14. 30	140	1. 3	31, 33, 199	2. 26	113, 140, 148, 149, 176
14. 31	96, 97	1. 6	181		
14. 35	66	1. 7	220	2. 27	145, 151, 176, 234, 336
14. 36	49, 330	1. 9	141		
14. 39	80	1. 14	233	2. 30	14
14. 41	24, 291, 336	1. 15	96, 180	2. 31	25
14. 42	82	1. 17	23, 257	2. 34	87
14. 44	41, 70, 83	1. 18	37, 268	2. 35	105
14. 47	55, 196	1. 20	48, 88, 89	2. 38	194
14. 49	95, 330	1. 21	146	2. 41	22, 67
14. 54	54, 266	1. 26	258	2. 42	81, 154
14. 55	143, 166	1. 29	123, 131	2. 43	145, 166
14. 58	161, 267	1. 31	86	2. 44	212
14. 60	49	1. 33	25	2. 47	66
14. 60 f.	67	1. 35	21, 87	2. 48	62
14. 63	27	1. 36	192	2. 49	261
14. 64	233	1. 37	196	3. 2	174, 207
14. 65	241	1. 38	185	3. 5	16, 253
14. 67	166	1. 39	16	3. 6	14
14. 71	137	1. 42	31	3. 8	168
14. 72	52, 137, 140	1. 43	45, 139, 240	3. 9	63, 199
15. 2	183	1. 44	254	3. 13	151, 216
15. 4	50	1. 45	35, 42	3. 14	27, 57, 151
15. 6	48, 67, 93, 268	1. 48	185	3. 15	23, 123, 130

INDEX TO REFERENCES

LUKE—continued		LUKE—continued		LUKE—continued	
	PAGE		PAGE		PAGE
3. 16	. . 240	6. 45	. . 14	9. 23	. . 76
3. 18	. 197, 337	6. 47	. . 233	9. 24	. . 43
3. 21	. . 145	6. 47–9	. . 79	9. 25	. 43, 80, 157
3. 23	. . 321	6. 48	. . 152	9. 27	. 96, 233
3. 23 f.	. . 168	7. 1	. 159, 321	9. 28	. 231, 335
4. 1	. 159, 257	7. 2	. . 89	9. 29	. 87, 145
4. 3, 9	. . 183	7. 3	. . 106	9. 32	. 71, 265
4. 10	. . 141	7. 4	. . 139	9. 33	. 117, 149
4. 16	. 27, 151	7. 6	66, 139, 157, 216	9. 34	. . 148
4. 17	. . 173	7. 8	. . 64	9. 36	. 70, 324
4. 19	. . 211	7. 12	. . 335	9. 37	. 235, 267
4. 20	. 158, 200	7. 17	. . 257	9. 38	. . 149
4. 22	. . 213	7. 18	. . 195	9. 40	. . 312
4. 23	. . 161	7. 22	58, 154, 331	9. 41	. . 35
4. 24	. . 89	7. 28	. . 30	9. 42	. . 322
4. 25	. . 21	7. 32	. 153, 179	9. 44	. . 24
4. 26	. . 330	7. 35	. . 73	9. 45	. 102, 234
4. 29	. . 136	7. 36, 42	. . 209	9. 46	123, 130, 182
4. 34	. . 13	7. 39	. . 48	9. 47	. . 23
4. 35	. . 246	7. 45	17, 159, 226	9. 48	. 30, 31
4. 36	. . 318	7. 47	. . 319	9. 49	. . 65
4. 41	183, 292, 313	7. 49	. . 312	9. 52	134, 136, 169
4. 43	. . 197	8. 2	. 53, 292	9. 54	. . 99
5. 1	. . 335	8. 5	. . 36	9. 55	. . 49
5. 3	. 50, 52, 154	8. 5 f.	. 36, 145	9. 58	. . 109
5. 4	. 52, 159	8. 6 f.	. . 197	9. 59	. 149, 197
5. 5	. 199, 272	8. 9	. 123, 131	9. 61	. . 197
5. 7	141, 198, 273	8. 10	. . 102	10. 1	41, 187, 266, 311
5. 10	. 89, 239	8. 12, 15	. . 23	10. 4	. . 77
5. 12	. . 179	8. 16	. . 279	10. 6	. 52, 208
5. 13	. . 156	8. 17	. . 96	10. 7	. 15, 194
5. 14	. 40, 326	8. 18	. . 284	10. 19	. . 97
5. 17	. . 143	8. 23	. . 72	10. 20	. 25, 313
5. 19	. 16, 235	8. 25	. . 318	10. 21	. . 194
5. 21	26, 156, 226	8. 26	. . 216	10. 23	. . 18
5. 22	. . 23	8. 27	. . 244	10. 23 f.	. . 38
5. 24	. . 75	8. 28	. . 156	10. 25	. 157, 232
5. 33	. . 56	8. 29	. 65, 67, 243	10. 27	. . 199
5. 37	. . 41	8. 30	. 296, 313	10. 29	. . 157
5. 39	. . 31	8. 35	. 208, 313	10. 35	. 145, 148
6. 2	. . 195	8. 37	. . 65	10. 37	. 56, 152
6. 4	. 137, 149	8. 40	. . 145	10. 39	. . 44
6. 7	. . 55	8. 46	. 160, 161	11. 2	. . 112
6. 8	. . 186	8. 47	. . 137	11. 3	. . 77
6. 11	. 123, 130	8. 48	. . 35	11. 4	77, 151, 200
6. 16	. . 168	8. 50	. . 75	11. 5	. 99, 320
6. 22	. 72, 285	8. 52	. . 76	11. 6	. 109, 320
6. 24	. . 206	8. 54	. . 52	11. 7	. . 99
6. 25	. 35, 153	8. 56	. . 151	11. 8	. 284, 330
6. 29	. . 235	9. 1	. . 55	11. 9	. . 75
6. 30	. 76, 151	9. 3	. . 78	11. 11	. 247, 258
6. 31	. . 293	9. 8	. . 305	11. 13	. . 25
6. 32	. . 115	9. 9	. 37, 46, 62	11. 15	. . 210
6. 37	. . 96	9. 10	. . 18	11. 18	. . 116
6. 38	240, 291, 293	9. 12	. . 52	11. 19	. . 37
6. 39	. . 283	9. 14	. 187, 266	11. 20	. . 180
6. 42	. 41, 94, 139	9. 16	. . 67	11. 21	. 43, 112
6. 44	. . 293	9. 18	. 18, 87, 89	11. 22	. . 112

INDEX TO REFERENCES

LUKE—continued		LUKE—continued		LUKE—continued	
	PAGE		PAGE		PAGE
11. 24	. 312	13. 7	. 62	16. 16	. 58
11. 26	. 313	13. 11	. 266	16. 19	66, 247
11. 28	. 338	13. 16	90, 231	16. 20	. 86
11. 29	. 214	13. 19	. 253	16. 23	27, 168
11. 32	. 266	13. 22	56, 154	16. 24	. 225
11. 33	. 21	13. 23	. 333	16. 25	. 44
11. 34	. 112	13. 25	149, 325	16. 26	14, 226
11. 35, 36	. 305	13. 28	168, 226	16. 31	. 284
11. 39	. 35	13. 29	26, 172	17. 1	141, 292
11. 41	. 247	13. 31	. 194	17. 2	32, 92
11. 42	90, 211	13. 32	17, 63	17. 3	. 42
11. 46	. 246	13. 33	. 17	17. 4	. 14
11. 49	. 209	13. 34	42, 43, 317	17. 6	. 92
11. 51	. 182	13. 35	96, 111, 112	17. 8	49, 77
11. 53	. 52	14. 1	55, 145	17. 11	170, 267
11. 54	. 30	14. 4	39, 232	17. 12	. 322
12. 2	. 286	14. 5	209, 342	17. 17	. 178
12. 3	. 258	14. 7	. 137	17. 20	. 156
12. 5	. 143	14. 8	. 89	17. 21	. 216
12. 6	. 58	14. 8 f.	. 99	17. 27	. 66
12. 7	. 24	14. 10	100, 154	17. 31	. 325
12. 8	. 110	14. 12	112, 335	17. 33	. 110
12. 9	. 58	14. 13	. 112	18. 1	. 144
12. 11	. 112	14. 17	. 173	18. 5	. 266
12. 12	185, 194	14. 18	18, 21, 162, 246	18. 6	. 213
12. 13	. 149	14. 19	. 63	18. 7	56, 96, 235
12. 14	. 33	14. 23	76, 181	18. 8	56, 330
12. 15	. 146	14. 24	. 233	18. 9	. 153
12. 16	. 156	14. 26	. 43	18. 10	. 134
12. 17	. 117	14. 29	. 322	18. 11	44, 57
12. 20	239, 293	14. 31	87, 154, 241	18. 12	. 235
12. 22	. 24	14. 33	43, 209	18. 13	57, 173
12. 23	. 311	15. 6, 9	. 55	18. 14	31, 45, 216
12. 26	. 31	15. 7	. 32	18. 17, 29 f.	. 96
12. 28	. 227	15. 12	52, 152	18. 30	. 193
12. 30	181, 190, 313	15. 13	282, 286	18. 31	. 238
12. 31	. 338	15. 14	21, 268	18. 36	65, 123, 131, 161
12. 32	. 72	15. 16	. 66		
12. 33	42, 151	15. 18	. 154	18. 39	. 41
12. 34	. 23	15. 19	320, 321	18. 40	. 322
12. 35	24, 89, 190	15. 20	42, 154, 322	18. 41	95, 99, 305
12. 36	. 322	15. 22	. 256	19. 4	16, 235
12. 38	. 321	15. 23	. 80	19. 7	. 273
12. 44	64, 151	15. 25	. 154	19. 8	63, 210
12. 45	. 139	15. 26	65, 123, 130	19. 9	. 305
12. 47	. 247	15. 29	. 62	19. 11	148, 227
12. 47 f.	18, 246	15. 30	. 44	19. 15	145, 149, 335
12. 48	39, 293, 316, 324	15. 32	. 71	19. 17	31, 89, 345
		16. 1	. 158	19. 20	. 197
12. 50	. 138	16. 4	74, 235	19. 23	. 92
12. 52	. 89	16. 6	. 154	19. 29	. 230
12. 54	63, 172	16. 8	43, 208, 213, 216, 250	19. 30	. 76
12. 56	. 193			19. 33	. 22
12. 57	. 258	16. 9	213, 260, 293	19. 37	. 274
12. 58	76, 99	16. 10	. 31	19. 41	. 72
12. 59	. 96	16. 11 f.	. 98	19. 42	180, 331
13. 1	. 194	16. 13	. 36	19. 46	. 246
13. 2	. 31	16. 15	23, 305	19. 48	. 182

LUKE—continued		LUKE—continued		JOHN—continued	
	PAGE		PAGE		PAGE
20. 2	156	23. 2	147	1. 25	156
20. 6	137	23. 3	183	1. 27	139
20. 7	148	23. 5	155	1. 28	87
20. 9	55	23. 6	336	1. 29	151, 231
20. 10	100	23. 12	41, 43, 159, 227	1. 30	32, 37, 216, 279
20. 11 f.	227	23. 13	55	1. 32	156, 161
20. 13	322	23. 14	158	1. 33	46, 135, 325
20. 20	136, 147	23. 15	240	1. 37, 38	161
20. 22	149	23. 19	89	1. 39	183
20. 24	136	23. 26	232	1. 40	135, 273
20. 25	16, 340, 347	23. 28	338	1. 42	37
20. 26	72	23. 31	99, 293	1. 44, 45	259
20. 27	286, 316	23. 33	36	1. 47	75
20. 33	209	23. 37	183	1. 48	275
20. 35	193, 232	23. 42	241	1. 49	144, 183, 184
20. 36	79, 208	23. 45	225	1. 50	161, 345
20. 46	227	23. 49	185	1. 51	82
20. 47	45	23. 50 f.	40, 45	2. 1	210
21. 6	316	23. 55	137	2. 1 f.	27
21. 7	112	24. 1	187, 235	2. 5	106
21. 14	23, 139	24. 4	56	2. 5–8	77
21. 16	7, 209	24. 6	137	2. 6	87, 266
21. 17	89	24. 7	24, 325	2. 10	31, 37, 113
21. 18	24, 96	24. 10	168, 206	2. 11	192
21. 24	27, 89, 240	24. 15	167	2. 16	76, 77
21. 25	172, 175	24. 19	166, 185	2. 18	318
21. 28	24	24. 20	49	2. 19	76
21. 32	96	24. 21	66, 291	2. 23	171
21. 33	97	24. 22	225, 335	2. 24	41, 142, 148, 194
21. 34	23, 225	24. 25	33, 141	2. 25	139
21. 37	67, 230	24. 26	90	3. 2	259
22. 1	27, 215	24. 27	15, 43, 155	3. 7	77
22. 4	181	24. 28	138	3. 15	237, 263
22. 8	156	24. 29	52, 179	3. 16	136, 197
22. 11	109	24. 31	39, 251, 349	3. 19	45, 216
22. 15	144, 148, 241	24. 32, 38	23	3. 22	87, 170
22. 16	96	24. 33	146	3. 23	27, 87
22. 17	155	24. 35	137	3. 25	208
22. 18	96	24. 39	232, 350	3. 27	89
22. 19 f.	87	24. 44	217	3. 28	46, 326
22. 19	191	24. 45	139	3. 29	242
22. 20	143, 301	24. 47	78, 155, 316, 343	3. 30	46
22. 23	89, 123, 131			3. 32	70, 85
22. 34	113			3. 34	282
22. 40	75	JOHN		4. 1	216
22. 42	115	1. 1, 4	183	4. 2	41
22. 45	258	1. 3	70	4. 3	167, 170
22. 46	75	1. 5	73	4. 5	167, 216, 256, 324
22. 49	16, 86, 98, 270	1. 8	95, 183	4. 6	260
22. 50	195, 196	1. 9	87	4. 7	135
22. 53	190	1. 10	71	4. 9	37, 169
22. 57, 60	33	1. 12	139, 153	4. 10	37, 135
22. 58	33, 210	1. 13	27	4. 14	97
22. 61	137, 140	1. 14	315	4. 16	76
22. 67, 68	96	1. 15	32, 216, 279	4. 17	269
22. 69	89	1. 16	258	4. 18	225
22. 70	183	1. 18	254	4. 21, 23	139
22. 71	233	1. 21	304	4. 27	272

INDEX TO REFERENCES

JOHN—continued		JOHN—continued		JOHN—continued	
	PAGE		PAGE		PAGE
4. 29, 33	283	6. 71	168	9. 25	64, 81
4. 31	67, 156, 277	7. 2	214	9. 26 f.	231
4. 32	135	7. 3	100	9. 27	78
4. 34	139	7. 4	115, 146	9. 28	46, 156
4. 35	17, 63, 76	7. 11	46	9. 29	149
4. 36	335	7. 12	36	9. 30	331
4. 38	135	7. 17	338	9. 33	90, 92
4. 41	29	7. 18	45	9. 37	46
4. 48	96	7. 22	304	10. 1	46
4. 49	140	7. 23	199, 217	10. 5	97
4. 50	324	7. 24	245	10. 7	212
4. 51	322	7. 27	112	10. 10	180
4. 52	65, 72, 226, 248	7. 30	173	10. 12	285, 342
4. 53	304	7. 34	342	10. 15	63
5. 2	18, 152, 171	7. 35	212, 226	10. 16	48
5. 6	62	7. 38	316, 320	10. 18	139
5. 8	77	7. 39	324	10. 21	26
5. 11	37, 46	7. 40	208, 234	10. 22	27, 171
5. 15	26	7. 45	46	10. 28	96, 286
5. 20	100	7. 47	335	10. 29	39
5. 24	175	7. 51	283	10. 30	37
5. 25	139	7. 52	63	10. 32	63
5. 27	49, 56	8. 7	159, 226	10. 36	183
5. 28	139	8. 9	155, 198, 268, 276	10. 37	284
5. 31	116	8. 12	96, 183	10. 39	24
5. 34	64	8. 14	334	11. 1	259
5. 35, 37	183	8. 15	177	11. 2	80
5. 36	135, 186	8. 18	42, 151	11. 6	324
5. 38	37, 45, 283	8. 19	92	11. 12	115
5. 39	37, 45	8. 22	259	11. 18	172
5. 44	13, 37, 226	8. 23	14	11. 19	16, 270
5. 45	76, 80	8. 24	26	11. 26	96
6. 6	41	8. 25	49	11. 27	183
6. 9	196	8. 26	135, 257	11. 28	62, 156
6. 10	221	8. 30	322	11. 31	135
6. 13	186	8. 38	38	11. 35	72
6. 14	26	8. 39	92, 168, 208	11. 36	66
6. 17	179	8. 44	40, 112, 177, 206, 208, 227	11. 36 f.	68
6. 21	227			11. 42	268
6. 22	67	8. 45	345	11. 43	304
6. 26	26	8. 51	96	11. 44	86
6. 30	37	8. 52	96, 233	11. 47	98
6. 31	135	8. 53	47	11. 48	63, 190
6. 32	70	8. 55	216, 321	11. 49	195, 196, 235
6. 33	217	8. 56	102, 138	11. 51	235
6. 35	96	8. 57 f.	168	11. 55	135
6. 37	21, 39, 97	8. 58	62, 140	11. 56	96
6. 39	39, 95, 179, 197, 316	9. 2	102, 156	11. 57	105
		9. 3	95, 304	12. 1	248, 260
6. 40	139	9. 4	110, 321	12. 4	89
6. 43	76	9. 5	112, 183	12. 8	42
6. 45	89, 234	9. 7	77	12. 9	186
6. 46	45, 304	9. 13	41	12. 10	54
6. 52	135	9. 14	324	12. 12	153, 186
6. 63	151	9. 16	26	12. 15	35
6. 64	86	9. 18	67	12. 11	81
6. 65	89	9. 21	41	12. 20	135
6. 70	55	9. 22	86, 162	12. 23	139, 155

INDEX TO REFERENCES 361

JOHN—*continued*		JOHN—*continued*		JOHN—*continued*	
	PAGE		PAGE		PAGE
12. 29	. . 291	16. 21	. . 112	19. 32	. . 187
12. 30	. . 268	16. 22	. . 23	19. 35	. . **46**
12. 32	. . 21	16. 24	. . 89	20. 1	. . 187
12. 38	. . 304	16. 25	. . 139	20. 11	. . 274
12. 40	. 23, 52, 70	16. 27	. 41, 259	20. 12	, 17, 274
12. 43	. . 216	16. 30	139, 253, 259	20. 14	. . **167**
12. 46	. . 196	16. 32	. . 198	20. 17	. 63, **76**
12. 47	. . 234	16. 33	. . 151	20. 19	27, 187
13. 1	70, 139, 215, 266	17. 2	. 21, **40**, 70,	20. 20	. . 160
13. 2	. . 139		100, 317	20. 23	. . 63
13. 3	. . 70	17. 3	. 139, 324	20. 25	. . 97
13. 4	. . 27	17. 5	. . 144	20. 26	. . 27
13. 6	. . **63**	17. 11	. . 35	20. 29	. . 345
13. 8	. 96, 97	17. 12	. . 208	20. 30	. 88, **337**
13. 10	. . **139**	17. 17	. . 177	20. 31	. 88, **183**
13. 13	. . 230	17. 19	. . 89	21. 2	. . 207
13. 15	. . 70	17. 20	. . 87	21. 3	. . 135
13. 18	. 95, 304	17. 21	. . 35	21. 10	. . 75
13. 19	. . 144	17. 23	. . 89	21. 21	. . 304
13. 21	. . 156	17. 24	. 21, 35, **100**	21. 22	37, 111, 303,
13. 22	. . 56	17. 25	. 35, **335**		304, 321
13. 24	. 123, 130	17. 26	. 245, 304	21. 23	. **45**, 63, 111
13. 24 f., 26	. 46	18. 1	. . 172	21. 25	86, 137, 285
13. 27	. **30**, 63	18. 3	. . **154**		
13. 29	. 195, 318	18. 9	58, **95**, 304, 325	ACTS	
13. 34	. 139, 225	18. 10	. 217, 296	1. 1	32, 56, 167, 227
13. 38	. . 111	18. 11	. 39, 96	1. 2	. . **350**
14. 1	. . 23	18. 13	. . 235	1. 3	143, 148, 267
14. 2	. 63, 135	18. 14	. . 149	1. 4	137, 233, 326
14. 3	. 63, **334**	18. 15	. . 89	1. 5	**193**, 240, 282, 286
14. 6	. . 178	18. 16	. . 274	1. 6	. . 333
14. 9	. 62, 244	18. 17	. . 210	1. 7	. . 27
14. 12	. . 63	18. 20 f.	. . 70	1. 10	. . 335
14. 21	. 41, 46	18. 25	. . 156	1. 12	. 152, **218**
14. 23	. . 56	18. 28	. . 226	1. 13	. . 168
14. 25	. . 26	18. 30	. 87, 89, **92**	1. 14	. . 174
14. 27	. 23, 185	18. 32	. 95, 304	1. 15	. . 338
14. 29	. . 140	18. 33	. 37, 183	1. 16	. 33, 185
14. 31	. 94, 95	18. 34	. . 42	1. 16 f.	. . 45
15. 2	39, 157, 316	18. 36	. . **92**	1. 18	. . 213
15. 5	. . 45	18. 37	. 37, **337**	1. 19	. 151, 191
15. 6	. **73**, **74**	18. 38	. . 37	1. 21	. . 71
15. 8	. 73, 74, **139**	18. 39	. 99, 139	1. 22	. . 155
15. 16	. . 129	19. 3	. . 66	1. 24	. . 80
15. 18	. . 32	19. 6	. . 182	1. 24 f.	. . 135
15. 19	. . 345	19. 11	. . 92	2. 1	. . **145**
15. 21	. . 256	19. 12	. . 156	2. 2	. . 158
15. 24	. . 92	19. 13	. . 234	2. 4	. . 176
15. 25	. 95, 304	19. 16	. . 135	2. 6	. 161, **233**
15. 27	. . 62	19. 18	. . 225	2. 9 f., 10	. **170**
16. 2	139, 321, 330	19. 19	. . 88	2. 12	. 44, **123**
16. 3	. . 71	19. 21	, 46, 76, 183	2. 14	. . **33**
16. 6	. 23, 345	19. 22	. . 85	2. 17	. . 241
16. 8	. . 154	19. 23	. . 27	2. 18	. . 185
16. 12	. . 135	19. 24	54, **95**, 304, 337	2. 20	. 140, 174
16. 17	. . 209	19. 25	. 169, 273	2. 23	. . 24
16. 19	. . 64	19. 28	. . 344	2. 24	. . 139
16. 20	. . 253	19. 31	. 313, 344	2. 27	. . 43

INDEX TO REFERENCES

Acts—*continued*		Acts—*continued*		Acts—*continued*	
	PAGE		PAGE		PAGE
2. 29	88, 304	5. 24	123, 130	8. 18	176, 255
2. 36	200	5. 25	88	8. 19	139
2. 37	23	5. 27 f.	66	8. 20	**122**
2. 38	214, 266	5. 28	172, 241	8. 22	251
2. 39	15, 239, 254	5. 29	216	8. 23	64, 161, 213,
2. 40	30	5. 32	218		253, **254**
2. 45	67, 93, 125	5. 34	210	8. 24	159
3. 1	**179**	5. 36	147, 216, 253	8. 26	44, 156
3. 2	41, 55, 93, 180,	5. 38 f.	115	8. 27	87, 154, 157
	195	5. 39	99	8. 30	330
3. 3	65	5. 41	37, 66	8. 31	65, 116
3. 10	33, 41, 149	6. 3, 5	315	8. 35	155
3. 12	33, 141, **158**	6. 4	89	8. 40	58, 144, 148
3. 13	45	6. 7	312	9. 1	166
3. 14	185	6. 8	**159**	9. 3	145, 171
3. 16	221, **267**	6. 9	15, 170	9. 4	161
3. 17	**154**	6. 11	213, 315	9. 5	27
3. 18	25	6. 13	315	9. 6	49, 154, **330**
3. 19	27, 52, 144	7. 2	140	9. 7	**233**
3. 20	105	7. 4	143	9. 9	88
3. 21	25, 174	7. 5	285	9. 11	154, 155
3. 25	208	7. 7	110	9. 12	105, 315
3. 26	146	7. 8	168	9. 13	233
4. 1	322	7. 10	206	9. 15	141, 213, 239
4. 4	315	7. 11	171	9. 16	50
4. 7	37, 65	7. 12	161, **254**	9. 18	57
4. 9	212, 258	7. 14	241, **265**	9. 20	183, 325
4. 11	44	7. 19	136, 141, 143	9. 24	55, **235**
4. 12	153, 264	7. 20	**239**	9. 27	232
4. 13	55, 149	7. 21	39, 322	9. 31	241
4. 16	30, 304	7. 26	17, 65	9. 34	64, 154
4. 17	241	7. 29	253	9. 38	171, 216
4. 18	141	7. 30	213	9. 39	55, 154
4. 19	216	7. 33	56	9. 42	171, 237
4. 21	117, 182	7. 34	94, 157	10. 2	315
4. 22	**216**	7. 35	70, **156**, 185	10. 3	**248**
4. 25, 27	181	7. 36	171	10. 6	206, 273
4. 29	200	7. 39	23	10. 14	196
4. 30	146, 148	7. 40	45, 316	10. 15	37
4. 32	191	7. 42	52	10. 17	123, 130, 335
4. 33	**350**	7. 43	26	10. 18	65, 152
4. 34	67, 81	7. 45	25	10. 20	154, 155, 330
4. 35	93, 125	7. 48	**287**	10. 24	55
4. 36	208, 220, 221,	7. 51	23, 220	10. 25	142
	258	7. 52	209	10. 28	30, 137
5. 3	136	7. 53	**255**, 266	10. 30	**248**
5. 7	231, 335	7. 54	23	10. 31	58
5. 9	149, 174	7. 56	25	10. 33	80, 135, 159
5. 12	24	7. 58	38	10. 34	55
5. 14	237	7. 60	72, 77	10. 36	324
5. 15	**100**	8. 2	**56**	10. 37	316
5. 16	58	8. 3	166	10. 38	72, 137, 240
5. 17	151, 152, 154	8. 5	40	10. 41	143
5. 19	27, 179	8. 6	52	10. 43	151
5. 20	57	8. 9	148, 159, 195	10. 44	176
5. 21	138, 275	8. 11	243	10. 48	65, 149, 256
5. 22	52	8. 15	106, 146	11. 1	313
5. 23	27	8. 16	159	11. 4	155

INDEX TO REFERENCES 363

Acts—continued		Acts—continued		Acts—continued	
	PAGE		PAGE		PAGE
11. 7	154, 161	14. 13	151, 152	17. 6	62
11. 13	137	14. 14	42	17. 11	48, 127, 131
11. 14	37	14. 16	241	17. 13	159, 171
11. 16	240	14. 17	23, 41	17. 14	321
11. 17	89, 237, 335	14. 19	66	17. 15	31, 139
11. 18	72	14. 21	53	17. 16	161, 171
11. 19	225, 271	14. 21 f.	80	17. 17	151
11. 26	72, 149, 199	14. 27	50, 158, 212	17. 18	36, 147
11. 28	21, 86	15. 1	242	17. 20	123, 130
12. 1	15, 268	15. 2	149, 181	17. 21	30, 169, 200
12. 2	240	15. 3	66	17. 22	30, 57, 161
12. 3	27, 227, 311	15. 4	258	17. 23	88
12. 4	56	15. 5	15, 217	17. 24	174, 175
12. 5	337	15. 9	23	17. 26	27
12. 6	27, 79, 260	15. 10	37, 136	17. 27	127, 157, 232
12. 8	77	15. 11	137	17. 28	36, 165, 221,
12. 9	331	15. 12	71		268
12. 10	178, 225	15. 13	143	17. 31	262
12. 11	200	15. 14	181	18. 2	85, 171
12. 12	206	15. 16	52	18. 3	221, 345
12. 14	331	15. 17	40, 105, 325	18. 4	65
12. 15	148, 322	15. 19	242	18. 5	220
12. 16	159, 226	15. 20	181	18. 6	24, 27
12. 25	206	15. 21	62	18. 7	27
13. 1	151, 152, 206	15. 23	24, 78, 305	18. 8	67, 237
13. 2	333	15. 27	267	18. 10	141, 318
13. 3	39	15. 28	139	18. 11	72
13. 5	246	15. 29	85, 157, 181	18. 14	33, 89
13. 8	31	15. 32	267	18. 15	86, 268
13. 10	208	15. 36	333	18. 17	232
13. 11	51, 89, 216	15. 37 f.	79	18. 19	41, 66
13. 13	16, 170, 270	15. 38	65	18. 21	52
13. 14	27, 171	15. 39	136	18. 22	158
13. 16	35, 153	16. 3	149	18. 23	80, 158
13. 19	53	16. 4	52	18. 25	15, 220
13. 20	243	16. 5	220, 239	18. 26	30
13. 21	168	16. 6	80	18. 27	80
13. 22	28, 156, 168,	16. 7	282	19. 1	145
	247	16. 8, 11	171	19. 3	255
13. 23	190	16. 12	178, 210	19. 4	325
13. 25	49, 137	16. 13	27	19. 5	255
13. 28	149	16. 14	139, 215	19. 7	201
13. 32	246, 325	16. 15	39, 65	19. 13	166
13. 33	80, 206	16. 16	22, 56, 185	19. 15	155, 166
13. 36	243	16. 17	40, 53	19. 16	158
13. 39	151, 217	16. 18	64, 194	19. 19	17
13. 41	96	16. 19	22, 232	19. 20	350
13. 42	277	16. 22	65, 78, 138	19. 21	139, 143, 148
13. 46	42	16. 23	221	19. 22	52
13. 50	259	16. 25	225	19. 24	56, 152
14. 3	24, 337	16. 26	27	19. 26	196, 235
14. 4	36	16. 29	55	19. 27	22, 138, 235
14. 5	139	16. 31	237	19. 28	316
14. 6	182	16. 34	160, 237	19. 30	322
14. 8	180, 220	16. 37	18	19. 31	239
14. 9	141	16. 39	15, 65, 259, 268	19. 32	30, 31, 198
14. 10	186, 225	17. 1	171	19. 33	209
14. 12	41	17. 4	282	19. 34	316

INDEX TO REFERENCES

Acts—continued		Acts—continued		Acts—continued	
	PAGE		PAGE		PAGE
19. 35	17, 162	21. 36	312	25. 14	15, **268**
19. 36	88, 157, 159, 322	21. 38	183	25. 16	58, 113, 130, 140
19. 37	157, **159**	21. 39	171, 282		
19. 38	**26**	22. 2	64	25. 17	56
19. 40	138, 231	22. 3	171, 185, 210	25. 20	55, 127, 131
20. 1	143	22. 5	87, 157	25. 21	42, 148
20. 2	170	22. 6	**149**	25. 22	65, 91, 120
20. 3	89	22. 7	161	25. 23	15, **268**
20. 4	168	22. 8	39	25. 24	312
20. 5	171	22. 9	**233**	25. 25	55
20. 6	171, 225	22. 10	39, 75, 149, 154	26. 1	58, **64**
20. 7	17, 179, 187	22. 13	194	26. 2	169
20. 9	258	22. 14	13, 233	26. 3	149, 162, 169, 221, **316**
20. 11	154	22. 15	70, 85, 200		
20. 12	282	22. 16	154	26. 4	169, 200
20. 13	171	22. 17	**149**	26. 5	31
20. 15	17, 171, **277**	22. 19	237	26. 7	33, 86, 169
20. 16	127, 149, **248**	22. 22	**90**	26. 9	42, 147
20. 18	179, 201, 226	22. 24	138, 149, 156	26. 11	**65**
20. 20	137	22. 30	58, 182, 273	26. 12	**218**
20. 21	86	23. 1	200	26. 13	225, **235**
20. 22	63	23. 3	138	26. 14	27, 161, **304**
20. 24	56, 105, 246	23. 10	99, 138	26. 16	330, 339
20. 26	215, 222, **333**	23. 12, 13	**56**	26. 17	87
20. 27	253	23. 14	42, 233	26. 17 f.	142
20. 28	78, 135	23. 15	30, 141, 144, 158	26. 18	221
20. 30	194			26. 21	169
20. 32	**264**	23. 18	65, 157	26. 22	221
20. 33	232	23. 19	18, 65	26. 23	**260**
20. 35	31, 154, 216	23. 20	30, 158	26. 25	31
21. 1	171	23. 22	326	26. 26	137, 285
21. 2	87	23. 23	195	26. 28	63, 147, **262**
21. 3	66, 171	23. 26	78, 305	26. 29	46, 91
21. 4	149	23. 27	187	26. 30	182
21. 5	174	23. 30	73, 85, 86	26. 31	62
21. 8	16	23. 31	171	26. 32	90, **91**, **92**
21. 11	190	24. 2	267	27. 3	149
21. 12	149	24. 3	232	27. 5	171
21. 13	52, 139, 226	24. 4	**344**	27. 8	216
21. 14	156, 315	24. 7	24	27. 9	345
21. 15	216	24. 10	162	27. 6	86, 149
21. 16	80, 109, 206, 209, 210	24. 11	17, 87, 135, 157	27. 12	30, **127**
		24. 15	86	27. 13	30, 52, 172, 232
21. 17	322	24. 16	253	27. 14	52, **268**, 282
21. 18	17	24. 17	87, 157, **236**	27. 15	17
21. 20	50, **66**	24. 19	90, 126	27. 17	53, 99, 154
21. 21	241	24. 21	193	27. 18	56
21. 23	154	24. 22	30	27. 19	17
21. 24	24, 57, **100**	24. 26	30, 154	27. 20	52, 140, 172
21. 25	181	25. 3	56	27. 21	33
21. 26	17, 57	25. 4	**147**	27. 22	138
21. 28	26, **69**	25. 4 f.	137, 326	27. 26	53
21. 29	66	25. 7	322	27. 27	51, 137, 172, 225
21. 30	27, **66**	25. 8	169		
21. 31	199	25. 9	155	27. 29	53, 99
21. 32	154	25. 10	30, 88, 169	27. 30	158
21. 33	65, 123, 130	25. 11	62, 140	27. 33	65, **159**
21. 34	198, 322	25. 13	80, 157	27. 34	226, **274**

INDEX TO REFERENCES 365

Acts—continued		Romans—continued		Romans—continued	
	PAGE		PAGE		PAGE
27. 37	201	2. 18	151	6. 14	177
27. 38	233	2. 19	137, 148	6. 15	72
27. 39	127	2. 23	253	6. 16	334
27. 40	17, 154	2. 26	40	6. 19	185
27. 41	65	2. 27	187, 267	6. 20	238
27. 42	139	3. 1	22	6. 23	27
27. 43	52, 72, 235	3. 4	105, 145, 148	7. 2	212
27. 44	36, 272	3. 5	98, 152, 211	7. 3	141, 215, 239
28. 2, 3	56	3. 6	318	7. 4	143, 239
28. 6	89	3. 8	14	7. 5	187
28. 7	15	3. 9	56, 287	7. 6	213
28. 11	243	3. 11 f.	151	7. 7	92, 339
28. 12	244	3. 20	177, 196, 287	7. 7 f., 9 f.	39
28. 13	172, 225	3. 22	211, 212	7. 15	45
28. 14	72, 171	3. 24	190, 221	7. 16	115
28. 16	58	3. 25	180, 190, 253,	7. 17	37
28. 17	24, 55, 151		263, 268	7. 18	140
28. 19	158	3. 26	15, 143, 212,	7. 20	115
28. 22	89		222, 260	7. 24	214
28. 23	217	3. 28	137, 240	8. 1	187
28. 24	36	3. 29 f.	181	8. 2	39
28. 26	97	4. 1	98, 168	8. 3	13, 253
28. 27	23	4. 3	253	8. 4	285
28. 28	14	4. 4, 5	58	8. 11	115
28. 30	72	4. 7	296	8. 12	141, 238
		4. 8	96	8. 13, 14	240
Romans		4. 11	143, 211, 214,	8. 17	335
1. 1	211		267	8. 18	79, 350
1. 2	33	4. 13	140, 175, 211	8. 21	213
1. 4	260	4. 14	15, 260	8. 22	200
1. 5	28, 335	4. 15	344	8. 23	24, 41, 42
1. 7	174, 206, 234	4. 16	15, 47, 143,	8. 24	241
1. 9	137		260	8. 25	267
1. 11	143, 231	4. 17	246	8. 26	182, 194, 268,
1. 14	169, 239	4. 18	143, 226		320
1. 15	247, 268, 302	4. 20	242, 266	8. 27	268
1. 16	151	4. 24	58, 237	8. 28	151
1. 17	211	4. 25	268	8. 29	143, 215
1. 19	14	5. 2	70, 262	8. 32	331
1. 20	14, 143, 148, 240	5. 3	173, 253	8. 34	17, 26, 86, 151
1. 21	23	5. 5	23, 173	8. 35	211
1. 22	23, 146	5. 7	86, 173, 180	8. 37	265
1. 24	141, 262	5. 9, 11	253	8. 39	187, 197
1. 25	89	5. 12	272	9. 3	65, 91, 146
1. 26	213	5. 13	177	9. 4	27
1. 26 f.	339	5. 15	240	9. 5	15
1. 30	234	5. 17	220, 240	9. 6	47
2. 1	35, 151, 253	5. 18	214	9. 7	345
2. 3	35, 37	5. 20	344	9. 8	58, 313
2. 4	14, 63	6. 1	72	9. 11	268, 334
2. 5	213	6. 4	213, 221	9. 17	45, 105
2. 7	153, 212	6. 5	220	9. 20	33, 153, 226, 338
2. 8	317	6. 6	141	9. 21	36
2. 13	177	6. 10	238	9. 22	14
2. 14	40, 112, 185, 313	6. 11	137, 148, 246,	9. 22 f.	213
2. 15	23		264	9. 25	261, 282
2. 17	39, 253, 343	6. 12	76	9. 30	221
2. 17 f.	115	6. 13	42, 76	9. 33	237

ROMANS—continued		ROMANS—continued		1 CORINTHIANS—contd.	
	PAGE		PAGE		PAGE
10. 1	. 191	14. 9	. 71	3. 10	. 13
10. 6	. 135	14. 11	. 333	3. 13	. 49
10. 9	. 162	14. 13	. 140	3. 15	. 41
10. 10	. 291	14. 14	46, 137	3. 18	. 147
10. 11	. 237	14. 15	46, 242	3. 21	. 265
10. 14 f.	. 99	14. 16	. 189	4. 2	. 265
10. 17	. 330	14. 17	176, 221	4. 3	31, 139
10. 17 f.	. 283	14. 19	. 16	4. 4	42, 253
10. 18	338, 347	14. 20	. 267	4. 5	14, 111
10. 19	225, 282	14. 21	141, 253	4. 6	182, 271
10. 20	58, 156, 264	14. 22	. 265	4. 8	72, 91
11. 2	. 261	15. 2	. 72	4. 13	. 321
11. 6	. 318	15. 6	. 252	4. 15	115, 330
11. 8, 10	. 141	15. 7	. 335	4. 18	. 158
11. 11	. 190	15. 12	. 181	4. 20	. 265
11. 12	. 175	15. 13	145, 265	4. 21	. 241
11. 12 f.	. 181	15. 15	30, 73	5. 2	. 95
11. 13	. 149	15. 16	. 211	5. 5	. 46
11. 15	. 175	15. 19	. 221	5. 9	. 73
11. 17	. 115	15. 23	. 141	5. 10	. 318
11. 20	. 242	15. 24	. 112	5. 11	73, 149
11. 20 f.	. 99	15. 26	170, 209	5. 12	. 240
11. 21	. 221	16. 1	. 187	5. 13	. 194
11. 22	. 318	16. 2	41, 265	6. 1	. 274
11. 24	. 18	16. 3 ff.	. 47	6. 2	31, 253
11. 25	111, 238	16. 10	. 169	6. 3	. 283
11. 26	. 200	16. 11	15, 169	6. 5	. 23
11. 27	. 221	16. 13	. 77	6. 6	. 45
11. 28	. 268	16. 15	. 221	6. 7	43, 57
11. 30 f.	. 243	16. 16	. 212	6. 8	45, 51
11. 32	. 266	16. 18	. 23	6. 11	. 53
11. 33	. 33	16. 25	. 243	6. 15	. 24
11. 36	. 267	16. 27	. 343	6. 16	. 253
12. 1	28, 267			6. 18	. 216
12. 2	57, 240	1 CORINTHIANS		6. 19	. 23
12. 3	. 143	1. 5, 7	. 265	6. 20	. 333
12. 5	15, 198, 268	1. 8	. 186	7. 2	28, 191
12. 6	. 333	1. 9	. 267	7. 5	13, 95, 321
12. 7	177, 302	1. 10	89, 265	7. 6	. 268
12. 9 f.	. 177	1. 11	16, 169	7. 7	36, 191
12. 10	. 239	1. 12	. 38	7. 8	. 321
12. 15	. 78	1. 13	. 270	7. 9	. 79
12. 18	. 14	1. 18	212, 217, 239	7. 10	. 95
12. 19	. 173	1. 22	. 55	7. 12	. 37
12. 21	. 62	1. 25	14, 21	7. 13	. 325
13. 1	52, 152	1. 26	. 282	7. 14	262, 313, 318
13. 3	14, 22, 319, 342	1. 27 f.	14, 21, 55	7. 15	262, 263, 265
13. 5	. 148	1. 28	55, 151	7. 17	75, 262, 264
13. 8	. 140	1. 29	105, 196	7. 18, 22, 24	. 264
13. 9	42, 182, 197	2. 2	. 335	7. 21	. 76
13. 11	45, 139, 335	2. 3	. 37	7. 25	. 158
13. 12	. 52	2. 5	. 253	7. 26	. 140
13. 13	76, 158, 243	2. 6	. 264	7. 28	74, 219, 238
14. 1	. 22	2. 8	70, 99	7. 29	95, 303
4. 2	36, 137	2. 13	211, 234	7. 31	. 51
14. 4	57, 153, 238	3. 2	246, 330	7. 34	. 220
14. 5	. 36	3. 4	. 112	7. 35	14, 151
14. 6	. 238	3. 8	182, 191	7. 36	75, 115, 116

INDEX TO REFERENCES 367

1 CORINTHIANS—contd.		1 CORINTHIANS—contd.		1 CORINTHIANS—contd.	
	PAGE		PAGE		PAGE
7. 37	45	12. 23	30, 137	16. 15	325
8. 4, 5	175	12. 24	56	16. 17	190
8. 6	325	12. 28	36, 55	16. 21	186
8. 7	187	12. 31	221	16. 22	122
8. 10	143, 153	13. 1	246		
8. 12	189	13. 2	116, 200	2 CORINTHIANS	
8. 13	96	13. 3	100	1. 3	296
9. 1	283	13. 13	177	1. 4	200
9. 4 f.	139, 283	14. 4	176	1. 6	190
9. 5	246	14. 5	135, 138, 216, 321	1. 8	141
9. 8	283			1. 9	42, 70, 89, 175
9. 10	141	14. 7	151, 337	1. 10	28
9. 11	115, 190	14. 9	89, 151	1. 15 f.	257
9. 12	211, 231	14. 10	125, 127, 175	1. 17	14, 102
9. 15	100, 135, 139, 265	14. 11	264	1. 19	349
		14. 15	241	1. 20	14
9. 17	225, 247	14. 16	14	1. 22	23
9. 18	100, 143	14. 18	160	1. 23	191
9. 19	30, 157, 215	14. 19	32	1. 24	303
9. 20	169	14. 20	177, 220, 239	2. 1	45, 141, 238
9. 21	100, 215	14. 26	112	2. 2	45
9. 25	46	14. 27	31	2. 4	267
9. 26	158, 285	14. 28	116	2. 6	30, 46, 311
10. 3	186	14. 32	313	2. 7	46, 242
10. 4	67	14. 34	58	2. 11	282
10. 5	30, 253	14. 35	261	2. 12	82, 171
10. 6	67, 143	14. 39	140	2. 13	70, 142, 146, 148, 219, 238, 242
10. 7	135	15. 2	321		
10. 8	262	15. 3	5, 69	2. 14	53
10. 11	25, 46, 67	15. 7	200	2. 15	239
10. 14	173	15. 8	321	2. 16	36
10. 16	324	15. 9	31	2. 17	158
10. 17	231, 303	15. 11	46	3. 2	23
10. 18	215	15. 12	210	3. 3	214, 287
10. 20	215, 313	15. 18	330	3. 5	303
10. 24	197	15. 19	228	3. 10 f.	151
10. 27	151	15. 22	262	3. 11	267
10. 30	40, 241	15. 24	112	3. 13	144
10. 33	151, 190	15. 25	111	3. 15	23, 112
11. 5	21, 186, 220	15. 26	63	3. 16	113
11. 6	57, 140	15. 28	265	3. 17	344
11. 13	88, 149, 253	15. 32	63, 239	3. 17 f.	174
11. 14, 15	239	15. 37	86, 125, 127	3. 18	218
11. 18	62	15. 38	191	4. 3	264
11. 21	36	15. 39	196	4. 4	218
11. 22, 25	143	15. 41	172, 265	4. 6	23
11. 23	37, 259	15. 42	180, 291	4. 8	56
11. 26	111, 175	15. 45	253	4. 10	24
11. 31	42	15. 47	175	4. 10 f.	167
11. 34	94, 112, 261	15. 49	333	4. 11	217
12. 2	93, 125	15. 51	287	4. 13	194
12. 6	265	15. 58	265	4. 15	30
12. 8	36, 267	16. 2	187	4. 16	190, 243
12. 8 f.	197	16. 3	27, 135, 267	4. 17	14
12. 11	18, 191	16. 4	139, 141	4. 18	323
12. 13	247	16. 5 f.	63	5. 1	214, 218
12. 15, 16	210	16. 6	322	5. 4	272
12. 22	31	16. 9	82	5. 5	214

2 Corinthians—contd.		2 Corinthians—contd.		Galatians—contd.	
	PAGE		PAGE		PAGE
5. 7	267	10. 12	42, **160**	1. 13	186, 191
5. 10	201, 302, 333	10. 13	324	1. 16	264
5. 11	63	10. 14	285, 287	1. 22	212, 221
5. 12	343	10. 15	343	1. 23	81, 151
5. 13	238	10. 16	216	2. 3	157
5. 14	211	10. 18	45	2. 4	99, 100
5. 19	40, 89, 137, 175	11. 1	91, 330	2. 4 f.	343
5. 20	158	11. 2	55	2. 5	**220**
6. 3	343	11. 3	99	2. 6	49, 196, 343
6. 4	28	11. 4	197	2. 7	211, 247
6. 7	180, 186, 207	11. 5	137, 250	2. 9	37
6. 8	267	11. 6	343	2. 10	95
6. 11	23, 82	11. 8	27	2. 11	58
6. 13	**245**	11. 9	187	2. 12	144, 259
6. 14	89	11. 10	178	2. 13	136
6. 17	76	11. 14	300	2. 14	63
6. 18	253	11. 15	321	2. 15	181, 220
7. 3	23	11. 16	137	2. 17	330
7. 5	28, 70, 343	11. 18	177	2. 18	40, 115
7. 9	72, 260, 268	11. 20	256	2. 20	246, 264
7. 11	50, 140, 148	11. 21	70, 137, 268	3. 1	33, 187
	220, 239, 268, 330	11. 23	28, **250**, 271	3. 2	259
7. 12	144	11. 24	18	3. 5	53
7. 13	29, 258	11. 25	70, 72	3. 7	208, 260
7. 15	211	11. 26	181, 212	3. 8	**260**
8. 1	264	11. 29	38	3. 9	168, 260
8. 2, 3	268	11. 31	151	3. 10	136, 260
8. 6	143	12. 1	88	3. 14	168, **253**
8. 7	95, 259	12. 2	25, 46, 162, 178,	3. 15	337
8. 8	14, 217		221, 260	3. 16	158
8. 9	71, 72	12. 3, 5	46	3. 17	143
8. 10 f.	140	12. 4	88	3. 18	70
8. 11	141, 144	12. 10	28, 112	3. 19	58, 111, 267
8. 12	268, 320	12. 11	90, 250	3. 21	152
8. 13	95	12. 12	58	3. 22	21
8. 14	46, 105	12. 14	52, 139, 226	3. 23	79, 144, 350
8. 15	13	12. 16	157	3. 28	334
8. 17	30, 73	12. 17	70	3. 29	168
8. 18	73, 343	12. 18	173, 283	4. 6	23, 345
8. 19	217	12. 19	62, 190	4. 10	55
8. 22	29, 73, 162	12. 20	28, 58, 99,	4. 11	99, 325
8. 24	343		283, 302	4. 13	30, 267
9. 1	140	12. 21	322	4. 15	92
9. 2	30, 170, 190, 259	13. 4	260	4. 17	194
9. 3	73, 89, 187	13. 5	321	4. 18	55, 145
9. 4	95, 99	13. 9	45, 112, 195	4. 19	111
9. 5	73	13. 12	75	4. 20	56, 65, 91, 120
9. 7	63	13. 13	211	4. 23	70
9. 11, 13	343			4. 24	187
9. 11 f.	219	Galatians		4. 25	182
10. 2	140, 146	1. 1	267	4. 26 f.	47
10. 3	157	1. 4	186	4. 27	31
10. 4	238, 274, 343	1. 5	25	4. 30	96, 97
10. 6	139	1. 6 f.	197	5. 1	242
10. 7	15, 137, 268	1. 7	153, 321	5. 2	246
10. 8	339	1. 8 f.	122	5. 4	63, 73, 74
10. 9	267, 321	1. 9	115	5. 5	214, 317
10. 10	293	1. 10	92	5. 11	92

INDEX TO REFERENCES

Galatians—contd.		Ephesians—contd.		Philippians—contd.	
	PAGE		PAGE		PAGE
5. 12	57	4. 9	182, 215	1. 22	117, 264
5. 13	239	4. 10	25, 55	1. 23	29, 143
5. 14	42, 182, 201	4. 11	36	1. 24	140
5. 16	75	4. 13	111, 218	1. 26	191
5. 18	240	4. 14	89	2. 1	316
5. 20 f.	28	4. 16	190, 200	2. 2	189
5. 21	325	4. 17	75	2. 3	44, 52
5. 25	75	4. 18	23, 89, 235	2. 4	100, 197
5. 26	94	4. 21	167, 178	2. 6	21, 140, 226
6. 4	190	4. 22	148	2. 7	220
6. 6	200	4. 24	268	2. 11	236, 302
6. 8	190	4. 26	76	2. 12	42
6. 9	159, 182, 285	4. 28	81, 151	2. 15	175
6. 10	14	4. 29	25, 196, 274, 287	2. 18	246
6. 11	50, 73	5. 2–8	75	2. 20	270
6. 12	63, 100, 242	5. 4	90, 282	2. 23	15, 43, 270
6. 14	149, 175	5. 5	47, 85, 157, 196, 287, 303	2. 27	216
6. 16	110			2. 28	30, 73, 160
6. 17	235	5. 11	39	2. 30	218, 239
Ephesians		5. 12	40	3. 2	162
		5. 13	55	3. 3	239
1. 1	152, 263	5. 14	180	3. 4	157
1. 4	55	5. 18	76, 240	3. 5	220
1. 6	180, 218	5. 19	23, 43	3. 6	151
1. 10	271	5. 28	24	3. 7	246
1. 12	143	5. 32	37	3. 8	14, 52, 137, 338
1. 14	215	5. 33	15, 95	3. 9	191, 221
1. 15	263	6. 3	100	3. 10	136, 141, 142
1. 15 f.	28	6. 5	23	3. 11	221
1. 16	159	6. 7	158	3. 13	137, 148, 250
1. 17	100, 128	6. 8	333	3. 16	75, 78
1. 18	23, 100, 218	6. 9	25	3. 20	190, 206
1. 19	218	6. 10	235, 336	3. 21	41, 141, 214, 220
1. 20	26	6. 11	28, 144	4. 3	180, 335
2. 2	208	6. 14	24	4. 5	14, 226
2. 3	28	6. 16	186	4. 6	241
2. 5	176, 240	6. 17	14	4. 7	23
2. 8	45, 176	6. 18	267	4. 10	140, 270, 272
2. 10	190	6. 18 f.	270	4. 11	37, 146, 303
2. 12	27, 215, 235, 243	6. 19	129	4. 14	159, 189
2. 13	226	6. 21	344	4. 17	303
2. 14	215, 242	6. 22	23, 73	4. 18	15, 140
2. 15	265	Philippians		Colossians	
2. 16	43				
2. 20	181	1. 3	200, 207	1. 2	181, 263
2. 21	200	1. 4	30	1. 3	28, 206, 206, 228
3. 4	187	1. 5	179, 187, 256	1. 4	187
3. 5	243	1. 6	39, 45, 246	1. 5	180, 213, 252
3. 6	215	1. 7	23, 39, 143	1. 6	17, 55
3. 8	31, 139, 200	1. 8	137	1. 7	259
3. 11	25	1. 9	29	1. 9	17, 159, 247
3. 12	263	1. 10	89, 143, 151	1. 10	55
3. 15	175	1. 11	232, 247	1. 12	154, 206
3. 16	129, 256	1. 12	15	1. 13	214
3. 17	23, 230	1. 14	222, 242	1. 15	200, 210
3. 18	55	1. 16	36	1. 16	14, 70, 253, 256
4. 1	37, 230, 343	1. 17	137	1. 17	40
4. 4	263	1. 18	241, 330, 333	1. 18	41, 89

COLOSSIANS—contd.		1 THESSALONIANS—continued		1 TIMOTHY—contd.	
	PAGE		PAGE		PAGE
1. 20	43, 212	2. 19	190	1. 9	45
1. 21	89	3. 3	141	1. 10	197
1. 22	267, 331	3. 5	99, 143, 266	1. 12	80
1. 23	200	3. 7	190	1. 13	150, 151, 154
2. 1	50	3. 8	116	1. 17	25
2. 2	23, 206, 211, 230	3. 10	143, 189	1. 18	30
2. 4	95, 102	3. 11	41	1. 19	270
2. 5	189, 239	3. 13	23, 189	1. 20	210
2. 6	75, 167	4. 1	182	2. 6	42, 258, 271
2. 8	153	4. 3	139	2. 10, 15	267
2. 12	180, 218	4. 6	141	3. 1	232
2. 13	39	4. 7	263	3. 13	263
2. 14	219, 242	4. 9	139, 143	3. 14	30
2. 15	40, 51, 55, 265	4. 12	75	3. 15	303
2. 16	27	4. 14	167, 267	3. 16	57
2. 18	246	4. 16	41	4. 5	189, 267
2. 20	57, 251	5. 1	27	4. 8	274
2. 22	181	5. 3	112	4. 13	111, 321, 344
3. 1 f.	14	5. 5	208	4. 14	76, 267
3. 5	47, 311	5. 8	157	4. 15	265, 303
3. 6	208	5. 9	55	5. 13	160, 322
3. 8	25	5. 10	100	5. 19	321
3. 9	76, 94	5. 11	187	5. 22	76
3. 12	28	5. 13	43	5. 24	195
3. 13	44, 234	5. 15	78, 98	6. 2	39
3. 14	212, 317	5. 23	41	6. 4	270
3. 15	23, 264	5. 27	149	6. 5	235
3. 16	23, 43, 230			6. 8	58
3. 17	206	2 THESSALONIANS		6. 12, 14	77
3. 18	90	1. 4	264	6. 15	243
3. 20	263	1. 8	213, 316	6. 17	193
3. 23	158	1. 10	57	6. 20	33, 77
4. 2	265	1. 12	105	6. 21	235, 270
4. 3	154, 212	2. 2	137, 158		
4. 5	75	2. 3	208	2 TIMOTHY	
4. 7	15	2. 4	149, 151	1. 4	189
4. 8	23, 73	2. 6	21, 151	1. 9	27
4. 12	57	2. 7	21	1. 13	185, 221
4. 16	95	2. 15	77, 247	1. 14	77
4. 18	189	2. 16	41	2. 2	77, 267
		2. 17	23, 189	2. 3	77
1 THESSALONIANS		3. 5	23, 189, 211, 212	2. 7	111
1. 1	206	3. 8	144	2. 10	232
1. 3	190, 211, 218	3. 9	25, 303	2. 12	115
1. 5	50, 175	3. 10	190	2. 14	78, 272
1. 7	25, 182	3. 11	62, 161	2. 15	77
1. 8	182, 187, 221, 286	3. 13	159	2. 18	235, 270
1. 9	49, 137	3. 14	187	2. 20	36
1. 10	180	3. 15	161	2. 22	269
2. 3	270	3. 16	41	2. 25	98, 99, 129, 178
2. 4	23, 147, 247			2. 26	194, 266
2. 6	259	1 TIMOTHY		3. 1	179
2. 8	231	1. 1	206	3. 4	216
2. 9	144	1. 3	95	3. 7	178
2. 10	137, 226, 239	1. 3 f.	343	3. 8	270
2. 12	143	1. 4	216, 221	3. 11	50
2. 14	212	1. 6	235	3. 15	62, 176, 263
2. 16	143, 189	1. 7	49	3. 16	199

INDEX TO REFERENCES

2 Timothy—contd.		Hebrews—contd.		Hebrews—contd.	
	PAGE		PAGE		PAGE
4. 2	77	3. 6	**311**	8. 1	175
4. 3	139	3. 8	23	8. 2	27, 324
4. 5	37, 77	3. 10	193	8. 3	109, 117, 143
4. 6	37	3. 11	333	8. 5	70
4. 7	84	3. 12	146, 213	8. 6	232
4. 8	213, 226	3. 13	42	8. 10	23
4. 9	30	3. 14	115	8. 11	30
4. 13	171	3. 15	23	8. 12	96
4. 15	227	3. 16	267	9. 1	186
4. 17	313	3. 18	86, 137	9. 2	27, 47
		4. 1	99	9. 2 f.	**31**
Titus		4. 2	58	9. 3	27, 269
1. 1	178	4. 3	153, 157, 333	9. 5	**21, 270**
1. 2	27, 325	4. 4	17, 52	9. 7	235
1. 5	37	4. 7	23, 261	9. 8	**212**
1. 12	**192**	4. 10	52	9. 9	47, 268, 311
1. 15	190	4. 11	**257**	9. 12	267
1. 16	146	4. 12	216	9. 24 f.	27, 135
2. 4	101	4. 13	274, 331	9. 25	241
2. 7	270	4. 14	232	9. 26	**90**, 272
2. 9	192	5. 1	221	10. 1	293
2. 10	217	5. 7	**18, 251**	10. 2	92, 143, 159, 318
2. 11	186	5. 8	157	10. 7	141
2. 12	193	5. 11	28, 220	10. 12	269
2. 13	**181**	5. 12	89, 139, 141, 146	10. 13	111
3. 5	190, 324	5. 13	**213**	10. 15	143
3. 9	28	6. 1	28, 215	10. 16	23
3. 14	**266**	6. 2	**218**	10. 17	97
		6. 3	28, 114	10. 19	**212**
Philemon		6. 4 f., 5	**233**	10. 22	23
5	189, **256**	6. 9	28, 247	10. 25	42, 43, **190**
7	267	6. 10	136	10. 26	143, **178**, 269
8, 9	157	6. 11	28	10. 27	195
12	73	6. 12	232, 331	10. 29	220
13	65, 91	6. 13	**80**, 268	10. 31	140
14	**13**	6. 14	157, **336**	10. 33	45, **215**
19	95, 191	6. 15	232	10. 34	148
		6. 16	268	10. 37	**50**
Hebrews		6. 17	14, 241, 253	10. 38	**43**
1. 2	25	6. 18	72, 153, 232	10. 39	**208**
1. 3	**214**	7. 1	45, 168	11. 1	307
1. 4	46, 181	7. 2 f.	**159**	11. 2	157
1. 5	209	7. 4	**50**	11. 3	25, 143, 287
1. 6	200	7. 5	157	11. 4	146
1. 9	215	7. 6	70, 168	11. 5	141
1. 13	111, 209	7. 7	**21**	11. 11	220
2. 1	52	7. 8	**152**	11. 12	**45**
2. 4	190	7. 9	70, 136, 151	11. 15	46, 52, 139, 259
2. 6	234, **318**	7. 13	146	11. 17	**65**
2. 8	**145**, 146	7. 15	29, 115	11. 21	225
2. 10	80, 149, 267	7. 16	268	11. 23	17, 225
2. 13	89	7. 18	14, 190	11. 27	**320**
2. 14	231, 232	7. 20 f.	36	11. 29	**17**
2. 15	45, 140, 144	7. 23	**30**	11. 32	157
2. 17	143, 221	7. 23 f.	36, 143	11. 33	47, 232
2. 18	253	7. 24	148, 186	11. 34	259
3. 1 f.	161	7. 26	147	11. 36	**197**
3. 5	87	7. 27	**191**	11. 40	55

INDEX TO REFERENCES

HEBREWS—contd.		JAMES—continued		1 PETER—continued	
	PAGE		PAGE		PAGE
12. 1	. 347	2. 10	. **110**	1. 20	. 27
12. 3	. 221	2. 11, 12	. 177	1. 22	. 77
12. 7	174, 267	2. 14	114, 146, 173	1. 24	. 73
12. 9	. 334	2. 15	114, 159	2. 1	28, 200
12. 10	36, 151	2. 16	. 210	2. 4	. 258
12. 11	. 151	2. 17	. 114	2. 6	97, 237, **292**
12. 15	99, 213	2. 19	. 184	2. 12	213, 260
12. 16	. **307**	2. 20	. 33	2. 13	52, 200
12. 17	85, 157	2. 25	. 241	2. 14	. 267
12. 18	. 232	3. 1	. **287**	2. 15	148, 226
12. 23	. 350	3. 2	45, 174	2. 16	. 52
12. 25	. 175	3. 3	24, 144	2. 17	. 77
12. 26	. 225	3. 4	. 31	2. 20	. **115**
12. 27	158, 182	3. 6	. 183	2. 24	. **22**
13. 2	159, 226	3. 7	. 240	2. 25	. 52
13. 3	. 234	3. 8	. **316**	3. 1	100, 192, 217
13. 4	. 27	3. 10	. 90	3. 3	. 186
13. 5	58, 96, 97, 343	3. 11	. **18**	3. 5	. 192
13. 6	. 148	3. 13	. 49	3. 8	. **218**
13. 7	. 47	3. 14	. 23	3. 13	87, 114
13. 8	. 25	3. 18	215, 238	3. 14	**212**, 245
13. 10	. 139	4. 2	143, 147, 148	3. 19	. **153**
13. 11	27, 190, 267	4. 2 f.	. 55	3. 20	**153**, 254, 267
13. 13	198, 340, 347	4. 8	. 23	4. 3	. 28
13. 16	57, 242	4. 9, 10	. 76	4. 5	139, 181, 226
13. 17	87, 158	4. 11	. 177	4. 6	. **102, 291**
13. 18	62, 75	4. 12	. 153	4. 11	25, 101, 158
13. 18 f.	. 28	4. 13	. 192	4. 12	158, 242
13. 19	. 30	4. 14	. **16**	4. 13	. 320
13. 20	. 186	4. 15	45, 114, **144**	4. 14	126, 187
13. 21	. 25	4. 17	. 39	4. 15	. 76
13. 22	. 267	5. 3	179, **264**	4. 17	126, 139, 217
13. 22 f.	. 28	5. 4	. 258	4. 18	. **13, 22**
13. 23	30, 162	5. 5, 6	. 23	5. 1	215, 217
13. 24	. **15**	5. 7	18, 77, 111	5. 2	. 77
		5. 8	23, 77	5. 3	. 139
JAMES		5. 9	. 27	5. 4	. 213
1. 1	78, 186	5. 10	. 246	5. 8	. **206**
1. 3	. **14**	5. 12	75, **76**	5. 9	55, 238
1. 4	89, 101	5. 13, 14	. 210	5. 10	39, 154, 186, 190
1. 6	. 175	5. 15	. 89	5. 11	. 25
1. 7	. **76**	5. 16	**56**, 106	5. 12	. 256
1. 11	. 73	5. 17	52, 142, 291		
1. 12	213, 296	5. 19	115, 210	2 PETER	
1. 13	215, 258			1. 1	181, 220
1. 13–15	. 63	1 PETER		1. 4	. 215
1. 18	. **195**	1. 1	170, 235	1. 5	. 45
1. 19	85, 143	1. 2	. 262	1. 7	. 192
1. 24	49, 73	1. 3	. 190	1. 8	. 217
1. 25	177, 213, **218**	1. 4	25, 213, **236**	1. 9	. 190
1. 26	. 147	1. 5	. 179	1. 10	. 160
1. 27	139, 215	1. 6	. **322**	1. 12	. 157
2. 1	. 28	1. 7	**14**, 153	1. 17	174, **183**
2. 2	23, 115	1. 11	. 48	1. 19	23, 52, 111, 159
2. 3	. 37	1. 13	24, 77	1. 20	. 196
2. 4	. **213**	1. 16	. 86	1. 21	. 258
2. 5	55, 238	1. 17	77, **247**	2. 3	. 325
2. 6	**13, 23**	1. 18	. 186	2. 6	**215**, 240

INDEX TO REFERENCES

2 Peter—continued		1 John—continued		Revelation—contd.	
	PAGE		PAGE		PAGE
2. 7	. 217	5. 6	226, 267	2. 14	151, 232, **246**
2. 12–5	. 158	5. 8	. 254	2. 15	. 232
2. 13	. 87	5. 10	. 267	2. 16	. 238, 239
2. 14	215, 233	5. 14	. 55	2. 17	. 325
2. 15	. 213	5. 15	. 116	2. 19	. 190
2. 16	. 192	5. 16	. **281**	2. 20	. 314
2. 19	. 240	5. 20	13, **44**	2. 22	. 116
2. 20	. 62	5. 21	42, 77	2. 24	. 187
2. 21	90, 149			2. 25	. 77
2. 22	16, 54	2 John		2. 28	. 70
3. 1	. 192	1	. 178	3. 2	. 79, 89
3. 2	217, **218**, 349	3	. 178, 304	3. 3	69, 115, 248
3. 4	17, 62	4	. 178, 209	3. 8	. 325
3. 5	175, 267	6	. 45	3. 9	100, 148, 325
3. 6	. 222	7	81, 153, 162	3. 10	. 345
3. 10	. 174	8	. 316	3. 12	97, 171, 314
3. 11	. 48	9	. 45, 51	3. 14	. **14**, 210
3. 14	. 239	12	. 267	3. 15	. **91**
3. 16	. 39	13	. 313	3. 16	. 79, 345
				3. 17	. 183
1 John		3 John		3. 18	. 101, 149
1. 1	. 232	1, 3	. 178	3. 19	. **173**
1. 4	28, 89	2	. 270	3. 20	. 115, 335
1. 5	. 233	4	29, 161, 191	4. 1	. 315
2. 1	. 72	6	. 80, 159	4. 3	. 185
2. 3	45, 139	8	. 178	4. 4	. 23
2. 5	. 88	9	. **40**	4. 5	. 311
2. 6	139, 146	12	. 57, 178	4. 8	. 266, 314
2. 9	62, 146	15	. 304	4. 9	. 112
2. 12, 14	. 73			4. 9 f.	. 86
2. 16	. **213**	Jude		5. 5	. 136
2. 19	**91**, 95	1	174, 240, **264**	5. 6	311, 314
2. 21	196, 287	2, 9	. 121	5. 7	. 67
2. 27	. 139	4	. 153	5. 8	. 311
3. 4	. 183	11	234, **238**, 242	5. 9	. 253
3. 8	. 62	13	. 28, 175	5. 11	. 210
3. 9	. 72	14	. 238, 241	5. 12	. 315
3. 10	. 313	15	. 56	6. 1	. 187
3. 11	45, 139	18	. 27, 89	6. 4	. 39, **100**
3. 14	. 161	22 f.	. 36	6. 6	. 27
3. 15	. 196	25	. 25	6. 11	25, **100**, 111
3. 16	. 139			7. 1	. 101, 196
3. 17	. 98	Revelation		7. 2	26, 172, 325
3. 19	23, 260	1. 4	. **230**	7. 3	. 111
3. 20	23, 189	1. 5, 11	. **314**	7. 4	. 314
3. 21	. 23	1. 8	. 174	7. 9	. 314, 325
3. 23	. 139	1. 13	. 274	7. 14	. 69
4. 2, 3	. 162	1. 15	27, 158, 314	7. 16	. 97, 196
4. 4	. 216	1. 18	. 89	7. 17	. **218**
4. 6	**260**, 260	1. 19	. 313	8. 1	. **93**
4. 10, 14	. 70	1. 20	. **324**	8. 3	. **100**
4. 12	. 88	2. 2	. **325**	8. 4	. **238**
4. 15	. 183	2. 5	115, 238, **239**	8. 5	. 69, 70
4. 21	. 139	2. 8	. **71**	8. 9	. 312, 314
5. 2	45, 112, 139	2. 9	. 148	9. 4	. **100**, 196
5. 3	. **139**	2. 10	. 209, 213	9. 5	. **100**, 113
5. 4	. 21	2. 11	. 96	9. 6	. 63, 97
5. 5	. 183	2. 13	. 273, 314	9. 7	. **24**

INDEX TO REFERENCES

REVELATION—contd.		REVELATION—contd.		REVELATION—contd.	
	PAGE		PAGE		PAGE
9. 10	220	14. 1	315	18. 12	17, 31
9. 11	17, 230	14. 2	27	18. 14	97
9. 12	188	14. 4	110	18. 15	190
9. 14	314, 315	14. 6	53	18. 16	17
9. 17	24	14. 7	246, 315	18. 19	24
9. 18	312	14. 8	218	18. 20	35
9. 19	24	14. 9	272	18. 22	196
9. 20	100, 209	14. 10	213	18. 24	27
10. 6	137	14. 11	25	19. 3	70
10. 7	53, 112	14. 13	100, 102	19. 5	35
11. 1	315	14. 15	334	19. 6	315
11. 4	314	14. 18	215	19. 15	40, 218
11. 5	25, 116	14. 19	314	20. 2	314
11. 6	101, 139	15. 2	240, 260	20. 3, 5	111
11. 8	22	15. 7	209	20. 4	24, 71
11. 9	209	15. 8	111	20. 8	325
11. 13	210	16. 6	27	20. 10	81
11. 15	315	16. 9	136, 245	21. 2	238
11. 17	69	16. 10	89, 260	21. 6	39
11. 18	139, 313	16. 12	26, 172	21. 9	94, 186, 314
12. 4	79	16. 13, 14	313	21. 11	31
12. 5	315	16. 15	101	21. 13	26
12. 6	46, 258	16. 18	46	21. 16	240
12. 7	141	16. 19	58, 218	21. 21	198
12. 9	152	17. 1	27, 94	21. 24	313
12. 12	35	17. 2	325	21. 25	325
12. 14	46, 101, 210	17. 3	213, 233, 315	21. 27	196
13. 1	213, 272	17. 4	314, 315	22. 2	188, 198
13. 3	175, 214	17. 9	46	22. 3	196
13. 5	139	17. 10	178	22. 5	172
13. 8	325	17. 15	26, 27	22. 14	102
13. 11	220, 315	17. 16	40	22. 15	151
13. 12	100, 175	17. 17	23, 111	22. 18, 19	115
13. 14	71, 315	18. 7	345		
13. 16	24, 100	18. 9	112		

(b) SEPTUAGINT.

GENESIS		GENESIS—continued		GENESIS—continued	
	PAGE		PAGE		PAGE
1. 6	23, 226	13. 14	26	21. 14	154
1. 9	226	14. 11	22	21. 22	108
1. 11	226	14. 19	240	22. 3	154
3. 19	144	15. 7	136	22. 14	104
3. 24	212	16. 2	142	22. 17	157
4. 2	227	16. 5	70	23. 6	235
5. 4	143	17. 17	333	24. 12	56
6. 3	96	17. 19	336	24. 15	154
6. 17	108	18. 1	322	24. 30	70
7. 1	193	18. 9	155	24. 33	144
7. 3, 9	187	18. 13	50	25. 1	227
8. 13	187	18. 21	95	26. 5	55
10. 19	144	18. 33	159	26. 11	215
11. 2	26, 145	19. 16	145	26. 12	162
11. 8	159	19. 22	144	26. 28	70, 157
12. 12	112	20. 6	142	27. 36	193
13. 10	144	20. 15	108	28. 6	145

INDEX TO REFERENCES

GENESIS—continued

	PAGE
28. 15	144
29. 20	144
29. 34	70
30. 8	95
30. 33	108
30. 42	93
30. 38	143
31. 1	70
32. 16	18, 23
33. 3	144
35. 18	145
37. 9	93
38. 23	70
38. 26	31
39. 3	107
39. 15	145
41. 19	325
41. 55	70
42. 2	254
42. 15 f.	336
42. 30	70
43. 16	248
43. 25	144
44. 1	108
44. 12	155
44. 31	145
44. 34	95
45. 28	154
47. 19	95
49. 12	32, 216
49. 15	143

EXODUS

	PAGE
1. 10	113
2. 2	17
3. 2	213
3. 6	306
3. 7	157
3. 14	230
4. 21	322
5. 22, 23	70
6. 4	70
6. 11	104
8. 6	22
8. 23	213
8. 29(25)	44
9. 15	213
9. 18	248
12. 21	154
14. 11	144
17. 3	232
18. 11	32
19. 24	342
20. 10	27
20. 17	232
27. 20	143
29. 29	213
31. 3	232

EXODUS—continued

	PAGE
33. 8	93
34. 3	283
34. 24	232
40. 2	187

LEVITICUS

	PAGE
10. 16	44
11. 43	97
20. 8	55
21. 17	49
23. 29	284
23. 32	27
27. 12	110

NUMBERS

	PAGE
1. 1, 18	187
7. 6	154
9. 14	335
11. 4	154
11. 15	95
12. 3	32
14. 22	193
14. 40	44
16. 29^b	287
16. 31	159
21. 9	93
21. 27	95
22. 6	32
22. 20	154
23. 7	26
24. 14	246

DEUTERONOMY

	PAGE
1. 42	97
1. 45	154
4. 21	104
5. 14	95
5. 21	232
6. 2	104
6. 14	97
7. 12	113
7. 16	97
9. 28	144
21. 8	40
31. 6	286
32. 21	282

JOSHUA

	PAGE
1. 11	231
22. 24	95
23. 1, 2	220

JUDGES

	PAGE
6. 15	30
7. 5	21
11. 35	35
13. 2	230
16. 15	193

JUDGES—continued

	PAGE
19. 2A	17
19. 6	155
20. 47A	17
Ru. 2. 11	143
„ 2. 22	35

1 KINGDOMS

	PAGE
1. 8	32
1. 9	143
1. 26	146
2. 19	144
3. 11	322
4. 7	21
5. 9	143
8. 5	55
10. 24	333
14. 34	40
14. 47	141
16. 4	151
17. 13, 14	30
20. 3	85, 157

2 KINGDOMS

	PAGE
7. 7	50
7. 10	208
11. 15	156
23. 3	99
24. 14	97

3 KINGDOMS

	PAGE
1. 1	220
1. 20	314
5. 14 (28)	317
17. 20	142
19. 5, 7	155
19. 7	342

4 KINGDOMS

	PAGE
1. 3, 6, 16	144
2. 24	7, 245
8. 14	50
10. 6	156
19. 4, 6, 22	245

1 CHRONICLES

	PAGE
9. 25	141
17. 6	50
21. 3	95
21. 18	104

EZRA-NEHEMIAH

	PAGE
1 Esd. 1. 15	61
3. 13	154
4. 18	196
4. 46, 47, 50	104
4. 49	238
6. 27, 31	104

Ezra-Nehemiah—continued	page	Job—continued	page	Tobit—continued	page
8. 21	144	7. 9	96	6. 13	27
2 Esd. 6. 8	141	12. 5	250	6. 15, 18	104
Ne. 7. 65	104	27. 1	227	8. 4B	104
		29. 1	227	8. 12B	95
Psalms		32. 13	95	8. 19	27
1. 20	122	36. 1	227	10. 7B	235
4. 9	18			10. 12B	22
6. 2	283	Wisdom		11. 16	161
13 (14). 1 ff.	151	1. 8	96	12. 13	226
17. 33, 35	343	2. 12	245	13. 2, 4, 7, 11	25
21. 2	72	3. 1	96	14. 9	104
23 (24). tit	187	6. 6	52		
27. 3, 4	21	6. 22	96	Minor Prophets	
32. 6	21	8. 21	242	Hos. 9. 13	141
38. 2	142	12. 10	96	Am. 3. 5	144
38. 5	95	13. 5	218	5. 25	35
38. 14	104	13. 6	337	5. 27	26
44(43). 22	210	14. 4	104	6. 12	215
45. 6	250	16. 3, 20	40	7. 2	114
45 (44). 8	32			8. 10	212
60 (61). 4	213	Sirach		Jon. 1. 3	40
60. 5	25	prol. 9	215	3. 3	239
68. 24	142	4. 13	232	Soph. 2. 3	213
74. 18	21	6. 1	232	Hag. 2. 4	35
76. 8	25	11. 7	113	2. 9	32
77. 22	238	13. 24	284	Hab. 1. 5	96
78. 24	135	15. 15	213	Sach. 3. 8	35
83. 5	23	16. 8	40	Mal. 1. 7, 12	145
88. 23	208	18. 1	25	1. 9	104
88. 53	25	28. 1	151	Ze. 3. 6	144
90. 11	142	29. 25	250		
102. 19	21	35. 21, 23	238	Isaiah	
105. 12, 24	238	36. 15	187	3. 9	70
106. 3	26	37. 15	104	10. 16	98
117. 23	21	38. 14	104	11. 11	258
118. 50, 56	21	39. 18	213	13. 4	70, 216
119. 7	93	44. 18	104	20. 3	70
142. 2	196	45. 24	104	22. 3	70
				24. 13	114
Proverbs		Esther		26. 20	307
3. 9	215	1. 5	58	27. 12	187
4. 17	240	2. 18	27	30. 12	89
21. 26	232	5. 3	210	33. 24	98
		5. 13	113	36. 12	104
Ecclesiastes		9. 22	27	38. 14	215
2. 9	32			40. 7	72
2. 16	231	Judith		40. 17	253
3. 15	141	7. 28	104	42. 21	104
9. 4	32	9. 12	336	45. 23	333
		12. 19	154	48. 10, 16, 17	70
Canticles				49. 1	259
1. 8	31	Tobit		49. 6	71
1. 16	250	2. 9	194	51. 22	71
5. 1	104	3. 6	32	52. 11	76
		3. 15	104, 239	53. 4	40
Job		3. 17	194	53. 5	70
6. 1	157	5. 7, 9	104	54. 6	71
6. 9	155			54. 17	215

INDEX TO REFERENCES

ISAIAH—continued

	PAGE
57. 18	70
57. 19	254
60. 1	71
61. 1	71
66. 8	70
66. 9, 19	71

JEREMIAH

11. 5	156
11. 6	109
11. 21	97
12. 6	238
15. 17	18
17. 8	159
20. 13	236
29. 11	100
34. 10	144
51 (44). 18	159
Ba. 3. 28	144
Ep. Je. 65	7, 245

EZEKIEL

9. 11	155
10. 11	93
14. 4	213
16. 49	232
29. 9	144
34. 7–9	144
36. 3	144
37. 23	95
39. 14	17
44. 12	213

DANIEL

2. 8 O′	71
2. 10	196
2. 31, 34, 41, 45	71
3. 33	314
3. 92 (25)	44
4. 22, 28, 29	292
4. 30b O′	69
5. 52	25
6. 27 θ′	25
7. 8 O′	196

DANIEL—continued

	PAGE
12. 1 θ	70
Su. 28	100
Su. 33	16
Su. 37	161
Bel. 3. 4	173
Bel. 12	113

1 MACCABEES

1. 9	95, 143
1. 11	17
1. 20	143
2. 15	16
2. 47	208
2. 52	253
2. 54, 58	144
3. 33	144
4. 2	136, 258
4. 28	136
5. 19, 54	144
5. 29	321
7. 7	154
7. 45	144
8. 6	154
9. 37	27
9. 44	16
10. 3	136
10. 38	144
10. 58	27
11. 57	156
11. 58	241
12. 10	144
12. 36	18, 143
13. 16	185
13. 20	93
14. 41	144
15. 28	80
16. 9	144

2 MACCABEES

1. 3	143
1. 9	95
2. 6	136
2. 13	268

2 MACCABEES—contd.

	PAGE
2. 27	337
2. 31	14
3. 16	14
4. 4	14
4. 5	18
4. 13	282
4. 27	58
4. 34	26
4. 36, 45	144
4. 40	220
5. 11	220
5. 18	92
5. 27	144, 159
6. 18	65, 220
7. 7	333
7. 9	140, 190
7. 24	26
10. 33	225
11. 22	52
14. 18	337
14. 21	18
14. 32	26
14. 42	32
15. 3	333
15. 5	337
15. 36	187

3 MACCABEES

1. 16	241
4. 5	276
4. 11	144
5. 20	70
5. 32	92
5. 34	198
6. 6	143
7. 3	143
13. 27	337
15. 11	337

4 MACCABEES

6. 13	14
10. 19	144
16. 7	17
18. 8	14

(c) OTHER VERSIONS OF OLD TESTAMENT.

AQUILA

	PAGE
Ge. 12. 9	52
17. 1	279
Dt. 33. 3	250
Jg. 5. 27	277
1 Km. 22. 4	279

AQUILA—continued

	PAGE
2 Km. 6. 14	279
3 Km. 15. 6, 32	277
Isa. 7. 2	279
Ezk. 1. 17	250
7. 23(22)	250

SYMMACHUS

	PAGE
Ps. 57 (58). 10	113
Je. 40 (47). 5	113
49 (42). 22	85

(d) Pseudepigrapha of Old Testament.

Test. XII Patr.—

Test. Levi.		PAGE
8. 3		11
		25
„ 14. 1		25
„ 18. 4		17
Test. Jud. 5. 2		26
Test. Naphth. 7. 1		
		27
Test. Benj. 7. 4		188

Greek Enoch—

3. 1	.	50
9. 4	.	25
10. 6–10		91
98. 12, 99. 10		97

Orac. Sibyll.—

3. 50	.	25
3. 308	.	27
3. 767	.	25

Ps. Sol. 1. 5 . 96

Epist. Aristeas—

		PAGE
51	.	16
59	.	124
126	.	26
137	.	159

Vitae Prophet.—

Elisha 2	.	70
Dan. 6	.	70
Nah. 2	.	70
Mal. 2	.	70
Jer. 13 f.	.	70
Jer. 14	.	96

Test. Solomon (T.Sol.)

| D 4. 4 | . | 124 |
| 17. 15 | . | 208 |

Test. Abraham (T.Abr.)
(M. R. James, *Texts and Studies*, II 2)

Rec. A p. 82		
line 11	.	320
Rec. B p. 106		
line 4, 11, 18		156

Test. Abraham—*contd.*

	PAGE
Rec. B p. 107	
line 1	. 156
Rec. B p. 108	
line 1, 21, 23	156
Rec. B p. 110	
line 7, 16, 21	156
Rec. B p. 110	
line 20	. 155
Rec. B p. 111	
line 18	. 156
Rec. B p. 112	
line 6, 9	156
Rec. B p. 113	
line 9	. 156
Rec. B p. 113	
line 29	. 194
Rec. B p. 114	
line 6	. 156
Rec. B p. 116	
line 27	. 194
Rec. B p. 118	
line 15	. 156
Rec. B p. 118	
line 26	. 320

(e) Early Christian Writings.

Clement of Rome (i/A.D.)

	PAGE
1 Cl. 2. 1	. 58
2. 4	. 53
4. 8, 10	. 279
10. 1	. 146
10. 4	. 26
12. 2	. 168
12. 4	. 16
12. 5	. 157
12. 7	. 227
18. 11	. 279
19. 3	. 137
20. 12	. 25
21. 3	. 137

1 Cl—*continued*

	PAGE
27. 5	. 96
28. 3	. 279
30. 4	. 137
32. 4	. 25
34. 3	. 279
34. 5	. 137
35. 3	. 25
35. 4	. 58
35. 10	. 279
37. 2	. 137
38. 2	. 109
38. 4	. 25

1 Cl.—*continued*

	PAGE
39. 5, 6	. 144
42. 4	. 247
43. 6	. 25
48. 6	. 29
50. 1	. 137
50. 3	. 192
51. 3	. 31
55. 2	. 162
55. 6	. 25
60. 2	. 86
61. 2	. 25
63. 2	. 192

Epistle of Barnabas (i/ii A.D.)

	PAGE
Barn 4. 3	. 100
5. 9	. 216
5. 13	. 139
6. 9	. 279
8. 5	. 50
8. 6	. 58
10. 1	. 50

Barn—*continued*

	PAGE
10. 3	. 216
10. 4	. 97
11. 1	97, 137
11. 7	. 279
11. 8	. 110
12. 2	30, 93

Barn—*continued*

	PAGE
14. 6	. 137
17. 2	. 96
18. 2	. 25
19. 1	. 94
19. 2 ff.	. 86
19. 8	. 232

INDEX TO REFERENCES

Shepherd of Hermas (i/ii A.D.)

V *Visions* M *Mandates* S *Similitudes*

	PAGE		PAGE		PAGE
V I. 1. 2	172	VII. 5	46	VIII. 7. 1	39
I. 4. 1, 3	26	VIII. 2	136	IX. 2. 3	187
II. 1. 3	148	IX. 2, 5	97	IX. 2. 5	42
II. 2. 6	86	X. 1. 6	30	IX. 4. 5	93
III. 1. 2	194	XII. 3. 1	86	IX. 5. 1	146
III. 3. 1	15	S I. 4	246	IX. 6. 4	93
III. 6. 1	208	I. 5	97	IX. 6. 8	148
III. 7. 2	142	I. 11	191	IX. 7. 6	100
III. 10. 10	30	II. 1	42	IX. 8. 3	138
III. 12. 3	74	II. 3	110	IX. 9. 1	98, 135
III. 13. 2	74	II. 5	190	IX. 10. 5 f.	111
IV. 1. 5	42	IV. 5	94, 190	IX. 10. 7	31
IV. 1. 6	137	V. 2. 2	111	IX. 11. 1	111
IV. 2. 1	17	V. 4. 3A	190	IX. 12. 4	126
IV. 3. 7	243	V. 7. 3	39, 99,	IX. 12. 8	17
M III. 2	74		113	IX. 13. 2	58
III. 5	45	VI. 1. 5	148	IX. 17. 3	93
IV. 1. 7	148	VI. 5. 3	17	IX. 18. 3	148
IV. 2. 2	146	S VIII. 1. 4	17, 49	IX. 19. 3	273
IV. 3. 7	116	VIII. 1. 14	273	IX. 20. 4	27
IV. 4. 3	17	VIII. 2. 5, 9	148	IX. 26. 2	74
V. 1. 2	116	VIII. 2. 8	187	IX. 28. 4	29
VI. 2. 2	190	VIII. 6. 1	148	IX. 28. 5	100
VI. 2. 10	100	VIII. 6. 6	17		

Ignatius, bp. of Antioch (ii/A.D.)

	PAGE		PAGE		PAGE
Eph. 2. 2	124	10	136	Rom. 5. 2	124
4. 2	101	Pol. 1. 2	27	5. 3	49
5. 3	73	Pol. 2. 2	279	10. 2	162
11. 1	78	5. 1	58	Sm 2	136
15. 3	279	6. 2	124	7. 2	18
Magn. 2. 12	124	8. 3	94	12. 1	91
Tral. 3. 2	137				

Martyrdom of Polycarp (ii/A.D.)

	PAGE		PAGE		PAGE
12. 1	30	16. 2	27	31. 7. 4	227

Didache (ii/A.D.)

	PAGE		PAGE		PAGE
3. 1	216	4. 3	136	8. 2	25
3. 8	89	4. 10	286	11. 7	86

Epistle to Diognetus (c. A.D. 150)

	PAGE		PAGE		PAGE
2. 3	140	6. 1	136	12. 1	53
4. 3	27				

Justin Martyr (ii/A.D.)

	PAGE			PAGE
Apology I 22; 32	70		67. 8	248

Clement of Rome: so-called Second Epistle (ii/A.D.?)

	PAGE			PAGE			PAGE
2 Cl. 1. 2	. 49	14. 2	.	137	20. 4	.	92
3. 1	. 245	2 Cl. 17. 3	.	30			
10. 5	. 159	19. 4	.	27			

Clementine Homilies (ii/A.D.? v/A.D.? vi/A.D.?)

	PAGE			PAGE			PAGE
1. 7	. 137	9. 1	.	17	15. 4	.	197
1. 7, 11	. 190	9. 21	.	240	16. 6, 7	.	137
1. 9	85, 91	9. 22	.	141	17. 18	.	42
1. 14	. 30	10. 2	.	146	19. 1	.	197
2. 25	. 136	10. 15	.	190, 241	19. 2	.	99
3. 8	. 190	11. 3	.	98	19. 6	.	49
3. 68	. 240	11. 28	.	137	19. 23	.	240
3. 69	. 282	12. 1	.	136	20. 13	.	136
6. 11	. 49	14. 7	.	137	ep. ad Jac. 3	.	89
8. 11	. 136	14. 8	.	159	„ 9	.	30
8. 14	. 284	14. 10	.	42			

Gospel of Peter (ii/A.D.)

	PAGE			PAGE			PAGE
2. 5	. 92	11	.	240	35	.	187

Apocalypse of Peter (ii/A.D.)

	PAGE			PAGE
2. 3	. 208	4	.	227

Apocryphal Acts (ii/A.D. onwards)

	PAGE		PAGE		PAGE
Andr. et Matth.		Pet. et Paul.—		Thom. 41. 39 .	316
90. 9 f. .	58	17 .	135	116. 4 f.	58
Barn. 7 .	142	186. 4 .	135	175. 2 f.	58
Ex Act. Andr.		187. 1 .	256	198. 17 .	39
45. 26 f.	14	209. 14 .	95	218. 25 ff.	138
Gesta Pil. 12. 2	58	Phil. 10 .	227	253. 6 ff.,	
John 90 .	241	Phil. 39. 1 ff.	95	10 ff. .	95
170. 29 f. .	138	62. 9	50	254. 6 ff.	95
Paul et Thecl. 8	231	86. 21 ff.	95	Xanth. 76. 32 ff.	58
		Pionii 11. 4	196		

Gospels of Thomas and of the Naasenes (ii/A.D.)

	PAGE			PAGE
Ev. Thom. 15. 2	312	Ev. Naas. 2	.	53

INDEX TO REFERENCES 381

Passions and Martyrdoms (iii/A.D. onwards)

	PAGE		PAGE		PAGE
Pass. Andr. alt.		Mart. Dasii 5	136	1. 1	99
28. 14 ff.	13	Mart. Matth.		Mart. Petr. 4	135
Pass. Barth.		243. 18 ff.	138	82. 20	13
133. 29 f.	138	Mart. Pelag. 26. 15	89	88. 7	135
141. 31	39	Pass. Perp. et Fel.			

Later Christian Greek texts

	PAGE		PAGE		PAGE
Orig. c. Marc.		Ev. VI. 7	50	65. 105c	50
(ed. Wetst.) 35	227	Epiph. Haer.		65. 377	58
Apost. Const. 4.3	32	43. 2	208	93. 1708	52
Euseb. Praep.		Migne *P.G.*			

(f) Inscriptions and Papyri

Please see vol. II pp. 503–12 for abbreviations not explained here.

	PAGE		PAGE		PAGE
Archiv iii. 173	29	416. 3	153	1300. 4	16
IG XII. 5. 590	32	417. 16	339	1764. 9	255
Kaibel 642. 10	10	417. 17	335	CPR 22. 15	198
Preis. Samm		417. 28	30	P. Fay.	
620. 6 f.	146	423. 11	35	I. col. III. 16	112
5216. 11	15	436. 9	285	III. 14	293
5827. 17	29	451. 11	30	XCI. 28	151
SIG (Syll.)		467. 15	154	P. Flor. I 6, 7	91
1240. 25	239	512. 2	152	P. Giss. 1. col. 1, 8	55
Ditt. Syll.		523. 6	155	23. 4	316
344. 59	48	523. 17	112	36. 10	44, 155
834. 10	144	530. 35	284	39. 9	53
410. 4, 24	17	543. 13	157	P. Grenf. I 33. 33	52
442. 3, 17	17	596. 11	157	53. 29	227
647. 17	220	615. 9, 28	30	P. Hamb. I.	
705. 57	276	624. 15	155	27. 4	17, 66
807. 9	18	625. 28	142	27. 9	159
1112. 25	26	813. 15	18	P. Hib. 27. 167	293
1157. 10	18	822. 4	49	29. 41	48
1173. 1	194	844. 15	318	38. 8	52
P. Amh. 34(c) 6	56	846. 15	32	46. 13	90
37, 8	62	909. 3	27	54. 23	26
78, 4	53	909. 8	154	59. 2	112
111–113	315	948. 13	49	63. 3	39
BGU (or BU)		1049. 8	26	75. 79	179
36. III. 3	255	1078. 2	162	96. 6, 23	27
46	185	1078. 5	315	110. 65, 100	179
69	238	1078. 8	91	P. Leip. 40. 10	162
86	42	1078. 10	162	40. 20	161
246. 12	242	1079. 6	336	108. 5	157
362. V. 9	151	1081. 3	101	P. Lille 26. 6	149
380. 3	17	1081. 5	138	29. 11	152
388. II. 36 f.	340	1103. 11	247	P. Lond. no.	
388. II. 41	30	1158. 17	304	21	51
388. III. 8	220	1247. 13	58	879, 21	48
388. III. 16	151	1253. 10	125	897, 20	91

INDEX TO REFERENCES

P.Lond.no.—*continued*		P. Par.—*continued*		PSI IV.—*continued*	
	PAGE		PAGE		PAGE
1343. 38	291	51. 9	68	484. 7	30
1394	93	51. 23	155	495. 8	99
P. Ox.		51. 25	315	495. 23	45
2. B 6	167	51. 39	35, 63	584. 30	26
6. 3	231	60. 4	48	P. Strass. II	
33. col. II 14	138	62. 2, 6	49	III. 23	52
37	192	63	45, 245	P. Teb. 5. 5	27
40	221	63. 11, 56	58	6. 32	58
43. B IV 3	277	63. 16	178	6. 43	76
111	27	P. Petr.		12. 23	15
119	96	I. 21	30	14. 10	181
120. 11	80	29. 4	16	17. 14	51
131	58	II. 10 (2) 5	179	22. 11	62
188	187	11 (1)	49	24. 65	125
292. 6	162	13 (17) 4	48	33	30
413. 184	94	13 (18b) 11	29	43. 22	99
472. 17	49	13 (19)	45	45. 17	31
475. 16	17	16. 13	30	46. 14	31
482. 1–2	70	18 (2b) 15	125	47. 11	31
526. 3	136	20. 2. 5	26	50. 12	52
528. 14	194	40 (a) 12	77	56. 11 f.	105
658. 8	226	40 (a) 27	43	61 (b) 29	36
886. 19	187	45	17, 27, 43	61 (b) 35	55
929. 12	254	P. Petr.		105	213
1162	39	III. 56 (b) 12	17	309	152
1189. 7	36	78. 13	17	331. 16	138
1678. 16	48	P. Rein. 18. 5	38	411. 3	194
1680. 11	257	P. Ryl. II.		421. 12	157
1831. 1	137	112. 13	315	793. XI 8	266
1833. 1	137	113. 12 f.	196	798. 16	256
P. Par.		140. 7	169		
8. 16	157	144. 14	37	P. Tor. I. 2. 17	52
12. 20	51	174. 15	266	4. 73	65
12. 21	157	PSI II. 286. 22	18	8. 21	51
15. 4	51	III. 167. 18	125	8. 65	29
18. 3	230	IV. 313. 8	37	UPZ	
22. 20	58	326. 4	39	I. 1. 12 f.	125
22. 25	135	340. 9	322	6. 30	155
22. 29	52	353. 16	76	31. 7	98
23. 9 ff.	62	372. 12	189	41. 25	232
23. 12	53	380. 4	312	42. 32, 33	197
23. 22	135	380. 6	17	71. 18	112
23. 23	101	383. 8	15	113. 12	189
26	149	391. 4	17	II. 161. 61	220
26. 35	51	392. 6	136	162. VIII 29	220
26. 48	29	402. 4	312	W. Chr. 10. 6	16
27. 33	318	402. 7	222	26. II 32	80
32	98	408. 9	17	46. 15	18
34. 9	48	425. 28	48	122. 4	286
35. 30	155	432. 5	27	167. 21	48
38. 11	58	433. 7	325	P. Alex. 4. 15	15
42. 3	227	434. 12	18	Pap. ptol. du Musée	
45	99	435. 19	29	d'Alexandrie,	
46. 7	27	442. 14 f.	226	G. Botti 1899.	
46. 12	43	443. 18	51	P. Eleph. 1. 9	256
47	63, 92, 178	443. 19	43	13. 7	48
48. 12	161	444. 11	30	23. 13	22
49. 33	58	571. 15	196	45. 1. 16	61

INDEX TO REFERENCES 383

Elephantine-Papyri, O. Rubensohn 1907.	Vol. II)	G. Zereteli 1925-35.
P. Goodsp. 3 . . 49	48. 15 . . 30	P. Vat. A 15 . 51
6. 5 . . 48	51. 9 . . 18	(see MM Vocab.
A Group of Gk Papyrus Texts, E. J. Goodspeed 1906.	130. 5 . . 51	p. xxix)
	132. 12 . . 22	SB (see Mayser II
	139. 21 . . 101	1.p.xv)
	186. 6 . . 62	3444 . . 22
P. Hal. I. 30 . . 17	737. 7 . . 18	4631 . . 26
167, 177 . 62	P. Path. (see R. C. Horn, *Use of Subj. and Opt. in the non-literary Papyri* 1926)	5627. 11 . 113
Dikaiomata herausgeg. v. der *Graeca Halensis*, 1913		5680 . . 22
		Zen. P. (see Mayser II 1.p.xiii)
	I . . 105	
P. Mich. Zen. 77. 13 . . 97	P. Prk. (see Horn, above)	59037. 7 . 230, 296
		59084. 9 . 96
ed. C. C. Edgar, 1931	5232. 32 . 105	59148. 2 . 230
P. Magd. 4. 6 . 51	5357. 9 . 105	59396. 4 . 96
9. 3 . . 99	P. Rev. L. 4. 2 . 52	59610. 21 . 97
21. 6 . . 31	5. 1 . 51	ZP or Zen. P. Cairo (*Zenon Papyri*. C. C. Edgar 1925, 1926, 1928, 1931)
27. 6 . . 58	17. 6 . 52	
29. 4 . . 55 f	*Revenue Laws of Ptol. Philad.*, B. P. Grenfell 1896.	
29. 9 . . 52		II. 7 . . 136
42 . . 125		28. 3 . . 58
Pap. de Magdola, J. Lesquier 1912	P. Ross. Georg. III 2, vol. 27 . 35	762. 6 . . 27
Or.Gr. (= OGIS, in	*Papyri russischer...*,	1038. 22b 15 . 25

(g) GREEK LITERATURE.

i. *Classical*.

Sophocles	Menander	Xenophon
	PAGE	PAGE	PAGE
Ajax 464 f. . 213	Epitr. 26 f. . 192	Anab. 1. 2. 21 . 170
554 . . 145	Fr. 425. 2 . 144	3. 5. 11 . 142
1400 . . 91	**Herodotus**	5. 2. 24 . 322
Ant. 369 . . 215		7. 7. 48 . 141
Oed. Rex. 1458 . 190	1. 69 . . 22	Hell. 5. 1. 14 . 136
1471 . 195	1. 80 . . 22	5. 4. 54 . 26
Ph. 442 ff. . 92	2. 99 . . 47	Cyr. 3. 3. 20 . 35
Trach. 865 . 195	2. 124 . . 17	6. 2. 33 . 46
	4. 25 . . 49	7. 1. 44 . 58
Euripides	4. 50 . . 187	Hier. 6. 5 . . 28
Andr. 757 . . 97	5. 76 . 136, 192	Mem. 1. 2. 49 . 147
Bacch. 389 . 213	6. 92 . . 53	3. 5. 26 . 62
914 . . 58	8. 140 . . 63	3. 7. 4 . 18
Cycl. 567 . . 58	9. 26 . . 32	**Isocrates**
El. 982 . . 97	**Thucydides**	4. 44 . . 109
Hipp. 213 . . 97	1. 32. 5 . . 18	4. 82 . . 15
Iph. T. 962 f. . 198	1. 114. 1 . . 322	15. 30 . . 71
Med. 737 . . 215	2. 4. 2 . . 22	**Plato**
Suppl. 1066 . 97	2. 45 . . 282	Crito 50B . . 98
Aristophanes	3. 14 . . 21	Gorg. 459. 6 . 282
Ach. 166 . . 97	3. 22 . . 58	Leg. 629D . . 198
Nu. 367 . . 97	3. 59. 1 . . 274	Meno 99A . . 176
Ra. 521 . . 34	4. 52. 2 . . 316	99E . . 176
866 . . 91	6. 78. 1 . . 22	100B . . 176
V. 397 . . 97	6. 84. 3 . . 22	

Plato—continued

	PAGE
Phaed. 246E	25
Rpb. 532C	186
Symp. 214A	98
Theaet. 147C	195

Aristotle

Metaph. 1071^{a}2	276

Demosthenes

1. 9	71

	PAGE
8. 67	169
18. 21	303
19. 30	179
23. 93	49
27. 58	179
54. 10	248
56. 4	55

Andocides

1. 125	32

Lysias

	PAGE
12. 16	179
19. 57	153

Lycurgus

79	22

Hyperides

Lycophr. 13	195

ii. *Hellenistic.*

Polybius

	PAGE
1. 29. 1	321
1. 48. 5	144
1. 71. 1	18
3. 10. 1	71
4. 1. 1	71
4. 15. 11	18
4. 32. 5, 6	93
4. 36	16
4. 84. 8	18
5. 13. 8	255
5. 18. 4	51
6. 21	16
6. 34. 3	17
11. 2	16
13. 7. 8, 10	93
27. 7. 2	17
39. 9. 12	141

Dionysius of Halicarnassus

de Plat et Pomp. 756	196
de Thuc. 8	57
Opusc. 1. 3. 6	31

Strabo

2. 5 (p. 133, Casaubon)	71

Philo Judaeus

5. 170. 8	18
6. cont. 15	16
Sacr. Abel 136	18
Spec. Leg. 3. 187	26
3. 121	49
Abr. 28	27

Josephus

Ant. 1. 1. 1	187
1. 33	27

Josephus—continued

	PAGE
1. 37	26
1. 100	49
1. 193	16
3. 272	26
6. 287	227
7. 294	26
8. 175	15
11. 104	52
11. 206	240
11. 293	144
13. 187	16
14. 170	144
15. 148	144
15. 370	16
17. 225	31
17. 336	18
19. 48	227
B.J. 2. 124	15
2. 199	18
3. 7. 3	226
6. 326	18
c. Ap. 1. 77	26
1. 217	284

Plutarch

2. 120 d	18
3. 231 d	160
Cat. min. § 18	32
Mor. 169 c	27
Pyrrh. 20. 1	16
Tranqu. c. 13	195

Epictetus

1. 9. 15	94
1. 22. 15	240
1. 24. 10	30
3. 1. 12	102
3. 22	32
3. 22. 33	96
4. 1. 50	136
4. 1. 97, 100	99

Epictetus—continued

	PAGE
4. 6. 8	136
4. 10. 27	74
4. 13. 15	137
Ench. 7	117

Arrian

Ep. ad Traj. 5	17
Epict. 4. 1. 120	50

Aelian

Anim. 2. 38	32
8. 1	216
8. 12	32
14. 37	226

Lucian

Herm. 28	17
Char. 3	17
Peregr. 39	26
Eunuch. 6	43
Dial. Mort. 10. 1	53
13. 3	192
Somn. 15	154
D. Deor. 2. 1	160
Consecr. Hist. 2	187

Vettius Valens

71. 22	18
181. 22	243

Philostratus

Ap. 1. 356. 17	49
3. 19	32

Sextus Empiricus

Phys. 1. 62	25

Diogenes Laertius

3. 2	27
6. 27	52

Aesop

	PAGE
121 . .	32

Apollonius Discolus

de Synt. 1. 14 .	196

Diodorus Siculus

1. 16 . .	16
1. 21 . .	18
1. 37 . .	16
2. 43 . .	26
4. 51. 16 . .	18
11. 16 . .	190
16. 1. 6 . .	71

Diodorus Siculus—(continued)

	PAGE
19. 19 . .	16
20. 1 . .	221

Dio Cassius

58. 4. 5 . .	231
987. 32 . .	26

Achilles Tatius

7. 11. 2 . .	192

Athenaeus

10. 438 . .	49

Marcus Antoninus

	PAGE
9. 3. 7 . .	117
10. 30 . .	52

Xenophon of Ephesus

5. 7. 9 . .	155
p. 393. 29 .	135

Tiberius Gracchus

2. 3 . .	16

INDEX OF SUBJECTS

A modern author is included for special indication, not when mentioned bibliographically.

A.V. 55, 65, 181, 270.
Abbott, E. A. 283
Abel, F. M. 26, 56, 65, 235, 314 f., 316.
Abraham, Testament of 203, 205, 332.
Absolute verbs 51.
Abstract nouns, neuter expressions for 13 f.
Accent query 36, 40, 41, 230, 250, 337.
Accusative: adjectival 220 f.—absol. 322—adverbial 247—cognate 245 f.—double 246 f.—extent 247 f.—ext. obj. 244 f.—point of time 248—predic. 253—w. ἀκούω 161—w. pass. 247—w. inf. 147, 148 f.—w. verb 244–8. S. Gk. Index under ἀνά, εἰς, ἐπί, διά, κατά, μετά, παρά, περί, πρίν, πρός, ὑπέρ, ὑπό.
Active 53—f. pass. 53, 292 f.—mid. or pass. f. 56 f.—intr. act. as causative 52 f.
Acts—s. Luke.
Acts, apocryphal 39, 50, 58, 138, 142, 196, 208, 227, 231, 241, 256, 316, 95 (imper. ἵνα,) 128 (fin. opt.), 135 (fin. inf.).
Adjectives: attrib. 185 f.—f. adv. 225 f.—gen. of qual. f. 212 f.—in -μηνος and -ήμερος 17—possess. 191—predic. 225 f.—pronom. 197-201—position 8, 185, 349—substantivized 13 f., 16-8.
Adverbs : adj. instead of 225 f.—adverbial vbs. 226 f.—as predic. 226—combined w. prep. 278 f.—depend. on prep. 250—position 227–9—w. art. (attrib.) 222.
Adversatives—s. Conjunctions.
Aelius Aristides 96.
Aeschines 52, 97.
Aeschylus 52, 96, 97.
Agent : dat. of, w. pass. 240—prep. w. gen. 258, 274.
Agreement 311-7—*constr. ad sens.* 311 f.—gender 311—number 312 f.—solecisms : Rev 314 f., rest 315–7—several co-ord. words 313 f.
Aktionsart 59, 60, 64, 65, 67, 68, 71, 72, 73, 74, 75, 77, 78, 81 f., 89, 91, 94, 107, 114, 145.
Alciphron 118, 122, 124, 127, 129, 130, 131.
Alexandrinus, codex 62.
Allo, E. B. 115, 314.
Ambiguity : refl. or pers. pron.? 43—refl. or recipr. pron.? 43.
Ambrose 26.
Ammonius 55.
Anacoloutha 342 f.—after rel. clause 325.
Anaphora 166, 167, 169, 171, 172-4, 178—οὗτος 44—ἐκεῖνος 46.
Aorist : indic. 68–74—ind. w. ἄν 91, 93—ind. w. ὅταν 124—ind. in wishes 91—ind. w. ὀλίγου 91—imper. 74 f., 76 f., 78—subj. 74, 76-8, 94, 95, 96, 97, 98, 99, 101, 107, 108 f., 111, 112, 114 f.—opt. 118, ch. 9—inf. 78 f., 145—ptc. 79–81—*Aktionsart* 59 f., 71-4 (ind), 74–8 (other moods), 107, 60 (stem used f. punct. action in pres. time)—constative (complexive) 70, 71, 72, 77—epistolary 72f.—ingressive (inchoative, inceptive) 70, 71 f., 75, 77—gnomic 73–4—perfective (effective, resultat.) 5, 68, 71, 72, 75—proleptic 74—w. descript. impf. 66 f.—different meaning from pres. 72—aorist. pf. 68–71.
Apollodorus 29.

386

INDEX OF SUBJECTS

Apollonius Dyscolus 102, 173, 174, 180, 196.
Appian 159.
Apposition 206.
Aquila 52, 250, 277, 279.
Aramaic—s. Semitisms.
Aratus 118, 121, 124, 125, 127, 129.
Aristeas 16, 26, 124, 159, 245.
Aristophanes 18, 34, 91, 96, 97, 106.
Aristotle 233, 270, 276.
Arrian 61.
Article 36 f.—anaphoric 166, 167, 169, 171, 172-4, 178—adjectiv. and predic. 165-84—demonstr. force 36—generic 180 f.—forming adv. accus. 14—individualizing 36, 165-80—less prolific in higher Gk. 36—never as rel. pron. 37—non-class. use 2—not w. ἕκαστος 198—substantival or pronominal 36 f.—vocative 34—w. adj. 13 f.—w. astron. names, etc. 172—w. attrib. adv. 14—w. attribute after anarthr. noun 218—w. gen. of nouns 16, 166, 168, 179 f.—w. geogr. names 169-72—w. ind. interrog. 117, 182—w. names of peoples 169—w. neut. adj. f. abstr. noun 2—w. numerals 178 f.—w. ptc. 150-3—w. personal names 165-9—w. prep. phrases 14, 15, 221—w. pred. 182-4—w. quotns. 182, 261—w. several nouns connected together 181—w. ἀλήθεια 177 f.—w. αὐτός 41, 183, 194—w. γράμματα 176—w. ἐκκλησία 176—w. ἄλλος and ἕτερος 197 f.—w. θάνατος 175—w. θεός 34 (LXX), 174—w. κύριος 174—w. νόμος 177—w. ὅλος, πᾶς (ἅπας) 199 f.—w. οὐρανός, γῆ, θάλασσα, κόσμος 174 f.—w. οὗτος, ἐκεῖνος 192—w. πνεῦμα 175 f.—w. σάρξ 177—w. τοιοῦτος, τοσοῦτος 46 f., 193 f.
Omission of: w. abstracts 176—w. adv. if gen. follows 14—w. ordinals 178 f.—w. pred. 173, 182-4—theolog. significance? 175—like Heb. constr. state 34, 173, 179 f.—after prep. 179.
Article, indef. (εἷς) 4, 195 f.
Articular infin.—s. Infinitive.
Aspect 59-86.
Asyndeton 9, 340 f., 342.
Attic Greek 31, 33, 34, 36, 37, 40, 41, 45, 47, 52, 53, 55, 56, 57, 82, 91, 94, 98, 105, 118, 126, 128, 135, 136, 152, 165, 173, 264, 265, 267, 273, 279, 286, 294, 295, 296, 312.
Attic inscriptions 106, 118, 122, 128, 169, 170, 198.
Atticisms, Atticists 7, 28, 30, 36, 106, 119, 126, 127, 128, 129, 130, 132, 187, 220, 240, 277, 338—inf. 135—opt. 119, 125, 128, 129, 130, 131 f., 313, 319—scribes and 6, 82, 119, 129, 135, 152, 245, 271, 313, 339.
Attraction of relative 324.
Attributives: art. w. several 186 f.—advs. 222—prep. phrases 221 f.—position 185, 217.
Augment 73—meaning of 59 f.
Augustine 26.

Babrius 245.
Barbelenet, D. 294.
Barnabas 332—s. Index of Ref.
Barrett, C. K. 343.
Bauer, W. 21, 26, 40, 55, 237, 244, 254, 270, 278, 285, 291.
Beginnings 337, 350.
Behm, J. 27, 233.
Bertram, G. 300.
Bezae, codex 41, 173.
Biblical Greek 3, 4, 6, 7, 8, 9, 26, 38, 42, 61, 74, 82, 86, 120, 131, 142, 144, 145, 153, 154, 155, 156, 175, 178, 196, 209, 212, 237, 240, 241, 258, 271, 275, 277, 295, 318, 320, 321, 322, 331, 335, 347, 349—unity of 5, 9, 95, 108, 123, 127, 129, 201.
Björck, G. 87.

INDEX OF SUBJECTS

Black, M. 194, 209, 258.
Blass, F. 50, 281, 285.
Blass-Debrunner 41, 169, 284, 315, 316.
Boobyer, G. H. 291.
Bover, J. M. 258.
Brown, J. A. 338.
Büchsel, F. 18, 52, 215, 240, 296.
Burkitt, F. C. 333.
Burton, E. de W. 62, 142, 143.

Cadbury, H. J. 47, 301.
Callimachus 118, 121, 124, 125, 127, 129.
Cardinals for ordinals 17, 187.
Case 230–80—after verbs 7, 161, 231–48.
Causal clauses 318 f.—negation 284—position 345—w. ptc. 157—ἀνθ' ὧν 258—ἀντί τοῦ w. inf. 144—διά τό w. inf. 142 f.—ἐάν (causal) 115 f.—εἰ (causal) 115—εἰς 266—εἰς τό w. inf. 143—ἐν τῷ w. inf. 145—ἐπεί 318—ἐφ' ᾧ 319—καθότι 318—καθώς 320—ἵνα 102 f.—ὅτι, διότι 318—οὗ χάριν 319—παρά τό w. inf. 144—τῷ w. inf. 142—ὡς 158, 320.
Causative verbs : from intransitives 52 f.—w. double accus. 246.
Cavallin, A. 336.
Chambers, C. D. 79, 80.
Chantraine, P. 5, 68, 71.
Chiasmus 345–7.
Chronicles (LXX) : non-fin. ἵνα 104—s. Index of Ref.
Chrysostom 14, 35, 135.
Circumstantial (adv.) participle 150, 153–5.
Classical Greek, differences from NT in syntax 2, 3, 18, 29, 30, 31, 33, 36, 37, 38, 47, 49, 50, 51, 53, 54, 64, 71, 79, 84, 85, 88, 90, 91, 92, 93, 94, 97, 98, 100, 109, 114, 117, 124, 128, 134, 135, 136, 137, 138, 142, 144, 147 f., 153, 158, 161, 197, 200, 207, 216, 220, 221, 226, 233, 235, 257, 261, 267, 273, 281, 282, 284, 285, 286, 311, 312, 331, 338, 341.
Clause order 344–7—καθώς-clause 320—ὥσπερ-clause 320.
Clement of Alexandria 31.
Clement of Rome 96—s. Index of Ref.
Coleman, N. D. 333.
Colwell, E. C. 178, 183–4.
Commands, pres. and aor. 74 f.
Comparatives 29–32—elative 3, 29, 30—comp. form of a comp. 29—f. pos. 30 f.—heightened 29—instead of superl. 2, 29—levelling of comp. and superl. 29—pos. f. 29—reduction of μᾶλλον ἤ to ἤ or παρά 32—use of παρά and ὑπέρ w. pos. or comp. 7, 29, 31, 216.
Comparative clauses 319–21—καθάπερ 319 f.—καθώς 319 f.—ὡς, ὥσπερ 320.
Concessive clauses 153, 157, 321—conjunctions 116—w. ptc. 153, 157.
Conditional clauses 91 f., 109, 113–6, 319—conjunctions 113—negation 283 f., 319—opt. 119, 125–8, 319—parataxis instead 319—tenses 114—w. ptc. 157, 319—ἐάν 113, 114 f.—ἐάν w. impf? 116—εἰ 91 f., 115 f., 125 ff.—ἐπί 272.
Congruence—s. Agreement.
Conjunctions : position 329—less rigid connection w. mood in Hell. Gk. 2, 107—co-ordinating 329–40—copulative 334 f., 338 f.—adversative 338, 340—causal 102 f., 158, 266, 318, 320—consec. 106, 336, 337—disjunctive 334—compar. 319 f.—concess. 116—condit. 113—temp. 110–13, 321.
Consecutive clauses : ἐπί 272—ἵνα 102—ὅθεν 337—ὅτι 318—οὖν 336—τοῦ w. inf. 141, 142—ὡς 136—ὥστε 106, 136.
Constructio ad sensum 40, 311 f.
Coptic 326.
Copula, omission of 294–8.
Copulative conjunctions—s. καί, οὐδέ, οὔτε, τε.

Corpus Hermeticum 33.
Correlative : conjunctions 320, 334, 339—pronouns 46 f.
Couchoud, P.-L. 347.
Countries, names of (partit.) 210, 259—w. art. 169-72.
Daniel (LXX or Th.) 61, 71, 104 (non-fin. ἵνα), 203 ff. (πᾶς), 332 (μέν)—s. Index of Ref.
Dates 17.
Dative : declining 7, 236, 249—added to vbs. 236-44—adjectival 219 f.—as attribute of nouns 219, of adjs. 220—associative dat. 240—credit and discredit 239—dat. absol. 243—*dat. sympatheticus* (ethical) 239—" happen to " 240—indir. obj. 236-8—instrumental 240—interchange w. accus. 7, 243—locative 242 f.—modi 241—of accomp. circumstances 241—of adv. and disadv. 238—of agent 240—of cause 242—of duration of time 243 f.—of possession 239 f.—of ref. 238—of respect 220—" relationis " 220, 238 f.—temporal 243—verbal noun 241 f.—εἰς and ἐν encroaching 236, 251-3—Hebrew inf. absol. 241 f.—w. cmpd. vbs. 242—w. πρός 237, 251—s. ἐν, ἐπί, παρά, σύν.
Debrunner, A. 116, 141.
Declarative clauses : w. διότι, ὅτι, ὡς, ὡς ὅτι 134, 137, 148, 161—negation 284.
Delling, G. 232.
Demonstrative pronouns : substantival 44-7—attributive 192-4—adverbial uses 45—anarthr. not necessarily predic. 4—art. as 34, 36 f.—position 193, 349—οὗτος followed by inf., ἵνα, ὅτι, etc. 45—αὐτός 7, 40-2. 194—ἐκεῖνος 45 f., 192 f.—ὅδε 44, 192—οὗτος 44 f., 192 f.—τοιοῦτος, τοσοῦτος 46 f., 193 f.
Deponents : now prefer pass. forms 54, 57—pass. of trans. deponents 58.
de Zwaan, J. 87.
Diatribe 293.
Dibelius, M. 183.
Didache 96, 332—s. Index of Ref.
Dio Cassius 26, 231, 245.
Dio Chrysostom 299.
Diodorus Siculus 57, 58, 71, 118, 126, 128, 130, 266, 279, 299—s. Index of Ref.
Diogenes Laertius 27, 52, 57, 96.
Dionysius of Halicarnassus 55, 61, 118, 130—s. Index of Ref.
Direct questions—s. Questions.
Disjunctive conjunctions 334.
Distributive : numerals 266—distrib. doubling 187—art. w. prep. phrase 14—distrib. sing. 23 f.—ἀνά 265 f.—εἰς 266—κατά 268.

Ecclesiastical Greek 50, 208, 248.
Elatives 3, 29, 30.
Ellipse : of apodosis 91, 319, 333—of subject 291-3—of εἶναι 231, 294-310—of ἡμέρα 17, 18—of χείρ 17—of ὥρα 17—of others 17— w. ἀλλ' ἵνα 304, 307, 330—w. ἵνα 304, 305—w. οὐχ ἵνα 308—w. εἴτε ... εἴτε 333—s. δυνατόν, ὄνομα.
Emendation 246.
Enoch, Greek 26.
Epexegesis, methods of : inf. 78, 139—inf. w. τοῦ 141—ἵνα 103 f., 129—εἰς τό w. inf. 143—ἐν τῷ w. inf. 146—καί 335.
Epictetus 33, 91, 126, 128, 303.
Esdras, I : non-fin. ἵνα 104—πᾶς 202 ff.—s. Index of Ref.
Esther (LXX) 130 f.—s. Index of Ref.
Euripides 52, 96—s. Index of Ref.
Euthymius 52.
Exclamations 33, 50.
Exodus (LXX) 202 ff., 332—s. Index of Ref.
Ezekiel (LXX) 132, 203 f., 275, 279, 332—s. Index of Ref.

Feminine : to form adv. phrases 21—f. neut. (pron.) 21.
Field, F. 93.
Final Clauses 95, 100–06, 111—position 344—w. ptc. 157 f.—opt. 128 f.—
εἰ w. opt. 127—εἰς τό w. inf. 143—ἐν τῷ w. inf. 146—ἐπί 272—πρὸς τό w. inf. 144—τοῦ w. inf. 141.
Final conjunctions : enlarged use of ἵνα 94 f.—ἵνα 95, 100–05—ὅπως 105 f.—ὡς 105, 136—ὥστε 106—μή, μήπως, μήποτε after statement of fear 99.
Foerster, W. 211, 269.
Fridrichsen, A. 147.
Friedrich, G. 53.
Future tense 86 f.—opt. 128—inf. 86—ptc. 86 f., 135, 150, 153—after εἰ 115—after ἵνα 100—deliberat. 86, 98—for imperat. 86—gnomic 86—lit. tr. of Heb. impf. 86—periphrasis f. 89—w. ὅπως 105—w. μήπως 99—w. οὐ μή 96 f.—no *Aktionsart* 86—interchanging w. aor. subj. 97.

Gender 21–2—agreement 311—fem. f. neut. 6 f., 21—masc. f. fem. (and reverse) 21—neut. of persons 21—anomalies 210—variation 21, 22.
General epistles : position of adj. 8.
Genesis (LXX) 108 f., 202 ff., 237, 332, 341—s. Index of Ref.
Genitive : addition to vb. 231–6—adjectival 207–19—after preps. (proper and impr.) ch. 18 *passim*—art. w. gen. of nouns 16, 166, 168, 179 f.—art. w. gen. of origin, etc. 16—art. w. partit. gen. of country 210—compar. 216—appositive (*materiae, epexegeticus*) 214 f.—local and temporal 235—objective or subjective 207, 210–12—partit. 7, 208–12—position of 217 f.—possessive 207 f., 231—price 258—quality 7, 212–4—separation 215 f., 235 f., 258 f.—w. adjs. and advs. 215 f.—w. ἀκούω 161—chain of 218, 335—in Mark 219.
Genitive absolute, misused and extended 4, 322 f.
Geographical names : country in partit. gen. 210, 259—w. and without art. 169–72.
Ghedini, G. 84.
Gildersleeve, B. L. 166, 170, 171.
Goodspeed, E. J. 336.
Goodwin, W. W. 96, 105.
Gospels : κύριε *sir* 34—γέγονα 70—πέποιθα etc. 82—fin. inf. 135—art. w. Ἰησοῦς 166 f.—position of adj. 349.
Green, E. L. 191.
Greenlee, J. H. 255.

Harry, J. E. 192, 309.
Harsing, C. 131.
Hauck, F. 211.
Hebrew influence—s. Semitisms.
Hebrews, epistle to : neut. adj. w. dependent gen. 14—ἡμεῖς f. ἐγώ 28—fut. inf. 86—fut. pass. ptc. 87—periphr. tenses 89—ἵνα never imperat. 95—οὐ μή 96—φοβέομαι μή (semi-lit.) 99— ἵνα w. subj. 101—opt. 119, 120, 121—inf. abs. 136—style 137—inf. w. vbs. of believing, etc. 137—artic. inf. 140 ff.—εἰς τό w. inf. (final) 143—supplem. (predic.) ptc. 158—position of πᾶς 203, 205—partit. gen. w. vbs. 231 f.—ἐν 257—aversion to σύν 265—to παρά w. dat. 273—ἕως, ἄχρι, μέχρι 276—μή w. ptc. 285—ellipse of εἶναι 299, 307 f.—καθάπερ 319—μέν . . . δέ 331—ὅθεν 336—τε 338—δήπου 339—asyndeton 340—position of compar. clauses 345—word-order 347, 350.
Hellenistic Greek *passim*.
Hendiadys 335.
Hermas : πρωΐα and ὀψίας unclass. 17—comparison 30—οὗτος and ἐκεῖνος 45—artic. inf. w. pron. 148—*schema Atticum* 312—s. Index of Ref.
Herodotus 6, 13, 96, 106, 155, 170, 171, 270, 272, 274, 294, 295, 296, 299.
Hesychius 50.

INDEX OF SUBJECTS

Hiatus 28.
Historical books, later (LXX) 61—s. Index of Ref.
" Holy Ghost language " 9.
Homer 22, 28, 32, 36, 106, 195, 252, 337.
Horn, R. C. 105, 115, 119, 120, 122 f., 125, 126.
Howard, W. F. v, 8, 72, 80, 182, 209, 240, 293, 315, 333.
Howes, G. E. 284.

Ignatius 96—s. Index of Ref.
Imperative : pres. and aor. 74–8—perf. 85, 89—periphr. f. 89—replaced by subj. 93–8; by fut. 86 ; by ἵνα-clause 94 f., 102, 129, 305 ; by inf. 78 ; by ptc. 293, 303, 308, 310, 343—f. opt. 118—negation 282—asyndeton w. 342.
Imperfect 64–8—retreat before aor. 2, 64—confusion w. aor. 2, 64, 67—conative or desiderative 65, 72—incohative 65—linear 65—descr. impf. woven w. aor. in narrative 66 f.—iterative 67—f. Engl. plupf. 67—periphr. f. 87—to express necessity 90 f.—impossible wish 91—" unreal indic." 91—condit. clauses 91 f., 116—w. ἄν to express repetition 124—w. ὅταν 124.
Impersonal constructions : in pass. 291—" they " 292 f.—scil. " the Scripture " 293.
Impersonal verbs 291-3.
Indeclinable : personal names w. art. 167 f.—πλήρης 315 f.
Indef. pronouns : attributive 195–7—ἄνθρωπος 195—τις 195—εἷς 4, 195 f.— -ουν and -ποτε 196—οὐ . . . πᾶς 196 f.
Indicative 90–3—*Aktionsart* 91—to express necessity 90 f.—wishes w. ἄν 91—unreal ind. w. ἄν 91 f.—condit. clauses 91 f.—f. opt. w. ἄν 92—w. ἄν in subord. clauses in iterative sense 92 f.—impf. ind. after ὅταν 92 f., 124 ,125—pres. ind. after ὅπου ἄν 93 ; after ἐάν 115 f.—fut. ind. w. οὐ μή 97, 282 ; f. imperat. 86 ; in dubitat. or deliberat. questions 98 ; after ἐάν 116 ; after ὅς ἄν 110 ; after ὅταν 112—pres. and fut. ind. after ἵνα 100 f.—relat. clauses 109—after ὥστε 136—negation 281 f.—s. Present, Imperfect, etc.
Indirect questions : opt. 130 f., 132—s. Questions.
Indirect statement : opt. 129 f.—ὅτι f. accus. w. inf. 148—mixed w. direct 325 f.
Infinitive 134–49—non-class. usage 2, 90, 134, 137, 148, 149—articular 2, 78, 134, 140–6—fin.-consec. 2, 78, 105 f., 134–6—replaced by ἵνα or ὅτι 2, 134, 137, 138, 139, 148 f.—after prep. 8, 78, 85, 105 f., 142–6—ἐν τῷ 8, 144 f.— εἰς τό 8, 143—πρὸς τό 144—τό 140 f.—τοῦ 8, 141, 142—w. πρίν 78, 140—of wish (epistol.) 78—imperat. 78—πρὸ τοῦ 78—epexeget. 78, 139—*Aktionsart* 78 f.—pres. and aor. 78 f.—fut. 79—w. μέλλω 79—pf. 85—w. function of dat. 134–6—w. various case-functions 136–46—infin. abs. (Gk) 136—w. vbs. *perceive, believe, say*, etc. 136–40—as dir. obj. 137 f.—in impers. phrases 139—w. nouns and adjs. 139—cases w. (nom., acc.) 146–9—negation 281, 285 f.
Inscriptions 22—s. Index of Ref.
Instrumental—s. Dative and ἐν.
Interrogative conjunctions : οὐ (οὐχί) and μή 282—οὐκοῦν 282, 337—μήτι (γε) 283—οὐ μή 283—ἆρα(γε) 330—εἰ 319, 333—ἤ 334.
Interrogatives: confused w. rel. (Hell. Gk.) 4, 49 f., 195—dir. interrog. pron. in indir. qu. 4, 48—pronouns 48–50—is ὅ interrog.? 50—exclam. 50—ποῖος = τίς 48—w. καί 334.
Intrans. verbs 51–3—used transitively 2, 51 f.—causative sense 52 f.
Ionic Greek 31, 94, 265, 269, 294, 295, 296, 304.
Ionicism in NT : ὅστις f. ὅς 47—ἀνατέλλω causat. 53—σύν with 265—copula 294—ὡς 321.
Isaiah (LXX) 132, 140, 203 ff., 271, 272, 274, 279, 332—s. Index of Ref.
Isaeus 97.
Isocrates 18, 170, 171—s. Index of Ref.

INDEX OF SUBJECTS

James, epistle of : ὥσπερ 320—periphr. tenses 88 f.—ἵνα never imperat. 95—artic. inf. 140—τοῦ w. inf. 142—position of πᾶς 203, 205—ellipse of εἶναι 299, 308.
Jannaris, A. 312, 315.
Jeremiah (LXX) 203 ff., 230, 332—s. Index of Ref.
Jeremias, J. 63, 237, 345.
Jerome 26—s. Vulgate.
Jewish Greek, spoken 4, 9.
Job (LXX) 62, 131, 202 ff.—s. Index of Ref.
Johannessohn, M. 33, 335.
John, gospel and epistles : style 1, 5, 25 (like Rev), 34 (artistry), 38 (class. correct), 157 (variety)—πρωΐα and ὀψία unclass. 17—*plur. sociativus* in 1 Jn 28—ὁ δέ rare 37—οὗτος foll. by ἵνα, ὅτι, etc. 45—ἐκεῖνος 45 f.—anaphora (οὗτος and ἐκεῖνος) 46—ὅστις rare 47—ὅς 47—ὑπάγω often intrans. 51—hist. pres. favoured (Jn) 60, 61 ; varied w. aor. 61, 62—epistol. aor. 73—strange use of tense 75, 85—pres. ptc. of relatively fut. time 80—pf. favoured 83, 84, 85—periphrasis f. pres., impf., pf. 87, 88, 89—imperat. ἵνα 95—οὐ μή 96 f.—ἵνα preferred to ὅπως 101, 103 f., 105—ὅταν w. subj. 112—ἄν and ἐάν 113—ἐάν w. subj. 114 f.— τοῦ w. inf. varied w. ἵνα 141—art. after prep. rare 142—art. w. prop. names 167—no ἀποκριθεὶς εἶπεν 155—ἀπεκρίθη λέγων 155—avoids redund. ptcs. 155—asyndeton 155—favours co-ordination 155—λέγων 156—ἀπεκρίθη καὶ εἶπεν 156—art. w. Ἰησοῦς 167—favours ἐμός 191—ἕτερος rare 197—position of πᾶς 203, 205—τις never w. gen. 209—κοινωνέω w. dat. 232—case w. ἀκούω 234—εἰς f. ἐν 255—favours ἐκ 260—ἐκ to denote sects, etc. 260—theological ἐν 263—σύν and μετά 265—παρά w. accus. absent 273—ὑπό w. acc. rare 275—prep. repeated 275—ἕως, ἄχρι, μέχρι absent 276—ἐνώπιον rare 277—οὐ varied w. μή 281—meanings of οὐ πᾶς 282—οὐ 285—copula inserted 294, 299, 303 f.—ellipse before ἵνα 298—καθώς 320—temp. ὡς 321—ὅτι *recit.* 326—οὖν 329, 337—τε rare and uncertain 338—asyndeton 340 f.—γάρ rare 331—μέντοι 340—τότε 341.
Josephus 13, 26, 33, 60, 61, 135, 144, 172, 191, 227, 243, 245—s. Index of Ref.
Jude, ep. of 119, 203, 205, 273, 308—vol. opt. 121.
Judges (LXX) 132, 202 ff., 332—s. Index of Ref.
Jülicher, A. 316.

Katz, P. 277.
Kennedy, H. A. A. 262.
Kilpatrick, G. D. v, 191, 209, 229, 279, 320.
Kingdoms (LXX) 62, 132, 202 ff., 279—s. Index of Ref.
Klostermann, E. 50, 156, 168, 316.
Knabenbauer, J. 316.
Knox, R. A. 335.
Koine : literary 45—and literary language 81—Ptolemaic period *passim*—Imperial 66, 68, 89, 96, 105, 111, 112, 113, 115, 116, 119, 125, 138, 255, 257, 258.
Krebs, F. 143.

L.S. 96.
Lagrange, M.-J. 18, 32, 38, 61, 87, 226, 252, 316, 334, 340, 341.
Laird, A. G. 284.
Lamentations (LXX) 52.
Latin versions 49, 58, 86.
Latinisms (alleged) : γάμοι 27—voc. without ὦ 33—aoristic pf. 71—epistol. aor. 72 f.—plupf. 83—σὺ ὄψῃ (and pl.) 86—subj. in rel. clauses 109—pass. inf. f. act. w. verba iubendi 138—accus. refl. pron. in accus. w. inf.-construction 147—omission of art. 173—πόλις w. gen. of name 215—ὅμοιος w. gen. 216—κονδύλοις ἔλαβεν 241—ὀψέ 278—impers. pass. 291—τί πρός σε ; *quid hoc a te?* 303.

INDEX OF SUBJECTS

Lightfoot, J. B. 55, 56.
Linear action 59, 64, 67, 71, 77, 86, 89.
Literary features in NT : ὅδε 44—τοῦτ' ἐστιν 45—pf. 83—s. Optative, and *passim*.
Ljungvik, H. 39, 316, 321.
Lobel, E. 125.
Local clauses, position 344.
Locative—s. Dative.
Lohmeyer, E. 102 f., 177.
Lucian 245, 269.
Lucianic text 80.
Luke-Acts : style 2, 8, 137, 158—τοῦ w. inf. 8, 142—Septuagintisms 8, 142, 145, 156—art. inf. 8, 140, 141, 142, 143, 144 f., 262—τὰ κατά (of general relationship) (Ac) 14—τὰ περί 15—scil. ἡμέρᾳ in dates 17—pl. of ὄχλος 26—meaning of πρῶτος 32—voc. 33—prol. Lk. 33—Latinism 33, 147—word-order 33—Semit. ὁ εἷς ... ὁ ἕτερος 36—(ὁ) μὲν οὖν (Ac) 37, 337—Semit. redund. of αὐτοῦ (Lk 1) 38—favours unemph. αὐτός 40—demonstr. αὐτός 194—more fond than Mt of ἑαυτοῦ 42—reads ψυχή as refl. pron. 43—removes anaphoric οὗτος 45—ὅς and ὅστις confused 47—correcting Mt? 49—ἐκλέγομαι 55—ποιέομαι 56—avoids histor. pres. 60 f.—φησίν 61—subtelty 75 f.—tenses and Mt 77 f.—fut. inf. (Ac) 79, 86—pres. pf. 82—use of pf. 84—fut. ptc. 86 f.—periphr. f. pres., etc. 87-9—οὐ μή 96 f.—φοβέομαι μή (semi-lit.) 99—ἵνα w. ind. 100—ἵνα w. subj. 101—imperat. ἵνα 95—stylistic ὅπως (Ac) 106—epexeg. ἵνα 103—ὅπως ἄν 105—ἕως 111—ὅταν w. subj. 112 f.— ἐάν w. subj. 114 f.—atticisms 131—opt. 119, 121, 123, 130 f.—inf. f. result 136—inf. w. vbs. *believe, say* 137—stylistic inf. (Ac) 138—τοῦ w. 2nd fin. inf. 142—τοῦ μή consec. 142—aor. inf. of anterior action 145—pleon. ἐγένετο 145—accus. w. inf. 149—avoids ptc. 154—λέγων 156—predic. ptc. 158—rule w. anaphor. art. 166—ἀκούω w. gen. and ptc. (Ac) 161—art. w. place-names (Ac) 170 f.—use of πνεῦμα 175 f.—τό before indir. qu. 182—ἀνήρ f. τις 195—ἕτερος 197—ἅπας 199—πάντες ἄνθρωποι 200—position of πᾶς 203, 205—adj. gen. 207—κρατέω 232—εἰς f. ἐν 254—σύν 265—κατά w. gen. 268—repetition of prep. 275—παρά 272—ἕως, ἄχρι, μέχρι 276—ἐνώπιον 277—οὐ w. ptc. 285—καθώς 320—temp. ὡς 321—ὡσεί 321—δέ and καί 322—ὅτι *recit*. 326—gen. abs. 322—ἀλλά 329—ἄρα (γε) 330—γάρ 331—μέν ... δέ 331—εἰ in dir. qu. 333—διό (Ac) 333—οὖν 337—τε (Ac) 338, 339—πλήν 338—τότε 341—ellipse of copula 295, 299, 301, 304 f.
Lund, N. W. 345.
Lyonnet, S. 272.

Maccabees, I 104 (non-fin. ἵνα), 274 (ὑπό)—s. Index of Ref.
Maccabees, II 60 (hist. pres,.) 130 (opt.)—s. Index of Ref.
Maccabees, II-IV 274.
Maccabees, IV 33, 123,129, 140, 332—s. Index of Ref.
McNeile, A. H. 341,
Malalas 134, 298.
Mantey, J. R. 266 267, 337.
Marchalianus, codex 44.
Marcus Aurelius 58.
Marcus, R. 267.
Margolis, H. 334.
Mark, gospel of: C. H. Turner and 2, 254, 292, 342—correct use of pf. 5, 69—πρωΐα and ὀψία unclass. 17—ὅ ἐστιν 48—change of subj. marked by ὁ (οἱ) δέ 37—favours hist. pres. 60, 61, 62—H. St. J. Thackeray and 62—impf. 66, 67—aor. 67—periphr. f. pres., impf. 67, 87, 88, 89,—pres. pf. 82—pf. 83—scribes and 87—position of copula 89—imperat. ἵνα 95—οὐ μή 96 f.—ἵνα frequ. 101, 103—non-fin. ἵνα 104—rel. clauses 108—ἕως 111, 276—ὅταν w. subj. 112—ἐάν w. subj. 114 f.— opt. 119—

wish opt. 121—ὅταν w. ind. 125—εἰ w. fut. ind. (wish) 127—M. Zerwick and 137, 341, 342—ἄρχομαι 138—artic. inf. 141—ἰδεῖν w. ptc. or ὅτι 161—art. w. Ἰησοῦς 166 f.—ἕτερος absent 197—word-order w. gen. 217—attrib. and partit. gen. 219—word-order of εὐθύς and πάλιν 229—G. D. Kilpatrick and 229, 320—constr. w. ἔρχομαι 257—παρά 272—παρά w. acc. only local 273—repet. of prep. 275—ἐνώπιον absent 277—impers. " they " 292 f.—insertion of copula 294—ellipse of copula 299, 306—pl. vb. w. ὄχλος 312—καθώς 320—gen. abs. 322 f.—ὅτι *recit*. 326—δέ or καί 329, 332, 334—μέν . . . δέ 331 f.—τότε 341—position of verb 348.

Mary of Bethany, identification 80.
Masculine : f. fem. or neut. 21—masculinizing of πέτρα 22—pl. incl. masc. and fem. components 22.
Matthew, gospel of : πρωΐα and ὀψία unclass. 17—meaning of πολλοί 26—pl. of ὄχλος 26—oblique αὐτός 38—avoids refl. pron. 42—anaphora : prefers οὗτος to ἐκεῖνος 46—ὅς and ὅστις confused 47, 48—ὅ ἐστιν 48—λέγει 61, 340—style 66, 158—γέγονεν f. pf. 70—Chantraine and pf. 71—tenses and Lk. 77 f.—periphr. f. pres., impf. 88, 89—imperat. ἵνα 94—οὐ μή 96 f.—epexeg. ἵνα 103—non-fin. ἵνα 104—rel. clauses 107, 108—and LXX 108—ἕως 111—ὅταν w. subj. 112—ἐάν w. subj. 114 f.—artic. inf. 135, 141—fin. inf. (cp. Mk) 135—ἄρχομαι 138—τοῦ w. 2nd fin. inf. 142—Semit. εἰς 196—ἕτερος 197—position of adv. 228—καὶ ἰδού 229—εἰς and ἐν correctly distinct 254—παρά w. accus. only local 273—repet. of prep. 275—ἕως, ἄχρι, μέχρι 276—ἐνώπιον absent 277—οὐ 285—ellipse of εἶναι 299, 309 f.— ὁ πᾶς w. ptc. 316—ὥσπερ 320—gen. abs. 322—ὅτι *recit*. 326—μέν . . . δέ 331 f.—γάρ 331—πλήν 338—asyndeton 340—τότε 341.

Mayser, E. *passim*.
Meecham, H. G. v, 81, 268, 343.
Meisterhans, K. 122, 128.
Menander 18—s. Index of Ref.
Michaelis, W. 212.
Middle voice 53–7—in class. Gk. 54—rarely refl. in NT 54—mid. f. act. 54–6—forms tend to merge w. pass. 54—not recipr. in NT 54—pass. f. mid. 56 f.—act. f. mid. 56 f.—not very significant 56—disappearing 56–7.
Milligan, G. 25, 293.
Milligan, W. 345.
Minor Prophets (LXX) 203 f., 274, 279, 332—s. Index of Ref.
Modern Greek 3, 17, 18, 26, 31, 32, 36, 40, 51, 52, 53, 58, 60, 68, 69, 74, 75, 91, 94, 95, 99, 103, 107, 138, 166, 171, 192, 212, 216, 225, 235, 236, 249, 250, 251, 253, 254, 261, 270, 284, 286, 295, 304, 312, 315, 336, 342, 347.
Moffatt, J. 317, 336.
Moule, C. F. D. 73, 86, 152, 178, 211, 233, 234, 245, 249, 267, 269, 271, 291, 292, 317, 337.
Moulton, J. H. v, 1, 9, 16, 34, 63, 70, 77 f., 86, 96, 143, 147, 168, 194, 233, 248, 261, 269, 293, 308, 315, 316, 343.
Multiplicatives 187.

N.E.B. (New English Bible) 95, 102, 137, 143, 143, 145, 146, 151, 176, 181, 187, 212, 335, 336, 348, 350.
Nauck, W. 337.
Negatives 94, 95, 281–7, 286 (double).
Neuter : substantival expressions 13 f.—neut. adj. w. sing. or pl. of persons (collective) 14, 150—plur. adverbially 21—masc. f. 21, 312, 314 f.—fem. f. (Heb.) 21—ὅ ἐστιν 48—pronom. pred. in neut. (τι, οὐδέν, ὅ, etc.) 311—predic. adj. in neut. 311—sg. and pl. vb. w. neut. pl. 312 f.—Οὐαί 315.
Nissen, Th. 307.

Nominative 230 f.—f. voc. 3, 34 f.—*ad sensum* 230—prop. nouns without syntax 230—parenthet. (ὄνομα) 230—incongr. ptc. in nom. 230, 314, 316, 317—of time 231—absol. (*pendens*) 314, 316—indeclinable πλήρης, εἶς, ἔχων, λέγων, λέγοντες 315.
Norden, E. 347.
Noun : substitutes f. 13–8—ellipse of 16 ff.—as attribute 185.
Number 22–28—agreement 311–4—distrib. sing. 7, 23, 25—collective sing. 22 f.—dual 29, 32—eccentric usage 210, 317—*constr. ad sens.* 311 f.—collective noun w. pl. vb. 311 f.—ἕκαστος w. pl. vb. 312—neut. pl. subj. w. pl. vb. (*schema Atticum*) 312 f.—of vb. w. several co-ord. words 313 f.—pl. (not neut) subj. w. sing. vb. 315—s. Singular, Plural.
Numerals 187 f.—art. w. 178 f.—Aram. use 187—w. τις 195—s. Distributives, Cardinals.

Oepke, A. 255, 263.
Omission—s. Ellipse.
Optative 6, 114, 117, 118–33—periphrastic 88—survival in LXX and NT 90, 127, 132—dying out 90, 94, 118 f., 120, 124—πρίν 113, 140—fut. opt. 118—aor. opt. 118—potential 118 f., 120, 122–4, 132 f.—iterative (oblique) 119, 124 f., 126, 128—volitive 118 f., 120–2, 127—Byzant. period 119, 125, 126, 130—artificial revival 119, 125, 130, 134—classified 119—main clauses 119, 120–4—subord. clauses 119, 124–32—LXX 119, 120 f., 122, 123, 126, 129—condiational 119, 125–8—comparat. 119, 132—final 119, 127, 128 f.—temp. 119—ἄν 120, 122, 124—" urbane " 122—set phrases 123, 131, 132—replaced by indic. 125—indir. speech 129 f.—indir. qu. 130 f., 132—negation 281, 283.
Orators, Attic 91, 106.
Ordinals, cardinals f. 187.
Origen 14, 177, 227, 316.
Ottley, R. R. 93.
Owen, E. C. E. 50.

Pallis, A. 137, 291.
Papyri 7, 8, 22 and *passim*.
Parataxis 9, 155, 334 f., 342.
Parenthesis 127, 342.
Participle 150–62—predicative 150, 158–60—position 79—*Aktionsart* 79, 151—pres., aor. 79–81—pf. 85—fut. 86 f., 135, 150, 153, 158—pres. ptc. f. fut. ptc. 87—in periphr. 87–9, 158—w. ἄρχομαι 138—w. χαίρω 138—attributive 150–3—circumstantial (adv.) 150, 153–8—w. art. 150–3—substantival 150 f.—co-ordinate w. fin. vb. 150, 343—imperatival 150, 293, 303, 308, 310, 343—πᾶς ὁ w. ptc. 151—redundant ὤν 151 f.—absolute 153, 322 f.—particles w. 153, 154, 157, 158—supplem. 153—modal-temporal 154–7—f. *with* 154—pleonastic 154, 155—f. Heb. inf. absol. 156—concessive 157—causal 157—oblique cases 160—negation 281, 284—anacoloutha w. 312, 314, 316—indecl. λέγων, etc. 315—incongruencies w. 315 f.
Particles 329–40—new compound 4, 329—reduced number and use 4, 329—s. Conjunctions.
Partitive expressions as subj. or obj. 7, 208 f.
Passive 57 f.—of vbs. w. indir. obj. 57 f.—trans. depon. vbs. w. pass. sense 58—w. dat., not ὑπό 58—of vbs. w. double accus. 247.
Pauline epistles and Pastorals : adnom. gen. 1—correct use of pf. 5, 69—position of adj. 8—artic. inf. 8, 140, 141 (τοῦ), 141 (εἰς τό, πρὸς τό), 143 (εἰς τό)—neut. adj. w. depend. gen. (not in pap.) 13, 14—neut. expressions f. abstr. noun 13—οἱ ἐκ -ists 15, 260—τὰ κατά f. general relationship 14—τὰ περί 15—αἰῶνες *eternity* 25—ἡμεῖς f. ἐγώ (*pl. sociat.*) 28—vocative 33—use of ἐγώ, σύ 39—οὗτος foll. by ἵνα, ὅτι, etc. 45—αὐτὸ τοῦτο 45—ὅς and ὅστις rule 47—ὁ ἐστιν 48—ἐνεργέομαι 56—epistol. aor. 73—μή τις w. aor. subj. (f. imper.) 77—prefers pres.

to aor. in commands 77—periphr. tenses 88 f.—imperat. ἵνα 95—οὐ μή 96—φοβέομαι μή (semi-lit.) 99—ἵνα w. ind. 100—ἵνα w. subj. 101— epexeg. ἵνα 103 f.—ὅταν w. subj. 112—temp. ὡς ἄν 112—ἐάν w. subj. 114 f.—opt. 119—wish opt. 121—μή γένοιτο 121, 330—εἰ τύχοι 125, 133—inf. w. vbs. *believe, say* 137—style 137, 158—λέγων 156—supplem. (predic.) ptc. 158—'Ιησοῦς and Χριστός without art. 167—pf. f. aor. 170—ὁ κύριος 174—νόμος 177—Colwell's rule 184—ἕτερος 197— πάντες ἄνθρωποι 200—οἱ πάντες 201—position of πᾶς 203, 205— mystic gen. 212—σῶμα 213—several genitives together 218—dat. of cause 242—εἰς and ἐν distinct 256—mystic ἐν 262 f.—σύν 265—repet. of prep. 275—ἕως, ἄχρι, μέχρι 276—μή οὐ in qu. 283—μή w. ptc. 285 —ellipse of copula 295, 299, 300–3—χάρις ὑμῖν, οὐχ οἶον ὅτι, etc. 300—καθάπερ 319—καθώς 320—gen. abs. 322—οὐχί 329—ἀλλά 329 f.— ἄρα, ἄρά(γε) 330—γάρ 331—μέν.. δέ 331 f. —νυνί δέ 331—δέ and καί 332—διότι, διό, εἴτε... εἴτε 333—πλήν weak 338—τε 338— asyndeton 340—parenthesis 342—anacoloutha 343—chiasmus 346.
Pentateuch (LXX) 61, 132, 202 ff., 271, 272, 274, 279—s. Index of Ref.
Peoples, names of, w. art. 169.
Perfect: unique features in NT 5, 69, 85—Aram. infl. 5—disappearance through assumption of aoristic functions 2, 68 f., 81—resultative (act., trans.) 5, 69, 82, 83, 84, 85—rarer in NT than Koine 5—Koine 68, 81— aoristic 68–71, 81, 85—Imp. and Byzant. period 68 f.—periphr. f. 69, 81, 88 f.—intrans. in origin 69, 81—stem assumes aor. endings 69, 81— MGr 69—gnomic 73—ptc. 81, 85—*Aktionsart* 81 f., 85—indic. 81–5— pres. meaning 82, 85—pres. forms coined 82—exegesis 84 f.—moods 85.
Periphrasis in verb 5, 69, 81, 85, 87–9.
Pernot, H. 135, 297, 304, 335.
Perry, A. M. 175.
Personal construction 291 f.
Personal pronouns: non-class. insertion 3, 4—instead of reflex. pron. (Hell. and Semit.) 3, 41, 42 (even after prep. 42 f.)—gen. preferred to possess. pron. 4—pleonast. after rel. 9, 325—in nom. 37 f., 40—oblique cases 38–40—ἐγώ, σύ in Paul 39—LXX use of nom. 40—*constr. ad sens.* 40—αὐτός = οὗτος (demonstr.) 41—position of dat. 309.
Peter, epistles of: atticism in 2Pt 30—tenses of imperat. (1 Pt) 76— prefers aor. to pres. in commands 77—fut. ptc. 87—periphr. tenses 88 f.—ἵνα not imperat. 95—οὐ μή 97—opt. 119, 126 f.—wish opt. 121— ἕτερος absent 197—artic. inf. 140 ff.—position of πᾶς 203, 205— φείδομαι w. gen. (class. 2 Pt) 235—ὑπάρχω w. dat. (2 Pt) 240—μή w. ptc. 285—ellipse of εἶναι 299, 308—καθώς 320.
Philo 26, 125, 126, 180—s. Index of Ref.
Philostratus 159, 299—s. Index of Ref.
Phonetic confusion 6, 94, 98, 101, 129, 130, 132.
Phrynichus 158, 232, 320.
Plato 96, 97, 98, 106, 118, 171, 180, 228, 279.
Pleonasm: μᾶλλον 3, 29—pleonastic pers. pron. after relat. 9, 325— ἄρχομαι 138, 154 f.—ἐγένετο 139, 145, 148 f., 291, 335—λαβών, λέγων, ἔχων, etc. 154, 155—negatives 286.
Pluperfect 86—periphr. f. 88 f.
Plural 7, 25–8—f. one pers. (allusive) 7, 25, 26—place-names 26—festivals 26 f.—Sabbath 27—towns 27—pl. f. sing. (class. and non-class.) 27— *pl. poeticus* 27 f.—*pl. modestiae* 28—" cases of " 28—*pl. sociativus* 28— *pl. auctoris* 28—pl. or sing. vb. w. neut. pl. subj. 312 f.—w. several subjs. 313 f.
Plutarch 16, 53, 128, 191, 279—s. Index of Ref.
Polybius 5, 6, 52, 57, 70, 71, 82, 106, 118, 122, 124, 128, 144, 179, 251, 267, 269, 271, 273, 274, 275, 276, 277, 278, 279, 291, 340—s. Index of Ref.
Positive: f. superl. (Heb.) 3, 31—w. παρά, etc. 7, 29, 31, 32—f. compar. 29, 31—compar. f. pos. 30 f.

INDEX OF SUBJECTS 397

Possessive pronouns 189-192—gen. of pers. pron. f. 4, 189—word-order 189—ἴδιος 191 f.
Prayer, significance of grammar f. 75, 77.
Predicate : anarthr. demonstr. prons. not necessarily predic. 4—nominal and verbal 11—ptc. 159—predic. adj. without art. 182-4—w. art. 183—position of predic. adj. 183—Colwell 183—pred. noun w. εἶναι and dat. 239—ὡς with pred. 246, 321—εἰς w. pred. 246, 253—predic. accus. 253—τί, οὐδέν, ὅ 311—*schema Atticum* 312 f.
Prepositions 6, 249-80—fluidity in meaning and use 2, 3, 261—theology of 3—increase in number 3—cases w. 6, 249 f., 258—w. inf. 8, 78, 85, 105 f., 142-6—w. proper nouns 170 f.—prep. phrases as attribute 221 f.—improper 250—anomalies 254-7—repetition or non-repet. w. 2nd noun 275—circumlocutions f. 279 f.—w. adv. 250—position of prep. phrase 349 f.
Present : *Aktionsart* 59 f., 64, 73, 74-6, 107—indic. 60-4, 98, 100 f., 115—subjunc. 94 f., 97, 101, 107, 108 ff., 112, 114—imperat. 74-6—inf. 72, 78 f., 145—ptc. 79-81—in indir. speech ref. to past 2, 64—historic 5, 60-2—perfective 62—futuristic 63—gnomic 63—conative 63, 72—expresses relat. time 80—periphr. f. 87—delib. 98—after ἵνα 100 f.—after ἐάν 115 f.—in -σκω 71.
Prévot, A. 58.
Procopius of Caesarea 119.
Prolepsis 3, 9, 41, 74, 325—proleptic attraction 226.
Pronouns : extended use in Koine 3, 50—indir. pron. disappearing 4—substantival 37-50—proleptic 41—distinctions blurred 50—attrib. 189-97—s. Demonstr., Interrog., Indef., Pers., Possess., Refl., Relat., Recipr.
Proper nouns w. and without art. 165-9.
Proverbs (LXX) 131 f., 202 ff.—s. Index of Ref.
Psalms (LXX) 132, 202 ff., 272—s. Index of Ref.
Psichari, J. 266.
Punctiliar action 59, 64, 67, 71, 72, 73, 74, 77, 86.

Q 332.
Quality, expressed by art. w. adj. 13 f.
Questions, direct : ὅτι 49 f.—prons. 48-50—dubitat. and delib. qu. 98 f.—οὐ 282 f.—w. οὐ μή 283—conjunctions 282, 283, 319, 330, 333, 334, 337. indirect : 116 f.—and relat. clause 4, 49 f., 195—use of dir. interr. pron. 4, 48.

RSV 30, 95, 137, 143, 145, 146, 151, 265, 335, 336, 350.
RV 55, 95, 137, 143, 151.
RVmg 40.
Radermacher, L. 120, 124, 125, 126, 128, 135, 283, 316, 321.
Rahlfs, A. 108.
Reciprocal pronouns 43 f.—refl. pron. f. 43—εἰς τὸν ἕνα 187.
Redundancy—s. Pleonasm.
Reflexive idea : expressed by act. rather than mid. in Hell. Gk. 54.
Reflexive pronouns : substantive 41-3—3rd pers. f. all pers. 4, 42—Semit. periphr. f. 7, 43—direct 41-3—indir. 43—accent query 41—not increasing in Hell. Gk. 41, 42—αὐτοῦ nearly dead 41—often a substit. f. ἐμός, σός 42.
Reinhold, H. 122.
Regard, P. F. 302, 303, 304.
Relative attraction 324.
Relative clauses 47 f., 106-110—and interrog. clause 4, 49 f., 195—f. fin. clause 107, 109—f. condition 107—f. consec. 109—negation 106, 284—w. ἐάν or ἄν 108—moods 109 f.—w. subj. without ἄν 110—ptc. equiv. to 151—include antecedent 324—continued by main clause 325.
Relative pronouns 47-8—confused w. interr. 4, 49 f.—pleon. pers. pron. in rel. clause 9, 325—w. μέν . . . δέ not class. 36—confusion in Koine

of ὅς and ὅστις, ὅσος and ὁπόσος 47—rules 47 f.—general rel. 47, 107—ὅσπερ 48—ὅ ἐστιν (i.e.) 48—ὅ interrog.? 50—ὅς ἄν f. ἐάν τις 107 f.—constr. ad sens. 312—rel. attract. and inverse 324.
Repetition : of prep. 275—distrib. doubling 187.
Revelation : usage and style like Jn 25—αἰῶνες eternity 25—repet. of pers. pron. 39—τάδε λέγει 44—ὅ ἐστιν 48—pf. f. aor. 69, 70—periphr. tenses 88 f.—fut. f. Heb. impf. 86—imperat. ἵνα 95, 102—οὐ μή 96 f.— ἵνα w. fut. ind. 100—ἵνα w. subj. 101—epexeg. ἵνα 104—τοῦ w. inf. (imper.) 141—anarthr. Ἰησοῦς 167—ἕτερος absent 197—position of πᾶς 203, 205—προσκυνέω w. accus. 245—εἰς and ἐν not confused 255— ἐκ against ἀπό 259—σύν absent 265—παρά w. acc. absent 273—ὑπό w. acc. absent 275—repet. of prep. 275—ἄχρις 276—ἐνώπιον frequ. in 1st part 277—ellipse of εἶναι 299, 310—solecisms 314 f.—ὥσπερ 320— γάρ 331—μέν lacking 332—δέ or καί 332—οὖν 337—few particles 341—parataxis 341—μετὰ τοῦτο (ταῦτα) 341.
Rhetoric 39.
Rhythm 39.
Rife, J. M. 347, 348.
Robertson, A. T. 80, 255, 283.

Schema Atticum 312 f.
Schlatter, A. 316.
Schmid, W. 135.
Schmidt, K. L. 27, 176.
Schneider, J. 26.
Schrenk, G. 213, 267.
Schwyzer, E. 33.
Scribes' corrections 25, 26, 27, 35, 38, 39, 43, 44, 52, 56, 68, 70, 71, 76, 77, 82, 83, 87, 91, 96, 97, 98, 100, 109, 116, 129, 132, 135, 136, 138, 140, 142, 152, 167, 178, 184, 190, 200, 209, 218, 228, 243, 245, 264, 286, 287, 312, 314, 319, 321, 322, 324, 325, 333, 335, 338, 340, 341, 342, 343.
Selwyn, E. G. 235.
Semitic influence 4, 8, 23, 88, 96 and *passim*—in MGr 32.
Semitisms 4—interchange of εἰς and ἐν 2, 249, 251, 254-6, 257—pers. pron. : unemph. nom. 3, 37 f. ; oblique cases frequ. and unemph. 3, 38 ; f. refl. 42—pos. f. superl. (Heb.) 3, 31—proleptic pron. (Aram.) 3, 9, 41, 209—reduced number and use of particles 4—hist. pres. 5, 61, 61—perf. aor. (Heb. stative pf.) 5, 72, 73—periphrasis 5, 85, 87-9— partit. expression as subj. or obj. (Heb.) 7, 207 f.—αὐτός demonstr. 7, 41—gen. of qual. f. adj. 7, 212 f.—ἀπὸ μιᾶς (Aram.) 7, 18, 21—ψυχή refl. pron. 7, 43—οὐ . . . πᾶς 7, 196 f.—πᾶς . . . οὐ, εἰς . . . οὐ 196 f.— anarthr. πᾶς 199 f.—case w. vbs. 7—distrib. sing. 7, 23, 25, 187—τοῦ w. inf. 8, 141, 142—ἐν τῷ w. inf. 8, 144 f.—εἰς τό w. inf. 8, 143— position of adj. 8—pleon. pers. pron. after rel. pron. 9, 325—word-order 9, 193—parataxis 9, 155, 334 f., 342—asyndeton (Aram.) 9, 341—fem. f. neut. (Heb.) 21—εἰς κρυπτήν (Aram.) 21—pl. f. sing. (αἰῶνες, οὐρανοί) 25—true superl. almost dead 31—ἀπὸ προσώπου 25, 279—pl. of ἡμέρα (Heb.) 27—periphr. w. πρόσωπον, στόμα, χείρ 25, 279, 280— pos. f. compar. (Heb.) 29, 31, 32—compar. expressing exclusion (ἤ or παρά f. μᾶλλον ἤ) 32—vocat. 33, 34 f.—Aram. emph. state 34—Heb. constr. state 34, 169, 170, 173, 179 f.—uses of εἰς 36, 187, 195 f.—ὅδε f. οὗτος 44—causatives in—-εύειν 52 f.—act. form w. pass. meaning (Aram.) 53—ποιέομαι ἔλεος (Heb.) 56—fut. ind. for Heb. impf. (Rev) 86 ; f. imper. 86—pres. ptc. f. fut. ptc. 87—imperat. ἵνα 95, 102, 129, 305—compar. opt. 132—τίθημι ἐν τῇ καρδίᾳ, etc. 139—use of inf. (without ὥστε) to express result 134-6—artic. inf. 134—pleon. ἄρχομαι 138, 154 f.—complem. inf. 138 f.—ἐγένετο constrs. 139, 145, 148 f., 291, 335—πρὸς τό w. inf 144—artic. ptc. as proper noun (Heb.) 150 f.— ptc. f. rel. clause 152 f.—pleon. λαβών, λέγων 154, 155—ἔγραψεν λέγων 156—ὁδόν as prep. 175, 212, 247—ptc. f. Heb. inf. abs. 156—ἐν in

multiplic. 188—distrib. doubling 187—ἄνθρωπος f. τις 195—εἰς in post-pos. 196—πᾶς ὁ frequ. 201, 316—υἱός 207 f.—μυριάδες μυριάδων 210—partit. ἐν 210—obj. gen. 212—appos. gen. or gen. of content 214— pron. added to gen. of qual. properly belonging to 1st noun 214—οὕτως predic. 226—fill w. accus. 232 f.—γεύομαι w. accus. 233—σπλαγχνίζομαι 234, 272—gen. w. verbal adj. 234—κωλ ύω ἀπό 235—eth. dat. 239— ἔρχεταί σοι 239—ἀστεῖος τῷ θεῷ 239—γίνομαι w. dat. 239 f.—dat. of agent w. pass. 240—dat. f. Heb. inf. abs. 241 f.—ἡμέρᾳ καὶ ἡμέρᾳ 243— φοβέομαι ἀπό 244—ὄμνυμι ἐν 244, 252, 255—accus. of content 245— καλέω τὸ ὄνομα w. accus. 246—εἰς predic. 247—ἄφαντος ἐγένετο ἀπό 251—ἐν instr. 252 f.—τοῖς εἰς μακράν 254—εἰς ὄνομα 255—δίδωμι εἰς place on 256—δὸς ἀντὶ ἐμοῦ καὶ σοῦ 258—ἐπ' ἐσχάτου τῶν ἡμερῶν 271— pre-position of ἕνεκα 276—ἐν μέσῳ etc. w. gen. 277—ὀπίσω as prep. 277—ἔμπροσθεν, ἐναντίον, ἐνώπιον 277 f.—impers. "they" (Aram.) 292 f.—ὄνομα without copula 295—οὐαί 296—ellipse of εἶναι 300— τί ἐμοὶ καὶ σοί; 303, 309—τί πρός σε; 303, 309—indecl. λέγων, λέγοντες 315—πᾶς ὅς 316—ὁ πᾶς w. ptc. 316—consec. ὅτι 318— weakening of ἐπεί 318—εἰ f. οὐ in oaths 319, 333—εἰ w. dir. qu. 319, 333—ὡς to soften 320—tempor. conj. instead of gen. abs. 321— anacolouthon after rel. clause 325—ὅτι recit. 326—εἰ μή interchanged w. ἀλλά (Aram.) 330—καί introd. subord. clause 334—τότε (Aram.) 341—chiasmus 345-7—particle 1st word 347—vb's position in sentence 347 f.—art. close to noun 348 f.
Sentence building 11, book I—sentence complete book II.
Septuagint: ὅδε more common than in NT 44—τῇδε 44—ὅστις confined to nom. and acc. 47—hist. pres. 61—aor. pf. 70—pf. 82 f., 84—periphr. tenses 89—ὄφελον 91—imperat. ἵνα 95—οὐ μή 96 f.—fin. ἵνα 102— non-fin. ἵνα 104—ἐάν w. impf. 116—opt. 120 f., 122, 123, 125, 126, 127, 130, 131, 133—inf. of purpose 135—τοῦ w. inf. 141—ἐν τῷ w. inf. 145 f.—ptc. 156—rendering of Yhvh 174—position of πᾶς 202 ff.— piecemeal transl. 237, 337—and passim.
Septuagintisms 8, 142, 145, 156.
Sibylline Oracles 25, 26, 27.
Singular 22-5—distrib. sing. 7, 23, 25—w. collectives (generic) 22 f.— ἕκαστος w. pl. 312—vb. w. neut. pl. subj. 312 f.—w. cmpd. subj. 313 f.— w. fem. pl. 315.
Sirach (LXX): πρίν 140—πᾶς 202 ff.
Slavery (Paul's advice) 76.
Slotty, F. 95.
Soffray, M. 35.
Solecisms 93, 314-7.
Solomon, Psalms of 96, 203 ff.
Sophocles 49, 96, 97—s. Index of Ref.
Sophocles, E. A. (lexicographer) 58.
Souter, A. 22.
Stählin, G. 245.
Stauffer, E. 40.
Strabo 13, 14, 71, 118, 159, 299.
Style 137—desire f. variety 67, 105, 109 f., 113, 135, 142, 157.
Subject 11—absence of 291-3, change of, marked by ὁ (οἱ) δέ 37.
Subjunctive 93-117—more often without ἄν in Hell. Gk. 2—Aktionsart 74-8, 107—periphrastic 88-9—confused w. opt. in wishes 94, 120— πρίν 113, 140—as substitute for opt. 119.
  Use in main clauses 93-9—prohib. subj. 74, 76-8, 94, 95—as substit. f. imperat. 93-8; f. fut. 98—jussive 94—hortat. 94—imperat. ἵνα 94 f.—οὐ μή w. aor. subj. (prohib. and denials) 96 f., 97; w. pres. subj. 97—w. μή f. cautious statements 98—in dubit. or delib. qu. 98 f.—οὐ μή in qu. 283.
  Subord. clauses 99-117—fearing 99—after μή 99 f.—after ἵνα 100-5— neg. μή 100, 105, 106—fin. clause 100-6—w. ὅπως, ὡς 105 f.—w. ὥστε

106, 136—in rel. clauses (futuristic) 106-10—in temp. clauses 110-13—
    w. ὅτε (late) 112—condit. clause 113-6—w. εἰ 116—indir. qu. 116 f.
Subordination 318-23, 342 f.
Swete, H. B. 221.
Superlative: elative 3, 31—true superl. almost dead 31—comparison of
    31—f. comparat. 32.
Symmachus 85, 113, 330.
Synagogue 6, 132.

Temporal clauses 92, 110-3, 321—ὡς ἄν in Paul 112—πρίν 113, 140,
    144—μετά τό w. inf. 143—πρό τοῦ 140, 144—ἐν τῷ 144 f.—w. ptc.
    154-7—ἐπί 272—position 344 f.—negation 284.
Temporal conjunctions 110-3, 321.
Tense 59-89—s. Time, *Aktionsart*.
Text of NT 31 f., 40, 70, 84, 86, 92, 97, 122, 152, 167, 181, 184, 295, 346—
    readings rejected 37, 38, 41, 70, 106, 110, 129, 139, 141, 167, 170, 171,
    209, 229, 331.
Thackeray, H. St. J. 61, 62, 279, 315, 335.
Theophylact 52.
Thomas, D. W. 239.
Thompson, F. E. 96.
Thucydides 13, 84, 88, 96, 106, 171, 228, 275, 340—s. Index of Ref.
Time : kinds of 59—ambiguity in Gk 60—pres. and aor. ptc. 79-81.
Tischendorf, C. 183.
Tobit : non-fin. ἵνα 104—πρίν 140—πᾶς 203 ff.—s. Index of Ref.
Tragedians 27.
Transitive verbs 2, 51-3—from intr. 2, 51 f.—used absol. 51—pass. sense
    of trans. depon. 58.
Trenkner, S. 334.
Turner, C. H. 2, 254, 271, 326, 342.
Turner, N. 2, 97, 192, 201, 252, 275, 276.

Unreal indicative 91 f.

Venetus, codex 44.
Verbal adjectives 89, 91.
Vettius Valens 128, 245—s. Index of Ref.
Vocative 3, 33-5—use of ὦ 33—emotion in 33—nom forms f. 3, 34 f.—
    position 33—κύριε *sir* 34—explan. of anarthr. nom. 35.
Voice 2, 51-8—s. Active, Middle, Passive.
von Soden, H. 93.
Vulgate 30, 35, 50, 65, 73, 181, 208, 256, 259, 272, 333.

Wackernagel, J. 22, 63, 265, 270, 271, 273, 276, 293.
Weiss, J. 345.
Wellhausen, J. 347.
Westcott, B. F. 143, 143.
Westcott and Hort 183.
Western readings 17.
Winter, P. 325.
Wishes : infin. 78—indic. 91—opt. 118 f., 120-2—ἵνα w. subj. 120.
Word-order 344-50—unique in Bibl. Gk. 9—prep. and case 5, 276, 278—
    voc. 33—copula in periphr. tense 89, 348—ἄν 92, 93, 107, 110—ἵνα-
    clause 105, 344—ptc. and adjuncts 152—adj. attrib. 189 f., 349—poss.
    adj. and gen. of poss. pron. 189 f., 191—ἴδιος 192—attrib. pron. 193—
    οὗτος, ἐκεῖνος 193—τις 195—εἷς 196—πᾶς 201-5—prep. phrase 209,
    349, 350—attrib. and partit. gen. 217 f.—adv. 227-9—several gens.
    218—main and depend. gen. 218/349—negative 286 f.—attrib.-subj.
    296—καθώς-clause 320—ὥστε-clause 320—gen. abs. (Mk) 322—antec.
    of rel. clause 324—rel. pron. 324—conj. 329, 330, 340, 347—μενοῦν

338—τε 339—τοιγαροῦν, τοίνυν 340, 347—fin., local, temp. clauses 344—causal and comp. clauses 345—chiasmus 345-7—subj.-obj.-vb. 347 f.—in the clause 347-50—normal 347—set phrases 350—art. close to noun 348—oratory and 350—ambiguity 350.

Xenophon 16, 61, 65, 96, 97, 106, 118, 143, 170, 171, 228—s. Index of Ref.

Zerwick, M. 26, 35, 42, 50, 50, 56, 57, 65, 72, 75, 79, 80, 87, 114, 115, 127, 145, 178, 201, 207, 210, 212, 214, 215, 233, 236, 255, 256, 259, 263, 285, 316, 341, 342, 347.
Ziegler, J. 44, 230.
Zorell, F. 316.

INDEX OF GREEK WORDS

Ἀβραάμ 168
ἀγαθόν, τό 13, 14—τὰ ἀγαθά 14
ἀγαλλιάω w. ἵνα 138—w. ptc. 160
ἄγαλμα, ellipse of 17
ἀγανακτέω περί w. gen. 269
ἀγαπάω, ingress. aor. 72
ἀγάπη w. gen. 211, 214
ἀγαπητός 214—w. gen. 234
ἀγγαρεύω ἵνα 138
ἄγγελος anarthr.174, 180
ἄγε 51, 231
ἅγιος, ὁ 13—τὸ ἅ. 2—τὰ ἅ. 27, 31 (superl.)
ἁγιάζομαι, aor. imperat. 77
ἁγνίζω pass. 57
ἀγνοέω not w. ptc. 161
ἀγορά anarthr. 179
ἀγριέλαιος 18
ἀγρός anarthr. 179
ἄγω: intr. 2, 51—aor. imper. 76—impf. 66—fut. ptc. 87—ἄγει τρίτην ταύτην ἡμέραν 291
ἀγωνίζομαι pf. 84
ἀδελφός, scil. w. gen. 168— plur. 22
ἀδικέω intr. 51—pass. "submit to fraud" 57—perfect. pres. 62
Ἀδρίας 172
ἀδυνατόν, τό 13—scil. ἐστιν 295, 306, 307, 309
ᾄδω 236
ἄζυμα 27
ἀθεμιτόν ἐστιν 149
Ἀθῆναι 27—Ἀθηναῖοι w. art. 169
ἀθῷος ἀπό 215
Αἴγυπτος anarthr. 171
αἵματα 27—ἐν τῷ αἵματι 241
αἰνέω 236
αἱρέομαι 78
αἴρω, intr. 52—gen. w. 232—aor. imper. 76, 77
αἰσθάνομαι w. acc. 234—not w. ptc. 161

αἰσχρόν (ἐστιν) 149, 295, 300
αἰτέω: act. and mid. 54 f.—futuristic pres. 63—constr. w. 149—pres. imper. 75
αἰών: pl. 25—ὁ ἀ. οὗτος, ἐκεῖνος 193
ἀκατάπα(υ)στος w. gen. 215
ἀκμήν 247
ἀκολουθέω: constr. 241—impf. 66— pres. imper. 76, 77—aor. pf. 82
ἀκούω: case w. 2, 161, 233—perfect. pres. 62—aor. pf. 82, 84 f.—ptc. 160f.
ἀκριβέστερον 3, 30— -έστατος 31
ἀκροβυστία w. gen. 211
ἄκρος: predic. 225—τὸ ἄ. w. gen. 224
ἅλατι instr. 240
ἀλείφομαι 54
ἀλεκτοροφωνίας 235
ἀλήθεια: anarthr. 177f.—ἐπ' ἀληθείας 253
ἀληθινός, ὁ 13
ἀλλά 329 f.—w. γε 331—w. ἵνα 304, 307, 330—w. καί 330
ἀλλήλων 43 f.
ἄλλος: f. ἕτερος 32, 197—position 187—ἄ. πρὸς ἄλλον 44—ἄλλοι ἄλλο 197
ἀλλότριος w. gen. 235
ἅμα: w. ptc. 153 f.—w. dat. 276
ἁμαρτάνω: ingr. aor. 72—pres. imper. 76
ἁμαρτία anarthr. 177
ἀμετάθετον, τό 14
ἀμήν, τό 14
ἀμύνομαι f. -ω 55
ἀμφί absent 249
Ἀμφιπόλη 171
ἀμφότεροι: f. more than two 32— w. art. 197
ἄν 107 f.—w. ind. 2, 91 f., 93, 110 —w. subj. 2, 108—ἄν f. ἐάν 91,

INDEX OF GREEK WORDS

113—w. opt. 91, 120, 122-4, 127, 130f.—position 92, 93, 110— ὅπως ἄν 94, 105—w. fut. ind. 110 —w. ἕως ἄχρι μέχρι 110, 111— ὡς ἄν 112 f., 321
ἀνά: τὸ ἀ. 14—ἀ. μέσον 23, 251, 265—distrib. 187—uses curtailed 249—not w. dat. 249—w. acc. 265
ἀναβαίνω: pass. meaning 53—futur. pres. 63—ἀνέβη ἐπὶ τὴν καρδίαν αὐτοῦ 292
ἀναγινώσκω constr. 137
ἀναγκάζω impf. 65
ἀνάγκη: pl. 28—constr. 148—no ἐστιν 295, 300, 307, 309
ἀνακάμπτω intr. 52
ἀναμιμνῄσκω constr. 234
ἀναπαύομαι constr. 235
ἀναπληρόω: w. ἵνα 102—w. dat. 238
ἀναστρέφω(-ομαι) intr. 52
ἀνατέλλω: causat. 53—gnom. aor. 73
ἀνατίθεμαι w. dat. 242
ἀνατολή: sg. and pl. 26—anarth. 26, 172
ἀναφαίνω causat. 53
ἄνεμος ellipse 17
ἀνένδεκτόν ἐστιν τοῦ w. inf. 141, 286, 305
ἄνεσις w. dat. 219
ἄνευ w. gen. 275 f.
ἀνέχομαι constr. 234
ἀνέῳγα 5, 82
ἀνῆκεν 90
ἀνήρ: ὦ ἄνδρες 33—f. τις 195
ἀνομολογέομαι w. dat. 236
ἄνθρωπος: οἱ ἄ. one 180—f. τις 195 —πάντες ἄ. 200
ἀνθύπατος 26
ἀνίστημι: ἀναστάς 154
ἀντέχομαι w. gen. 232
ἀντί: use curtailed 249—ἀντὶ τοῦ w. inf. 144—w. gen. 258—ἀνθ' ὧν (ὅτι) 258, 345—compound vbs. constr. 242
ἀντικρύς w. gen. 277
ἀντιλαμβάνομαι w. gen. 232
ἀντιπέρα w. gen. 216
ἀντλάω pf. 84
ἄνω 279—τὰ ἄ. 14
ἀνωφελές, τό 14
ἄξιος constr. 139, 141, 295
ἀξιόω constr. 149—ἠξίου 65

ἀόρατα, τά 14
ἀπάγχομαι 54
ἀπαιτέω 292
ἀπαλλοτριόω constr. 235
ἀπαρνέομαι 58
ἅπας 199
ἀπειθέω constr. 237
ἀπειθής constr. 220
ἀπείραστος κακῶν 215
ἀπεκδύομαι 55
ἀπέναντι w. gen. 6, 278
ἀπελθών pleon. 154
ἀπέχω intr. 52—f. ἀπείληφα 62— ἀπέχει 291, 336— -ομαι constr. 235
ἀπιστέω constr. 237
ἀπό: f. partit. gen. 7, 208 f.—ἀπὸ μιᾶς 7, 18, 21—οἱ ἀπό 15—ἀπὸ προσώπου 25—w. adj. 215 f.— gov. nom. 230—w. vbs. 233, 258 f.—f. παρά w. ἀκούω, etc. 233 f., 258 f.—ἀπὸ τοῦ στόματος 233—f. gen. of sep. 235, 251— ἀπὸ τότε 250—f. far from 251— encroaches on ἐκ, ὑπό 251, 259— w. φεύγω 244— f. ὑπό (causat.) 258 —w. gen. 258 f.—f. country of origin 259—f. after 259—ἀφ' ἧς 17
ἀπογράφομαι act. 57
ἀποδίδωμι: futur. pres. 63—fut. pf. 87
ἀποθνῄσκω: pass. sense 53—futur. pres. 63
ἀποκόπτομαι 57
ἀποκρίνομαι: constr. 237—ἀποκριθεὶς εἶπεν, etc. 61, 79, 155 f.—ἀπεκρίθη 54, 79
ἀποκτείνω pass. 53
ἀπολλύω 82
Ἀπολλωνία 171
ἀπολογέομαι w. dat. 236
ἀπολούομαι mid. 54
ἀπολύω impf. 67
ἀπόλωλα 82
ἀπορέομαι 56—constr. 244
ἀπορίπτω intr. 52
ἀποσπάω act. f. mid. 56
ἀποστέλλω: aor. pf. 70, 84—constr. 266
ἀποστερέω: intr. sense 51, 52—pass. submit to loss 57—constr. 235
ἀποστρέφω intr. 51 f.

INDEX OF GREEK WORDS

ἀποτάσσομαι w. dat. 236
ἅπτομαι: pres. imper. 76—w. gen. 232
ἄρα, ἄραγε 330, 347—ἄρα οὖν 330
ἆρα, ἆρά γε 330, 333
'Αραβία: art. 170, 171
ἀργύριον 17—pl. 27
ἀρέσκω: constat. aor. 72—constr. 236
ἀριστερά (χείρ) 17
ἀρκέομαι 57 f.
ἀρκετόν 139, 295, 309—ἀρκετός 220
ἁρμόζω mid. f. act. 55
ἀρνέομαι: aor. imper. 76—s. ἀπαρνέομαι
ἄρτι position 228
ἄρχομαι: pleon. 138—ἀρξάμενος 154 f.—adverbial 227
ἀρχήν; τήν 49 f., 247
ἀσεβής, ὁ 13, 22
ἀσθενές, τό 14, 21
ἀσθενέω pf. 70
'Ασία, ἡ 170
ἀσπάζομαι: pres. 73—aor. imper. 75, 77
ἄσπιλος ἀπό 216
ἆσσον 30
ἀστεῖος τῷ θεῷ 239
ἀστήρ anarthr. pl. 172
ἀστοχέω constr. 235
ἄστρον anarthr. pl. 172
αὐλίζομαι impf. 67
αὔρα ellipse 17
αὔριον: ἐπαύριον 17
αὐτόματος adj. f. adv. 225
αὐτός: not emph. 3, 40—demonstr. 7, 41, 194—confusion of αὐτός etc. w. αὑτός 41; of αὐτοῦ and ἴδιος 2; of αὑτοῦ and ἑαυτοῦ 41—αὐτοῦ frequ. and pleon. 38 f.—he emph. 40 f.—possess. gen. 40, 189 f.—in reflexives 41 f.—αὐτὸς ὁ 41, 194 —αὐτὸ τοῦτο 45—ὁ αὐτός constr. 183, 194—τὸ δ' αὐτό constr. 246 —position of dat. 349
ἄφες w. subj. 94
ἀφίημι: futur. pres. 63—aor. imper. 77—constr. 138—οὐκ ἀφίω 287
ἀφίσταμαι constr. 235
ἀφυπνόω ingress. aor. 72
'Αχαΐα: art. 170
ἄχρι(ς): w. gen. 276—conj. 110 f.— ἄ. οὗ 276, 345

βάαλ, ἡ 21
βάλλω: intr. 51, 52—futur. pres. 63 —impf. 67—gnom. aor. 73— proleptic aor. 74—aor. and pf. 84— fut. f. impf. 86
βαπτίζω: mid. and pass. 57—impf. 67—periphr. tense 87—ptc. 151
βάπτισμα w. gen 211
βασιλεία ἐν 241
βασιλεύω 2, 52, 62, 64, 71—ingress. aor. 72—pres. imper. 76
βασιλεύς voc. 34
βαστάζω pres. imper. 77
βάτραχος, ἡ 22
βιάζομαι pass. 58
βιβλίον art. 173
βλασφημέω 245
βλασφημία 26
βλέπω: constr. 138, 160 f.—βλέπετε 78
βορρᾶς anarthr. 172
βούλομαι: constr. 78—impf. 65, 91 —βούλεσθε w. delib. qu. 98
βουλὴ ἐγένετο ἵνα 139
βραδύνω w. gen. 235
βραδύς constr. 141
βρέχει: trs. and intrans. 52—impers. and pers. 291
βροντὴ γέγονεν 291
βρῶμα ἵνα 139
βύσσινος 17

Γαλιλαία, ἡ 170
γαμέομαι: w. dat. 238—Aktionsart 79 — -ίζομαι get married 57
γάμος pl. 27
γάρ 331, 347
γε 331, 347
γέμω, γεμίζω: constr. 233: aor. imper. 77
γενέσια 27
γεννάω: futur. pres. 63—τὸ γεννώμενον, τὸ γεγεννημένον 21—aor. pf. 70—γεννητός w. gen. 234
γένος: τῷ γένει 221
γεύομαι w. acc. and gen. 233
γῆ: ellipse 16, 170—w. 'Ιούδα, 'Ιουδαία 170—w. 'Ισραήλ 169— art. w. 174 f.
γίνομαι: γέγονα 5—γέγονεν f. ἐγένετο 70—futur. pres. 63—ἐγενήθημεν 54—aor. imper. 77—μὴ γένοιτο 118, 120-2—w. ptc. in periphr. 87,

INDEX OF GREEK WORDS

89—w. τί 130—ἐγένετο w. inf.
139, 148 f., 291; w. fin. vb. 335;
ἐν τῷ w. inf. 145—fut. ptc. 86 f.—
w. adv. 226—w. gen. 231—w. dat.
239 f.— w. εἰς 253
γινώσκω: pass. 58—pf. 70, 84—
  ingress. aor.71—gnomic aor. 74—
  constr. w. 160 f.
γλῶσσα ellipse 17, 18
γνήσιον, τό 14
γνώμη τοῦ w. inf. 141 f.
γογγύζω pres. imper. 76
γονεῖς, οἱ 22
γράμματα 176
γράφω: impers. pass. 5, 292—in
  epistles 73—pres. imper. 76—pf.
  84, 85—constr. 149—w. λέγων
  156
γρηγορέω: pres. imper. 75, 77—
  new verb 82
γυνή: art. w. 173 f.—f. τις 195

δαιμόνια schema Atticum 313
δακρύω ingress. aor. 72
δαμάζομαι pass. constr. 240
δέ 329, 331 f.—position 347
δεῖ constr. 139, 148, 291—supply w.
  inf. 78—δέον (ἐστιν) 88, 291,
  295, 305, 308, 322—ἔδει 90, 148,
  291
δειγματίζω intr. 51
δέω w. double accus. 247—δέομαι
  constr. 146, 149
δεισιδαίμων comp. 30
δέκα, οἱ 178
δεκάμηνος, ἡ 17
δέκατον, τό 17, 210
δεξία 17
δέρω: πολλάς, ὀλίγας 18, 246, 247
δεσμεύομαι impf. 67
δεσπότης, ὁ (voc.) 34
δεῦρο, δεῦτε: w. subj. and imper. 94
δευτεραῖος 225
δή 333
δῆλον ὅτι 295, 300
δημοσίᾳ 18
-δήποτε 196
δήπου 339
διά: encroaches on simple case 236—
  w. gen. 267—w. acc. 267 f.—διά
  τοῦ w. inf. 144—διά στόματος 25,
  280—διά χειρός 280—διά τό w.
  inf. 85, 142 f., 147, 345

διαθῆκαι 27
διαγρηγορέω linear aor. 71
διακονέω: pres. imper. 77—impf. 67
  —w. dat. 236—pass. 57
διαλέγομαι impf. 66
διαλείπω w. ptc. 159, 226
διάλεκτος ellipse 17
διαμένω 82
διαμερίζομαι: impf. 67—mid. 54
διαρρήγνυμι f. mid. 56
διατελέω w. ptc. 159, 226
διατρίβω constat. aor. 72
διαφημίζω perfect. aor. 72
διδακτός w. gen. 211, 234
διδάσκαλος, ὁ (voc.) 34
διδάσκω: aor. pf.70—w. double accus.
  246—pass. w. accus. 247
δίδωμι: futur. pres. 63—impf. 66, 67
  —aor. pf. 70, 83, 84—aor. and
  pres. imper. 76, 77—fut. f. impf.
  86—opt. δῴη 100,128 f.—w. εἰς 256
  —impers. δώσουσιν 293—δὸς ἐργασίαν 76, 99
διέρχομαι: futur. pres. 63—impf. 66—
  constat. aor. 72
δίκαιος, ὁ 13, 22, 23—δίκαιόν ἐστιν
  295, 300
δικαιοσύνη: constr. 211—ἐν δ. 252
δικαιόω gnom. aor. 73
διό 333
διόπερ 333
διοπετές, τό 17
διότι 161, 318, 333, 345
διψάω w. accus. 232, 244
δογματίζομαι submit to rules 57
δοκέω: constr. 78, 137, 147—pres.
  imper. 76
δοκιμάζω constr. 147, 160, 162
δοκιμεῖον, τό 14
δόλῳ, ἐν 252
δοξάζω: impf. 66—prolept. aor. 74—
  constr. 242, 246
δουλεύω: perfect. pres. 62—ingress.
  aor. 71—w. dat. 236
δουλόω 56
δραχμή ellipse 17
δύναμαι: constr. 78, 138—ἐδύνατο
  could have 90
δυνατός: constr. 78, 139, 147, 238
  —δυνατόν (scil. ἐστιν or ἦν) 295,
  297, 300, 305, 306, 309—τὸ δυνατόν 14
δύο δύο 187

δύο *second* 315
δυσμαί anarthr. 26, 172
δωρεάν 247
δῶρον 295, 309

ἐάν 109, 113 f., 115 f.—instead of εἰ (w. indic.) 107, 115 f.—ὅς ἐάν 107 f.—ἐάν καί 321—f. ἄν 2
ἐάω: οὐκ ἐῶ 287
ἑαυτός f. 1st or 2nd p. 42
ἑαυτοῦ: f. ἀλλήλων 43 f.—and αὐτοῦ 41—indir. refl. 43—in Lk 42—position 190
ἑβδόμη, ἡ 17
ἑβδομηκοντάκις ἑπτά 187
ἐγγίζω: pf. 5, 82—ingress. aor. 72—constr. 241
ἐγγύς: case 216—as predic. 226
ἐγείρω: intrans. 52—pass. w. act. meanings 57—futur. pres. 63—ἐγήγερται *he is risen* 69—pres. imper. 75—ἐγρήγορα 82—ἐγερθείς 154
ἐγκαίνια 27
ἐγκακέω w. ptc. 159
ἐγκαλέω: pass. 57—constr. 236, 242
ἐγκαταλείπω perf. aor. 72
ἐγκόπτω constr. 245
ἐγώ: μου f. ἐμός 4—literary pl. 28—use of nom. 37 f.—μου and ἐμοῦ 38, 189—emph. obl. cases 39—ἐμοῦ f. ἐμαυτοῦ 42—possess. gen. 189—position of μου 189
ἔθνη: anarthr. 180—*schema Atticum* 313
ἔθος ἐστίν constr. 149
εἰ 115 f.—wish-clause 91—f. ἐάν (w. subj.) 107, 116—εἰ καί 115, 321—w. opt. (final) 127—εἴ γε 319—*whether* 319, 333—oaths, etc. 319, 333—εἰ οὐ 319—dir. quest. 319, 333—εἰ μή 333—εἰ μή f. ἀλλά 330—εἰ δὲ μή (γε) 331
εἰδέναι: constr. 160, 162—οἶδα perf. pres. 62, 82
εἴθε w. ind. 91
εἰθισμένον, τό w. gen. 234
εἰμι, εἶναι: perf. pres. 62—imperat. fut. 86—fut. ptc. 86—in periphr. 5, 85, 88 f., 153—ὁ ὤν καὶ ὁ ἦν 230—ptc. redund. 151 f. — ellipse 231, 294-310—w. dat. 240
εἴπερ 319, 330

εἶπεν: and ἔλεγεν 64—εἰπών 155 f.
—w. ἵνα 103— πρός 237
εἴπως 127
εἰρήνη w. dat. 304, 308
εἰς: εἰς κρυπτήν 6—εἰς τό w. inf. 8, 85, 106, 135, 141, 142, 143—ὁ (οἱ) εἰς 15—εἰς χεῖρας 24, 280 — encroaches on simple case 236, 251, 253— w. λογίζομαι 246—w. ἔχω, etc. (predic.) 246, 247—γίνομαι, εἰμι 253—f. ἐπί, πρός 256 local 266 — distrib. 266— final 266 —causal 266 f.— confused w. ἐν, see ἐν
εἷς: indef. art. 4, 195 f.—ἀπὸ μιᾶς 7, 18, 21—μία f. πρώτη 17, 187—ἕν fem. 21—ὁ εἷς . . . ὁ ἕτερος 36 —εἰς τὸν ἕνα 187—ἕν τριάκοντα 188— w. partit. gen. 195—εἷς τις 196—καθείς 197—εἷς ἕκαστος 198 —cmpd. vbs. constr. 242
εἰσάγω aor. 69
εἰσακούω 251
εἰσέρχομαι linear aor. 71
εἰσφέρω aor. imper. 77
εἴτε . . . εἴτε 302, 319, 333
εἴωθα 82
ἕκαστος 198—anarthr. 198— diff. from πᾶς 199—w. pl. vb. 312
ἐκβάλλω futur. pres. 63
ἐκδίδομαι mid. 55
ἐκεῖ: redund. after ὅπου 46—f. ἐκεῖθεν 226—temp. 226
ἐκεῖθεν: οἱ ἐ. 14—f. ἐκεῖ 226
ἐκεῖνος 5, 45 f., 192 f.—ἐκείνης (scil. τῆς ὁδοῦ) 16—anaph. 46—simply *he* 46—meaning 45 f.—ἐκείνου possess. 190—art. 192
ἐκκλησία: anarthr. 176—*constr. ad sens.* 312
ἐκκλίνω intr. 52
ἐκκόπτομαι 63
ἐκλέγομαι mid. 55
ἐκλεκτός w. gen. 234
ἐκπίπτω: f. ἐκβάλλομαι 53—gnom. aor. 73
ἐκπλήσσομαι impf. 66
ἐκτός: w. gen. 216, 277—ἐ. εἰ μή 321
ἐκχέω: w. gen. 234—w. dat. 238
ἐλαία ellipse 18
Ἐλαιῶν ὄρος 230
ἔλαττον, τό f. persons 14, 21
ἐλαύνω impf. 67

INDEX OF GREEK WORDS

ἐλαφρόν, τό 14
ἐλάχιστος 31— -ον w. ἵνα 139—
 -ότερος 31
ἐλεέω: trans. 234, 244—aor. 69
ἐλεύθερος: ἀπό, ἐκ 215— w. dat. 238
 ἐλευθερόω ἀπό 235
Ἑλλάς w. art. 170—Ἕλληνες 26,
 169—ἑλληνική, ἡ 17
ἐλπίζω: impf. 66— w. fut. inf. 79—
 ἤλπικα 82, 84—constr. 238
ἐμαυτοῦ 41—position 190
ἐμαυτῷ f. μοι 42
ἐμβάπτομαι mid. 55
ἐμμένω constat. aor. 72
ἐμός: disappearing 42, 191—μου f.
 4, 189
ἐμπαίζω constr. 242
ἐμπορεύομαι tr. and intr. 244
ἔμπροσθεν 6, 278 f.
ἐμφανής constr. 220
ἐν 260 f.—confused w. εἰς 2, 249,
 251, 254-6, 257—extension 6—f.
 partit. gen. 7, 208, 210—ἐν τῷ
 w. inf. 8, 142, 144 ff.—οἱ ἐν 15
 ἐν χειρί 24, 280—encroaches on
 simple case 236, 241, 251-3, 264
 f.—f. instrum. dat. 240, 252 f.—
 w. accompanying circumstances,
 forces, etc. 241, 252—adv. 250—
 temp. 252, 262—manner 252—f.
 gen. of price 253—of cause 253—ἐν
 μέσῳ 257—in quot. formulae 261—
 local 261 f.—ἐν Χριστῷ κυρίῳ 262
 —Christian use 262 f.—other uses
 265—compound vbs. constr. 242
ἔναντι w. gen. 278
ἐνάντιος: constr 220—ἐξ ἐ. 16—
 -ιον w. gen. 251, 277
ἐνδέχομαι constr. 291 f.
ἐνδιδύσκω: constr. 247—impf. 66
ἐνεδρεύω trans. 244
ἕνεκα(-εν) 276—ἕ. τοῦ w. inf. 144—
 position 5, 276
ἐνεργέω trans. and intr. 244—
 -έομαι 56
ἐνέχω: intr. 52—w. dat. 242
ἐνθυμέομαι w. accus. 245
ἔνι 308
ἔνοντα, τά 247
ἐνορκίζω constr. 244
ἔνοχος constr. 175, 215
ἐντέλλομαι constr. 142
ἐντολή ἵνα 139

ἐντός: w. gen. 216, 277—τὸ ἐντός
 14
ἐντρέπομαι w. accus. 234, 245
ἐντυγχάνω constr. 242
ἐνώπιον 251, 277
ἐξ, ἐκ: extended use 249—f. partit.
 gen. 7, 208-10, 233—οἱ ἐκ 15,
 260—ἐκ τοῦ w. inf. 144—ἐλεύθερος ἐκ 215— w. buy 234—f. dat.
 of sep. 235—f. country of origin
 259—causal 259 f.—confused
 w. ἀπό 259—as subj. gen. 259—
 instrum. 260—w. fill 260—w.
 στόμα, χείρ 24, 280
ἐξαμαρτάνω causat. 52
ἐξαπορέομαι τοῦ w. inf. 141
ἐξαυτῆς 17
ἐξέρχομαι: linear aor. 71—aor.
 imper. 76—w. fin. inf. 134
ἔξεστιν: constr. 149—ἐξόν (scil.
 ἐστιν) 88, 291, 295, 300, 304,
 309, 322—ἐξῆν absent 91
ἑξῆς, (ἐν) τῇ 17
ἐξίστημι impf. 66
ἐξομολογέομαι w. dat. 236
ἐξουσία constr. 139, 141, 211
ἔξω: w. gen. 216, 277—ἔξωθεν
 w. gen. 216
ἑορτή 243
ἐπαγγέλλομαι 58—constr. 236
ἐπάν 112 f., 344
ἐπανάγω intr. 51
ἐπάνω: f. ἐπί 251—w. gen. 279—
 ἐπάνωθεν f. ὑπέρ 251
ἐπεί, ἐπειδή 318, 321, 344, 345
ἐπέκεινα 26
ἐπερωτάω impf. 65, 67
ἐπέχω intr. 52
ἐπηρεάζω w. dat. 7, 245
ἐπί 6, 250—w. accus. 272—ἐφ' ὅσον
 272—w. gen. 271—ὁ ἐπί 15—ἐ.
 στόματος 280—w. dat. 271 f.—
 ἐφ' ᾧ 134, 272, 345—cause 272—
 cmpd. vbs. constr. 242
ἐπιβάλλω intr. 52
ἐπιδείκνυμι mid. 55
ἐπιεικές, τό 14
ἐπιθυμέω: constr. 232, 244—impf.
 66
ἐπικαλούμενος, ὁ 152, 206
ἐπιλαμβάνομαι w. gen. 232
ἐπιλανθάνομαι: constr. 58, 234—
 gnom. aor. 73—pres. imper. 76

ἐπιμένω w. ptc. 159, 226
ἐπιοῦσα, ἡ 17
ἐπιποθία w. τοῦ w. inf. 141
ἐπίσταμαι constr. 160, 162
ἐπιστέλλω τοῦ w. inf. 142
ἐπιστολαί, αἱ 27
ἐπιστρέφω, -ομαι intr. 52
ἐπιτάσσω constr. 149
ἐπιτελέομαι 55—w. dat. 238
ἐπιτρέπω 58—punctil. pres. 64
ἐπιτυγχάνω constr. 232
ἐπιφαίνω intr. 52
ἐπιχορηγέω constr. 236
ἑπτάκις, τό 14
ἑπτάμηνος, ἡ 17
ἐργάζομαι pass. 58
ἐργασίαν, δός 76, 99
ἔργον w. gen. 211
ἔρημος, ἡ 13, 16
ἔρις pl. 28
ἐρρέθη ὅτι 291
ἔρρωσο 85
ἔρχομαι: perfect. pres. 62—ὁ ἐρχόμενος futuristic 63, 151—aor. pf. 70—ἔρχου, ἐλθέ 75—ἔρχου καὶ ἴδε 75—impf. 66—aor. 69—w. fin. inf. 134—w. dat. 238, 239
ἐρωτάω: impf. 65, 67—aor. 65—w. ἵνα 138—w. inf. 149
ἐσθίω constr. 244
ἑσπέρα anarthr. 179
ἕστηκα meaning 5, 53, 82
ἔσχατος 32—ἐπ' ἐ. τῶν ἡμερῶν 271
ἔσω 216, 276
ἑταῖρε 50
ἕτερος: confused w. ἄλλος 32, 197—ὁ ἕ. 197
ἔτι 333—w. comp. or pos. f. comp. 29, 31—position 228
ἑτοιμάζω aor. imper. 77—pf. 84
ἕτοιμος constr. 139, 141, 142
εὐαγγελίζω: causat. 2, 53— -ομαι 58, 291—constr. 245, 246
εὐαγγέλιον constr. 210, 211
εὐαρεστέομαι pass. 57
εὐδοκέω: ingress. aor. 72—constr. 244
εὐδοκία 213
εὐεργεσία constr. 212
εὐθύς, -έως 153—in Mk 229
εὐκαιρία τοῦ w. inf. 141
εὐλογημένος: superl. 31—w. gen. 234 —scil. ἐστιν 296, 305
εὐλογητὸς ὁ θεός 296, 308

εὐπάρεδρον, τό 14
εὑρίσκω: pass. 58—act. f. mid. 56— pf. 84—impf. 66—fut. ptc. 87— constr. 160, 162
Εὐρώπη, ἡ 170
εὐσεβέω trans. 244
εὔσχημον, τό 14
εὐχαριστέω constr. 160
εὐχαριστία w. dat. 219
εὔχομαι: impf. 65, 91—εὐξαίμην ἄν 91—constr. 236
ἕως: conj. 344—ἕ. τοῦ w. inf. 144
Ἔφεσος 171
ἔχω: τῇ ἐχομένῃ (ἡμέρᾳ) 17—intr. w. adv. 51, 52—ἔσχηκα f. aor. 70, 83—ingress. aor. 72—imperat. inf. 78—have to, know 138—ἔχων with 154—ἔχων indecl. 315—w. ptc. 160, 162—have as w. double acc., ὡς, εἰς, ὅτι 226, 246—ἔχομαι w. gen. 232
ἕως: w. gen. 276—conj. 110 f., 321 —w. ἄν, οὗ, ὅτου 111

ζῆλοι pl. 28
ζηλόω mid. 55
ζάω: ingress. aor. 71—constr. 264
ζητέω: futur. pres. 63—pres. imper. 75

ἤ 7, 216, 334—w. positive 31—f. μᾶλλον ἤ 32, 216—ἤ . . . ἤ 334
ἤ 333
ἡγέομαι: w. acc. and inf. 137—w. ptc. 162—w. double acc. 246— ἥγημαι pres. 82, 84—ἡγούμενος noun 151
ἥκω 62, 82
ἡλίκος excl. 50
ἥλιος 172
ἡμεῖς: f. ἐγώ 28—use of nom. 37— position of ἡμῶν 189
ἡμέρα: ellipse 17, 18—pl. f. sing. 27 —art. 179—w. gen. of qual. 213— (ἐν τῇ) ἡμέρᾳ 243—ἡμέρα καὶ ἡμέρα 243—τὴν ἡμέραν per day 247—(τὸ) καθ' ἡμέραν 247
ἡμέτερος 191
ἥμισυ, τὰ ἡμίσεια, w. gen. 210
ἡνίκα 112 f., 321, 344
ἤπερ 32
ἡσυχάζω ingress. aor. 72

INDEX OF GREEK WORDS

θά 138
θάλασσα art. 174 f.
θάνατος anarthr. 175—θάνατοι 28
θάπτομαι 62, 69
θαυμάζω: aor. imper. 77—constr. 234, 244, 269
θεά 22
θεάομαι 58—constr. 160 f.
θελήματα 28—θέλημά έστιν ίνα 139
θέλω 78—impf. *I would like* 65, 91
  —periphr. fut. 89—w. ίνα 103, 138—adverbial 227—w. accus. 244
θεμέλιον 13
θεός: gender 22—voc. 34, 35—anarthr. 174—θεοῦ 212
θεοστυγεῖς 234
θερμαίνομαι 54
θεωρέω constr. 160 f.
θησαυρίζω pres. imper. 76
θλῖψις w. dat. 219, 238
θνήσκω: pf. τέθνηκα 5, 69, 82
θριαμβεύω causat. 53, 244
θυγάτηρ 35
θυμόω ingress. aor. 72
θύρα sing. and pl. 27—w. gen. of direction 212

ίάομαι pass. 58—punctil. pres. 64
ίδε 231
ίδιος 2, 4, 191 f.—ίδίᾳ 18—κατ' ίδίαν 18
ίδού: καί ί. 229—ίδε without syntax 231—without fin. vb. 296, 303, 306, 309
Ίεροσόλυμα 27—Ίερουσαλήμ 171 f.
ίερουργέω trs. 244
Ίησοῦς art. 166 f.
ίκανός constr. 139, 147, 220—ίκανόν 305
ίκετηρία 18
ίλάσκομαι: *be merciful* 57—constr. 244
ίλεως (σοι) 309
ίμάτιον: ellipse 17—pl. 27
ίνα 2, 2, 8 f., 128, 134, 138 f., 141—imperat. 94 f.—final 100 f., 105 f. —w. indic. 100 f.—ecbatic 102—causal 102 f.—epexeg. 103 f., 129 —άλλ' ίνα 304, 307, 330—elliptical 304, 305—temporal 321—position 344
Ίόππη art. 171
Ίορδάνης, ὁ 172

Ἰουδαία, Ἰούδα 170—Ἰουδαῖοι art. 169—Ἰουδαῖος, ὁ 22
ίππος, ἡ 22
ίσα 21—ίσος 220
Ἰσραήλ, ὁ 169
ίστημι aor. imper. 77
ἰσχύω constr. 138
ἰσχυρά, τά 21
Ἰταλία, ἡ 170

καθά 345—καθάπερ 319, 320, 345
καθαιρέομαι constr. 235
καθάπτω f. mid. 56
καθαρίζω άπό 235
καθαρός: άπό 215—w. dat. 220, 239
καθ' εἰς 197, 268, 317—τὸ κ.ε. 197
καθεύδω impf. 66
καθῆκεν 90
κάθημαι impf. 66
καθίζω: perf. aor. 72—constat. aor. 72—aor. and pf. 70—aor. pf. 82
καθό 320
καθότι 318, 345
καθώς 320, 345—scil. έστιν 297, 307
καί: κ. ταῦτα w. ptc. 157—art. w. nouns connected by κ. 181—ὁ κ. 206—καί... καί, τε... καί 329, 334, 335—varies w. δέ 329, 332, 334—ἤ κ. 334—introducing apodosis 334—copula 334 f.— after έγένετο 335—κ. ιδού 335—epexeg. 335—καί τίς *who then?* 335—κ. νῦν 335—εἴ κ., s. εἰ—έάν κ., s. έάν—κ. ἄν, κ. έάν, s. κάν
καίγε 331
καίπερ w. ptc. 153, 157
καιρός: pl. 27—constr. 139, 141—anarthr. 179—w. ούτος and νῦν 193
καίτοι (γε) 157, 339
κακά, τά 14—κακόν (scil. έστιν) 295
κακόω fut. ptc. 87
καλέω: linear aor. 71—pf. 84 imperat. fut. 86—ὁ καλούμενος 152, 206—w. double acc. 246—w. εἰς, έν 264
καλλιέλαιος, ἡ 18
καλόν 90, 295, 309—constr. 139, 149—τὸ καλόν 13—τά καλά 2, 14 —καλός superl. 31
καλῶς constr. 245—κάλλιον 30
κάν 100, 321
καρδία, distrib. sing. 23

INDEX OF GREEK WORDS

καρποφορέω act. and mid. 55
καρτερέω trans. 244
κατά: w. accus. 268—as adv. 187—
  κ. μόνας 18, 21—κ. ἰδίαν 18—κ.
  πρόσωπον 25—τὸ (τὰ) κ. 15, 247
  —οἱ κ. 15—w. gen. 268
καταβραβεύω w. acc. 234
καταγινώσκομαι pass. 58
καταδικάζω 236, 245
καταδουλόω 56
κατακληρονομέω causat. 53
κατακλίνω w. double acc. 247
κατακρίνω: fut. ptc. 86—constr. 236
  —w. θανάτῳ 240
καταλαμβάνομαι mid. 55
καταλείπω futur. pres. 63
καταμανθάνω pres. imper. 76
κατανεύω constr. 142
κατανοέω: gnom. aor. 73—w. ptc. 160 f.
καταπαύω: intr. 52—constr. 235
καταράομαι w. accus. 7, 245
καταργέομαι futur. pres. 63—prolept. aor. 74
κατέναντι 6, 278
κατεργάζομαι 58
κατηγορέω pass. 58—w. πρός 237
κάτω 279—τὰ κ. 14
καυματίζομαι w. acc. 245
καυχάομαι constr. 236
κε, κεν 124
Κεδρών, ὁ 172
κείρομαι have one's hair cut 57
κεῖμαι perf. pres. 62, 82
κελεύω: impf. 65—constr. 78, 148, 236
κενόν, εἰς 266
κέντρον pl. 27
κεφαλή distrib. sing. 24
κηρύσσω: impf. 67—imper. inf. 78
Κηφᾶς 22
Κιλικία art. 170, 171
κινδυνεύω constr. 138
κλαίω: pres. imper. 76—aor. imper. 76—imperativ. inf. 78—constr. 244
κλέπτης, ὁ 180
κληρονομέω constr. 232, 244
κλίνω intr. 52
κλοπαί 28
κοιμάομαι 62—ingress. aor. 72
κοινωνέω w. gen. 232, 241
κοινωνία constr. 211
κοινωνός constr. 215
κοινόω pf. 69
κολλάομαι w. dat. 241
κόλπος pl. 27
κοπιάω aor. pf. 82
κόπτομαι constr. 244
κόσμος : anarthr. 174 f.—w. οὗτος 193
κράζω and κέκραγα 82
κρατέω: pres. and aor. imper. 77—ingress. aor. 72
κράτιστε voc. 31
κρεῖττον ἦν 90
κριθαί 27
κρίνω: constr. 78, 238—pf. 84—mid. 142
κρούω pres. imper. 75
κρυπτά, τά w. gen. 14—εἰς κρυπτήν 6, 21
κτίζω pf. 70
κυκλόθεν 277—κύκλῳ 221, 251
κυλίομαι 66
κύριος: pl. 22—κύριε sir 34—ὁ κ. (voc.) 34—anarthr. 167, 174
κωλύω constr. 235

λαγχάνω constr. 141
λάθρᾳ 226, 277
λαλέω: impf. 67—aor. pf. 70, 84—fut. ptc. 87—constr. 237, 238
λαμβάνω: aoristic εἴληφα 69 f., 82, 84—gnom. aor. 73—pleon. λαβών, λάβετε 154— -ομαι w. gen. 232
λάμπω ingress. aor. 72
λανθάνω w. ptc. 159, 226
λαός: ὁ λ. μου (voc.) 34— w. constr. ad sens. 311 f.
λατρεύω w. dat. 236
λέγω: λέγει hist. pres. 5, 60 f.—τάδε λέγει 44—asyndetic λέγει 61, 340 —ἔλεγεν 67, 68; and εἶπεν 64, 68 —aoristic εἴρηκα 69, 70, 83—imperat. fut. 86—w. ἵνα 103—w. double accus. 147—w. pers. accus. 149—ὁ λεγόμενος 152—λέγων, λέγοντες 155 f., 315—impers. ἔλεγον 292—ellipse of subject 293
λεγιών 21
λείπομαι w. gen. 235
λίαν position 227 f.
Λιβύη, ἡ 170
λιμός gender 7, 21
λογίζομαι: w. inf. (ὅτι) 137—w. double acc. 246—w. εἰς 246—pass. 58

INDEX OF GREEK WORDS 411

λογομαχέω imperat. inf. 78
λόγος constr. 180, 212, 220
λοιπόν, τό 336—τοῦ λοιποῦ 235
λούω: mid. 54—constr. 235
λύω: impf. 65—aor. imper. 76—
　constr. 235—act. f. mid. 56
λυπέομαι ingress. aor. 72
λυσιτελεῖ constr. 292
λυτρόω constr. 235

μαθητεύω causat. 53, 244
μακάριος without vb. 102, 296, 300,
　303, 305, 310
μακράν 247—w. gen. and ἀπό 216
　—predic. 226
μακροθυμέω aor. imper. 77
μαλακοί, οἱ 13, 17
μᾶλλον: pleon. 3, 29—w. pos. 31—
　ellipse of 32, 216
μανθάνω constr. 146, 160
Μαρίαμ, -ία art. 168
μαρτυρέω: aor. pf. 82—constr. 146,
　238—parenthet. 342—pass. 57
μαρτύριον, τό 14
μάχαι 28
μάχαιρα: ἐν μ. 252
μάχομαι constr. 241
μέγας superl. 31—μέγιστος 29 f.
μεθίστημι constr. 235
μεθοδεῖαι 28
μεθύσκομαι 240—pres. imper. 76
μείζων: as superl. 29—μεῖζον 21
μέλει constr. 269
μέλλω: w. inf. f. impf. 79—w. fut.
　inf. (Ac) 79—w. inf. f. fut. 89
μέν ... δέ 165, 331 f., 347—μὲν οὖν
　37, 337—μενοῦν γε 338, 347
μένω: constat. aor. 72, 77—aor.
　imper. 77
μεντοί 340
μεριμνάω: pres. and aor. imper. 76,
　77—constr. 238
μέρος: ellipse 17—pl. f. district 26
μεσονύκτιον: anarthr. 179—temp.
　gen. 235
Μεσοποταμία, ἡ 170
μέσος: predic. 225—τὸ μέσον 14—
　ἀνὰ μέσον 23—ἐν μέσῳ w. gen.
　257—w. ἐκ, διά 267
μεστός w. gen. 215
μετά 6—not w. dat. 249—w. acc.
　269—μετὰ τό w. inf. 85, 143—
　asyndetic μετὰ ταῦτα 341—w. gen.

268 f.—and σύν 265, 268 f.—w.
λέγω, etc. 237—encroaching on
　simple dat. 236—in composition
　269
μεταδίδωμι w. acc. 231
μεταίρω intr. 52
μεταλαμβάνω w. gen. 231
μεταμορφόομαι w. dat. 240
μετανοέω pres. imper. 75
μεταξύ w. gen. 277
μετέχω constr. 231
μετοικεσία constr. 212
μέτρον: (ἐν) ᾧ μέτρῳ 253
μέχρι(ς): conj. 110 f., 276, 345—
　μ. οὗ 111, 276, 345—τοῦ w. inf.
　144—prep. w. gen. 276
μή 4, 281-7—w. aor. subj. (prohib.)
　74, 76-8, 94—μὴ οὐ 98, 283—
　μὴ γένοιτο 118, 120-2—τὸ μή w.
　inf. 141—τοῦ μή w. inf. 142—
　interrog. 282 f.—in hesit. qu. 283—
　πᾶς ... μή 287
μηδέ 286, 340
μήν 336
μήποτε 98, 99—neg. 98
μήπως 99
μήτε ... μήτε 340
μήτηρ scil. 168
μήτι(γε) 283
μικρόν (ἐστιν) 295, 303—μικρότερος
　30
Μίλητος 171
μιμνῄσκω: constr. 234—ἐμνήσθην
　pass. 58—μέμνημαι 82
μισέω: ingress. aor. 72—pf. 84
μνημονεύω constr. 234
μοιχάομαι ἐπί 272
μοιχεῖαι 27
μόνος: and adv. μόνον 225 f., 228—
　οὐ μόνον ... ἀλλά 295—ὁ μ. 13—
　κατὰ μόνας 18, 21
Μυσία, ἡ 170
μωρά, τά of persons 14, 21—τὸ
　μωρόν 14

νά 95, 103
ναί 286, 336—τὸ ναί 14
νεκροί anarthr. 180
νέος comp. 30
νή 336
νικῶν, ὁ perfective 62
νίπτομαι aor. imper. 77
νοέω constr. 240

INDEX OF GREEK WORDS

νομίζω: impf. 66—aor. imper. 77— w. inf. or ὅτι 137
νόμος: anarthr. 173, 177—constr. 212
νότος anarthr. 172
νῦν 153—τὸ νῦν 14—as adj. 222—position 228
νυνὶ δέ 331
νύξ 179, 235—νυχθήμερος 17

ξηρά, ἡ 16, 17
ξηραίνω: gnom. aor. 73—prolept. aor. 74
ξυράομαι 57

ὁ, ἡ, τό: s. Article—as voc. 34—as pron. 36—ὁ μέν ... ὁ δέ 36—ὁ δέ 37—ὁ καί 206—ὁ, τό, οἱ, τά w. gen. 16, 166, 168, 179 f.—οἱ ἐκ 15, 260—τὸ, τὰ ἐκ 14—τὸ, τὰ κατά 14—τὸ, τοῦ, τῷ w. inf. 8, 78, 85, 105 f., 139, 140 f., 142–6
ὅδε 44, 192
ὁδός ellipse 16, 18—ὁδόν w. gen. versus 175, 212, 247—ὁδῷ w. πορεύομαι 241
ὅθεν f. where 226—conj. 336, 344
οἶδα, s. εἰδέναι
οἴδε 43
οἴομαι: pres. imper. 76—constr. 137
οἰκία constr. ad sens. 311 f.
οἶκος, voc. w. art. 34
οἰκουμένη, ἡ (scil. γῆ) 17
οἰκτιρμοί 28
οἷος 46 f., 49—w. superl. 31—excl. 50—οὐχ οἷον ὅτι 295, 300
ὀλίγος: τὸ ὀλίγον 13—ὀλίγας δέρομαι 18, 246—ὀλίγου w. aor. absent 91—ἐν ὀλίγῳ 262
ὅλος art. 199—δι' ὅλης νυκτός, etc. 199
ὁμιλέω: impf. 66—constr. 241
ὄμνυμι: pres. and aor. imper. 75, 76—constr. 137, 244
ὅμοιος case 216, 220
ὁμολογέω constr. 162, 236, 291
ὅμως 337
ὀνειδίζω w. acc. 245
ὄνομα: τοὔνομα 239—ᾧ ὄ., οὗ τὸ ὄ., καὶ τὸ ὄ. αὐτοῦ, ὄ. αὐτῷ, ὀνόματι 220, 230, 295 f., 303, 304 f., 306, 310
ὄπισθεν w. gen. 277

ὀπίσω w. gen. 6, 277
ὁποῖος 49
ὁπόσος 47
ὁπόταν 124
ὁπότε 321, 345
ὅπου 46, 109, 116—scil. ἐστιν 297—ὅπου ἄν w. ind. 93
ὅπως 49, 94, 102, 105 f, 128, 138—w. ἄν 94, 105
ὁράω: pass. ὀπτάνομαι, ὤφθην 58—aor. pf. 70—ὅρα (ὁρᾶτε) μή 78—pf., plu pf. 84, 85—σὺ ὄψῃ and pl. 86—constr. 160
ὁρατά, τά 14
ὀργίζομαι: ingress. aor. 72—constr. 234
ὀρεινή, ἡ 16
ὁρκίζω constr. 244
ὅς, ἥ, ὅ: confused w. ὅστις 2, 47 f., 117; w. ὅσος 47; w. τίς (is ὅ dir. interr.?) 49 f.—ἀφ' ἧς 17—ᾖ w. superl. 31—ὅς μέν ... ὅς δέ 36—ὅ ἐστιν 48—ὅτι dir. interrog. 49 f.—f. τίς 50—ὅς ἐάν 108—ὅς ἄν w. indic. 110—ὅς γε 331
ὅσος: confused w. ὅς 47; w. τίς 49—w. ἐάν 108—excl. 50
ὅσπερ 48
ὅστις 110—confused w. ὁπόσος 47; w. ὅς 47 f.—ὅ τι w. indir. qu. 49—dir. interrog. 50—w. subj. without ἄν 108
ὀσφύς distrib. sing. 24
ὅταν 2, 112 f.—w. ind. 92 f., 107, 112, 124, 125—position of clause 344
ὅτε 321—w. subj. 107, 112
ὅτι: s. ὅστις—declarative 134, 137, 148, 161, 306—f. inf. 2, 137—w. superl. 31—why? 49 f.—negation 284—scil. ἐστιν 297, 309—οὐχ (οἷον) ὅτι 298, 303—consec. 318—causal 318, 345—recit. 325 f.—clause-order 344
οὐ 4, 281–7, 338—τὸ οὐ 14—οὐ μή w. subj. 95–8; w. fut. 96 f.—οὐ ... πᾶς (πᾶς ... οὐ) 196 f., 287—in questions 282 f.—οὐ 286—οὐ ... οὐ 286—οὐ ... οὐδέ (μή ... μη δέ) 286—οὐ πάντως 287—οὐ ... ἀλλά 329—οὐ μόνον ... ἀλλά 329
οὐαί 260, 296, 306, 308, 309, 315

οὐδέ 340
οὐκοῦν 282, 337
οὖν 329, 337 f.—ἆρα οὖν 330—position 347— -ουν 196
οὐρανός: sg. and pl. 25—anarthr. 174 f.
οὔτε . . . οὔτε 340
οὗτος 192 f.—αὕτη f. τοῦτο 21—αὐτή and αὕτη confused 40—deictic 44—w. anaphora 44 f., 46—pronominal 44 f.—αὐτὸ τοῦτο 45—pointing forward to ὅτι, ἵνα, ἐάν, infin. 45, 139—τοῦτο μὲν . . . τ. δέ 45—elliptical τοῦτο δέ 45—τούτου possess. 190—art. 192—asyndetic μετὰ τοῦτο (ταῦτα) 341
οὕτω(ς): w. ptc. 154—as predic. 226, 303—ὡς . . . οὕτως 320
οὐχί 96, 282, 286, 329
ὀφείλω: intr. 51—ὤφειλον 90—ὄφελον 91, 295, 300—constr. 141
ὀφειλέτης constr. 238
ὀφθαλμός anarthr. 179
ὄχλος: constr. ad sens. 311—ὄχλοι πολλοί 7, 26
ὀψέ: ἐγένετο 226—ο. σαββάτων 278
ὀψία 17
ὄψιμον scil. ὑετός 18
ὀψώνιον pl. 27

παῖς, ἡ (voc.) 34—οἱ παῖδες 22
πάλαι, ἐκ 250
πάλιν in Mk 229
Παμφυλία art. 170
παντότε position 228
πάντως οὐ (οὐ πάντως) 287
παρά 6, 250, 272—w. acc. 273—w. pos. and comp. 3, 7, 29, 31, 216, 251—w. inf. 144—w. gen. 273—οἱ π. 16—τὰ π. 15—ἀπό f. 233 f. 258 f.—w. dat. 273—cmpd. vbs. constr. 242
παραβιάζομαι 65
παραγγέλλω: punctil. pres. 64—impf. 65, 67
παράγω intr. 51
παραδίδομαι: futur. pres. 63—aor. pf. 83—fut. ptc. 86, 151
παραινέω constr. 149
παρακαλέω: impf., aor. 65—constr. 142, 149
παραλαμβάνω Aktionsart 79
παραπλήσιον case 216

παρατηρέομαι 55
πάρειμι perfective 62
παρέχομαι 56
παριστάνω pres. and aor. imper. 76, 77
παρρησία constr. 241
πᾶς: position 5, 201-5—πᾶς . . . οὐ (οὐ . . . πᾶς) 7, 196 f., 287—πᾶς ὅστις (ὅς) 21, 316—ὁ πᾶς and pl. 21, 201—πᾶς ὁ w. ptc. 151, 197, 316—anarthr. 199 f.—w. art. 200 f.—πάντων f. fem. 316—anacolouthon w. 316
πάσχα, τά 27
πάσχω: pres. imper. 76—aor. pf. 82—w. ὑπό 53
Πάταρα 27
πατήρ: voc. 34, 35—art. 174
παύομαι mid. constr. 159, 235
πειθαρχέω constr. 7, 237
πείθω, -ομαι: constr. 137, 138, 237—perf. pres. 62—πέπεισμαι 82, 137—s. πέποιθα
πεινάω w. acc. 232, 244
πέμπω epistol. aor. 73
πενθέω: trans. and intr. 244—aor. imper. 76
πενθεροί, οἱ 22
πέποιθα: constr. 237, 242—pres. sense 5, 82
πέραν w. gen. 216, 278
περί 6—not w. dat. 249—w. acc. 270—οἱ π., τὰ π. 15, 16, 270—w. gen. 269 f.—w. σπλαγχνίζομαι, μεριμνάω, μέλει 269—w. ἐγκαλέομαι 231—w. θαυμάζω 269—interch. w. ὑπέρ 270—τὰ π. w. gen. 15, 269
περιάγω: intr. 51—w. double acc. 246
περιβάλλω: aor. imper. 77—w. double acc. 246
περιβλέπομαι mid. 55—impf. 66
περιέχω intr. 52, 292
περικύκλῳ f. περί 251
περίοδος ellipse 17
περιπατέω: pres. imper. 75, 77—aor. imper. 76
περίχωρος, ἡ 16
πέτρα, πέτρος 22
πηλίκος exclam. 50
πίνω constr. 244
πίπτω: impf. 66—fut. f. impf. 86

πιπράσκω: impf. 67—pf. 70, 84
πιστεύω: constr. 137, 237 f., 247, 263—pass. 57, 247, 291—impf. 67—ingress. aor. 71—pres. and aor. imper. 75 aor. pf. 82
πίστις constr. 211, 263
πιστός constr. 220
πλεῖστος, ὁ 30—τὸ π. at most 31
πλείων: (οἱ)πλείονες 30, 172— πλεῖον 21
πλεονεκτέω trans. 244
πληγή ellipse 18
πλῆθος w. constr. ad sens. 312
πλήν prep. w. gen. 278—advers. conj. 338
πλήρης: constr. 215—indecl. 315 f.
πληροφορία w. gen. 211
πληρόω: act. and mid. 55—pass. 58— pass. w. acc. 233, 245, 247—pf. 84 —ἵνα πληρωθῇ 102
πλησίον w. gen. 216
πλούσιοι, οἱ 13, 34
πλουτέω ingress. aor. 72
πνέω: τῷ πνέοντι and τῇ πνεούσῃ 17
πνεῦμα: pl. w. sing. or pl. vb. 313— constr. ad sens. 312—π. ἅγιον art. 175 f.—(ἐν) πνεύματι 241
πνίγομαι impf. 67
ποιέω: constr. 138, 142, 246—mid. 56—ἔλεος μετά 56—ποιέομαι σπουδήν, etc. 56—futur. pres. 63— impf. 66—pf. 69, 70, 83, 84— ingress. aor. 72—pres. imper. 75, 76, 77—aor. imper. 77—fut. ptc. 87—w. ἵνα 104—w. inf. 138—w. ptc. 159—καλῶς (εὖ) π. 245
ποῖος: f. τίς 48—f. ὁποῖος 48—ποίας (scil. ὁδοῦ) 16
πολεμέω constr. 241
πόλις w. gen. of name 215
πολύς: οἱ πολλοί 13, 31—τὸ πολύ 13 —πολλάς δέρομαι 18, 246, 247— πολλοί great 26—ὁ ὄχλος π. 26, 186—πολύ, πολλῷ w. comp. 29— (τά) πολλά adv. 247 f.
πονηρός, ὁ 13, 14—πονηρά, τά 14
πορεύομαι: impf. 66, 67—futur. pres. 63—aor. pf. 70—πορεύου, πορεύθητι 75—πορευθείς 154
πορνεῖαι 27
πόρρω predic. 226
πόρφυρος 17
πόσος: f. ὁπόσος 48—exclam. 50

πόταμος, ὁ 172
ποταπός 48
ποτέ 153— -ποτε 196
πότερος: confused w. τίς 32—πότερον ... ἤ 338
ποτίζω: w. double acc. 246—pass. w. acc. 247
ποῦ 109, 235
πούς: πόδες καί χεῖρες 350
πρασιαί 231
πράσσω perf. pres. 62
πρέπει, πρέπον ἐστίν: 88, 149, 292, 295, 309—personal constr. 147
πρεσβύτερος 30
πρίν: constr. 78, 113, 140, 345— π. ἤ 78, 113, 130, 140—prep. w. gen., acc. 260, 270
πρό: w. gen. 248, 260—πρὸ τοῦ w. inf. 78, 140, 144, 345
προάγω intr. 51
πρόβατον neut. pl. w. sing. vb. 313
προβλέπομαι mid. 55
πρόδηλον ὅτι 295
προέχομαι 56
προηγέομαι trans. 245
προθυμία τοῦ w. inf. 141
πρόϊμος 18
προκόπτω intr. 52
προλαμβάνω w. inf. 138, 227
πρός 6, 273—cmpd. vbs. constr. 242 —adv. use 250—w. gen. and dat. 273 f.—w. acc. 274—πρός με 39— πρός τό w. inf. 105 f., 141, 144—w. λέγω, etc. 237—encroaches on simple dat. 251—f. παρά 254, 274 —εἰς f. 256 f.
προσάγω intr. 51
προσεύχομαι: impf. 66—pres. imper. 75—w. ἵνα 103—w. τοῦ w. inf. 142—w. dat. 236—περί w. gen. 269
προσέχω: intr. 52—constr. 138
προσήκει absent 91
προσκυνέω 7, 236, 245—impf. and aor. 65—fut. f. impf. 86—fut. ptc. 87
προσποιέομαι constr. 138
προστάσσω: aor. 65—constr. 149
προστίθεμαι: constr. 138, 155, 227 —προσθείς εἶπεν 227
προσφέρω pres. imper. 75
πρόσωπον: anarthr. 179—Hebraisms 25, 279

INDEX OF GREEK WORDS

πρότερον, τό 30
προϋπάρχω w. ptc. 159
προφθάνω w. ptc. 159
πρωΐ: τό π. adv. 14, 247—ἦν π. 226
πρωΐα, ἡ 17
πρῶτος f. πρότερος 32
πτωχεύω ingress. aor. 71, 72
πτωχός, ὁ 13, 23
πυκνότερον 3, 30
πύλη: ellipse 18—sing. and pl. 27
πυνθάνομαι impf. 65—aor. 65
πῦρ: w. φλόξ 213—(ἐν) πυρί 240, 252, 253
πῶς 117, 123, 137—f. ὡς, ὅτι 137

ῥαβδίζω constat. aor. 72
ῥάβδος: ellipse 18—ἐν 241
ῥίπτω intr. 52
ῥομφαία, ἐν 252
ῥύομαι: pass. 58—constr. 235
Ῥώμη, ἡ 171

σάββατον: sing., pl. 27—(δὶς τοῦ) σαββάτου 235—(ἐν) τῷ σ., τοῖς σ. 243—ὀψὲ σ. 278
σαλπίζω: aor. imper. 77
Σαμαρίτης art. 169
σαπρά, τά 14
σάρξ: anarthr. 177—τῇ σ. 239—(τὸ) κατὰ σ. 268
σεαυτοῦ 41—position 190
σελήνη art. 172
σημεῖον 26, 214
σήμερον, ἡ 17
σιγάω ingress. aor. 71 f.
σιωπάω impf. 66
σός disappearing 42, 191
σπάω 55
σπέρμα constr. ad sens. 312
σπλαγχνίζομαι constr. 234, 269, 272
σπουδαῖος comp. 30
σταυρόω aor. and pf. ptc. 85
στήκω 82
στηρίζω w. πρόσωπον τοῦ w. inf. 142
στοιχέω: imperat. inf. 78—pres. imper. 75
στολή distrib. sing. 25
στόμα Hebraism 25, 280
στρατεία constr. ad sens. 311 f.
στρ φω: intr. 2, 51, 52—aor. imper.

σύ: nom. 37—possess. gen. 38 f. 189—σου f. σεαυτοῦ 42 f.—position of μου, σου, ἐμοῦ 189
συγκαλέομαι 55
συγκληρονόμος w. gen. 215
συλλαμβάνω pf. 84
συλλέγω impers. pl. 293
συμβαίνω: aor. pf. 82—συνέβη 139, 148, 292
συμβουλεύω, -ομαι constr. 149
συμπόσια 231
συμφέρει: constr. 103, 139, 149, 292 —συμφέρον scil. ἐστιν 88, 295, 300
σύμφυτος w. dat. 220
συμφωνέω constr. 149, 234
σύν: encroaches on simple dat. 236 —and μετά 265, 269—οἱ σὺν αὐτῷ 265
συνάγω intr. 51
συναίρω λόγον 56
συναντάω fut. ptc. 86
συναρπάζω pf. 84
συνέπομαι constr. 241
συνεργέω 244
συνέρχομαι linear aor. 71
συνίημι constr. 160
συντίθεμαι constr. 142
Συρία art. 170
σύρω 66
συσχηματίζομαι to conform 57
σῴζω constr. 235, 240—pf. 69, 83, 84—aor. 69—fut. ptc. 87
σῶμα: distrib. sing. 7, 23, 24— w. gen. of qual. 213—schema Attic. 313
σωτήριος constr. 220—τὸ σωτ-ήριον 14

ταπεινόω aor. imper. 77
τάσσω constr. 149
ταχύς: τάχιον 30—ἐν τάχει 252
τε ... καί, τε ... τε, etc. 329, 338 f., 347—τε γάρ 339
τέκνον ellipse 21—τὰ τ. voc. 34
τελειόω: futur. pres. 63—w. ἵνα 102
τελέω: pf. 85—w. ptc. 159
τελευτάω aor. pf. 82
τέλος, εἰς 266
-τεος 91
τέταρτον, τό 17
τηρέω pf. 84
τίθημι: act. and mid. 55—ἔθετο 56 —impf. 67—pf. 84—constr. 246

INDEX OF GREEK WORDS

τιμιώτατος 31
τίς: f. δστις 4, 48, 49, 117—f. πότερος 32—varying w. δσος and δς 49—τί έμοί καί σοι 240, 303, 306 —εις τί 267—τί γάρ (μοι) 301— τί οδν 301—τί πρός ήμας (σε) 303
τις 195—indecl. 316—είς τις 195— w. partit. gen. or έν 209—ού (μή) ... τις 77—εί τις 321—position 195
τοιγαροΰν 340, 347
τοίνυν 340, 347
τοιοΰτος 21, 46 f., 193 f.—ό τ. 46 f., 193 f.
-τος verbal adj. w. gen. 89
τοσοΰτος 46 f., 194
τότε 341—as adj. 222—άπό τ. 250
τουτέστιν 45
τρέμω w. ptc. 160
τρίζω trans. 244
τρίμηνος, ή 17
τρίτη, τη 17
τρόπος: (καθ') δν τρόπον 247—παντί τρόπω 241
Τρωάς art. 171
τυγχάνω: constr. 158, 227, 232— aor. pf. 82—εί τύχοι 125, 133— τυχόν 322
τύπος distrib. sing. 25
τυφλόω pf. 70, 84

ύβρίζω trans. 244
ύδωρ: pl. 27—ellipse 18
ύετός ellipse 18
υίός: voc. 34—scil. 168—anarthr. 173 f.—figurat. 207 f.
ύμεις: nom. 37 f.—ύμιν f. έαυτοις 42 —position of ύμων 189, 190— ύμων f. ύμέτερος 190
ύμέτερος 190, 191
ύπάγω: intr. 51—ΰπαγε 75, 77, 342 —w. ίνα or inf.? 135
ύπακοή w. obj. gen. 211
ύπακούω w. dat. 237
ύπάρχω: w. dat. 240—w. ptc. 158 f.
ύπέρ: w. pos. and comp. 3, 7, 31, 216 —τοΰ w. inf. 105—as adv. 250, 271—w. acc. 270—interchanged w. περί 270—w. gen. 270 f.
ύπεράνω: w. gen. 279—f. ύπέρ 251
ύπερέκεινα w. gen. 216
ύπερέχων, τό 14
ύπερλίαν 250

ύπήκοος 220
ύπηρετέω w. dat. 236
ύπό 274—not w. dat. 249, 274— άπό f. 258—cases 275
ύποκάτω: w. gen. 279—f. ύπό 251, 279
ύποκρίσεις 28
ύπολαβών 62
ύπομιμνήσκω, -ομαι constr. 234
ύπομονή constr. 173, 211, 212
ύπονοέω constr. 137
ύστερέω: mid. 56—constr. 235

φαίνομαι 58—w. ptc. 159—πέφηνα 82
φανερός: constr. 220, 227, 304— φανερότερον 30—scil. έστιν 295, 304
φανερόω 55
φείδομαι w. gen. 235
φέρω: impf. 67—imper. of pres. and aor. 75, 77, 231—φέρων 154
φεύγω: futur. pres. 63—trans. and w. άπό 244
φησίν: hist. pres. 60 f.—asynd. έφη 61, 340—without subj. 293
φθονέω 245
φιλέω: impf. 66—pf. 84
Φίλιπποι 27
φιμόω: πεφίμωσο, φιμώθητι 85
φοβέομαι: pres. and aor. imper. 75 f., 77—w. μή 99 f.—trans. and w. άπό 244
φόβοι 28
φόνοι 27
φορά ellipse 18
φορτίζω w. double acc. 246
φρονέω constr. 238
φρόνιμαι, αί 13
Φρυγία art. 170
φυλακή 243
φυλάσσω φυλακάς 245— -ομαι ίνα (μή) 104, 138
φύσει 220
φωνή ellipse 17, 18

χαίρω: constr. 160, 305, 308—pres. and aor. imper. 76—χαίρειν wish- inf. 78—w. χαρά, χαρά 242
χαρίζομαι 58—aor. pf. 70
χάρις: art. 176—χάριν prep. w. gen. 278—ού χάριν 278, 319—χ. ύμιν χ. ειρήνη 300, 310—τω θεω 298

INDEX OF GREEK WORDS

χειμῶνος gen. of time within which 235
χείρ: ellipse 17—distrib. sing. 24—πόδες καὶ χεῖρες 350—Hebraism 24, 280
χειρόγραφον 219
χερουβείν gender 21
χιτῶνες 27
χορηγέω constr. 244
χρεία constr. 103, 104, 139
χρή 295, 308
χρηματίζω: pass. 57—gnom. fut. 86 —constr. 149
χρῆσαι aor. imper. 76
χρηστόν, τό 14—χρηστός comp. 31
χρίω constr. 240
Χριστός 212—art. 167
χρόνος: pl. 27—w. ἵνα 104—τοῦ w. inf. 141
χώρα ellipse 16
χωρίζω constr. 235
χωρίς w. gen. 278

ψάλλω constr. 236
ψεύδομαι: pres. imper. 76—constr. 236
ψηλαφάω w. acc. 232
ψυχή reflex. pron. 43—τῇ ψυχῇ 221

ὤ, ὦ 3, 33
ὧδε 44
ὥρα 243—ellipse 17—w. ἵνα 103—constr. 139—art. 179—acc. for time-when 248—scil. ἐστιν 295, 300
ὡς 135, 137, 161—w. superl. 31 (ὡς τάχιστα)—final 105, 136—consec. 136—w. inf. abs. 136—declarative 137—w. ptc 158—w. predic. 246, 321—no longer prep. 249—position w. neg. 286 f.—scil. ἐστιν 297 —to soften a statement 320—causal 320—*as if* 320—correlative 320—temp. 321—f. ἕως 321—clause-order 344
ὡσάν, ὡς ἐάν 112 f., 321
ὡσεί 158, 321
ὥσπερ 158—scil. ἐστιν 297, 310—correlative 320—ὡσπερεί 321
ὥστε 106, 134, 135, 136, 137 f., 139 —final 106, 136
ὠφελέω constr. 246, 292
ὠφέλιμος constr. 220

www.ingramcontent.com/pod-product-compliance
Lightning Source LLC
Chambersburg PA
CBHW050133240426
43673CB00043B/1647